COLLECTED PAPERS

VOLUME I

COLLECTED PAPERS

□□

GILBERT RYLE

Formerly Waynflete Professor of
Metaphysical Philosophy in the
University of Oxford

VOLUME I
CRITICAL ESSAYS

BARNES & NOBLE, Inc.
NEW YORK
PUBLISHERS & BOOKSELLERS SINCE 1873

HUTCHINSON & CO (*Publishers*) LTD
178-202 Great Portland Street, London W1

London Melbourne Sydney
Auckland Wellington Johannesburg Cape Town
and agencies throughout the world

Published in the United States of America
by Barnes & Noble, Inc.

First published 1971

*This book has been set in Garamond type, printed in Great Britain
on antique wove paper by W. Heffer and Sons Ltd, Cambridge*
ISBN 389 04112 2

CONTENTS

CONTENTS

INTRODUCTION

In this volume are resurrected most of the thoughts that I had, by 1968, written and published about individual thinkers.

One other member of this genre, namely 'Mr. Collingwood and the Ontological Argument' which should have appeared in this volume, in fact, owing to muddled instructions to the Printers, appears as No. 7 in the second volume of these Collected Papers.

Several lesser things, such as reviews and obituary notices, which are not revived here, are listed in the bibliography at the end of *Ryle*, in the series *Modern Studies in Philosophy*, published by Doubleday & Co., Inc., N.Y., 1970, and by Macmillan, London, 1971.

To these may be added some pieces written by me but published too late for inclusion here, namely: (1) 'G. E. Moore's "The Nature of Judgement" ' (11 pp.) in *G. E. Moore: Essays in Retrospect*. Ed. Alice Ambrose and Morris Lazerowitz, Muirhead Library of Philosophy, George Allen and Unwin, 1968.

(2) A lecture on Alexius Meinong delivered to the Meinong-Colloquium at the University of Graz in October, 1970. A collection of the lectures given at this Colloquium, edited by Prof. R. Haller, should be published soon.

(3) An obituary appreciation of Bertrand Russell in *The Listener*, 12th of February, 1970.

(4) An obituary appreciation of Bertrand Russell delivered to the Aristotelian Society, on 7th of December, 1970, will appear in the *Proceedings of the Aristotelian Society*, 1970–1, (8 pp.).

(5) 'Autobiographical;' (15 pp.), an introductory contribution to *Ryle* (mentioned above).

(6) Interview with Bryan Magee in the Series 'Conversations with Philosophers', published in *The Listener*, 21st of January, 1971. Publication in book form is planned for the whole Series of 'Conversations with Philosophers'.

Not all, but most of these Critical Essays issue from a common exegetic policy, which I shall shortly expound.

(1) One exception is No. 4 'The "Timaeus Locrus" '. This was written as a 'Who Dun It'. It attempts to credit the young Aristotle with a composition which scholars have relegated to a much later age. If this attempt were successful, it would indeed reinforce certain hypotheses about the careers and the philosophical thinkings of both Plato and Aristotle. But the question whether the detective-work was a failure or a success could not be determined by consideration of the dividends which would accrue if it were a success.

(2) Nos. 5 and 6 on Dialectic aimed to provide a cultural, pedagogic and tool-shop background for the elucidation of Plato's and of Aristotle's thought, without providing much of that elucidation itself. Incidentally, the former piece, apart from its wind-up and appendix, reappeared, with trivial differences, as Chapter IV of my book *Plato's Progress*, so its revival in this volume is probably gratuitous.

(3) Three of the Critical Essays are undisguisedly—and unrepentantly—polemical, namely (*a*) (from Volume II) No. 7 'Mr. Collingwood and the Ontological Argument,' with its rider, No. 9, 'Back to the Ontological Argument'; (*b*) No. 15, 'Logic and Professor Anderson'; and (*c*) No. 14, 'Discussion of Rudolf Carnap: Meaning and Necessity'.

(*a*) The vehemence of my onslaught on Collingwood came partly from a local patriotism. We Oxford philosophers were, I thought, by the mid-thirties, sufficiently abreast of the century's advances in logic and in meta-philosophical theory to have the right to dissociate ourselves from the Ontological Argument that Collingwood had recently exhumed. We were not *ex officio* dedicated to this lost cause.

(*b*) Professor Passmore invited me to discuss the philosophical contributions of Professor John Anderson, of Sydney University. As he had reserved his publication for an antipodean philosophical journal, he had not got any currency for his thoughts in the northern hemisphere. Nor had he embroiled himself in discussions of issues stemming from the logical doctrines of Frege and Russell or from the meta-philosophical teaching of either Wittgenstein or the Logical Positivists.

The electrifying younger generation of antipodean philosophers owed much to Anderson's unromantic and uncompromising teaching. But, I thought, by 1950 it needed to hear other voices than 'His Master's Voice'. In Sydney, especially, discipleship was having the same sterilising effect that another discipleship was visibly having in Cambridge. I wanted to provoke, even to infuriate, Anderson into open debate; but still more did I want to chivvy Australian philosophers-in-the-making into sorting out for themselves what in Anderson's thinking was in motion from what was stuck.

(*c*) The heat in my review of Carnap's *Meaning and Necessity* had a different origin. Carnap was by now the *doyen* of the old Vienna Circle as well as a devoted adherent of Frege. He was in the vanguard of those who wished to rigorise philosophy by formalising its theses and its arguments in apparatus like that of modern Mathematical Logic. The authoritative promise of a technology and, therewith, of a scientific standing for philosophy was already tempting some of us to shirk our impasses for the firm pavement of algebra. Yet, as I harshly objected, Carnap's own handling of the crucial notions of Sense and Nonsense was, in large measure, a relapse into muddles of pre-Wittgenstein, pre-Russell and even pre-Frege sorts. His scientific-seeming apparatus had not helped to solve, but merely to screen the cruces.

Through nearly all of the other Critical Essays, and also through these three polemics, there runs a common strategy, or, it may be, a common *idée fixe*. From the time of the *Tractatus* the question had been a live and insistent one:— What sort of an enquiry is philosophy as distinct from Natural Science, Mental Science, Mathematics, Theology and Formal Logic? What, if any, is its proprietary subject-matter? What, if any, is its peculiar method?

By the early 1930's, if not the late 1920's, I had shaken off the central article of faith of the historians of philosophy, that philosophers, like theologians, are campaigners for and against 'isms'. The 'School of Thought' that flourishes a philosopher's name is the creation of his loyal and therefore inferior pupils. I had shaken off, too, the modern notion that, (say), Kant's three *Critiques* are (like a set of *Minds*) a random assortment of 'analyses' of detachable little tangles. A Kant, a Hume or an Aristotle seeks to eradicate *one* briar-patch—which necessarily consists of a multiplicity of briars. To elucidate the thoughts of a philosopher we need to find the answer not only to the question 'What were his intellectual worries?' but, before that question and after that question, the answer to the question 'What was his overriding Worry?'

Naturally the fact that this is the question to ask does not ensure success for the attempts to answer it. There are two pieces here about John Locke, of which the second, I now think, gets nearer to the right answer than did the first. I think, too, that my latest critical examination of Phenomenology yields a more radical diagnosis than did my earlier examinations.

None the less, it needs to be realized and remembered that my exegeses are exercises of a fairly definite theory about the nature of philosophy, one according to which it is always proper to look, whether in Plato or in Locke or in Mill, for dialectical moves of the same sorts as those which we, in the same quandary, would be tempted or proud to make.

It will be fairly objected that in expositions that are governed by this, or by any other, controlling theory of philosophy, the author must necessarily have an axe to grind. The risk is a real one. But the alternative policy of expounding a thinker's thoughts without reference to his puzzles and difficulties is what has given us our standard histories of philosophy, and that is calamity itself, and not the mere risk of it.

GILBERT RYLE

March, 1971

I

PLATO'S 'PARMENIDES'

Reprinted from 'Mind', vol. XLVIII, *1939*

I

The following observations are arguments in favour of a certain interpretation of Plato's dialogue, the *Parmenides*. According to this interpretation the dialogue is philosophically serious, in the sense that its author thought that its arguments were valid and that its problem was one of philosophical importance. Further, it will be maintained that he was right on the latter point and predominantly right on the former point. The problem is important and most of the arguments are valid.

It will be suggested that the obvious obscurity of the dialogue is due to a very natural cause, namely that Plato could not with the logical apparatus accessible to him propound in set terms what is the general conclusion or even the main drift of the dialogue. For the construction of the required logical apparatus could not be taken in hand until after the inevitability of the sorts of antinomies which the dialogue exhibits had been realised.

If this interpretation is correct, or even if some interpretation of a kindred type is correct, then the interpretation suggested by Burnet and Professor A. E. Taylor is wrong. My main object is to show what the true interpretation is, but a brief résumé of other reasons for rejecting the Burnet–Taylor theory may not be out of place.

Burnet and Professor Taylor declare the dialogue, or the dialectical part of it, to be a joke. Plato's object was to ridicule certain philosophers or philosophasters by parody. None of its arguments are valid or thought by Plato to be so. And its pretended problem or set of problems is a sham one. The butts of the ridicule are either the philosophers of the Eleatic school or those of the school of Megara or both. They merited such ridicule because the logic employed by them was vexatious and fallacious. They had exercised this corrupt logic against certain doctrines which Plato accepted; consequently Plato in this dialogue is paying them back in their own coin.

The main objection to such a theory is of course that the arguments of the dialogue are either valid, or else plausible enough for their author to have taken them to be so. Other objections are as follows. If the intended butts of the alleged mockery were Parmenides and Zeno, it is hard to explain why in the two adjacent dialogues, the *Theaetetus* and the *Sophist*, Plato goes out of his way to express his admiration for the former; or why the Zenonian method of argument by antinomy is declared by Professor Taylor himself[1] (I think correctly) to be that recommended to philosophers by Plato in the *Republic* as well as in the *Sophist*.

Moreover, Professor Taylor recognises not only that Plato thought that the Zenonian pattern of ratiocination was valid, but also that it is valid. He recognises, too, that it is important, since by means of it Zeno had shown that there were hidden absurdities in the premisses of Pythagorean mathematics—which absurdities were acknowledged and partly remedied by Plato's own circle.

In the *Sophist* and the *Politicus* the leader of the discussion is described as an Eleatic Stranger, and his arguments are notoriously intended to be taken seriously. And the Megarian philosopher Euclides is introduced as a sympathetic character at the opening of the *Theaetetus*. The Eleatic Stranger who conducts the argument of the *Sophist* is expressly praised as a genuine philosopher and not a mere tripper-up of unsubtle persons.

So slight a part does Socrates play in the *Parmenides*, *Sophist* and *Politicus*, and so slight also is the positive role given to any known Socratic theories in those dialogues or in the *Theaetetus*, that the natural inference would surely be that Plato had discovered that certain important philosophic truths or methods were to be credited not to Socrates but to the Eleatics. Zeno is the teacher now and not Socrates.

Doubtless there were (long after the time of Parmenides) Megarian thinkers who loved to lay logical traps and pose logical riddles. Maybe some of them prosecuted this search from motives of mischievousness, though generally the collectors of fallacies and puzzles in logic (like Lewis Carroll) do so from the more serious motive of desiring to discover the rules of logic which will provide the rebuttal of the fallacies and the solution of the riddles. But the theme of the *Parmenides* has (unlike Aristotle's *Topics* and *De Sophisticis Elenchis*) no obvious connection with any such posers. Nor could Plato have preserved any historic unities and represented Parmenides as the victim of the posers garnered by this yet unborn band of formal logicians.

[1] In *Plato: The Man and his Work*, p. 290.

But in any case the supposed joke would have been a very poor one. For Parmenides and his followers are supposed to be rendered a laughing-stock by the ascription to Parmenides' own lips of arguments which he never used. He is made to talk nonsense by Plato. Yet this joke would only have succeeded—and then how lamely!—if the words put into his mouth were almost parallel to words which he was known to have uttered. The comicality of the former would be transferred to the latter by the closeness of their analogies. But Parmenides is not known to have produced either fallacious or valid specimens of Zenonian dialectic, and Zeno is known to have produced valid specimens of it. Was Plato perhaps being silly enough to poke fun at a valid method of ratiocination, mistakenly thinking it to be fallacious? This would have made only Plato ridiculous.

Moreover, Parmenides in the dialogue, so far from being an innocent victim, unwittingly entrammelled in an absurd argument, himself draws attention to the untenability of certain of the conclusions of the dialectic. It is he who brings out and draws attention to the contradictions which he has deduced. He underlines the antinomies here as vigorously as Zeno underlined the antinomies which he disclosed as resident in the Pythagorean premisses. He is a poor butt who is both the author of a joke and the commentator upon its absurdities.

It is small wonder that it took two and a half millennia before anyone was found to give vent even to a laboured chuckle at the supposed fooling. Further, in the *Sophist*, which is accepted as a sober dialogue, a certain stretch of the dialectic of the *Parmenides* is echoed as a constituent of the argument. Was it conscious sophistry in the *Parmenides* and serious reasoning in the *Sophist*?

Later on we shall see that the central crux of the second part of the *Parmenides* was recognised by Aristotle to have been a serious philosophical puzzle, and one which he thinks he can, with the aid of his logical apparatus, resolve. This will also be evidence that this issue was not a sham issue and the intricacies of the argument not gratuitously manufactured.

The one piece of internal evidence which seems to be in favour of Professor Taylor's theory is the passage where Parmenides prefaces his antinomian operations with the expression 'since we have committed ourselves to the laborious sport'. I think that παιδία is here 'play taken as exercise or practice' rather than 'fun' in the sense of 'jest' or 'ridicule'. But even if it were taken in the latter sense, the whole alleged joke would be killed. Parmenides could not be the

3

unwitting butt of ridicule while himself recognising that he was being ridiculed. Don Quixote does not say 'Let me pretend for fun to be a gallant knight'. He is a figure of fun because he takes his acts and attitudes seriously.

Finally, the first part of the dialogue, where Socrates is being cross-questioned, is taken by Professor Taylor to be serious. He holds that the arguments which silence Socrates are not really conclusive (in which point I think that he is mainly wrong), but that the discussion is one which has a genuine philosophical problem and moves by a method which is meant to be taken seriously. It is therefore only the second and longer part of the dialogue which has to be construed as a parody. Yet so far from there being any detectable relaxation here in the sobriety of the dialogue, it is generally felt that liveliness and dramatic qualities, not to speak of humour, vanish from the very beginning of this second part.

It reads as if it were sober, professional, systematic, arid and in conformity with set rules—and it reads so, I suggest, because it is so. Moreover, there is a clear connection between the two parts. In the first part Socrates several times over proclaims a challenge, and Parmenides more than once declares that he takes it up. What the challenge is, we shall see later. But if in a serious part of the dialogue a task is set, and if in the second part the task is performed, it is hard to reject the inference that the second part of the dialogue is also serious.

It is now time to give an analysis and interpretation of the dialogue based upon the assumption that Plato thought that it dealt with a real problem and that its arguments were valid. I shall begin with a discussion of the first part of the dialogue, where Parmenides is in discussion with the young Socrates.

Socrates has been listening to the reading of an argument written by Zeno, in which Zeno had been controverting certain opponents of the Monism of Parmenides by demonstrating that their position entailed that one and the same subject had incompatible predicates. Namely, they maintained the existence of a plurality (no matter of what), and Zeno argues that the members of a plurality must exemplify both similarity and dissimilarity; and as these are opposite attributes, it is impossible that there should exist a plurality.

Socrates then urges that Zeno's argument is answerable. For according to the theory of Forms, since Forms and the instances of them are distinguishable, it is possible for there to exist things which are instances of several Forms at once and even, in a certain fashion, instances of opposite Forms at the same time. Things may exemplify

4

similarity and dissimilarity at the same time, or unity and plurality, as a person is one person but a plurality of limbs and bodily parts. It is to be noticed that Socrates does not try to explode the apparent contradictions by distinguishing relational from other predicates, a distinction of which Plato is well aware in other dialogues. He might have shown that there is no contradiction in saying that something is bigger than one thing while smaller than another, or similar to one thing and dissimilar to another, while there would be a contradiction in describing a thing as having and not having a given quality at the same time. Instead the young Socrates maintains that the apparent contradictions vanish or lose their menace when it is seen that Forms and their instances are to be distinguished from one another and that a particular may, without absurdity, be an instance of several Forms and even opposing Forms at the same time.

However, Socrates repeats four times between 129b and 130a that he would be gravely perturbed if it were shown that not the instances of Forms but Forms themselves underwent opposite predicates. And we shall see that in the second part of the dialogue Parmenides takes up just this challenge.

Meanwhile, however, Socrates' theory of Forms has to undergo an examination. And as Socrates has proposed to upset Zeno's assertion that the existence of a plurality entails that the members of such a plurality would have opposite predicates, by referring to the relation between Forms and the instances of Forms, it is to this alleged relation that chief attention is paid.

Socrates accepts as specimens of Forms similarity, unity, plurality, magnitude, justice, beauty and goodness. He boggles at the suggestion that there are also Forms of hair-ness, mud-ness and dirt-ness, and is uneasy even about Forms of natural kinds such as men, fire and water would be instances of. He is advised not to be squeamish, but the general theoretical question is at once embarked on: What sort of a relation is it which holds between instances and what they are instances of? To put it roughly, a Form is taken to be something answering to any general predicate, noun, verb or adjective, in such a way that any significant abstract noun will be the proper name of such a something. And it is because there exist such somethings that many ordinary objects can be characterised by a common predicate. To ascribe a predicate to something is to assert that this something stands in some relation to a Form. So if a thing is an instance of something, there exist two objects, the instance and that of which it is an instance. And there is the special relation between them which constitutes the former an instance of the latter. For example, my body, being one body, exemplifies or is an instance of unity. This, according to the theory, entails that there exist two things, namely my body and unity, and there obtains too the relation answering to the word 'exemplifies' or the phrase 'is an instance of'. We might say, for nutshell effect, that the theory of Forms is the theory that abstract nouns are proper names or that being-an-instance-of is a proper relation.

What sort of a relation is this relation of exemplification? Socrates essays different answers to this question, all of which collapse. We shall see later that any answer must collapse, since the question itself is logically vicious, which entails that the theory of Forms, in its present shape, is logically vicious.

Socrates first suggests that the relation is that of participation, and Parmenides proceeds to examine the concept expressed by this word taken in its natural and literal sense. To participate in something is to possess or occupy a part of something. You and I participate in a cake if you take half of it and I take the other half. So if to be an instance of something is to participate in it, it must be to possess or occupy a fragment. If a thousand objects exemplify circularity by being circular, then on this literal rendering of 'participation' each must somehow have one-thousandth of circularity. Now it already sounds absurd to speak of fractions of attributes, such as slices of yellowness or quotas of similarity. But Parmenides does better than rely upon our nose for the ridiculous; he explores a set of cases where the notion generates flat contradictions. He operates, namely, upon predicates of magnitude and relative magnitude. For example, the existence of many large things would imply that each possessed a very small fraction of largeness, a fraction very much smaller than that of which it was a fraction. And things equal in size will possess fragments of equality which are much smaller than and so not equal to equality. Smallness will vastly exceed in dimensions the fractions of itself that render their possessors small.

Our reactions to such reasoning naturally take two forms. We object at once that of course concepts like magnitude, equality, smallness and the rest do not themselves have magnitudes. Bigness is not bigger or smaller than anything else, nor equal in size to anything else. It is nonsense to ascribe predicates of size to concepts of size. Attributes such as quantitative dimensions are not instances of themselves. Indeed, like Professor Taylor and Mr Hardie, we are ready to declare with confidence that no 'universal', i.e., no quality, relation, magnitude, state, etc., can be one of its own instances. Circularity is not circular nor is proximity adjacent. Nor even are such concepts capable of being instances of other concepts of the same family as themselves. It is nonsense to describe circularity as circular *or* of any other shape; and it is nonsense to describe redness as of *any* colour, or equality as of *any* dimensions. We are right to make such objections. The theory of Forms is logically vicious if it implies that all or some universals are instances of themselves or of other universals of the same family with themselves. And Plato had, apparently, once thought that beauty was beautiful and goodness was good; maybe he had thought that circularity, and circularity alone, was perfectly circular.

But that such descriptions of qualities, magnitudes, relations, etc., are illegitimate has to be shown and not merely felt. Plato is either showing it or on the way to showing it in this part of the dialogue. The very next stage in the argument proves that no universal can be an instance of itself.

Another objection that we feel disposed to make is that Plato is treating such concepts as smallness, equality, similarity and otherness as if they were qualities, instead of seeing that they are relations. To be small is simply to be smaller than something, or than most things or than some standard thing. But we are here trading upon the distinction, worked out in part by Aristotle, between universals of different sorts. Yellow is a universal in the category of quality, equality is one in the category of relation. But how do we establish such categorial differences? Not on the authority of Aristotle or by native instinct or whim, but by exhibiting the contradictions or other absurdities which result from treating universals as all of one type. The theory of Forms was logically vicious in so far as it did, unwittingly, treat all universals as if they were of one type. Plato is proving the need for a distinction between the different types of universals.

In 132a Parmenides briefly shows that if instances of largeness and that of which they are instances are alike considered and compared in respect of largeness, an infinite regress is at once set on foot. If largeness is a large something, it must be an instance of largeness Number 2, and this will be an instance of largeness Number 3 and so on for ever. So 'largeness' will not be the name of one Form but of an endless series of Forms. It is only our generalisation of this to say that it is logically vicious to treat any universal as one of its own instances. We shall see that interesting consequences follow from this.

Socrates now toys for a moment, still within the confines of the participation theory, with the conceptualist theory that Forms are thoughts or notions, so that the relation between instances and that

7

of which they are instances either is or is a species of the relation between our thinkings and what we think about. To this Parmenides gives two different but both fatal objections. The thinking of that of which instances are instances must be the thought of something, and that which is the object of such thinking must be real or exist. And this will be a Form, the existence of which will not be the occurrence of that thinking but presupposed by it as its object. Moreover, if universals were bits of thinking, their instances (on the literal participation theory) will be fragments of those bits. So everything whatsoever will be a piece of thinking, unless we are ready to swallow the alternative of saying that there exist thoughts which are never thought. The latter of these objections would not hold necessarily, if some account of 'being-an-instance-of' other than the literal participation account were given.

Socrates now abandons the literal participation theory and suggests in its place the similarity theory. For one thing to be an instance of a Form is for it to copy or resemble it in one or more respects; or if there exist several instances of a Form they all copy or resemble it, and from this resemblance is derived their resemblance to one another. Historically it is probable that this theory had seemed the obvious theory to hold when attention was being focused upon the concepts of mathematics and especially of geometry. The squares and circles which we draw are not exactly square or circular. They are nearly but not quite good copies of ideal or perfect squares and circles, though these never exist in nature. At this stage, probably, philosophers failed to distinguish ideal circles from circularity and ideal squares from squareness. It was only later seen that they are or would be instances of those attributes and so are or would be particulars even though not ones existing in nature.

Parmenides swiftly refutes this theory. Resemblance is a symmetrical relation. If A is similar to B in a certain respect, B is similar to A in that respect. (We must be careful not to say that 'being a copy of' signifies a symmetrical relation, since in the notion of being a copy there is, over and above the notion of resemblance, the quite different notion of origination. A portrait is a copy of a face, but a face is not a copy of a portrait.)

But for two things to resemble each other in a certain respect, both must have at least one common attribute, or both must be instances of at least one common universal. So if a Form and its instances are similar, both must be instances of at least one higher Form. And if their being instances of it entails, as according to the theory it must entail, that they and it have some point of similarity, then all must be instances of a still higher Form, and so on *ad infinitum*. So, even if there is some sense in which a drawn circle is rather like an ideal circle, there is no sense in which either is similar to circularity.

Socrates is now bankrupt of any answer to the question, What sort of a relation is being-an-instance-of? But the debate is so far inconclusive that the fact that Socrates cannot answer the question does not imply that there is no answer. Other 'friends of the Forms' might assimilate the relation to some other as yet unexamined familiar relation. I propose here to go beyond my text and argue that there can be no answer to the question, since the question itself is illegitimate.

To show this, it is convenient to consider Cook Wilson's answer to the question. His view is that the relation of being-an-instance-of is a relation *sui generis* capable of no analysis and in need of none. It is a mistake in principle to look for some familiar relation which holds between one particular and another, and to try to show that the relation of being-an-instance-of is a case or species of that. None the less, there is no mystery about the relation of being-an-instance-of; it is one with which any ability to think presupposes familiarity. Indeed no ordinary relation or quality or state could be familiar to us without our being familiar with this unique relation.

Let us, for brevity, call this alleged relation, as Cook Wilson does not, 'exemplification' and, ignoring the question whether or not it is assimilable to any other known relation, consider whether the assumption that there exists such a relation contains any logical vice. On this view a thing-quality proposition will assert that a thing is in this relation of exemplifying to the quality; and a relational proposition will assert that the two or more terms jointly exemplify the relation.

Thus every thing-quality proposition will be a relational proposition, and every ordinary relational proposition will be a doubly relational proposition, since it will be asserting that the relation of exemplification holds between the terms and the special relation, say that of being-neighbour-to.

Now if one thing is in a certain relation to another, the latter will be in some, not necessarily the same, relation to the former. If 'this is green' is more fully expressed by 'this exemplifies greenness', there will be another relational proposition of the form 'greenness is exemplified in (or inheres in) this'. Forms will be the subjects of relational propositions: i.e. there will be significant and irreducible relational sentences each with an abstract noun denoting at least one of the terms in the relational proposition.

9

Now what of the alleged relation itself, which we are calling 'exemplification'? Is this a Form or an instance of a Form? Take the two propositions 'this is square' and 'that is circular'. We have here two different cases of something exemplifying something else. We have two different instances of the relation of being-an-instance-of. What is the relation between them and that of which they are instances? It will have to be exemplification Number 2. The exemplification of P by S will be an instance of exemplification, and its being in that relation to exemplification will be an instance of a second-order exemplification, and that of a third, and so on *ad infinitum*.

(This is not the same regress, though reminiscent of it, as that which Bradley thought he had found in the necessity of there always existing a further relation to relate any relation to its terms.)

This conclusion is impossible. So there is no such relation as being-an-instance-of. 'This is green' is not a relational proposition, and 'this is bigger than that' only mentions one relation, that of being-bigger-than.

There are no genuine simple relational propositions having for their terms what is denoted by abstract nouns. Forms are not terms in relational propositions with their instances acting as the other terms. And if (what is a further point which is not here being argued) Forms are also incapable of having qualities or dimensions or states or places or dates, etc., it follows (what is true) that Forms cannot be the subjects of any simple propositions, affirmative or negative, attributive or relational.

Now when we say such things as that there is no relation between greenness or circularity and its instances, we seem to be saying that there exists an intolerable remoteness or alienation between universals and particulars. It sounds like saying that two men have no dealings with each other, or that two bodies are debarred from ever coming into contact. But this is not what is meant. What is meant is that abstract nouns are not proper names, so that to ask what is the relation between the nominee of such a noun and something else is an illegitimate question. The semantic function of abstract nouns is something other than that of denoting subjects of qualities, states, dimensions or relations. To enquire after the qualities, states, positions, sizes or relations of circularity or unity or civility is to ask a nonsensical question. Abstract nouns are not the names of entities (solemn word!), for they are not names at all in the way in which 'Julius Cæsar' is the name of someone.

So when we say that there is no relation between a universal and its instances we are only saying the same sort of thing as when we say that yellowness has no colour or circularity has no shape. These assertions suggest that yellowness is woefully anaemic and that circularity is gravely amorphous; but what is meant is simply that such sentences as 'yellowness is yellow or green' and 'circularity is circular or square' are illegitimate, since the abstract nouns are not the names of things possessing qualities.

It is important to see that this is all quite consistent with the admission that there are plenty of significant sentences of the noun-copula-adjective or the noun-copula-noun pattern, the grammatical subjects of which are abstract nouns. 'Yellow is a colour' and 'unpunctuality is blameworthy' are significant and true sentences. Only they do not express singular attributive propositions about one entity of which the proper name is 'yellow' and one of which the proper name is 'unpunctuality'.

The theory of Forms maintained that Forms are terms in relational propositions; namely, that about any Form there will be the true proposition that something does or might stand in the relation to it of exemplification. So this was a doctrine of Substantial Forms, for according to it each Form would be a substance, since it would be an 'entity' possessing at least one relational property.

It is commonly said that where the young Socrates went astray was in treating universals as if they were particulars. How does one treat a quality or a relation or a dimension as if it were a particular? Not by falsely asserting of it that it has the quality of particularity, for there is no such quality. Treating a universal as if it were a particular can only be speaking as if there could be significant sentences of the simple, singular, attributive or relational patterns having abstract nouns (roughly) for their nominatives; as if, for example, given a sentence like 'This has such and such a quality or relation or magnitude', an abstract noun could replace the 'this' and leave the resultant sentence significant. And this is illegitimate, partly for the reasons already given by Parmenides, partly for reasons yet to come in the dialogue, and partly for reasons which I have suggested.

The reasons are all of one type, namely that contradictions or vicious regresses arise out of assertions which assume the validity of the practice in question.

Parmenides now produces a general argument against the possibility of there existing any relation between Forms and their instances. I am not sure that the argument is valid; it would certainly require a much profounder enquiry into the varieties of relations than Parmenides supplies to establish the point. The argument is as follows.

If instances and that of which they are instances, namely Forms, both exist, they will be existences of different orders. Now when a relation holds between terms, those terms are correlates of each other. And these correlates must be of the same order of existence. A slave-owner is the correlate of the slave whom he owns. He owns a slave and not slavery. The correlate to servitude is ownership, while the correlate to a slave is an owner. If there are the two orders of existence—'existence' and 'subsistence' are the titles recently coined—then what exists is correlated with what exists, and what subsists with what subsists. There is no cross-correlation of something existing with something subsisting.

Thus instances of knowing, namely the cases of knowing which we enjoy, are correlated with their objects, namely instances of truth. But knowledge (that of which cases of knowing are instances) is correlated not with truths but with trueness. Hence if there are Forms, they cannot be what our knowings are knowings of. We cannot know the Forms. And if knowledge—in the sense of that of which knowings are instances—belongs to God, then God cannot know us or any of our concerns. (This step is unwarranted. Parmenides is speaking as if that of which knowings are instances is itself a knowing of something and one which God enjoys. I think he is also assuming or pretending that God, because supramundane, must be a Form, and yet a possessor of knowledge. But if God knows anything, he is a particular, whether supramundane or not; and his knowings will be instances of knowledge.) This last conclusion is rather shocking than convincing; but the general point is of some logical importance, though it is too elliptically presented to carry much weight as it stands. I think that it is true that a relation can only be conceived to hold between terms that are of the same type or level; and if instances and what they are instances of are not of the same type or level, no relation can hold between them. But the notion of types or levels is still a very obscure one, and was much more so in Plato's time when even the much more elementary distinctions of Aristotelian categories had yet to be worked out.

There is now left a big question. It is apparently illegitimate to assert that Forms have this, that or any relation to their instances; it is illegitimate to assert that any quality, relation, magnitude, state, etc., is an instance of itself or of any attributes of the same family with itself. What sorts of propositions can then be asserted about Forms? Are there any cases where it is legitimate to describe one Form as an instance of any other? Are there any attributive or relational propositions about Forms at all? Or is Socrates to be disconcerted in the

way in which he repeatedly said that he would be disconcerted by the
discovery that propositions about Forms are or entail self-
contradictions?

Parmenides says that the young Socrates has got into difficulties
because he has not been put through a certain sort of philosophical
discipline; namely, he has not learned to explore questions by the
Zenonian method of dialectical reasoning. We know well what this
method was. Zeno had shown that the premisses of Pythagorean
mathematics were illegitimate, since incompatible consequences
could be rigorously deduced from them. Those premisses had seemed
innocent and plausible, but their hidden viciousness was exposed by
the derivation of antinomies from them.

But the method requires a certain expansion. Zeno had shown
that certain propositions or hypotheses entailed contradictory
consequences; but it is also required to see whether the contradictories
of such propositions or hypotheses entail contradictory consequences.

For prima facie we should expect that if a given proposition is
shown to be logically vicious, its contradictory must be automatically
validated. But if both a proposition and its contradictory are logically
vicious, both entailing contradictory consequences, then the viciousness of those propositions is of a more radical order.

For instance, ' Jones is a childless parent' contains a contradiction,
but ' Jones is not a childless parent' contains none, though it contains
a 'trifling proposition'. But 'a line is an assemblage of a finite
number of points', as well as 'a line is an assemblage of an infinite
number of points', generates contradictions. There is an illegitimacy
common to both which is first revealed when both are shown to
entail contradictory propositions.

Parmenides is prevailed on to give a specimen exhibition of
this sort of two-way Zenonian operation, in which he is also to
take up Socrates' challenge to show that Forms have incompatible
predicates. Namely, he is to take up a proposition or hypothesis
about a Form, and show that this hypothesis and also the contradictory of it entail that contradictory propositions are true about that
Form.

He gets Socrates to allow that it is an integral part of his theory of
Forms, that if there exist instances of something, that of which they
are instances itself exists and is something other than they. Goodness,
similarity, circularity and the rest are terms of which it is not only
significant but true to say that they exist (or are 'entities', if we relish
terms of art). It is also taken to be an integral part of the theory that
Forms have attributes, i.e. that abstract nouns can be the subject-

13

words in significant and true sentences, of which the predicates signify the having of qualities, relations, magnitudes, states, etc.

Parmenides is going to perform a dialectical operation upon a selected Form; namely, he is going to discover whether a certain hypothesis about that Form, as well as its contradictory, generates contradictions. Which Form will he choose? The list of alternatives out of which he selects is 'plurality (or manifoldness), similarity, dissimilarity, change, changelessness, becoming, annihilation, existence, non-existence and unity (or singleness)'. And he picks on the last on the pretext that it was his philosophical perquisite. The proposition which and the contradictory of which he is going to subject to Zenonian dissection both have for their subjects the Form or concept of Unity or Singleness, that, namely, of which 'all these buildings are one college' embodies an instance.

And here I must differ from Professor Taylor, Mr Hardie and many others on a point of translation. For they render τὸ ἕν as 'The One'. Now this phrase is objectionable on other grounds, for any man of sense will be provoked to say 'the one what'? As it stands, the phrase is incomplete and meaningless. However, the suggestion is that we are to take it as analogous to 'the Almighty', i.e. as a terse description of a being of which singleness (like omnipotence in the analogous case) is a leading property. But Plato makes it perfectly clear that τὸ ἕν is the name of a Form side by side with ἰσότης or σμικρότης. The English abstract noun 'Unity' is its proper translation. If the Greek language had possessed the word—as it did later on—ἑνότης would have been employed instead.

The collocation of the particle τὸ with a neuter adjective is a perfectly familiar way of expressing what we express by an abstract noun, and the only excuse for rendering it by 'the one' in this dialogue is the presupposition that of course Parmenides must be discussing his Monistic theory, for which there is no internal evidence whatsoever.

While on this matter of translation, we may also complain of Professor Taylor's constant use of such phrases as 'the just equal' and 'the just similar' as translations for τὸ ἴσον and τὸ ὅμοιον or αὐτὸ τὸ ἴσον and αὐτὸ τὸ ὅμοιον. Actually these phrases are only the equivalent of our abstract nouns 'equality' and 'similarity'; but Professor Taylor's phrases are nearly senseless and quite misleading. When we use the word 'just' adverbially we usually mean 'nearly not', as when I reach the station just in time. Or sometimes we use it in the sense of 'merely' as when I call someone 'just an ignoramus'. If either sense were appropriate, phrases like 'the just equal' would be descriptions of particulars characterised as 'nearly not equal' or 'merely equal'—silly descriptions of nothing at all. But in fact, the Greek phrases are used to denote Forms; they mean 'equality' and 'similarity', and the sentences in which they occur make no sense unless they are so taken.

What then are the propositions or hypotheses about Unity which are to be shown to entail contradictory conclusions? And here, unfortunately, there is a real ambiguity in the Greek.

There are three alternatives.

(1) Each hypothesis is the existence-proposition 'Unity exists' or its contradictory 'Unity does not exist'.

(2) Each hypothesis is the attributive proposition 'Unity is unitary (or single)' or its contradictory 'Unity is not unitary (or single)'.

(3) Some of the hypotheses are of type (1) and some of type (2).

If we are primarily interested in the logic of existence-propositions or in the theory of the substantiality of the Forms, we shall be tempted to render all the hypotheses as of the first pattern. If we are primarily interested in the logical question whether any universal can be an instance of itself, we shall be drawn towards the second.

Both would be natural topics for Plato to explore, after what has already transpired in the first part of the dialogue. The *Theaetetus* and the *Sophist* show that Plato was at this time deeply concerned with the logic of existence-propositions, and they contain no suggestion that he was much exercised about the problem whether a term can be one of its own instances. The prefatory remarks of Parmenides (135–6) strongly suggest that the hypotheses will be of the form 'that so and so exists' and 'that so and so does not exist'. But the internal evidence of the earlier dialectical movements, though equivocal when taken by itself, points as strongly to the second alternative or to the third as to the first.

The difficulty is this. ἐστί can be used as a copula or to mean 'exists'; ἕν can be used as an abbreviation for τὸ ἕν, i.e. substantivally, or it can be used adjectivally, so that it can mean 'Unity' or it can mean 'unitary' or 'single'. And Greek permits the predicate adjective to precede the copula. So the little sentence ἕν ἐστι can mean 'Unity exists' or 'it (i.e. Unity, which has been previously mentioned) is unitary'.

And this is complicated by the fact that Plato is ready to infer from a proposition of the form S is P to 'S exists', since if S has a certain sort of being it must have being, i.e. exist (see *Theaet*. 188–9, *Parm*. 161–2, *Soph*. 252). That is, an ἐστί in the sense of 'exists' follows from an ἐστί, in the sense of 'is . . .'. And conversely, if it is true to say that Unity exists, it is plausible to infer that it is unitary. (This begs a big question—but we cannot say yet that Plato realised that it begs it.)

I am convinced that the correct interpretation is the existential one; that is, that in the first two of the four 'operations' the hypo- thesis under examination is 'that Unity exists' and in the second two it is 'that Unity does not exist'.[1] When, as sometimes occurs, especially in the first operation, he is deducing consequences from the proposition 'Unity is unitary (or single)', this itself is taken to be an obvious consequence of the original one 'Unity exists'. It has to be admitted that, especially in the first operation, the Greek does not square any better with this interpretation than with the other. But the following considerations make it necessary, if it is possible.

The general pattern of the argument is simple. There are two main operations upon the affirmative hypothesis, and two main operations upon the negative of it. Let us label them A1 and A2, N1 and N2 ('A' for 'affirmative', 'N' for 'negative'). Next, A1 answers to N1, and A2 to N2, in this way: In A1 and N1 Parmenides is seeing what propositions *about Unity* are entailed by the hypothesis; in A2 and N2 he is seeing what propositions *about terms other than Unity* follow from the hypothesis. (There are subordinate divisions within these operations, which do not matter for our present purpose.)

Now, though the actual formulation of the hypothesis and the development of the argument in operation A1 leaves it in doubt whether the hypothesis is 'Unity exists' or 'Unity is single', the formulation of the hypothesis and the argument of N1 make it perfectly clear that here the hypothesis is 'Unity does not exist'.

It is fairly clear too, though less so, that the hypothesis of N2 is 'Unity does not exist'. But from this it follows that the hypotheses of operations A1 and A2 *must* be 'Unity exists', else the promised two-way application of the Zenonian method would be broken. Moreover, this alone is consistent with Parmenides' sketch of the task of the dialectical method in the passages from 135a to 136c. And as I have said, it is corroborated by the facts (1) that in the *Theaetetus* and the *Sophist* Plato is acutely concerned with existence- propositions and (2) that, as we shall see, Aristotle recognises that

---

[1] V. Brochard construes the hypotheses in this way in his essay 'La Théorie Platoni- cienne de la participation' in his book *Études de Philosophie Ancienne et de Philosophie Moderne*.

there was or had been a major philosophical crux about the two concepts of Unity and Existence. And (anyhow later) ὑπόθεσις normally meant the assumption of the *existence* of so and so.

Professor Taylor's translation hinders rather than assists us in this matter. For he rings the changes upon such formulations as, 'if it (i.e. the one) is one' 'if there is one' 'if the one is' 'if the one is not' and 'if there is no one'. None of these is consonant with English idiom, and hardly with English syntax; but anyhow the very variety of them is inconsistent with Parmenides' self-announced task. His task is to explore *one* proposition with its contradictory, and not several. And this proposition and its contradictory must have Unity for their subjects.

Evidence that the single word ἕν is used as a simple substitute for the phrase τὸ ἕν is as follows: καλόν, δίκαιον and ἀγαθόν are so used in 130b and 135c, ἀνόμοιον in 136b. ἕν is indubitably used substantivally at 143b2, 143c5–7, 144a4, 149c7, 160b5–7 et seq., 161b9, 163c1, 164b3, 164d and e, 165b6, 166b1. Cf. also *Theaetetus* 185d1, 186a8, *Sophist* 238e1, 239a10, *Phaedo* 76 and 77. On my view there are lots of places in the *Parmenides* where this idiom is employed; but I cannot use most of them as evidence, since it is just the conclusion that it is being employed there for which I adduce these other passages as evidence.

There are, of course, plenty of passages where ἕν is certainly being used adjectivally or predicatively.

Before embarking upon the exegesis of the main drift of the Zenonian exercise, there is a matter of some general interest to notice. Why does Plato make Parmenides choose to operate upon such rarefied concepts as Unity and Existence? Or, when making his selection of his victim, why does he only mention as candidates for the post such rarefied concepts as Manifoldness, Similarity, Dissimilarity, Change, Changelessness, Existence and Non-existence? Would not the operations have worked if applied to beauty or justice, circularity or squareness, humanity or animality?

No hint of a reason is given in the dialogue. The answer may simply be that he assumed that what is true of the more generic Forms will cover the more specific ones; the general logical properties of universals will come out most swiftly from an inspection of those which are nearest the peak of the pyramid. That is, Plato may have thought that as Figure is higher than Plane Figure, and that than Triangle, so Similarity, Plurality, Existence and the rest are higher than Figure, i.e. that they are Summa Genera. If he did think this, he was mistaken. This seems to be Professor Cornford's explanation for the selection; he does not recognise that Existence is not a sort-concept.

In fact, these concepts or most of them, and several others, differ from most ordinary concepts not just in level of generality but in type. They are formal concepts, not peculiar to any special subject matter, but integral to all subject matters. They belong, so to speak, not to this or that special vocabulary of knowledge, but to its general syntax. Now in the *Theaetetus* and the *Sophist* we find Plato recognising just such a feature of certain concepts. The mode of arrangement of letters which constitutes them a syllable is not itself a letter; and Plato uses this analogy to explain how certain concepts like existence and non-existence have a different sort of logical behaviour from most ordinary concepts, just (as I construe him) because they are not terms in the propositions which we think but the forms of the combinations of those elements into propositions. He does not and cannot fully develop this view. But as it is true and important and was in Plato's mind at this period, it is agreeable to conjecture that it entered into his motive for selecting the concepts which he does select for subjection to his Zenonian operation.

As what I wish to show is that the *Parmenides* is an early essay in the theory of types, this suggestion has some relevance to what will be my general thesis. I shall take it up again later on.

Another possible motive should be considered. What were the salient properties of Forms according to the strict theory of them? Plainly two; first, that a Form is single whereas its instances are or might be plural. The whole problem was: How can a plurality of objects different from one another be given one name or be spoken of as if there was one identical something in them? It is the prime business of a Form to be single. And, second, a Form had to be real or existent, in order to infect its instances with such meagre contagions of reality as they enjoy. It is by referring to a Form that we answer the question What really *is* this particular?

Now, if Forms, to resolve any of our difficulties, have to exist and to be single, what sort of Forms will these be, namely, Existence and Singularity? Will they too be existent and single? Or not? Clearly the menace of an infinite regress or else a flat contradiction stares us in the face. (Cf. *Philebus* 15.)

For this to have been Plato's motive in selecting for inspection the hypothesis that Unity exists *or* that Unity is single (or their contradictories), he would not have had to suppose that Unity and Existence are Summa Genera, nor yet would he have had to see or half-see that Unity and Existence are *not* Summa Genera but form-concepts. His concentration upon them would have had the historical reason that just these concepts were the sheet-anchors of the whole theory of Forms. He operates upon them, because the whole argument is an *argumentum ad homines*. I think that in fact, if not in Plato's consciousness, this suggested line of approach is only a special case of the one previously mentioned. For what it is tempting to construe as the essential properties of universals will in fact turn out (since universals cannot have properties) to be formal features of propositions, in which of course universals will be factors.

The one motive which I feel fairly sure did not much influence Plato is the one usually mentioned, namely that he wished to discuss Parmenidean Monism. This insipid unitarianism has no special bearings on the truth of falsity of the theory of Forms, and no special bearings on more general questions of logic, and I see no reason why Plato should have interested himself much in it, or much evidence that he did so, whereas there is plenty of evidence internal to this dialogue and adjacent dialogues that he was very much interested in the theory of Forms and very much interested also in more general questions of logic.

Parmenides has opted to practise his Zenonian operations upon one selected concept; that of Unity. But he does not suggest that the resultant antinomies are peculiar to this concept. The implied suggestion is, rather, that antinomies of the same type could be shown to result from operations either upon any other concepts or upon some other concepts. Parmenides nowhere says which. Either discovery would provide the young Socrates with the disturbance which he had said would trouble him. Whether it is shown in the case of one concept, or of several, or of all, that contradictions arise in their description, it will be enough to show that the promise of the perfect knowability of the supposed supramundane entities has been delusive.

The most tempting reading of the position is that Plato realised or nearly realised that antinomies necessarily arise from the attempt to make any concept whatsoever (from the most specific to the most categorial) a subject of attributes. To assert or to deny that a concept does or does not exemplify itself or another concept is to assert something illegitimate, no matter what that concept may be. A quality or a relation neither has nor lacks any quality or relation. The name of a quality or relation cannot significantly occur as the subject of an attributive or relational sentence. Abstract nouns cannot assume the roles of proper names or demonstratives.

In particular, there is a deep-seated irregularity in sentences of which the verb is the verb 'to exist', and the subject is an abstract noun or the name of an εἶδος. Contradictions arise as well from the denial as from the assertion that Unity or any other εἶδος exists. So the hallowed doctrine that it is only of such subjects that we can with knowledge or truth assert that they really exist is baseless.

This, I say, is the most tempting construction of the message of the *Parmenides*. For, for one thing, it is true. And for another thing, it is completely general. And, thirdly, it rounds off very neatly Parmenides' criticism of the young Socrates' simple theory of Substantial Forms. It had been shown already that Socrates could say nothing of the relations between his Forms and their instances, or between his Forms and our knowings and thinkings. And now it is shown that he can say nothing of the relations between one Form and another Form.

None the less, I am not satisfied that this is the message of the dialogue. I think that Plato thought that the antinomies which he exhibits result from the application of the Zenonian operation to certain concepts, and no such antinomies would have arisen from its application to certain others. There is something logically eccentric about certain concepts, such as Unity and Existence, which does not infect all concepts, though it may infect a few others.

I shall try to formulate this interpretation more accurately later on. For the moment I wish to mention the grounds which make me dubious of the truth of the more tempting interpretation. First, the dialogue the *Sophist*, which is certainly closely connected with the *Parmenides* in date and style, and in certain stretches also in method and topic, nowhere handles any general theoretical difficulties in the theory of Forms; but it does deal very intensively with the logical properties of a few concepts which are of a very formal sort, namely, those of existence, non-existence, similarity, difference, change and changelessness. And it picks up two threads which are already to be found in the *Theaetetus*, namely (1) that there is something logically peculiar about the concepts of existence, and non-existence, and (2) that the modes of combination of elements, like that of letters in syllables or words in sentences, are not themselves elements. And it is suggested that some concepts (but not all) are somehow analogous not to letters or words but to the modes of combination of letters and words, so that the contradictions which perplexed us over these formal concepts arose from the fact that we were trying to treat as 'letters' or 'words' what are in truth modes of combination of 'letters' or 'words'. Or to use the language of Kant and Wittgenstein, we were trying to treat formal concepts as if they were 'proper' or material concepts.

Finally, it seems to me unquestionable that Aristotle (in *Metaphysics* 1001a, 1003b, etc., *Physics* 185–7, *Topics* 121a and b, 127a, and *De Sophisticis Elenchis* 182b) is referring to notorious cruces about the special concepts of Unity and Existence—whether he actually has his eye on the *Parmenides* does not matter. There were clearly difficulties about them which were not thought to attach to most other concepts; they were clearly closely affiliated to each other; and something important is thought by Aristotle to be revealed about them when it is said of them not merely that they are not substances (which is true of all Forms alike), but also that they are not genera and do not fall under any one of the categories as opposed to any other, but in some way pervade them all—in which respect they are unlike most concepts.

These considerations suggest to me the following way of rendering Plato's line of thought in the *Parmenides* and the *Sophist* (and in lesser degree the *Theaetetus*).

He was beginning to see that there are different types of concepts. (As always happens, a philosophical problem is, at the start, dominated by a status-question. Later, this status-question surrenders its primacy and even its interest to a network of constitution-questions.) (*a*) One difference between types of concepts, specimens of which Plato explores with almost tedious pertinacity in the *Sophist* and the *Politicus*, is that between generic and specific concepts, or between the more generic and the more specific concepts. Thus, living creature —animal—man, or figure—plane figure—plane rectilinear figure— triangle—isosceles triangle, are scales of kinds or sorts, which scales exhibit differences in degree of generic-ness or specific-ness. But this sort of difference is not directly important for our purpose, save in so far as the negative point, to which Plato was, I think, alive in the *Sophist*, is relevant, namely that Existence and Non-Existence are not co-ordinate species of a genus, nor themselves genera having each other or other concepts as subordinate species. The same would be true of Unity and Plurality. (*b*) Another distinction, which Plato himself draws elsewhere, is that between qualities and relations. Relational predicates, with the possible exception of identity, require the existence of at least two terms, whereas qualitative predicates only require one. (*c*) A third distinction, which I think Plato never attends to, is that between simple and complex concepts, or between simpler and more complex concepts. Thus, 'danger' is less simple than 'harm', for it combines the notion of harm with that of likelihood. Completely simple concepts would be indefinable, and definable concepts are complex. It is odd that the Socratic hunt for definitions did not lead to the realisation that some concepts must be simple and so indefinable. Perhaps the cryptic theory, expounded and criticised in the *Theaetetus*, that the ultimate elements of what exists are simples which can be named but not asserted, is an indication that somebody had noticed the point. But it is probable that by 'simple elements' Plato understood atomic particulars, like sense-data, rather than elementary concepts like 'yellow'. (*d*) Quite other than these differences of type between concepts is the difference between formal concepts and 'proper' concepts. A formal concept is one which may have a place in a proposition about any subject-matter you please, and some formal concepts or other will be present in any proposition. But non-formal concepts will only occur in propositions with this as opposed to that special topic. 'Triangle' occurs in propositions of geometricians or surveyors, and 'catapult' in propositions describing shooting. But 'not' 'exists' 'some' 'other' 'single' 'several' 'is an instance of' 'is a species of' 'and' 'implies' and many others are not peculiar to any special topics.

Such formal concepts are not subject or predicate terms of propositions—they are not 'letters', but rather the modes of combining terms. What the spelling of a word is to its letters, or what the syntax of a sentence is to the words in it, that a formal concept is to the non-formal concepts in a proposition.

So it may be that the laborious operations of this dialogue are intended, perhaps only half consciously, to bring out the difference between formal and ordinary concepts by showing that the logical behaviour of some of the former is anomalous.

II

I have said that the Parmenidean dialectic contains four main stages or operations which I have labelled A1, A2, N1 and N2. Each of these contains two movements. Let us call these M1 and M2, so that we can refer to a given movement as A1 (M2) or N2 (M1) ('M' for movement).

The references to them are as follows:

A1(M1)	137c4	N1(M1)	160b5
A1(M2)	142b1	N1(M2)	163b7
A2(M1)	157b6	N2(M1)	164b5
A2(M2)	159b2	N2(M2)	165e2

The general relation between the two movements within one operation is this, that while M1 (say) proves that the subject under investigation, namely Unity (or, in the other cases, what is other than Unity), possesses both of two antithetical predicates, the other movement M2 proves that that same subject possesses neither of two antithetical predicates. Or rather, in each movement the label of which is M1, say, it is proved that there are numerous pairs of antithetical predicates both of the members of all which pairs characterise the subject, while M2 establishes that the subject is characterised by neither of the members of these several pairs of antithetical predicates. And in general the predicate-couples considered in M1 are more or less the same as the predicate-couples in the corresponding M2.

Actually, in A2, N1 and N2, the first of the two movements in each case proves that the subject possesses both of the members of the pairs of antithetical predicates, while the second movement proves that it possesses neither; but in A1 the order is the other way round, M1 proving that it has neither and M2 proving that it has both.

A1(M1). The first movement of the first operation, namely A1(M1), is (according to my interpretation) as follows:

If Unity exists, it cannot be manifold and therefore must be unitary or single. It cannot therefore be a whole of parts. It will not therefore have outer or inner parts, and so it will have no figure. It will have no location and no surroundings and so no change of position or stationariness of position. Change and fixity of relations are forbidden to it. It cannot be numerically different from anything or identical with anything: it cannot be identical with anything else or different from itself, for obvious reasons; and it cannot be different from anything else, because being different is different from being single, so that if it is single it cannot be that *and* be different from anything. Equally it cannot be identical with anything, even itself. For unity is one thing and identity is another. (This seems a dubious step. Certainly unity is not the same as either identity or difference. But it does not seem to follow that it cannot *enjoy* identity or difference, save on the assumption that unity is single *and* has no other properties than singleness. However, this point is now affirmed.) If Unity has any other attributes than that of being unitary, then it is *ipso facto* shown to be several things, which severalness is inconsistent with its unitariness. Unity cannot be *both* unitary *and* anything else at all, even identical with itself. Since similarity and unlikeness are identity and difference of attributes, Unity cannot enjoy either similarity or unlikeness, and so neither equality nor inequality of dimensions. So it cannot have equality or inequality of age with anything, and so cannot have an age at all, and is therefore not in time.

Its existence therefore is existence at no date, and this is non-existence at every date. It cannot, therefore, exist, and if it does not exist it cannot carry its alleged special property of being single, since there would be nothing in existence for the property to characterise. So Unity neither exists nor is it single. No name can be the name of it, no description the description of it, and there can be no knowledge, opinion or perception of it. It cannot be talked or thought about (since there isn't any 'it'), which is absurd.

Comment. This, like all the other operations, smells highly artificial. There must be something wrong with the several deductions. We are inclined to say that the starting-point was illegitimate, and to write off 'Unity exists' and 'Unity is unitary' as bogus sentences—the latter for making a universal one of its own instances, the former for tacking the verb 'to exist' on to what is supposed to be a logically proper name. We may also suspect that the argument presupposes that singleness is a quality, when it is nothing of the sort. Doubtless we are correct on all these scores—but how can the illegitimacy of such procedures be established? Not by prima facie unplausibility, for the Theory of Forms did seem plausible and did entail (1) that every universal is single; (2) that every abstract noun is not only possibly but necessarily the subject of a true affirmative existence-sentence; and (3) that being single is a case of having an attribute.

The illegitimacy of the starting-point is established by the impossibility of the consequences that must follow if the original propositions are taken to be both legitimate and true. We must not be superior and appeal to sophisticated distinctions between formal and non-formal concepts or to professionalised classifications into 'categories' or 'types' of the various sorts of logical terms; for the necessity of such distinctions and classifications had first to be shown. Plato is showing it, though it may well be that he could not formulate what it was that he was showing. Of necessity he lacked the language of categories and types. That there are different forms of judgement and what their differences are could hardly be familiar at a time when the very notion of 'judgement' had yet to receive its introductory examination, e.g. in the *Sophist.* And little progress could be made in the former enquiry until principles of *inference* became the subject-matter of specialised research.

We can say, glibly enough, that qualities do not have qualities and also that existence and unity are not qualities. For we have been taught these lessons. But what first made it clear to whom that these lessons were true, unless some such ratiocinations as these?

To say that a term is of such and such a type or category is to say something about its 'logical behaviour', namely, about the entailments and compatibilities of the propositions into which it enters. We can only show that terms are not of one type by exhibiting their logical misbehaviour when treated alike. And this is what Plato is here doing.

To complain that the several conclusions are absurd is to miss the whole point. Plato means to prove that the premisses must be illegitimate because the conclusions are absurd. That is the sole and entire object of *reductio ad absurdum* arguments, which is what all these arguments are.

A1(M2). This, the second movement of the first operation, is the longest of them all. And it is insufferably tedious. Its object is to prove that Unity has both of the members of all the predicate-couples, the lack of both of the members of which had been established in A1(M1).

If Unity exists, it must partake in or be an instance of existence. So being unitary is one thing and being an existent is another. So the Unity to which existence belongs will be a compound of Unity and Existence, a compound having those two parts or members. The whole containing these parts will itself be unitary and existent, and so also each of its members will be both unitary and existent and thus will be another compound of these two elements over again, and this will continue forever. So if Unity has existence, it must be an infinite manifold.

Next 'Unity' and 'Existence', not being synonymous, must stand for different things. So both will be instances of difference or otherness, which is consequently a third term over and above those original two. We can now speak of one couple consisting of Unity and Existence, another couple consisting of Unity and Otherness, and a third of Existence and Otherness.

And the constituents of a couple are units both of which must be unitary in order to be instances of unit. A couple plus the third unit will make three objects, and as couples are instances of even-ness, and threes of odd-ness, the Forms of Even-ness and Odd-ness are also now on our hands. And as multiplying consists in, e.g. taking couples three at a time, or threes twice at a time, we can get any number in this way. All arithmetical concepts are automatically generated; from the existence of unity the existence of every number follows, i.e. an infinite number of objects must exist. Every number yields an infinity of fractions, so Unity is fractionised by its inter-locking with Existence into as many members as there could be arithmetical fractions, i.e. an infinite number.

Being a whole of parts, it must contain its parts. There must be a distinction between what is and what is not contained by it. So it must have limits and consequently be finite, for all that there is an infinite number of parts which it contains.

If it has limits or boundaries it must have a beginning and an end as well as a middle: and it must have a configuration or shape. (Parmenides here unwarrantably jumps to the conclusion that it must have a *spatial* configuration.) Being a whole of parts, Unity cannot be a part of any of its parts, nor can it be just one of its own parts. It cannot therefore be one of the things that it itself contains. To be anywhere it must be in something other than itself; yet since every-thing countable is among its parts, it must be contained in itself. This is supposed, I think invalidly, to imply that it must, *qua* self-containing, be immobile, and, *qua* contained by something else, be mobile.

Next, Unity, not standing to itself as part to whole or as whole to part, must be identical with itself, fully and not partially, and it must also be fully and not partially other than whatever is not Unity. But the next stage seems very paradoxical. For it is to be argued that Unity is *not* different from what is other than it and also is *not* identical with itself.

For a container is not where its contents are, since they are inside it, which it cannot be. Now Unity has just been shown to be both content and container, so it must be elsewhere than itself and so not be identical with itself.

The opposite point, that Unity is identical with what is not Unity, is shown in this way. Otherness cannot characterise anything, for everything is 'itself and not another thing'. So neither Unity nor what is not Unity can possess otherness. And as what is not Unity cannot be either a part of Unity or a unitary whole of which Unity is a part, it is only left for Unity and what is not Unity to be identical. (This argument pretends, for the moment, that 'otherness' is the name of a quality. Of course it isn't a quality—but why not?)

Next, since Unity is other than what is not Unity, and vice versa, both Unity and what is not Unity must exemplify otherness. But in their both being instances of the same attribute, namely that of otherness, they must be similar in that respect. For that is what similarity is, the possession by two things of the same character.

Now identity is the opposite of otherness. But it has been shown, in an earlier argument, that Unity must be identical with what is not Unity (146-7); consequently, as the possession of identity is the non-possession of otherness, there must be this respect of dissimilarity between Unity and what is not Unity. For by this argument a suggested shared property is not shared. It follows that Unity is both similar and dissimilar both to what is not Unity and to Unity itself.

I skip the detail of the next few stages of the argument. It is argued that Unity must be both in and out of contact with itself and with the 'field';[1] that it must be both equal and unequal to itself and the 'field', that it must be greater and smaller than itself and the 'field' and also older and younger than itself and the 'field', and also be neither of these.

Then, to controvert the end conclusion of A1(M1) it is shown that Unity does exist at every time and is there to be named and described, known and thought about.

Finally, since the only way in which a subject can be conceived both to have and to lack a given property is that it *alters* having the property at one date and lacking it at another, it is argued that Unity changes, develops, decays, and moves as well as being immutable and static, and that the time of its changings and movings must be a time which takes no time—at which time it is in neither of the conditions from or to which its transition is. (This looks like a variant of a Zenonian paradox about motion.)

Comment. Naturally we feel that most of the foregoing assertions, with the arguments leading to and from them, are absurd. Concepts are being played with fast and loose. Those of one type, with one sort of logical role, are being made to understudy or deputise for others of quite different sorts. Different concepts should not be treated as if the rules of their co-functioning were all similar. Precisely—but only absurdities reveal the different rules, and the *reductio ad absurdum* argument marshals the absurdities.

A2(M1). Parmenides now enquires: From the assumption that Unity exists, what consequences follow about τὰ ἄλλα? He will argue that this subject too must possess opposite predicates. What exactly does τὰ ἄλλα denote? We have no reason to restrict it, for example, to the objects of sense or opinion; nor yet to the Forms other than Unity. It must be taken to cover all terms whatsoever, of whatever sorts, which are other than Unity. So Circularity as well as Alcibiades,

---

[1] Meaning by this the totality of all that is distinguishable from Unity.

the Equator as well as my present pang of pain, will be members of this *omnium gatherum*: let us just call it, in racing parlance, 'the field'.

The field is other than Unity, yet it embodies it. For it has members, being a plurality, and so must be *one* aggregate or whole of those members. Moreover, each of those parts of members must be one part or member. A whole is a plurality of units, so it is a unit and each of them is a unit.

But though or because they exemplify it, it is not and none of them is Unity. A thing is not that of which it is an instance. So since the field is not Unity is must be a plurality or manifold. And the argument, which I skip, is developed that such a plurality must be both a finite and an infinite plurality, so each of its members will be so too.

Being both limited and unlimited, the field and its several members are similar to one another, since they all co-exemplify limitedness and unlimitedness; yet since these are opposite predicates, what exemplifies one must be unlike what exemplifies the other, as what is black is unlike what is white. Similarly it could be shown, though it is not shown, that the field and its several members must enjoy both identity and otherness and both change and changelessness, etc.

A2(M2). Unity and the field are an exhaustive disjunction; there can be nothing which does not belong to the one camp or to the other. So there can be no superior camp, to which both these camps are subordinate as members. Hence Unity will have no truck with the field, either so as to constitute it *one* whole of parts, or as an assemblage of *unitary* parts. So the field cannot be a plurality, nor will any number be applicable to it, or to any part or feature of it. So the field cannot possess either similarity or dissimilarity or both at once. For both together would be a pair and each by itself would be single, and these are applications of number. For the same reason the field cannot be identical or different, stationary or mobile, coming into or going out of existence, greater or smaller or equal.

The conclusion of all the movements of both operations A1 and A2 is thus summed up. If Unity exists it both has every predicate and lacks every predicate, including that of unity. And the same holds good for the field too.

N1(M1). We now turn to the consequences of the hypothesis that Unity does not exist. The proposition that Unity does not exist clearly differs in having a different subject from the propositions that largeness or that smallness does not exist. So we know what 'Unity' denotes and that it denotes something other than what these other nouns denote, whether our judgement is that there does or that there does not exist such a thing. So Unity is something which we apprehend, and it possesses and is known to possess the attribute of being other than the terms which we have distinguished from it. Consequently Unity, for all that it does not exist, is an instance of various things. The word 'it' applies to it. Being distinguished, it has dissimilarities from what it is distinguished from, and as it is not so distinguishable from itself, it must have the opposite of dissimilarity, namely, similarity to itself. (We may grumble at this step. The inference 'I am not unlike myself, therefore I must be like myself' contains a fallacy. But what sort of fallacy? The inference is valid if I am compared with my father, so why does it not hold good in this case? If we say 'because the terms to the relations of likeness and unlikeness must be numerically different', then we are asserting a very special sort of 'must'. Namely, we are saying that 'I' and 'like/unlike' are terms which are of such formal constitutions that absurdity results from their juxtaposition in this way. And that *is* a discovery about the formal properties of certain sorts of terms. It shows that similarity is not a quality. But the distinction of quality-concepts and relation-concepts is a distinction between types of concepts.)

Being unlike the field, it cannot be equal to it or its members; so it must be unequal to them. But inequality is in respect of largeness and smallness (since for two things to be unequal in size one must be relatively large and the other relatively small). So Unity possesses largeness and smallness (the argument would only prove that it must possess at least one of the two); but as being big is the opposite of being small, Unity must, by way of compromise, have what is betwixt and between the two, i.e. equality with itself. (This is fallacious—but why?) Unity therefore is an instance of bigness, smallness and equality.

But if it has all these predicates, Unity must, though non-existent, still enjoy being in existence in some fashion. For if the above descriptions were true, they described it as being what it really is. Unity must be there for us to be able to say or think that it does not exist. But also it must not be there, for its non-existence to be truly predicated of it. But hovering in this way between existence and non-existence is change, and change or transition is motion. (This is illegitimate—but to see why it is illegitimate is to see something important about the concepts of existence, non-existence and change.)

Yet since it does not exist it cannot be anywhere or move anywhence anywhither. And the other sort of transition, from state to state, is also ruled out; for if unity changed in this way it would cease to be Unity and become something else.

But to be exempt from movement and change is to be stationary and immutable. So Unity both is and is not mobile, and both is and is not mutable. And it also follows both that it is and that it is not subject to generation and annihilation.

Comment. The interesting parts of this movement are the stages where we find the famous argument that that of which it is true that it does not exist must be *there*, in some sense, to accept this ascription of non-existence and also to be distinguishable from other terms, existent or non-existent. We are enlightened enough to say (with Kant) that 'exists' is not a predicate or (with latter-day logicians) that the nominatives to verbs of existence do not function as demonstratives or logically proper names; but the penalties of not saying so are here exhibited. Doubtless the rules governing the logical behaviour of verbs of existence are still obscure to Plato; but that there are such rules, and that they are different from those governing ordinary predicates, is here being realised by him. For absurdities result from treating them alike. Plato seems to be ahead of Meinong here.

N1(M2). If Unity does not exist, it is lacking in all modes, departments or sorts of existence. It can enjoy neither coming-to-be nor annihilation; it cannot be subject to mutation or motion, nor, being nowhere, can it be stationary anywhere.

Indeed, it can have no attributes or properties, neither largeness, smallness, nor equality, neither similarity nor difference. It cannot even be correlated with a field, for its having such a correlate would be a relational property of it. It has no attributes, parts, relations, dates, and it is not there to be known, thought or talked about, perceived or named. There is no 'it' at all.

Comment. It seems to follow from this that all negative existence propositions must be nonsense if they are true, since there is nothing left to support the negative predicate. So the name of the subject of predication is the name of nothing. From this it is a short step, which Plato does not take (any more than Meinong did), to seeing that the nominatives to verbs of existence are *not* the names of anything, and 'exists' does not signify a quality, relation, dimension or state, etc.

N2(M1). If Unity does not exist, what predicates attach consequentially to the field? Plainly, the field must by definition be other, yet it cannot be other than Unity, since this, by hypothesis, does not exist for the field to be demarcated against it. The field must be other in the sense that its members are other than one another.

Yet, since Unity does not exist, the members of the field cannot be unitary or be units; so the field can only be a manifold of manifolds without end. Only of such manifolds can we say that they are other than each other—since there is nothing else to say it of. Each manifold of manifolds will seem to be single, though not really being so. And numbers will seem to be applicable to them, though the seeming will be illusory. Derivatively, the concepts of odd and even, greater, smaller and equal, limit and unlimitedness will appear to have application, together with those of unity and plurality, similarity and dissimilarity, etc., etc. Yet if unity does not exist, none of these concepts can really have application to the field.

N2(M2). If Unity does not exist, the field cannot be single, nor can it be a plurality, else it would be *one* plurality and its members would be units. Nor could the field seem to be either single or a plurality. For since there is no Unity, there is nothing of the sort for the field to exemplify or participate in in any respect whatsoever. So the field cannot be thought, even, to be single or plural or to be an instance of anything else, such as similarity or dissimilarity, identity or otherness, contact or separation, or anything else at all. The field could not therefore be thought to exist. So if Unity does not exist, nothing exists. So, whether Unity exists or not, Unity and the field both have and lack every predicate and its opposite. 'Very true' is the last word of the dialogue.

What is the outcome of all this tiresome chain of operations? First, *ad hominem* it seems to have been proved, in the case of at least one extremely eminent Form, what Socrates was reluctant to believe could be proved, that a Form does undergo hosts of incompatible predicates, and that these disagreeable consequences flow not only from the palatable hypothesis that that Form exists but also from the unpalatable hypothesis that it does not exist.

But what does Plato think to be the important lesson of the whole dialogue? Here we can only make more or less plausible conjectures.

(1) Plato might think that the whole argument proves that no universal can be the subject of an attributive or relational proposition; and he may have confused with this the quite different point that no universal can be the subject of an affirmative or negative existence-proposition. (For he may have thought wrongly, as Descartes and Meinong did, that 'exists' is a predicate of the same category, i.e.

with the same sort of logical behaviour, as 'is square' or 'is green'.) Universals are not substances, or abstract nouns are not proper names, and sentences in which we talk as if they were are logically vicious.

This conclusion is true, and relevant to the question of the truth of the Theory of Forms. So it may be what Plato had in his mind.

(2) But Plato may be apprising himself and us of a seemingly more parochial discovery, namely that some concepts do not behave in the same way as some others.

He may, for example, be making the discovery that 'exists' and 'does not exist' do not have the same sort of logical behaviour as 'breathes' or 'resembles' or 'is square'. If we consider the concepts which occur in our ordinary descriptions and classifications of things, they seem to fit reasonably well into scales of genera and species. And we can imagine a table depicting all the ladders or pyramids of generic and specific concepts, such that any descriptive or classificatory concept would have its place fixed for it somewhere in one and not more than one such ladder or pyramid. But there are some concepts which can be peculiar to no one ladder or pyramid but must somehow pervade them all. Such are the concepts answering to expressions like 'not', 'exists', 'same', 'other', 'is an instance of', 'is a species of', 'single', 'plural' and many others. Some concepts are 'syncategorematic'.

At first sight we may be tempted to take such concepts, which are obviously of very general application, to be merely highly generic concepts, perhaps actually Summa Genera. But if we do so take them, our enterprise collapses, for just these concepts are again required when we attempt to describe the affiliations or non-affiliations between Summa Genera themselves, and also between the sub-divisions, not of one but of all the sort-hierarchies.

Formal concepts, as we may now call them, differ from generic ones not in being higher than they in the way in which they are higher than specific concepts, but in some other way. They differ from generic concepts not, for example, as 'Even Number' differs from '2', but as ' + ' and '√' differ from either.

Or again, to pick up again the two analogies which Plato uses in the *Theaetetus* and the *Sophist*, formal concepts differ from generic and specific concepts not as one letter of the alphabet differs from another or as one bunch of letters differs from another bunch of letters, but as the mode in which letters are arranged into a syllable or word differs from the letters which are so arranged: or else as the way in which nouns, verbs, adjectives, etc., are combined to form a significant sentence is different from those elements or even from the way in which one such element, like a noun, differs from another, like a preposition. What a grammatical construction is to the words of a sentence embodying that construction, that a formal concept is to the terms (particulars and ordinary universals) which enter into the proposition or judgement.

Now when we treat a formal concept as if it were a non-formal or proper concept, we are committing a breach of 'logical syntax'. But what shows us that we are doing this? The deductive derivation of absurdities and contradictions shows it, and nothing else can. Russell's proof that, in his code-symbolism, φ cannot be a value of x in the propositional function φx is only another exercise in the same genre as Plato's proof that 'Unity' cannot go into the gap in the sentence-frame '. . . exists' or '. . . does not exist'.[1]

I feel fairly sure that this is something like the point which Plato was trying to reveal in this dialogue. I feel this partly because the imputed doctrine is true and important and partly because, so construed, the dialogue then links on directly to the later parts of the *Theaetetus* and to almost the whole of the *Sophist*. Whereas the first interpretation which I suggested has no echoes of importance in either dialogue.

Moreover, we know that Aristotle was alive to the fact that there was a special crux about Unity and Existence; and also that these concepts with some others (e.g. Good) did not come under any one of the Categories but exhibited themselves in all of the Categories: nor were they concepts of the genus–species sort.[2]

And (in *Met.* 1003b and 1053b) he uses for both 'existence' and 'singleness' the argument which Hume and Kant used for 'existence', to show that they do not signify attributes; namely that the descriptions of a man, an existent man and a single man are not descriptions of different sorts of men.

And lastly I am tempted to prefer this interpretation to the other on the score that it does more credit to Plato's powers of discerning the important in logical questions. There is, indeed, an agreeable sweepingness in that suggested message of the dialogue according to

[1] It is worth noticing that the concept of being-an-instance-of, about which the discussion turned in the first part of the dialogue, is in fact a form-concept, and not a proper concept; the contradictions and circles which embarrassed Socrates did arise from his attempt to treat it as if it was from the same basket with ordinary relations. However, Plato does not point this out. We can conjecture that the second part of the dialogue does contain (between the lines) the answer to the problem of the first part; but we cannot say that Plato was aware of it.
[2] And *cf. De Interpr.* 16b, where Aristotle explicitly says that 'is' and 'is not' only function significantly in the assertion of some synthesis, and cannot be thought except together with what is combined in such a synthesis.

which Plato was proving the general point that universals are not subjects of qualities or relations. But its sweepingness would only be *sanitary*, for it would only be establishing the negative point that there was something wrong with the foundations of the theory of Forms.

It would have small instructive effect on thinkers who had never adopted the belief that abstract nouns are the names of substances.

It would leave open and, worse, it would leave almost unformulated the profounder question, What is wrong with those foundations? *This* question requires the discovery of the difference between formal and non-formal concepts—and this discovery is required for all sorts of logical problems, and not only this special historical one of the nature of the fallacy underlying the special doctrine of Substantial Forms.

One objection to the foregoing interpretation of the dialogue is sure to be made. It is incredible, it will be said, that the central doctrine of Platonism, namely, that Circularity, Unity, Difference, etc., exist, should be shown by Plato himself to be logically vicious, even though he mitigates the cruelty of his exposure of his earlier children by showing that there would be a precisely parallel viciousness in the doctrine that they do *not* exist. On minor points, doubtless, Plato's second thoughts might be expected to be improvements on his first thoughts, but that he should overtly demonstrate the untenability of the very principles of the system from which his whole influence upon subsequent thinking derives is too shocking a supposition.

But such an objection does less than justice to a great philosopher. Kant is felicitated for being capable of being awoken from dogmatic slumbers; Aristotle is permitted to be fonder of truth than of Platonism; those of Russell's contributions to logical theory are considered important which belong to the periods after his affiliation to Kant, Bradley, and Bosanquet. Why must Plato alone be forbidden the illuminations of self-criticism?

Moreover, it has long been recognised that in the whole period which includes the writing of the *Theaetetus*, the *Sophist*, the *Politicus*, and the *Philebus*, Plato's thinking is not entirely, if at all, governed by the premisses of the Theory of Forms.

He attends to the theory on occasions, but he does so in a dispassionate and critical way. In the *Sophist* (246) the exponents of the theory of Forms are treated in the same way as are the materialists; neither can answer the Eleatic Stranger's puzzles about existence and non-existence. Similarly in the *Philebus* (15). Moreover, if it is true that the theory of Substantial Forms embodied radical fallacies, to praise Plato as a great philosopher, as we do, would be consistent with crediting him both with the acumen to recognise and the candour to expose them.

But more important than these considerations is this fact. Whatever its sublimity and inspiration-value, the Theory of Forms had been from the start, *inter alia*, a doctrine intended to resolve certain puzzles of a purely logical nature. How can several things be called by one name or be of one sort or character? And how is it that only those systems of propositions express certain knowledge which contain neither the names nor the descriptions of actual instances of sorts or characters—namely mathematics and philosophy?

The Theory of Forms was intended to answer both these questions. It fails to be a satisfactory theory, for the reason, mainly, that exactly analogous questions arise about Substantial Forms to those questions about the instances of Forms which the theory had been intended to resolve. And in so far it was the wrong sort of answer.

But something remains. It remains true that every judgement or proposition embodies at least one non-singular term or element. It remains true that the propositions of mathematics are universal propositions. And it remains true that in some sense, some or all philosophical questions are of the pattern 'What is it for something to be so-and-so?' (where 'being-so-and-so' is a universal).

The criticisms of the doctrine of Substantial Forms given in the dialogue have no tendency to upset these positions even if they do not directly yield an answer to the problems which they raise. But the road is cleared for an answer to them, a road which was blocked by the fascinating but erroneous theory which they dispose of. Nor could the new advances have been begun save by someone who had himself gone through the stage of being at least very familiar with the theory of Substantial Forms.

In particular, I shall suggest, the road is now cleared for the advance which was partially made in the *Sophist*, where for the first time the possibility and the need of a theory of categories or types is realised.[1] The distinction between generic concepts and formal concepts is here seen or half-seen, and logical enquiries are at last capable of being begun.

In fine, on my theory, the *Parmenides* is a discussion of a problem of logic—as part of the *Theaetetus* and most of the *Sophist* were discussions of problems in logic. Not that Plato *says*, 'Let us turn back from Ethics, Metaphysics, Epistemology and Physics and

---

[1] I use the word 'category' in a less misleadingly precise way than Aristotle.

consider some questions belonging to the province of Logic', for these titles did not exist.

But his questions and his arguments in this dialogue should be classified by us as belonging to the same sphere to which belong, for example, Aristotle's theory of Categories, Kant's separation of formal from non-formal concepts, Russell's theory of types, and Wittgenstein's and Carnap's theories of logical syntax.

Whether, if I am right, the dialogue is interesting is a question of taste. The central problem seems to me of radical importance and therefore interesting, potentially, to any philosopher who cares to get down to the roots. But the detail of the argument is arid and formalistic and so sustained that everyone must find it tedious—in the same way as the methodical dissection of Vicious Circle Fallacies is tedious if it is thorough.

I do not think that the dialogue could or should be interesting to a student who is primarily anxious to know Plato's later views about the human soul, or God, or immortality, or physics, or Parmenidean Monism. For, as I read it, the dialogue contains no references to such topics and no premisses from which conclusions about these topics can be deduced.

The dialogue is an exercise in the grammar and not in the prose or the poetry of philosophy.

To corroborate the foregoing theory about the programme of the *Parmenides*, I append some remarks about the *Theaetetus* and the *Sophist*, in which, I think, the same or kindred lines of thought are to be traced. These dialogues were certainly composed close to the date of the *Parmenides*. The *Sophist*, which is a sort of sequel to the *Theaetetus*, was certainly written after the *Parmenides*, to which indeed it makes one or two undoubted allusions and of which, in an important stretch, it partly echoes and partly presupposes a part of the dialectical operations. The *Theaetetus* was almost certainly in part, and perhaps as a whole, composed after the *Parmenides*, and it contains what is probably a reference to it.

THE 'THEAETETUS'

With the main problem of this dialogue I have here no special concern. It is an enquiry into the nature of knowledge. It begins with a sustained exposition and criticism of the theory that to know something is to have sense-acquaintance with it or memory of sense-acquaintance with it. It is soon shown that neither this theory nor a more generalised analogue to it can account for our knowledge about the future, or of the truth of theories about what is right or expedient, especially of the truth or falsehood of this theory of knowledge itself, or even of mathematical truths. And it is briefly indicated that even within the field of the objects of sense-acquaintance it will not do. For to know that sense-given objects exist or do not exist, are similar or different, single or plural is to do or experience something more than merely having sense-acquaintance. So a new hypothesis is considered, the gap between which and the previous view is of the greatest importance not only for the theory of knowledge, but also for our special problem. For it is now suggested that to know is to judge, or is a species of judging. And this means—to bring together threads from earlier and later parts of the dialogue—that knowledge requires for its expression not just a name but a sentence or statement. And what a sentence or statement expresses always contains a plurality, at least a duality, of distinguishable elements or factors. Knowledge, as well as true and false belief and opinion, cannot be expressed just by a proper name or demonstrative for some simple object, but only by a complex of words which together constitute a sentence.

At this point Socrates does something which at first sight seems to be deserting the direct path in order to follow up a side-track. For he suddenly opens up a prolonged enquiry into the nature of false beliefs or mistakes, and is of necessity at once led to debate how we can either think or state that which is not. How can I either think or describe something which is not there to be the object of a thought or description? But I think that this is in fact no digression at all. For, first, it is true that I can only be described as knowing the same sort of things as I could be described as mistaken about. To know is, at the least, to be under no mistake. And, second, any description of any actual or possible mistake automatically reveals the complexity both of what is falsely judged and, correspondingly, of what would be truly judged. For to mistake is to take something for something instead of for something else.

So a 'simple' could never be the object of a mistake. I could mistakenly think that $7 + 5 = 11$, and unmistakenly judge or know that $7 + 5 = 12$. But 7 could not be the total object of a mistake, and so, by implication, not the total object of a piece of true belief or knowledge either. And this is what was at bottom wrong with the equation of knowledge with sense-acquaintance. This noise or that stench is not the sort of thing that could be described as what I mistakenly believe, and therefore it is not the sort of thing which could be described as what I correctly believe or know. There must

37

be a complex of distinguishable elements as well in what I know as in what I mistakenly or correctly believe. What I know are facts, and facts always have some complexity. So 'simples' could not be facts, though they would be elements in facts. Only a proper name could directly stand for a simple, and only a sentence could state a fact.

Now, without raising for the moment the question what are the simples or elements of which what I know or believe are complexes, or even whether there are any such elements, we can see that a complex of elements must be one of two things. Either it is just a lot or assemblage of elements or it is some sort of union of or fabric embodying them. *Either* the required complex of elements A, B and C just is A and B and C, so that to know the complex would just be to know A and to know B, and to know C, which would merely be to go back on the result already arrived at and to suppose that what can be named but not stated could be what I know. *Or* the required complex is some sort of an organised whole, of which the principle of organisation is distinguishable from the elements which it combines. And in this case the principle of organisation is something unitary and not to be resolved into a plurality of elements; that is, it is a new 'simple', somehow superadded to the original elements which it organises into the single complex. But if we may not say that simples are what we know, we may not say it either of this new combining simple.

This point is brought out by means of the analogy of letters in syllables. A syllable is a complex of letters, which themselves are not complexes. Now *either* a syllable is nothing but the lot of letters in it, in which case to know it is just to know each of them, an illegitimate hypothesis if what I know must always be a complex. *Or* a syllable is some ordered arrangement of letters. But in this case the order of arrangement *is* not a lot of letters but something unitary and irresoluble. And then it is an extra simple element (though not, of course, one of the same type as a letter). Finally it is argued, on the tacit assumption that by a 'complex' can only be meant either a conjunction of similar elements ('letters') or a conjunction of some elements of one sort ('letters') plus at least one element of a different sort ('order of arrangement'), that in fact such conjunctions or assemblages are not more knowable but less easily knowable than what they are conjunctions of.

If knowing was inventorying collections, certainly simple elements could not be known. But in fact, whatever knowing is, collections are not more accessible to knowledge than their members are. Moreover, inventories are just as well capable of being the objects of true or false beliefs as of knowledge. So the differentia of knowledge is not to be found in this direction.

Now this discussion reveals at least two extremely important points.

(1) It is true that if the universe contains simples, such that for each there could be, in principle, a proper name, the utterance just of this proper name could not be the expression of true or false belief or of knowledge (in the sense of 'knowledge that . . .'). What I believe or know requires a whole sentence for its expression, and what a sentence states is *in some sense* a complex. It is always possible to find for any sentence another sentence the signification of which is *partly* similar and *partly* dissimilar to that of the given sentence, i.e. what a sentence says contains parts or factors distinguishable from each other and capable of some independent variations by substitution.

Now, though Plato does not make this application, Substantial Forms were supposed to be just such simple namables. And if we ask ourselves: What would it be like to be knowing Equality or knowing Justice or knowing Existence?, and, still more, if we ask: What would it be like to be mistaken about Equality or Justice or Existence?, we find ourselves bothered and bothered for the very reason that Plato here gives, namely that we know that when we describe ourselves as 'believing or knowing so and so', a proper name cannot go into the place of the accusative to those verbs.

Oddly, Professor Cornford, who approves of the refutation of the view that knowing is having sense-acquaintance, since knowing is, or is a species of, judging, still believes that Plato's real theory of knowledge, unexpressed in this dialogue, was that Substantial Forms are what knowledge is of. Yet this would involve that 'Equality' and 'Circularity' do express knowledge, for all that it would be nonsense to assert that any such abstract noun could express either a mistaken or a true belief.

Socrates draws attention to an important affiliated point when he asks how we can mistake one thing for another either when we know both (supposing still that we may speak of knowing 'things'), or when we know neither, or when we know one and not the other. And he asks: Who has ever mistaken the number 11 for the number 12 or vice versa, for all that plenty of people have taken 7 + 5 to equal 11? No one has ever told himself that an ox must be a horse or that two must be one, that beauty is ugliness or justice is injustice. By analogy we might ask (though Socrates does not): Who ever told himself the infallible tidings that 11 is not 12 or that 11 is 11, that justice is not injustice or that ugliness is ugliness?

It is tempting to suggest that the moral of this puzzle and of later developments of it is something like this, that while a mistaken or a true judgement must contain some plurality of elements, this requirement as it stands is too hospitable. Not any combination of any sorts of elements constitutes a possible mistake, or in consequence, a possible truth. '$7 + 5 = 11$' is a possible mistake, but '12 is 11' is not. 'Theaetetus is Theodorus' is not a possible mistake, but 'Theaetetus is the son of Theodorus' is. The elements of what I know or believe will not all be of the same type. But Plato does not here allude to any such lesson.

(2) But anyhow it is unquestionable that Plato is in this dialogue alive to the following matters. What I know or truly believe or falsely believe is some sort of a complex of elements, and one the verbal statement of which requires not a name only, nor even a conjunction of names, but a complex expression of which the special form of unity is that of a sentence. What constitutes a complex, like a syllable, a unity is some feature of it other than any one or the mere lot of its elements, such as letters.

That is, Plato is now considering the places and roles of 'terms' in truths and falsehoods, with his eye on the underlying question of what are the principles of organisation which govern the combination of such 'terms'. He does not say, nor are we warranted in inferring from the contents of this dialogue that he saw, that there are some concepts, namely form-concepts, which cannot do duty for proper concepts or ordinary 'terms', much less that he saw that 'exists', 'not', 'one', 'several' and others do express such form-concepts. But it is clear that he is consciously developing a method of inspecting the formal properties of such complexes of elements as constitute truths and falsehoods. He knows that names are not true or false, that sentences are not names, that sentences are not just assemblages of names or composite names resoluble without residue into several component names; and he knows that nothing less than sentences will express what we know or truly or falsely believe. A mere inventory of namable simples would not only not be all that we know, or wish to know, it would not even be any part of what we know or wish to know.

In any truth or falsehood there must be some multiplicity of distinguishable factors, and of these at least some perform a different sort of function from some others—the order of arrangement of letters in a syllable does not play the same sort of role and so is not the same type of factor as the individual letters. Of course, Plato has not got a substitution-method, or, what this involves, a code-symbolism with which to indicate those similarities and differences of factor-types which sanction or veto particular substitutions. But that there is a co-functioning of distinguishable factors in truths and falsehoods and that their functions are not all similar is, I suggest, a thing which Plato is here clearly realising.

THE 'SOPHIST'

This dialogue begins with an attempt to arrive at a clear definition of what constitutes a Sophist. Its method is that of dichotomous division. Some highly generic concept, which is assumed without proof to be the correct one, is divided into two species, one of these is then similarly divided into two sub-species, and so on until a point is reached where the concept under enquiry is seen to be such and such a sub-sub-species of the original genus. Many commentators regard this method of Dichotomous Division as a grand discovery of Plato, and some even identify it with the Method of Dialectic for which Plato makes his famous claims. It is clear to me that the Method of Dialectic as this is described in outline in the *Republic* and in detail in the *Parmenides* and the later parts of the *Sophist*, and is actually exercised in the second part of the *Parmenides*, has almost nothing to do with the Method of Division. The Method of Dialectic has links with Zeno's antinomian operations, or it may just be an expansion of them; but this process of Dichotomous Division is an operation of quite a different sort. In particular, it is not a process of *demonstration*, as Aristotle points out.[1]

Whether Plato did or did not believe that the Method of Division was a powerful philosophic instrument, we can be quite clear that it is not so. No philosopher, including Plato, has ever tried to employ it for the resolution of any serious philosophical problem, and if they had done so they would not have succeeded. For first of all it can only be applied to concepts of the genus-species or determinable-determinate sort, and it is not concepts of this sort that in general, if ever, engender philosophical problems. And, next, most generic concepts do not subdivide into just two polarly opposed species; usually there are numerous species of a genus or sub-species of a species.[2] And the question whether a sort divides into two or seventeen sub-sorts is, in general, a purely empirical question. So nearly any case of a philosopher's operation by Division could be upset by the subsequent empirical discovery of sorts lying on neither

[1] In *Prior Analytics*, 46a, *Posterior Analytics*, 91 b and 96 b.
[2] *Cf.* Aristotle's criticism of the programme of dichotomous division, *De Part. An.* 642.

side of the philosopher's boundary lines. And, finally, there is room for almost any amount of arbitrariness in the selection from the ladders of sorts *en route* for the definition of a given concept. Except in artificial hierarchies, such as library catalogues and regimental ranks, there are few, if any, rigid scales of kinds. So there are many tolerable and no perfect ways of defining most of the sort-concepts that we employ.

Had Plato wished to exhibit these and kindred blemishes in the programme of definition by Dichotomous Division, he could have chosen no more effective procedure than that of exhibiting several definitions of one and the same concept, all achieved by descending different scales of kinds. And this is what in fact he does. He gives six or seven different definitions of 'sophist', all arrived at by different paths. However, he does not say that he is revealing defects in the method, and the subsequent dialogue, the *Politicus*, is another exercise in it; so some of his commentators may be right in believing that Plato thought well of its potentialities.

However, there is a pair of concepts which are forced upon our notice in the course of the operations which turn out to require a very different sort of elucidation, namely those of non-existence and existence. For a Sophist is a pretender who either thinks or says that what is not so is so. The puzzle which arose in the *Theaetetus* arises again here. How can what does not exist be named, described or thought of? And if it cannot, how can we or Sophists talk or think of it, falsely, as existing? So the question is squarely put: What does it mean to assert or deny existence of something?

What do Pluralists *or* Monists mean when they assert that there exist a lot of things or that there exists only one thing? What do materialists *or* idealists mean when they assert or deny that bodies or that Forms are real?

Now, it is of the first importance for our main question to notice certain points. (1) With reference to Parmenidean Monism it is shown that the concepts of Unity and Existence interlock in an important way, without being identical. And part of the argumentation of the *Parmenides* is echoed here upon just this matter. (2) No attempt is made to elucidate the concepts of existence and non-existence by the Method of Division. The heroic attempt of Meinong to show that they are co-ordinate species of a generic concept is not anticipated by Plato. And we can see—so perhaps Plato saw—that the Method would not work just because these concepts are *not* sort-concepts, but that there is an important difference between sort-concepts and these two which is the source of the inapplicability of the Method of Division to them. (3) There are some other concepts, identity, otherness, change and changelessless which have to be operated upon alongside of existence and non-existence. (4) The procedure of investigating the interrelations of these concepts is called Dialectic—which, I think, is only remotely connected with the operation of tracing out sort-hierarchies which is called Division.

Now in attempting to elucidate the concepts of existence and non-existence, Plato makes use of two analogies, one of which he had used in the *Theaetetus*. Namely, he compares the ways in which some concepts will combine in only certain ways with certain others (*a*) to the ways in which letters will only admit of certain sorts of alliances so as to form syllables, and later (*b*) to the ways in which words will admit only of certain sorts of alliances so as to form sentences.

For a syllable to be constituted vowels must be there as well as consonants, and for a sentence to be constituted a noun must be conjoined with a verb and not a noun with a noun or a verb with a verb. If we like to build metaphors from these analogies we can say that some, but not all, concepts must be 'vowel'-concepts, or that some, but not all, concepts must be 'syntax'-concepts as opposed to 'vocabulary'-concepts. And existence and non-existence are of these new types.

It is further indicated (253, 259, 260b) that these two concepts of existence and non-existence, together with certain others which are associated with them, namely changes and changelessness, otherness and identity, are in an important way pervasive—they crop up, that is, in all the Division-scales in which we locate other concepts, in the same sort of way, I take it, as 'non-existence' cropped up in one of the definitions of 'sophist'. We are reminded of Aristotle's assertion that Existence and Unity and Goodness belong to no one of the Categories but pervade them all, though his Categories are not, of course, Summa Genera.

There appears, then, to be quite good internal evidence in the *Sophist* for the view that Plato was now discerning an important difference between types of concepts or universals, and in particular that concepts of sorts, which can be scaled with or without precision in hierarchies of genera, species and sub-species, obey very different rules from some others, like existence and non-existence. And the concepts of this latter class perform what I may call a logical role which is analogous to the role of vowels in syllables or that of syntax-rules in sentences. They function not like the bricks but like the arrangement of the bricks in a building.

Now the interesting thing is that it is true that existence and non-existence are what we should call 'formal concepts', and further that if modern logicians were asked to describe the way in which formal concepts differ from proper or material or content-concepts, their method of exhibiting the role of formal concepts would be similar to that adopted here by Plato. But we need not go further than to say that Plato was becoming aware of some important differences of type between concepts. There is no evidence of his anticipating Aristotle's enquiry into the principles of inference, which enquiry it is which first renders the antithesis of formal and other concepts the dominant consideration. There is, consequently, in Plato, no essay at abstracting the formal from the contentual features of propositions, and so no code-symbolisation for the formal in abstraction from the material features of propositions.

There is, of course, always a considerable hazard in attempting to elucidate a doctrine of an earlier philosopher in the light of subsequent and especially of contemporary doctrines. It is always tempting and often easy to read palatable lessons between the lines of some respected but inexplicit Scripture. But the opposite policy of trying to chart the drift of some adolescent theory without reference to the progress of any more adult theories is subject not to the risk but to the certainty of failure. We cannot even state what was a philosopher's puzzle, much less what was the direction or efficacy of his attempt to solve it, unless subsequent reflections have thrown a clearer light upon the matter than he was able to do. Whether a commentator has found such a light or only a will-of-the-wisp is always debatable and often very well worth debating.

Thus I may be wrong in believing that there are affinities between Plato's enquiries in these dialogues and Hume's and Kant's accounts of assertions of existence, Kant's account of forms of judgement and categories, Russell's doctrine of propositional functions and theory of types, and, perhaps, more than any other, nearly the whole of Wittgenstein's *Tractatus Logico-Philosophicus*. I may be wrong in construing these dialogues as, so to speak, forecasting most of the logical embarrassments into which the infinitely courageous and pertinacious Meinong was to fall. But at least my error, if it is one, does not imply that Plato's puzzles were so factitious or ephemeral that no other serious philosopher has ever experienced any perplexity about them.

2

REVIEW OF F. M. CORNFORD:
'PLATO AND PARMENIDES'

Reprinted from 'Mind', vol. XLVIII, *1939*

In his new book Professor Cornford tackles the long-vexed question of the interpretation of Plato's baffling dialogue, the *Parmenides*. It will be welcomed by all students of Greek thought on many scores, but above all because it not merely suggests a quite plausible construction of the dialogue, but supports it by a detailed analysis of the intricate stages of its argument.

In the first sixty pages of the book, Professor Cornford brings together all that is known or can reasonably be conjectured about the Pythagorean cosmogony and about Parmenides' own 'Way of Truth', together with an examination of the historical setting and bearings of Zeno's famous dialectical operations. These chapters are valuable in themselves and especially useful for showing in what ways problems close to the heart of the dialogue, which seems so strained and arid to us, were very much burning questions in Plato's time.

When he comes to the *Parmenides* itself, Professor Cornford adopts the method which he has employed elsewhere, of giving a translation of the dialogue interspersed with exegesis. This ensures that the detail of the arguments is not relegated to semi-oblivion before the discussion of their sources, validity and relevance is entered upon. The lesson and the sermon go hand in hand.

The *general* position taken up is as follows. The dialogue is intended to be a serious discussion of an important problem or tissue of problems. There is in it nothing of the skit which some scholars have professed to find—and to find diverting. Nor, on the other hand, is there any foretaste of a Neoplatonic theology in it. Rather, to use a terminology which could not be pre-Aristotelian, it is a discussion of a *logical* problem or set of problems. And the problem under discussion is one known to and discussed by Aristotle. He recognised its importance and its difficulty; and his answer to it is, anyhow in part, already in Plato's mind, though Plato does not formulate the

REVIEW OF F. M. CORNFORD: 'PLATO AND PARMENIDES

REVIEW OF F. M. CORNFORD: 'PLATO AND PARMENIDES

answer so much as force his hearers and readers towards it by exhibiting the untenability of any more simple-minded position. The logical problem is closely connected both with the very roots of the doctrine of Substantial Forms and with the premisses and conclusions of Parmenidean Monism. And, lastly, it is affiliated to central issues in the adjacent dialogues, the *Theaetetus* and the *Sophist*. All these points seem to me to be true and important and even if there remain, as I think there do remain, certain residual matters where there is room for differences of opinion, the progress already made is notable. For now, at last, the force and the drift of the actual arguments of the dialogue have become discussible. It is no longer a question of decoding an inscription in an unknown tongue, but of debating alternative translations of a clause in a passage from a language of which we are already familiar with both the vocabulary and the grammar.

Professor Cornford's *special* thesis is this, that after showing that there were genuine logical difficulties in the doctrine of separately existing Forms, which he does in the first part of the dialogue, Plato then goes on to give a fully worked out exercise in a particular sort of philosophical method, namely, one the object of which was to show that certain terms, especially 'one', 'existent' and 'non-existent', are the residences of numerous dangerous equivocations. To yield to the natural temptation to treat them as univocal is to slide down a slippery slope into logical absurdities. The early doctrine of separately existing Forms had been subject to this peril, for it had been wont too naïvely to glorify these Forms as being unitary (as against the plurality either of their instances *or* of their constituent Forms which definitions would reveal) and as existent (as against the relative unreality of their instances). But still more deeply involved had been Parmenides' own Monism, since it had asserted that only what was absolutely unitary really existed. 'Unity' and 'Being' came, virtually, to being alternative proper names for the same thing, and that the only thing. That there are ambiguities in these terms is shown by the procedure, which apes but is not the same as Zeno's *reductio ad absurdum* method, of deducing from *apparently* the same premiss sets of *apparently* conflicting conclusions. What these arguments really show, though Plato leaves this to be understood, is that the premisses from which these apparently conflicting conclusions flow, are not identical, save in diction. 'One' and 'exist' are being used in one sense in one operation, and in another in the next, and so on. So each separate argument is, or is intended to be, valid. And the conclusions do not really conflict, since their premisses have, save verbally, different subjects and predicates. Aristotle often formulates (though without using this method of argumentation) what Plato shows by his argumentation (but does not formulate), when he says that 'one' and 'exist' are 'used in many senses'.

I believe this special thesis to be mistaken; but it is following the wrong scent in the right country and with the right sort of pack. In criticising it with detailed arguments, therefore, I mean it to be clear that I regard the question as being, at last, the proper question. It is because, after too many false starts, the hunt is now nearing its end, that I want to lift the pack off what I think is a false scent.

And in particular, though I dispute Professor Cornford's account of both the goal and the procedure of the dialectic, I know of no discussion which throws anything like so much light as his does upon the meanings, sources and affiliations of the multifarious steps of the whole complex of deductions. And if I concentrate solely upon what I dispute in his thesis, it is because this is the only way that I know of treating it as seriously as it deserves.

My first objection is this. The dialogue begins with a rejoinder by Socrates to a particular specimen of Zeno's *reductio ad absurdum* method. His rejoinder having been shown to contain either fallacies or lacunae, Socrates issues the challenge to be shown that Forms can themselves be proved to be subject to incompatible predicates, i.e. that the *reductio ad absurdum* method can be applied to the hypothesis that there exist Forms. Parmenides urges Socrates to undergo a certain sort of logical discipline before launching out into constructive theories, and the discipline recommended is the practice of the Zenonian *reductio* method, but with a certain expansion. Zeno had, perhaps from polemical motives, torpedoed a given hypothesis by deducing absurdities from it. Socrates is urged to try the same procedure upon *both* a given hypothesis *and* its negative. And Parmenides is persuaded to give an example of this two-way Zenonian enquiry. Now, unless the whole of this preface is conscious and pointless deception on Plato's part, the second part of the dialogue must (1) be a *reductio ad absurdum* argument; and (2) be an application of it to *one* hypothesis and its negative. The identity of this hypothesis in half the operations and the identity of its negative in the other half must be not merely a delusive identity of diction, but be, or be thought to be, a real identity. And this means that 'one' and 'exist' must be supposed by Plato to be univocal throughout the whole argument.

In corroboration of this, it should be noticed that according to Professor Cornford one, but only one, of the various meanings of the subject-term in all the hypotheses is Unity, the Form or universal, that of which there are or could be instances. But it was only about Forms that Socrates was concerned to discover whether or not there could be produced conflicting predications; and it was only from a collection of Forms that Parmenides selected what was to be the subject of his hypothesis. Indeed the whole preliminary inquest upon Socrates' doctrine of Forms would, I think, have been a complete red-herring if the lengthy remainder of the dialogue was not going, save *per accidens*, to be about Forms at all, but primarily about certain quite different sorts of assumptions resident in Parmenidean Monism. The evidence of Aristotle, I think, really supports this. For whole certainly Aristotle professes—I think unsuccessfully—to resolve certain logical difficulties about 'one' and 'existent' by finding that they have a variety of significations, the various significations which he distinguishes are still different *universals*. It is the various *predicative* uses of these adjectives to which he draws attention, as when he points out that the phrases 'a man', 'an unitary man' and 'an existent man' mean the same thing, which would not be the case with ordinary adjectives.

And, again, when he points out that 'existence' and 'unity' are not co-ordinate species of a genus, and neither is a species of the other, and that an ascription of either entails the ascription of the other, he is noticing that these 'universals' behave in a very different way from the ways in which ordinary universals behave, those, namely, which accept classification as being of this or of that category.

To come more closely to the special point of Professor Cornford's view. He maintains that Plato is compelling the realisation that certain words are ambiguous. Now we should distinguish, as perhaps Aristotle partly does, between two sorts of ambiguity. There is the uninteresting *local* sort, which I may call 'dictionary-ambiguity', where in a particular language like Greek, a given noise or mark has different and unconnected uses (as 'malo' does in Latin). And this seems to be the sort of ambiguity which Professor Cornford has in mind, for he says that the ambiguities which Plato is revealing are 'owing to certain peculiarities in Greek grammar'. And he admits, what his practice shows, that it is not easy to find in English correspondingly equivocal expressions. On this showing Plato was only trying to show that the Greek language contained some unsuspected founts of puns; though this might be quite a useful if humdrum task, since philosophical theories certainly can be perverted by local ambiguities of this type. Yet to employ so elaborate and systematic a procedure for achieving this end would be like using all the resources of a smithy in order to crack nuts.

But there are ambiguities of another sort, which are, I suspect, nearer to what Aristotle had in mind; and ambiguities of this type can be expected to show themselves similarly in all languages, however different their vocabularies may be. I refer to what are sometimes called 'systematic ambiguities'. An expression undergoes systematic modifications in its significance according to the type of context in which it is used. For example, both 'very' and 'punctual' undergo these modifications in the three assertions: 'You were very punctual for breakfast to-day', 'You are a very punctual sort of man', and 'Naval officers are a very punctual class'. The first says, 'You arrived almost exactly at breakfast time—and this is unusual'; the second says, 'You are more prone than most people to keep appointments on time'; and the third says, 'Naval officers as a class are more prone than most other classes to be on time for appointments'. And these uses are different, but connected, and connected in the same sort of way as would be the corresponding uses of 'rather irritable' or 'pretty tidy'. That 'very punctual' has different significations here is easy to show. For it would be absurd to say 'You were more punctual for breakfast to-day than most men are', or 'than the class of naval officers is'. Now, certainly 'one' and 'existing' are subject to systematic ambiguities of this sort, for all expressions are so subject. But even if they are, and even if, what is dubious, this is something like what Aristotle had in mind, it is not the case that all the puzzles about 'unity' and 'existence' would be cleared up by distinguishing between the multifarious context-modifications to which they are liable. For it will still be true that in none of these distinguishable uses will they behave in the way we expect predicate-expressions to behave, if we are predisposed to expect all predicate-expressions to behave like 'green' or 'punctual' or 'irritable'. They still will not behave like 'ordinary' subjects or predicates. They misbehave if treated like 'ordinary' subjects of attributes or attributes of subjects. To this extent Aristotle's solution was inadequate. For even if these terms are shown to have several roles, yet still these roles are unlike the roles of 'ordinary' words, i.e. those expressing concepts falling under this or that Aristotelian category. However, it could well be that what Aristotle did not see, Plato had not seen either; and that what Aristotle thought, if wrongly, was an adequate clue to the riddle, Plato had thought also, if wrongly, to be an adequate clue.

Next, Professor Cornford admits that it is odd that Parmenides, having promised to produce a dialectical operation having four main stages, should then produce one having in fact eight (or nine) stages. On his showing, these eight (or nine) stages have to be separate, else the first operation, say, would be proving the precise opposite of what the second operation proves, and so on; whereas his interpretation requires that each of the eight or nine movements should be, or be intended to be, a valid argument for a set of true conclusions, in only seeming, because merely verbal, conflict with the results of the other movements. Now he is here maintaining two different, though connected, positions. (1) First he is denying that the second part of the dialogue is what had been promised in the first part and what seems from the wording and the arrangement of the deductions to be fulfilled, namely, a quadrupedal *reductio ad absurdum* argument, each quarter of which consists of two 'claws' such that the conclusions of the one are the direct antitheses of those of its counterpart. We were promised and seem to have been given a series of pairs of arguments, of which the former establishes the possession by a given subject of both and the second establishes its possession of neither out of several couples of opposite predicates. According to Professor Cornford, no such antinomies are really produced or intended to be believed to be produced. The semblance of the contradictions is intended only to advertise the plurality of meanings of the original premisses. (2) But this involves him in denying something further. Plato *seems* to have exhibited not only contradictions between the several conclusions of one 'claw' and the corresponding conclusions of its counterpart 'claw', but also contradictions in each 'claw' taken by itself. For it looks as if it is self-contradictory to ascribe both of two antithetical predicates to a subject, and also self-contradictory to deny both of a disjunction of antithetical predicates to it.

For if we take a pair of opposite predicates, say 'male' and 'female', *if a given subject has a sex at all*, then it seems absurd to say either that it has both sexes or that it has neither. Now most subjects have, of course, no sex, so to deny that they have either is true and not absurd. But there seem to be some high-level disjunctive pairs of predicates, of which we think that one *or* the other (not both and also not neither) must characterise any subject you please. And just these are the sorts of predicate-couples with which Plato is working. He is, in some cases, I think, mistaken in thinking that the option 'neither-heads-nor-tails' is ruled out; and in others he is, I think, mistaken in thinking that the option 'both-heads-and-tails' is ruled out. But in general it seems to me that the complex conclusion of each of the

REVIEW OF F. M. CORNFORD: 'PLATO AND PARMENIDES'

eight movements is logically impossible on its own account, besides being controverted by the directly opposite conclusion of its counter-part movement.

But if this is so, then Professor Cornford's position is impossible. For in his view each movement is a valid argument for a set of *true* conclusions, and the semblance of logical absurdity only arises from the naïve belief in the univocality of, particularly, the subject word in the conclusions of the different movements *vis-à-vis* each other. And obviously the conclusions of a single movement cannot all be true *and* in contradiction with each other. So Professor Cornford tries to show that the seeming contradictoriness between the parts of the conclusion of each movement taken by itself is also unreal. And this he does by discerning (between the lines) the frequent interpolations of new quasi-definitions demarcating new distinctions of meaning of the terms involved. Thus he tries to show that in no case is one and the same subject either asserted to have both or denied to have either of two contrary predicates. The contrariness of the predicates is what establishes the real non-identity of the subjects to which they are severally ascribed or denied. He has to speak of 'definitions disguised as deductions', and has to find such a disguised definition wherever the argument seems to establish a both-heads-and-tails or a neither-heads-nor-tails conclusion—and that is in nearly every link of the chain of deductions. I shall content myself with saying that I do not think him successful—and not *only* because I think him mis-taken in denying that the total argument is intended to be a grand *reductio ad absurdum*.

One last point. Professor Cornford is continually forced to trans-late certain Greek expressions by such English phrases as 'a one being', 'the One Being', 'one-entities', and so on. Now it is impor-tant to notice that *except for translation purposes* no one would ever dream of using these phrases either in colloquial or in philosophical discourse. The child in the nursery would wriggle and feel inarticu-lately that something had gone wrong with the works of the speech of anyone who talked in these ways. But why cannot these phrases be used? The grammar is normal, for 'one' is a familiar adjective, and 'being' is a common substantive, and 'entity' an established pedantic one. So why does the total phrase 'a one being' cause us any more discomfort than, say, 'a wise man'? And the answer, which the child would feel but could not articulate, is that 'one' does not signify an attribute as 'wise' does; and that 'being' does not stand for a sort or kind as 'man' does. Now Professor Cornford, like many philosophers, does think, for he repeatedly says, that 'one' and 'existent' do signify attributes. And he even thinks, as Meinong and the early Russell did, that being an entity or being is an attribute which is possessed by some objects which nevertheless lack the specific attribute of existing. Else how could negative existence-propositions be significant? There must *be* something, for us to be able to say of *it* that it does not exist. Consequently the phrases, 'a one being' and 'the one-entities', *ought* to be just as proper expressions as 'a wise man' or 'the ingenious Eleatics'. But they are not proper expressions, and they are not so for the reason that the roles of 'one', 'existent', 'being', and some others are different from the roles of attribute-words and sort-words. And it is just these differences of role which generated the puzzles which Aristotle was alive to, though I do not think he solved them. And, I urge, it is just these differences of which Plato was becoming aware in the *Parmenides*, the *Theaetetus* and the *Sophist*. The puzzles are not peculiar to one language or epoch; they can be found, for example, still unsolved and still central, in Russell's *Principles of Mathematics*.

I suggest, therefore, that while Professor Cornford is completely right in holding that Plato is, in this and the adjacent dialogues, concerned with genuine problems and problems of the sort which we should describe as 'logical', and completely right, again, in holding that these problems are identical with those to which Aristotle continually recurs, he has failed to put his finger upon just what these problems were, because he has not himself realised that or how the concepts of unity, existence and non-existence refuse to behave like ordinary attribute-concepts and kind-concepts. He has not *felt* the paradoxes which, in my view, are the nerves of the *Parmenides* and the *Sophist*.

To clinch the issue—and that the issue can be clinched itself shows that the problem of the interpretation of the *Parmenides* is at last becoming definite—I lay down the following theses. The second part of the dialogue is or is intended to be a *reductio ad absurdum* argument. The two propositions to which it is applied, namely, *Unity exists* and *Unity does not exist*, are intended to be univocal. There are four main operations in the argument, and each operation has two 'claws'; and the two 'claws' of each operation are intended to demonstrate antithetical conclusions. And the conclusions of each 'claw', taken by itself, constitute, for the most part, logically impossible conjunctions. The subject of the hypotheses is a Form or 'universal'. The purpose of the second part of the dialogue is to show that some presupposition of the theory of Forms contains a radical logical flow. And the argument is successful.

I do not claim that there remain no difficulties. For example, it is difficult to explain why the argument is put into the mouth of Parmenides, especially if, as I think, the general course of the argument is, while closely relevant to the theory of Forms, not very closely relevant to Monism, save in so far as this doctrine did depend upon special and illegitimate inferences from the natures of the concepts of unity and existence. Then there are plenty of places in the argument where logical tricks are played with other concepts than unity and existence; for example, with the concepts of similarity, dissimilarity, identity, otherness, change, time, and so on. Doubtless the expansion of these absurdity-producing operations would reveal important truths about the logical roles of these concepts, but the introduction of them into the specific inquest upon unity and existence does leave the impression that we are losing both the bone and the shadow.

And, finally, I suspect that Professor Cornford is right in detecting in a lot of the turns and twists of the argument of the second part of the dialogue echoes of special controversies about the foundations of arithmetic and geometry; and this would indicate that the concept of unity demanded investigation, not only because of its cardinal position in the theory of Forms and, perhaps, in Monism, but also because of its connexion with the notion of arithmetical units and with the general question of what it is that numbers characterise or belong to (which is also Russell's problem in the *Principles of Mathematics*). And if questions of this special sort are dominant and not merely interjected, the problem of what the whole *reductio ad absurdum* argument is intended to reveal will become a lot more complicated. It will mean that Plato is attending not just to the logic of predication but also to that of counting, measuring, and calculating. However, at present, I am disposed, though with qualms, to believe that these special questions are not dominant here. They do not seem to control the arguments of the *Theaetetus* or the *Sophist*.

3

LETTERS AND SYLLABLES IN PLATO

Reprinted from 'The Philosophical Review', vol. LXIX, *1960, by permission of the editors*

In his later dialogues Plato makes a lot of use of the notions of letters of the alphabet and the spelling of syllables out of these letters. He frequently uses these notions for the sake of analogies which help him to expound some more abstract matters.

There is one of his uses of the letter-syllable model which is not of special interest to me, namely, for the exposition of some merely chemical theories about the combinations of a few material elements into multifarious compounds. Plato employs this model in this way in the *Timaeus* (48 B–C), though he says that the analogy is not a good one. Here he is stating what is essentially an Empedoclean theory. Sextus Empiricus says that *stoicheion*, used thus to denote an ultimate material element, was a Pythagorean term.

My interest is in Plato's use of the alphabet model in expounding his logical or semantic views, namely his views about the composition of the thoughts, that is, the truths and falsehoods that we express or can express in sentences (*logoi*).

I. LETTERS

First, I have to make a dull but necessary distinction. When we run through the alphabet viva voce we produce the *names* of letters, that is, made-up words like 'Alpha', 'Queue', 'Double-U', 'Ess', 'Omega', 'Aitch', and so forth. If, on the other hand, we have to write out the alphabet, we write the letters themselves and not their names. We inscribe the character 'H'; we do not inscribe the five characters of its English name, 'a-i-t-c-h'. The word 'Double-U' is a trisyllabic name of a letter which is not itself a trisyllable or even a monosyllable. The word 'Queue' rhymes with the word 'few', but the letter that it is the name of does not rhyme with anything. The American proper name 'Zee', the English proper name 'Zed', and the Greek proper name 'Zeta' are three names for the same letter. These letter names are just as much words as are the names of people, dogs, or days of the week. Plato discusses the names of letters in the *Cratylus* (393).

Well, then, what *is* the letter of which the proper name 'Zed', say, is the English name? Is it (1) the zigzag character that we inscribe at the beginning of the written word 'zebra', or (2) the semi-sibilant beginning of the uttered dissyllable 'zebra', or (3) both that zigzag character and that semi-sibilant consonant? It will turn out to be crucially important to consider whether, when Plato refers to the particular letter of which the word 'Beta', say, is the name, he is thinking primarily of a noise or primarily of a character; whether, for example, he is thinking of the beginning of the noise 'Basileus', or thinking of the left-hand-most character in the written word 'Basileus'. We nowadays naturally think first of a printed or written character. I hope to show that Plato, on the other hand, naturally thought first of the explosive beginning of uttered words like 'Basileus', that is, that the letter names like 'Beta' and 'Sigma' were, for him, names primarily of phonetic elements or phonemes. So when Plato speaks of a child learning the letters called 'Beta' and 'Sigma', he is not, according to me, thinking first of all, as we should be, of the child being taught to inscribe and decipher characters, but of him learning to recognize by ear, name, and pronounce the consonants and vowels.

Platonic Greek had two words for 'letter', namely *gramma* and *stoicheion*. Sextus Empiricus, in *Against the Grammarians* (99), says that *stoicheion* may mean (1) a character; (2) the phonetic element that a character stands for; or (3) the name of the letter, for example, the word 'Beta'. It is the phonetic element that is accounted by the grammarians the *stoicheion* proper. Sextus Empiricus himself avoids using *gramma* for a phonetic element or *stoicheion* for a character.

The sole philological use of *stoicheion* given by Aristotle in *Metaphysics* Δ (1014a) is that of 'phonetic element'—as is that given in the '*Platonic*' *Definitions* (414E)—and Aristotle sticks to this in his own practice with only rare exceptions, for example, in *De Soph. Elench.* (177b) and in *Metaphysics* (1035a). Correspondingly, a *gramma* is for Aristotle a character and hardly ever, if ever, a phoneme, though in *Problems* (10, 90, and 11, 30 and 57) we hear of people who lisp being unable to utter certain *grammata* and of animals that can utter just a few *grammata*, among the other noises they make.

I hope to show (*a*) that Plato uses *stoicheion* nearly uniformly for 'phonetic element', though in the *Theaetetus* (206A) *stoicheia* are both things uttered and things written; (b) that Plato uses *grammata* quite impartially for phonetic elements and for characters. *Gramma*, despite its etymology, did not for Plato connote writing. *Grammata* are, of course, written characters in the *Republic* (368 and 402) and in the *Phaedrus* (274–5), where Plato also, for once, uses *typos*. Unlike Sextus Empiricus, he and Aristotle never use the ambiguity-removing word 'character'. 'Syllable' is regularly used as a phonetic term by Plato, Aristotle, and Sextus Empiricus for the minimum pronounceable. Consequently letters, when mentioned as elements of such pronounced syllables, have to be audible consonants and vowels and cannot possibly be characters.

Plato says a good deal in the *Cratylus* (especially 424–7, 434–5) about the phonetics of letters and syllables, but it is especially in the *Theaetetus* and *Sophist*, and more cursorily in the *Politicus*, that he makes philosophical use of the model of letters and their combinations in syllables. He uses it in the *Theaetetus* in order to throw light on the differences between what is said in a sentence (*logos*) and what is named by a separate word, between a truth-or-falsehood and a named thing, between a proposition and a term, and between what we can know or believe and what we can see or touch.

In the *Sophist* he uses the alphabet model for a more abstract task. He emphasizes the differences between vowels and consonants and the necessity for at least one vowel being present to enable consonants to combine together. By means of this analogy he tries to show at least this, that some Forms are unlike the rest in being vowel-like, that is, in being necessary for the combining of terms into truths and falsehoods. I think he has in mind here those notions which are expressed (a) by verbs as distinct from nouns and adjectives and (b) by certain radical verbs such as the verbs 'to be' and 'to become', in distinction from all other verbs.

This brings us to the important ambiguity that I have mentioned in all that Plato says about letters and syllables. Is he, as I formerly took for granted and as the commentators whom I have consulted take for granted, referring only or primarily to written characters and written syllables, or is he, as I now think, referring only or primarily to the uttered consonants and vowels in uttered syllables? Or is he referring indiscriminately to both? For example, to take the three letters of the English monosyllabic word 'box', is Plato thinking only or primarily of the three characters written left to right, of which the second is nearly circular and the third consists of two straight lines cutting one another at something less than a right angle? Or is he thinking only or primarily of what these three written letters stand for in the realm of pronounced noises, that is, of what the monosyllable 'box' sounds like? The reason why it is important to clear this matter up is this. There are some very important differences between what can be said about inscribed characters and what can be said about the phonemes or noise elements that they stand for, and these differences make all the difference to our interpretation of the doctrine which Plato uses the alphabet model to expound. The written word 'box' contains three parts or components, namely, the 'b' and 'o' and 'x', any one of which could survive when the other two were deleted. We could write these characters down at different times, on separate bits of paper, and then paste the pieces together in one order, take them apart again, rejoin them in a new order, and so on. Characters are separate inscribables; they can be separately read; and they can be combined in any order or left uncombined. But what, in the phonetic field, the three characters stand for could not be similarly separated or shuffled. We could not make a noise at all answering to the sequence of the three characters 'OXB'.

More than that; while we could indeed pronounce by itself the vowel-noise answering to the character 'o', we could not pronounce by themselves separate noises answering to 'b' and 'x', though we might do so for a few hissable or hummable consonants like 's', 'r', 'm', and 'l'. In short, most separately inscribable characters of the written alphabet do not stand for separately pronounceable noises, and these were known to Plato by the technical terms *aphona* and *aphthogga*, that is, 'mutes'. These are not sounds but only *con*-sonants. The uttered monosyllable 'box' is one noise, a monosyllable and not a trisyllable. It is not a sequence of a 'b' noise and an 'o' noise and an 'x' noise. There are no such noises as 'b' and 'x', and if there were, the sequence of them would not be the monosyllable 'box' but a trisyllable. Certainly the uttered monosyllable 'cox' differs audibly in one respect from the monosyllable 'box', though resembling it in two respects, but the audible difference does not consist in the monosyllables being made up out of different and separately pronounceable component noises. We cannot therefore say that the vowel 'o' enables us to co-utter the consonant noises 'b' and 'x', since there are no consonant noises 'b' and 'x' to be uttered by themselves at all. We cannot speak of the vowel as linking some components that could exist without that linkage. A spoken monosyllable is not a phonetic molecule of which its consonants and vowels are the atoms. In short, while characters are graphic atoms, phonemes are not phonetic atoms. Chinese writing and 'Linear B' do not contain even graphic atoms.

We have to say instead that what the characters 'b' and 'x', say, stand for are ways or respects in which one monosyllable may resemble other monosyllables, though not resembling them in other respects; they stand for distinguishable aspects or features of integral noises but not for integral noises. Borrowing from Frege, we might say that the phonetic element for which the character 'b' stands could and, for certain purposes, should be graphically symbolized not just by 'b', but by 'b ...' or '... b' or '... b ...', where, with qualifications, the gaps are vacancies to be tenanted by some vowel character or other, no matter which; and ditto for 'x' and 'q' and any other consonant; and for that matter, *mutatis mutandis*, ditto for vowels too, save that the gaps flanking them could be flagged as optional.

I bring this point out at once, because the phonetic model of letters and syllables would be an almost perfect model by means of which to express Frege's difficult but crucial point that the unitary something that is *said* in a sentence or the unitary sense that it expresses is not an assemblage of detachable sense atoms, that is, if parts enjoying separate existence and separate thinkability, and yet that one truth or falsehood may have discernible, countable, and classifiable similarities to and dissimilarities from other truths and falsehoods. Word meanings or concepts are not proposition components but propositional differences. They are distinguishables, not detachables; abstractables, not extractables—as are the audible contributions made to the voiced monosyllable 'box' by the consonants 'b' and 'x'.

But did Plato mean us to construe his model in phonetic terms? Prima facie the answer is 'no'. If he had meant this, he would surely have told us that he was talking phonetics and not graphology. The few commentators whom I have read have assumed that Plato is talking about characters and collocations of characters and have not even mentioned the alternative possibility. On the other hand, there are things which Plato says which cumulatively point so strongly in the affirmative direction that I think 'yes' is the right answer. I also hope that it is, since the semantic view which results is both true and important. So now for the evidence.

(1) In the *Theaetetus* (from 202E) after expounding his 'dream' in which simples, that is, elementary or atomic namables, are contrasted with the complexes which entire sentences (*logoi*) express, Socrates goes very thoroughly into two main kinds of complexes, those which are pure pluralities or totalities and those which are organic unities.

He suggests that syllables may be of this latter kind. If so, then a syllable cannot have letters for its parts; indeed it cannot be divided up into parts at all. Now this, as we have seen, is perfectly true of monosyllabic noises, but it is totally false of their written symbolizations in Greek or English script. Socrates does not commit himself to this view, but at least Plato was explicitly considering the idea that uttered monosyllables do not have parts. Next, quite shortly before this passage, Theaetetus had been asked how he would break up the first syllable of the word 'Socrates', and he naturally replies, 'Into "s" and "o".' Then when asked how the 's' can be broken up, he says, '"s" is one of the consonants (aphonon) nothing but a noise, like a hissing of the tongue; while "b" not only has no articulate sound, but is not even a noise (oute phone oute psophos); and the same is true of most of the letters.'

Here, then, Plato is certainly talking phonetics and not graphology; he sees that to most of the consonant characters no separately pronounceable noises correspond and he considers whether a syllable is a plurality of separately utterable parts, or is an organic unity, not divisible into parts. The letters that he is talking about are not characters but elements of voiced syllables. He uses *stoicheion* and *gramma* interchangeably for these phonetic elements.

Two pages later (207 D) Plato, discussing the learning of spelling, says that a child who writes down the correct characters for the first syllable of 'Theaetetus', but then writes down incorrect characters for the first syllable of 'Theodorus', does not really know (the spelling of) that shared syllable. He got the first one right without knowledge. But Plato does not consider the possibility that the child might, when examined viva voce, have sung out 'theta epsilon' perfectly correctly for the first two phonemes of both names, while still being muddled about what character to write down for theta. He might, that is, know the spelling without yet knowing his characters. When shown the mark θ he might have said first, 'That is tau,' later on, 'That is theta.' The point is only of importance in that it shows that Plato could confuse knowing what phonetic element a given letter name designates with knowing what written character symbolizes a given phonetic element. The ambiguity of 'letter' was not fully realized by him.

(2) In the *Sophist* (253 A), after some talk about the blendings and nonblendings of Forms, the Eleatic Stranger says, 'They might be said to be in the same case with the letters of the alphabet (*grammata*). Some of these cannot be conjoined, others will fit together.... And the vowels are specially good at combination,

a sort of bond (*desmos*) pervading them all, so that without a vowel the others cannot be fitted together.' Now so far as this passage by itself goes, Plato might be saying one of two quite different things. (*a*) The rules of Greek orthography forbid you to run consonant characters side by side in certain collocations on the page, without some vowel character or other going next to or between them. (*b*) It is phonetically impossible to pronounce even a monosyllable without pronouncing at least one vowel. Plato unquestionably meant the second.

Later on (261 D), he says, 'Remembering what we said about Forms and letters, let us consider words in the same way.' He goes on to distinguish nouns from verbs, and to show that a statement or sentence cannot be a string just of nouns or just of verbs. It must, at the least, marry one verb with one noun. I think Plato means us to think of verbs as the *analogon* to vowels, and to think of nouns, and so forth, as the *analogon* to consonants.

What I vainly wish he had said explicitly is this. Vowel characters correspond to verbs, but the vowels that these vowel characters stand for correspond to what verbs mean, that is, to what they contribute to statements. Similarly, consonant characters correspond to nouns, and so forth, but the consonants that these characters stand for correspond to what nouns and so forth mean, that is, to what they contribute to statements. As the atoms of writing do not stand for atoms of noise, so the atoms of speech do not stand for atoms of meaning. Conversely, as an atom of writing—a character—does stand for a respect in which one uttered monosyllable may resemble other monosyllables, while differing from them in other respects; so an atom of speech—a word—does stand for a respect in which one statable truth or falsehood may resemble others, while differing from them in other respects.

To put this point in another idiom: what characters stand for are not noises but noise functions, that is, abstractable noise features or noise differences. We learn what they stand for not by meeting them on their own, since they are not there to meet on their own, but only by comparing partly similar, partly dissimilar, integral mono-syllables which we do hear and pronounce on their own. Similarly, what isolated words convey are not atomic thoughts, but propo-sitional functions, that is, abstractable thought features or thought differences. We learn what they convey not by apprehending their meanings on their own, but only by comparing partly similar, partly dissimilar, integral truths and falsehoods. In both cases abstraction is possible, extraction impossible, and the abstracting requires noticing the constancy of something through ranges of variations in its settings.

(3) There is an important passage in the *Politicus* (277E–8D), in which the Eleatic Stranger discusses the teaching and the learning of letters, in order thereby to formulate a philosophical thesis concerning our knowledge of the elements of reality. He reminds his hearers of the way in which a child, who is just beginning to recognize certain letters in the shortest and easiest syllables, may still be puzzled or muddled about those same letters when incorporated in other syllables. For example—this is my example—the child may recognize and name correctly the letter 'r' as this occurs in 'roy' and 'rat', and yet fail to identify the letter 'r' as this occurs in 'cry'. To get him beyond this point, he has to be got to compare the syllables 'roy' and 'rat', say, which he has got right, with lots and lots of other syllables, including 'cry', which still baffle him; thus he learns to recognize the letter 'r' not just in one or two but in all possible juxtapositions with other letters where it is constant and the rest are varied.

Once more Plato's vocabulary leaves it quite open whether he is thinking of a child learning to read and write his characters or of a child learning to distinguish and label phonetic similarities and dissimilarities. But here Plato must be thinking of the latter and not of the former, since what he says would be a patent falsehood if he were talking about characters. For a child to master the character 'r', say, he would normally be drilled in writing this character down, by itself, again and again, and in naming the character correctly when it was pointed out to him by itself on paper. The character 'r' is a graphic atom which can be produced and encountered by itself. It can therefore be and usually is in fact learned by itself, without the confusing proximity of neighbours. It is just because this is not the case with the phonetic value of the character 'r', that is, the consonant 'r', that the child can master the noise difference that the character 'r' stands for only by comparing lots of entire uttered syllables in which what 'r' stands for is constant and all the rest is varied. There is no question here of his first uttering and hearing the noise 'r' by itself and then going on to collocate it and recognize collocations of it with other noises. For the character 'r' does not stand for a noise but only for a common feature of a range of otherwise different monosyllabic noises. Being incapable of extraction it can be learned only by abstraction. This passage in the *Politicus* is explicitly linked to the passage in the *Theaetetus* in which Plato had discussed the knowability of simples and complexes. This contrast of simples and complexes was connected with the contrast between what is expressed by individual words and what is expressed by complete sentences. So we have in this passage a good warrant for saying that Plato did realize that word meanings stand to sentence meanings not at all as characters stand to written syllables but as phonemes stand to uttered syllables.

It still puzzles me why Plato did not bluntly tell us that he was describing not how the child learns to read and write his characters, but only how he learns to discriminate by ear and with his tongue the phonetic values of the letters of the alphabet, i.e. the audible vowels and consonants. Can it be that Greek children were introduced to writing only quite a long time after they had learned to distinguish and name the phonemes into which spoken syllables are analysed?

(4) In the *Philebus* (17 A–B), we are given another account of the learning of letters. Socrates, in expounding the notions of *Peras* and *Apeiron*, says, 'Surely my meaning is made clear in the letters of the alphabet which you were taught as a child; so learn it from them. . . . Sound (*phone*) which passes out through the mouth of each and all of us is one and yet again it is infinite in number. . . . And one of us is no wiser than the other for knowing that it is infinite or that it is one; but that which makes each of us a grammarian is the knowledge of the number and nature of sounds.' Here Socrates equates the learning of letters with the acquisition of phonetic expertness. Nothing whatsoever is said about marks inscribed on papyrus or wax tablets. A little later (18 B–C) Socrates credits the Egyptian wizard Theuth with the systematic discrimination first of the vowels from one another and then of the vowels from other vocal noises which were not quite vowels and yet could be sounded, that is, noises like 'ssss' and 'mmmm', I suppose; and these, too, he discriminated from one another. Both these classes he discriminated from the mutes, that is, from most of the consonants, which he then discriminated from one another. He called each and all of them 'letters' (*stoicheia*). Then, 'Perceiving, however, that none of us could learn any one of them alone, by itself, without learning them all and considering that this was a common bond which made them in a way all one, he assigned to them all a single science (*techne*) and called it grammar.' Aristotle gives a very similar classification in *Poetics* 20.

Here too nothing is said about letters (*grammata* or *stoicheia*) being things written or read. They are vowels or mutes or else semi-vowels. Theuth had classified pronounceables, not inscribables. So when Socrates says that Theuth perceived 'that none of us could

learn any one of them alone by itself, without learning them all'
he is not saying what would obviously be false, that a child could not
learn to write and read six characters of the alphabet without learning
to write and read the other twenty. He is saying what is true, that the
child does not really know either the consonant 'b' or the consonant
'd' if he cannot *inter alia* distinguish by ear and tongue 'bog' from
'dog', 'cab' from 'cad', and so forth.

(5) The *Cratylus* is a thoroughly philological dialogue and in the
course of it a good deal is said in several places about letters. On most
occasions the letters are described in purely phonetic terms; we hear
how the breath is expelled or checked in the pronunciation of them,
what the tongue and the lips do. An onomatopoeic theory is built up
according to which letters (*grammata* or *stoicheia*) sound like things or
happenings and so qualify to function as their names. There is, I
think, no passage in this dialogue in which a letter-name like 'Alpha'
or 'Sigma' is the name of a character.

In sum, then, I maintain that Plato regularly thinks of letters not as
things written and read, but as things pronounced and heard.
'Syllable' is, for Plato, as for Aristotle and Sextus Empiricus, a
regular phonetic term, and when letters are mentioned in association
with syllables, they are in these contexts phonetic elements and not
characters, no matter whether they are called *grammata* or *stoicheia*.

II. VERBS

I shall now take it as established that Plato's model of letters and
syllables was the phonetic model. What did Plato intend to explicate
by means of this model? I canalize my answers to this question through
a discussion of Plato's treatment of live verbs. I mean by 'live verbs'
expressions like 'assassinated', 'believes' and 'will wake up', not
verbal nouns like 'assassination', 'belief', 'waking', or 'wakefulness',
and not participles like 'walking' or 'bereaved.' Incidentally, it has
been maintained that Plato, when he uses the word *rhema*, does not
restrict himself to what we call verbs, like 'assassinated' and 'will
wake up', but includes also complete predicating phrases like
'assassinated Caesar' or 'was a snub-nosed philosopher' or 'believed
that the earth is flat'. I think the evidence points in the other direction;
but I do not mind. It will not matter for the points that I wish to make.

Plato, in the *Sophist* (261 D), links what he has to say about verbs
and nouns to what he had said about vowels and consonants; and
I think, though I may be co-operating here, that Plato means us to
liken the role of verbs in sentences to the role of vowels in syllables.

A vowel supplies a syllable in which it occurs with its breath and so collects the consonants with itself into a unitary utterance. A verb supplies the sentence in which it occurs with its asserting force and so collects the nouns and other parts of speech with itself into the telling of a unitary truth or falsehood.

For an assertion to occur there must, at the least, be someone or something of whom or which something is asserted, and there must be something which is asserted of that subject. A sentence conveying an assertion must, that is, marry a nominative expression with a live verb—somewhat as in a syllable a consonant must be married to a vowel. A string of nouns say nothing, nor does a string of verbs, nor a noun by itself or a verb by itself. Plato does not pause to make allowances for one-word sentences like 'Badizo'. Plato is perfectly clear that a sentence, though consisting of two or more words, says just one thing, true or false. Saying one thing in two words is not to be equated with mentioning-by-name two things. He distinguishes saying from naming in the *Theaetetus* (202) and in the *Sophist* (262). He sees, that is, that the live verb 'flies' in the two-word sentence 'Theaetetus flies' does not do the sort of thing that the name 'Theaetetus' does (for example, mention someone); it does the asserting of something *about* Theaetetus without which we should not have a truth or falsehood about Theaetetus. Further, Plato sees that, given the sentence 'Theaetetus flies', we may replace the verb 'flies' with some other verb, and another true or false sentence will result—much as the consonant 'b' will accept the company of the vowel 'a' *or* 'e' *or* 'i' *or* 'o' *or* 'u'. It demands vowel-company, but it does not demand the company of this vowel as against that vowel. Nouns and verbs, like consonants and vowels, can vary independently, but they cannot function by themselves. As an integral sentence is the minimum vehicle of a truth or falsehood, it is also the minimum expression of knowledge, belief, and conjecture. A noun by itself or a verb by itself does not convey what I know or think, any more than a consonant-character stands for something that I can pronounce. What I know or think is something sayable and not something merely mentionable-by-name. This is brought out in, *inter alia*, Socrates' 'dream' in the *Theaetetus* (202). So a live verb is an indispensable element in the expression of knowledge or opinion.

I am going, somewhat arbitrarily, to split up my account of Plato's treatment of verbs into five heads.

(1) *Etymology*. In the *Cratylus* Plato proffers, surely with his tongue in his cheek, a great number of etymological derivations of Greek

words. It has not, I think, been noticed that, especially from 411 B, nearly all of the suggested root words are verbs. Socrates does not, unless by a hint or two (for example, in 411 C), avow that this is the principle of his etymologizing, though he does avow that he is doing his best for the Heracleiteans. So Plato was toying with the idea that the original seeds of language were expressions for happenings, undergoings, doings, havings, gettings, startings, stoppings—that is, verbs. He was perhaps pretending that what the Heracleitean flux theory amounted to is that what is real is wholly expressible by tensed verbs of happening, doing, and so forth.

(2) *Tenses*. Plato attends to the time indications of tensed verbs in many places (for example, *Timaeus* 37–8; *Philebus* 39–40, 59; *Cratylus* 439 D; *Theaetetus* 178; *Sophist* 262 D). In the *Parmenides* (141 D–E) he actually distinguishes eight or nine tenses in place of the hackneyed trinity of past, present, and future. Plato is now taking time very seriously. Not only the timeless is real (*Sophist* 248–9, 262 D). Not only the timeless is knowable (*Philebus* 61 D, 62 B; *Theaetetus* 201 B–C). It is worth noticing, too, that about a third of the dialectical operations in Part II of the *Parmenides* are or include operations upon temporal concepts. Pardonably, Plato is not alive to the fact that there could be languages in which time indications were not given by inflections of verbs. He did not know Chinese or the stories of Damon Runyon. Nor does he notice that time indications can be given by the participles of verbs.

(3) *Active and passive voices*. Plato frequently, from the *Euthyphro* (10) on, contrasts *poiein* with *paschein*, acting with being acted on. I suspect, but do not pause to argue, that when he draws this distinction he often has one eye on the grammatical distinction between a verb in the active voice and the same verb in the passive voice. Loving and being loved are not the same thing though the verbal noun 'love' is the same for both.

(4) *Saying*. Unlike Protagoras, who had apparently distinguished asserting from inquiring, commanding, beseeching, and the like, Plato attends only to those sentences in which we assert or deny that something is the case, that is, to those which convey truths and falsehoods. A sentence expresses the termination of an inquiry. When we have something to state, we have terminated a stretch of wondering (*Theaetetus* 190 A; *Sophist* 262 D, 264 A). In stating something we combine, at the least, a verb with a noun. By the noun we mention some subject by name; by the verb we assert something about that subject. So the sentence is not just a list of two mentioned subjects. Statements are either assertions or denials, that is, either

affirmative or negative (*phasis* or *apophasis*, *Sophist* 163 E; cf. *Theaetetus* 190 A). The notion of the verb as a copula seems to be at least nascent in *Parmenides* (162 A) where the use of *desmos* (bond) for the verb 'to be so and so' echoes, I guess, the use of *desmos* in the *Sophist* (253 A) for the linking function of vowels in syllables. Plato saw that there begin with saying, as distinct from naming, both asserting and denying and truth and falsehood, though in the *Cratylus* (385 B–C) Socrates pretends that the parts of a true sentence must themselves be true. Moreover, only things said can contradict or be contradicted. A word could not be the contradictory of another word, though it might be its opposite. If I say that Socrates is not tall, I contradict the assertion that he is tall, but I do not assert that Socrates is short (*Sophist* 257 B). Consequently, I think, though I am co-operating here, that Plato realized that 'not' operates only where live verbs are functioning. It makes its particular contribution to the *saying-about* that the verb in a sentence does, not to the *mentioning-of-the-subject* that the nominative of the sentence does. 'Not' cannot appear, either by itself or in harness with another word, in a list of things. In the *Sophist* (237–9) Plato emphasizes the queer-seeming but important point that we cannot speak about the nonexistent, since the expression 'the nonexistent' is debarred from being either singular or plural. We cannot say 'it is so and so' or 'they are so and so', for 'it' and 'they' refer to what is and are there to be referred to, not to what is and are not there. There cannot be many or even one of what there is none of.

In the *Theaetetus* Socrates' puzzle was, How can we think what is not, when what we see or hear are things that are? The source of the trouble is this. We see and hear *things*, for example people. But what we believe are propositions *about* people, that is, sayables and not namables. Now among things, for example visible things, there are indeed no non-things, but among believables and sayables there are things which are the right and the wrong things to believe and say *about* a given subject term. The work that 'not' does it can do only in collusion with a live verb or, more generally, with a live predicative expression that is doing its work in a full sentence. In the *Sophist* (243) Plato sees clearly that his perplexities about '. . . is not . . .' and '. . . does not exist' are just as much perplexities about '. . . is . . .' and '. . . exists'. Of course 'not' is not itself a verb. But what it means is somehow internal to what is meant by the live verb with which it goes. Parmenides' trouble with 'not' derived, I suggest, from his assumption that 'not' would, if admitted at all, have to be a component of subject-denoting expressions like 'the not-real' or 'the not-existent'. Plato, on my interpretation, rightly transfers the locus of 'not' to the asserting side of sentences, that is, roughly, to their verbs. There are no negative things to make true or false assertions about, but about anything you please there are true or false denials to make. What I declare can be negative. What I mention cannot be negative or, of course, affirmative either. It must be singular or plural; it cannot be zero.

This suggests a line of interpretation of the baffling doctrine of the 'Greatest Kinds' in the *Sophist* (254 et seq.). The explicit object of the inquiry is to find a home for 'not'. The concepts collected as 'Greatest Kinds' are those of *kinesis, stasis, being, identity*, and *otherness*. Now what are these supposed to be supreme kinds *of*? They are not, I suggest, adduced as *summa genera* of namable things, that is, of the subject terms about which true and false assertions can be made. Instead, I suggest, they are *summa genera* of what is assertible about subject terms, that is, very crudely, they are basic *verb forms*. *Kinesis* (which Plato, like Aristotle, explicitly uses for any kind of change, not only motion) is the generic verbal noun for all live verbs and verb inflections of happening, doing, beginning, stopping, and the like. *Stasis* is the verbal noun for all verbs and verb inflections of continuing and remaining. 'Being' is the verbal noun for existing and for being so and so. 'Identity' is the abstract noun for 'is', where this is the 'is' of identity. 'Otherness' is the abstract noun for the verb phrase 'is not' where this is the 'is not' of nonidentity. Plato's aim is, I suggest, to show that the notion of 'not' is, via the 'is not' of nonidentity, internally constitutive of, without being equivalent to, what is asserted in assertions of all the various types. 'Not' is not an external appendage which just happens now and again to attach to this or that verb. It is, in different ways, an internal part of the force of any verb. For example, if Socrates is now waking up (*kinesis*) it follows that he is not still remaining asleep (*stasis*) and vice versa. To say something is to deny some other things.

Plato's intricate argumentation about the Greatest Kinds is followed immediately by his treatment of nouns and verbs. Having satisfied Theaetetus that any truth or falsehood must be about someone or something, the Stranger finds falsehood to consist in something being asserted about the subject other than what is the right thing to assert about him; that is, the crucial notion of otherness is brought in to mark off one assertible from another assertible, for example, the right one from a wrong one. The otherness that we heard so much of among the Greatest Kinds is here controlling assertibles, for example, the sense of different live verbs. If it is false to assert about Theaetetus that he is flying, then it is true to assert about him that he is not flying; and if it happens also to be true to assert of him that he is sitting, *part* of the force of 'is sitting' is 'not flying'. If we discover that he is sitting, then we do not have to make a second discovery, that he is not flying. 'Is not flying' is part of what 'is sitting' says. However, I do not want to thrash out this very conjectural line of elucidation. But if this or something like this was in Plato's mind, then he was aiming at the right target, though I think that he was not aiming at its bull's-eye.

It is worth while now to consider briefly a point which worried the young Russell in his *Principles of Mathematics* (at the end of chapter IV). Russell realized, rather reluctantly, that between the statement 'Brutus assassinated Caesar' and the list 'Brutus, assassination, Caesar' there was some vital difference. The first tells a truth or falsehood; the second tells nothing at all, though it mentions three things. Yet surely the verbal noun 'assassination' expresses the same concept as the verb 'assassinated' and, if so, it ought to be able to replace the live verb in a sentence *salvo sensu*—which it patently cannot do. This little crux is of great importance. For if asked 'What does "assassinated" mean?' or 'What does "will prosecute" mean?' we see automatically that we are being asked for the elucidation of the common core of all full sentences of the pattern 'Blank assassinated Blank', or 'A will prosecute B'. Live verbs unmistakably advertise themselves as being cores cut out of full sentences. To ask what a given live verb means is to ask what a speaker would be saying if he said something with it. Live verbs are snatches from speech, that is, from the *using* of words. Live verbs could not feature in lists. They occur only in contexts; indeed they are the lifebreath of those contexts. This is even more obvious in Greek than in English, since a Greek verb indicates not only time, but also the singularness, dualness, or plural-ness of the subject, and the subject's being the first person, second person, or third person. Very often a Greek verb is by itself an entire sentence. What we automatically see to hold of the meanings of live verbs, we can then without difficulty see to hold also of 'and', 'if', 'therefore', 'not', 'some', 'any', 'a', and 'the'. It would be as vain an enterprise to try to examine the meanings of these words out of any sentence context as to try to examine the noise for which the character 'b' stands, out of the phonetic context of any syllable.

Russell was forced by this sort of consideration of the senses of live verbs, as opposed to the meanings of the corresponding verbal nouns, to realize, with Frege, that the notion of the sense of an integral sentence, that is, what it says, is prior to the notion of the senses of at least some of the words in it. To ask after the meaning of a live verb or of a conjunction or of 'not' is to ask what *would* be being said with it if someone did put it to work. It is to ask what the word contributes to the senses of the integral sentences in which it occurs. The sense of the sentence is not an amalgam of separately thinkable word meanings. The meanings of its live verbs and so forth are abstractable features, not detachable parts of the senses of the sentences in which they occur. To paraphrase Frege, a live verb or, more generally, a predicative expression flourishes gaps or lacunae around it, namely, lacunae for such other expressions as would, with it, constitute an integral statement. These lacunae are, of course, hospitable. Any expression of the right sort would be welcome. We could fill the lacuna in '. . . flies' or 'Blank flies' with 'Theaetetus' or 'Plato' or 'Bucephalus', and so forth, and each time a significant though usually false sentence will result. The alternative fillings of the lacuna are, in this way, substitutable for one another; and the lacuna can be called, therefore, a 'substitition-place'. What the verb contributes to the sentence 'Plato flies' it contributes to the sentence 'Bucephalus flies'—but 'Blank flies' says, as yet, nothing, and *a fortiori* just 'flies' says nothing. Nor, of course, does it name anything or anyone.

Now Plato, though he is, I maintain, very clear about the saying function of verbs and clear that this function is quite different from the naming function of nouns, says not a word about Russell's special problem: just how is the sense of a live verb different from the meaning of the corresponding verbal noun, for example, how is the sense of 'Blank assassinated Blank' different from the meaning of 'assassination'? There is, however, one fact, besides the *a priori* probabilities, which makes me think that Plato had seriously considered this question or part of it. The second part of the *Parmenides* is an entirely abstract discussion in which hardly a single concrete or even specific word is used. About a third of the dialectical operations are operations upon temporal concepts. Yet, with the exception of *ousia*, hardly a single verbal noun is employed. Abstract nouns in general are also pretty rare, but there are three or four stretches of the discussion in which Plato is quite lavish with such terms as 'equality', 'similarity', 'smallness', and so on. But verbal nouns like 'motion', 'rest', 'alteration', 'termination', 'becoming', and 'cessation' virtually do not occur. This is refreshingly unlike the discussion of the Greatest Kinds in the *Sophist*, in which the reader is presented with a stodgy pudding of verbal and other abstract nouns, together with opaque metaphors like 'participate', 'merge', 'blend', and 'pervade', with nothing to indicate whether we are to translate these culinary metaphors (1) in terms of 'ingredient' and 'compound' or (2) in terms of 'if' and 'therefore', that is, whether they stand for (1) relations between what can be named or (2) connections between what can be said. In the second part of the *Parmenides* we get instead of verbal nouns, such as 'motion', 'continuance', 'alteration', 'cessation', and so forth, integral sentences and clauses the live verbs of which are such verbs as 'moves', 'alters', 'began', 'will cease', and the like. Apparently Plato was now, for some reason, deliberately abstaining from using verbal nouns, as if he thought, as he would have been right to think, that there are important things which operations with live verbs display which verbal nouns would conceal. But what?

(5) *Implications.* Implications hold only between assertibles. 'If' and 'therefore' link sentences, not names. Where 'if' or 'therefore' occurs, there at least two verbs occur. Old Parmenides, in the *Parmenides* (136A–C), repeatedly states the programme of looking to see what must be the case, if something else is the case, or what has got to go with what, or what follows from what. All the subsequent dialectical operations are derivations, legitimate or illegitimate, of consequents from antecedents. Now it is an obvious point that the formulation of antecedents and consequents involves the production of integral sentences or clauses incorporating, necessarily, live verbs. But there is a further point, not so obvious, and presumably not noticed at all by Plato. Take the implication 'If Plato is the uncle of Speusippus, then Plato is the brother of one of Speusippus' parents'. Clearly this implication holds good if for 'Plato' we substitute 'Robinson' or 'Voltaire' and if for 'Speusippus' we substitute 'Brutus' or 'Trotsky'. The implication is quite indifferent to whom in particular the antecedent and the consequent are about. But it is not at all indifferent to what is said about them. We cannot *salva implicatione* substitute 'is the employer of' for 'is the uncle of', or substitute 'is the neighbour of' for 'is the brother of'. Implications are the gift not of the subject terms of sentences, but of their asserting or denying bits, namely their verbs or more generally their predicative expressions. Hence, when formal logic begins, expressions like 'Plato' and 'Speusippus' are algebraized away, that is, they are replaced by '*a*' and '*b*'. But the verbs or predicate expressions are not algebraized away, nor are the words 'not', 'all', 'some', 'if', 'and', and so forth. I think Plato realized that implication, like negation and contradiction, lives only where *saying* lives, and therefore where

live verbs live. I do not think that he had any idea how to detach what implications are indifferent to from what they are not indifferent to. Algebra did not yet exist.

CONCLUSION

Plato in his late dialogues was concerned with some of the same cardinal problems as those which exercised Frege and the young Russell, problems, namely, about the relations between naming and saying; between the meanings of words and the sense of sentences; about the composition of truths and falsehoods; about the role of 'not'; about the difference between contradictories and opposites; and in the end, I think, about what is expressed by 'if' and 'therefore'. His admirable model, which Frege lacked, of the phonetic elements in syllables enabled Plato to explain more lucidly than Frege the notion of the independent-variability-without-separability of the meanings of the parts of sentences. On the other hand, lacking the apparatus of algebra, he was nowhere near abreast of Frege's and Russell's symbolization of substitution places. Plato could not extract implications from their particular contexts or therefore codify implication patterns. A blackboard would have been of no use to him.

Plato says nothing about the bearings of the alphabet model on the Theory of Forms, or of the Theory of Forms on the alphabet model. So I shall not say much. If the Theory of Forms had maintained or entailed that Forms are just subject terms of a superior sort, that is, just eminent namables, then this theory could contribute nothing to Plato's new question, What does a sentence convey besides what its subject name mentions? But if the theory of Forms had been meant or half-meant to explain the contributions of live predicates, including tensed verbs, to truths and falsehoods about mentioned subjects, then in his operations with the model of letters and syllables, Plato has raised to maturity things which, in his Theory of Forms, had been only embryonic. To his terminal questions about the composition of *logoi* and, therewith, about the roles of live, tensed verbs, the Theory of Forms was either quite irrelevant or else quite inadequate.

4

THE 'TIMAEUS LOCRUS'

*Reprinted from 'Phronesis', vol. x, 1965, by permission of the editors
and Royal Van Gorcum Ltd*

The *Timaeus Locrus* (= TL) is a *précis*-paraphrase of Plato's *Timaeus*.
It tries to be in the Doric dialect, and it essays eloquence. It by-passes
much of the *Timaeus*, and its vocabulary is largely non-Platonic. It
also frequently diverges from the *Timaeus* in content. Like Aristotle
and Plutarch the author of the *TL* renders Plato's doctrine of Place
in terms of Hyle, Morphe and Hypokeimenon. He also improves on
Plato's natural science. The *TL* omits Plato's Theory of Forms.
God constructs his world after an 'Idea', but this word is never used
in the plural.

A. E. Taylor examines the *TL* in an appendix to his *Commentary
on Plato's 'Timaeus'* (1928), R. Harder in *Pauly–Wissowa* (1936). See
also Holger Thesleff's *An Introduction to the Pythagorean Writings of the
Hellenistic Period* (Acta Academiae Aboensis), Abo, 1961.

I. THE TAYLOR–HARDER THESIS

Taylor argues that the *TL* was written in about the 1st century A.D.
He allocates it to the *genre* of the Neo-Pythagorean forgeries of the
1st century A.D. That the *genre* even existed is disputed by Thesleff,
who argues that most of the members of this supposed *genre* were not
forgeries and were composed in the 4th and 3rd centuries B.C. Taylor
finds in the *TL* astrological ideas and Stoic philosophical legacies,
particularly fatalism.

Taylor acknowledges that there is no Neo-Pythagoreanism in the
TL, which, indeed, is less Pythagorean than the *Timaeus*, in that it sniffs
at transmigration (104D). He points out that the *TL* is never named
by Plutarch and is first named by Nicomachus in the 2nd century A.D.

Harder accepts Taylor's dating, though he rightly rejects most of
Taylor's reasons for it. He finds no astrology in *TL*, no fatalism or
other Stoic thought.

72

Harder argues that as the *TL* is first explicitly mentioned in the 2nd century A.D., it came into existence not long before that mention. Yet this argument would dispose at one blow of scores of lost works by Speusippus, Xenocrates, Aeschines, Aristippus, Antisthenes, Aristotle, etc., the first extant mentions of which are found in post-Christian authors. Neither Taylor nor Harder worries that Nichomachus treats the *TL* as a pre-Platonic composition, never dreaming that it had been composed during his own lifetime.

Harder, like Taylor, classifies the *TL* as a forgery, and therefore as belonging to the golden age of Neo-Pythagorean forgeries. Neither explains what the *TL* might be a forgery of. It does not pretend to be by any named individual, since it is anonymous. Nor does it purport to be by a member of a School, like that of the Pythagoreans. It makes no pretences at all, unless its being in quasi-Doric is taken to be a pretence to antiquity, which would beg the question. Of what could an anonymous *précis* be a counterfeit?

Harder recognises that a lot of the *TL* is much earlier than the 1st century A.D. He therefore valiantly postulates an earlier *précis* of the *Timaeus*, 'Q', on which the *TL* drew. The fact that 'Q' is unmentioned by anybody at all, A.D. or B.C., does not embarrass Harder. Nor does he show why, if 'Q' did exist, the *TL* should not be simply identified with it.

So far we have found no evidence for or any sense in the view that the *TL* was a forgery at all, or specifically a 1st century forgery. It was composed after the *Timaeus*, and before Nicomachus, but we have only the hazardous argument from its being unmentioned before the 2nd century A.D. to its having been composed late in that half-millennium. Thesleff says that the *TL*'s brand of Doric died out some two centuries B.C.

II. THE COUNTER-THESIS

I shall argue that the *TL* was written in the 4th century B.C., during Plato's lifetime. It is certainly not mentioned by Plutarch or Aristotle, but they make lots of draughts on it.

A. VOCABULARY

The *TL*'s vocabulary is largely non-Platonic. It contains lots of out-of-the-way words, including over 30 ἅπαξ λεγόμενα and about a dozen words peculiar to *TL* and Plutarch.

Of about 160 out-of-the-way non-Platonic words in the *TL* that I have collected, over 80 are found in Aristotle, many of them only in

Aristotle and the *TL*. A moderate number are found in and sometimes only in the Hippocratic writings, and about a dozen in and
sometimes only in Theophrastus. A few are used by Speusippus.
A few seem to be Archytean words; and a few may hail from
Democritus.

Apart from ὕλη, μορφή and ὑποκείμενον, the Aristotelian words
in the *TL* are not logical or metaphysical, but e.g. medical, astronomical, geometrical and zoological words. Its vocabulary coincides
scores of times with that of the *De Caelo*, *De Anima*, *De Partibus
Animalium*, *Meteorologica*, etc., but not with that of the *Organon* or the
Metaphysics. Categories, Contraries, Four Causes, Potentiality,
Actuality, Peras and Apeiron, Syllogisms, Premisses, Predicates, etc.,
are unmentioned in the *TL*.

With one or two doubtful cases, no Stoic words, logical, philosophical or scientific, are in the *TL*. Where Plutarch draws from
Plato, Aristotle, the Stoics and the Epicureans, the *TL* speaks in the
voice of 4th century 'physiology'. The exceptions are these: τονόω
('brace') is used by a minor Stoic or two and by the *TL* (103 E), and
Plutarch; we have no proof that these Stoics coined it. εὔροια (*TL*,
104 C) in an ethical sense is a Stoic use, though it had been used
hydraulically, medically and phonetically by Plato and Aristotle.
There is also in the *TL* (97 C) a queer verb ἐκτυλίσσει, where I
conjecture Aristotle's and Plutarch's [ἕλικας] ἐξελίσσειν. It has
been argued that ἐκτυλίσσειν, not found elsewhere, ought to be
Archimedean in derivation. The MSS. are not unanimous about it.
The *TL* uses ἀντίληψις, which sounds Stoic but might be Democritean. Its σκῆνος (tent) for the body could be Hippocratic or
Democritean.

B. CONTENT

The *TL* is a digest of the *Timaeus*, but not a slavish digest. On several
points the *TL* improves on Plato's natural science. These all belong
to the 4th century B.C.

(*a*) The *Timaeus*, 79, explains inhalation/exhalation by a circulating
pressure, περίωσις as Aristotle calls it, who attacks this account in
his *De Respiratione*, 427 b. He likens breathing to the in–out action
of the blacksmith's bellows, 474 a; the *TL*, 102 A, to the ebb and flow
of the tide, εὔριπος.

(*b*) The *Timaeus*, 38–9, describes the relative positions of the Sun,
Moon, Earth, Venus and Mercury; the remaining planets it leaves
unplaced and unnamed. The *TL*, 97 A, names and, more doubtfully,
places Saturn, Jupiter and Mars. This arrangement, called by H.

Lorimer the 'Pythagorean' arrangement, adopted by Eudoxus and Aristotle, was replaced by the 'Chaldean' arrangement in about 200 B.C., some three centuries too early for Taylor and Harder.

(c) The TL, 96 C, parades the fact that the Morning Star and the Evening Star are often one and the same planet, namely Venus. Plato does not mention this in the Timaeus, and is still unaware of it in the Laws, 821. It is in the Epinomis, 987 B.

(d) Where the Timaeus, 47, talks of the intellectual values of sight and hearing, the TL, 100 C, and Aristotle in De Sensu, 437 a, add that people born blind are more intelligent than those born deaf, since the latter are cut off from human discourse.

(e) The Timaeus, 56 A–B, accounted for the penetrating and consuming character of fire by the fire-pyramids having the 'cuttingest' shape. The TL, 98 E, explains the phenomena by the fire-particles being the finest or smallest. Aristotle in De Caelo, 304 a, criticises Plato and then discusses the subtler account.

(f) The Timaeus, 62 A–B, connects the difference between Cold and Hot with the fact that the grosser particles cause blockages, where the finer particles penetrate and permeate. The TL, 100 E, says that cold blocks up the pores. Plato had said nothing about pores. Aristotle in De Caelo, 307 b, criticises, presumably, Plato for making Cold and Hot differ in the sizes, instead of in the shapes of particles, and mentions the blocking up of pores.

(g) The TL, 100 D, departs from the account of Above and Below in Timaeus, 62–3, for one in terms of Away from the Centre and Towards the Centre, like Aristotle in De Caelo, 308.

(h) Where the Timaeus, 52 B, said that we apprehend Place only by a 'bastard sort of reasoning', the TL, 94 B, says that Matter is apprehended by a bastard sort of reasoning helped by analogy. In Physics I, 191 a, Aristotle allows Matter to be known by analogy.

(i) In the TL, 100 C, God kindles sight in us for the contemplation of the heavenly bodies and the acquisition of science. This is not said in the Timaeus, though it was Plato's view that in seeing the eye emits light (Timaeus, 45–6). Aristotle retained this doctrine in De Caelo, 290 a, but not in De Sensu, 437 b, or Topics, 105 b 6.

(j) In the TL, 102–3, the ἀρεταί of the body, namely health, beauty and strength, with their opposite κακίαι, are accounted for by 'symmetries' and 'asymmetries' between Heat and Cold, Wet and Dry. This is not in the Timaeus, but it is in early works of Aristotle, namely Eudemus, Topics, esp. 116 b, and Physics VII, 246 b 4–8.

(k) The TL expounds Place and its occupants in terms of ὕλη, μορφή and ὑποκείμενον, like Aristotle, e.g. in Physics IV.

(*l*) The *TL*, 101 D, refers to Natural Heat, φυσικὴ θερμότης. This was cardinal in Aristotle's physiology, e.g. in *De Resp.* It hailed from Philistion. It is not in the *Timaeus*.

(*m*) The 'Pneuma' theory, cardinal to Aristotelian physiology and psychology, is present in *TL*, 101 et seq. It was Philistion's theory. It is not in the *Timaeus*.

Of these thirteen points where the *TL* improves on the *Timaeus*, not one presupposes any post-Aristotelian speculations or discoveries; and nearly all are made by Aristotle, often in early works.

C. ECHOES

There are many passages in *TL* between which and passages in other works there are certain or probable echo-relations.

Plutarch

(1) In his *Platonic Questions* and *De Animae Procreatione in Timaeo* Plutarch construes the *Timaeus* in the hylemorphic way in which both Aristotle in *Physics* IV and *TL* construe it. In his *In Timaeo*, 1014F, he says: τὴν ὕλην . . . ἄμορφον καὶ ἀσχημάτιστον . . . (See also *Platonic Questions*, 1007 C, and *Quaest. Conviv.* VIII, 2719 D.) *TL*, 94 A, says: ταύταν δὲ τὰν ὕλαν . . . ἀμόρφωτον δὲ καθ' αὐτὰν καὶ ἀσχημάτιστον . . . ὕλη as a metaphysical term and ἀσχημάτιστος are not in the *Timaeus*.

(2) In his *Divine Vengeance*, 550 D, Plutarch professes to find Plato saying καὶ τὴν ὄψιν αὐτὸς οὗτος ἀνὴρ [Plato] ἀνάψαί φησιν τὴν φύσιν ἐν ἡμῖν ὅπως ὑπὸ θέας τῶν ἐν οὐρανῷ φερομένων . . . ἡ ψυχὴ . . . ἀπέχθηται τοῖς ἀναρμόστοις . . . This sentiment does not occur in the *Timaeus*. It does in *TL*, 100 C: . . . τὰν μὲν ὄψιν ἁμὶν τὸν θεὸν ἀνάψαι εἰς θέαν τῶν ὠρανίων καὶ ἐπιστάμας ἀνάλαψιν . . .

(3) On p. 580 of his *Commentary on Plato's 'Timaeus'* Taylor notices that Plutarch's mechanical explanation of the attracting powers of cupping-glasses and of amber is that of *TL*, 102A. The *Timaeus*, 80, provides no such explanation. Taylor speculates where Plutarch got his explanation from; he does not suggest the *TL*.

(4) In his *Quaest. Conviv.* VIII, 2719 E, Plutarch, obviously paraphrasing the *Timaeus*, 53, mentions ὀκταέδρων καὶ εἰκοσαέδρων. Plato had mentioned eight-sided and twenty-sided solids, but not given them names. The *TL*, 98 D, gives them their names, namely ὀκτάεδρον and εἰκοσίεδρον. The latter word is found only in *TL* and Plutarch; the former is also in Aristotle's *De Caelo* and in Euclid. Here Plutarch again uses ἄμορφος . . . καὶ ἀσχημάτιστος,

where *TL*, but not the *Timaeus*, gives ἀμόρφωτον and ἀσχημάτιστον.

(5) At 720A–B Plutarch refers to the trinity of Creator, Pattern and Matter rather like the *TL* in its first two pages. There is nothing conspicuously similar in the *Timaeus*, 48E, though Plutarch refers explicitly to the *Timaeus*.

(6) Of over two dozen very out-of-the-way non-Platonic words in both the *TL* and Plutarch, a dozen would be ἅπαξ λεγόμενα in either if they were not in the other.

Zeno (of Citium)

Sextus Empiricus (in *Adv. Phys.* I, 107) cites Zeno as saying, in unison with the *Timaeus*, τὸ πᾶν...κατὰ τὸν εἰκότα λόγον ζῷον ἔμψυχον νοερόν τε καὶ λογικόν. Λογικός does not occur in Plato at all, νοερός only in [?] Plato's *Alcibiades I*.

In *TL*, 94D, God made the Cosmos ... ἕνα, μονογενῆ, τέλειον ἔμψυχόν τε καὶ λογικόν. At 99E one part of the soul is ...τὸ μὲν λογικὸν καὶ νοερόν.

Aristotle

(1) In the *De Anima*, 406b28, Aristotle ascribes a certain theory to Plato's *Timaeus*. He says: ... συνεστηκυῖαν γὰρ ἐκ τῶν στοιχείων καὶ μεμερισμένην κατὰ τοὺς ἁρμονικοὺς ἀριθμούς, ὅπως αἴσθησίν τε σύμφυτον ἁρμονίας ἔχη καὶ τὸ πᾶν φέρηται συμφώνους φοράς, τὴν εὐθυωρίαν εἰς κύκλον κατέκαμψεν· καὶ διελὼν ἐκ τοῦ ἑνὸς δύο κύκλους δισσαχῆ συνημμένους πάλιν τὸν ἕνα διεῖλεν εἰς ἑπτὰ κύκλους... ἁρμονικός does not occur in Plato; it is found occasionally in Aristotle and is credited by Philo, as an arithmetical term, to Archytas. μεμερισμένη does not occur in the *Timaeus* 36B–D. *TL*, 96D, says: ἁ δὲ τῷ ἑτέρῳ φορὰ μεμερισμένα καθ᾽ ἁρμονικὼς λόγως ἐς ἑπτὰ κύκλως συντέτακται. The phrase κατ᾽ ἀριθμὼς ἁρμονικώς occurs in *TL*, 96A.

(2) In *Physics* A, 191a8, Aristotle, arguing for ὕλη, says ἡ δὲ ὑποκειμένη φύσις ἐπιστητὴ κατ᾽ ἀναλογίαν. As bronze is to statues, etc., so the ὑποκειμένη φύσις is to what has substantial existence. *TL*, 94B, says: ... τὰν δ᾽ ὕλαν λογισμῷ νόθῳ τῷ μήπω κατ᾽ εὐθυωρίαν νοῆσθαι ἀλλὰ κατ᾽ ἀναλογίαν.

Plato's *Timaeus*, 52B, gives us the 'bastard reasoning', with no mention of 'analogy'.

In the same passage Aristotle had used the rather rare word ἀσχημάτιστος. This occurs, also on p. 94A, in *TL* but not in the *Timaeus*.

(3) In his *De Sensu*, 437a3–17, Aristotle, like the *Timaeus*, 47,

assesses the intellectual values of sight and hearing, Plato's phrase, 47 C, μεγίστην συμβαλλόμενος εἰς αὐτὰ μοῖραν being echoed by Aristotle's πρὸς φρόνησιν ἡ ἀκοὴ πλεῖστον συμβάλλεται μέρος. Aristotle adds that those who have been blind are more intelligent than those who have been deaf from birth. *TL*, 100 C, makes this addition too; and Aristotle's τῶν ἐκ γενετῆς ἐστερημένων rings like that in *TL*: . . . ἀκουᾶν . . . ἃς στερισκόμενος ἐκ γενέσιος ὁ ἄνθρωπος οὐδὲ λόγον ἔτι προέσθαι δυνάσεται.

(4) In *De Gen. et Corr.*, 329 a 13, Aristotle says, 'What is written in the *Timaeus* is not accurately defined; for Plato has not clearly stated whether his 'omnirecipient' (τὸ πανδεχές) has any existence apart from the elements (στοιχείων) nor does he make any use of it, after saying that it is a substratum (ὑποκείμενον) prior to the so-called elements, 'as gold is to objects made of gold'. Plato does not use ὑποκείμενον in the *Timaeus*, in 51 A or anywhere else. *TL*, 97 E, uses ὑποκείμενον of ὕλη, though Aristotle's purported citation as a whole is not in *TL* or in the *Timaeus*.

(5) In Περὶ φιλοσοφίας, Fr. 12 *b* (Ross), 1476 a 27 (quoted by Sextus Empiricus) Aristotle says: . . . θεασάμενοι ἥλιον μὲν τοὺς ἀπὸ ἀνατολῆς μέχρι δύσεως δρόμους σταδιεύοντα . . . This resembles *TL*, 97 B, τὸν ἅλιον, ὃς ἀμέραν ἀποδίδωτι τὸν ἀπ' ἀνατολᾶς ἐπὶ δύσιν αὐτῶ δρόμον. No such phrase occurs in the *Timaeus*, 38–9.

(6) In [?] Aristotle's *Magna Moralia* (1204 b 38) Plato's notion of pleasure as a restoration is criticised. The noun and verb used are ἀποκατάστασις and ἀποκαθίσταναι, completed by εἰς φύσιν. Plato does not use this noun or verb in the *Timaeus*, *Republic* or *Philebus*. Nor does Aristotle in *EN* or *EE*. *TL*, 100 C, paraphrases the *Timaeus*' account of pleasure by ἀποκαθίσταντι ἐς αὐτάν (sc. φύσιν).

(7) In *Topics* E, 130 a 11–13, 132 b 21 and 31, Aristotle comments on certain unnamed persons' ascriptions of Properties. Fire was σῶμα τὸ εὐκινητότατον εἰς τὸν ἄνω τόπον, σῶμα τὸ λεπτότατον τῶν σωμάτων, σῶμα τὸ λεπτότατον καὶ κουφότατον. Fire had the property τοῦ λεπτομερεστάτου σώματος. It was a property of Earth to be βαρύτατον τῷ εἴδει.

In the *Timaeus*, 56 A–B, τὸ εὐκινητότατον [εἶδος] was ascribed to Fire, as well as τὸ σμικρότατον σῶμα and τὸ ἐλαφρότατον ἐξ ὀλιγίστων . . . τῶν αὐτῶν μερῶν. So presumably Aristotle has the *Timaeus* in mind. But the vocabulary used by Aristotle coincides less closely with that of the *Timaeus* than with that of *TL*, 98 D, where λεπτομερέστατον, βαρύτατον, and εὐκινητότατον all occur; only the last occurs in the relevant passage in the *Timaeus*.

(8) In *De Respiratione*, 472 b and 474 a, Aristotle dismisses the

Periosis theory of breathing in the *Timaeus*, 79, for an 'in–out'
motion, like that of the air in the blacksmith's bellows. *TL*, 102 A,
says nothing about *periosis*, but likens breathing to the ebb and flow
of the tide, *euripus*. Aristotle uses this simile in a different physiological
context in *De Somn. et Vig.* 456b21.

(9) In *De Caelo*, 304 A, Aristotle, referring presumably to the
Timaeus, 56 A–B, criticises the argument that Fire must be composed of
pyramids, since Fire is the 'cuttingest' (τμητικώτατον) of bodies,
and the pyramid is ditto of shapes. He then discusses the 'subtler'
argument from the fact that Fire is the *finest* (λεπτομερέστατον) of
bodies, and the pyramid is ditto of solid shapes. *TL*, 98 E, gives this
'subtler' theory and not that of the *Timaeus*. λεπτομειρία and
λεπτομερέστατος do not occur in the *Timaeus*; they do in *TL*,
98 D–E.

(10) In *De Caelo*, 307b11–16, Aristotle criticises, presumably,
Plato's account of Cold and Hot in terms of the sizes of the fire-
pyramids: φασὶ γὰρ εἶναι ψυχρὸν τὸ μεγαλομερὲς διὰ τὸ συνθλίβειν καὶ
μὴ διιέναι διὰ τῶν πόρων. δῆλον τοίνυν ὅτι καὶ τὸ θερμὸν ἂν εἴη τὸ διιόν·
τοιοῦτον δ' ἀεὶ τὸ λεπτομερές. ὥστε συμβαίνει μικρότητι καὶ μεγέθει δια-
φέρειν τὸ θερμὸν καὶ τὸ ψυχρόν, ἀλλ' οὐ τοῖς σχήμασιν.

This tallies well with *TL*, 100 E, τὸ μὲν ὦν θερμὸν λεπτομερές τε καὶ
διαστατικὸν τῶν σωμάτων δοκεῖ εἶμεν, τὸ δὲ ψυχρὸν παχυμερέστερον
καὶ συμπιλατικὸν πόρων ἐστί. Cold is πιλητικός in [Aristotle] *Problems*,
14, 8, 909b18. The *Timaeus*, 62 A–B, has nothing about pores. It
does, however, contain μεγαλομερέστερα like Aristotle's μεγαλομερές,
where *TL* has παχυμερέστερον. Aristotle and the *TL* have λεπτομερές
where Plato has only λεπτότητα and σμικρότητα.

(11) In *De Caelo*, 279a7–11, Aristotle says: ἐξ ἁπάσης γάρ ἐστι
τῆς οἰκείας ὕλης ὁ πᾶς κόσμος. . .ὥστε οὔτε νῦν εἰσὶ πλείους οὐρανοὶ οὔτ'
ἐγένοντο, οὔτ' ἐνδέχεται γενέσθαι πλείους· ἀλλ' εἷς καὶ μόνος καὶ τέλειος
οὗτος οὐρανός ἐστιν.

This resembles *TL*, 94 C–D, [ὁ θεὸς] ἐποίησεν ὦν τόνδε τὸν κόσμον ἐξ
ἁπάσας τᾶς ὕλας, ὅρον αὐτὸν κατασκευάξας τᾶς τῶ ὄντος φύσιος διὰ τὸ
τἆλλα πάντα ἐν αὐτῷ περιέχεν, ἕνα, μονογενῆ, τέλειον, ἔμψυχόν τε καὶ
λογικόν. Aristotle says that the οὐρανός is ἔμψυχος in *De Caelo*, 285 a 30,
where Plato had called the cosmos ζῷον ἔμψυχον ἔννουν in *Timaeus*,
30 B.

(12) In his *Aristotle: Physics*, p. 17, Ross, following Jaeger, argues
for the earliness of *Physics* VII from its reference, 246b4–8, to the
ἀρεταὶ τοῦ σώματος, namely ὑγίεια, κάλλος and ἰσχύς. These bodily
ἀρεταί are mentioned together in Aristotle's *Eudemus* and *Topics*;
they do not appear thus in Aristotle's later writings, like his *EN*.

They had been mentioned together in Plato's *Republic, Philebus* and *Laws*, though only in the *Republic* are they treated as ἀρεταί. They are not mentioned together, nor are bodily ἀρεταί mentioned in the *Timaeus*.

In the *TL*, 103 C, the ἀρεταί and κακίαι of the body are mentioned generically; ὑγίεια, κάλλος and ἰσχύς, plus εὐαισθησία, are the specific 'virtues' mentioned. The account in the *TL* is fuller than that in *Physics* VII, *Eudemus* and *Topics*. The *Physics* talks of the 'symmetry' of warm and cold [humours], where the *TL* talks of the 'asymmetries' of warmness, coldness, wetness and dryness. These four 'humours' are mentioned in connection with 'symmetry' in *Topics*, 116b18–22; and cf. 139b21 and 145b8. Plato, in the *Timaeus* and elsewhere, has the four Empedoclean elements; but not the four humours.

Incidentally the passage in the *Physics* VII, 246b9, says that each of the bodily ἀρεταί and κακίαι ...εὖ ἢ κακῶς διατίθησι τὸ ἔχον. *TL*, 103 A, has the markedly similar phrase ...εὖ ἢ κακῶς ἀμὲ διατίθητι. A little later, 247a7, Aristotle says that all ethical virtue is concerned with bodily pleasures and pains. *TL*, 102 E, says that the ἀρχαί of badness are pleasures and pains, desires and fears, ἐξαμμέναι μὲν ἐκ σώματος, ἀνακεκραμέναι δὲ τᾷ ψυχᾷ. In *EN* Aristotle had given up this extreme physiological account.

(13) Vocabulary-coincidences between *TL* and Aristotle are very frequent. Between 80 and 90 out-of-the-way non-Platonic words in *TL*, about 5 per page, are found also and often only in writings of Aristotle, like *De Caelo, Meteorologica, De Partibus Animalium*, etc.

The 'Platonic' Definitions. In vol. v of Burnet's *Opera Platonis*, there is the collection of Definitions erroneously labelled 'Platonic'.

(1) On the first page, a definition of 'God' runs: Θεὸς ...τῆς τἀγαθοῦ φύσεως αἰτία.

In the second sentence of *TL* we find, δύο αἰτίας εἶμεν τῶν συμπάντων, νόον μὲν...ἀνάγκαν δὲ...τουτέων δὲ τὸν μὲν τᾶς τἀγαθῶ φύσιος εἶμεν θεόν τε ὀνυμαίνεσθαι.

(2) On the same page a definition of 'Day' runs: ἡμέρα ἡλίου πορεία ἀπ' ἀνατολῶν ἐπὶ δυσμάς. *TL*, 97 B, has τὸν ἄλιον, ὃς ἀμέραν ἀποδίδωτι τὸν ἀπ' ἀνατολᾶς ἐπὶ δύσιν αὐτῶ δρόμον.

We have then, besides lots of vocabulary-coincidences, a score of apparent passage-echoes between the very short *TL* and other works; few of them can be dismissed as fortuitous. Which way does the echoing run?

My view is that the *TL* preceded even the *Definitions*, Aristotle's *Eudemus*, *De Philosophia*, *De Caelo* and *Topics* and, *a fortiori*, his later works and those of later writers. Aristotle's, Zeno's and Plutarch's memories of the *Timaeus* were blended with their memories of the *TL*, which was short enough to memorise. Since, as I shall argue elsewhere, the *Timaeus* was not given to the world but only to the Academy, so that during his lifetime the only text of the *Timaeus* was in Plato's custody, Aristotle, until he was over 37, may have had no regular access, if any, to this text, though he must have often heard it and made full notes of what he heard. But he possessed his own copy of the *TL*.

My reasons are these:

(1) As said earlier, the *TL*'s non-Platonic vocabulary is, save for ἅπαξ λεγόμενα, almost wholly Aristotelian, Hippocratic, Speusippan, Archytean and Theophrastan. Only three of its words look like Stoic words, and possibly the Stoics got them from the *TL*.

(2) The writings of Plutarch, the Stoics, and, of course, our Aristotle himself are full of Aristotelian logical and metaphysical terms. So are the '*Platonic*' *Definitions*. How could the postulated late writer of the *TL* have gleaned vocabulary and ideas from the Stoics, Plutarch, Theophrastus and Aristotle without picking up any Category-parlance or making any mentions of Contraries, Privations, Actualities and Potentialities, Four Causes, Peras and Apeiron, etc? The *TL* reads as if its author did not know the *Categories*, *Topics* or *Metaphysics*, or the writings of anyone who did. It reads so because he did not.

(3) What customers wanted a digest of the *Timaeus*? The dialogue, though longish, is short compared with the *Republic* and the *Laws*.

Elsewhere I shall argue that the *Timaeus* is identical with the single lecture given by Plato to Dionysius in 367–6 (see the *Seventh Letter*, 341 and 344). Now this composition was not to be given to the public, in speech or in writing (341 D–E), but only to those who knew how to research, i.e. to the members of the Academy. Galen says that the *Timaeus* was not published to the world by Plato (Kühn, vol. IV, 757 ff.). The *Timaeus* was indeed ill suited for general dissemination. Its theology was unorthodox; and its second half was pure medical students' pabulum. Above all, much of its substance was not Plato's own, but drawn from Archytas and Philistion. The description of Timaeus in the *Timaeus* is the description of Archytas. Plato would not steal.

So if the *Timaeus* was unpublished during Plato's lifetime, there might well have then existed a demand for a *précis*-paraphrase of it.

The *Timaeus* was published soon after Plato's death. Aristotle often refers to what is 'written' in the *Timaeus*, and occasionally cites its *ipsissima verba*. Theophrastus knew it and Crantor wrote a commentary on it. It was the time while the *Timaeus* was confined to the Academy, before Plato's death, that was the right period for the production of a digest of it, to serve as an 'exoteric' deputy for it.

(4) If so, then only an Academic who had been taught from it would yet be equipped to write a digest of it. That his non-Platonic vocabulary should largely be Aristotelian, Hippocratic and Theophrastan is just what we should then expect. The *TL*'s author studied in the Academy and also knew things deriving from Archytas and Philistion other than what is in the *Timaeus*.

(5) If all or several of my alleged echoes are genuine, then the hypothesis of a post-Plutarch *TL* would be the hypothesis that the author of a brief *précis* of an only moderately long and, by now, basic Platonic dialogue, ransacked, jackdaw-like, works by Plutarch, Zeno, 'Hippocrates', Speusippus, Archytas, Philistion, Theophrastus, Democritus, and especially Aristotle, plus the *Definitions*, for non-Platonic sentiments and vocabulary with which to de-Platonize the *Timaeus*. Moreover, his ransackings were highly selective. No Stoic ideas or terms, save perhaps two, were to be used; no Aristotelian logical terms or ideas; and only three Aristotelian metaphysical terms or ideas. For what customers could such a curious concoction be designed? For studious readers of the *Timaeus*? Then why did the author not simply paraphrase the *Timaeus*? And why did he attempt eloquence? On this hypothesis *TL* would be echoing some non-Platonic doctrines which Aristotle had held in early writings (e.g. *Physics* VII and above all *De Caelo*), but had modified in later writings (e.g. *EN* and *De Sensu*).

(6) The interval between Plutarch's and Nicomachus' floruits cannot be a long one and might be a short one. The *TL*, if it appeared during this interval, would have been known by Nicomachus to be a very recent production or resurrection. Yet he regarded it as a genuine antique. If he did not suspect it of borrowing from his near-contemporary Plutarch, we should suspect the idea that it did so.

III. ARISTOTLE

We now have enough pointers to surmise that Aristotle himself, when a very young man, wrote the *TL*, if only the objection that the *TL* is in imitation Doric can be circumvented. E. Frank, in his *Plato u. die Sogenannten Pythagoreer*, shows that Speusippus and Xenocrates also doricised. But it is just its being doricised that has inhibited the idea of Aristotle's authorship of the *TL*.

Diogenes Laertius ascribes to Aristotle a single book called *Extracts from the 'Timaeus' and the Works of Archytas*, Τὰ ἐκ τοῦ Τιμαίου καὶ τῶν 'Αρχυτείων. This, I suggest, is the *TL*, which is brief enough to be 'one book'.

Well, then, how could a composition by Aristotle be in would-be Doric? In 361 Plato made his third visit to Syracuse. Though the *'Platonic' Letters* hush this up, there were with him Speusippus, Aristippus and Aeschines; Xenocrates was almost certainly there; Eudoxus was probably there. There was a delegation of intellectuals from Athens and Dionysius had invited them all, probably in concert with Archytas. I had already wondered why Aristotle should *not* have been in this delegation, with Xenocrates, when it struck me that Aristotle's early writings do have a markedly Italian bias.

When pretty young he wrote a book about the Pythagoreans. In the *Fragments* we have several snippets from this book. As these seem to be the sorts of things to hail from oral traditions, perhaps Aristotle collected them in person in the 'boot' of Italy. One batch of stories comes from Pythagoras' region of Croton, Sybaris and Metapontum. In his *Politics* VII, 1329b, Aristotle seems to draw, quite gratuitously, on some contemporary traveller's topographical knowledge of this region, and so, perhaps, on his own knowledge. Maybe some of the numerous yarns about Sicily and southern Italy in the *De Mirabilibus Auscultationibus* are out of Aristotle's own travel-diaries. In his *Politics* Aristotle draws a surprising number of his examples from the Greek cities of the Mediterranean and Adriatic. Aristotle's early *On Contraries* is said by Simplicius to have been powerfully influenced by Archytas. Aristotle also wrote three books on Archytas. His *Extracts from the 'Timaeus' and the Works of Archytas* is likely to have been fairly early, if the *Timaeus* was not published during Plato's lifetime, so that it would be during this period that there would be a demand for a digest of it. Perhaps Aristotle could have acquired his interest in the Pythagoreans and the ideas of Archytas and Philistion without leaving Athens. But perhaps he acquired his interest and knowledge in Syracuse and Tarentum. The strong influence of the Sicilian doctor Philistion upon Aristotle, described in C. Allbutt's *Greek Medicine in Rome* (Macmillan, 1921) and W. Jaeger's *Diokles von Karystos* (1938), was too deep and wide to have been the product of transported lecture-notes or the reminiscences of go-betweens. Aristotle sat at Philistion's feet, somewhere;

maybe he sat at his feet in Syracuse and at Archytas' feet in Tarentum in 361–0.

No authority lists the members of the delegation. Plutarch tells us of Plato, Speusippus, Aristippus and Aeschines; Diogenes Laertius of Plato, Xenocrates, Aeschines and Aristippus; Aelian (*Var. Hist.* VII, 17) of Plato and Eudoxus. No one tells us that Aristotle was there or gives a roster of the visitors which excludes him. Aristotle nowhere gives us an atom of autobiography.

This is, as yet, speculation, but let us, for the moment, assume its truth. Then it would have been proper for Aristotle to present his host with a discourse. The visitors were expected to 'sing for their supper'. If so, then Aristotle, aged 24, would have been likely to deliver something reproductive rather than original. Diogenes Laertius says that Aristippus both presented compositions to Dionysius and wrote some compositions in Doric. Presumably Aristippus' Doric compositions were his gifts to Dionysius. It was a courtesy to discourse to a Syracusan audience in its dialect. Consequently, if the *TL* was Aristotle's gift to Dionysius, we should have a simple explanation why it is in amateurish Doric. Aristotle wished to do the courteous thing but did not know the dialect very well. The amateurish doricising of Speusippus and Xenocrates might be similarly explained.

So far my picture is this. The delegation arrives in Syracuse in the early summer of 361. Dionysius, who had heard Plato delivering the *Timaeus* five years before, wishes to have a *précis* of this unpublished dialogue. Plato permits or desires Aristotle to compose such a *précis*. No copy of the *Timaeus* is in Syracuse, so Aristotle has to produce from his memory, helped out perhaps by that of Xenocrates, the gist of the dialogue that he has studied and restudied during his last five years in the Academy. Plato desires him to put his digest in his own words. The *TL* contains not a sentence and hardly even a phrase quoted *verbatim* from the *Timaeus*, and its eloquence is not Plato's.

The delegates are eagerly absorbing Italian and Sicilian philosophy and science. Archytas' disciple, Archedemus, was a resident in Syracuse, and Plato lived in his house for part of the year. Plato lets Aristotle incorporate in his digest Archytean improvements upon the *Timaeus*, which had itself expounded doctrines of Archytas and Philistion. The *Timaeus* was a scientific and especially a medical manual for the Academy, so it was proper for it to be brought up to date. We might guess that where the astronomy of the *TL* improves on the *Timaeus*, Archedemus had taught Aristotle and Eudoxus new doctrines of his master. Conceivably the Hylemorphism of the *TL* and of Aristotle derived from Archytas, whom, in *Met.* H, 1043 a 21, Aristotle credits with a Matter–Form doctrine. Among the out-of-the-way words in the *TL*, three or four are said to be Archytean, including 'harmonic' in its arithmetical sense. The Eurytus story in Ar. *Met.* N, 1092 b 10, came from a *talk* by Archytas (Theophrastus, *Met.* 6 a 19, ἔφη). *Extracts from the 'Timaeus' and the Works of Archytas* would then be a proper title for the *TL*.

I must now both complicate and corroborate this story. I have been identifying the *TL* with Aristotle's *Extracts* but there remains to be accounted for a, seemingly, second paraphrase of the *Timaeus*, if this really is the single lecture which according to the *Seventh Letter* Plato delivered to Dionysius in 367–6. For Dionysius himself is said, coached by unnamed persons, to have produced a version of this single lecture.

The *Seventh Letter* is a Dionist forgery, but where Sicilians would have first-hand knowledge it would need to be veracious, else the gaff would be blown. So presumably Dionysius did deliver a version of the *Timaeus* and some Dionist addressees of the *Seventh Letter* heard him deliver it.

I now suggest that the *TL*, the *Extracts* and Dionysius' version are all one and the same composition. The *Seventh Letter*'s unnamed 'lesser or greater men', 344 D, and the 'certain others (who) have written about these same subjects, but what manner of men they are not even themselves know', 341 B, are Aristotle, who by the year 353 really could be described as γεγραφότων καὶ γραψόντων and as εἴτ' ἐμοῦ ἀκηκοότες εἴτ' ἄλλων εἴθ' ὡς εὑρόντες αὐτοί, 341 C. It might be very significant that 'Plato' mentions pupils of his own in Syracuse. Who could they be save Xenocrates and, hypothetically, Aristotle? Presumably Dionysius took no hand in the composition of the *TL*. Aristotle composed it for Dionysius to deliver, as Isocrates composed the *Nicocles* for Nicocles and the *Archidamus* for Archidamus to deliver. This rather than mere courtesy is the reason why the *TL* is in would-be Doric. If their high-brow tyrant was to discourse to Syracusans it would be in Doric. This too would explain why the *TL* was never ascribed to Aristotle. Not only was it in quasi-Doric; but his hearers credited it to Dionysius. His 24-year-old visiting ghost-writer was not yet a name to them.

To reverse the argument. If Plato's single lecture in 367–6 was the *Timaeus*, then we have contemporary evidence in the *Seventh Letter* that a version of the *Timaeus* was produced by Dionysius before he was ousted in 356. The *TL*, being in would-be Doric and having a

4th century vocabulary and scientific content, has a strong claim to be identical with this version. Two 4th century Doric versions of the *Timaeus* would be one too many.

His *Extracts* would be naturally dated early in Aristotle's career, while he is influenced by Archytas and while the *Timaeus* is still unpublished. To identify the *Extracts* with the Syracusan *Timaeus*-paraphrase requires just one very big historical premiss, namely that, though extant Greek literature is silent on the matter, Aristotle did go to Syracuse in 361, did act as Dionysius' ghost-writer, and did study under Philistion and Archytas. Jaeger, in his *Diokles von Karystos*, accounts for the influence of Philistion upon Aristotle by bringing Philistion to the Academy. He adduces as evidence the mention of the Sicilian doctor in the fragment from Epicrates, the invitation to Philistion from Speusippus in the forged *Second Letter*, and the statement of Diogenes Laertius that Eudoxus studied under Philistion (and Archytas). Jaeger overlooks the possible visit of Eudoxus to Syracuse in 361. At least the influence of Philistion upon Aristotle requires *either* Philistion visiting Athens *or* Aristotle going to Syracuse when quite young. Jaeger does not ask, Where and when did Eudoxus and Aristotle learn the doctrines of Archytas? Archytas did not come to Athens, though Archedemus did.

Style. The TL is not in Aristotle's lecture style, but nor are his dialogues, or his *De Philosophia* or *Protrepticus*. The TL essays eloquence as if intended for an audience. One high-falutin word χειρόκμητος is also in Aristotle's *De Caelo, De Philosophia* and *Meteorologica* and in Democritus.

Aristotle has a penchant for words ending in '...ikos' and '...ike'. Only in two late dialogues does Plato acquire this habit. It is not strong in the *Timaeus*, or, surprisingly, in the *Characters* of Theophrastus. There are 22 such words in the 17–18 pages of the TL, a higher ratio even than in the *Rhetoric* or the *Eudemian Ethics*. Aristotle loves verbs with biprepositional prefixes, like συνεπι-τείνειν. There are over a dozen such verbs in the TL. Jaeger, in his *Diokles von Karystos*, adduces both idioms as evidence that Diocles learned his Attic from the late Plato and Aristotle. He also adduces Diocles' use of καθάπερ *vice* ὥσπερ, when hiatus was to be avoided. The TL uses ὥσπερ once, where there is not, and καθάπερ once where there is a hiatus to be avoided.

Aristotle uniformly prefers φοινικοῦς for 'red' to Plato's ἐρυθρός. So does the TL. Aristotle prefers φωσφόρος to Plato's ἑωσφόρος. So does the TL. The *Epinomis* uses ἑωσφόρος.

IV. TWO DIFFICULTIES

(1) Simplicius, in a passage cited in the *Fragments* 'On the Philosophy of Archytas', says: '[Aristotle] epitomising Plato's *Timaeus* writes "................".' The quotation which follows is not from the *TL*. Simplicius seems to quote Aristotle *verbatim*, so if 'epitomising Plato's *Timaeus*' meant 'in his epitome of Plato's *Timaeus*', i.e. 'in his *Extracts from the "Timaeus" and the Works of Archytas*', the *TL* would not be identical with the *Extracts*, since a sentence found by Simplicius in the latter is not in the former.

I suggest that 'epitomising Plato's *Timaeus*' need not mean 'in his Epitome of Plato's *Timaeus*', but only 'putting succinctly what the *Timaeus* says at greater length'. Aristotle's *Extracts* were not *entitled* 'Epitome of . . .'.

If so, Simplicius could be quoting from any lost work of Aristotle, perhaps from the *De Philosophia*, which he did know. ἐπιτέμνειν is used for 'abbreviate' or 'curtail', and not for 'write an epitome of', in *De Soph. Elench.* 174 b 29.

The idea that Aristotle's *Extracts* was other than the *TL* would leave it unexplained why nowhere else does Simplicius use it in expounding the *Timaeus*. In my view, the commentators, including Plutarch, did use it; for it was what we know as the *Timaeus Locrus*; they had no idea that Aristotle wrote it. There did not exist an additional *précis* for them to use. They do not mention the *TL* by name because it had no name, or even a namable author. It was just a handy *Timaeus-précis* of unknown origin and of a date which they knew or believed to be early. I guess that some people, including Nicomachus, identified the *TL* with the Pythagorean work from which they uncharitably supposed that Plato lifted his *Timaeus*.

(2) On p. 97 c the *TL* speaks of the sun advancing one degree *per diem*, κατὰ μίαν μοῖραν ἐν ἀμερησίῳ χρόνῳ. If by 'one degree' were meant one 360th of a circle, then the *TL* would be post-Hipparchus, who, in the 2nd century B.C., introduced this metric into geometry. However, Hipparchus was merely generalising from the Chaldean astronomers' division of the Zodiacal circle in particular into 12 equal 'signs', and of each 'sign' into 30 equal sections. These yielded the 12 months of the year and the 30 days of the month. So the Zodiac is divided into 360 sections, or 'Chaldean degrees'.

When did the Greeks get to know this Chaldean division of the Zodiac? Its division into 12 'signs' was known in Greece before Plato's day. Both Democritus and Eudoxus might have brought back from the Orient the Chaldean degree with the astronomy that they amassed there, but we have no proof that they did so. Aristarchus, in the 3rd century B.C., must have known it, since he speaks of 1/30 of a right angle, 1/15 of a Zodiacal 'sign', and 1/720 of the Zodiacal circle.

Eudemus mentions a pre-Aristotelian astronomer who divided the Zodiac into fifteenths. This is a nicely sub-divisible fraction of 360, so conceivably he was working with the Chaldean metric.

I claim that the *TL* shows rather that the Chaldean degree was known in Greece or Italy a century before Aristarchus, than that the *TL* is as late as Aristarchus. Or is the *TL* merely saying, tautologically, that the Sun moves through the Zodiac at the rate of 1/36oth of its year's progress *per diem*?

5

THE ACADEMY AND DIALECTIC

Reprinted from 'New Essays on Plato and Aristotle', edited by R. Bambrough, 1965, by permission of Routledge & Kegan Paul Ltd and Humanities Press Inc.; the title there was 'Dialectic in the Academy'

I. ARISTOTLE'S 'ART OF DIALECTIC'

A treatise called *The Art of So and So* was a body of general rules, explanations, examples, warnings and recommendations, the study of which was calculated to help the student to become proficient in the practice in question. It was a training manual. Protagoras is said to have written an *Art of Wrestling*. Some people may learn to wrestle well from mere flair, habituation and imitation; but there is much to be learned also from the technical theory of wrestling. The same thing is true of medicine and navigation. Rule of thumb is not enough.

Between the time of Protagoras and that of Aristotle in his early teaching years, there had appeared a considerable number of *Arts of Rhetoric*. This is quite understandable since intelligent and ambitious young Greeks who looked forward to careers in public life needed to be taught how to compose forensic and political orations. Nor, save for a few specialists like mathematicians, astronomers and doctors, was any other higher education provided, until the Academy began. Not all, but many, of the sophists of whom anything is known were, or were *inter alia*, teachers of rhetoric. The training manuals of rhetoric that Plato mentions in his *Phaedrus* (especially 266-7) were all composed by sophists. Some of these *Arts* were versified to aid memorisation by students. Aristotle, too, wrote an *Art of Rhetoric*, which we possess. But what concerns us is something different. He also wrote an *Art of Dialectic*, known to us as his *Topics*. What was the practice of dialectic of which Aristotle's *Topics* is the Art? We know what the practitioners of rhetoric practised, in what circumstances and for what professions or careers. We are not so sure what a student of the art of dialectic hoped to become a practitioner of. We know the kind of career that a Demosthenes had. Was there a corresponding kind of career for a dialectician? If not, then for whom was Aristotle providing a training manual, and for what vocation?

I mention Aristotle's *Art of Rhetoric* alongside his *Art of Dialectic* partly because Aristotle himself closely associates the two practices (*De Arte Rhet.* Book I (1) 11, 12, 14; (2) 7, 8, 9, etc.; *Topics* 164a5, 167b8, 174b19, 183b). Moreover, as we shall see, the exercise which Aristotle calls 'dialectic' had been taught for a long time before Aristotle, anyhow sometimes as an ancillary to rhetoric.

What, then, is this exercise of dialectic, for which the *Topics* is a training manual? There is a special pattern of disputation, governed by strict rules, which takes the following shape. Two persons 'agree to have a battle'. One is to be questioner, the other answerer. The questioner can only ask questions; and the answerer can, with certain qualifications, answer only 'yes' or 'no'. So the questioner's questions have to be properly constructed for 'yes' or 'no' answers. This automatically rules out a lot of types of questions, like factual questions, arithmetical questions, and technical questions. Roughly it leaves us only conceptual questions, whatever these may be. The answerer begins by undertaking to uphold a certain 'thesis', e.g. that *justice is the interest of the stronger*, or that *knowledge is sense-perception*. The questioner has to try to extract from the answerer, by a series of questions, an answer or conjunction of answers inconsistent with the original thesis, i.e. drive him into an 'elenchus'. The questioner has won the duel if he succeeds in getting the answerer to contradict his original thesis, or else in forcing him to resign, or in reducing him to silence, to an infinite regress, to mere abusiveness, to pointless yammering, or to outrageous paradox. The answerer has won if he succeeds in keeping his wicket up until the close of play. The answerer is allowed to object to a question on the score that, for example, it is two or more questions in one, like *have you left off beating your father?*, or that it is metaphorical or ambiguous. The duel is fought out before an audience (cf. *Sophist* 230c); and apparently it is sometimes left to the audience to judge whether the questioner or the answerer has won. Certain debating tricks and manoeuvres are recognised as fouls (*Topics* 171b20; 172b20; cf. Plato, *Theaetetus* 167E). The exercise has to have a time-limit, or else the answerer can never win. I think the 'time's up' is referred to in *Topics* 161a10 and 183a25.

In the Greek world in general, elenctic duelling is normally called 'eristic', but this word has acquired pejorative connotations for

Plato and Aristotle. They use this word and its variants for commercialised and debased forms of the exercise practised by certain sophists, who stoop to all sorts of tricks in order to make sure of winning. Plato's *Euthydemus* depicts such sophists in action. Aristotle uses the word 'dialectic' for the exercise as practised with intellectual seriousness and without conscious trickery. I shall show that Plato does so too. The word 'eristic' continues to be used, often with no pejorative connotations, after Plato's and Aristotle's time, and I shall regularly use it myself. The word 'dialectic' now carries too many daunting and uplifting associations for us to rely on it.

Why do people engage in eristic Moots? Aristotle gives several reasons:

(*a*) There is the pedagogic or tutorial motive. A student's wits are sharpened if he is made to practise argumentation by trying to defend his own theses against criticisms and by trying to think up and organise criticisms of other people's theses. So the teacher may either himself engage his pupil in eristic bouts, or else pit one pupil against another, subject to his own tutorial criticisms of their arguments. This is dialectic conducted with a *gymnastic* purpose. Obviously students may, for fun and for extra practice, conduct their own matches without tutorial supervision.

(*b*) Sometimes people are intellectually complacent or reckless. They need for the good of their souls and wits to be deflated. When they discover that they can quickly be driven, without trickery, into acknowledging things patently inconsistent with other things which they had felt perfectly sure of, they become warier and intellectually humbler. This is what Aristotle calls the *peirastic* or probing purpose. It is a part or species of the pedagogic or tutorial dialectic.

(*c*) The exercise is an absorbing game—difficult, exciting, and competitive. It has much in common with chess and fencing. It is fun to win, and fun even to try to counter one's opponent's stratagems. Aristotle calls this the *agonistic*, i.e. the match-winning, purpose of the exercise. Aristotle says, what we could have guessed anyhow, that even those who dispute for intellectual gymnastic cannot be stopped from trying to win (*Topics* 164b8–14). The students are, after all, young men; and their instructor, Aristotle, is not very old.

From Plato's *Republic* VII (537–9) (and cf. *Apology* 23 C) it appears that by the composition date of this book the eristic game had acquired an unhealthy vogue; and that this had led to scandal or crisis. (See also Isocrates, *Helen* 1.) Socrates refuses to let young men engage in the exercise, though their sober seniors may do so.

Apparently this really was the initial policy of the Academy. At the end of his *De Sophisticis Elenchis* Aristotle claims to have had to work out the entire *techne* of dialectic by himself. He draws on Plato's dialogues for specimens, but he acknowledges no debts to Platonic tuition in the theory of dialectic. He received no such tuition. Plato did not teach Aristotle philosophy. This ban on eristic for young students has, however, been lifted by the time of the *Parmenides* (Part II). Now Aristotle is already teaching much of the contents of the *Topics*, and teaching it to young men.

(*d*) Some of the sophists, on occasions, put on public tournaments in which, debatably, they take on challengers from the audience, or else challenge one another. Their object is to win at all costs, and so build up such a reputation for invincibility that they will make money—make money, presumably, from the fees of the pupils who will flock for coaching in such duelling, and, conjecturally, from the gate-money paid by the audiences who come to hear the champion performing. This is the prize-fighting or *eristic* purpose, in the pejorative sense that the word has for Plato and Aristotle.

(*e*) Finally, serious philosophers engage in duels with each other from an interest in philosophical issues themselves. Though Euthydemus and Dionysodorus may use as a mere booby-trap the question *Does not he who says that something is the case say something that is the case?*, i.e. *Are not all significant statements true?*, a Plato or an Aristotle will examine this very same question in order to bring out into the light of day the relations between *significance* and *truth*. We may call this the *philosophical* purpose of the dialectical exercise. I shall have more to say later on about this function of dialectic.

In whichever of these five spirits the exercise is conducted, its rules are the same. Certain dodges, employed in sophistic duels, are disallowed in an Academic *milieu* (*Topics* 164b8, 171b21). We cannot from internal evidence fix the date when Aristotle composed the *Topics*. But in 354/3 B.C., i.e. some seven years before Plato's death, Isocrates, in his *Antidosis* (258–69; and cf. his *Panathenaicus* 26–9), makes it clear that the teaching of eristic is, with geometry and astronomy, already a part of the curriculum of the Academy. In the *Panathenaicus* and in his *Letter to Alexander* of 342 he is likely to be sneering at Aristotle in person as a teacher of eristic. Plato, in what must be a late, and I think is his latest finished, composition, the *Parmenides* (Part II), represents the venerated old Parmenides as demonstrating to the young Socrates the intellectual gymnastic which he must practise if he is to become a philosopher. He then produces the most unrelieved and formalised model of a two-way eristic question–answer exercise that has come down to us. The model conforms well with the rules and prescriptions collected in Aristotle's *Topics* for a philosophically serious exercise in dialectic. Plato himself does not here use the words 'dialectic', 'dialectician', or 'dialectical', or, of course, 'eristic', or 'eristical' either. There can be no reasonable doubt, then, that what Isocrates calls 'eristic' and Aristotle calls 'dialectic' is, despite the veto in *Republic* VII, being taught to young men in the Academy in or before the middle 350s; that Plato approves of this teaching; and that Aristotle teaches it, in fairly close connection with his teaching of rhetoric. It is not by coincidence that Plato unearths a coeval of Socrates called 'Aristotle' to be Parmenides' answerer. Xenocrates too must have been closely associated with the teaching of this *gymnastic*. Of his numerous writings the titles of which are recorded by Diogenes Laertius at least five have to do with dialectic, including one, in twenty books, *Of Theses*, another, in fourteen books, τῆς περὶ τὸ διαλέγεσθαι πραγματείας. At least two of the writings of Heracleides Ponticus must also be of this *genre*. That the exercise continues to be an important ingredient of university education throughout the succeeding centuries is shown by, among other things, the book-titles of the later Academics, Peripatetics and Stoics.

II. THE EARLIER HISTORY OF DIALECTIC

The eristic Moot was far from being the invention of Aristotle in particular or of the Academy in general. Its history goes well back into the fifth century. I set down here what I have been able to collect of its history. I shall often use the title 'eristic' for the exercise, though without the pejorative connotations which it acquired for Plato and Aristotle. It was these connotations, I guess, that made Plato coin, as Favorinus says he coined (D. L., *Plato*, 24), the noun 'dialectic', and therewith 'dialectician' and 'dialectical', from διαλέγεσθαι; this last was the general verb for 'discuss', 'debate', and, specifically, 'discuss by the method of question and answer'. There are two other recurrent titles for eristic disputation. It is sometimes called '*antilogike*', and its practitioners are described as 'antilogical' when emphasis is being laid on their readiness to argue impartially for and against any given thesis. It is sometimes called '*agonistike*', to emphasise the fact that its practitioners are primarily out to win their matches. This match-winning spirit is regularly called φιλονικία by both Plato and Aristotle. We could call it 'eristic gamesmanship'.

Diogenes Laertius credits a number of people with the invention of the eristic duel.

(a) *Zeno*. Diogenes Laertius quotes Aristotle as saying that Zeno was the inventor of dialectic; and Sextus Empiricus tells us that Aristotle said this in his *Sophist* (see Aristotle: *Selected Fragments*). Plato virtually says the same thing in the *Parmenides* where he makes old Parmenides tell the juvenile Socrates that if he is to become a philosopher he must put himself through a certain sort of training, namely in the method of reasoning of which Zeno has just produced an example. This method, however, requires a certain expansion. The argumentation should be two-way argumentation, deriving consequences both from a given proposition and from its negative. Parmenides then demonstrates the method in full question–answer style, with his answerer duly responding with 'yes' and 'no'. Commentators sometimes grumble at the unconversational role given to Parmenides' young interlocutor. But it is one of the first rules of the eristic exercise that the answerer has, with certain exceptions, to confine himself to assent and dissent. Cornford, in his translation of the *Parmenides*, omits the young Aristotle's responses, and thus obliterates the eristic procedure and intention of the dialogue. Now Zeno's own argumentation had not, apparently, taken the form of a questioner driving an answerer into elenchus after elenchus. It had been a chain of *reductiones ad absurdum*; and this is probably what Aristotle has in mind. An eristic elenchus is, so to speak, a two-person incarnation of a *reductio ad absurdum*. But it was not Zeno who invented this incarnation. He pitted arguments against arguments. It was someone else who first pitted questioners against answerers. If Zeno was the father, he was not also the mother of dialectic.

(b) *Euclides*. According to Diogenes Laertius, Euclides of Megara studied the writings of Parmenides; his followers were called 'Megarians', 'Eristics', and, later, 'Dialecticians' because they put their arguments in the form of question and answer. Euclides, we are told, rebutted demonstrations by attacking, not their premisses (λήμματα), but their ἐπιφορά, which I think must mean the inference from those premisses to their alleged conclusions. Eubulides, a follower of Euclides, is reported to have produced many dialectical arguments in interrogative form, including the famous and important crux 'the Liar'.

Plato and other Socratics are said to have taken refuge with Euclides at Megara after the execution of Socrates in 399. Plato brings old Euclides into the stage-setting of his *Theaetetus*; i.e. as still alive in 369. He is made to say that he had frequently had conversations with Socrates on his visits from Megara to Athens.

Suidas says that Bryson, together with Euclides, introduced the eristic dialectic.

We know very little about the Megarians, but we know enough to satisfy us that they had very sharp noses for important logical cruces. They consequently get short shrift from commentators on Plato, as does Zeno, of whose earthshaking discovery of the *reductio ad absurdum* the Megarians may well have been the transmitters.

(c) *Protagoras*. Diogenes Laertius says that Protagoras was the first to say that there are two opposite λόγοι about every subject; and was also the first to argue in this way, by means of questions (συνηρώτα). He was also the first to institute λόγων ἀγῶνας, i.e. eristic matches or duels; he introduced the Socratic Method; and he was the father of the whole tribe of eristical disputants. Protagoras is also reported to have written an *Art of Eristic*, and this may be hinted at in Plato's *Sophist* (232 D–E). It seems to me that we have good reasons for thinking that Protagoras did introduce the exercise into Athens; and that he was the first to give coaching in its techniques and to do so for a fee. As a teacher of rhetoric, wishing to train his pupils for forensic advocacy, he might well have invented the questioner–answerer Moot. The title of his *Art of Eristic* is strong evidence for the association of Protagoras with eristic; Diogenes' explicit statements are weak evidence. But we also have ample corroboration in both Isocrates and Plato.

At the beginning of his *Against the Sophists*, which can be dated *circa* 390, Isocrates scolds the teachers who devote themselves to disputation (τῶν περὶ τὰς ἔριδας διατριβούντων). They profess to search for the truth; they promise to teach the young what to do and how to prosper; they inculcate virtue and self-control; they claim to be able to foretell the future; they charge fees which have to be deposited with a person of trust before the course of instruction begins. Now Protagoras did write a famous lecture-treatise called 'Truth', and Plato tells us in the *Theaetetus* (178 D–9 A) that he claimed to foresee the future. All the rest of Isocrates' charges fit Protagoras, though maybe not only Protagoras. So Isocrates almost certainly associates Protagoras with eristic and the teaching of it. Isocrates in his *Helen* (2) again associates Protagoras with eristic.

Plato associates Protagoras with eristic in the *Protagoras*, *Theaetetus*, and *Sophist*. In the *Theaetetus* (167 D–8), Socrates, acting as spokesman for Protagoras, makes Protagoras say that his critics may either set up a doctrine in opposition to his own, or 'if you prefer the method of questions, ask questions; for an intelligent person ought not to reject this method, on the contrary he should choose it before all others'. He goes on to distinguish the mere match-winning eristic from the serious, truth-hunting eristic and urges his critics to pursue the latter, since familiarisation with the match-winning eristic nauseates the young with philosophy (cf. *Rep.* 537–9, and *Phaedo* 89–90). In Plato's *Protagoras* (329 B), Protagoras is described as being able to deliver a long and excellent speech, but also as able when questioned to reply briefly; and after asking a question to await and accept the answer. When Socrates at a later stage asks Protagoras to confine himself to brief replies, Protagoras huffily says, 'I have undertaken in my time many disputation-matches (ἀγῶνα λόγων) and if I were to do what you demand and argue in just the way that my opponent (ὁ ἀντιλέγων) demanded, I should not be held superior to anyone. . . .' The expressions ἀγῶν λόγων and ὁ ἀντιλέγων were standard parts of the parlance of the eristic exercise. The dialogue largely consists of regulation question–answer moves, which duly result in Protagoras being driven to contradict his original thesis, but result also in Socrates' own position being turned upside down. At one point, when Protagoras has lost his temper (337 A–B), Prodicus exhorts Protagoras and Socrates ἀμφισβητεῖν μεν, ἐρίζειν δὲ μή (cf. *Theaetetus* 167 E–8 A). Hippias urges the appointment of an umpire (ἐπιστάτης). The idea is rejected as unworthy of serious thinkers, but it is interesting as suggesting, what would *a priori* seem necessary, that at least in the students' Moots and in the exhibition bouts staged by sophists the contests may have been umpired. In the *Sophist* (225 E) Plato may, but need not, be alluding to Protagoras, *inter alios*; at 232 E, Protagoras is mentioned as the author of *Arts* of wrestling and of a lot of other things; and, since what is in question is the possibility of anyone writing an *Art* which could teach people how to dispute on any subject whatsoever, it may be that Protagoras' *Art of Eristic* is being alluded to. Though Plato thus associates Protagoras with the eristic exercise, he nowhere hints that he invented it or even introduced it into Athens. Protagoras probably died in about 411 B.C., aged seventy. So the eristic exercise must have been a familiar thing well before the last decade of the fifth century.

(d) *The Dissoi Logoi*. At the end of Diels-Kranz' *Fragmente der Vorsokratiker* there is a little piece, entitled '*Dissoi Logoi*' from a phrase occurring both in its first sentence and elsewhere in the piece. '*Dissoi Logoi*' means 'Arguments Both Ways'. The *Dissoi Logoi* is, for the most part, a sequence of theses, generally shocking ones, about each of which are marshalled first an array of arguments *pro* and then an array of arguments *contra*. Among the arguments *contra* the thesis that *Virtue is not teachable* there is one shrewd argument which, together with an illustrative example, Plato also employs, putting it into the mouth of Protagoras in his *Protagoras* (327E–8C). This, with some corroborative evidence, strongly suggests that the backbone of the *Dissoi Logoi* derives from Protagoras himself, though some stretches, including a mention of the result of the Peloponnesian War, which was posterior to Protagoras' death, must be additions by a later hand. The whole piece is highly pemmicanised, somewhat jumbled, and fragmentary. It is written in amateurish Doric, with plenty of Ionicisms.

These arrays of *pro* and *contra* arguments seem to be designed for memorisation by students as ammunition for their questionings and answerings in eristic Moots. The piece as a whole may, therefore, have been or belonged to a primitive *Art of Eristic*. Aristotle alludes scathingly to such primitive *Arts of Eristic* at the end of his *De Sophisticis Elenchis* (183b35–184a10). His description of them fits the *Dissoi Logoi* well. It teaches arguments; not how to argue. At the least the *Dissoi Logoi* shows us not only that, but also in some degree how, students were being trained for participation in eristic Moots before the end of the fifth century B.C. They committed to memory batches of recommended points for and against some standard theses. It is worth noticing that the author of the piece, speaking of himself as 'I', sides with the arguments *contra* the cynical or nihilist theses. Like the Socrates of Plato's Socratic dialogues, he wants the arguments *pro* and *contra* to be fairly pitted and weighed against one another, but he does not want the cynical or nihilist theses to win. He marshals the Worse and the Better Reasons, but his heart is with the Better Reasons.

(e) *The Hippocratic Writings*. *The Nature of Man*[1] is thought to date between 440 and 400 B.C. Its author begins by criticising some people, not physicians, who discourse on What Man is Made Of. They are eristic debaters (αὐτοῖσιν ἀντιλέγουσιν).

Given the same debaters and the same audience, the same man never wins in the discussion three times in succession, but now one is victor, now another, now he who happens to have the most glib tongue in the face of the crowd. Yet it is right that a man who claims correct knowledge about the facts should maintain his own argument victorious always, if his knowledge be knowledge of reality and if he set it forth correctly. But in my opinion such men by their lack of understanding overthrow themselves in the words of their very discourse. [Tr. W. S. H. Jones.]

---

[1] Hippocrates, Loeb edition, vol. IV, p. 5.

97

This passage shows or suggests several interesting points. Eristic matches were familiar things before and perhaps well before the end of the fifth century B.C. They were conducted before audiences, and it was the audience that decided who had won. A given thesis would come up again and again for discussion, and the same debater might attack or alternatively defend the same thesis on several successive occasions. So he could and presumably would re-employ, discard, or reshape arguments that he or others had used in previous Moots. Thus we can infer that as theses were, in some measure, stock topics, the arguments for and against them would enjoy an evolution by the progressive mending of proven weaknesses. The deliberate study of the profits and losses of particular eristic tactics was possible and expedient. Two or three generations later Aristotle was to provide a theoretical basis for such study. In his *Topics* (105 b 12; and 163 b 17) Aristotle gives concrete tutorial advice to students on how to prepare for debates upon the themes that regularly crop up.

Against this background, the recurrence of the problem *Is Virtue Teachable?* in Plato's *Laches, Protagoras, Euthydemus, Meno,* and [*Alcibiades*] becomes explicable. It had been canvassed in the *Dissoi Logoi,* and Isocrates gives his own negative answer to it at the end of his *Against the Sophists.* There were compositions on this theme by Crito, Simon, Antisthenes, and Xenocrates. It was a constant Moot point, and consequently the arguments to it were in development. The frequent phrase λόγον διεξίεναι might therefore mean 'go through a sequence of argument-moves'. Chess-players call their analogous sequences 'combinations'.

Conceivably, too, if Plato composed his early dialogues with *antilogike* going on under his nose, then, some of their argumentative content reflects the actual argumentation of recent Moots. Perhaps these dialogues were, in part, dramatised 'documentaries' of 'combinations' recurring there.

This would explain (1) why the *Protagoras* contains a well-organised argument for the Hedonistic Calculus, though adjacent dialogues exhibit little interest in Hedonism; (2) why the *Protagoras* repeats argument-moves already made in the *Dissoi Logoi* and the *Laches.* Effective 'combinations' become stock-in-trade of the Game; (3) why these pre-*Republic* dialogues culminate not in doctrines but only in eristic checkmates. If a Moot has a finish, it ends in an elenchus.

(*f*) *Euthydemus and Dionysodorus.* Early in the *Euthydemus* Socrates says that the two sophists learned their brand of eristical all-in wrestling only a year or two before the dramatic date of the dialogue, i.e. before *circa* 402 B.C. They give exhibitions of their art and also, for a fee, tuition in it. They are exponents of the match-winning eristic from which Protagoras dissociated himself. The sophist Dionysodorus may have been a pupil of Protagoras.

At 275 C the lad Cleinias is described as having already had a good deal of practice in disputing (διαλέγεσθαι) and the answering of questions. This suggests that the uncorrupted eristic exercise had become popular with the young men by the last decade of the century. What was new to them was eristic prize-fighting, though they could swiftly pick up the tricks of it. In the course of the dialogue Socrates exhibits a couple of pieces of philosophically serious and edifying eristic. He does not even altogether despise the sophists' eristic tricks. He thinks that he and others ought to find out how to cope with them. Aristotle, in his *Topics*, does deal fairly carefully with a number of the 'Sophistical Elenchi' that fill the *Euthydemus*.

(g) *Socrates*. Nearly all the specimens that we possess of eristic exercises are the elenctic question–answer operations with which, in his early dialogues, Plato credits Socrates. We have to distinguish, as commentators have not always distinguished, between, on the one hand, mere philosophical discussions and, on the other hand, the rule-governed concatenations of questions, answerable by 'yes' or 'no', which are intended to drive the answerer into self-contradiction. The latter is what should be meant by 'the Socratic Method'. Socrates himself is made to say in the *Apology* (27), ἐὰν ἐν τῷ εἰωθότι τρόπῳ τοὺς λόγους ποιῶμαι, before notionally driving his prosecutor into an elenchus by a duly concatenated sequence of questions. With much or little dramatic or merely conversational relief, eristic exercises dominate, or at least feature largely in *Laches*, *Lysis*, [*Alcibiades*], *Euthyphro*, *Charmides*, *Hippias Major* and *Minor*, *Protagoras*, *Ion*, *Euthydemus*, *Gorgias*, *Meno*, and *Republic* I. There is a short stretch in the *Symposium*; a little in the *Phaedo*; and the short stretch, just mentioned, in the *Apology*. The bulk of the *Cratylus* is not eristic in method, but the last twelve pages are. By contrast, there is virtually none of it in the *Crito*, in the last nine books of the *Republic*, in the *Philebus*, *Phaedrus*, or *Theaetetus*. There is no place for it in the *Timaeus* or *Critias*; or in the *Laws*, which last makes few pretences to being more than lectures. In the *Parmenides*, Part II, of course, we get our one full-scale, undramatised, even unmitigated, model of a two-way eristic exercise; but here the questioner is Parmenides, not Socrates. The *Sophist* and *Politicus* are conducted not by Socrates but by the Eleatic Stranger, and he does not discuss eristically, even in the debate about the Greatest Kinds in the *Sophist*. It is interesting to speculate why a pattern of argument which had dominated the Socratic dialogues prior to Book II of the *Republic* was abandoned almost altogether from then until the *Parmenides* (II). Which Platonic Socrates are we to believe in, if either, the one who does or the one who does not employ the Socratic Method?

A propos this question, there is a curious feature of the *Theaetetus*. At the beginning and the end of the dialogue Socrates declares, almost apologetically, that his sole intellectual power is the 'maieutic' one. He can extract ideas from his answerer and test them, if necessary, to destruction. In Aristotle's parlance, he is capable only of *peirastic* cross-questioning, or what the Eleatic Stranger describes as the 'cathartic' elenchus, in the *Sophist* (230–1). Yet in his actual discussion Socrates does not handle Theaetetus as his ἀντιλέγων. Certainly some of Theaetetus' suggestions are examined and demolished, but so are some of Socrates' own suggestions and those of Protagoras who is not there to defend them. There is excellent debate, and the debate generates ἀπορίαι; but they are ἀπορίαι for Socrates as much as for Theaetetus. Save in a few very brief stretches the argumentation has not got the eristic shape or style. So we seem to be presented with an emphatic and repeated apologia for Socratic eristic accompanying a variety of philosophically admirable arguments which are not typically eristic or characteristically Socratic. The rules of the eristic Moot are almost audibly in control in, e.g., the *Protagoras*, *Euthydemus*, *Gorgias*, and *Republic* I. They are not easily, if at all, audible in the rest of the *Republic*, the *Phaedrus*, the *Theaetetus*, the *Philebus*, the *Sophist*, or the *Politicus*.

Did the real Socrates, as distinct from the Platonic Socrates of the pre-*Republic* dialogues, practise the eristic method? We do not believe Plato when he represents old Parmenides as giving a full-scale demonstration of what Aristotle's *Topics* is the *Art* of; so perhaps we should not believe Plato when he represents Socrates as repeatedly forcing elenchi by concatenations of questions. Here we are without any relevant testimony from Isocrates or, surprisingly, from Diogenes Laertius; and we are without the evidence of treatise-titles. The fact that two presumably loyal Socratics, Plato and Antisthenes, both propagated the eristic technique, one in dialogues, and the other, probably, in primitive training manuals, is some evidence for their common master having taught them the use of it. When Aristotle credits Socrates with the invention of 'Induction' in his *Metaphysics* (1078b), he credits him with one of the dialectical procedures that he describes in his own *Topics*. Certainly

Socratic Induction could have been used independently of eristic cross-questioning, but its incessant employment in Plato's early dialogues, and Aristotle's treatment of it as a part of dialectic suggests that it did, in fact, first live as a specifically dialectical procedure.

Subject to the debated proviso that Xenophon's ideas of the Socratic Method may all derive from Plato's dialogues, his *Memorabilia* supports the view that Socrates did practise the eristic method. Xenophon employs the semi-technical terminology of the eristic exercise in his *Memorabilia* (III, viii, 1; IV, iv, 9; IV, v, 12 to vi, 1; IV, vi, 13–15; and IV, viii, 11). I do not suppose that Xenophon understood this parlance, or that he would have recognised an elenchus if he had met one. Even more significantly, he consistently represents Socrates as asking one question after another. But, with a few exceptions, the questions are rhetorical questions, Socrates' positive views expressed in interrogative form. Their sequence does not depend on whether the answerer says 'yes' or 'no'. His interlocutor is not an adversary, and the questions do not drive him into checkmate, but merely lead him to a wiser view. It looks as if the unphilosophical Xenophon is garbling something that he has heard and misunderstood about Socrates' conduct of discussions; and this is some independent evidence that Socrates had used the Socratic Method, though independent only if Xenophon was not merely garbling the Platonic representations of Socrates at work. At least he was not plagiarising Plato.

In the slender fragments from the dialogues of Aeschines given in chapter XI of G. C. Field's *Plato and His Contemporaries*, Socrates is represented as plying his interlocutors with chains of questions. Unlike Xenophon, Aeschines is known to have been a close associate of Socrates. Aristophanes, in the *Clouds*, certainly accuses Socrates of pitting the Worse against the Better Reason, i.e. of teaching the young men to argue as forcibly against a respectable thesis as in its favour. But this does not prove that the argumentation was of the question–answer pattern. Anyhow, Aristophanes might be pinning on to Socrates things that belonged elsewhere, e.g. to Protagoras, as he certainly pins 'physical' theories about Air on to Socrates which belonged to Diogenes of Apollonia. However, Aristophanes employs a few of the semi-technical dictions of the eristic exercise; and both the Worse Reason and Pheidippides assail their interlocutors with tail-twisting interrogations. So I think that by 423, or else by the time when he revised his *Clouds*, Aristophanes did associate Socrates with something like the Socratic Method.

If the earlier argument is allowed, that eristic was practised and taught by Protagoras, then Socrates would have been familiar with it before he was elderly. If so, then it seems likely that he would have realised at least its *peirastic* potency.

In sum, I think we are warranted in taking it that the Socratic Method was the method of the real and not only of the Platonic Socrates. We have good reason to think that he did not invent it or introduce it into Athens; but probably he improved its armoury and techniques. Possibly he emancipated it from rhetoric. But if we doubt the biographical authoritativeness of Plato's dialogues, Protagoras seems more important in the history of dialectic than was the real Socrates.

(*h*) *Antisthenes*. We know little about Antisthenes. He is thought, but not known, to have died, aged ninety, in about 366 B.C. He probably studied rhetoric under Gorgias, and he had pupils of his own, some of whom he took with him to sit at the feet of Socrates, i.e. before 399. His school is likely to have been, in the first instance, a school of rhetoric, since a good many of his writings appear from their titles to deal with standard rhetorical themes. What is of interest to us, however, is that his titles include περὶ τοῦ διαλέγεσθαι ἀντιλογικός, Σάθων ἢ περὶ τοῦ ἀντιλέγειν, περὶ ὀνομάτων χρήσεως ἐριστικός, περὶ ἐρωτήσεως καὶ ἀποκρίσεως and δόξαι ἢ ἐριστικός. All or some of these were probably training manuals, and show that the teaching of eristic, presumably as an ancillary to the teaching of rhetoric, had become an established thing well before Aristotle came to the Academy. Aristotle himself, at the end of his *De Sophisticis Elenchis*, speaks witheringly of the quality of the training manuals of eristic that his fee-taking predecessors had composed. We have no reason to suppose that he here has Antisthenes particularly in mind. I think the reference to fee-taking indicates that it is Protagoras whom he has chiefly in mind. But Aristotle's statement corroborates the impression given by the titles of Antisthenes' writings that there had for quite a long time been a market for technical instruction in eristic. Even if the training manuals that preceded Aristotle's *Topics* were merely cram-books of *pro* and *contra* arguments, written down to be memorised by the students, and quite devoid of any general theory, still the fact of their existence shows us the pre-Aristotelian beginnings of an interest, however vocational, in the Art of elenctic argumentation. It had become a proficiency to be acquired and a subject to be studied. It had a careers-value. But it was also interesting. This interest was to develop into what we know as 'philosophy'.

(i) *Plato*. Diogenes Laertius in his *Plato* (48), confusing, as others have done, the production of dialogues with the production of dialectical arguments, says 'in my opinion Plato, who brought this form of writing to perfection, ought to be adjudged the prize for its invention as well as for its embellishment. A dialogue is a discourse consisting of question and answer on some philosophical or political subject, with due regard to the characters of the persons introduced and the choice of diction. Dialectic is the art of discourse (τέχνη λόγων) by which we either refute or establish some proposition (ἀνασκευάζομεν τι ἢ κατασκευάζομεν) by means of question and answer on the part of the interlocutors.' Later (79) he says that Plato 'was the first to frame a science for rightly asking and answering questions, having used it himself to excess'. In his *Arcesilaus* (28) he says, obviously erroneously, that Arcesilaus was the first to argue on both sides of a question (εἰς ἑκάτερον ἐπεχείρησε), and the first to meddle with the system handed down by Plato and by means of question and answer to make it more clearly resemble eristic. So it looks as if a tradition grew up according to which dialectic was a Platonic invention. I think that the word 'dialectic', with its inflections, was invented by Plato. The eristic or dialectical exercise was not invented by him, or even by his own master, Socrates. When Aristotle says that Plato's forerunners did not participate in dialectic (*Metaphysics* A 987b), he cannot mean merely that they had not got the word 'dialectic'. But Aristotle is surely here referring only to the forerunners whom he had just been describing, namely the Pythagoreans, not to Plato's forerunners in general.

III. PLATO'S DIALECTIC VIS-A-VIS ERISTIC

We have seen that what Aristotle means by 'dialectic' is just what other people meant by 'eristic', save that Aristotle is, in the main, concerned with those question–answer matches which are conducted in a pedagogically or philosophically serious spirit. But what about Plato? His accounts of dialectic in *Republic* VII, *Phaedrus*, *Philebus*, and *Sophist* give such lofty places in knowledge to the results of dialectical thinking that he seems to be talking about something entirely different from what the *Topics* is the Art of. We get the impression that in the Academy, at the same moment, the word 'dialectic' is being used in two entirely different ways, in one of which dialectic has everything, in the other nothing, to do with the Moots that are held, so to speak, on Wednesday evenings between a young Coriscus and a young Theophrastus, with the not very old

Aristotle or Xenocrates acting as coach, umpire, and time-keeper. I shall try to establish that for Plato, as for Aristotle, the concrete or, so to speak, Wednesday evening activity of prosecuting dialectic *is* the eristic match conducted in an academic spirit; that where Plato differs from Aristotle—and also from himself—is in his accounts of the philosophical profits of the exercise; and that even here some of Plato's accounts of these profits are not more disparate from those given by Aristotle than we should expect from our knowledge of Aristotle's addiction to logical and methodological enquiries, as well as from our knowledge of the growth and systematisation of the special sciences in the Academy.

In the *Cratylus* (390 C) Socrates says, 'And the man who knows how to ask and answer questions you call a dialectician?' In the *Meno* (75 C–D) he says, 'If my questioner were a professor of the eristic and contentious sort (εἰ μέν γε τῶν σοφῶν τις ἔίη καὶ ἐριστικῶν τε καὶ ἀγωνιστικῶν ὁ ἐρόμενος) I should say to him: I have made my statement; if it is wrong, it is your business to examine and refute it (ἐλέγχειν). But if, like you and me on this occasion, we were friends and chose to have a discussion together, I should have to reply in some milder tone more suited to dialectic (πρᾳότερόν πως καὶ διαλεκτικώτερον). The more dialectical way, I suppose, is not merely to answer what is true, but also to make use of those points which the questioned person (ὁ ἐρωτώμενος) acknowledges that he knows.' Here we get the contrast, credited to Protagoras and constantly made by Plato and Aristotle, between the match-winning and the truth-hunting spirits in which the question–answer exercise may be conducted, with the adjective 'dialectical' used just as Aristotle uses it.

In the *Republic*, VII (534), dialectic is set up in a sovereign position over the so-called sciences. But in 537–9 we are told of the immense evil of insubordination that at present accompanies dialectic. For a young man of twenty or so, 'when met by the question What is beauty? and, having given the answer which he used to hear from the legislator, is confuted by the dialectic process (ἐξελέγχῃ ὁ λόγος); and when frequent and various defeats have forced him to believe that there is as much deformity as beauty in what he calls beauty, and that justice, goodness, and all the things which he is used to honour most are in the like predicament' he will become cynical and lawless. So only selected thirty-year-olders are to be introduced to dialectic. 'Whenever boys taste dialectic (τῶν λόγων) for the first time, they pervert it into an amusement and always employ it for purposes of contradiction, imitating in their own persons the artifices of those who study refutation (τοὺς ἐλέγχοντας) delighting, like puppies, in pulling and tearing to pieces with logic (τῷ λόγῳ) anyone who comes near them.' The senior men, however, will imitate those who are resolved to discuss and examine truth, rather than those who play at contradiction (παίζοντα καὶ ἀντιλέγοντα) for amusement. Here, too, Plato is distinguishing dialectic from match-winning eristic by the different spirits in which the same question–answer disputation exercise is conducted.

In the *Phaedo* (75 C–D and cf. 78 D) we hear of '. . . absolute beauty and the absolute good and the just and the holy and, in short, with all those things which we stamp with the seal of "absolute" both in our questions when we are questioners and in our answers when we are answerers.' Plato does not here use the word 'dialectic'; but he is surely referring to some regulation question–answer disputations and saying that the Theory of Forms is common to both sides in these disputations. So apparently these disputations were philosophically serious, and conformed to the pattern described by Aristotle. In the *Republic*, V (454A) Socrates distinguishes the Art of *antilogike* from dialectic, those who employ ἔριδι from those who employ διαλέκτῳ against one another. The former are content with making empty verbal points. But both are in pursuit of τοῦ λεχθέντος τὴν ἐναντίωσιν. The concrete procedure of dialectic is for Plato just what it is for Aristotle. It is the *proper* employment of the method of driving an answerer into elenchi by strategically arranged sequences of questions. See also *Philebus* (17A) and *Theaetetus* (161E).

Next, Plato and Aristotle are in complete or considerable agreement about the subordinate values of elenctic cross-questioning.

(*a*) What Aristotle calls 'peirastic' (e.g. *Topics* 169b26) is the dialectical method as employed to prick the bubble of an individual's intellectual conceit. He thinks he knows things, but is driven to concede propositions which he recognises to be inconsistent with what he thought he knew. Plato does not use the noun '*peirastike*', but he and Aristotle both use the phrase πεῖραν λαμβάνειν (Aristotle's *Topics*, 171b4; Plato, *Gorgias*, 448A; *Protagoras*, 348A; *Euthydemus*, 275B; cf. *Theaetetus*, 157C). In his *Sophist* (229–30, especially 230B–D) Plato gives a full account of how his last variety of sophist, who merits a better title than 'sophist', purges, by cross-questioning, the false conceit of knowledge. At the beginning of the *Theaetetus* (149–51D and cf. 210C) Socrates explains at length how his powers are only 'maieutic', emphasising that his kind of midwifery involves the extinction of sham offspring.

(b) The *gymnastic* value of dialectic, mentioned by Aristotle (e.g. *Topics* 159a25, 161a25, 164a12), is what old Parmenides gives as the reason why the young Socrates should practise the two-way Zenonian method. This training exercise is indispensable for the young man who wishes to become a philosopher (*Parmenides*, 135–6). It is an interesting fact that Socrates must be about twenty years old, just the age at which in the *Republic*, VII, Plato had found it dangerous for people to get a taste of dialectic. Plato seems to have changed his mind. Probably dialectic practised under tutorial surveillance was proving less demoralising than he had previously feared or found. Or there may be an explanation of a quite different kind. In the *Phaedrus* Plato acknowledges, what he had denied in the *Gorgias*, that there is teachable Art of Rhetoric, but he requires that the student of it must also learn psychology and, more conjecturally, dialectic (265–6, 269E–72B, 273D–4A, 277B–C). Presumably, such a student would be of the normal age of a student of rhetoric, i.e. a young man. Even Isocrates, whose educational ideals were far from Platonic, admits the gymnastic value of astronomy, geometry, and eristic, in *Antidosis* and *Panathenaicus* (loc. cit.). These studies should, however, be dropped when student days are over. When he speaks of these studies as being good training for 'philosophy', he means by 'philosophy', 'rhetorical and literary culture'.

(c) Both Plato and Aristotle rank *agonistic* eristic low. Aristotle's strictures, however, are less wholehearted than Plato's, though even Plato now and then lets Socrates score by fairly unscrupulous argumentative tricks. Aristotle allows himself to give a good many tips in eristic gamesmanship. He is, after all, a much younger man than Plato, and probably by nature more of a controversialist. (On eristical gamesmanship see *De Sophisticis Elenchis*, *passim*; also *Topics* 111b12; 112a10–15; 134a3; 142a32; 148a21; 155b25–7a5; 158a25–30; 159a16–25; 163b–4b.)

(d) Plato and Aristotle are entirely at one in their contempt for sophistical eristic, i.e. eristic prize-fighting.

(e) *The Philosophical Value of Dialectic*. First for a verbal point. When Aristotle uses the word 'philosophy', save when he speaks of First Philosophy, he normally has in mind what we mean by 'science'. Thus arithmetic, geometry, astronomy, and medicine are for Aristotle branches of philosophy. In this sense of 'philosophy' dialectic is not the whole or even a part of philosophy, though it is in important ways ancillary to scientific knowledge. Plato, on the other hand, sometimes equates the dialectician with the philosopher, as we ourselves would nowadays do; though sometimes he talks in

Aristotle's idiom and treats, e.g., geometry as a branch of philosophy (*Theaetetus* 143 D and *Philebus* 56 D–E, 57 C–D). We have recently, though only recently, come to use 'philosopher' in contrast with 'scientist', and are therefore surprised to find the Aristotelian non-equation 'dialectician ≠ philosopher'. Realisation of this partial terminological divergence of Aristotle from Plato by itself reduces a good deal the apparent gap between their views about the major value of dialectic.

Next, Plato and Aristotle agree almost completely that the dialectician's concern is with what is 'common' to, i.e. shared by and neutral between, the various special branches of knowledge. He is concerned with those 'common' concepts which are ubiquitous or trans-departmental; or with those truths which are in some way presupposed by all alike of the proprietary truths of the special sciences. The concepts of *existence, non-existence, identity, difference, similarity, dissimilarity, unity,* and *plurality* are such 'common' or ubiquitous concepts (see Plato, *Theaetetus* 185–6; *Sophist* 254–9; and *Parmenides*, 136; compare Aristotle, *Metaphysics* 995 b 19–26; 998 b; 1004 a; 1004 b–5 a 18). But in the main Aristotle's emphasis is less on the ubiquitous *concepts* than on the trans-departmental *truths*. Even here, however, he has, or may have, Plato with him in one of his moods; for in *Republic* VII (532–3), arguably, the 'hypotheses' of the special sciences and, presumably, the unpostulated first principle or principles are truths and not concepts. (For the trans-departmental truths with which the dialectician is concerned see Aristotle: *Topics* 101 a 34–b 4; 115 b 7–15; 170 a 20–170 b 11; 171 b 35–172 b 8; *Met.* 1005 a 19 et seq.; *Rhet.* I (1), 14; ii, 21; iv, 6.) Nor is there a total disparity between Aristotle's view of the role of dialectic *vis-à-vis* the special sciences and the view that Plato had held in *Republic* VII. True, for Aristotle the special sciences rest on their special axioms, and these departmental axioms are not the mere postulates which Plato held them to be. So for Aristotle there is no question of dialectic being a hunt for trans-departmental axioms from which the departmental principles of the special sciences will be deducible. Apparently Plato, at one time, did hold this view, though he gives us no specimens of his super-axioms. So far Aristotle does differ from Plato and, to put it bluntly, is right where Plato had been wrong. From completely topic-neutral premisses, the truths of the special sciences *could* not follow.

On the other hand, it really is the business of dialectic, according to Aristotle, to be in some way analytical or critical of the departmental axioms of the special sciences; though he does not clearly explain how or why these axioms require or benefit from such criticism. Some trans-departmental principles, which do not function as axioms, are presupposed by the special axioms of all the sciences, and the Principle of Non-Contradiction is one such principle. The establishment of such underlying and neutral principles is still eristic in pattern. (See *Met.* 1004b15–27; 1005a19 et seq.; 1006a16–28; 1012a17–28; *Topics* 101a35–b4; 155b10–16; 163b8–12.) In *Met.* 1005b7 Aristotle requires the philosopher to study, *inter alia*, the principles of syllogistic reasoning, though 'syllogistic' may here have, not the highly determinate sense that it gets in the *Prior Analytics*, but only the very broad sense that it has throughout the *Topics*. As we might put it, there are trans-departmental Formal or Logical principles presupposed by the departmental truths of the special sciences; and these logical principles need to be extracted, and can be extracted only by dialectic.

So Plato and Aristotle both credit dialectic with the task of discovering some very important trans-departmental principles which hinge on the ubiquitous, non-specialist, or 'common' concepts. They differ about the status of these principles. Plato and Aristotle are talking about the same exercise, but Aristotle is controverting an important error in what Plato had said about its philosophical proceeds. Even so, when Aristotle comes to speak of First Philosophy as the Science of Being *qua* Being, he seems to be moving nearer to Plato's position in the *Republic*.

However, in his *Phaedrus* (265–6), *Politicus* (286) and, more debatably, *Philebus* (16–18), Plato seems to give a role to dialectic quite different from that given in the *Republic*. We hear no more of the discovery of non-hypothetical first principles functioning as super-axioms for all the special sciences; nor is any reason given for the disappearance of this view. Perhaps daily intercourse with mathematicians, astronomers, and other researchers had taught him that no such super-axioms were to be looked for, since their absolute generality or formality would prevent special or material consequences from being derivable from them. Nor had the lack of them prevented new geometrical, astronomical, or physiological truths from being discovered. Plato, now, in the *Phaedrus*, the *Politicus*, and, debatably, the *Philebus*, seems closely to connect the task of dialectic with the tasks of Definition and especially Division, i.e. the tasks of articulating higher or more generic kinds into their lower, more specific kinds. He is tempted to treat this articulation as being necessarily dichotomous, though he prudently resists this temptation some of the time. In the *Sophist* and *Politicus* we are presented with detailed Kind-ladders, on the bottom rungs of which are the concepts of *sophist* and *statesman*. The pedagogic value of trying to build such ladders of kinds was doubtless considerable. The ideal of systematic Definition probably derives from such exercises in Division. But it is immediately clear that eristic cross-questioning cannot be the way of constructing such ladders of kinds. The answerer could not be driven into elenchus by rejection of a suggested division. Aristotle saw this (*Posterior Analytics* 91 b). Nor, for that matter, does Plato make his Eleatic Stranger try to establish his divisions by eristic argumentation. A chain of *summa genera*, *genera*, *species*, *sub-species*, and *varieties* is not a chain of axioms, theorems, and riders. But what is more, it cannot, in general, be deductively established or established by *reductio ad absurdum*. The work of a Linnaeus cannot be done *a priori*. How could Plato, who knew exactly what question–answer arguments were really like, bring himself to say, if he did say, that the philosophically valuable results of such arguments are Kind-ladders? In the jewelled examples of the Socratic Method that fill, e.g., the *Protagoras*, *Gorgias*, and *Republic* I not a single Kind-ladder is or could have been established. Quite often, of course, Socrates has to draw attention to differences between different species of a genus, just as, very often, he has by means of his Induction to draw attention to their generic affinity. But until we get to the *Sophist* we have nothing reminding us of the contribution of Linnaeus to botany; nor should we have been grateful or philosophically enlightened if we had. No such divisions result out of the dialectical operations in the *Parmenides* (Part II).

Before trying to assess the claims made by Plato for Division and for Definition (in *Phaedrus* 265–6), let us consider what place is actually occupied by Division and Definition in the curriculum of the Academy. In his *Topics*, especially Book VI, Aristotle describes carefully various failings to which debaters' definitions are liable. But he does not here introduce his students to the Rules of Definition. They know them already. Similarly, in his *Rhetoric*, though he frequently employs division and constantly produces definitions, mostly very good ones, of virtues, passions, temperaments, etc., he does not have to explain what he is doing.

The so-called '*Platonic*' *Definitions* contains nearly two hundred definitions or would-be definitions. For some of the terms to be defined half a dozen or a dozen different definitions are provided. Quite a lot, though far from all, of the definitions are or try to be of the Genus–Differentia pattern; and quite a lot of them embody semi-logical or semi-philosophical parlance, apparently of Aristotelian provenance. Two or three of the definitions have been culled from Plato, and eight or nine may have been culled from Aristotle. But most of the terms defined are unsophisticated terms of so little scientific or philosophical interest that any adolescent would be familiar with them; and a large number of the definitions offered are amateurish or even puerile. Over a dozen of the definitions are or closely resemble definitions which are justly demolished in the *Topics*.

It seems plausible to suppose, and I shall boldly assume, that the *'Platonic' Definitions* is a class album of definitions, partly culled from Plato, Aristotle, and maybe Xenocrates, etc., but mostly subscribed as beginners' essays by Aristotle's pupils themselves. To put it anachronistically, Definition was a Pass Moderations subject for freshmen in the Academy. These beginners were not yet supposed to know any science or dialectic. They were not yet even being taught rhetoric. Not one of the scores of definitions in Aristotle's *Rhetoric* has been garnered into the album, though two or three dozens of the terms defined, often very badly, in the album are terms defined, usually very well, in the *Rhetoric*.

At the end of Diogenes Laertius' *Plato*, we have ten pages of divisions, erroneously said to have been collected by Aristotle out of the works of Plato. Many, though not all, of these divisions are again amateurish and even puerile attempts at the division of frequently unsophisticated and unimportant generic concepts. I take them to be specimens from a class album of divisions, i.e. a collection of, mostly, students' early essays in division assembled for tutorial criticism.

Diogenes Laertius credits Xenocrates with eight 'books' of Divisions; Aristotle with seventeen; Theophrastus with two; and Speusippus perhaps with one. Speusippus is given one 'book' of Definitions; Aristotle seven; Theophrastus three or perhaps five.

It looks to me, therefore, as if, whatever Plato promised or dreamed for Division and Definition, in mundane curricular fact they were taught to young, even very young, students in the Academy before they were qualified to study the Arts of Rhetoric and Dialectic—and a very sensible preliminary course this could have been. We can well imagine that the *Sophist*'s half-dozen Kind-ladders terminating in the notion of *sophist*, though philosophically quite unrewarding, were intended to serve as exemplary models for the propaedeutic course on which the eighteen-year-olders were embarked. As the ladders are apparently alternatives to or rivals of one another, these could stimulate some educative comparisons and criticisms.

Similarly with the *Politicus*. Here the Stranger's voice and manner are markedly, even irksomely, those of the schoolmaster. The political concepts to which he applies his division procedures are concepts familiar to any bright lad. Save for some discussion of the notion of the Mean, the dialogue imposes no philosophical puzzles upon its recipients. It was not written to interest or profit those more senior students who were equipped to cope with the philosophical core of the *Sophist* or with either part of the *Parmenides*. Dialectic is alluded to only twice (285 D and 287 A), and then only in the Stranger's explanation of the preparatory role of the intellectual exercises that he is giving. So Plato may have composed the *Politicus* for the special benefit of the philosophically innocent novices who were at that moment getting their freshman training in the ABC of thinking. Perhaps it was the curricular needs of this special class of recipients which made Plato forget to give to the dialogue even a vestige of dramatic life.

The *Sophist* consists, queerly, of a stretch of highly abstract and sophisticated philosophical reasoning sandwiched between some division operations which presuppose no philosophical sophistication whatsoever. In the philosophical stretch, dialectic, here equated with philosophy, is described (at 253 C–D), as the science which discovers how the 'Greatest Kinds' are 'joined' with and 'disjoined' from one another. Among a lot of other metaphors the term 'division' occurs once or twice. This makes it tempting to infer that Plato thought that the task of constructing Kind-ladders was not only a propaedeutic to the philosopher's or dialectician's task; it was a part of it, or the whole of it. But then we have to recognise that the Stranger's exploration of the mutual dependences and independences of the Greatest Kinds does not yield one Kind-ladder, however short. For the Greatest Kinds are not related to one another as genus to species, or as species to co-species. Aristotle seems to be saying this in *Metaphysics* III (998 b). Even to render γένη by 'kinds', and *a fortiori* by 'classes', is to prejudice the interpretation of the Stranger's operations. *Existence*, *identity*, and *otherness* are not Sorts or Sets of things, embracing sub-sorts or sub-sets of things. The Stranger produces here neither dichotomous nor trichotomous divisions, for he produces no divisions at all.

In the *Parmenides* (Part II), between which and this stretch of the *Sophist* there are probable echo relations, scores of implications, real or apparent, are traced between propositions anchored in, *inter alia*, the Stranger's Greatest Kinds. But again no Kind-ladders are generated. At least Plato did not work as if he thought that his own dialectical operations were of a piece with his own exercises in division.

There is, however, one argument, besides the natural interpretation of *Phaedrus* (265–6), for the view that Plato did assimilate Division to Dialectic, namely that Aristotle does scold some unnamed person or persons for failing to see that a division is not, and is not the product of, demonstration. There need be nothing illogical in refusing to accept a recommended division (*Posterior Analytics* 91 b, and cf. *De Partibus Animalium* 642 b–4 a). This point would assuredly not have been an obvious one in the days when Aristotle himself had not yet pre-envisaged the science of Formal Logic. So maybe Plato did fail to see that Dividing is not Reasoning and is therefore not Dialectic.

None the less, the actual propaedeutic place of division and definition in the curriculum of Plato's own Academy, together with Plato's own non-production of Kind-ladders in his *Parmenides* (Part II) and in the philosophical core of his *Sophist* itself, satisfy me that Plato knew quite well that to be good at division did not by itself amount to being good at dialectic, and so that in the *Phaedrus* passage he means but omits to say explicitly that division is only a preparation for dialectic. If this is so, then Plato, after *Republic* VII, gives us only one statement of what kind of contribution dialectic makes to human knowledge, namely the statement in the *Sophist* (253) that dialectic reveals the mutual associations and dissociations of the Greatest Kinds. As these Kinds seem partly to coincide with what Aristotle calls the πρῶτα γένη (*Met.* B 998 b, 999 a), and with what he elsewhere calls the 'common' terms or notions, Plato's present account of the role of dialectic seems to have some close affinities with that of Aristotle (e.g. *Rhet.* I, II 20–22, *Met.* B 995 b 21).

It is difficult to extract a hard-edged doctrine out of the metaphors in which Plato talks of those relations between the Greatest Kinds which it is the task of dialectic to disclose. But as in the *Parmenides* (Part II) old Parmenides is all the time drawing consequences, legitimately or illegitimately, from propositions that hinge on the formal or 'common' concepts, including those listed as 'Greatest Kinds' in the *Sophist*, it is possible that in the *Sophist* itself Plato is gropingly beginning to isolate for consideration such trans-departmental propositional connections as *implication, incompatibility, contradiction,* and *compatibility*. If so, then here in the *Sophist* and with fuller awareness in the *Parmenides* (Part II), he is ascribing to the dialectician enquiries which Aristotle ascribes to the dialectician, namely what we can now call 'logical' enquiries. Plato is, perhaps, adumbrating the route on which in his *Topics* lectures Aristotle is already toddling, and in his *Analytics* will before long be marching.

I say that in his *Topics* Aristotle is, as yet, only toddling, for though his purpose is to construct an Art which shall enable eristic questioners and answerers to force and rebut elenchi, he is still very unclear about the difference between (1) an argument generating an absurd conclusion because the *inference is fallacious* and (2) an argument generating an absurd conclusion because the answerer has not noticed that at least one of the *questions* put to him was equivocal, or many questions in one, or unrestrictedly general, or metaphorical, etc. There is one and only one logical fallacy about which Aristotle is perfectly clear in the *De Sophisticis Elenchis*, namely the Fallacy of the Consequent. An answerer may erroneously think that having conceded that *if p then q*, and having also conceded *q*, he must concede *p*. But in the main, Aristotle tries to diagnose the treacherousness of arguments in terms only of internal trickinesses in their premisses. It is worth noticing that nowhere in the *Topics*, not even in the reputed Handbook of Fallacies, the *De Sophisticis Elenchis*, does Aristotle mention such formal fallacies as Undistributed Middle. His *Art of Dialectic* is not yet a work of formal logic. The *Topics* could have been taught without the Academic equivalent of a blackboard. The *Prior Analytics* could not.

Aristotle makes it a defining property of a dialectical argument that the thesis which the answerer undertakes to uphold is an 'endoxon' and not a paradox. It should be a truism, or something attested by the experts, or something obvious to the man in the street. Now, certainly, it would be a sensible piece of practical advice to a participant who wants to win an eristic duel to tell him to defend only those theses of which he and the members of the audience feel quite sure. It is much easier to think of points supporting what one believes than to think of objections to it, or to think of points supporting what one disbelieves. But Aristotle is wrong in making this a defining property of the exercise. For one thing he himself allows, what old Parmenides insists on, that the would-be philosopher should practise constructing and rebutting arguments both *pro* and *contra* each thesis and its negative. But if a thesis is an endoxon, its negative will be a paradox, so the defender of this negative will be arguing for something which he does not believe, and yet will still be operating dialectically (see Aristotle, *Topics* 101a34; 163b1-15). I suspect that Aristotle overstresses the importance of the unparadoxicalness of theses for another reason. I think that his grasp of the notion of fallaciousness of reasoning is still so unsure that he is inclined to assume that a paradoxical conclusion must generally derive (validly) from something overtly or else covertly paradoxical in a premiss. The answerer must have conceded something inadvertently, so that the truism that he meant to uphold has been replaced by a paradox that he never meant to uphold.

I believe that the correct answer to the question 'What is the philosophical value of elenctic argumentation?' is much the same for both Plato and Aristotle. Both know in their bones that ἀπορίαι are the driving force of philosophical, as distinct from scientific, thinking; but neither is able to state to himself why this should be so, or what sort of knowledge or insight comes from the unravelling (λύσις) of an ἀπορία. Aristotle says, with his enviable pungency, 'the resolution of a perplexity is discovery' (ἡ γὰρ λύσις τῆς ἀπορίας εὕρεσίς ἐστιν) (*Nic. Eth.* 1146b6; cf. *Met.* 995a24–b5); and in his practice he regularly first marshals ἀπορίαι and then moves to their λύσεις. But he never explains clearly why the person who has never been in an ἀπορία at all is to be pitied rather than envied. It is, however, not for us to complain. We, too, know in our bones how philosophical problems differ in kind from scientific problems; but our statements of the differences continue to be inadequate. Wittgenstein's 'fly-bottle' is the ἀπορία of the Academy. But what has the fly missed that has never got into the bottle, and therefore never looked for or found the way out of it?

CONCLUSION

Our study of the eristic or dialectical exercise has shown us something of what is going on in the Academy during the last ten or twelve years of Plato's life and the first ten or twelve years of Aristotle's teaching life. Eristic contests have become a part of the curriculum even for fairly junior members of the Academy, and both Plato and Aristotle are keenly interested not only in its gymnastic utility but also in its philosophical productiveness, in our sense of 'philosophical'. Aristotle's pedagogic interest in the Art of constructing and rebutting elenchi leads him into the pure theory of valid versus fallacious argument, but only at a later stage. The idea of confutation-without-cheating precedes the idea of validity.

APPENDIX

By the time Aristotle had completed his *Topics* the eristic exercise had collected a fairly large technical and semi-technical vocabulary. Some of this vocabulary was doubtless deliberately coined by Aristotle, his colleagues and students. But a good deal of it had grown up before. We find a fairly copious vocabulary in Plato's dialogues, largely but not entirely coinciding with that of the *Topics*. I append, in no special order, the words and phrases that Plato seems to associate with elenctic cross-questioning. Nearly all of them are standard terms in Aristotle's *Topics*. ἀπορία, ἀπορεῖν, etc.; εὐπορεῖν; ἔλεγχος, ἐλέγχειν, etc.; θέσις (*Rep.* 335), τιθέναι, etc.; ὑπόθεσις, etc.; λύειν, λύσις, etc.; ἐρωτᾶν, ἐρώτησις, ἐρώτημα, etc.; ἀποκρίνειν, ἀπόκρισις, etc.; ἀντιλέγειν, ἀντιλογική, etc.; ἐρίζειν, ἐριστική, etc.; ἀγών, ἀγωνιστική, etc.; διαλέγεσθαι, διαλεκτική, διαλέκτος, etc.; συλλογίζεσθαι; λόγον διεξίεναι, etc.; ἀμφισβητεῖν; συμβαίνειν; ἀκολουθεῖν; ληρεῖν (= *Ar.* ἀδολεσχεῖν); ἀδικεῖν, ἀδικία, etc.; γυμνασία, etc.; πεῖραν λαμβάνειν, etc.; ἐξετάζειν; φιλονικία, etc.; ἐναντία λέγειν; ἐναντίωσις; ὁμολογεῖν, ὁμολόγημα, etc.; ἀπόδειξις; ὀνόματα θηρεύειν; ἀνατιθέναι (revoke an earlier concession); παραδέχεσθαι τόν λόγον (cf. *Topics* 159b34); ἄτοπον; ἀπολόγημα.

Plato's phrases for the (so-called) Fallacy of Many Questions are δύο ἅμα με ἐρωτᾶς and οὐχ ἁπλοῦν τοῦτο ἐρωτᾶς (*Gorg.* 466c; 503A). Aristotle's regular phrase is τό τά πλείω ἐρωτήματα ἕν ποιεῖν.

This so-called Fallacy of Many Questions is not a fallacy at all, since it is not an argument. It is a trick-*question*. The only person who can be guilty of this foul is a questioner. The provenance of the trick was the eristic exercise. So was the provenance of the foul, miscalled the 'Fallacy', of Begging the Question, of which also only the questioner can be guilty. He begs the question, only 'begs' is a hopelessly misleading translation, when he, in effect, asks the answerer to concede the direct negative of the thesis that it is the answerer's job to defend. Even if by skilful rewording the questioner does trick the answerer into admitting the negative of his thesis, still he has not argued him into an elenchus, and *a fortiori* he has not fallaciously argued him into an elenchus.

6

DIALECTIC IN THE ACADEMY

Reprinted from 'Aristotelian Dialectic', Proceedings of the Third Symposium Aristotelicum, 1965, by permission of the Clarendon Press, Oxford

(1) Isocrates, in his *Antidosis* of 354/3 (258–69), commenting on the curriculum of what is obviously the Academy, concedes a limited pedagogic value to the studies of astronomy, geometry, and eristic. He repeats this concession a dozen years later in his *Panathenaicus* (26–9), with acidities at the expense of some unnamed teachers of these subjects; it has been conjectured that he has Aristotle particularly in mind. In his *Letter* to the young Alexander, of 342, he refers to teachers from Athens from whom the princeling is learning eristic. Here Isocrates can hardly not be alluding to Aristotle.

Anyhow the *Antidosis* proves that dialectic, or what Isocrates always calls 'eristic', had been a part of the Academy's curriculum for young men for at least a little while before 354/3.

No one, I fancy, doubts that Aristotle began to teach parts of the contents of our *Topics* in his quite early teaching years in the Academy. The *Topics* is an 'Art' or training-manual in the questioner–answerer disputation-exercise, and both in his *Topics* and in his *Art of Rhetoric* Aristotle closely associates the study of rhetoric with the study of dialectic. In his *Art of Rhetoric* Aristotle frequently talks as if his rhetoric students are quite familiar with the terminology and the practice of dialectic, i.e. as if they are learning both 'arts' together. Both book III of the *Topics* and *Rhetoric* I 6–7 give instruction in the types of arguments to be employed in order to establish the goodnesses and the comparative goodnesses of various types of things; their instructions are pretty similar and in several points identical. The version in the *Topics* shows only slightly greater technical sophistication than the version in the *Rhetoric*.

So Aristotle may have begun to give instruction in elenctic disputation nearly as soon as he began to teach rhetoric, well before the middle 350s. This connexion between the teaching of rhetoric

116

and the teaching of dialectic may have been of long standing. Antisthenes seems to have taught both, and in the mistier past Protagoras seems to have done so too. Political and forensic success both require not only fluency and elegance of diction, but also readiness and cogency in argumentation and counter-argumentation.

Among the writings credited by Diogenes Laertius to Xenocrates there are the *Solutions of Logical Problems* in ten books, *Solutions* in two books, eight books of *Divisions*, twenty books of *Theses*, the *Study of Dialectic* in fourteen books, and nine *Logisticon Biblia*. So Xenocrates must also at some stage have done a lot of teaching of dialectic. Perhaps he collaborated with Aristotle.

At the end of his *De Sophisticis Elenchis* Aristotle, in almost his sole statement about himself, says that where the authors of *Arts of Rhetoric* built on foundations laid by their predecessors, he, Aristotle, had had to start the theory and methodology of dialectic from absolute scratch. He does, of course, adduce concrete examples of dialectical arguments from Plato's dialogues and elsewhere. He also mentions, very scathingly, some earlier *Arts* of eristic disputation, which had done nothing but present, in memorizable form, particular arguments *pro* and *contra* particular theses, as if learning by heart particular arguments amounted to learning how to argue. The *Dissoi Logoi* is our solitary surviving specimen of such manuals of *pro* and *contra* argumentation. It really does just assemble particular arguments *pro* and *contra* particular theses, compressed and, once, numbered off for memorization, without a serious trace of diagnosis, comparison, or classification. Plato and Aristotle certainly know and draw on the *Dissoi Logoi*, so it is quite likely that this composition is one of the *Arts* of eristic of which Aristotle is complaining.

Even in his *Euthydemus*, a dramatized collection of sophistical elenchi, from which Aristotle draws several of his examples, Plato makes no positive contributions to the theory of cogent, as opposed to merely tricky, argumentation. Its author is interested in what we should classify as logicians' teasers; but he is not yet a logician. The author of the *Topics* teaches generalities about the forms and ingredients of arguments and misarguments. He is beginning to answer general technical questions which even in the *Euthydemus* were not yet being asked.

(2) Was dialectic a part of the Academy's curriculum before Aristotle taught it? In particular had Aristotle himself, during his student years, been coached in at least the match-winning tactics of questioner–answerer disputation? Was the Socratic Method taught to the young men in the Academy during the 360s?

At first sight we naturally suppose that this must have been so. (*a*) Plato frequently identifies or very closely associates dialectic with philosophy, and we all have the congenial picture of the Academy as, above everything, a school in which Plato taught philosophy to the young men. (*b*) In his *Parmenides* Plato makes old Parmenides urge the youthful Socrates to train himself for philosophy by going through Zenonian exercises, and the second part of the dialogue is presented as an exemplar of these exercises. (*c*) All Plato's early dialogues up to the *Gorgias* or the first book of the *Republic* have their dramatic life in questioner–answerer duels; and the young Cleinias, Lysis, Menexenus, Polus, Alcibiades and Charmides are subjected to Socratic questioning, as if this is indisputably of benefit to them. (*d*) Whether or not the young men, including Plato, around the historical Socrates were in any formal sense his pupils, they seem, from the *Apology*, to have learned from his example to practise the Socratic Method. Surely Plato would have transmitted to the students in his own Academy what Socrates had transmitted to him. What else, indeed, had Plato to teach?

But though tempting, this is not the right answer. In Book VII of the *Republic* (537–9) Socrates sternly forbids anyone under the age of thirty years to participate in questioner–answerer disputation. Young men are demoralized by the fun of tearing and shaking their opponents to bits. Elenctic disputation is reserved for the selected thirty-year-olds.

Plato adhered to this ban. He did not any longer teach dialectic, or therefore teach philosophy to the young men, though it was with his full approval that Aristotle introduced the teaching of dialectic into the Academy's curriculum fairly early in the 350s. It *could* be that Plato did teach the scientific contents of the *Timaeus*. But his own darling subject, the Socratic Method, he did not teach, though, we may suspect, not at all for the reasons given in Book VII of the *Republic*.

In support of this idea that Plato did not teach, *inter alios*, the young Aristotle dialectic or philosophy, we have evidence besides that given by Book VII of the *Republic*. (*a*) First of all we have Aristotle's own statement at the end of the *De Sophisticis Elenchis* that he had himself to start from scratch the Art of dialectic. If Plato had, however pragmatically, taught the Socratic Method, he could not have done so without at least sometimes discussing, especially with the young Aristotle, some moderately general methodological questions. Although in his *Topics* Aristotle pretty often draws on or alludes to things in Plato's early, middle and late dialogues, he never once refers to any tutorial injunctions, diagnoses, or even tactical tips from Plato. The *Topics* contains not a single identifiable echo of Plato's pedagogic voice. (*b*) Not even in Plato's late dialogues do we find more than two or three of the very numerous technical terms which Aristotle uses in his anatomy of dialectical arguments. The only ones that I can think of are '*poiotes*' in the *Theaetetus*; '*phasis*' and '*apophasis*' in the *Sophist*; and '*koina*' in the *Theaetetus*. (*c*) There is a passage in the *De Sophisticis Elenchis*, 182b22–7, in which Aristotle, possibly referring to Plato's *Parmenides*, mentions two rival views, according to one of which the *aporiai* in the arguments of Zeno and Parmenides about Unity and Existence are to be resolved by finding pluralities of senses in the terms 'one' and 'exists'. It is not even suggested that anyone asked Plato for his solution of the puzzles that, conjecturally, he had himself composed. We are reminded of passages in Aristotle's *Politics*, 1264a29, 1264b34, 1316a1, where Socrates (*sic*) is reproached for leaving undetermined certain important arrangements in his Ideal State. Neither Aristotle nor anyone else seems to have asked Plato which of the open alternatives he intended. This point has no weight if Aristotle's reference is not to Plato's *Parmenides*. (*d*) In the *Gorgias* and Book I of the *Republic* Plato reached the peak of his genius in the dramatic representation of questioner–answerer duelling; yet just then he abandons this whole type of dialogue. From the *Phaedo*, the bulk of the *Republic*, and all the later dialogues, save the highly formalized *Parmenides*, Part II, the Socratic Method has vanished, save for stray spasms, e.g. in the *Cratylus* and *Theaetetus*. The answerers are now mostly nodders and not defenders of theses. The elenchus has vanished. It seems reasonable to suppose that Socrates' veto on dialectic for the young men in Book VII of the *Republic* was connected somehow with Plato's abandonment of the dialectical dialogue. (*e*) Isocrates' *Busiris*, which scholars have surely grossly antedated, seems (in 15–23) to credit to Egypt policies recommended in Plato's *Republic*, including the Academy's curriculum. Astronomy, arithmetic, and geometry are the young men's studies. Eristic is not mentioned.

If Plato did not teach Aristotle dialectic, then he did not teach Aristotle philosophy, in anything like Plato's or our sense of the word. But if not, then the much canvassed question How, When, and Why did Aristotle break away from being the loyal disciple of Plato that he must have begun by being? becomes an unreal question. Aristotle never was a philosophical pupil or *a fortiori* a philosophical disciple of Plato. He knew and learned much from the dialogues of Plato. He also knew some of the writings of Zeno,

Heraclitus, Democritus, and Empedocles. But he did not sit at the feet of any of these authors. It was partly because Aristotle had to work out for himself the theory and methodology of dialectic that he made himself into the first logician-philosopher. He never ceased to be anyone's echo, for he never had been anyone's echo. He stood to Plato as Wittgenstein to Frege, and not as Bosanquet to Bradley, or as Theophrastus to Aristotle. To trace the intellectual growth of Aristotle we must cease to locate its germ in something called 'Platonism', or even in something called 'anti-Platonism'.

(3) In *Republic* VII Socrates, though forbidding the under-thirties to participate in dialectic, 'the coping-stone of the Sciences', requires the over-thirties, or the best of them, to do so. Do the senior members of the Academy hold their own questioner–answerer disputation-matches? (*a*) *A priori* it seems likely that their discussions of philosophical issues would take this form. (*b*) In Aristotle's *Peri Ideon* and, for example, in his assemblage of the cruces about the nature and worth of Pleasure in Book x of the *Nicomachean Ethics*, he makes such constant use of the technical terminology of dialectic that it is natural to suppose that he is giving us digests of actual elenctic disputations between Speusippus, Xenocrates, Eudoxus, himself and others. (*c*) In the *Peri Ideon* the arguments supporting and the arguments controverting the thesis that Forms have a separate existence are too abstract and sophisticated to derive from the disputations of mere twenty-year-old novices.

(*d*) In the *Topics* (101 b 22) Aristotle says that the term '*idion*' or 'property', i.e. 'peculiarity', is the title universally employed. This may show that at least one of Aristotle's regular technical terms had been taken over by him from elsewhere. But the passage may not carry this weight. (*e*) Several times in the *De Sophisticis Elenchis* he reports some anonymous other people as proffering rival diagnoses of and remedies for specific sophistical elenchi. At 182 b 23 Aristotle mentions two parties, those who deny and those who assert that the *aporiai* in the discourses of Zeno and Parmenides derive from the plurality of senses of 'one' and 'exists'. The technical instrument of *Many Senses* is being used by people other than Aristotle. (*f*) The Third Book of the *Metaphysics* is a catalogue of *aporiai* that need to be resolved. These *aporiai* are usually referred to quite impersonally; but in 995 a 26 and 1000 a 5 some of them are ascribed to contemporary persons other than Aristotle himself.

(*g*) In *Metaphysics* M 1079 b 21 the Mixture theory of the relation between Forms and particulars is credited to Eudoxus, who ἔλεγε διαπορῶν. Whether διαπορῶν means 'raising an *aporia*', or 'tackling an *aporia*', or 'going through a set of *aporiai*', the conjunction of the participle with ἔλεγε strongly suggests both that Eudoxus produced the theory in the course of elenctic disputation and that the theory was not one which Eudoxus necessarily agreed with.

The rules and codes of the elenctic disputation-match did not require that the defender of a thesis believed it to be true. His business was to produce the best possible case for it. Nor did the questioner have to believe the thesis to be false. His business was to produce the best possible case against it. In the *Topics* (163 a–b) Aristotle recommends his students to be, on different occasions, attackers and defenders of the same thesis, and this not only for the sake of developing dexterities, but still more for the sake of developing the philosophically valuable capacity to survey the implications both of the thesis and of its contradictory. Two or three generations earlier Protagoras and Socrates had laboured under the reproach of teaching students to argue both for and against theses. The *Dissoi Logoi* does exactly this. The same interchange of disputation-roles seems to continue to be a standard feature of the elenctic exercise. So it is probable that in the Academy's discussions of, for example, the Theory of Forms, Aristotle, Speusippus, Xenocrates, Eudoxus, Heracleides, and others all try their hands both as attackers and as defenders of the Theory. Aristotle knows well, since he has himself often had to marshal and develop, the numerous arguments against the Theory of Forms that we find in, for example, the fragments of the *Peri Ideon*. He also knows well, since he has himself had to marshal and develop, the numerous non-Platonic arguments for the Theory of Forms.

En passant, this might give us an explanation of the 'we' in Aristotle's *Metaphysics* different from that given by Jaeger. 'We' might mean not 'we Platonists' but 'we (whoever we are and whatever doctrines we hold) when we are acting as answerers in defence of the thesis that Forms are separate entities'. It would still be arguable that Aristotle uses the word 'we' at the time when these disputations are currently in progress inside the Academy, and that he drops it when he leaves the Academy, or when he and his colleagues have exhausted the potentialities of the problem.

There is a further point to be noticed about the conduct of elenctic disputation. A given thesis is commonly debated again and again; and sometimes the same person acts as defender of it or else as attacker time after time. Written minutes or abstracts of the argument-sequences deployed are kept and consulted. Consequently the arguments for and against a given thesis undergo a progressive development and crystallization. I, in attacking the thesis, say, that Virtue is teachable, redeploy question-chains that I and others have deployed before, as well as try progressively to fortify them against past or present rebuttals, misinterpretations and exceptions. Like chess-players' 'combinations', lines of argumentation are public property, and a tactical improvement made by myself becomes henceforth a part of anyone else's stock of arguments for or against the same thesis. We can see a partial analogy in the more or less standardized question-chains which are employed in the opening moves in the radio game of *Twenty Questions*. Aristotle gives some advice about the memorization and the composition of minutes or abstracts of lines of argument in *Topics* 105 b 12 and 163 b 17 ff., and in the latter passage he speaks of the disputation-issues that crop up again and again. When we think, therefore, of the Academy's disputations about Pleasure, or about the Theory of Forms, we should not suppose that these are just single or occasional discussions. They are deliberately repeated over and over again, with the same or with different questioners and answerers; and the course of today's debate largely repeats, with condensations, that of yesterday's debate or last week's debate, save in so far as the participants reinforce, repair, or clarify argument-sequences that were gone through yesterday and last week. To ask whether the finally crystallized refutation of the thesis *that pleasure is not a good* is the handiwork of Aristotle or of someone else is to ask an unanswerable question. It has passed between all the millstones. Dialectic is a co-operative and progressive polemic—a polemic not between persons, but between theses and countertheses. Theses are not personal property, nor arguments.

(4) Aristotle frequently distinguishes between those notions which are proprietary to specific disciplines, like medicine or geometry, and those which are ubiquitous or 'common' to all subject-matters alike. Among such 'common' or ubiquitous concepts are *existence, identity, similarity, unity, alteration, coming-to-be*, and their opposites. The proper dialectician investigates these common or neutral concepts. (See *Rhet.* 1, 1; 1, 2, 1358a2–32; *Topics* 170a34–b11; 172a7–b4, cf. *Met.* 995b20–6; 998b14–27; 1004a9–5a18; also *Met.* Δ *passim.*)

In three of his late dialogues Plato seems also to isolate a set of neutral concepts, and in his *Theaetetus*, 185–6, he too calls them 'common'. He instances *existence, identity, difference, unity, plurality, likeness, unlikeness*, and *odd* and *even*, and associates with these the notions of *beauty, ugliness, goodness*, and *badness*. For his present purposes, at least, he pits their neutrality not, as Aristotle does, against disparate disciplines, but against the disparate qualities apprehended by the different sense-organs. In the *Sophist*, from 254C, Plato examines the concepts of *existence, non-existence, 'motion'* and *'rest', identity*, and *otherness*. He calls them the 'greatest kinds'; he does not here use the word 'common'. In 253b–4b he allots to the dialectician the task of exploring the connexions between these summit-concepts. In his *Metaphysics*, 998b15–22, Aristotle speaks in a similar way of 'the first kinds', and of 'the highest of the kinds', instancing only *existence* and *unity*. In the *Parmenides*, 129, Socrates mentions together *unity, plurality, likeness, unlikeness, 'rest'* and *'motion'*; and later on old Parmenides, describing the exercises required by the would-be philosopher, instances as concepts to be explored by the two-way Zenonian method *unity, plurality, likeness, unlikeness, 'motion', 'rest', becoming* and *ceasing to be, existence* and *non-existence*. No general epithet, like 'common' or 'greatest', is here applied to these concepts; nor are the words 'dialectic' or 'dialectician' employed. In the Second Part of the *Parmenides*, while all the dialectical operations are operations *upon* the concept of *unity*, the operations themselves are very largely operations *with* the concepts of *existence, non-existence, identity, otherness, likeness, unlikeness, coming to be, ceasing to be, unity, plurality, part, whole*, and so on. What Aristotle says that the dialectician ought to concern himself with, namely the ubiquitous concepts, coincides with what Zeno's master is made to concern himself with. It seems, then, that, however strenuously Aristotle criticizes Plato's Ontology of Forms, he and Plato are in perfect agreement about the differences between 'common' or ubiquitous concepts and all the other concepts. They are in perfect agreement too that it is these ubiquitous notions which constitute the proper or the basic subject-matter of dialectic.

The dialectical part of the *Parmenides* is prefaced by the advice of old Parmenides to the youthful Socrates to train himself for philosophy in exercises of the Zenonian pattern; with the qualification that he should examine the implications not only of a given positive thesis, but also of its contradictory. After Zeno has explained that an exhibition of the exercise would be unsuited to *Hoi Polloi*, old Parmenides launches into his dialectical exploration, in lifeless questioner–answerer style, of the consequences following from the theses (*a*) that Unity exists, (*b*) that Unity does not exist.

For whose benefit did Plato compose this second part of the *Parmenides*? Explicitly for the benefit, not of *Hoi Polloi*, but of the young men who hoped to become philosophers, and therefore presumably for the young men in the Academy. Clearly the abstractness and subtlety of its argumentation would render it totally obscure and uninteresting to young men who had had no or little practice or coaching in dialectic. If Aristotle inaugurated the teaching of dialectic in the Academy, then the second part of the *Parmenides* was composed for the pedagogic benefit of Aristotle's pupils, and of his relatively advanced pupils. The young men to whom Aristotle is teaching some of the contents of our *Topics* are the young men for whom Plato composed the dialectical part of the *Parmenides*. That Parmenides' young interlocutor is a namesake of our Aristotle is no accident; and that Parmenides says of him that 'he is not the one to make trouble (for his questioner)' is surely a collegiate joke. For this to be true, Plato would have had to compose this part of the *Parmenides* at least some way on in the 350s. Part I of our *Parmenides* had surely been substantially composed several years earlier than Part II, and had not been planned to have for its completion anything like our Part II. Nor had our Part II been originally planned to be the completion of our Part I. For Part I is in *oratio obliqua*, while Part II, save for one opening 'he said', is in *oratio recta*. This suggestion that Part II of our *Parmenides* was composed fairly well on in the 350s clashes violently with the dating-scheme into which scholars commonly coerce the composition of the Platonic dialogues and the foundation of the Academy. So much the better, since, for reasons which cannot be given here, this scheme must as a whole be massively antedated.

(5) We are left with one major historical puzzle. If Plato so approves of Aristotle's *Topics*-classes that he composes for them his *Parmenides*, Part II, as an instructional exemplar of philosophically fertile dialectic, then why has he not himself taught dialectic in the Academy? All the more since not only were all his early dialogues dramatized elenctic disputations, but his *Euthydemus* in particular was a brilliant assemblage of sophistical elenchi, intended to stimulate the young Cleiniases to inquire what was wrong with these insidious elenchi. Why does Book VII of the *Republic* forbid the young men to participate in exercises of the Socratic Method, when almost all the pre-*Phaedo* dialogues are spurs to them to do so? In the *Apology* Socrates admits that the young men of his circle learn from his example to practise the Socratic Method, and he denies that he corrupts or spoils them. Yet in the *Republic*, Book VII, which is dramatically earlier than the *Apology*, Socrates says that participation in the Socratic Method is the ruination of young men. Why the yawning gap between Plato's *Euthydemus* on the one side and Plato's *Parmenides*, Part II, and Aristotle's *Topics* on the other? Why is it left

to the young Aristotle to teach dialectic to the young men in the Academy? Why, if Plato approves of this teaching in the 350s, had he vetoed it in the early days of his Academy?

In his *Memorabilia* I (31–8) Xenophon says that two members of the Thirty made it illegal for Socrates in particular to subject young men under thirty to Socratic questioning. Plato's *Apology* contains no such story; in the *Euthydemus*, of which the dramatic date is only two or three years after the fall of the Thirty, the two sophists interrogate the young Cleinias and Ctesippus, and are willing, for a fee, to give young men tuition in their Art, with nothing said of the recent or present existence of any politicians' veto; and Isocrates, in his *Helen*, scolds the teachers of eristic, but not as contravening any law against it. In the *Republic* the veto on dialectic for the young men is Socrates' own veto. Apparently Xenophon knows of an *ad hominem* veto on the teaching of dialectic to the young men, but invents a fifth-century provenance for it.

7

JOHN LOCKE ON THE HUMAN
UNDERSTANDING

Originally delivered as the John Locke Tercentenary Address, in the Hall at Christ Church, October 1932, and reprinted by permission of the Oxford University Press

My purpose in this address is not to discuss or even to mention a great number of the views which Locke puts foward in the *Essay*, but solely to try to state what in my view is the important contribution to philosophy which he made and for which he deserves to be ranked among the great philosophers. I shall, in consequence, squander no time in appraising him as an historical influence or as the founder or offspring of this or that philosophical school. For I shall, I think, be doing him a greater honour if I can point out how he threw new light where darkness was before.

The minds of thinking men in the late seventeenth century were woefully harassed by the numbers of disparate bodies of propositions which demanded their acceptance. Even within the field of theology —interest in the cruces of which was then more widespread among educated men than is even now interest in the cruces of the natural sciences—traditional revelation, personal illumination, authority, and faith were all severally acclaimed as sure grounds for the truth of most important propositions about God and human destiny. And besides theology, the newly developed mathematical disciplines were hardly distinguished, even by the masters of them, from the physical and metaphysical speculations which they thought demonstrable by simple extension of the methods of mathematics, with the result that general propositions based on experimental evidence, no less than the hypothetical constructions of dogmatic ontologies, pretended to the same sort of logical necessity as that which, whatever it is, holds between the successive steps of a mathematical deduction.

Worse still, the atomic hypothesis of the physicists had already been translated by Hobbes into a materialist metaphysic with paradoxical and alarming corollaries in his political, moral, and epistemological theories. Nor did his first and chief philosophical opponents, the Cambridge Platonists, make any lower claims to logical impregnability for their idealistic than he had done for his materialist conclusions.

Small wonder then that Locke discovered that before 'coming any nearer a resolution of those doubts which perplexed us'[1] 'it was necessary to examine our own abilities and see what objects our understandings were or were not fitted to deal with'. His object was 'to inquire into the original, certainty and extent of human know-ledge, together with the grounds and degrees of belief, opinion and assent',[2] and for this end it was necessary to give a general classifi-cation of the main sorts of subject-matters about which we think and formulate propositions, the main sorts of propositions that we make about them, the main sorts of evidence upon which our propositions can be based, and the main sorts of conditions of mind in which we accept these propositions. And if, as turns out to be the case, there are found differences of kind in all these respects between the pro-positions of mathematics, those of the inductive sciences, those of history, those of theology, those of common-sense experience, those of moral philosophy, and those of dogmatic metaphysics, there will be an end to a great part of the disputes which arise when the credentials of one method of discovery are purloined to bolster up the con-clusions of another.

Two convictions underlie his method of inquiry. The first is, to parody the title of Toland's heterodox book, his supposition of 'The Human Understanding not Mysterious', by which I mean that he consistently refused to accept any account of the ways or workings of the human mind which relied on the miraculous, the magical, or the transcendent. This shows itself both in his sustained criticism of the doctrine of Innate Ideas, which was in his own day the chief weapon of the Cambridge Platonists against the Hobbists, and also in his unsentimental exposure of the claims made in theology for traditional revelation and for the direct illumination appealed to by 'enthusiasts'. It shows itself too in the treatment he accords to the Scholastic doctrines of Substantial Forms, Essences, and the like.

The second underlying conviction is that the philosophical inquiry into such subjects as the human understanding should not embody 'the physical consideration of the mind', i.e. the attempt to discover by experiment or hypothesis causal laws governing the occurrence of mental states and happenings. The analysis of the concepts of knowledge, probable judgement, belief, guesswork,

[1] Epistle to the Reader.   [2] Bk. I, chap. I, §2.

127

faith, sensation, perception, discernment, comparison, abstraction, and the rest, is not laboratory work—though what the nature of the process is he does not directly elucidate.

The pity is, as we shall see, that the one doctrine which above all others we tend to regard as Locke's central and official teaching, namely 'the new way of ideas', is partly and disastrously the product of just the sort of causal hypothesis which he abjures.

THE NEW WAY OF IDEAS

That human knowing and thinking are to be described as consisting in or, at any rate, containing 'ideas' is something which it never occurs to Locke to question. It was, after all, common ground to the Cartesians and the Cambridge Platonists, and it was natural, though most regrettable, that Locke should have deemed it his task merely to elaborate the theory and not to reconsider it. For, as I shall try to show, while the term 'idea' is used by Locke in a number of completely different senses, some of which embody no philosophical nuisance save brachylogy, there is one sense in which he uses the term, and one which is cardinal, for what are, in my view, the most damaging errors in the theories of knowledge of Locke and his successors, in which it must be categorically denied that there are such things as 'ideas' at all. And had this been the only sense in which Locke used the term, then his whole *Essay* would have been, what it is not, a laboured anatomy of utter nonentities.

Let us consider some of the main uses to which he puts this Pandora's box of a word.

(*a*) In his account of sense-perception Locke gives the usual treatment to the data of the five senses, and treats the sensible 'qualities', such as softness, hardness, coldness, warmth, white, red, sweet, stinking, and the rest as affections or states of the perceiving mind (on all fours with pains) caused by some physical impulse from the minute constituents of the external body upon the minute constituents of the appropriate organs of the percipient's body. He does not observe that the arguments which prove that these sensible qualities are relative to the percipient prove only that they are relative to the physical situation and condition of the percipient's body, and so he lightly assumes it for certain that they are dependent on the percipient in the special sense of being modifications of his *mental* condition. However, as pain, for example, or fear presumably are mental states, and can without too much peril be described therefore as being 'in the mind' as distinct from 'in physical objects', it makes sense (even if it is false) to say that colours, tastes, noises, smells, and 'feels' are in the same way 'in the mind', namely as being special conditions in which a mind may be on an occasion of perception.

Therefore, when Locke calls sense-data or sensible qualities 'ideas', while his theory may be false, there is no special objection to his using the term 'idea' as a special term of art to denote states of mind of this sort, namely feelings or sensations.

(b) Sometimes, though relatively rarely, Locke uses the term 'ideas' to denote 'images' or pictures in the mind's eye. This is, of course, the normal use of the word by Berkeley and Hume. Of images it is at least plausible to say that they are somehow mental, though it is hard to describe the precise way in which they are in the mind. They are, however, at least not directly the effects of external impact and so are not homogeneous with sense-data as Locke describes these.

(c) Sometimes, by 'idea' he simply denotes an act of thinking about something. For example, in his chapter 'Of the Association of Ideas'[1] he refers to many cases, which all of us could multiply indefinitely, where we are set thinking of one topic by the thought of another, even though neither has any real relevance to the other. This sense remains in use in ordinary speech today. We say 'the idea of so-and-so has just occurred to me', meaning no more than that something or other has just caused or occasioned us to think of the thing in question. In this use the term 'idea' denotes just acts of attention or consideration, and these are certainly acts of mind, but they have nothing special to do with sensations or with images, both of which we have already seen to be referred to by the term 'ideas'.

(d) Next, Locke explicitly uses the term 'ideas' as his paraphrase for the more academic 'notions', 'species', 'conceptions', and 'terms'; and he continually describes 'ideas' as what words are the signs of, or what words stand for or are the names of, or what e.g. are expressed by the words 'whiteness, hardness, sweetness, thinking, motion, man, elephant, crazy, drunkenness'.

In this use he is clearly referring to what we technically call 'concepts'. Now a 'concept' is nothing more or less than an apprehended attribute, property, quality, or character, and conception is the apprehension of an attribute, property, quality, or character.

This use divides into two. (1) In one sense 'having an idea' is simply knowing or thinking something to be of a certain character. When I know or think that something is moving, or that something is an elephant, I can go on, if I like, for the purposes of such inquiries

---

[1] Bk. II, chap. 33.

as logic, to consider in abstraction the character which I have been considering the object to have, namely being in motion, or being an elephant.

Now *usually* when Locke uses the term 'ideas' (except where his special representative theory of ideas is under consideration, which it pretty seldom is), he is simply referring to the mental acts of considering something to be of a certain character. And the acts of considering are certainly 'in the mind', in the sense of being acts performed by the mind. But the characters are not mental acts or states. No one in his wits could think that being an elephant is an occurrence in a person's mental life.

(2) And in the other sense not infrequently[1] when Locke speaks of 'ideas', he is referring not to the apprehending of a character but to the character or attribute itself. And this is clearly his meaning in the lengthy analyses that he offers of space, time, number, infinity, power, substance, activity, identity, personality. He is inquiring what it is to be in space, to be infinitely extensible, to be a substance, to be a person, etc., and not what it is to think of things as being one or other of these. And, as we shall see later, his famous definition of knowledge as the perception of the connexion and agreement or disagreement and repugnancy of any of our ideas is translatable simply into the assertion that knowing consists in seeing that a given character implies or excludes (i.e. implies the absence of) another character. He is not saying that knowing consists in a species of introspection.

So far we have no special objection to any one of the five given uses that Locke gives to the term 'idea'. They are all quite different from one another, so to call them all by one title is ruinously ambiguous; and each by itself is complex enough to make the term 'idea' a dangerous condensation. But none of these five uses conceals any special hypotheses or presuppositions.

(e) But there remains the last and most notorious use of the term—and the one with which Locke's name is peculiarly closely associated. The term 'ideas' is used to denote certain supposed entities which exist or occur 'in the mind'. But they are 'in the mind' not, apparently, as states or operations of the mind, nor yet are they merely 'in the mind' in the way in which the battle of the Marne is 'in my mind' when I am thinking about it. For they are clearly supposed to be dependent on minds for their existence. Later exponents of the theory speak of them as 'contents', as if the mind was a container in some (non-spatial) sense analogous to physical

[1] Bk. II, chap. 8, §8; Bk. II, chap. 28, §1; Bk. IV, chap. 1, §6; Bk. IV, chap. 6, §5, &c.

objects which spatially contain other physical objects. But this metaphor—which Locke does not employ—sheds only a deeper darkness.

However, the theory supposes that in some sense minds do support these 'ideas', and further that these ideas are objects for them, i.e. that minds attend to ideas and think about them. It also supposes that minds cannot immediately attend to or think about any other things save 'ideas'. So whenever we think of or are awake to anything, it is to these supposed mind-dependent entities to which we are attending and never directly to any real existence outside of (which I suppose means independent of) our minds. An idea is 'whatsoever is the object of the understanding when a man thinks . . . or whatever it is which the mind can be employed about in thinking . . .'.[1]

There is supposed to be some relation between some of our ideas and real existences, for ideas of sensation are said to be produced in us by bodies; and 'ideas of primary qualities of bodies are resemblances of them, and their patterns do really exist in the bodies themselves'.[2] Ideas of secondary qualities are unlike but are the effects of powers in bodies.

Moreover, ideas are distinguished into 'real' and 'fantastical', of which the former are 'such as have a foundation in nature; such as have a conformity with the real being and existence of things or with their archetypes'. 'Our complex ideas of substances, being made all of them in reference to things existing without us and intended to be representations of substances as they really are, are no farther real than as they are such combinations of simple ideas as are really united, and coexist in things without us.'[3] Again he speaks of 'simple ideas which are ἔκτυπα, or "copies"', and 'the complex ideas of substances are *ectypes* or "copies", too; but not perfect ones, not adequate'.[4] And in his chapter 'Of True and False Ideas'[5] he says: 'Thus the two ideas of a man and a centaur, supposed to be the ideas of real substances, are the one true and the other false; the one having a conformity to what has really existed, the other not.' He states the first and most obvious difficulty in the theory in his chapter 'Of the Reality of Human Knowledge':

It is evident the mind knows not things immediately but only by the intervention of the ideas it has of them. Our knowledge therefore is real only so far as there is a conformity between our ideas and the reality of

[1] Bk. I, chap. 1, §8.   [2] Bk. II, chap. 8, §15.
[3] Bk. II, chap. 30, §5.   [4] Bk. II, chap. 31, §§12, 13.
[5] Bk. II, chap. 32, §5.

things. But what shall be here the criterion? How shall the mind, when it perceives nothing but its own ideas, know that they agree with things themselves? This, though it seems not to want difficulty, yet I think there be two sorts of ideas that we may be assured agree with things.[1]

This relation between ideas and real things he describes elsewhere thus:[2] 'For since the things the mind contemplates are none of them, besides itself, present to the understanding, it is necessary that something else, as a sign or representation of the thing it considers, should be present to it; and these are ideas.'

The theory is then this: that the world contains a number of real things or substances. Some of these are minds. A mind cannot directly know other substances, but in lieu of this it has dependent on itself certain objects called 'ideas'. These are not, apparently, states in which the mind is (with the exception of sense-data which are) nor are they acts of thinking performed by the mind, but something else, the status of which is not (and could not be) specified. These, or some of them, are present proxies or 'ghosts' of absent substances or of absent qualities, meaning by 'present' 'capable of direct inspection' and by 'absent' 'incapable of direct inspection'. By means of these vicarious objects we can and without them we cannot think some thoughts and even get some knowledge about other substances. Finally, sense-data, images, acts of attention, the apprehensions of characters, and characters themselves (all of which were severally called 'ideas' in completely different senses of this word) are now classified as species of 'ideas' in this special sense of mind-dependent objects, functioning, sometimes, as *locum tenentes* for independent realities.

But it needs now no prolonged argument to show (1) that there is no evidence for the existence of these supposed mental proxies for independent realities, (2) that the assumption of them throws no light on the problem (if it is one) how we can think about or know things, but only multiplies gratuitously the number of things to be thought about or known; and (3) that it embodies a theory, unplausible in itself, which, if true, would make knowledge or even probable opinion about independent realities quite impossible.

(1) If they existed or occurred, there should be empirical evidence of their existence or occurrence. But in fact introspection does not reveal them, and (I put it dogmatically) there is no causal inference to them. The argument on which Locke seems chiefly to rely, namely that the words which express our thoughts have meanings, proves nothing. For the word 'square', e.g., means a

shape which physical objects do or do not have and not a mental something.

(2) The assumption of 'ideas' does not explain how we think about or have knowledge of objects; for they are themselves described as objects about which we think and of which and the relations between which we have knowledge. If there is no difficulty in seeing how we can think about or have knowledge of ideas, then there is none in seeing how we can do so with respect to other objects like the moon or Julius Caesar. There is a prejudice that minds can only attend to what is part of or attached to their own being, but it seems to be due either to the futile superstition that minds are a species of container or to the popular mistake in logic of supposing that relations are not genuine in the way in which qualities and states are genuine characters of things.

(3) Even if there did exist such things as 'ideas' were supposed to be, it is almost impossible so to describe them as to make sense of the assertion that some of them 'resemble' or 'represent' realities, and quite impossible to explain how we could ever know or even opine with probability that they do so, unless it is granted that we can have the same direct knowledge of realities as of the ideas of them. And if this is granted, there is no need to assume the existence of the mental 'ectypes'. Not a few philosophers have tried to evade representationism by denying the existence of the supposed archetypes of the ideas and thus populating the world with nothing but minds and their ideas. And others have tried to accord to ideas truth of a non-representationist type by such dodges as internal coherence, systematic connectedness, and the like. But the problem which they try thus to solve is a sham one, since the alleged 'contents' for the objective validity of which they proffer such devious defences have no existence and so no properties or relations. They belong where 'phlogiston' belongs and where 'substantial forms' belong, namely to the folk-lore of philosophy.

The theory did, however, secure for Locke one important positive advantage in enabling him to draw what we shall see is a really crucial distinction between certain generically different types of propositions and consequently between certain generically different types of inquiry. For, as I have said, it was a part of Locke's purpose in writing the *Essay* to expose the nerves of the differences between the pure mathematical sciences, the natural or experimental sciences, moral and political philosophy, and theology. And for this purpose it was quite necessary not only to distinguish the sorts of evidence upon which are based the conclusions of these several types of inquiry, but much more to discover and find some way of formulating the differences between the sorts of subject-matters about which these propositions are. And this his theory of ideas partially enables him to do. For he is now in a position to say that the subjects of the propositions in arithmetic and geometry, for instance, are merely the species of ideas which he calls simple modes and are therefore not real existences or substances. Numbers, ratios, square roots, pentagons, circumferences, and tangents are in fact being negatively described as not things in nature when Locke describes them in the seemingly positive term of 'ideas'. It is not, of course, a finally adequate analysis of mathematical propositions to say that they are only about 'ideas', for not only are they plainly not psychological propositions, but 'ideas' themselves are only psychological fictions. But as a provisional step, it does mark an important step away from the insidious indulgence of the Schoolmen of hypostasizing the terms of propositions of all sorts and thus, by multiplying entities without limit, of obscuring the distinction between propositions about matters of fact and propositions of quite other sorts.

All the discourses of the mathematicians about the squaring of a circle, conic sections, or any other part of mathamatics, concern not the existence of any of those figures; but their demonstrations, which depend on their ideas, are the same whether there be any square or circle, existing in the world, or no. In the same manner, the truth and certainty of moral discourses abstracts from the lives of men, and the existence of those virtues in the world whereof they treat . . .[1]

We could, it may be hoped, find some other and less question-begging way of stating how it is that such propositions as those of mathematics and philosophy are about something, and yet are not about things in nature, than by saying that they are about ideas in our minds. But if we take Locke's account sympathetically, as a purely negative one, elucidating merely what such abstract propositions are *not* about, we shall find that a great part of Locke's treatment of the nature and relations of the several sorts of human inquiry only requires a little purely verbal translation to be seen as a successful, even revolutionary re-charting of the fields of human knowledge and opinion.

Similarly the consideration of those propositions containing terms which seem to denote fictitious objects, such as propositions about centaurs, unicorns, and sea-serpents, has tempted logicians to suppose that, as these nouns are not meaningless, reality must in some unexplained fashion contain centaurs, sea-serpents, and uni-

[1] Bk. IV, chap. 4, §8.

corns. And to this extent it is a healthy if incomplete manipulation by Locke of Occam's razor when he denies the real existence of such supposed objects by his device of describing them as 'fantastical ideas' or as 'ideas' simply. Positively, of course, it is false that a sea-serpent is a mental state or operation; for sea-serpents have (or rather would have) scales and swim (or rather would swim) in the sea—attributes which could not possibly characterize 'ideas'. But negatively taken it is half-way to the true account of such propositions seemingly about fictitious objects, to say that they are about ideas. For it is true that they are *not* about things in nature. But this line of interpretation must be expanded later.

THE ORIGIN OF IDEAS

The historians of philosophy, abetted, it must be confessed, by those who set examination papers in philosophy to students, love to allocate philosophers to 'schools of thought', and Locke has suffered more than most from this facile pigeon-holing. He is generally written off not merely as an Empiricist but as the founder of the School of English Empiricism.

It is not quite clear what an Empiricist is, but it is quite clear that most of the doctrines which an Empiricist (as ordinarily defined) should hold are strenuously denied by Locke. That the evidence of particular perceptions can never be a foundation for true knowledge, that true knowledge is both completely general and completely certain and is of the type of pure mathematics, that inductive generalizations from collected observations can never yield better than probable generalizations giving us opinion but not knowledge, are doctrines which Locke's whole *Essay* is intended to establish. He even goes so far with the rationalist metaphysicians as to hold that the existence of God is demonstrable, and he is at one with the Cambridge Platonists in arguing that the principles of morality are demonstrable by the same methods and with the same certainty as any of the propositions of geometry.

But he shows the cloven hoof, it is alleged, in his assertion that 'the materials of all our knowledge, are suggested and furnished to the mind only by those two ways . . . viz. sensation and reflection'[1] (i.e. introspection); and 'Our observation, employed either about external sensible objects, or about the internal operations of our minds, perceived and reflected on by ourselves, is that which supplies our understandings with all the materials of thinking'.[2] He makes, of course, a sharp distinction between the materials of thinking and

---

[1] Bk. II, chap. 2, §2.   [2] Bk. II, chap. 1, §2.

the constructions, combinations, comparisons, and abstractions which we make out of those materials. But it is ordinarily supposed that Locke's delimitation of the sources of the 'materials of thinking' should have forced him to the conclusion that there can be nothing more in thinking or knowing than the bare serial reception of these materials. But we must not vault to the conclusions which Locke did draw or should have drawn from this premiss until we have discovered what this premiss really is. To clear possible interpretations out of the way: by 'materials of thinking' and 'source of our ideas' (1) he *might* have meant (but in fact did not) the data, i.e. evidence, on which all the conclusions of our inferences are founded. Such a view would imply that all inference is inductive and, eventually, that no conclusions of inferences are certain. But it is clear that in fact he means something much more innocuous than that. (2) Or again he *might* have meant that images never occur unless we have previously experienced directly in sensation or introspection data of which they are reproductions; i.e. that images can only echo sense-data. This was certainly Hume's way of taking Locke's principle that the materials of our knowledge originate in sensation or reflection. But I find no evidence that Locke meant this. All that he seems to mean is this: (*a*) that we can never think of anything as being of a given character, unless we have met with an instance of this character, where the character is a simple unanalysable one. Where it is a composite character, we must at least have met with instances of the simple characters, of which the composite character is compounded; and (*b*) that the only ways in which human beings can be directly acquainted with instances of characters are by sense-perception and introspection. The former proposition is plausible if not true; and is anyhow only an Aristotelian orthodoxy. The latter is also plausible and (if the former proposition be accepted) can only be rejected by any one who can show that there is at least one other species of perception. (It could be debated whether introspection really is a species of perception, but I cannot discuss this question here.) And if the former proposition (*a*) is rejected, there seems no alternative but to accept some sort of doctrine of innate ideas.

Of course Locke was handicapped by his physiological theory of sense-perception from giving any plausible account of how in particular perceptions we can come to know that *relations* of any sort hold between the objects which we perceive; for he had to hold that perceiving is barely acquaintanceship with our internal affections, with which such relational characters as 'intenser than', 'between', 'after', etc. could plainly not be classified. Nor, for the same reason, could he explain how particular perceptions introduce us to such principles of form as the substance-attribute form, the term-relation form and, perhaps, the principle of cause and effect. But these serious defects have no tendency to prove either that Locke was wrong in maintaining that we can only learn that there is such a thing as being of a given character from first meeting in perception with instances of it (where the character is a simple one), or that his acceptance of this view logically committed him to what I take to be the full empiricist position that all reasoning is induction.

Perhaps I should just allude here to another rather hollow objection which is popularly levelled against Locke's account of the source of our ideas. He says that in sensation the mind is passive, though active in the operations of combination, comparison, abstraction, etc., which it performs upon the data of sensation. And it is held to be highly wicked for a philosopher to say that the mind is passive. I do not myself think that the disjunction activity–passivity is of great importance—or even of much luminousness. However, Locke does seem to be confusing two quite different senses in which the mind is said to be passive in sensation which are worth distinguishing.

That I cannot choose but see what I see or hear what I hear or, for example, that it is not by an act of my will that onions smell as they do is true and obvious. And sometimes[1] by the distinction between passive and active Locke seems to be doing no more than referring to the distinction between those states of affairs which I bring about voluntarily and those which come about involuntarily. So 'passive' just means 'willy-nilly'. But generally Locke presupposes in his use of the term 'passive' his special causal theory of perception, by which the smell that I smell or the sound which I hear is a state of me caused by the impact upon me of something outside my skin. 'Passive' then means 'inflicted'. This causal theory may be false, but its refutation cannot be grounded upon a supposed *a priori* inappropriateness of the term 'passive' to states of mind. Before we can accept the supposed alternative doctrine that the mind is *active* in sense-perception, we should need to know whether 'active' means 'creating' or 'making a new combination of' or 'causing a change in', or whether it merely means 'tending to engender fatigue'.

I need not say much about Locke's treatment of the formation of derivative ideas, that is to say, of the operation of mind by which we come to apprehend compound characters, and to consider attributes in abstraction from the particular objects which we have found to

[1] Cf. Bk. II, chap. 30, §3.

exemplify them. For in the main his treatment of these topics is an unsatisfactory mixture of an attempt to give a logical classification of the types of general terms which occur in the propositions of the mathematical and natural sciences with a half-hearted attempt to button these subjects up into the straitjacket of his representationist theory of ideas. However, in his classification of space as a 'mode' as opposed to a substance, and especially in his not unimportant analyses of the concepts of extension, distance and place or relative position, and in his defence, against the Cartesians, of the distinction between space and body he does not merely introduce us into the very heart of the controversy between the Cartesians and the Newtonians, but is half-way to supplying a satisfactory account of the differences between pure geometry and physics as well as of the way in which geometry enters into physics. He seems even to be inclined to the relational theory of space, but the authority of Newton seems to have been a stronger influence in the contrary direction. And in his treatment of infinity in which he distinguishes the infinity of space, time, and number from the notion of *an* infinite space, of *an* infinite time, or of *an* infinite number, it may be that there do lie the seeds of the final solution of the perplexities upon these matters which have so long occupied men's minds.

We shall have to return to consider Locke's treatment of what sort of truth it is which is contained in geometrical and arithmetical propositions; but the rest of the topics which Locke deals with in this book must be passed over as not being indispensable for the understanding of Locke's main objects and main achievements.

KNOWLEDGE

The propositions in which we formulate what we know or think or guess are divided, in quite the traditional way, into particular and general or universal. Particular propositions profess to state particular matters of fact and to be about particular existences. General propositions fall first into two main types, those which are certain, being either self-evident or demonstrable by self-evident steps from self-evident premisses, and those which are not certain but at best probable. The latter rest on the foundation of particular observations of particular existences. The former are either trifling, i.e. identical or analytic, or else instructive or 'synthetic' (to use Kant's term).

Now 'scientific knowledge' must, he takes it, be of general truths; and to be 'certain' its truths must be either self-evident or rigorously demonstrable. Hence it follows that its propositions cannot be about particular existences nor founded on the evidence of propositions which are so. The propositions, therefore, of 'scientific knowledge'[1] can only be about the relations of 'abstract ideas' in the way of agreement or disagreement. As he has in mind here such propositions as that the internal angles of a triangle are equal to two right angles, it is clear that the mysterious-sounding phrase 'the agreement and disagreement of our ideas' refers simply to the propositions which assert that the having one general character implies (or implies the absence of) another character.

Locke was not enough of a logician to analyse very closely these notions of agreement and disagreement, i.e. implication and exclusion. But one point he makes quite clear. By the universal and certain propositions of science he does not mean either such propositions as 'what is green is green' or such propositions as 'what is green is coloured', or such propositions as 'a triangle is a plane figure bounded by three straight lines'. For a definition he regards as a proposition about the employment of a word; and what we call analytic propositions are for him only fragments of definitions. And these are, for him, 'trifling' propositions in the sense that nothing is learned, no new knowledge is got, when we see one of them to be true. It follows that the 'agreement' of which he speaks is not the 'is' of identity, nor yet is it the entailment of a generic character by a specific one, but something different. He thinks, namely, that there are some general propositions which we can know to be true which assert that the having one attribute implies the having of another, when these are not only different attributes but further when neither is entailed in the other as generic in specific.

And he thinks that the propositions of arithmetic and geometry as well as those of moral philosophy are of this sort; and indeed that 'scientifical knowledge' consists in the knowing of such implications.

So when he gives his notorious statement 'knowledge then seems to me nothing but the perception of the connexion and agreement, or disagreement and repugnancy, of any of our ideas. In this alone it consists. Where this perception is, there is knowledge; and where it is not, there, though we may fancy, guess, or believe, yet we always come short of knowledge,'[2] he is attempting not to give a definition of knowing as opposed, say, to guessing and believing, but to describe what it is that we know when we know something scientifically—namely, that it is never anything else but what we would call an implication (or exclusion) of one attribute by another. 'Ideas' here is just a synonym for 'quality' or 'attribute', and connotes, unless I am wrong, nothing at all of his 'proxy' theory of

[1] Bk. IV, chap. 3, §26.   [2] Bk. IV, chap. 1, §2.

139

ideas. He does, however, reintroduce this in a ruinous fashion,[1] where he says, 'Every man's reasoning and knowledge is only about the ideas existing in his own mind, which are truly, every one of them, particular existences; and our knowledge and reasoning about other things is only as they correspond with those our particular ideas.'

Locke is now in a position to show that the truth of the abstract general propositions of pure mathematics as well as of moral philosophy (which he is surely wrong in thinking homogeneous with mathematics) does not in the least depend upon whether there exist any objects having the properties the implications between which those propositions state. He is within an inch of saying that these propositions which express 'scientifical knowledge' are hypothetical. *They do not directly describe real existences*. They say what properties *would* follow, if something had certain other properties, and not that anything has them.

Now this seemingly unexciting discovery is of the greatest importance. For it proves that geometry does not (as the Cartesians thought) directly describe the world; and it proves that anyhow many philosophical statements have no ontological bearing—they do not describe transcendent entities, but merely say what *would* follow about any ordinary object if it was of such and such a character.

This is where Locke is an anti-Rationalist—not that he disputes our power to reach new certain and universal truths by pure reasoning (on the contrary it is in this process that, for him, science proper consists), but that he maintains, in effect, that all these truths are general and hypothetical and do not therefore give any description of what exists. Even the existence of God, demonstrable with mathematical certainty in Locke's opinion, must have for one of its premises the existence of the person making the demonstration, and *his* existence is perceived and not proved.

Knowledge of the highest type consists, then, for Locke in knowledge of what have since been called synthetic *a priori* truths, but these do not constitute either an ontology or natural science. But he makes no attempt to show wherein consist these rather mysterious relations of agreement and disagreement (or implication and exclusion) nor to prove that mathematical propositions are really synthetic.

[1] Bk. IV, chap. 17, §8.

KNOWLEDGE OF EXISTENCE

Besides the knowledge formulable in general or hypothetical propositions, in which field alone formal deduction or demonstration is possible, there is the field of matters-of-fact within which some little knowledge of an inferior sort and much probable opinion is possible. This divides into knowledge (*a*) of particular existences and of particular co-existences of qualities in particular substances on the one hand, and on the other (*b*) the judgement (it does not amount to knowledge) based on the evidence of particular instances that certain properties always accompany certain others.

(*a*) Locke offers no analysis of existential propositions, and so never even considers whether knowing that I, for example, exist is really a case of perceiving a relation between two qualities. He argues that this I can know in the full sense of the verb, namely that I exist. It needs no proof. 'We have an intuitive knowledge of our own existence and an internal infallible perception that we are.'[1] Whether this involves knowing who or what I am (ignorance or doubt about which would leave small significance to the existential proposition 'I exist'), Locke leaves it to Hume to discuss.

Next, we can prove the existence of God from our own existence, since 'what had a beginning must be produced by something else'. And lastly, though we can neither have intuitive nor demonstrative knowledge that anything else exists, yet we can have 'an assurance that deserves the name of knowledge'.[2] For, while quite ignorant *how* our data of sense are caused to arise in our minds, *that* they are caused by agencies outside us is so highly probable that we have the right to feel certain that an object exists at the time we are experiencing a sensation. But of course we can have no such assurance of the past or continued existence of external objects, or indeed of any moment of their existence except at the instant when the sensation is occurring. It will be seen thus that all our knowledge or assurance of the existence of other things, both God and bodies, presupposes our knowing that 'what had a beginning must be produced by something else'. Perhaps it was an interest in this special question of our knowledge of other existences that caused Hume to fix his criticism on the one (alleged) synthetic *a priori* proposition that every event must have a cause.

What exists is particular or, better put, the subject terms of existential propositions are not general or abstract terms but singular and concrete ones. It follows, therefore, that there can be

[1] Bk. IV, chap. 9, §3.　　　[2] Bk. IV, chap. 6, §3.

no question of our knowing synthetic *a priori* truths which are also existential.

No collocation of propositions of the form '*x*-ness implies *y*-ness' or 'whatever is *x* is *y*' can lead to a conclusion of the form 'Cicero exists' or 'Westminster Abbey has such and such mass'. Pure reason cannot inform us of a single particular matter of fact. So all the knowledge or assurance we can have about what exists or occurs in nature must either be or be based on the evidence of particular observations. If this is Empiricism then Locke is an Empiricist and, I would add, Empiricism is the truth.

THE NATURAL SCIENCES

But Boyle and Sydenham and 'such masters as the great Huygenius and the incomparable Mr Newton' do not merely list particular observations. The discoveries of the natural sciences are or are intended to be laws, i.e. general propositions holding good not only of all observed but also of all unobserved, all possible as well as all actual, instances of the type of phenomenon under examination. How do these differ from the general propositions of geometry and arithmetic?

Locke takes up this question by considering first of all how we come to classify things in nature into sorts. For the general propositions of the natural scientist will all be of the form that every object of such and such a sort has such and such properties. A living creature is classified as a lion or a body as a piece of gold because it is found to possess a certain set of qualities and is similar to many other objects which also have just the same or almost the same set of qualities.

But, unlike our procedure with abstractions which we can *define* to have such and such properties and no others, in respect of natural kinds we cannot arbitrarily coin our definitions of the properties essential to the kinds that nature provides. Even if, as Locke seems to think, things in nature are really members of real kinds, in such a way that in their inward constitution their properties are necessarily connected, yet we have no way of perceiving the necessity of the co-existence of the qualities which we observe to co-exist. When we come to distinguish lions from bears and tigers, we do not yet know why tawny fur goes with such and such a shape of head in the way in which we do know why in a right-angled triangle the square on the hypotenuse is equal to the sum of the squares on the other two sides.

We find several objects having in common a large set of qualities (though we can usually give no precise catalogue of these common characteristics), and so come to treat and name all the objects which have anyhow a large fraction of this set of qualities as members of the same sort. Moreover, we *suppose* that there is some principle, although we do not know it, necessitating that whatever has certain of these characteristics shall also have the rest.

Our faculties carry us no farther towards the knowledge and distinction of substances than a collection of those sensible ideas which we observe in them; which, however made with the greatest diligence and exactness we are capable of, yet is more remote from the true internal constitution from which those qualities flow than, as I said, a countryman's idea is from the inward contrivance of that famous clock at Strasbourg, whereof he only sees the outward figure and motions.[1]

So the definitions which we give of the natural kinds which we establish do no more than list the properties which we constantly find to be concomitant. Thus our definitions are only of 'nominal essences', that is, of the bunches of properties which we have chosen to unify under one name. But how many such properties ought to be treated as necessarily concomitant we cannot know. 'We can never know what are the precise numbers of properties depending on the real essence of gold; any one of which failing, the real essence of gold, and consequently gold, would not be there, unless we knew the real essence of gold itself, and by that determined the species.'[2] Often Locke speaks as if the difficulty is merely a consequence of his causal theory of sense-perception or, what comes to the same thing, of his theory that the secondary qualities of things are in the mind and not in things, namely that as all we can know of things is the sensations which they cause to occur in us, therefore the real internal constitution of things necessarily eludes our apprehension.

But in Book IV especially he puts his finger on the real nerve of the difficulty, which is, of course, the nerve of the whole problem of induction. The concomitance of what we take to be the 'sortal' properties of lions, say, or gold is generically different both from the relation of specific to generic quality ('entailment') and from the relations of agreement or disagreement (implication or exclusion) which we can know to hold between certain of our abstract ideas. So it is not merely that we do not yet see how to demonstrate by rigorous deduction that whatever has the other properties of gold must be soluble in *aqua regia*, but we can already see that there is no such logical implication. It is not an analytical proposition; it is not a self-evident synthetic one; and it is not one that can be

---

[1] Bk. III, chap. 6, §9.   [2] Bk. III, chap. 6, §19.

demonstrated in a chain of propositions each self-evidently consequent from its predecessor.

Thus though we see the yellow colour, and upon trial find the weight, malleableness, fusibility, and fixedness that are united in a piece of gold; yet because no one of these ideas has any evident dependence or necessary connexion with the other, we cannot certainly know that where any four of these are the fifth will be there also, how highly probable soever it may be; because the highest probability amounts not to certainty; without which there can be no true knowledge. For this coexistence can be no farther known than it is perceived; and it cannot be perceived but either in particular subjects by the observation of our senses, or in general by the necessary connexion of the ideas themselves.[1]

This gives Locke the generic difference which he requires between the pure deductive or *a priori* sciences and the experimental sciences. The general propositions of the physical and other inductive sciences rest on the evidence of regularly observed concomitances of properties; and these concomitances are not self-evident or necessary. So the conclusions of these sciences never can reach the certainty of mathematics, and in Locke's rigorous use of the term science, they cannot constitute scientific knowledge. They cannot rise higher than probability. 'We are not capable of a philosophical knowledge of the bodies that are about us, and make a part of us; concerning their secondary qualities, powers and operations, we can have no universal certainty.'[2]

THEOLOGY

It is likely that in Locke's mind and in the minds of his contemporaries, no more important or urgent question was discussed in the whole *Essay* than the question of the nature and certainty of the propositions of theology. Whether historical tradition can enable us to *know* that such and such things were revealed to certain of our forefathers, whether immediate revelation or inspiration yields a certainty of the same sort as our certainty of mathematical axioms, whether religious truths are above reason or according to reason or whether, although contrary to reason, they still demand unquestioning assent, these were questions of deep importance for Locke and for his age.

It seems not unlikely that it was from an inquiry into problems such as these that the *Essay* took its beginning. But, for us, Locke's treatment of these problems has by itself removed them from their pride of place in the forefront of philosophical interest. For we have

---

[1] Bk. IV, chap. 3, §14.　　　　[2] Bk. IV, chap. 3, §29.

no doubt now that historical testimony can yield nothing higher than probabilities; that whatever may be the authority of immediate inspiration, if and when it occurs, the claim that it has really occurred and not merely seemed to occur can never fully certify itself. Belief is belief and not knowledge; and no matter how transcendent its object or how elevated its effects may be, it can rise no higher than whole-hearted assurance. And we are sometimes whole-heartedly assured of what is not true. So the doctrines of theology rest on the fallible testimony of historians or the fallible testimony of the human heart, and may achieve indeed a degree of probability more than high enough for the confident and wise conduct of life; but they cannot emulate the demonstrability of mathematics nor even the broad statistical foundations of experimental science. From which follows the corollary, to which we are now well acclimatized, that it is in principle erroneous to seek to base or corroborate the premisses of mathematics, philosophy, or the natural sciences upon the conclusions of theology or the tenets of religious faith. These have their place in life, but they enjoy no precedence in rational inquiry.

What, then, was Locke's achievement? If I am not mistaken, it was something much greater than is usually allowed him. He was not merely the plain-spoken mouthpiece of the age or the readable epitome of its development; nor was it his task merely to anglicize and popularize the philosophical and scientific concepts and theories of his day. His title does not rest upon his rather frail claim to be the founder of psychology, nor yet upon his two-edged claim to be the founder of modern theories of knowledge. And to my mind there is no unkinder or unfairer testimonial to his philosophical writings than to say, what is often said, that in them the common-sense views of ordinary man find their best expression. Nor yet, in my view, is it a part of Locke's greatness as a philosopher that he expounded and popularized the theory (which he did not invent) of representative ideas. For I hold that the theory is not only an error, but the wrong sort of error, being in the main fruitful of nothing of positive value to the theory of knowledge.

Instead I claim for Locke that he did achieve a part of his ambition 'to be an under-labourer, in clearing ground a little, and removing some of the rubbish that lies in the way to knowledge' in that he taught the whole educated world the lesson (which might with profit be conned over in some quarters in our own day) that there are differences in kind, and roughly what these differences are, between mathematics, philosophy, natural science, theology, inspiration, history, and common-sense acquaintanceship with the world around us. In a word, his achievement is that he gave us not a theory of knowledge but a theory of the sciences. So that for which we should render him thanks is no exciting speculation or visionary promise of another world, no disclosure of startling secrets of earth or heaven or of human nature, but something else which, though it does not glitter, still is gold, namely a permanent emancipation from a besetting confusion. He taught us to distinguish the types of our inquiries, and thus made us begin to understand the questions that we ask.

8

JOHN LOCKE

Reprinted from 'Critica Revista Hispanoamericana de Filosfía', vol. I, by permission of the editors of that journal; originally delivered as a lecture in July 1965 to the Summer School at the University of Edinburgh

If we are asked to give a list of the ten most influential philosophers of all time, we are likely to have the name 'John Locke' in our list, even, perhaps, fairly high in the list. It is not much of an exaggeration to say that one cannot pick up a sermon, a novel, pamphlet or a treatise and be in any doubt, after reading a few lines, whether it was written before or after the publication of Locke's *Essay concerning Human Understanding*, which was in 1690. The intellectual atmosphere since Locke has had quite a different smell from what it had before Locke. If we could fly back in a time-rocket to England in 1700, we could already breathe its air, and we could already converse with our new acquaintances there without feeling lost. In the England of, say, 1600, we should gasp like fishes out of water. But if we are then asked what Locke's great contribution was, we find it very difficult to answer.

A good many years ago, I happened to be sitting with Earl Russell in the restaurant-car of a train to North Wales. Somehow our conversation turned to John Locke and I put to Russell this very question, perhaps with some hyperbole: 'Why is it that, although nearly every youthful student of philosophy both can and does in about his second essay refute Locke's entire Theory of Knowledge, yet Locke made a bigger difference to the whole intellectual climate of mankind than anyone had done since Aristotle?' Russell agreed that the facts were so, and suggested, on the spur of the moment, an answer which dissatisfied me. He said, 'Locke was the spokesman of Common Sense.' Almost without thinking I retorted impatiently, 'I think Locke invented Common Sense.' To which Russell rejoined 'By God, Ryle, I believe you are right. No one ever had Common Sense before John Locke—and no one but Englishmen have ever had it since.'

Now there was something true both in my unpremeditated retort and in Russell's unpremeditated rejoinder. But it is not at all easy to nail down this truth. The major thing I want to do in this talk of mine today is to try to nail it down.

Let me first of all, though, run through and dismiss three other more or less standard answers to that original question of mine, namely, 'What was Locke's great contribution?'

(1) The first of the four books into which Locke's *Essay* is divided is occupied almost entirely with the refutation of a theory, known as the 'Theory of Innate Ideas', the theory, namely, that we are born not only with arms, legs, eyes and ears, but also with a fund of truths and concepts. It hails originally from Plato's dialogues, the *Meno* and the *Phaedo*. Some philosophers, whose reading of Locke seems to have terminated at the end of this first book, speak as if what Locke achieved was just the demolition of this quaint but erroneous old theory. But this cannot be the right answer. A number of mostly rather small fry had indeed, in Locke's own day, given, with modifications, a brief revival to Plato's theory, often for theological ends; and the philosopher Descartes, who was not at all small fry, had given it a rather perfunctory and non-commital endorsement. But the Theory of Innate Ideas was not, in the 17th century, a dominant or even a very influential doctrine. It was not a doctrinal Goliath whose menace to mankind urgently needed to be dispelled by a stone from John Locke's sling. Moreover, we possess Locke's first draft of what was many years later to be his *Essay*, and in this draft the Theory of Innate Ideas goes almost, though not quite, unmentioned. He had begun to write his *Essay* without yet having even seriously attended to the Theory of Innate Ideas. It was only a secondary or tertiary target. He attacked it for interim tactical, not for ultimate strategic, ends. I think myself that he filled up too many pages on his demolition of the Theory.

(2) A quite different kind of answer to my original question is this. Locke, in his explorations into the workings of the human mind, and particularly into its workings when trying to acquire knowledge, was inaugurating the science of psychology. Yet Locke never claims to be doing anything of the sort. So far from aspiring, as Hume did aspire, to be a second Newton, namely the Newton of the mental world, he speaks as if his task was rather to remove certain intellectual obstructions to the progress of such natural sciences as Newtonian mechanics, chemistry, astronomy and medicine. Moreover, if it were true that Locke's chief legacy was his contribution to psychology, we should have to concede that this contribution was of

very little value. Next to nothing of Locke's terminology or of his theory of thought and perception survives in modern psychology. In fact psychology had to disembarrass itself of Lockeanisms before it could win its spurs as a science. A student who knew his *Essay concerning Human Understanding* and claimed to be well grounded in psychology would receive very short shrift from the Department of Psychology of his university.

(3) The third and the most favoured answer to my original question, and the last that I shall consider, is this. Locke was the champion of Empiricism against Rationalism. Philosophers, it is supposed, have to join one party or the other, and Locke was, if not the founder, at least the organiser and leader of the Empiricist Party. Yet Locke never calls himself an Empiricist, nor does he call Descartes, say, a Rationalist. Locke learned a lot from Descartes, and when he criticises Descartes's doctrines, it is only sometimes, though it is sometimes, for their abstract speculativeness that he takes them to task. Locke himself knew a good deal of medicine; he was a close friend of the chemist, Boyle, and he was an early Fellow of the Royal Society, which was dedicated to the advancement of knowledge by observation and experiment. He knew, by personal participation, the unseaworthiness of scientific theories which get no ballast from the laboratory, the operating theatre or the observatory.

Descartes, a mathematical genius, was indeed in his physics and his physiology much more of a pure theorist and much less of an experimentalist than Galileo, Harvey or Boyle. But even he never pretended that the science of human and animal anatomy, say, or astronomy, could be done, like geometry, in the armchair. Indeed he made some creditable though not very systematic observations of his own on the carcasses of animals in butchers' shops. Some of his *a priori* arguments for the existence of God are repeated, without uneasiness, by Locke himself. Indeed Locke's whole account of indubitable knowledge diverges only slightly from that of Descartes. If Descartes was a Rationalist, then in this matter Locke was a Rationalist too.

The historical truth is that the supposed two-party system of Rationalists versus Empiricists just did not exist. But even if it had existed, the principle that our knowledge of nature must be rooted in observation and experiment had been the overt maxim of the Royal Society for a generation or more before the publication of Locke's *Essay*. If this maxim is 'Empiricism' then Empiricism had long been the familiar and uncontroverted principle of the Royal Society. Locke would not have invented it or felt any special call to

champion it. Champion it against whom? The principle was in no
jeopardy; and the defence of it, if it had needed defence, would have
required no special originality.

I now turn to my positive task of specifying what Locke's contribution was.

We should, to start with, consider the seemingly trivial question—
for whom was Locke writing? His own prefatory Epistle to the
Reader makes it quite clear that he was writing for the general
public, or rather for the general literate public, that is, for all who
habitually read sermons, plays, histories, novels, books of travel or
essays. He was not writing for a handful of experts in theology,
scholarship or science; he was not, for example, writing exclusively
for the Fellows of the Royal Society, the Professors of Oxford or
the divines of the Church of England. Least of all was he writing for
professional philosophers—no professional philosophers existed in
the age of Locke. The whole first edition of his *Essay* was in fact
sold out in less than two years.

To say that the *Essay* was written for the general public is not to
say that it was a work of popularisation or vulgarisation. But it is to
say that Locke thought that its problems and his solutions of them
were germane to the intellectual interests of everyone, not just to the
professional interests of the learned. But what intellectual interests
are common to everyone? Surely some people get heated by political
issues who are lukewarm about theological issues; some people are
eager to hear about new discoveries in astronomy or medicine, while
others care nothing about these but love to study archaeology or to
read travel journals, essays or biographies. By what hook could
Locke have hoped to capture the attention, as he did capture the
attention, of literate folk in general? Even more, by what lessons
could Locke have hoped to improve the thinking, as he did improve
the thinking, of literate folk in general?

Notoriously, Locke in his *Essay* dissects the thoughts of which the
human mind is capable into their constituent ideas; and he traces
these constituent ideas to their sources in sense-perception and
introspection. He describes the compoundings of these elementary
ideas into complex ideas, and the distillation from them of abstract
ideas, the coupling of them into propositions, and so forth. But what
were the bearings of this quasi-mechanics of our intellectual operations
upon any, and *a fortiori* upon all, of the variegated intellectual interests
of literate people in general? If you were a passionate supporter
and I was a passionate opponent of the Arian Heresy, or of the
Divine Right of Kings, as at that time, we might well have been,

how possibly could we find in Locke's *Essay concerning the Human Understanding* a common illumination or a sharable lesson? Well, unless we were too bigoted or fanatical to be teachable at all, we could, I suggest, have found such a lesson, and Locke's actual readers found it too.

Violent controversy was a salient mark of Locke's age. In matters of religion above all, though followed closely by matters of politics, people who held opinions at all held them rabidly. The idea that opposing sects or opposing factions should or even could ever agree to differ, the idea, that is, of Toleration was as yet, save in Holland, hardly thought of or, if thought of, then generally deemed to be itself intolerable. Roman Catholics and Calvinists were at one on the duty of Intolerance, though they applied it very differently. If your opinions differ from mine, then to the scaffold or to exile or to Hell you should go. Conflicts between your and my opinions could be settled only by the elimination of you whose opinions must be wrong and pernicious. Locke himself lived for some years in Holland as a political refugee, and his Oxford college, Christ Church, was forced to deprive him of his Studentship because the King suspected Locke's politics. In the 20th century no one tried to deprive me of my Studentship at Christ Church, or was even perturbed about any of my views.

It is against this background of controversy without toleration that we need to read Locke's *Essay*. Men in general needed to learn, what the handful of Locke's scientific friends in England and theological friends in Holland had quite recently learned, to realise not just that their own opinions and surmises might be mistaken, but still more that their opinions deserved only that *degree of adherence* that was warranted by the ratio of the amount of their evidence to their scope. For example, historical and theological opinions resting on testimony were less or more secure as that testimony derived from few or many witnesses, uneducated or educated witnesses, biased or impartial witnesses, remote or recent witnesses, concordant or discordant witnesses. Analogously, the strength of our scientific opinions that rest on observation and experiment should be proportioned to the amplitude and the precision of those observations. In the fields of geometry and arithmetic, what is neither axiomatic nor proved by axioms is, as yet, mere hypothesis or else error. Here anything like a mere opinion, and *a fortiori* a stubborn opinion, is entirely unreasonable. 'Mathematical bigot' is almost a contradiction in terms.

Moreover, disputants often fail to consider the nature of the propositions that they espouse. Some propositions, though unquestionable, are only verbal or 'trifling' propositions, such as the proposition that a bachelor is an unmarried man. But their dull unquestionability is then covertly bestowed upon propositions of sorts which are not verbal and are far from trifling, like the proposition that for human beings there is a life after death. A person who rightly avers that he could not be wrong about the former proposition may easily go on to aver that he could not be wrong about the latter proposition.

Sometimes Locke seems to us unduly to narrow the field of what can be known for certain in order to widen the field of the propositions that can, at best, be reasonably opined, i.e. be of sufficiently high probability for us safely to act on them; and perhaps the intellectual modesty which he recommends does come a bit too close to intellectual defeatism. There are, according to him, very few sorts of truths that we can conceivably acquire real knowledge of. But I suggest that his prime concern was just with the areas where not concord on certainties but discord between certitudes prevails. It was for these cockpit areas, which on any showing, were and still are large enough, that he was prescribing. His prescription, which has been a blessedly trite one since 1690, is that men should learn to ask themselves what are the solidities and what are the frailties of the reasons they have for their opinions, no matter on what subject. They should learn to harness their opinions between the shafts of evidence and clarity. If this is what it is to have some degree of Common Sense, namely to have learned when it is silly and when it is reasonable to feel quite or fairly sure of things; when certitudes are unreasonable and when they are reasonable; then Locke's *Essay* does not only teach us what Common Sense is; it teaches us Common Sense. It teaches us how to be sensible or reasonable in our adoption, retention and rejection of opinions. It is, I suggest, chiefly for contrast that Locke concerns himself with Euclidean certainties. His business is with the territories in which, though Euclidean certainties are unattainable, die-hard certitudes are all too prevalent.

A cautionary word is needed here. Our hackneyed phrase 'Common Sense' is not Locke's phrase. Moreover, when we use the phrase nowadays, we think chiefly of sensibleness in common, i.e. everyday, matters, like not discarding winter clothing on a sunny morning in February. But for our purposes we should construe the word 'common' in a different way, namely to mean potentially common to or shared by all men alike, in respect of all their opinions alike, whether these opinions are theological or scientific or commercial or

political or moral or aesthetic, and so on. Locke is teaching us what
it is to be sensible, and what it is to be silly in anyone's adherence to
views of any sort about no matter what. It is no accident that Locke
wrote, besides his *Essay*, one thing on the *Reasonableness of Christianity*
and another on *Toleration*, i.e. the Toleration of religious differences.
Locke's *Essay* is, in intention and in effect, much less a theory of
knowledge than it is a theory of opinion. He is not, as Descartes had
been, primarily pointing out the strait and very narrow path to
certainties. He is teaching us how we can in some matters, and why
we cannot in other matters, make reasonably sure.

But now for a bit of trouble. If this is the central moral of his
Essay, how could Locke expect, and how could he have been correct
in expecting that his quasi-chemical account of the ultimate elements
of our thoughts would persuade people of this moral? How could
people be taught to become critical of their own previous opiniona-
tednesses by being told of the sources of our simple ideas in sensation
and introspection, of the compoundings of these simple ideas, of
their fixation by the attachment of them to words, of the different
types of the true and false propositions into which they are combined, and so forth? Can ordinary or even highly sophisticated
people be converted from bigots into fairly judicious and cautious
thinkers by examining, so to speak, the mechanics of their own
internal intellectual operations? We do not see better for knowing
about our retinas. We do not swim better for knowing about our
sinews, tendons, muscles and arteries. Why should we think less sillily
for knowing what mental atoms our thoughts are composed of and
how these mental atoms cohere into mental molecules? I think that
there is an answer to these questions, though I am not positive that
I have got it. But I shall try.

Even though we aim to be as factual or scientific as possible when
we start to think about our actions, thoughts, perceptions, memories,
resolutions and the rest, we still know, so to speak, in our bones that
our theories about them, because couched in factual idioms echoing
those of chemistry, mechanics, hydraulics, or physiology, have
inevitably omitted something; and omitted something that is
cardinal to their being actions, thoughts, perceptions, memories, or
resolutions at all. For such theories, couched in such idioms, are
necessarily silent about the *purposive* nature of our doings, thinkings,
perceivings, etc. It is essential to them that they merit good,
medium or bad marks. In our actions, unlike our mere reactions,
either there is success or there is failure, and either dexterity or
clumsiness. Some actions are obligatory; others are wrong; some

are prudent; others are imprudent. Even walking, unlike breathing, is something that the infant has to learn, by trial and error, to do, first on flat and firm floors, and later, perhaps, on loose stones or icy pavements. He learns, but of course sometimes forgets that in special situations it is necessary to walk *carefully*. Similarly with perception. However well equipped he is with sharp eyes or good ears, the child has to learn to estimate, and not to misestimate, distances, speeds, directions and sizes, and to recognise at a glance, and not to mis-recognise even slightly different kinds of objects and happenings. There is room for adeptness, precipitancy, imprecision and systema-ticness in our perceivings. It is not for optical reasons that the lynx-eyed Red Indian cannot detect misprints or see that a chessplayer's queen is in danger. If he has not learned to read or to play chess his lynx eyes cannot tell him these things. Now the same thing is true of thought. What a person thinks on a certain matter is true or else it is false; it is accurate or else inaccurate; it is definite or else it is vague; it is clear or it is muddled; it is well or else ill founded; it is expert or else it is amateurish, and so on. Some practice and often some tuition is a *sine qua non* of our being able to think out any problems at all, however simple, within certain fields. It is not from lack of quick-wittedness that my Red Indian cannot work out or even be defeated by a chess problem, but because he has not learned the game. Thinking, like fencing and skating, is a consortium of com-petences and skills. Like them, it has tasks which it may accomplish or may fail to do so. It has room in it, therefore, for high and low degrees of these competences and skills, i.e. of low and high degrees of stupidity and silliness. In our thinking we exercise good, moderate or bad craftsmanship. Thought is not something that just happens to us and in us, like digestion. It is something that we do, and do well or badly, carefully or carelessly, expertly or amateurishly.

As I said, we know these and kindred platitudes in our bones. So when we read Locke's chemical-sounding theory of thought and perception and try to apply his theory to our own thinkings and perceivings, we automatically re-instate between the lines of the *Essay* this element that he has so far omitted, this cardinal element of purposiveness or craftsmanship. These lines say only that our simple ideas, the prime elements of our thoughts, originate in sense-perception and introspection. But we forthwith construe this theory of origins into a maxim of intellectual craftsmanship, namely the maxim of the Royal Society that theories about what exists and happens in Nature are relatively good theories only in so far as they are relatively well vouched for by relatively copious, systematic, careful and precise observations and experiments. Nor, I suggest, are we advancing beyond Locke himself in reading this and other maxims of intellectual workmanship between the lines of his *Essay*. I think that Locke himself thought and meant his readers to think that his chemical-sounding analyses of thought and knowledge carried with them these maxims about how to think well rather than badly. He talks of the origins and the agglomeratings of ideas, but only in order to illuminate the notions of judiciousness and injudiciousness.

It may also be the case, though now I am not suggesting that Locke had the point in mind, that the factual or scientific sound and 'feel' of his anatomy of cognition helped his readers to draw the intended moral. In this way. Suppose you hold some opinion passionately and are then advised to examine its credentials dis- passionately and to examine the objections to it dispassionately, you, being human, will resent, passionately resent, the advice as partisan advice. It will feel like a traitor's advice to sell your fortress to its besiegers. But if someone, John Locke say, advises you to trace to their origins the complex ideas that are the materials of your opinion, to test for their precision and unambiguousness the words in which your ideas are fixed, then the advice does not feel to be partisan advice. It now feels like neutral advice from the laboratory. You may take this advice without suspecting treachery. So now you can allow yourself to practise some self-criticism—and from now on your opinion is no longer a passionate opinion. But, as I said, I am not suggesting that Locke thought of his anatomy of cogitation as a device for lulling suspicions. I am only suggesting that his *Essay* succeeded partly because its anatomical tone of voice did in fact have this temperature-lowering effect.

Examiners award to the candidates their alpha, beta and gamma marks for, among other qualities, the qualities of their thinking. We can all learn, in some measure, to be our own habitual examiners, though without any formalised marking-code. Locke, I think, meant to teach us to become our own examiners. His *Essay* was meant to be an *Ars Cogitandi*, or even, if you prefer, an Ethics of Thinking. Certainly he couched the principles of intellectual self-marking in idioms reminiscent of a fairly primitive atomic and molecular theory —and a theory which, as I said at the beginning, can be refuted by any youthful student of philosophy. But this does not matter very much, if, as I am urging, for Locke himself and his readers the lessons conveyed in these pretty factitious laboratory idioms were not laboratory lessons. They were lessons in the craftsmanship, in the economics and even in the ethics of the formation, retention and rejection of opinions. They were lessons in reasonableness. If Common Sense is reasonableness in opining, then Locke taught and was the first to teach Common Sense.

I can imagine that some of you may grumble: 'Then did Locke's great contribution just amount to his long-winded statement of the obvious truth that the tenacity with which people hold their opinions is not always, but ought always, to be proportioned to the quantity and quality of the reasons that can be adduced for them?' To this grumble I reply, 'Yes, yes, yes!—but who made this obvious if it was not John Locke?' Every philosopher of genius has made obvious to mankind things that, in his youth, had not been more than, if as much as, quaint speculations. Every philosopher of genius can be ridiculed for having once painfully excogitated and laboriously argued positions which we absorbed effortlessly with our mother's milk. This is their contribution. They, with sweat and worry, designed and laid the pavements on which we easily stroll. Our difficulty is that of re-discovering what on earth it was that prevented them from strolling on these good, old pavements. The idea that there was a time, namely their time, when these pavements were missing is an idea to which, precisely thanks to them, we are not accustomed. To his pupils their teacher, if he is any good, is always the sedulous transmitter of the obvious. Its obviousness is his gift to them. How could they discern behind the ease of their reception of it, the pains that had gone to his giving of it? Standing on his shoulders, they cannot conceive why his feet had not from the start been where theirs are now.

I must not be construed as saying that Locke's *Essay* has made all of us, in respect of all our opinions, cautious, unobstinate, unbiased or open to correction. There are bigots, fanatics and cranks in our midst in 1965; there are bigotries, fanaticisms and crankinesses under our own dear skins, still in 1965. But to all or nearly all of us the words 'bigot', 'fanatic' and 'crank' are now terms of condemnation or contempt. We know what it is like for people, including ourselves, to be or else to keep clear of being die-hards in opinion; and we know how, at least in most matters of opinion, to require for our opinions their due meed of backing in testimony, clues, experiments or statistics; and where there is room for differences of opinion, we do not habitually or naturally demand the extreme penalties for other peoples' dissents.

Oliver Cromwell in 1650, with characteristic forcibleness, had said to the General Assembly of the Church of Scotland, 'I beseech you, in the bowels of Christ, think it possible you may be mistaken'. This lesson—except alas! in matters of race and nationality—has been fairly widely learned. But Locke's lesson was harder and a profounder lesson than was Cromwell's. For Locke required of us not just that we remember, from time to time, the quite general lesson that we are fallible, but that we remember all of the time to subject our particular opinings to the disciplines appropriate to them. All of our opinions could be and ought to be *considered* opinions. None of us can claim with a good conscience that we always succeed in this labour of intellectual self-control. But the very fact that we have bad consciences about our lapses shows by itself how deep Locke's lesson has sunk into us. Of course, that our opinions should always be *true* cannot be secured. But that they should always be well weighed and tested can in principle be achieved. John Locke taught us to wish to achieve this and to be sorry when we fail. Certainly we do often fail, but certainly too we are sorry when we fall below our standards. It was Locke who gave us these standards.

9

HUME

Reprinted, in English translation, from the original French in 'Les Philosophes Célèbres' edited by M. Merleau-Ponty, 1956, by permission of Editions d'Art Lucien Mazenod

David Hume is apt to be regarded by English-speaking thinkers as a philosopher of genius; Continental thinkers tend to take him as a mere gadfly. This difference of estimation may be symptomatic of wider and deeper divergences of outlook. I shall not assess these, but shall content myself with trying to describe a transformation of the climate of ideas for which Hume deserves most of the credit. I shall also briefly suggest two causes for the tepidity with which Continental thinkers, other than Kant, tend to speak of him.

First let me put on one side three features of Hume's thought which, though salient enough to monopolise the attention of most historians of ideas, are not in my opinion cardinal.

(1) Hume thought of himself as the inaugurator of the natural science of the human mind. He was to be the Newton of the moral sciences, that is to say, of the sciences, or studies, which we know as psychology, sociology, political science, history, economics, ethics and literary and artistic criticism. The experimental methods by which Newton had disclosed what could be disclosed of physical nature would be applied by Hume to disclose what could be disclosed of human nature. What the *Principia* did for the one realm would be matched for the other realm by *A Treatise of Human Nature: being an Attempt to introduce the experimental Method of Reasoning into Moral Subjects.*

In fact Hume's would-be mechanics of mental operations had even less foundation in experiment and observation than had Hartley's. A present-day student of psychology would learn much from reading Hume, but he would learn no psychology. Whether, for the structure of his projected experimental science, Hume borrows concepts from mechanics or concepts from biology, whether he thinks in hydraulic or in physiological models, he not only establishes no laws, he hardly even isolates his phenomena. His particles of mental life, namely his impressions, ideas and passions, are the products of theory, not authentic data for theory. His organising principles of association, custom and vivacity are sham counterparts to attraction, inertia and active force.

Hume's Newtonian enterprise was an ambitious failure. His psychological theory certainly helped his philosophical achievement, but not by containing new scientific discoveries, or even fertile scientific mistakes. The examples set by the other sciences gave him a new horizon; his belief in the scientific nature of his own ideas gave him extra boldness.

(2) Hume preened himself on being a ruthless though not immoderate Sceptic. Like Sextus Empiricus, Montaigne, Bayle and Voltaire he loved to puncture convictions and to discomfit dignitaries. He was sincerely irreligious, but he also wanted to shock. Such *Schadenfreude* doubtless quickens a man's perception of vulnerable targets, but in itself it gives no more, though no less, of a title to intellectual eminence than does the desire to reassure. Both can be motives to good, both to bad thinking. But the quality of the thinking has to be judged by its results, not by its motives.

(3) Hume may certainly be classified as an Empiricist. More clearly than Locke and more uncompromisingly than Leibniz, he separated truths of fact from truths of reason, and argued that only the latter can be known *a priori*. Knowledge of what exists or happens cannot derive from knowledge of the logical connections between concepts. Only observation and experiment can yield the answers to questions, particular or general, about the actual contents of the world. The existence of God and the uniformity of nature are no exceptions. Pretended *a priori* demonstrations of either are demonstrable fallacies.

Some commentators base their esteem for Hume upon his guillotine-edged Empiricism. But I find something over-dramatic in the picture of Hume decapitating the Rationalists. Rationalism was not, in Hume's day, an organised or self-conscious school of thought. No one, I think, styled himself a 'Rationalist' in the way in which in the medieval university men styled themselves 'Realists' and 'Nominalists', or in the way in which in the 19th and 20th centuries men have styled themselves 'Idealists', 'Pragmatists', 'Neo-Kantians' and 'Existentialists'. Except for Kant, the great philosophers of the 17th and 18th centuries were not university teachers. They taught no scholars; they headed no schools. As Rationalism was not a creed, so Empiricism was not a crusade.

Certainly there was rationalism working powerfully in Descartes, Malebranche, Spinoza and Leibniz; in the Cambridge Platonists, and the Deists; in Hobbes, Clarke and even Locke. But their rationalisms were tendencies exhibited rather than principles promulgated, *un*questions rather than doctrines. Even so, they were mixed up with plenty of theoretical and practical respect for experimental methods of enquiry. The reputations of Galileo, Harvey, Boyle, Huyghens and Newton were not in any jeopardy; the scientific procedures espoused by the Royal Society were not in dire need of an advocate.

Endemic to the reasoning of philosophers, as distinct from scientists, there was indeed much confusing of factual with conceptual questions. But this discrimination of philosophising from scientific theorising was yet to be made by Kant. Hume was not knowingly legislating against mutual trespasses between empirical science and philosophy. He did not even know, as we know, which he himself was really doing. Moreover, even if there had existed a philosophical school of Rationalists for Hume to refute, his refutation of it could have been an unimportant victory in a merely local and ephemeral debate. For a counter-'ism' to matter, more is required than that its demolition of its adversary should be complete. Rationalism, if it had existed, might have been a silly school doctrine; in which case Empiricism, if it had existed, would have been only a momentarily interesting purge. We could then have forgotten Hume as we have forgotten both Herbert Spencer and the victorious critics of Herbert Spencer. But Hume refuses to be forgotten.

If Hume was not at all the Newton of the moral sciences, not merely the Sextus Empiricus of the British Isles, and only by retrospective dramatisation the executioner of Continental Rationalism, where did his genius lie? To this question there can be no single-stranded reply. A philosopher's genius lies not in his giving one new answer to one old question, but in his transforming all the questions. He gives mankind a different air to breathe. But the differences that he makes are as hard to describe as the differences made by growing up. The adolescent cannot realise what these changes will be like; the adult cannot recollect what they had been like.

I pick a single strand out of the total reply, hoping to accomplish by illustration what I could not accomplish by catalogue.

Hume lifted the notion of Reason off its pedestal and out of its shrine. He asked just what human beings can do, and also just what they cannot do, in virtue merely of their capacity for abstract reasoning. How much and in what concrete ways do men in their daily lives differ from animals, adults from infants, scientists from yokels, honest men from rogues? What kinds of truths are, but also what kinds of truths are not, accessible to a Euclid? Obvious questions to ask, assuredly; obvious, that is, since Hume first asked them. But to ask them then was to step out of a cleric's into a naturalist's work-room; out of the atmosphere of colleges into that of the Royal Society. The venerable hierarchical concept-system, recently shattered from the physical world, was now to be shattered also from the world of rational animals. Questions of relative efficacy displaced questions of relative dignity; causal questions displaced questions of precedence. The notion of rank was, at long last, dismissed even out of epistemology and ethics. Reason had lost its crown—or its mitre—and become just one among the many cause-factors in human living. It had become one corner of the field to be covered by the natural science of man.

What, then, can men do by abstract reasoning, and what can they *not* do? They can establish logically necessary truths, that is, they can deduce and demonstrate. The products of Reason, in its strict sense, are the propositions of mathematics. Certainly there are many other qualities for which human beings, at their best, are popularly but loosely described as 'rational'. Men make inferences from observed to unobserved matters of fact; they construct general scientific theories; they control their irritation or their alarm; they accept, teach and apply moral rules. But Hume will argue, *seriatim*, that not one of these mental operations is an operation of abstract or pure Reason. Both in questions of fact and in problems of action Reason is, by its constitution, causally inert. The anatomist of human nature must give an account of our factual beliefs, our feelings and our moral principles different from the account he has to give of our apprehension of logical implications.

The main plank on which Hume's fame rests is, as he would have wished, his separation of causal inference from demonstrative reasoning. A truth of reason is one the negation of which can be directly seen or indirectly shown to be absurd. No assertion of existence, and therefore no conjunction of different assertions of existence can be thus established. 'Hark, thunder, though there was no lightning' is surely false, but knowledge of its falsity comes by meteorological investigation, not, like fallacies, by unaided logical acumen. Logic teaches us no laws of nature. To predict or diagnose is not to deduce. In the strict sense of 'Reason', it is not in virtue of his Reason that the doctor diagnoses a fractured bone or the shepherd predicts the rising of the sun. Both are profiting from lessons learned, but these lessons were taught by unorganised or organised experience.

There are other things, besides the factual inferences of the sciences and daily life, which had traditionally been piously but erroneously credited to Reason. Moralists had spoken of the control of Passion by Reason, and of Reason as the source of moral rules. Theologians had endowed Reason with the power to prove the existence of God and the immortality of the soul either *a priori* from definitions, or *a posteriori* from the constitution of the cosmos. In each case Hume scrutinises the ascription and essays to demolish it. Certainly irritation and alarm may be curbed; but the curb is provided not by the inert thought of some premisses and conclusions, but by a countervailing passion, like self-interest or shame. Such passions may resemble Reason in being unperturbing or 'calm', but they differ from it in being dynamic. Certainly, too, it is in the light of moral rules that we approve or disapprove of people's actions and characters. But these rules are not axioms or theorems; they are the complex product, primarily, of habituation and sympathy. In a loose sense of 'rational', indeed, we have to be rational to have moral principles. For we have to be capable of reflecting on general rules. But such reflecting is not Euclidean reasoning.

The existence of God and the immortality of the soul are similarly removed from the class of things decidable by *a priori* reasoning. But they are virtually removed also from the class of things decidable by *a posteriori* inference. The particular inferences and the general laws of natural science, the curbing of passions, and the acceptance and application of moral rules, are all denied to be operations of Reason; yet all are granted alternative status. They are transplanted, not eradicated. But the propositions of religion are neither logically necessary nor yet experimentally well founded. The *a priori* arguments for them are fallacious; the *a posteriori* arguments for them are nugatory. Here Hume proffers, save by lip-service, no loose sense of 'reasoning' in which we are justified in claiming to reason to religious conclusions. He is not a sceptic of natural science or of ethics; a religious sceptic he is.

By what methods does Hume separate from the operations of Reason, in its strict sense, the factual inferences of natural science and daily life, the control of passions, and the acknowledgement of moral rules? Hume's own answer would, I think, be this: that as an experimental psychologist he collects the data of introspection and subsumes them under the laws of association and custom-formation.

This enables him to give a scientifically probable description and causal explanation of the specific differences between these different mental operations. If this were what Hume really did or were all that he did, the demise of his psychological mechanics would carry with it the demise of his philosophy; and this it is very far from doing.

I may indicate what, in my view, Hume really did, as distinct from what he supposed himself to be doing, in the following manner. Wanting to describe in psychological terms what takes place when a doctor, say, infers a wound from a scar, or a scar from a wound, Hume begins by describing the ways in which one thing commonly puts us in mind of another. The thought of Romulus leads to the thought of Remus or the thought or perception of lightning puts us in mind of thunder. But with his scrupulous nose for conceptual differences, Hume detects that this is not enough. There is no 'therefore' in the passage from the thought of Romulus to the thought of Remus. For thunder to be inferred from lightning, the passage of thought must be more than a mere case of being put in mind of thunder. To infer 'lightning, so now for thunder' requires the possession and application of a generalisation of the pattern 'Whenever lightning, then shortly thunder'. A factual 'therefore' flourishes the fiat of such a generalisation. Get someone to entertain doubts of the generalisation *Whenever an A, then a B*, and you get him to refuse to make or concede any factual inference from an actual observed A to an unobserved B, for all that he may well still be regularly put in mind of B's by his observation of A's.

What then is the origin of the knowledge or belief that *whenever an A, then a B*? Again Hume begins psychologically by describing the ordinary processes of familiarisation. We get used to A's being succeeded by B's and come to be surprised if an A occurs with no B following. But again Hume's scrupulous nose for conceptual differences prevents him from being contented. Sometimes we are satisfied that *whenever an A, then a B*, though we have encountered far too few instances of the conjunction of A with B to have become used to it; and sometimes we are not satisfied with a generalisation, though we have encountered very many instances of the conjunction. The intellectual operation of induction embodies some element over and above that of familiarisation. At our best, we generalise with discrimination. We have and we use tests for our generalisations. There are Rules for Judging of Causes and Effects, in virtue of which Rules we can be careful or careless. In mere familiarisation there is no place for care or the lack of care, for talent or the absence of it.

'Scientific' is a laudatory and not merely a descriptive adjective. A Newton is not just ridden by more blind habits of expectation than the layman or the dog; he thinks more shrewdly and experiments more extensively and deliberately. Here, as almost everywhere else, Hume's initial attempts to reduce some supposed operation of abstract Reason to a product of the interplay of blind mental forces are successful and his conceptual scruples are aroused by the smothering effects of his own levelling work. To use a gratuitous modern diction, his phenomenological left hand insists on bringing into relief just what his psychological right hand had tried to flatten down. Hume sees what more is needed in the very act of trying to make do with a bare minimum; and what he sees is very often what no one else had even considered. Induction is indeed not deduction, and Hume showed their differences. But induction is also not mere familiarisation, and again it is Hume who showed their differences. He showed these differences by means of philosophical arguments, the cogency of which derives not at all from his pretended Experimental Method. Again and again Hume was the hero of a double combat; first with the hierarchical system, and then with his own reductionist system. Yet the second victory does not invalidate the first.

Even in the 20th century we are capable of feeling a sense of grievance with Hume for bringing Reason so low. We object, perhaps, that Newton's thinking is surely a palmary example of human rationality at work. In his consideration and decision of his moral problems Mr Everyman is surely sometimes thinking with all the seriousness and independence that the most exacting epistemologist could demand. We grant that neither Newton nor Mr Everyman achieves, tries to achieve or should try to achieve the formal rigours of Euclidean demonstrations. But why limit the operations of Reason to deducing and demonstrating? Why sanctify just these highly specialised operations? Why put the *a priori* on a pedestal?

In part our attitude is itself the gift of Hume. He, in levelling abstract reasoning down, levelled the human understanding up to human stature. He did indeed show that induction, factual inference, and moral judgement are not operations of tracing logical implications. But he also taught us that this was no slur. Indeed he frequently allows us to use expressions like 'reasoning' and 'rational', in a loose and popular manner, to cover just what he denied to be reasoning or rational in their strict sense.

In part, too, our attitude derives from our almost complete emancipation from the venerable idea of human nature as a pyramidal system of Faculties. To Hume, and in some degree to Locke, this emancipation is chiefly due—though they did not entirely emancipate themselves. For them it was still, as it is not to us, a live question whether this or that element of experience was to be affiliated to Reason, Imagination, Sense, Memory, Understanding, Will or Passion, and this despite the fact that the whole picture of the Mind as a federation of Faculties had a function only inside the entire hierarchical world-scheme of which Hume was, not quite consciously, completing the demolition. Hume could still relapse, however heretically, into the old orthodoxy, as when he says, 'Reason is and ought only to be the slave of the passions.'

We, therefore, being unhampered by this scheme of ideas, feel neither republican glee nor royalist resentment at Hume's discrimination between different kinds of propositions and between different kinds of argumentative bases for them. Indeed on most days of our lives we now dispense altogether with such words as 'Reason' and 'rational'. There remains no special job for them to perform. Epistemological snobbery has been despatched by Hume and epistemological anti-snobbery has gone with it. We have learned, largely from Hume, to discuss human thought and conduct in terms of methods, efficacies and results, instead of in terms of badges and degrees.

Like all the great philosophers of the 17th and 18th centuries, with the exception of Kant, Hume was unacademic. He wrote in order to be read and discussed by the literate public. His writing had therefore to achieve and did achieve that peculiar magic that makes literature. His idioms are not the idioms of the lecture-hall. His doctrines are not supplementations of a curriculum. He wrote neither from a Chair nor for a Chair. He meant not to conciliate, but to shock, his seniors.

Unlike things written according to a didactic tradition, literature is impatient of translation and synopsis. Hume's philosophy does not lend itself to the sandwich-nutrition even of English-speaking lecture-audiences, much less to that of foreign lecture-audiences. The Hume who is sliced up for these audiences has to be grossly unlike and markedly inferior to the Hume who is read. But I guess that Hume is unsympathetic to foreign lecture-audiences not only because his voice does not easily survive transmission, but because the voice itself displeases Continental ears. It is too irreverent for some; and its irreverence is too cheerful for others. It conveys no tidings of hope, but also no tidings of despair. But through the youthful accents of the good-humoured iconoclast, there rings another accent which jars equally on those who severely disapprove and on those who severely approve of irreverence. This is the accent of the thinker to whom even beliefs or unbeliefs are less important and less interesting than cogency and trenchancy of argument.

10

PHENOMENOLOGY

Reprinted from 'Proceedings of the Aristotelian Society', vol. XI, *1932,*
by permission of the editor

I want to distinguish the question what Phenomenology is from certain special questions about certain special claims that are made for it.

What Phenomenology is

Phenomenology is not specially concerned with phenomena in the sense of sense-data. Nor is it, unless *per accidens* any sort of Phenomenalism.

The title (which is a misleading one) derives from the following historical source. Brentano, following Herbart, repudiated the psychologies which treated mental faculties as the ultimate terms of psychological analysis, and insisted instead that the ultimate data of psychology are the particular manifestations of consciousness. These he called 'psychic phenomena', not as being appearances as opposed to noumena or things in themselves, but as being directly discernible manifestations of mental functioning as opposed to being inferred or constructed mental 'powers'. So 'Phenomenology' only means, as it stands, the science of the manifestations of consciousness and might have been used—though it is not—as another name for psychology.

Brentano next distinguished between two radically different sorts of enquiry into mental functioning. One is empirical—or what he calls, oddly, 'genetic'—psychology, which is inductive, experimental and statistical, and the conclusions of which are only probable generalizations. The other is the enquiry into the concepts or presuppositions of any such empirical psychology, namely, such enquiry as 'What is it to be a case of remembering, judging, inferring, wishing, choosing, regretting, etc.?' It asks what ultimate forms of mental functioning there are to be exemplified in particular instances, and so is not concerned, e.g., with what it is that makes this or that man remember something, but with what it is for a mental act to be a case of remembering.

He got to this position, I gather, in this way. Convinced that the physiological and the associationist psychologies were radically false, he had to examine and reject their presuppositions—in particular, the presuppositions (1) that mental life is a mere avalanche of atomic 'ideas' and (2) that these 'ideas' are in no sense *of* anything. Instead, he argued, we can know *a priori* (1) that any case of consciousness of any form must be a case of consciousness *of* something and (2) that there are irreducibly different sorts of mental functioning, so that while 'ideas' may be necessary ingredients in judging and wanting, judging and wanting cannot be analysed without residue into 'ideas' or complexes of them.

Whatever his line of approach may have been, he and his pupils were always perfectly clear that the analysis of the root types of mental functioning is one thing and the experimental or statistical search for the natural laws governing the occurrence of mental acts and states is quite another. And I think that they were right.

Husserl uses the term 'Phenomenology' to denote the analysis of the root types of mental functioning. And he tries to show (1) that Phenomenology is anyhow a part of philosophy; (2) that it is an enquiry which can become a rigorous *science*; (3) that it is *a priori*. (1) and (3) seem to me to be true; (2) seems to me to be either false or an awkward terminological innovation. For I don't think that philosophy or any part of philosophy is properly called a 'science'. Philosophical methods are neither scientific nor unscientific. But this is not a question which I want to deal directly with here.

It is not a new discovery or a new theory that at least a part and an important part of philosophy consists in the analytical investigation of types of mental functioning. Theories of knowledge, belief, opinion, perception, error, imagination, memory, inference, and abstraction, which can all be classed together as epistemology, have ever since Plato constituted at least an important part of philosophy. And anyhow a large part of Ethics has, since Plato and Aristotle, consisted in the analysis of the concepts of motive, impulse, desire, purpose, intention, choice, regret, shame, blame, approbation, and the like. And while parts of the treatments given by historical philosophers to these subjects have been not analytical, but speculative or hypothetical or dogmatic, other parts have always been strictly analytical and critical and have therefore been proper cases of what Husserl describes as the phenomenological method. So nothing much save a rather misleading title would have been secured by Husserl had he merely asserted that these and such like enquiries are all phenomenological enquiries, in that all are enquiries into the nature of more or less radical types of mental functioning.

He does, of course, go a good deal further than this. First of all he argues, in opposition, I take it, to special schools of positivists and experimental psychologists as well as to the whole associationist theory of psychology, that the way in which types of mental functioning are analysed by philosophers or phenomenologists when they know their business is quite different from the way in which empirical psychology enquires into the causal laws governing the occurrence of mental states, acts and dispositions in the life-history of actual persons in the world. For (1) the method of philosophy proper is *a priori*, whereas that of the others is inductive; and (2) the very questions raised by empirical psychology embody the concepts the analysis of which belongs to phenomenology. So that in two connected ways phenomenology is independent of empirical psychology: (1) that, being *a priori*, phenomenology cannot employ as its premisses either the particular observations or the inductive generalizations of empirical psychology and (2) that, being analytical or critical, it enquires what any psychological proposition of this or that sort really means (whether it is true or false), and so throws light on and cannot derive light from the particular psychological propositions which psychologists put foward as true or probable.

This seems to me to be true and generalizable. Not only psychology, but all sciences and all sorts of search for knowledge or probable opinion aim at establishing particular or general propositions. But whether in any particular case such a proposition is true or false, the analysis of what it means, or of what would be the case if it were true, is different from and in principle prior to the discovery of what proves it or makes it probable. Thus, the philosophy of physics is indifferent to the answers that physicists give to the questions of physics, the philosophy of mathematics does not wait for the solution of all possible equations, and in ethics we must have some notion of desert, and one which we are already in principle ready to analyse, whether or not we are able to decide that a given defendant deserves a certain punishment.

No philosophical propositions are empirical either in the sense of being about this as distinct from that particular subject of attributes or in the sense of implying as premisses propositions which are so.

This does not, of course, involve that philosophical arguments should not contain references to particular cases as instances or examples. On the contrary, a good illustrative example is often of great utility. But an *exempli gratia* is not an *ergo*—as is shown by the fact that imaginary examples are often just as useful as actual ones, which would not be the case in a genuine inductive argument.

Husserl's apriorism is, perhaps, nothing very alarming. But, at the time of the last century, naturalism and empiricism were so fashionable that Husserl had to prosecute very difficult and painstaking logical enquiries in order to justify it. And we should first notice three cardinal points in his account of the *a priori* nature of philosophical propositions.

(1) He does not hold that philosophers should or can construct deductive systems. Demonstration *ordine geometrico* belongs to mathematics and not to philosophy. For Husserl Spinoza's notion of philosophy as a sort of metaphysical geometry is a completely mistaken sort of apriorism. And I think Husserl is right.

(2) Further, Husserl refuses to admit into phenomenology, or by implication into philosophy in general, any sort of metaphysical system-building or speculative construction. Dogmatic metaphysics is put out of court by Husserl just as much as by Kant. (It is, however, arguable that some of Husserl's conclusions are of the nature of metaphysical constructions. His half-solipsist and half-monadological account of the experienced world is not at all what one would expect to find deriving from a purely analytical enquiry into the *summa genera* of the manifestations of mind.) But with his official view, that the business of philosophy is not to give new information about the world but to analyse the most general forms of what experience finds to be exemplified in the world, I completely agree.

(3) On the other hand Husserl's special account of the nature of *a priori* thinking seems to me to be wrong. Rather like Meinong, he holds, or used to hold, that universals or essences, as well as propositions, are objects of a higher order. And of these we can have a knowledge by acquaintance analogous to (though of a higher order than) our perceptual acquaintanceship with particulars like this tree and that man. We can, he holds, perceive or intuit essences in the same sort of way as we can perceive or intuit particulars, except that the direct intuition of an essence requires to be founded in the direct intuition of a particular instance of it (which may be real or imaginary). Philosophy is, accordingly, a sort of observational science (like geography); only the objects which it inspects are not spatio-temporal entities but semi-Platonic objects which are out of space and time. These are correlates to acts of conception and judgment, though whether it is essential to them to be so correlative or whether it is accidental is left rather obscure in Husserl's writings.

I fancy that Husserl used to think of them as independently subsisting and now regards them as intrinsically contents of possible
acts of thinking.

I do not myself believe that phrases such as 'being a so and so',
'being such and such' and 'that so and so is such and such' do
denote objects or subjects of attributes. For I don't think that they
are denoting expressions at all. Consequently, though I can know
what it is for something to be a so and so, I think that this knowledge is wrongly described as an 'intuition of an essence'. For
intuition, which I take to be a synonym for knowledge by acquaintance or perception, does seem to be or to involve a relation between
two subjects of attributes, the perceiver and the thing perceived.
And I do not think that what Husserl calls 'essences' are subjects of
attributes at all. However, I do not think that the whole notion of
phenomenology hinges on this special theory, so I do not think
that it need be discussed here. But we shall have to discuss later a
more general question, which is connected with this one, concerning
the theory of intentional objects.

So much for the general plan of phenomenology. It is that part, or
those parts, of philosophy in which the root types of mental functioning are distinguished and analysed. And most philosophers have
talked phenomenology, as M. Jourdain talked prose. What Husserl
has done so far is (a) to distinguish, as his predecessors had largely
failed to do, between the philosophical and the psychological
methods of investigating consciousness; (b) to make clear that anyhow this part of philosophy is analytical and not speculative or
hypothetical; and (c) to name it with a rather unfortunate name.

Now for his main doctrines in phenomenology. It is an 'essential
intuition', that is, it can be known a priori that all consciousness is
consciousness of something. To wish is to wish for something, to
regret is to regret something, to remember, expect, decide and choose
are to remember something, expect something, decide something
and choose something. To every piece of mental functioning there
is intrinsically correlative something which is the 'accusative' of that
functioning. But though all consciousness is 'intentional' or
'transitive', it is not all intentional or transitive in the same way.[1]
The act of remembering may have the same object as one of
regretting, but they are different sorts of acts and 'have' their object

---

[1] 'Intentionality' has nothing special to do with intending in our sense of purposing.
It is a revival of a scholastic term and is used only as a name for the fact that mental
acts are of objects. I use the term 'accusative' to render 'Gegenstand'. 'Object' is
damagingly equivocal since it may mean 'entity' or 'subject of attributes' as well as
meaning 'object of . . .'.

in different manners. Moreover, some sorts of 'consciousness of' demand others as their platform. I cannot regret without remembering, though I can remember without regretting. And, again, I cannot remember without having once directly perceived, but I can perceive without having to remember. And so on.

Next, all intentional experiences, whatever their 'accusatives', must belong to an experiencing ego. *Cogito ergo sum* is a cardinal proposition in Husserl's phenomenology. 'What is it to be an "I"?' is perhaps, the most general way of formulating the question of phenomenology—indeed Husserl coins the unattractive alternative title for phenomenology of 'descriptive transcendental egology'.

These two marks of intentional experiences—namely, that in all of them there is a subject-pole and in all of them there is an object-pole—are not independent. They are intrinsically correlative. But the correlation can take as many different forms as there are different types of intentionality. For a type of intentionality is simply a not further analysable way in which an I may be about something.

On the other hand, the subject-pole is, for Husserl as for Descartes, something the reality of which is philosophically unimpugnable and presuppositionless, whereas any of its objects upon which it may from time to time be directed may have no other reality than that with which it is endowed by being what the self is dreaming, say, or expecting or believing in.

As we shall see, Husserl does, in fact, terminate in a subjectivist or egocentric philosophy, though he is at pains to argue that it is not a form of solipsism.

THE PHENOMENOLOGICAL REDUCTION

In our everyday frames of mind, and particularly in our scientific frame of mind, we treat the world and the things and happenings in it as independently existing. That is, we focus on their relationships to one another and ignore the fact that they all alike stand to us as pegs upon which we are hooking *our* interests, attentions, queries, emotions, decisions and volitions. They are—but we habitually fail to remember that they are—constituents of our variegated cognitive-*cum*-volitional-*cum*-emotional experiences. We think about things, but do not ordinarily notice that they are at least, whatever else they are, what we are thinking about.

Now, Husserl argues, of our experiences we can have direct and self-evident perception. Reflective inspection of our own *actus* of consciousness can give us knowledge in the strict sense of the term. I can know both that I am enacting an act of a certain description and what that description is. And he rather assumes than argues, following Descartes, that there is no other sort of self-evident (or knowing) inspection of particulars.

Let us, then, by a sort of Method of Doubt bracket out or shelve all that we accept in our everyday or scientific frames of mind over and above what reflective inspection can warrant. This will leave as one of our most important sets of data to be studied, such facts as that we accept the proposition that the sun is bigger than the moon, but will bracket out the fact (if it is one) that the sun *is* bigger than the moon. We are left with *Erlebnisse,* and that means that we are left with the whole experienced world. But what (if anything) exists or happens or is the case without being a constituent of experiences is not the theme of any phenomenological proposition.

What an 'object' is now is nothing save what sort of an 'accusative' it is to what sorts of intentional experiences. It is just that which constitutes particular mental functionings as the particular mental functions that they are. In a word, it is just the special character of an act or set of acts, or, to employ a misleading expression of which Husserl is fond, the object of an intentional experience, treated as such, is just the intrinsic meaning or sense of the experience.

We can now say that whatever may be the special objects of such studies and interests as physics, biology, astronomy, psychology, and the other natural sciences—history, sociology, economics and law, business, politics, and, in a word, of all intellectual, practical and emotional occupation, all alike have, and have essentially, the character of being constituents of experiences. They are the ways in which I or we function.

Consequently, Husserl argues, both the scientific search for the laws governing the existence of such things and the special philosophical analyses of the essences of them presuppose the philosophical analysis of the types of mental functioning in the several instances of which these objects present themselves as the specifying or individuating constituents.

So phenomenology is the first philosophy, or the science of sciences. It and it alone has for its topic the *summum genus* of the objects of all the other sciences and interests. It even has priority over logic.

It is therefore, for Husserl, part of the nature of all possible subjects of attributes to be constituents in the intentional experiences of an 'I'. But as persons in the ordinary sense of the term are only empirically discovered things in the world of objects, it is not empirical selves, but a pure or transcendental self whose 'intentions' are the home of the being of objects. And Husserl accordingly develops a Kantian or neo-Kantian doctrine of a pure or absolute subject which is other than you or I for the reason that you and I are merely items in the list of the possible accusatives of intentional experiences.

I think myself that Husserl is (with Kant) confusing 'I'-ness with a new 'I'. Propositions about '*Bewüsstsein überhaupt*' are really about what it is to be an 'I' having experiences, and not about an 'I' that has them. But I doubt if it would be profitable to let our discussion turn upon this question.

Husserl now seems to have reached the position that nothing exists—indeed, that it is nonsense to speak of anything existing— save, on the one hand, a pure subject of experiences, or several such subjects which exist in their own right, and, on the other hand, the entire realm of intentional objects, the being of which is their being 'intended'.

This conclusion seems to me to be false, and with it the conse- quential doctrine that phenomenology is logically prior to all other philosophical or scientific enquiries. Phenomenology seems to have turned in Husserl's hands into an egocentric metaphysic. But this seems to be the result of one or two false theories which need never, and should never, have trespassed into the analysis of types of mental functioning.

(a) The Doctrine of Intentional Objects

It was an assumption rooted in the Cartesian and Lockean theories of mental life that what I am aware of when I am aware of something must always be an 'idea'. We need not bother our heads about the definition of 'idea' (for nonentities are not necessarily definable), but at least it was held that an idea is a mental something and something existing or occurring inside the mind that is aware of it. The theory of intentionality is an attempt not to repudiate, but to modify, elaborate and reform the 'idea' epistemology. The first modification was the distinction between the act and its object, the *ideatio* and the *ideatum*, e.g., in the idea of a circle, the circle is some- thing with a centre but the ideating of it is not. But it was still supposed that the circle was really existing or occurring in the mind together with the act of which it was the 'content'. Similarly, the proposition which I judge and the desideratum which I desire, though distinguishable from the acts of judging and desiring, were still supposed to be actually resident where these resided.

Husserl, however, like Meinong in this respect, denies that what an act is 'of' is essentially contained in or adjoined to the act. 'Contents' are not real parts of mental functioning. Introspection cannot find them. (This is proved by the fact that two acts of different dates can have the same object.)

Nor can all possible 'contents' be lodged in the actual world of space and time. For what fancies, false beliefs, wishes, expectations and conceptions are of, are nowhere to be found there. And as Husserl seems, anyhow latterly, to reject Platonic or Meinongian subsistence theories, it becomes very hard to see in what sense he holds that 'intentional objects' really are genuine objects or subjects of attributes at all. He *should* hold (I believe) that what we miscall 'the object or content of an act of consciousness' is really the specific character or nature of that act, so that the intentionality of an act is not a relation between it and something else, but merely a property of it so specific as to be a differentia or in some cases an individualizing description of it. He does in fact, however, continue to speak as if every intentional act is related, though related by an internal relation, to a genuine subject of attributes.

I would urge against this view (1) that it is erroneous in itself and (2) that it originates from an erroneous assumption that 'consciousness of . . .' is a true *summum genus* of which the several forms of mental functioning (including knowing) are true homogeneous species.

(1) It is certainly a convenient and popular idiom to speak of 'the objects of' imagination, desire, belief, knowledge, etc. when we wish to refer to what someone imagines, desires, believes or knows. And as we often use 'object' as a synonym for 'thing', as when we call a Chippendale chair 'a handsome' or 'expensive object', we have anyhow this motive for supposing that some subject of attributes is being referred to when we speak of what Jones imagines or wants or believes or knows. But the supposition seems to be a mistake. For the phrase 'the object of Jones' desire or fancy', e.g., is not necessarily a referentially used 'the'-phrase, any more than the 'the'-phrase in 'Poincaré is not the King of France'. It is almost certainly a systematically misleading expression. For there is nothing of which we can say truly or even falsely '*that* is the object of Jones' desire or fancy'. We can indeed state which attributes Jones is imagining something to be characterized by or what are the features of his situation, the absence or alteration of which Jones desiderates. But these statements will not require us to employ descriptive phrases referring to queer non-actual objects. Such references could not be made, for they would be self-contradictory.

If, then, the doctrine of intentionality implies that to every case of mental functioning of whatever sort there must be correlative a special something describable as an 'intentional object', then this doctrine seems to be false.

(2) Husserl assumes that all forms of mental functioning are species or sub-species of a *summum genus* called 'consciousness of...'. And by 'consciousness of...' he means to denote not *knowing*, but something of which knowing is, with believing, guessing, dreaming, craving, etc., only a species. From this, of course, it has to follow that often I am 'conscious of' something which is not a known reality and so is not real at all. (It is not possible to state this sort of view in an unobjectionable way.)

Now in my opinion Cook Wilson has shown in a strictly phenomenological manner that this whole assumption is vicious. Knowing is not one definable species of 'consciousness of...' among others, it is something anyhow partly in terms of which believing, fancying, guessing, wanting and the rest have to be defined. Belief, e.g., is a state of mind involving *ignorance* of such and such a *knowledge* of so and so: it involves more than that, but at least it involves this double reference to knowledge.

Consequently the 'intentionality' of mental acts must be defined in terms not of 'consciousness of...' but of 'knowledge of...'. And as it is, if not self-evident, anyhow plausible to say that what I know to be the case is so whether I know it or not, a phenomenology operating with this modified notion of intentionality would not be obviously bound to terminate in an egocentric metaphysic, or to claim a priority over all other branches of philosophy, such as logic or the philosophy of physics. For it would no longer be essential to any subject of attributes to be 'accusative' to a mental act. Intentionality will not now be an internal relation.

(b) Immanent versus Transcendent Perception

An important premiss in Husserl's argument which helps to involve him in his quasi-solipsistic conclusions is his theory of the self-evidence of immanent perception and the fallibility of transcendent perception.

By 'immanent perception' he refers to the direct recognition or inspection that I can have of my own mental states and acts when these are concurrent with the inspection of them. I take it that he is referring to what we call introspection. When, which is fairly infrequent, I introspect upon my present *Erlebnis*, I can *know* in the strict sense that I am enjoying this *Erlebnis* and what sort of an

Erlebnis it is. Introspection tells the truth, the whole truth and nothing but the truth.

By 'transcendent perception' he refers to the perception of physical things and events, the mental acts and states of others, and those mental acts and states of my own which are not contemporary with the inspection of them. This, Husserl maintains, can never be or give *knowledge*. It is never self-evident, and the possibility of delusion is always present. It follows that sciences of 'the external world' cannot be or give knowledge, but that the science of the self can: and all that I can *know* about the world is what I can know about my fallible cognizings of the world and my resultant practical and emotional attitudes towards it. And if this were true, Husserl would, I think, have established some sort of primacy for phenomenology.

But (1), while I see no reason to doubt that we *can* inspect and recognize states and acts of our own minds, I think that this introspection is not really perception (save in an enlarged sense). I believe that introspection is merely remembrance controlled by a special interest. But whatever it is, it seems clear that we often make mistakes about our mental condition. Very likely these should not be attributed to 'mistaken introspection', but are mistakes due to an unnoticed omission to introspect. But then the same indulgence should be allowed to what is very likely miscalled 'mistaken perception' in the sphere of what Husserl calls 'transcendent perception.

(2) I can see no *a priori* grounds for supposing that perception can only be knowledge where the object perceived and the perceiving of it are conjoined parts of one stream of experience. It seems to me just the old prejudice that the thing known should be in some way very near to the knowing of it.

So I see no grounds for denying universally that we can have knowledge by perception of physical things and events. Husserl's arguments on this point, which I have not expounded, seem to me only to show that particular perceptions don't tell the whole truth about their objects. But if they can tell us the truth and nothing but the truth, no conclusions damaging to the world seem to arise from the comparison of this sort of perception with introspection.

My conclusion is, then, this: (1) There is an important part of philosophy describable as the philosophy of psychology. It is, like any other part of philosophy, *a priori* in the sense that its methods are not inductive and that its objects are not this as distinct from that particular matter of fact. It is an enquiry into the forms of certain classes of facts, or, to put it in another way, it enquires what is really meant by such propositions as 'Jones knows or believes such and such', 'Jones wanted this but chose that', 'Jones took what he saw to be a so and so', 'I am a such and such'. And we can, if we like, call this part of philosophy 'phenomenology'.

(2) The fact that Husserl concludes that the world consists of nothing but bi-polar mental experiences, and consequently that phenomenology is 'first philosophy' is the result of his acceptance of one or two theories which are not true and are not arrived at by genuine phenomenological analysis.

II

PHENOMENOLOGY VERSUS 'THE CONCEPT OF MIND'

Reprinted, in English translation, from the original French in 'La Philosophie Analytique', Cahiers de Royaumont Philosophie, no. IV, 1962, by permission of Editions de Minuit

PHENOMENOLOGY

Husserl's Phenomenology stemmed from Brentano's critique of the atomistic and associationistic psychology of Hume and Mill. Brentano realised that the then prevalent English theories of mental life were impotent to do justice to the notions of conception, judgement and inference, of the will and of the feelings. The attempt to reduce all mental operations, attitudes and states to sensations and their echoes, randomly coagulated by association, inevitably eliminated just what make the differences between thinking and mere wandering, between choice and mere impulse, between judgement and mere fancy, between inference and mere suggestion, between doubt and mere vacancy.

In introducing his doctrine of the essential intentionality of consciousness, and in demarcating the different levels and dimensions of this intentionality, Brentano was—and he knew that he was—laying down *a priori* principles for psychology. He was not formulating any hypotheses about what we might expect to find happening when a person makes up his mind that something is the case, or resolves to conduct his life in a certain way. He was bringing out what must be the case for a mental process to be one of judging or of resolving. There could be no empirical investigations into, say, the development of the child's power to count or to infer unless the enquirer already knew what would constitute an activity of counting or inferring.

In effect, Brentano was distinguishing conceptual enquiries from factual enquiries, and demanding that the factual enquiries of empirical psychologists should be preceded by non-empirical enquiries into the compositions and connections of the concepts under which fall the manifold manifestations of mental life.

179

Husserl gave to this field of conceptual enquiries the title of 'Phenomenology'. The title has always puzzled Anglo-Saxon students, who, while familiar with the Platonic and Kantian uses of the word 'phenomenon', are quite unfamiliar with Brentano's idiosyncratic use of it, to stand for whatever could carry the epithets 'conscious' and 'consciously', that is, for Cartesian indubitables.

Husserl adopted the Platonistic practice of describing what I have called conceptual enquiries as enquiries into Essences. This idiom, which by itself would have been merely over-portentous for Anglo-Saxon tastes, went with some special doctrines about the method of conceptual enquiries which English thinkers did not share.

Husserl at the turn of the century was under many of the same intellectual pressures as were Meinong, Frege, Bradley, Peirce, G. E. Moore, and Bertrand Russell. All alike were in revolt against the idea-psychology of Hume and Mill; all alike demanded the emancipation of logic from psychology; all alike found in the notion of meaning their escape-route from subjectivist theories of thinking; nearly all of them championed a Platonic theory of meanings, i.e. of concepts and propositions; all alike demarcated philosophy from natural science by allocating factual enquiries to the natural sciences and conceptual enquiries to philosophy; nearly all of them talked as if these conceptual enquiries of philosophy terminated in some super-inspections of some super-objects, as if conceptual enquiries were, after all, super-observational enquiries; all of them, however, in the actual practice of their conceptual enquiries necessarily diverged from the super-observations that their Platonising epistemology required. Husserl talked of intuiting Essences somewhat as Moore talked of inspecting concepts, and as Russell talked of acquaintance-ship with universals, but of course it was by their intellectual wrestlings, not by any intellectual intuitings, that they tackled their actual conceptual difficulties.

After his *Logische Untersuchungen* (1899), Husserl's interests focused upon the Philosophy of Mind or Phenomenology; as did the interests of Bradley, Moore, and many others. For Frege and Russell this interest was more peripheral. But already there were some big divergences—divergences which make me want to say that Husserl's path led him into a crevasse, from which no exit existed; whereas the epistemological travails of contemporary English thinkers led them, indeed, into morasses, but morasses from which firmer ground could be reached.

First, Husserl was so bewitched by his Platonic idea that conceptual enquiries were scrutinies of the super-objects that he called

'Essences', that he persuaded himself that these enquiries should
and would grow up into another science—grow up, indeed, not
just into one science among others but into the Mistress Science, to
which all other sciences would be in tutelage.

Next, for special reasons he was convinced that the philosophy
of mind was the basic part of philosophy. All other conceptual
enquiries were logically posterior to enquiries into the concepts of
consciousness, ideation, perception, judgement, inference, imagination, volition, desire and the rest. A Platonised Cartesianism would
be the science of the basic Essences; and so be the Mistress not only
of all the other sciences, but also of all the other parts of philosophy.
He certainly so padded and inflated his theory of meaning that it
came to cover at once (1) that which a linguistic expression signifies;
(2) that which we take a sensible appearance, like a noise, to be the
appearance of; (3) that which anything whatsoever *is*, i.e. the sort,
kind or nature which it is properly classified as belonging to or
possessing; and (4) that which constitutes what any given mental
act, state or condition has for its intentional object. Consciousness
was aggrandised into the source or donor not only of the significations of all significant expressions, but also of all that sensible
appearances are apprehended as being the appearances of and
ultimately of what anything at all is known to be, when we know
what it is.

This caricature of Husserl's Phenomenology is intended to show up
by contrast some of the predominant features of recent philosophy
and in particular of the philosophy of mind in the English-speaking
world.

(1) Apart from one or two brief flirtations, British thinkers have
showed no inclination to assimilate philosophical to scientific
enquiries; and *a fortiori* no inclination to puff philosophy up into the
Science of sciences. Conceptual enquiries differ from scientific
enquiries not in hierarchical rank but in type. They are not higher
or lower, since they are not on the same ladder. I guess that our
thinkers have been immunised against the idea of philosophy as the
Mistress Science by the fact that their daily lives in Cambridge and
Oxford Colleges have kept them in personal contact with real
scientists. Claims to Fuehrership vanish when postprandial joking
begins. Husserl wrote as if he had never met a scientist—or a joke.

(2) Even inside philosophy, no privileged position has with us
been accorded to the philosophy of mind. Certainly, with us as elsewhere, and in this century as in other centuries, many philosophers
have been primarily interested in problems of epistemology, of

ethics, of aesthetics, of politics, and of jurisprudence. But many others have been primarily interested in the philosophy of mathematics, of physics, and of biology. We have not worried our heads over the question Which philosopher ought to be Fuehrer? If we did ask ourselves this question, we should mostly be inclined to say that it is logical theory that does or should control other conceptual enquiries, though even this control would be advisory rather than dictatorial. At least the main lines of our philosophical thinking during this century can be fully understood only by someone who has studied the massive developments of our logical theory. This fact is partly responsible for the wide gulf that has existed for three-quarters of a century between Anglo-Saxon and Continental philosophy. For, on the Continent during this century, logical studies have, unfortunately, been left unfathered by most philosophy departments and cared for, if at all, only in a few departments of mathematics. Having indicated, by contrast with Husserl, how we tend not to assimilate philosophy to science, or *a fortiori*, to super-science, I must now try to show what have come to be our ways of conducting conceptual enquiries and our theory of those ways of conducting them.

THE CAMBRIDGE TRANSFORMATION OF THE THEORY OF CONCEPTS

First for a prefatory terminological warning. By 'concept' we refer to that which is signified by a word or a phrase. If we talk of the concept of *Euclidean point* we are referring to what is conveyed by this English phrase, or by any other phrase, Greek, French, or English, that has the same meaning.

So far this indication is entirely neutral between different philosophical theories about what sorts of things concepts *are*; whether, e.g. they are Lockean ideas or Platonic Essences. A child who understands something that he reads or hears gets what the words mean, though still totally incapable of following philosophical theories about the status of meanings. But already we have to notice a certain hesitation in ourselves about the natural reference of the word 'concept'. It seems more natural to speak, for example, of the concept of *equality* than of the concept of *equal to*; of the concept of *existence* than of the concept of *exists*; of the concept of *negation* than of the concept of *not*. When we need to mention that which is conveyed by an adjective, a verb, a preposition, a conjunction, or even by an ordinary concrete general noun like 'man', we tend to make use of some corresponding abstract noun. We find ourselves speaking of the concept of *pleasure* and not of the concept of *pleased* or the concept of *enjoys*; of the concept of *unity* and not of the concept of *one* or *single*. Perhaps this transference makes no difference. Does not the abstract noun 'pleasure' mean exactly what is meant by the corresponding verb 'enjoys' or the adjective 'pleased'? But it transpires that the answer must be 'no'. If I say 'I enjoyed that concert', I cannot simply replace the verb 'enjoyed' by the noun 'pleasure'; since no sentence would result. We shall see before long that an inevitable generalisation of this point led to most important results.

In the first three years of this century Russell was chiefly engaged in the development of mathematical logic, a task in which an essential element was his philosophical enquiry into the key-concepts of formal logic and of arithmetic. This enquiry occupies some of the early chapters of his *Principles of Mathematics* (1903), as well as many of his subsequent writings. These key-concepts were those of *all*, *some*, *any*, *a*, *the* (singular), *the* (plural), *not*, *is a . . . is identical with*, *exists*, *if*, *and*, *or*, *. . . such that . . .*, together with the concepts of the *variable* (or *x*) and the *propositional function*. Though still as unquestioning as Husserl in his general adherence to a Platonic theory about what concepts are, Russell was already being forced by considerations of logic itself to realise that it was not enough to allocate a separate Platonic universal or Essence to every meaningful word. The phrase 'Socrates and Plato' cannot be just a list of Socrates, Plato and 'and'-ness—since the conjunction of this postulated third member with the other two would require once again the notion of *and*. 'And' conjoins; it is not just a further item to be conjoined. *Mutatis mutandis*, the same kind of objection rules out the idea of treating any of the other key-concepts of logic as terms, i.e. as objects mentioned by the statements which incorporate such words as 'all', 'not', 'the' and the rest. 'All men are mortal' and 'Some men are not mortal' say different things; but they are not about different subject-matters. The former is not about *Allness*, nor the latter about *Someness* and *Notness*.

Russell was, at this stage, especially embarrassed by verbs. He saw that 'Brutus assassinated Caesar' is a significant sentence, while 'Brutus, Assassination, Caesar' is not a sentence at all, but just a list. But he was unable to express what distinguishes the meaning of the live verb '. . . assassinated . . .' from the meaning of the corresponding verbal noun 'Assassination', save by saying that that organic unity of a truth or falsehood which is contributed by a live verb is not in the gift of the corresponding verbal noun, nor even of this noun in collocation with any number of attendant verbal nouns. What is conveyed by an entire sentence cannot be conveyed by a sequence of names of objects, even Platonic objects. To examine what is meant by one of the logical words, or by any live verb, is to examine what it contributes to the entire statements in which it occurs. It is not merely to consider what it does by itself, since it does nothing by itself. It is *ex officio* auxiliary to the saying of true or false things as wholes.

This opened Russell's eyes to the possibility that many other sorts of expressions, simple or complex, might also be auxiliary to entire statements, instead of being designations of extra objects. It followed in fact, whether or not Russell saw it, that there could in principle be no such thing as intuiting or inspecting the concept of *not*, the Essence of *the*, or the notion of *assassinated*, since what is conveyed by the corresponding words is conveyed by them only in the total setting of some significant sentence or other. When we produce such a word, we are not mentioning an extra entity by name; we are in course of saying something unitary. Considering the meaning of such an expression is considering what is common to all the entire significant sentences in which this expression is constant and the rest is varied. Its meaning is an abstractible feature, not an extractible part of the unitary senses of the different sentences that incorporate it.

It was not Russell but Wittgenstein who, developing arguments of Frege, showed that the sense of a sentence is not, what had hitherto been tacitly assumed, a whole of which the meanings of the words in it are independently thinkable parts but, on the contrary, that the meanings of the parts of a sentence are abstractible differences and similarities between the unitary sense of that sentence and the unitary senses of other sentences which have something but not everything in common with that given sentence. To put it in epistemological terms, we do not begin with the possession of concepts and then go on to coagulate them into thoughts. We begin and we end with thoughts, but by comparative analysis we can discriminate ways in which something is constant *vis-à-vis* what else is varied between different unitary things that we think. A human face is not a molecule of which its profile, its complexion and its expressions are the atoms; yet still we can discern similarities and dissimilarities between different faces in respect of these features. Similarly an assertion is not a molecule of which the meanings of the words in which it is worded are the atoms; yet still we discern what features one assertion has and has not in common with another assertion.

Now, perhaps, we can begin to formulate the idea, familiar to us *ambulando* since Socrates, that philosophical enquiries are conceptual enquiries. Concepts are not things that are there crystallised in a splendid isolation; they are discriminable features, but not detachable atoms, of what is integrally said or integrally thought. They are not detachable parts of, but distinguishable contributions to, the unitary senses of completed sentences. To examine them is to examine the live force of things that we actually say. It is to examine them not in retirement, but doing their co-operative work.

When Aristotle was discontented with Plato's account of Pleasure, he would have got nowhere by, so to speak, just gazing hard at some insulated entity or Essence designated by this abstract noun 'Pleasure'. Instead he rightly considered what we are asserting or denying *in concreto* when we say that someone did or did not enjoy the concert; or that someone enjoys this piece of music more than that piece. Unlike the abstract noun 'Pleasure', the live verb '... enjoys ...' is here actively making just that specific sense-contribution to which it happens to be dedicated.

Similarly our examination of the notion of *existence* cannot consist just in acts of contemplating a rarefied object, withdrawn, like a coin in a museum, from its native commercial transactions. We must consider what we assert when we assert e.g. that there exists a prime number of a certain specification, when we deny that the sea-serpent or Father Christmas exists, when we ask whether mammoths still exist, when they existed and how long they existed for; and even when we tell someone to construct, destroy or preserve something. Especially we must consider wherein lies the absurdity of such questions as 'Do you exist?', 'How many satellites of Venus do *not* exist?' and 'Can a thing exist *fast* or *intermittently*?'

This last point deserves amplification. In the course of his enquiries into the logical foundations of Arithmetic Russell had found his path obstructed by some quite unforeseen contradictions or antinomies. Some of the key-concepts of logic had turned in his hands, and generated not the docile consequences that were to be expected, but propositions which were true only on condition that they were false, and vice versa. The 'I am now telling a lie' of Epimenides exemplifies the kind of rebellious statements that barred Russell's progress.

After many attempts to circumvent the rebels, Russell brought in a new weapon. Some sentences, whose syntax and vocabulary are impeccable, convey neither truths nor falsehoods, but are nonsensical. They have been composed, sometimes on purpose, but sometimes unwittingly, in contravention of some latent conditions governing the possible associations of concepts with one another. Some dicta, which conform perfectly to the rules of school-grammar, still say nothing. In the metaphor used both by Husserl and Wittgenstein, the rules of *logical* grammar forbid the elements of these dicta to co-operate.

Russell used this new weapon as a crowbar to dislodge only certain local obstructions. In Wittgenstein's hand, it became the fulcrum for inverting the whole notion of meaning. Making sense and failing to make sense belong first to entire sentences. The notion of the unitary sense of a sentence is logically prior to the notion of the meanings of the words of which that sentence is composed. If, in a given significant sentence, we replace one of its words by another word of the same grammatical kind, the new sentence will not necessarily be significant. Though the new word is grammatically fitting, what it means, i.e. what it would contribute, if it could, may not fit. If in the sentence 'Manchester is near Liverpool' we replace 'near' by 'between'; 'Liverpool' by 'Sunday'; or 'is' by 'occurs', the result is nonsense. A concept is, so to speak, already shaped for the assertions, questions, commands etc. into which it will fit; and shaped, therefore, not to go into other grammatically allowable vacancies. As Aristotle saw, in the sentence 'he began to eat his dinner, but was prevented from finishing', we cannot replace 'eat' by 'enjoy'. Eating is, but pleasure is not, a *kinesis*. A conceptual enquiry is, therefore, of necessity an enquiry not only into what can be significantly said but also into what cannot be significantly said with the word or phrase conveying the concept under investigation. Its métier is a determinate and rule-governed métier, and the examination of it has to be the examination of the sense-conditions in which it can and cannot make its contribution. To do its work, it must be where it *can* do its work. The word 'between' cannot make its contribution at all unless at least three towns (say) are mentioned; and the verb 'occurs' demands to be escorted by the mention of an event, an escort which cannot be tolerated by the verb 'exists'.

When Wittgenstein wrote the *Tractatus Logico-Philosophicus* (1921–22) he drew certain very startling consequences from his inversion of the traditional theory of concepts and propositions. We saw that the statements 'All men are mortal' and 'Some men are not mortal' are not about different objects or entities; that is, the logical words 'all' 'some' 'are' and 'not' have the meanings that they have, not *qua* designating extra subjects or terms, but only *qua* making their specific contributions to the structures of the unitary senses of the sentences in which they function. From this it seemed to follow inexorably that neither the logician nor the philosopher can construct significant sentences *about* what is conveyed by these logical words. We can say true and false things about Socrates, but we cannot say true or false things about what is conveyed by 'not' or 'and' or 'is'. Certainly we can say true or false things about the *words* 'not' or 'if', inside inverted commas, e.g. that they are monosyllables or polysyllables. But the attempt to say true or false things about what these words convey results of necessity in nonsensical dictions like 'And is not in London'. The word 'and', not inside quotation marks, cannot replace the noun 'Socrates' in any significant sentence. What must function as a conjunction, if it is to function at all, cannot function as a subject-term. The same is true of any other logical word; of any live verb, like 'assassinated'; of any predicative expression, like 'is a man'; and, finally, of any entire sentence, like 'Socrates is a man'. The senses of complete or incomplete sense-conveying expressions cannot have said about them any of the things that can be said about Socrates. The formal logician can indeed exhibit the way that 'and' and 'not' function, by displaying them operating inside the skeletons of complete sentences, from which all informative content has been algebraised away. Like a horse-dealer, he can put 'if' through its paces, without baggage, or rider, by, for example, producing the formula 'for any proposition p and any proposition q, the compound proposition *if p then q* is incompatible with the compound proposition *p but not q*'.

But such a formula is not, *per impossibile*, an informative assertion about a subject-term called 'if'; it is a sentence (or rather a blank cheque for sentences) asserting something *with* 'if'. It exhibits the work done by 'if', but it does not, *per impossibile*, ascribe attributes to that work since the word 'if' does not and could not occupy an object-mentioning place in that sentence-skeleton.

The conceptual enquiries that constitute philosophy are in an even worse plight than those that constitute Formal Logic. For the philosopher has apparently to try not just to deploy but to describe the concepts with which he is concerned. He has to try to say what Pleasure and Existence are. He has to try, necessarily in vain, to attach object-characterising predicates to non-object-mentioning expressions. But by no prestidigitation can the live verb 'enjoys' or the live verb 'exists' (except in inverted commas), be made grammatical subjects to live verbs. The philosopher's description of a concept is bound to terminate in a stammer. The Platonic dream of a descriptive science of Essences is shattered. The sense of a sentence and, therewith, the auxiliary senses of its parts are not describable things. They are not describable, for they are not things.

Some years after the *Tractatus* Wittgenstein was able, in practice if not in explicit doctrine, to disentangle the required notion of *elucidation* from the obsessive notion of *object-description* and so to rescue conceptual investigations from the menace of ineffability without re-assimilating them to inspections of entities.

But at this point let us cease to debate from the esplanade the art and possibility of philosophical swimming, and instead let us plunge into the water and feel for ourselves what it is like to be trying to swim. For this purpose I am going to reanimate three specific conceptual worries with which I attempted to cope in *The Concept of Mind*. Since I wrote this book some ten years ago, I have now attained the right seniority over my then self, to treat him not, of course, with the austerity of a judge, but with the candour of an elder brother.

THE PHILOSOPHY OF MIND

First a word or two about the programme of the book as a whole. Though it is entitled *The Concept of Mind*, it is actually an examination of multifarious specific mental concepts, such as those of *knowing, learning, discovering, imagining, pretending, hoping, wanting, feeling depressed, feeling a pain, resolving, doing voluntarily, doing deliberately, perceiving, remembering* and so on. The book could be described as a sustained essay in phenomenology, if you are at home with that label.

The book does not profess to be a contribution to any science, not even to psychology. If any factual assertions are made in it, they are there through the author's confusion of mind. Next, the book has a central strategic motif. The philosophy of mind had, I thought, been systematically distorted by a pervasive conceptual mistake—namely the mistake of regarding a person as consisting of two compartments, his mind and his body, the two compartments being the fields of two disparate kinds of causality. This assumption of a bifurcated causality seemed to me to result in a Janus-faced account of human life, according to which every slice of a man's life has to be a pair of slices of two synchronous lives, mysteriously united by causal connections bridging the gap between mechanical and psychical causation. So I tried to show how in the case of lots of specific varieties of human acts, propensities, powers and states, the traditional pattern of explication collapsed and needed to be replaced by an explication of a quite different pattern.

I mention this strategic motif chiefly to bring out a general feature of conceptual enquiries, namely that the philosopher's task is never to investigate the *modus operandi* just of one concept by itself; the task is always to investigate the *modi operandi* of all the threads of a spider's web of inter-working concepts. A problem about, say, the notion of *imagining* is *ipso facto* a problem about the notions of *perceiving, remembering, thinking, pretending, knowing, inventing, experimenting,* and so on indefinitely. To fix the position of one concept is to fix its position *vis-à-vis* lots of others. Conceptual questions are inter-conceptual questions; if one concept is out of focus, all its associates are also out of focus.

Let us now try to get the 'feel' of two or three live specimens.

(1) *Dispositions and Acts*

When I was a schoolboy I was taught that all active verbs signify actions; i.e. that what is true of active verbs like 'dig', 'walk', and 'build' is true of all active verbs. Patently this is false. *Sleeping, dying, neglecting, forgetting, resembling, undergoing* and *possessing* are not actions, although the verbs signifying these things are active verbs.

Now we employ for saying things about the mental life of people many active verbs which do signify acts of mind; and we are tempted to assume that this is the function of all the active verbs that we employ in these contexts. Having correctly listed *calculating, pondering* and *recalling to mind* as mental acts or processes, we go on to list *believing, knowing, aspiring,* and *detesting* also as acts or processes. If this listing were correct, then, given the statement that Socrates was occupied at a certain time in calculating or recalling something to mind, we could replace the participle 'calculating' or 'recalling to mind' by the participle 'knowing' or 'detesting'. But it is immediately apparent that these substitutions cannot be significantly made. We can say that Socrates knew, believed or detested something from, say, his twentieth birthday to the end of his days; but we could not say that at any particular moment he was occupied in knowing, believing or detesting. As Aristotle realised, *knowing, believing* and *detesting* have to be listed not as acts or processes but as 'hexeis'. Just as possessing a bicycle is not something that is happening or in process at a particular time, though the owner may remain in possession of the bicycle throughout a span of time, so *knowing* and *believing* are not incidents in a person's mental life, though they make an important difference, of quite another sort, to his mental life. Certainly I *acquire* a bicycle at a particular moment, and I *find out* or *become convinced* of something at a particular moment; but being in possession of something is remaining and not attaining; having and not getting.

There are, of course, lots of what I call 'dispositional' concepts which have nothing special to do with persons or, *a fortiori*, with their qualities of intellect and character. The flexibility of a piece of steel is a dispositional property which it possesses, perhaps, for years or for ever, though at few moments, if any, is it actually being bent or twisted or recoiling from having been bent or twisted. The habits into which a dog is trained may be kept for the rest of its life, though its particular acts of begging, say, which it does from habit, occur relatively infrequently and last for only a few seconds. But there is a special point in attending to those dispositional concepts which do apply specifically to the mental life of human beings, namely that if we inadvertently treat the active verb 'believe', say, as signifying an action, we are forced to regard the postulated acts of believing as peculiarly occult acts. For we never find other people or catch ourselves engaged in any such acts. Similarly, if the schoolboy is persuaded by his school-grammar that owning a bicycle is doing something, he is forced to suppose that owning a bicycle is an occult sort of doing, since he never meets anyone occupied in doing it.

It is a general mark of a dispositional concept as opposed to an activity-concept or a process-concept, that the time-qualifications which fit concepts of the one family will not fit concepts of the other. A man might have been calculating or running while the clock was striking twelve, but he could not have been engaged in knowing or believing or possessing a bicycle while the clock was striking twelve. Conversely, a man may have known something for the last twenty years, but he could not have been engaged in a particular task for the last twenty years. We can say of a sleeping man that he is a cigarette-smoker or that he believes that the earth is flat; although he is not now smoking a cigarette or now considering the shape of the earth.

Other qualifications also will fit concepts of the one family but not those of the other. A man may be doing something industriously or lethargically, fast or slowly, efficiently or inefficiently, continuously or intermittently. But none of these qualifications will fit his knowing, believing, aspiring, detesting or possessing. To resume an earlier metaphor, dispositional concepts and act-concepts are 'shaped' for different kinds of propositions. Where members of the one family will fit, members of the other will not fit. For subsequent problems, it becomes of first-rate importance to distinguish different kinds of dispositional concepts from one another. Skills are not of a piece with blind habits, and neither can be assimilated to tastes, to inclinations, to phobias, to inhibitions, to moral principles or to frailties. But for my present purpose it is enough to draw attention to the need to follow Aristotle in distinguishing the type of force that belongs to, e.g., the verb 'to calculate' from the type of force that belongs to, e.g., the verb 'to know'; and we need also methods of fixing their differences. A bare contemplation (if it could, *per impossibile*, take place) of the Essences of *Knowledge* and of *Calculation* would get us nowhere. We require systematically to unfold the disparities between the functionings of these concepts in live discourse; to be able, e.g., to say why the gap in 'Socrates . . . fast but carelessly' can be filled by 'calculated' or 'dug' but not by 'knew' or 'possessed'. We shall then, incidentally, be out of danger of supposing, as epistemologists often have supposed, that knowing and believing are very peculiar processes, namely occult processes.

One further point about dispositions. Although to say that someone is a cigarette-smoker, is honest or has a good musical ear is not itself to report that he is at a particular moment doing something, still what is said of him is intimately connected with mentions of his particular actions. We learn that a man is an habitual smoker from seeing him smoking on one occasion and then seeing him smoking on another occasion, and so on. We find out that he is honest by hearing him tell unpalatable truths on various particular occasions. Moreover, to know or believe that he has a good musical ear is, *inter alia*, to expect him to sing or play the correct notes on future occasions; to shudder when he hears the wrong notes; to applaud good music; and to switch off the radio when the music is bad. Potentialities, abilities and liabilities are potentialities to . . . , abilities to . . . , and liabilities to . . . ; and what fill these gaps are references to actual momentary doings, reactings, and abstainings. None the less a man who is asleep or at his office-desk can be truly described as being good at swimming, though he is not then engaged in swimming.

Now let us turn to consider some concepts of doing.

Here I want to draw your attention to an important, if somewhat subtle difference between two families of action-concepts. Consider what we are saying of a doctor (1) when we say that he has been treating an invalid and (2) when we say that he has cured him. At first sight we may suppose that these differ only, perhaps, as running differs from walking, or as drawing differs from scribbling. But the difference is more radical. When we say that the doctor cured the invalid, we are saying in one breath both that he treated the patient *and* that the patient was thereby restored to health. In a word the treatment was successful. Similarly the difference between my arguing with you and my convincing you is that the latter embodies the notion of my arguments having actually had the effect that they were meant to have. Winning a race differs in this way from running a race, hitting a target from shooting at the target, murdering from trying to murder, and purchasing an article from bargaining for it. This conceptual difference between trying to bring something about and succeeding can be shown in this way. Very often the attempt to bring something about fails just through bad luck or succeeds with good luck. A runner may win the race because he ran well or because his chief rival slipped in a patch of mud. So it makes sense to describe a success as lucky, or a failure as unlucky. But it would make no sense to describe the making of the attempt as due to good or to bad luck. In the sentence skeleton 'Socrates was lucky enough (or unlucky enough) to ...', the gap can be filled by a verb of success, or a verb of failure, but not by a verb of trying or undertaking. Conversely there are qualifications which fit concepts of trying or undertaking which will not fit concepts of succeeding or failing. A man may search busily, systematically or intermittently; but we could not say that he *found* something busily, systematically or intermittently. The doctor may treat the patient carefully or carelessly, but he cannot cure him carefully or carelessly.

The present importance of this conceptual distinction is that in our accounts of, e.g., intellectual operations, we use concepts of both kinds, and can easily mystify ourselves if we suppose that a concept of the one sort is of the other sort. For example, the notions of *proving, establishing, discovering, solving, seeing*, and *recollecting*, are all notions of success. It would be absurd to say that a thinker had solved a problem incorrectly, proved a theorem invalidly, recollected something that had not happened, or seen something that was not there. From the other family there are also scores of notions, like those of *pondering, enquiring, investigating, deliberating, listening*, and so on. These are activities which certainly can be conducted in vain, pertinaciously, methodically, and so on. They are what a person is at a time and for a time occupied in, as he cannot be occupied in solving, proving or seeing (as distinct from trying to solve, prove or see). If we treat the notion of *deducing* as if it belonged with *deliberating* or *examining*, we find ourselves confronted, apparently, with a mental activity mysteriously controlled by the laws of logic. For a deduction certainly is forbidden to be fallacious, as a cure is forbidden to be unsuccessful. Our theories of knowledge, inference, and perception are, *ex officio*, concerned with, among others, concepts of intellectual achievement and failure; so a great deal depends upon our distinguishing the logical behaviour of verbs of trying from that of verbs of succeeding and failing.

(2) *Imagination*

Now I turn to a very different field. In a late chapter of my book I discussed a battery of concepts falling under the general heading of 'Imagination'. Here my chief bother was with the moderately specific notions of visual and auditory imagination. We visualise or 'see in our mind's eyes', faces, buildings and landscapes, and we 'hear' voices and tunes 'in our heads'.

It was important for me to discuss these special mental acts of imagining since we are all strongly tempted to think of the human mind as a sort of private chamber, and to think of the things that we visually and auditorily imagine as, somehow, authentic occupants of this private chamber. *Imagining* then comes to be misconstrued as a special brand of *witnessing*, the objects of which happen to be internal and private to the witness. Sartre, in his *L'Imaginaire, psychologie phénoménologique de l'imagination* (1940), was partly concerned to attack this same conceptual misconstruction. There was another, connected conceptual mistake which I, like Sartre, tried to expose. Hume, and many others, have maintained that the difference between what is seen and what is visualised, between 'impressions' and 'ideas', was a difference in degree of intensity. So, presumably, very faint noises, such as barely heard whispers, would have to be auditory images or 'ideas'; and merely imagined shouts would have to be actually heard whispers. Which is absurd.

I shall not repeat the arguments by which Sartre and I exposed the absurdity of Hume's view or of the other view that imagining is witnessing things existing or occurring inside a private chamber. What is more interesting, at least to me, is that after these insidious conceptual misconstructions had been exposed, I was obliged to try to give the correct positive account, and in this conceptual search I got lost. I was, I think, on the right track in assimilating imaging, e.g. visualising, to the much more general notion of make-believe, about certain other varieties of which, like the notions of pretending and playing, I felt fairly clear. But when I found myself classifying visualising as 'make-believe seeing' I felt conceptual embarrassments, and these are always a sure sign that something has gone wrong. Part of these embarrassments derived from the fact that my previous treatment of visual perception proper had got stuck over the relations between the concept of seeing trees and stars, say, and that of having optical sense-impressions. This illustrates the way in which conceptual enquiries cannot be confined behind watertight bulkheads.

Through the lengthy stretch during which I floundered there did, however, run one idea which I still think is cardinal to the concept of imaging. It is this. A person at a concert may be listening to a piece of music that is strange to him, so that he is then and there trying to learn how it goes; but a person who goes over a tune in his head must already have learned and not yet forgotten how the tune goes; and more than this, not only must he already know how the tune goes, but he must be at the time *using* this knowledge; he must be actually *thinking* how it goes; and he must be thinking how it goes without the tune being actually played aloud to him or hummed aloud by him. He must be thinking how it goes, in its *absence*.

Nor do these 'musts' represent a psychological law. An act would not be one of going over a tune in one's head unless these conditions were fulfilled. Of this I feel fairly sure. But what stumps me is what more to say of this notion of *thinking how the tune goes*. For the man may say, even with surprise, 'it was almost as if I actually heard the notes.' The kind of 'thinking' that he was doing had a certain degree of vividness or lifelikeness which makes him want to liken his merely thought-of notes to heard notes, save for the crucial difference that the thought-of notes were *only* thought of, and not heard at all. He heard no notes; but he 'heard' them vividly. He was *non-*sensuously so alive to how they would have sounded, that it was almost as if they had been sounding in his ears. It is for this concept of the quasi-sensuousness or vividness of, e.g., auditorily imagined notes that I feel sure that I failed to fix the bearings.

(3) 'Cogito'

The last specimen of my phenomenology that I want to mention is this. There is, as has long been recognised, an important difference between certain first-person and the corresponding third-person pronouncements. If I declare of someone else that he is depressed, in pain or intending to travel, I may easily be wrong. But if I declare that I am depressed, in pain or intending to travel, then if I am not being insincere I must, it seems, be declaring something about which I could not be mistaken. I could not be wrong or even dubious about my present mood or my present intentions. This exemption from the possibility of uncertainty and error does not attach to my declarations of how I formerly felt or formerly intended, or to my declarations about my future moods or intentions. Nor does it attach to any diagnoses I may give of why I am depressed or in pain. Nor does it attach to any declarations in the present tense that I may make about the physiological state of any part of my body. I may, for example, be mistaken in thinking that I now have a high temperature.

It is present-tense, first-person declarations or 'avowals' of mental states and acts that seem to be exempt from any possibility of doubt or mistake.

At first sight we are inclined to follow Descartes in saying that such 'avowals' express the highest level of knowledge and certainty. No other truth could be better known to me than the truth that I now have a pain or that I now feel depressed. At the top of the list of the things that I not merely claim to know, but do really know and cannot but know are the things that at any given moment I may avow to others or to myself.

But there are some puzzling features in this notion of avowals being expressions of knowledge. Ordinarily when we grade statements on a scale of approximations towards certainty we use such adverbs as 'probably', 'presumably', 'unquestionably', 'patently', 'self-evidently'. But none of these, not even the highest of them can be used to qualify 'I am in pain'. Nor could we say 'I have proved or established or decided, beyond question that I am in pain' or 'I have the best of reasons for thinking that I am in pain'.

Even the verb 'to know' does not fit. To know something is to have discovered or learned something and not to have forgotten it. But 'I have found out that I am depressed' is absurd—where 'I have found out that she is depressed' and 'She has found out that I am depressed' are perfectly in order.

An avowal of depression seems to come, so to speak, directly out of the depression itself and not out of the settlement, however conclusive, of any questions about that depression. In avowing my depression I speak not as an angelically well-situated reporter on my depression, but simply as a depressed person.

In my book I half-assimilated avowals to the yawns which manifest the sleepiness of which they are signs or to the oaths by which the angry man vents his rage and shows others how angry he is. As an oath is not a report of anger, so, I was inclined to say, an avowal of depression is not a report of depression but an ejaculation of depression. It is exempt from uncertainty only for the reason that an ejaculation or a complaint cannot be qualified by 'perhaps' or 'indubitably'. But it is clear that this assimilation of avowals to ejaculations or complaints will not do. An avowal may be a reply to a question; it may even be meant to provide a doctor or an oculist with the information that he requires for his diagnosis. If I say 'I have a shooting pain in my eyes', while I may be complaining, I am also reporting. Avowals seem then to be like reports, and yet not to be reports of anything discovered or established, to merit being received as incontestable and yet not to issue from any kind of certitude on the part of their authors, or of course of incertitude either. In one way avowals are completely authoritative, and yet there is nothing about which their authors are special authorities. I am not an expert about my pain, nor an angelically well-situated observer of it; I am merely a person who is in pain and is saying so. You may conjecture, infer, believe or know that I am in pain; but I just have the pain—and the words for it. My avowals may be, for you, the best possible reasons for concluding that I am in pain; but they are not *my* reasons. I do not need reasons. I do not conclude.

Here, then, we have another puzzle or trouble-spot in the philosophy of mind. These first-person, present-tense declarations refuse to behave either like ebullitions of mental states or like testable reports of ordinary matters of fact. Above all they refuse to behave like infinitely well-certified reports of matters of solipsistic fact. Their conceptual location is not yet fixed; so the locations of the concepts of consciousness and self-consciousness remain unfixed; so what is conveyed by 'I', 'you' and 'he' remains unfixed. But perhaps we are clearer than we were about the sort of position-fixing that we desiderate.

I2

HEIDEGGER'S 'SEIN UND ZEIT'

Reprinted from 'Mind', vol. XXXVIII, *1928*

This is a very difficult and important work, which marks a big advance in the application of the 'Phenomenological Method'—though I may say at once that I suspect that this advance is an advance towards disaster.

Heidegger is probably the most original and powerful of Husserl's pupils; and this book, which is dedicated to Husserl and first appeared in his *Jahrbuch für Philosophie und phänomenologische Forschung*, Vol. VIII, presupposes a knowledge of the published works and refers explicitly to more recent teachings and writings, as yet unpublished, of that difficult author. Now if *Sein und Zeit* were nothing more—and it is more—than a re-exposition of the ideas of Heidegger's teacher, it would be hard enough for, anyhow, English readers to understand, since, save in chance quotations, not a word of Husserl has yet been translated and no adequate exposition in English of the cardinal positions of Phenomenology or even of the logical, epistemological and psychological doctrines contained in the *Logische Untersuchungen* (1900–1901 and re-edited with modifications 1913) has yet been given.[1] Moreover, to add to our difficulties, until recently there has been an additional historical obstacle to the understanding of Husserl, namely that no sure estimate could be formed of the nature and extent of the influence upon Husserl of Franz Brentano, though it was known that this was great; as, until Kraus and Kastil devoted themselves to the task, most of the psychological and philosophical teaching of Brentano remained unpublished and inaccessible. And finally the 'logical Realism' of Bernard Bolzano (1781–1848) which, with that of Frege, was so largely formative of Husserl's logical theories, must for the present remain unexplored country for most researchers in this field; since the first and only complete edition of his most important *Wissenschaftslehre* (1837) is

[1] But see Boyce Gibson's article in *Mind*, 1922; references and quotations in Bosanquet's latest writings; and Linke's article in *The Monist*, 1926.

unprocurable, and even Höfler's re-edition in 1913 of the first two of the four books is now out of print.

It is, however, now becoming possible to see in some sort of perspective what were the beginnings and what have been the stages in the growth of Phenomenology, and a short sketch of its genesis must preface my attempt to state even the programme and method of Heidegger—many of his conclusions for lack of comprehension I must abandon unexpounded.

Brentano was, like Bradley, a step-son of the 'Association philosophy'; for him, as for Bradley, the problems are largely set by Locke, Berkeley, Hume, and the two Mills, as well as by Herbart; and he, like Bradley, makes a partial escape from the conclusions of Hume by a theory of Judgement which denies the (for Locke) basic position that judging is a *coupling* or *having-together* two 'ideas'; instead, he asserts, a judgement contains one 'idea'-element *plus* another element irreducible to 'idea', namely the element of acceptance or rejection, affirmation or negation. Unlike Bradley's, Brentano's metaphysic was Aristotelian and Thomist rather than Hegelian, and, unlike him again, avoiding any attempt to *define* Judgement (e.g. in terms of Subject and Predicate) he contents himself with declaring judgement to be an ultimate, irreducible and indefinable psychic fact, differing qualitatively from the primitive psychic fact of 'having an idea' (*Vorstellung*) just in the presence to the former of the extra element of 'accepting or rejecting'.

He went on to find a third class of psychic facts, equally irreducible to 'ideas' or even to Judgements, namely Feelings of 'liking and disliking' or 'wanting and aversion'.

He thus broke with the English school by rejecting 'Association' as the one principle and 'Ideas' as the one element of psychic complexes, setting up instead a division of three irreducible types— capable, of course, of various inter-combinations—of psychic facts or 'phenomena'. This division was accepted as basic, anyhow at first, by all his pupils, and in particular by both Meinong and Husserl; and it has led them, with others, into profound and important investigations in the psychology and philosophy of thinking.

That, however, despite the improvements that he introduced, Brentano was fundamentally a member of the school of Locke, is shown by the fact that for him 'ideas' (*Vorstellungen*) are, if no longer the whole, yet still the substrate of all conscious experience; for while an act of 'having an idea' (*vorstellen*) may occur alone, an act of judging or feeling must always be founded in one of 'having an idea'. To judge is to have an idea and to do something with it; to feel is to have an idea and to take up an attitude towards it. We, made wise by the event, may already wonder whether such premisses will not in due course lead to a subjectivist or agnostic theory of knowledge.

There is a character shared by acts of *Vorstellung*, Judgement and Feeling in virtue of which they may all be classified as *psychical* as opposed to *physical* facts, namely the necessary presence to all of them of an 'immanent object' or 'content'.

There is no 'having an idea' that is not having an idea of something; no affirming that is not affirming something, no wanting that is not wanting something. This relation of a psychic act to its content or immanent object is named by Brentano, in loan from the schoolmen, the 'intentional' relation; and the content or immanent object that the act is of is the 'intentional' object. 'Intentionality' is the essential character of consciousness, and is what differentiates the psychical from the physical (a 'res cogitans' from a 'res extensa').

Two important things must be noticed about intentionality (which is, of course, ultimate and indefinable): (1) It has nothing to do with 'intending' in our sense of intending or purposing to do: its affinities are rather with the doctrine of 'first, and second intentions'. Heidegger in an earlier work on Duns Scotus showed that his use of 'intentio' was closely akin to Husserl's 'Meaning' (*Bedeutung*). (2) The 'intentional object' of an act of consciousness is not an extra-mental reality, but immanent in the consciousness of which it is the 'content'. Its status is psychical, and it exists, if it exists at all, when the act that 'has' it is in existence. Its being is to be 'accusative' to an act of consciousness.

That is to say, Brentano's theory of intentionality is not to be construed as a premiss to or conclusion from a Realist theory of knowledge but only as a clearing up of an ambiguity latent in the use of such terms as Idea, Judgement, and Feeling.

However, Brentano is not a Solipsist; so the further distinction has to be made, between the content or intentional object of a psychic act, and the real, extra-mental object, e.g. a 'thing' in space and time. All psychic acts have intentional objects; only some have also real objects. For instance, the 'idea' of a Golden Mountain has a content but no object; that of Mount Everest has both. Thus, too, the idea of 'the composer of the *Iliad*' and that of 'the composer of the *Odyssey*' have different contents, but (perhaps) the same real object.

As there are three ultimate types of psychic acts, so there are three ultimate types of intentionality; though those of Judging and Feeling are founded in that of *Vorstellung*.

The next important legacy of Brentano, and one which was a necessary condition and almost the sufficient condition for the birth of Phenomenology, was his theory of the absolute Self-Evidence (*Evidenz*) of 'inner perception' or the perception of our present psychic acts and states *with their intentional objects*.

Harking back to Descartes's Method of Doubt and his 'Cogito ergo sum', he asserts that while our judgements of external reality are contingent and problematic (since they are founded in 'ideas' the contents of which are different from and ultimately incomparable with their extra-mental real objects), our judgements of what is immanent in the consciousness of the judger are self-ratifying, since there is *identity* between the content and the object of the idea which, *qua* judging, we are asserting.

Thus I may doubt whether I am really seeing a ship, but I cannot doubt that what I see *really* looks to me as it *seems*, or that I am really believing it to be the look of a ship; I may doubt whether sardines are good food, but I cannot doubt that I like them.

He gives to the objects of 'inner perception' the general title of 'Psychic Phenomena' or the 'Phenomena of consciousness', using the term 'phenomenon' (it is important to note, to appreciate the meaning of 'Phenomenology') *not* in the sense of Kant but in that of Comte; i.e. to denote not an 'appearance' as *opposed* to a reality, but a *reality that appears,* i.e. manifests itself. So a 'psychic phenomenon' is simply a particular manifestation of consciousness. Often, indeed, the term means little more than 'fact' in ordinary parlance.

We have then in inner perception of our own psychic phenomena a fount of self-evident judgements which are both affirmative and existential; and we have no other such fount (though we may make self-evident *negative* judgements of the form 'no X is Y' or 'there is no X that is Y' simply from logical insight).

So all positive knowledge either is, or is founded in 'inner perception', and the science of the objects of inner perception acquires accordingly a priority over all other sciences.

Now the science of the objects of inner perception falls for Brentano into two major divisions. At first only in his practice but later also explicitly in his theory, he divides Psychology into 'genetic' and 'descriptive' psychology. Under the former he classed all forms of inductive, experimental, statistical, anthropological, evolutionary, and pathological or physiological psychology; but these all presuppose the findings of 'descriptive' psychology, the function of which it is to analyse and describe the general types of psychic phenomena or the general modes of intentionality which the particular data of 'genetic' psychology exemplify. The method of 'descriptive psychology' is intuitive, moving not by inference but by direct inspection of individual instances of psychic phenomena in which the universal type-structure can be read. We are told that Brentano, reserving the title 'psychology' for the inductive or 'genetic' branch, came later to call the descriptive science of psychic phenomena by the name 'Psycho-gnosis'. Kraus, more recently, has coined for it the name 'Phenomenognosis': but the title that will stick is that adopted by Husserl and his school—'Phenomenology'. It would have been more accurate, if less convenient, to call it 'Psycho-phenomenology' since its subject-matter is limited to psychic phenomena; but as, in the end, the conclusion is reached that *only* such entities as are psychic are self-manifesting, i.e. are proper 'phenomena', this precision would perhaps be extravagant.

These are, I think, the most important of the teachings of Brentano for the history of Phenomenology; they are not, however, his *only*, and in some respects they are not his final, teachings. For, alarmed by the erections made upon his foundations by his two leading pupils Husserl and Meinong, he came later to withdraw or re-fashion some of his theories. These later theories, however, need not be expounded here.

Husserl began his career as a theoretical psychologist of the school of Brentano; and a native interest in the theory of mathematics led to his first book *The Philosophy of Arithmetic* in which he applies the principles of Brentano to the special field of arithmetical 'ideas'. Hence, like Meinong, he was driven back to the general problem of the nature, status, and origin of 'abstract ideas', i.e. concepts and ideas of relations; and the early writings of both are accordingly largely composed of criticisms, amazingly acute and profound, of the treatment of these problems by the English Locke–Spencer school. And it is perhaps no coincidence that Brentano who claimed to be the pupil of Aristotle and the Schoolmen should be the teacher of pupils who re-affirmed the independent reality of 'entia rationis' and found in our thinking elements that were not 'sensations' or echoes of 'sensations'.

Husserl in particular came then to see the domain of the logical as no mere province in the domain of the psychological, and in the First Part of his *Logische Untersuchungen* he attacks root and branch the fallacy of 'psychologism', of which at that date almost all logicians were victims, the fallacy, namely, that the objects of Logic, universals, Facts, implications, relations, types, wholes, etc., are simply varieties of mental states, processes, and dispositions. His sustained and masterly demonstration of the self-ruinous character of all such 'psychologistic' theories and of the necessity of a 'pure' and independent science of Logic, to which parts of the Second Part of the *Logische Untersuchungen* are valuable contributions, have been of radical importance for German philosophy and psychology in the last quarter of a century.

But he had other fish to fry than merely to elaborate a 'Platonic' logical Realism, and though many would have preferred him to work along the lines of Bolzano and Frege in the direction of a pure Formal Ontology, like the *Gegenstandstheorie* of Meinong, he had no intention of abandoning his first love, the study of the phenomena of consciousness. Emancipation from 'psychologism' did not involve desertion of the task of analysing the types of 'intentional experiences': and clear ideas about the *objects* of knowing and thinking were an aid and not a hindrance to his study of what knowing and thinking in essence are.

Especially does he devote himself to the complex problem or cluster of problems of the nature and status of Meaning. For this general and even over-catholic title covers both the 'terms' and 'propositions' (i.e., roughly, the word-meanings and sentence-meanings) with which logic has to do and the 'ideas' or 'conceptions' and 'judgements' which are the objects of the psychology or Phenomenology of Thought. More, the theory of mathematics necessitates an understanding of what symbols and symbol-meanings are; metaphysics must have or give an account of the sort of being possessed by 'concepts', 'facts', and 'propositions' (or Meinong's 'objectives'); the philosophy of language and of grammar pivot on the idea of 'expression', and these are all problems of 'Meaning'. And lastly the characterisation of all conscious acts as 'intentional experiences', i.e. experiences in the essence of which it is that they are *of* something other than themselves, soon led to the adoption of the noun 'Meaning' to denote the 'intentional object' of a psychic act, and of the verb 'to mean' to denote the intending of its immanent object by such an act.

It is, then, in the first instance the Phenomenology of those psychic acts that have *logical* Meanings, i.e. of acts of thinking, that Husserl prosecutes; but concurrently he is developing the general theory of Phenomenology and the general theory of its subject-matter, the intentionality or meaningfulness of consciousness in general. And this general theory we may now sketch. Phenomenology is for Husserl the science of the 'phenomena of consciousness' (a phrase of Brentano's which Husserl for good reasons came to relinquish) or of 'intentional experiences'. But it is not a 'matter-of-fact' science: it does not deal with actual instances, in the sense that it first records and explores these and then makes inductive generalisations from them. Rather it is a science of Essences; it is the science of the character that any experience must have to be a case of doubting (say) or questioning or fancying or inferring. Its subject-matter is the type or type-structure of intentional experiences as discerned *intuitively* in some real or imaginary exemplary instance. In a word its subject-matter is Essences and not individuals and its method is by 'exemplary intuition': so that it stands to empirical psychology as geometry stands to geography.[1]

That there *are* Essences and that we can know them has been already established in the more purely logical parts of the *Logische Untersuchungen*.

Now as Phenomenology is the 'eidetic' science of intentional experiences, as such, it covers with its net in a certain sense *everything*. For whatever in any sense *is*, be it an existent or a subsistent, a fancy, a relation, the number 7, a hope, a piece of nonsense, the Equator, etc.; in a word, anything that could conceivably be named or thought about is potentially *for* me; i.e., it is potentially the objective correlate or intentional object of some or other act of my consciousness. I may know it or wonder about it or entertain it or be angry with it and so on, and it is therefore actually or potentially the 'accusative' (I borrow the metaphor from grammar, as we have no separate rendering for '*Gegenstand*' as opposed to '*Objekt*') of an intentional experience. And the sort of intentionality that makes my *Erlebnis* what it is, is in its specific detail as in its generic structure something the analyis of which belongs to Phenomenology. This leads to important and (I think) dangerous consequences; for the science of Phenomenology is given a primacy over all other sciences, and it, itself presupposition-less, is supposed to be sovereign over presuppositions which all other sciences must make.

For already in his *Logische Untersuchungen* Husserl, on the basis of what I regard as a serious error in his theory of Meaning (derived, I suspect, from Brentano's founding of Judgement and Knowledge in *Vorstellung*), had erected a theory of knowledge or self-evident judgement according to which such objects of knowledge as are not experiences 'enjoyed' by the knower of them are tissues of Meanings,

---

[1] A good statement in English of what are in fact the subject-matter, method and relations with empirical psychology of Phenomenology is given—of course unwittingly —by Cook Wilson, *Statement and Inference*, vol. I, p. 328, and the last sentence of §119 on p. 277. And his analyses, e.g., of Opinion, Conviction, and Belief are admirable applications of the 'Phenomenological Method'.

which Meanings are the *gift* of consciousness; so that consciousness is *constitutive* of all objects that are (or pretend to be) transcendent. This culminates in a doctrine explicitly formulated in his 'Ideen zu einer reinen Phänomenologie', which reminds us strongly of Kant or Green, that 'pure consciousness' is the only self-subsistent reality and the absolute *prius*. And he speaks accordingly of all objects of psychic acts, *including all objects of knowledge*, as 'correlates of consciousness'—things the being of which is to be 'accusative' to actual or possible intentional experiences.

There is thus a progressive trend visible in the philosophy of Husserl and his followers towards a rarefied Subjective Idealism or even Solipsism, a trend which, in my view, is not necessitated by the idea of Phenomenology, which I regard as good, but only by a particular elaboration of a part of a special theory of Meaning which is, if I am not mistaken, an evil legacy from the Locke–Brentano hypothesis of the existence of 'ideas'—certain mental entities out of which knowledge is somehow composed, though they are neither the objects known nor yet our acts of getting-to-know, but representatives between the former and the latter.

This very sketchy account of a few of the threads in the philosophy of Husserl—I can give here no exposition of the many other elements in it which I believe to be of really notable importance—must serve as a preface to Heidegger.

Heidegger's only previous published book was a little work on Duns Scotus whose doctrine of the Categories, Intentionality, and Meaning he expounds clearly, comparing them *en route* with kindred views of Husserl.

In *Sein und Zeit* however, he breaks new ground and in some 440 large pages he builds up what he himself only claims to be the threshold to the solution of a problem vastly more profound and radical than any that Husserl has yet formulated. Moreover, in the course of the book Heidegger sets himself to the construction of a new philosophical terminology, especially designed to denote unambiguously the basic categories of Meaning which he is trying to explicate.

Phenomenology must be presupposition-less; that is to say, phenomenological interpretations or analyses must take for granted no theories or observations made in a state of (phenomenological) naïveté. This is common ground. But in fact—so Heidegger thinks—previous phenomenologists had failed to disembarrass themselves of a weighty inheritance of presuppositions, the presence of which either cramps or vitiates their results. For instance, the historical genesis of Phenomenology from psychology, the survival in that psychology of the simple Mind-Matter dualism of Descartes, as well as the 'chemical' theory of atomic ideas, states, and dispositions, the universal domination of Platonic and Aristotelian categories over all contemporary philosophical and psychological thinking, have stood in the way of the strict application of the phenomenological method; with the issue that even the most radical of its exponents have been tackling, with tools that were not their own, objects that they could only see with a squint.

It is no longer, or rather it is not yet, the time for Phenomenology to analyse the types of psychic acts and their interconnexions, to examine the relation of 'act' to 'content' and of these to 'real physical things' and 'the world'; for the original isolation of such things as types, psychic acts, act-contents, physical things and the world, was one inherited from naïve predecessors and not *found* by Phenomenology.

The most fundamental presuppositions are ontological presuppositions; and it is to this field that Phenomenology must go, deliberately postponing the study of the twigs until it has completed its examination of the root. And the root is Being (*Sein*). The root problem of Phenomenology is the Meaning of Being—not in the sense that a *definition* is sought for it, for that would be a nonsensical demand, but that an insight of a new—phenomenological—sort is wanted, in possessing which we shall know 'with a difference' something which, of course, we must understand or know 'in a way' already. And by 'Being' is meant not this or that entity of which we can say that it is or that it is something, but the universal which these exemplify.

Now Husserl, though he reached the point of saying that *Sein* is nothing else than the Correlate of *Bewusstsein*, i.e., Being is just what Consciousness has as its 'accusative', had never quite emancipated himself from the Cartesian point of view that Consciousness and Being are *vis-à-vis* to one another in such a way that in studying Consciousness we are studying something on the outside of which and transcending which lies a region of absolute Reality.

And in this frame of mind he could *separate* the spheres of Phenomenology and Ontology by saying that the former is the science of Consciousness, the latter the science of—something else.

But Heidegger is critical of this naïve assumption; and Phenomenology must, he urges, so far from accepting the alleged cleavage between Consciousness and Being, select as its first task of all the analysis and description of that most primitive level of Experience in which is generated *for us* that seeming polar opposition. Our attitude of regarding Being as the opposite of Consciousness is itself one of the intentional experiences, and perhaps the most important of the intentional experiences that Phenomenology must examine.

In this way Heidegger turns the tables on the objection that a more orthodox phenomenologist would be certain to raise, namely, that Phenomenology, being by definition the science of consciousness, can only take Being into its province on the illegitimate assumption that Being is an *Erlebnis* or a component of an *Erlebnis*.

Next, as well the Husserlian as the Kantian or Cartesian accounts of Thought or Consciousness are stated in terms of the ontological categories of Plato and Aristotle. But as these categories were distilled out of a natural and naïve (i.e., pre-phenomenological) attitude towards the world and ourselves, they must be not indeed rejected but put, so to speak, in inverted commas; they must be accounted for with the naïve attitude from which they sprang. They cannot supply the terms in which we are to unpack the Meanings for which we are looking, for they are at least under suspicion of being metaphorical. Phenomenology is Hermeneutic and the categories which are the untested framework of our everyday world are among its primary *interpretanda*.

As a practical consequence of this view Heidegger imposes on himself the hard task of coining, and on us the alarming task of understanding, a complete new vocabulary of terms—mostly many-barrelled compounds of everyday 'nursery' words and phrases —made to denote roots and stems of Meaning more primitive than those in which Plato, Aristotle, and subsequent scientists and philosophers have so taught us to talk and think, that we, by the strong force of habit, have come to regard as ultimate and pivotal ideas which are in fact composite and derivative. Heidegger's ontological Phenomenology is to turn our eyes back again to contemplate with a new method and a new clarity the springs of Meaning from which flow our most familiar and most 'homely' conceptions and classifications. The principle on which he seems to be designing his new terminology is, I should judge, the hypothesis that certain 'nursery' words and phrases have a primitiveness and freedom from sophistication which makes them more nearly adequate expressions of really primitive Meanings than the technical terms which science and philosophy in the course of a long development have established.

The hypothesis seems to me a perilous one, for it is at least arguable that it is here, and not in the language of the village and the nursery, that mankind has made a partial escape from metaphor.

In *Sein und Zeit* Heidegger does not make the assault upon his final objective; he opens the campaign with a preliminary occupation of a terrain that is nearer home. Indeed it is of the essence of his starting-point that it is as near home as possible, for, before trying to interpret what is the Being which any entity as such has, he tries to examine what sort of Being *we* have who are making the examination.

Like Brentano and Husserl he goes back to Descartes's 'Cogito ergo sum' and enquires more deeply than Descartes could do not merely what is a 'cogitatio' or what can be done by or what can happen to a 'res cogitans', but what the 'I' is and must be for such actions and passions to be possible. The threshold to the Hermeneutic of 'Esse' is the Hermeneutic of 'Sum'; and if he can find out what it ultimately is to be an experiencer having experiences, a door, perhaps the only door, will be open for the next search after the innermost Meaning of Being.

The title that Heidegger appropriates for an 'I' who thinks and in particular is asking the questions, using the methods, and appreciating the answers that I am now doing, is '*Dasein*' (one of numerous loans from established *philosophical* terminology which, however necessary, are certainly confusing). The business, then, of the present work is the 'Hermeneutic' or 'Analytic' of '*Dasein*'; and as my being is not a timeless subsistence but a being-myself through a continuum of 'nows', the special problem of the work as indicated in the title is to analyse the intrinsic *temporality* of my being.

Perhaps also Heidegger's interest in the way in which time enters into conscious experience was stimulated by some lectures that Husserl was giving, in 1905 and later, on the inward experience of time. These have just been edited and published by Heidegger.

Now the most fundamental and 'primitive' moment of a '*Dasein*'s' being is 'being-in-the-world'—being in it not as a chair is in a room or a cow in a field but as having it or being through and through occupied with it and by it. The world that I am in in this sense is all that it means to me; it is what makes me an experiencer of experiences. 'Being-in-the-world' for a '*Dasein*' is just the tissue of its attitudes, interests, and utilisations. In a word, the world that I am 'in' is simply the sum of what I am *about*. The distinction between theory and practice, or thought and will, between thinking-about and doing-about is derivative from the primitive mode of a '*Dasein*'s' being— namely 'being-about . . .' (*besorgen*). Nor is it a mere chance attribute of a '*Dasein*' that it has this character of 'being-about . . .'. Rather it is the essence of its being what it is, to 'be about . . .'. And so, as the world, namely what I am about, belongs intrinsically to what I am, the pretended Subject-Object dualism is a pure fiction imported from the naturalistic attempt to see the relation between me and my world as akin to a relation between one fragment and another fragment of my world.

One of the derivative ways of 'being-about . . .' is 'thinking-about . . .': and of this one of the derivative modes is knowing; and that this is derivative and not primitive is shown by the fact that before knowing I must 'wonder about . . .' and before 'wondering about . . .' I must be 'interested in . . .' or 'concerned about . . .' which in the end turns out to be close to the most primitive mode of 'being-about . . .' and also of 'being-an-I' that there is.

Now while everything that I am-in-the-world-with has the character of being something that I am-about, this is not yet enough to characterise what we ordinarily term 'Things'. The Meaning of 'Thing' is not primitive but derived, and before the world that I 'have' is stocked with 'Things' it is stocked with *instruments* or *tools,* i.e. what I can 'work-*with*' in the performance of some task for some end. Later comes the conception of a 'Thing', namely what can't or needn't be worked with: the conception of 'Thing' is derived from the conceptions of 'unemployed' and 'instrument': so the mode of 'being-about . . .' which is *using* is primitive to the modes of 'being-about' which are knowing, classifying, and naming 'Things'.

(I may here interject that Heidegger seems to be confusing what is anthropologically primitive with what is logically primitive. It is perhaps a fact of human nature that I begin by being interested in things for what I can or can't do with them and only later do I want to know as a scientist what they are. But the former attitude involves equally with the latter the knowledge of things as having attributes and relations, though in infancy I restrict my interest to a few of those attributes and relations, namely those which bear on my business.

(I must leave till later my further and fundamental objection that all these so-called 'primitive' attitudes or ways of 'being-an-I' really involve *knowledge*, which knowledge necessitates universals and categories upon which the Analysis of *Dasein* throws—and can throw—no light at all.)

It is important to note that, in all the ways of being-about, being-in, being-with, and being-without that characterise a '*Dasein*', the *Dasein* has some sort of *understanding of* what it is being or doing. Not that it has scientific, 'thematic' *knowledge*—for this is a late product—but the moods, tenses, and inflections of its being-itself are 'illuminated' or 'transparent' to itself. If it were not so the Analysis of *Dasein* would have no self-evidence, and so would not be the proper approach to our ultimate problem.

The spatiality of the world is derived from such primitive attitudes as having-to-hand-convenient-for-using or not-having-to-hand; but apart from mentioning the similarity of Heidegger's treatment of Space and later of Time with that of Bergson and some anthropologistic pragmatists, I must pass quickly over this and several other important sections in which the constituents and structure of the world we 'have' are derived or analysed.

What in the end *is* a *Dasein*? What does 'sum' in 'Cogito ergo sum' ultimately denote? Behind the question 'What are the root types of my behaviour, my attitudes, my actions, and my passions?' lies the question 'What is it to *be* an I (*Dasein*)?

The answer rings at first strangely. 'Dasein ist Sorge.' What I am is Concern or Care (*cura*). Willing, wishing, wondering, reflecting, knowing, doing, with their 'accusatives', all are ways of 'caring' or 'caring about' or 'caring for'.

Heidegger tells us that he came to this conception of Care as the absolutely primitive Being that an 'I' as such has, through studying the Augustinian and other Christian philosophies of human nature; but I surmise, too, that there are legacies in it of the characterisation by Brentano and Husserl of Consciousness as what has intentionality. For by 'Care' Heidegger does not mean any particular emotion of fearing, or being anxious, or wishing, or any particular act of striving, or any particular inclination or impulse, but the primitive sort of being in which all such emotions and acts and states are founded; for they are all particular ways of 'caring'.

Next (what bears on the special problem of the *temporal* nature of an 'I'), what I am is not exhausted by what I have done and become up to date; rather it is of the essence of my being what I am that there are potentialities in me; I *can* be what I am not yet; and what I can be belongs just as intrinsically to my being as what I am already, i.e. that of my being which I have already realised. Care is accordingly as essentially care about what I might be as care about what I already am. This leads to an analysis of what my Being as a *whole* is, i.e. the whole structure of which what I am up to date and what I might be are integral moments. Now one of the characteristics of my whole being is that *qua* Life it terminates in Death—*terminates* in Death without finding its *completion* in it. So we have to investigate what sort of a whole it is which has both termination in Death and a completion (never fully realised) in being all that it has the potentiality of being. In this whole belong conscience—the certainty of what I might be—and the sense of sin or guilt—the certainty that I am not what I might have been. (Here Heidegger is reviving important Augustinian theses which lead one to wonder if the second part of this work will not be a sort of Eckhart philosophy in phenomenological clothing.)

But here, for the reviewer at any rate, the fog becomes too thick; and the results of the analyses of our intrinsic temporality, of the several concepts of time, historical becoming, history, and the criticisms of the theories of Dilthey and Hegel must go unexpounded.

A word about the *method* of Phenomenology. It is its boast that it does not make and does not presuppose 'logical constructions' or 'theories' or 'systems'. 'Phenomenology makes no hypotheses.' It does not move by making deductions from axioms or inductions from observed and recorded facts. Its method is that of 'exemplary intuition', i.e. the inspection of individual examples *qua* exemplifications of Essences or Types—this of course in the region of consciousness. We intuit in this or that feeling of anger, act of choice or imagination, that essential character lacking which the particular examined would be something other than a case of being angry, choosing, or imagining.

So here Heidegger claims simply to be revealing, unpacking or interpreting the essence of what we do and are. Accordingly, his sentences, which on first reading seem to be mere dogmatic assertions, have to be read as expressions of a Hermeneutic analysis to understand which is to see that it is true. He is simply telling us explicitly what we must have known 'in our bones' all the time. Similarly, e.g., Cook Wilson does not tell us anything *new* about Conception, Opinion, or Belief; he is telling us something which we, when told, recognise that we knew implicitly from the start.

The dangers lie in the undue extension of this method; if, for instance, our interpreter has, without realising it, a theory of knowledge, or a metaphysical system, he may easily come to interpolate into the interpretations that he gives something that could never have been intuited in the exemplary instance he is examining— since, even if it be true, yet it was never in the Essence of that example. Or else, under the same influence, he may omit to notice an integral element in that Essence. Thus I suspect that certain theories of human nature have been interpolated into Heidegger's analyses of it; and on the other side the basic place of knowing in being-in-the-world or in any experiencing of a Meaning has been forgotten.

And so an anthropologistic Metaphysic seems to have been read out of our everyday experience, of which both the positive element of Humanism and the negative sceptical element of Relativism and Solipsism appear to be derived from views interpolated into and not won by the Phenomenological Method.

It remains to make a few tentative comments and criticisms upon the general idea, and especially the method, of this approach to the Hermeneutic of Being via the Hermeneutic of 'being-an-I' ('*Dasein*').

(1) In the first place it is taken for self-evident that some sort of *understanding* what I do and am belongs essentially to my doing what I do and being what I am. This doctrine is, I suppose, the same as that of Brentano and Husserl that in 'inner' or 'immanent perception' I have a source of self-evident positive judgements and that I have no other such source; so that any degree of '*Evidenz*' in any positive judgement that I make must either be or be grounded in the self-evidence of 'inner perception'. But while there is no objection to the thesis that I can know my own experiences and the 'I' who has them, the assertion that this is all that I can know, or that if I can know anything else I can only know it if I first know my experiences and my 'I', is far from self-evident; indeed it seems to me to contradict itself. At any rate it presupposes a theory of knowledge and a metaphysic, and so a Phenomenology based on this theory is not presuppositionless. However it might still be the case that the analysis of what it is to be 'an I' and to experience my experiences was the best, though not the only, approach to the ultimate analysis of what Being as such is. 'I' might be the most accessible or the most transparent example of Being.

(2) Some would quarrel with the original assumption that there *is* a problem about the Meaning of Being. But as the (perhaps departmental) question of the relation between Being *qua* timeless 'subsistence' and existing *qua* existing in the world of time and space seems to me a real one, I do not take up this cudgel.

(3) But there is what I regard as a vital ambiguity present in that expanded theory of Phenomenology which makes it the logical '*prius*' of not only psychology but logic, metaphysics, and the mathematical and natural sciences. Accepting Brentano's improvement on the Locke-Hume theory of 'ideas' according to which the distinction was made between the act and the content (or immanent object) of a *Vorstellung*, the phenomenologists have very properly generalised the principle and find in every phenomenon of consciousness, i.e. in every intentional act or experience an act side and a

content or Meaning side. Then, looking at the world, they see that every thing or event, every relation or universal, every conceivable 'It' can be regarded as the objective correlate or content to an appropriate act of consciousness—knowing perhaps, or surmising, or being vexed at, or wanting, or being interested in.

And as it is the proper business of phenomenology to analyse states and acts of consciousness, everything is in this way drawn into its net; for anything and everything is or has a Meaning-for-me, and the meaning of the act or acts in which it has its Meaning-for-me is the proper subject matter of the science of intentionality.

But while it is a dangerous metaphor to speak of acts having 'meanings' or of things as being the 'meanings of acts', it is a fatal error to speak of a thing known as the correlate of a knowing-act as if that implied that we could get to the heart of the thing by analysing our experience of knowing it. A twin is a correlate to a twin but operations upon the one are at most operations upon the other one's twin, not operations upon the other one himself.

And this leads to dangerous results in the practice of the phenomenological method; it leads to them here in *Sein und Zeit*. For the presence of *knowledge* of some reality (which is surely present in any and every conscious experience) though it is not explicitly recognised is surreptitiously imported as well into such terms as 'understanding' and 'illumination' as into the countless nursery-terms which Heidegger is trying to build up into a new philosophical vocabulary.

For instance, the general characterisation of our conscious being as a 'being-in-the-world' surely implies that *underlying* our other reactions and attitudes there is *knowledge*. We 'have' or are 'in-the-world' only if we know that at least one 'something' exists. Similarly the attempt to derive our knowledge of 'things' from our practical attitude towards tools breaks down; for to use a tool involves knowledge of what it is, what can be done with it, and what wants doing.

And if we like to call things that we know 'correlates of acts of knowing', we must at least recognise that the analysis of what those things are is not in the least degree forwarded by an analysis of our acts of knowing them, but only by getting to know still more about the things themselves.

This ambiguity is especially well concealed, equally deeply involved, in the conception of Meaning. The thing which I know and which I signify with such symbols as sentences is in one sense of the word the 'Meaning' of my sentences: but it is not (except *per accidens*) an *Erlebnis* or an act of consciousness; nor is it anything constituted by an act of consciousness. Only in another sense of the word is 'Meaning' something derivative from a state or act of consciousness—namely when it is not the thing symbolised by a symbol but the fact that this symbol symbolises that thing. Certainly a symbol symbolises because we choose that it shall, so its meaning (i.e. meaningfulness) is the product of an act of consciousness, but the origin of the functioning of a symbol is no more the origin of the thing which it is its function to symbolise than the forest in which a sign-post grew is the parental home of the town to which the sign-post points.

And I stress these arguments against the Husserl–Heidegger treatment of Meaning for two connected reasons:

(*a*) I think it can be shown that Husserl's theories of Meaning (*Sinn* and *Bedeutung*) are primarily developments of Brentano's theory of 'ideas' (*Vorstellungen*). A Meaning is, at the start, just the intentional 'accusative' of an act of 'having an idea'; later the term also covers the intentional 'accusatives' of acts of Judging, so that propositions as well as concepts are Meanings. Now (as Representationism always ends in Subjectivism) this theory has in the end to say that the world of things and events *as I apprehend it* must be just a tissue of Meanings, which Meanings must be the contribution of acts of consciousness.

(*b*) I think, too, that it can be shown that the only reason why Heidegger's Hermeneutic of '*Dasein*' takes or promises to take the form of a sort of anthropologistic Metaphysic (smelling a little oddly both of James and of St Augustine) is because Heidegger presupposes that the Meanings which his Hermeneutic is to unravel and illuminate must be in some way man-constituted.

But though I deplore the damage wrought upon his Metaphysics by the presuppositions which Heidegger has unconsciously inherited, I have nothing but admiration for his special undertaking and for such of his achievements in it as I can follow, namely the phenomenological analysis of the root workings of the human soul.

He shows himself to be a thinker of real importance by the immense subtlety and searchingness of his examination of consciousness, by the boldness and originality of his methods and conclusions, and by the unflagging energy with which he tries to think behind the stock categories of orthodox philosophy and psychology.

And I must also say, in his behalf, that while it is my personal opinion that *qua* First Philosophy Phenomenology is at present heading for bankruptcy and disaster and will end either in self-ruinous Subjectivism or in a windy mysticism, I hazard this opinion with humility and with reservations since I am well aware how far I have fallen short of understanding this difficult work.

Sein und Zeit, it is worth mentioning, is most beautifully printed and the pages have generous margins.

13

REVIEW OF MARTIN FARBER:
'THE FOUNDATIONS OF
PHENOMENOLOGY'

Reprinted from 'Philosophy', vol. XXI, *1946, by permission
of the editors*

The major trends of philosophy of the past hundred years in both the
English and the German speaking world have derived directly or
indirectly from recoil against the British school of thought which
began with Locke and culminated in John Stuart Mill. Subsequent
theories of knowledge, perception, deduction, induction, probability,
mathematics and semantics (not to speak of ethics, politics and
political economy) can nearly all be traced back to revolts against the
conclusions and the premisses of this school. In particular Mill's
System of Logic (1843) stimulated (chiefly as an emetic) a galaxy of
original thinkers into reconsideration of the principles of logic,
epistemology and psychology.

The importation into England of the philosophies of Kant, Hegel,
Lotze and Herbart had for its main motive not love of the Teutonic
but nausea for Associationism. Jevons, Pearson and Venn were
similarly moved to relay the foundations of the theory of scientific
method. They with Caird, Green, Bradley, Cook Wilson, Grote,
Sidgwick, Moore and Russell were disunitedly united in the task of
refuting dogmas of the Church of Hume.

In Germany and Austria there were parallel revolts. In Germany
Frege's logical and epistemological theories were Platonic repudia-
tions of the English psychological idealism, as this was mediated
by Erdmann. In Austria Franz Brentano trained his whole school
of philosophical psychologists upon the critical study of Locke,
Berkeley, Hume, the Mills, Bain and Spencer.

Through his pupil Meinong (whose ultra-Platonism he repudiated)
Brentano exercised, at the end of the 19th century, a certain cross-
influence on English thought, particularly that of the early Russell.

He also exercised a powerful influence upon German thought through another pupil, Edmund Husserl, though him too he disinherited both for his ultra-Platonisms and for other later offences. It is with Husserl that we are here primarily concerned.

Brentano made two radical amendments to the '*Denkpsychologie*' of the British Empiricists. (1) Accepting, unfortunately, the dogma that the ultimate elements of thought are 'ideas', and that sense-data, images and concepts can all be classified as species of ideas, Brentano set up two other radically different modes of consciousness, namely judgment and feeling. These are founded in ideas, but are irreducible to ideas or amalgamations of ideas. This generic differentiation of feelings and judgments from ideas facilitated Brentano's rejection of the whole subject-predicate analysis of propositions, and he did in fact hold (*a*) that simple existence-propositions embody only one idea or term; (*b*) that most of the propositions hitherto construed as the ascriptions of predicates to subjects should instead be construed as linguistically veiled conjunctions of existence-propositions with attributive propositions; (*c*) that so-called universal affirmatives are really negative existence-propositions. On several scores, therefore, Brentano found that the grammatical structure of sentences is not an index to the logical structure of the propositions expressed by them. Epistemology and logic needed to discard the leading-strings of ordinary syntax. Both Meinong and Husserl were insufficiently influenced by this part of their master's teaching. (2) More important in his own eyes and in those of his pupils was Brentano's second amendment, namely his doctrine of 'intentionality'. All acts of consciousness, the having of ideas, judging and feeling are intentional (or as we might say 'transitive'). Each is necessarily the sensing, imaging, conceiving, judging and liking (or disliking) *of something*. The objects (or 'accusatives') of acts of consciousness were not supposed by Brentano to be independent reals, but rather 'internal accusatives', the description of which was still the task of philosophical or descriptive psychology. Brentano was not, at this stage at least, any sort of a Realist. None the less the properties of, say, the number 7 are quite other than those of the acts of conceiving it, just as the properties of propositions are quite other than those of the acts of judging them. In particular, numerically and qualitatively different acts on the part of the same thinker or of different thinkers can 'intend' one and the same concept or proposition. The contemporary British mishandlings of the special problem of 'abstract ideas' were due to their proper refusal to ascribe to mental acts the properties which they improperly failed to accept as characters of the intentional objects of those acts, since they failed to acknowledge the presence of these intentional objects.

Meinong took the Realist plunge of converting the internal accusatives of conception, judgment and feeling into Objects. Criticising the abstraction-theories of Locke, Berkeley and Hume on what he took to be Brentano's principles, he hypostatised all the *entia rationis* of which Plato had ever dreamed, as well as many which could never have occurred to him. Not only abstract nouns, but general nouns, all substantival verbal expressions, including descriptive phrases, sentences, optatives and the rest, were construed as being genuine proper names of higher-order entities. For all alike could be embodied in significant sentences as subjects of predication. There must *be* objects named by them, else we could not say true *or* false things about them. Unfortunately for Meinong, though most fortunately for the course of subsequent philosophy, he could not prevent some of his higher-order Objects from infringing the laws of logic. Like his contemporary Frege, who reached a similar position by an independent path, he had to accept as authentic the credentials of certain *entia rationis* which would not pass muster with the law of Excluded Middle.

In short, like Russell in his *Principles of Mathematics,* he swallowed whole the hallowed doctrine of Terms, and accordingly construed as names of genuine Terms all expressions which could stand with grammatical correctness as subjects of verbs. He merely de-psychologised by hypostatising whatever satisfied this inexacting test of what constitutes a term. In him and in general, the logical Objectivism which was rife from 1890 to 1910, was, very roughly, Mill's logic refracted through a Platonic prism.

It is of historical interest to note that at the time that Russell was working out his salvation by his (and Frege's) doctrine of 'incomplete symbols', Brentano and Marty were operating with what was in effect the same weapon. They found that Meinong's grotesque conclusions derived from the assumption that all grammatical nominatives are the names of authentic terms, and are, in the old parlance 'categorematic' or, as they put it 'autosemantic' ex-pressions. Instead, they argued, many such nominatives share at least part of the expressive functions of 'syncategorematic' or 'syn-semantic' expressions. They 'mean' not by denoting objects but by contributing to the expression of integral propositions. They belong to what is left in skeleton-sentences, after names have been struck out of them; or what they signify is part of what is common to formally similar propositions about different Terms.

They belong not to the directories but to the work-sheets of thought.

Husserl began publication as a loyal disciple of Brentano. His first concern was to improve from inside the empiricist psychology of mathematical thinking, which he tried to do by giving an intention-alist but still psychological account of the genesis and manipulation of mathematical ideas. At this stage, though interested in the work of Boole, Schröder and Frege, he was not effectively influenced by it. By 1900 he had seen the light. In the first edition of his *Logische Untersuchungen*, which he wrote with the intention of discovering the true bases of mathematics, his first task was to demolish the principles and procedure of 'psychologism'—meaning by 'psychologism' any theory which reduces the description of what we think to descriptions of the internal processes through which we come to think it. Like Frege and the long-forgotten Bolzano, and considerably influenced by them, he argued against any attempt to subordinate logic and mathematics to empirical psychology. His premisses and many of his results were, not unnaturally, closely similar to those of Meinong, though this similarity neither led to nor derived from any personal sympathies between the two scions of Brentano.

Husserl, like Meinong, resolved, in effect, the old problems of abstraction by denying that abstract ideas were either ideas in the mind or abstractions. They are higher-order entities, non-actual but authentic, subsistent Terms. There *are* numbers, universals, classes, relations and propositions. 'Abstraction' is just a misnomer for our procedures in coming to apprehend them.

Much of the later parts of this edition of the *Logische Untersuchungen* (in my opinion much his best written and best argued book) is devoted not to the classification of his higher-order objects but to the reconstruction of epistemology and '*Denkpsychologie*'. He repudiates 'psychologism' but is still largely if not chiefly interested in applying the consequential reforms to the theory of knowledge. It was, however, the earlier parts of the book which influenced German thought in the first decade of this century. His anti-psychologism and his ultra-Platonism won converts, while his philosophy of mind remained almost unnoticed. (He aroused almost no interest in the English-speaking world at this time. His thunder had been stolen by Meinong and Frege on the Continent, by Moore and Russell at Cambridge, and by Cook Wilson in Oxford. His message was *démodé* before it was heard of.) Husserl's next publications in and after 1913 caused both surprise and disappointment in Germany. He had changed direction once again. Weary, perhaps, of being treated as a partner or disciple of Meinong, or else perhaps half-hankering to come back to the disapproving Brentano's heel, he began to soft-pedal his ultra-Platonism (which he never, I think, disavowed) and returned instead to philosophical psychology, to the philosophical demarcation of the genera and species of acts of consciousness. He ennobled this branch of philosophical enquiry with the quaint title 'Phenomenology'; he credited it with a proprietary method which he calls 'essential' or 'exemplary intuition'; and he claimed for it an absolute logical priority over all other philosophical, scientific, or historical enquiries. These three points all require some elucidation. (1) Brentano had employed the word 'Phenomena', not in its customary disparaging sense, but in a new honorific sense. The acts and processes of consciousness being self-presenting (and not representatively perceived) are realities which necessarily also appear. They cannot be without being inwardly perceived; and the perception of them is incapable of being delusive. So psychology, unlike the physical sciences, starts with hard data or 'phenomena'. Even knowledge of the non-mental has to be mediated by the direct inner perception of the acts and states of their knower's own mind. This is why Husserl calls his philosophy of mind 'Phenomenology'. Its subject-matter coincides with or overlaps that of Descartes, Locke or Kant as well, of course, as with that of empirical psychology. But it differs from both in the sorts of problems it has to solve and especially in the special method it employs for solving them.

(2) Husserl retained enough Platonism to believe that some 'essences' or generic concepts, namely those the instances of which are self-presenting, can be explored by a process of direct inspection. Somewhat as I can study a daisy with my eyes, so I can with my intellect look hard at Memory, Creative Fancy or Contempt. I can detect by non-inferential inspection what it is that their actual or imagined instances exemplify. To do this I must discard pre-suppositions and hypotheses and, what is harder, train myself to look away from what usually interests me and concentrate on what I usually ignore. Namely, I must cease, for the moment, to participate in the world in order to study the various ways-of-participating-in-the-world. Daily life must be put into inverted commas, so that I may become able to consider what constitutes daily life. I must lower my telescope from my eye if I am to look at it.

It follows, as Husserl allows and insists, that different observers of these mental essences both can and should pool their results. There could and should be a central register of the (eidetic) observations made by all properly trained phenomenologists. Their results can only be false or discrepant if instead of recording observations they record the conclusions of theories. There is nothing in Phenomenology to argue.

This point merits some debate. It is common ground to Platonists and non-Platonists that we can first learn and finally know how to think *with* concepts. We can ask intelligent questions, we can intelligently debate answers to them, and in some cases we can decide these questions. Concepts are intelligently used in ordinary thinking. But according to Platonist theories the intelligent employment of concepts presupposes a prior non-judgmatic apprehension of some higher-order entities known as 'universals'. This apprehension would be something like Husserl's 'essential intuition' (his reasons for restricting this eidetic inspection to the generic and specific concepts of mental acts and attitudes need not here be considered).

Yet the moment we are told by Husserl that there is a process of directly contemplating universals we feel a certain scruple. For we know quite well not only that there do not in fact occur any such contemplations but, more, that there is some absurdity in supposing that there should. What is the source of this scruple? For the doctrine is widely regarded as at least respectable which holds that the using of concepts does presuppose the finding of special entities; yet explicit talk about this finding does cause a sense of intellectual embarrassment. Why is it not merely a tasteless metaphor but a flat impropriety to speak of 'peering at Remorse', 'gazing at Induction', 'taking a long look at Choice', or 'happening to light on Conscience'?

If we consider the intelligent use of some of the recognised syncategorematic words (sometimes called 'form-words' or 'logical constants') such as 'if', 'and', 'not', 'exists', 'some', 'all', etc. and ask whether they stand for Terms in the way in which 'Fido' stands for Fido, we have to reply that they do not. Else, among other objections, a sentence of seven words would be just a list of seven things and so not be a sentence. It would not express a proposition. None the less these words are significant, but *not* in the sense that they stand in the 'Fido'–Fido relation to anything. Moreover, their significations can be elucidated by a certain procedure, though this procedure does not consist in acquainting or re-acquainting ourselves with their nominees. For they are not names. The procedure consists in showing, e.g. how 'if'-propositions behave differently from 'because'-propositions; how 'or'-propositions behave differently from 'and'-propositions, and how 'any'-propositions behave differently from 'some'-propositions and from 'Socrates'-propositions. We elucidate their significations by fixing the rules of their uses and not by any operation of gazing at any wearers of labels. The elucidation of 'non-formal' conception-words is performed in the same way, for 'non-formal' concepts, like Conscience and Hope, differ from formal concepts not as flesh differs from bone, but as bodies differ from skeletons, or as partly filled cheques differ from blank cheques. They, too, are abstractions from integral propositions and they embody the logical structures of those propositions. Thought does not begin with a vocabulary and then trick this vocabulary out with a syntax; its vocabulary is syntactical from the start. The intelligent use of concepts in thinking does not, therefore, presuppose a pre-judgmatic finding of entities of which concept-words are names, for concept-words, formal or non-formal, are syncategorematic. It is, therefore, nonsense (as we felt in our bones) to speak of 'intuiting essences'. The proprietary method claimed for Phenomenology is a sham, and Phenomenology, if it moves at all, moves only by the procedures by which all good philosophers have always advanced the elucidation of concepts, including conscious-ness-concepts.

Husserl's practice bears this out. He does often produce acute and sometimes original and illuminating elucidations of such concepts. But he does so not by barely 'constatating'. He argues. Nor does he barely record the constatations of other Phenomenologists. If he mentions them at all, he champions them, and correlates them with the rest of his system.

(3) The large claims made by Husserl for Phenomenology as the one presuppositionless theory underlying all other theories naturally expanded in his later years, when what had been an ambitious methodology burgeoned into a full Cartesian metaphysic. Not merely was the theory of Mind logically prior to all the other branches of theory, but Mind became the source or home of all existence.

I think, but am not sure, that these conclusions issued from the following misreasoning.

(a) Accepting the (to me questionable) axiom of Brentano that acts of consciousness are and alone are self-presenting, it seemed to follow that my knowledge or probable hypotheses about other existences must rest on absolute knowledge of the existence of my mental processes and states. Hence the classification and anatomy of the genera and species of my mental acts is necessary for the proper understanding of my propositions about everything else. The verification of all other propositions entails the self-verification of various sorts of '*cogito*'-propositions and the ways or senses in which other things can be said to exist are pensioners of the self-established existence of my cogitatings. My world is what I think, perceive, imagine, lament, etc., and my thinking, perceiving, imagining, lamenting, etc. are not constituents of that world but its Constitution.

(*b*) Husserl, with other members of Brentano's school, early acquired the hazardous habit of assimilating the (supposedly simple) relations between acts of consciousness and their intentional objects to the (supposedly simple) relations between symbols and what they stand for. Indeed, it was assumed that to explore the signification of our symbols was to explore what are 'intended' by our intentional experiences. So yesterday's headache was described as the 'meaning' of to-day's memory of it. And as it is patent that our symbols mean what they do because we endow them with that function, it seemed to follow that our thinkings, etc. are responsible for their objects. As credits only exist if banks give credit, so the various objects of consciousness, including all higher-order objects, only exist because consciousness gives them their existence and their characters. Since intentionality or 'transitivity' is an internal property of consciousness, not only the having-of-objects but the objects-had are analytically contained in the descriptions of the experiences which have them. Brentano's Revised Version of Locke's theory of 'ideas' has developed into a Revised Version of Mill's.

Mr Farber's *The Foundations of Phenomenology* gives a very useful and thorough account of Husserl's development. Mr Farber is avowedly a loyal disciple of Husserl in all but his final Cartesian Solipsism, and his book is published under the auspices of the International Phenomenological Society. He endorses most of the large claims made by Husserl for his new science, and has made a gallant attempt to paraphrase for Anglo-Saxon readers the whole of Husserl's esoteric terminology. (But he should not render '*Evidenz*' by 'evidence'; only 'self-evidence' carries the intended force.) His well-documented account of Husserl's early interests and affiliations is of considerable historical interest. With a few minor exceptions the 570 odd pages of this book are expository and not critical.

I do not expect that even the corporate zeal of the International Phenomenological Institute will succeed in winning for Husserl's ideas much of a vogue in the English-speaking world. When Husserl inherited in the early years of this century his master's '*Messiasbewusstsein*' he lost what humour he had ever possessed as well as nearly all his original clarity and vigour of style. Dazzled by the independence and originality of his own new system, he ceased to take cognisance of the views or problems of any other philosophers. Deaf to the language of others, he found that the appropriate expressions for his own discoveries required an independent mint, and he accordingly coined a vast jargon of his own which subserves, apparently, the ends neither of brevity nor of perspicuity.

Had his writings and teachings consisted even largely of his positive analyses of psychological concepts, a good deal of value would have been got from them. For despite his erroneous conviction that his method was novel, many of his particular results are fresh. But instead, the great bulk of his labours was devoted to the profitless tasks of promising epoch-making results and of demarcating the sub-faculties of his new science. The drafting of constitutions for future research organisations does not stimulate those who have yet to be satisfied that the promised organisations have any function. We should have been better satisfied with bigger slices of pudding and fewer pots and pans.

In short, Phenomenology was, from its birth, a bore. Its over-solemnity of manner more than its equivocal lineage will secure that its lofty claims are ignored.

On the other hand there is now a vogue in Germany and, oddly, in France an offshoot of Phenomenology, known as 'Existentialism', which may well be smuggled overseas in someone's warming-pan. For it is a part of culture to believe that all culture comes from Paris, so Martin Heidegger's graft upon his former master's stock is not unlikely before long to be adorning Anglo-Saxon gardens.

Apparently what has happened is this (I do not vouch for the whole story): Husserl had, like Aristotle, discerned several different senses of the verbs 'to be' and 'exist'. Unlike Aristotle he correlated these differences with differences between the various moods and inflections of consciousness. The *radical* sense of 'exist' is that recorded in the slogan *Cogito ergo sum*. The most primitive and basic mode of consciousness is 'the having of ideas' (*Vorstellung*). All other modes of consciousness are founded in the having of ideas. Heidegger retained the intentionality dogma, but rejected, perhaps as over-intellectualistic, the axiom that consciousness first realises itself in the having of ideas. Feelings, for example, are at least as directly constitutive of my world as are ideas or concepts, and the latter are not presupposed in the former.

None the less he continued to speak of the 'meanings' of acts of consciousness and to equate my world with the conglomeration of these meanings (although in the beginning this incautious ascription of 'meanings' to acts of consciousness had been just an elaboration of the Lockean theory of ideas).

I *think* Heidegger or members of his school hold that ideas and judgments, so far from underlying feelings and volitions, are supervenient constructions or efflorescences of them. Not, therefore, 'in the beginning was the Word' but 'in the beginning was the cry'.

The Existentialists also (again, I *think*) adhere to the proprietary intuitions of Husserl, oblivious of the fact that the case for their existing rested upon a Platonised reconstruction of Mill's doctrine of Idea-Terms. At least the language of some of the members of the school has the Eleusinian ring of intuitionism. It is not made forensic by argument. Part of the popularity of the new creed is doubtless due to its momentary congeniality to the territories of despair. Lack of hope tends to result in the multiplication of faiths, so lands west of the North Sea may also be ripe for similar evangelisation.

14

DISCUSSION OF RUDOLF CARNAP: 'MEANING AND NECESSITY'

Reprinted from 'Philosophy', vol. XXIV, *1949, by permission of the editors*

Professor Carnap in his new book proffers a method for analysing and describing the meanings of expressions and, more briefly, discusses the theory of logical modalities, the concepts, that is, of logical necessity and possibility. His meaning-analysis is in the main intended as an improvement upon certain doctrines and practices of Frege. His account of the modal concepts of logic is in the main intended as an improvement upon certain doctrines of C. I. Lewis. Views of Quine, Russell, Tarski, Church and others are also discussed.

Students of Carnap's other writings will notice with interest that he has now swung still further from the extreme nominalism of his earlier years. Inverted commas are no longer his panacea, and he now makes alarming requisitions upon philosophy's stock of extra-linguistic entities. Indeed, he seems to need at least as many as Meinong needed, and for almost the same bad reasons. A more reassuring trend is his growing willingness to present his views in quite generous rations of English prose. He still likes to construct artificial 'languages' (which are not languages but codes), and he still interlards his formulae with unhandy because, for English speakers, unsayable Gothic letters. But the expository importance of these encoded formulae seems to be dwindling. Indeed I cannot satisfy myself that they have more than a ritual value. They do not function as a sieve against vagueness, ambiguity or sheer confusion, and they are not used for the abbreviation or formalization of proofs. Calculi without calculations seem to be gratuitous algebra. Nor, where explicitness is the desideratum, is shorthand a good substitute.

The only comment that I shall make upon his account of modal concepts is that he says nothing about most of our ordinary ways of using words like 'may', 'must', 'cannot', 'possible' and 'necessary'.

He discusses the 'mays', 'musts' and 'need nots' of logic, but not those of legislation, technology, games, etiquette, ethics, grammar or pedagogy. Above all, he says nothing about laws of nature or the concepts of natural necessity, possibility or impossibility.

The bulk of the book is concerned with what Carnap calls 'meaning-analysis', i.e. with the elucidation of the concept of 'the meaning of an expression' or of 'what the expression "so and so" means'. This elucidation diverges slightly from that of Frege. Carnap is solicitous not to seem to be accusing Frege of error; his views had led to inconveniences, from which Carnap hopes that his alternative account is exempt. I shall be less solicitous and shall argue that both Frege's and Carnap's theories are either erroneous or worse.

Frege, like Russell, had inherited (directly, perhaps, from Mill) the traditional belief that to ask What does the expression 'E' mean? is to ask To what does 'E' stand in the relation in which 'Fido' stands to Fido? The significance of any expression is the thing, process, person or entity of which the expression is the proper name. This, to us, grotesque theory derives partly, presumably, from the comfortable fact that proper names are visible or audible things and are ordinarily attached in an indirect but familiar way to visible, audible and tangible things like dogs, rivers, babies, battles and constellations. This is then adopted as the model after which to describe the significance of expressions which are not proper names, and the habit is formed of treating the verb 'to signify' and the phrase 'to have a meaning' as analogous relation-stating expressions. 'What that expression means' is then construed as the description of some extra-linguistic correlate to the expression, like the dog that answers to the name 'Fido'. (Similar reasoning might coax people into believing that since 'he took a stick' asserts a relation between him and the stick, so 'he took a walk', 'a nap', 'a job', 'a liking', 'the opportunity' or 'time' asserts a relation between him and a funny entity.)

Now a very little reflection should satisfy us that the assimilation to proper names of expressions that are not proper names breaks down from the start. (Indeed the whole point of classing some expressions as proper names is to distinguish them from the others.) No one ever asks What is the meaning of 'Robinson Crusoe'?, much less Who is the meaning of 'Robinson Crusoe'? No one ever confesses that he cannot understand or has misunderstood the name 'Charles Dickens' or asks for it to be translated, defined, paraphrased or elucidated. We do not expect dictionaries to tell us who is called by what names. We do not say that the river Mississippi is so and so *ex vi termini*. A man may be described as 'the person called "Robin Hood"', but not as 'the meaning of "Robin Hood"'. It would be absurd to say 'the meaning of "Robin Hood" met the meaning of "Friar Tuck"'. Indeed, to put it generally, it is always nonsense to say of any thing, process or entity 'that is a meaning'. Indeed, in certain contexts we are inclined not to call proper names 'words' at all. We do not complain that the dictionary omits a lot of English words just because it omits the names of people, rivers, mountains and novels, and if someone boasts of knowing two dozen words of Russian and gives the names of that number of Russian towns, newspapers, films and generals, we think that he is cheating. Does 'Nijni Novgorod is in Russia' contain three, four or five English words?

There are indeed some important parallels between our ways of using proper names in sentences and our ways of using some, but not many, sorts of other expressions. 'Who knocked?' can be answered as well by 'Mr Smith' as by 'the landlord'; and in 'the noise was made by Fido', 'the noise was made by the neighbour's retriever' and 'the noise was made by him' the proper name, the substantival phrase and the pronoun play similar grammatical roles. But this no more shows that substantival phrases and pronouns are crypto-proper names than they show that proper names are crypto-pronouns or crypto-substantival phrases.

Two exceptions to the 'Fido'-Fido principle were conceded by its devotees.

(1) Frege saw that the phrases 'the evening star' and 'the morning star' do not have the same sense (*Sinn*), even if they happen to apply to or denote (*bedeuten*) the same planet. An astronomical ignoramus might understand the two phrases while wondering whether they are mentions of two planets or of only one. The phrase 'the first American pope' does not apply to anyone, but a person who says so shows thereby that he understands the expression. This concession seems to have been thought to be only a tiresome though necessary amendment to the 'Fido'-Fido principle. In fact it demolishes it altogether. For it shows that even in the case of that relatively small class of isolable expressions, other than proper names, which are suited to function as the nominatives of certain seeded subject-predicate sentences, knowing what the expressions mean does not entail having met any appropriate Fidos or even knowing that any such Fidos exist. The things ('entities'), if any, to which such expressions apply are not and are not parts of what the expressions

mean, any more than a nail is or is part of how a hammer is used.

(2) The traditional doctrine of terms had required (confusedly enough) the analysis of proposition-expressing sentences into two, or, with heart searchings, three or more 'terms'; and these terms were (erroneously) supposed all to be correlated with entities in the 'Fido'-Fido way. But sentences are not just lists like 'Socrates, Plato, Aristotle', or even like 'Socrates, mortality'. For they tell truths or falsehoods, which lists do not do. A sentence must include some expressions which are not terms, i.e. 'syncategorematic words' like 'is', 'if', 'not', 'and', 'all', 'some', 'a', and so on. Such words are not meaningless, though they are not names, as all categorematic words were (erroneously) supposed to be. They are required for the construction of sentences. (Sometimes special grammatical constructions enable us to dispense with syncategorematic words.) Syncategorematic words were accordingly seen to be in a certain way auxiliary, somewhat like rivets which have no jobs unless there are girders to be riveted. I have not finished saying anything if I merely utter the word 'if' or 'is'. They are syntactically incomplete unless properly collocated with suitable expressions of other sorts. In contrast with them it was erroneously assumed that categorematic words are non-auxiliary or are syntactically complete without collocations with other syncategorematic or categorematic expressions, as though I have finished saying something when I say 'Fido', 'he', 'the first American pope' or 'jocular'. Russell's doctrine of incomplete symbols was a half-fledged attempt to re-allocate certain expressions from the categorematic to the syncategorematic family. It was half-fledged because it still assumed that there were or ought to be some syntactically complete categorematic expressions, some 'logically proper names' which would brook being said *sans phrase*. To call an expression 'incomplete' was erroneously supposed to be saying that it did not function like a name, as if the standard of completeness were set by names and not by sentences; in fact it is saying that it is only a fragment of a range of possible sentences. So ordinary proper names are (save perhaps in some of their vocative uses) as incomplete as any other sentence-fragments.

Frege had, in consistency, to apply his modified 'Fido'-Fido principle to expressions of all sorts, save those which are patently syncategorematic. So he had to say, for example, that a full indicative sentence both names an entity and has a sense (*Sinn*). Its sense is what is sometimes called a 'proposition'; its nominee is a queer contraption which he calls a 'truth value'. To use Mill's language (from which, perhaps, Frege's *Bedeutung* and *Sinn* were adapted), an indicative sentence denotes a truth value and connotes a proposition (or *Gedanke*, as Frege calls it).

Carnap diverges slightly from the 'Fido'-Fido principle—or rather he thinks he diverges from it. (But his divergence is not due to recognition of any of the difficulties that I have adduced above.) Instead of speaking of expressions as 'names', he gives them the intimidating title 'designators'. (He likes to coin words ending in '... tor'. He speaks of 'descriptors' instead of 'descriptions', 'predicators' instead of 'predicates', 'functors' instead of 'functions', and toys with the project of piling on the agony with 'conceptor', 'abstractor', 'individuator', and so on. But as his two cardinal words 'designator' and 'predicator' are employed with, if possible, even greater ambiguity and vagueness than has traditionally attached to the words 'term' and 'predicate', I hope that future exercises in logical nomenclature will be concentrated less on the terminations than on the offices of our titles.) By a 'designator' Carnap means 'all those expressions to which a semantical analysis of meaning is applied', i.e. 'sentences, *predicators* (i.e. predicate expressions, in a wide sense, including class expressions), *functors* (i.e. expressions for functions in the narrower sense, excluding propositional functions), and individual expressions; other types may be included, if desired (e.g. connectives, both extensional and modal ones). The term "designator" is not meant to imply that these expressions are names of some entities. . .but merely that they have, so to speak, an independent meaning, at least independent to some degree' (*sic*) (p. 6). Thus everything goes to the laundry in the same washing-basket, from '(declarative) sentences', which have 'a meaning of the highest degree of independence', down to 'expressions with no or little independence of meaning ("syncategorematic" in traditional terminology)' (p. 7). It is an inauspicious start, particularly since the notion of independence is not only left perfectly vague but is repeatedly spoken of as something of which there are degrees.

It is, however, clear from his practice, though not from his statement, that 'designator' is generally equivalent to the word 'term' of the (I had hoped, moribund) tradition.

Instead of saying, after Frege, that what a designator means is, in the first instance, that to which it stands as 'Fido' stands to Fido, Carnap says that what a designator means is two things at once, namely the intension that it has and the extension that it has. The intension corresponds with Frege's sense (*Sinn*); the extension is what the designator actually applies to. Knowing the intension of a designator is understanding it; knowing its extension is knowing some facts about both the designator and the furniture of the world, namely that the designator applies to certain bits of that furniture. Carnap says a little, though not enough, about fictitious and non-sensical designators, i.e. those which do not in fact have and those which could not conceivably have extensions. He wrongly says (on p. 202), what, in effect, he rightly denies (on pp. 21 and 30), 'We must realize that every designator has both an intension and an extension.'

As a senseless designator cannot and a fictitious designator does not apply to anything, it is clear that the question whether a designator does apply to anything cannot arise until after we know what, if anything, it means. The things it applies to, if any, cannot there-fore, for this and other reasons, be ingredients in what it means. It should be noticed that we hardly ever know and hardly ever want to know how many things, if any, our designators apply to. We do not have inventories of stars, ripples or jokes; nor do we try to get them. But we can talk sense and follow talk about stars, ripples and jokes. So we are not missing anything we want to know about the uses of expressions if we do not know their extensions (in this sense).

But these supposedly twin notions of 'having an intension' and 'having an extension' need further examination. Carnap professes in his use of them to be merely clarifying a traditional usage. Yet not only have there been several discrepant usages (as Joseph and Keynes showed long ago), but the usage to which Carnap attaches himself belonged to the muddled doctrine of terms, which itself rested on the 'Fido'-Fido principle which he disclaims. I think he actually confuses two nearly disconnected usages when he assimilates the sense in which truth-functions are called 'extensional' while modal functions are called 'intensional', to the sense in which certain nominatives are said to have extensions and intensions. The use of 'extensional' and 'intensional' to mean 'non-modal' and 'modal', derives from the debate about the ambiguity of the word 'all' as meaning sometimes 'every one of the . . .' and sometimes 'any . . .'. No one, I think, ever couched this debate in the dictions of 'denotation' and 'connotation'. On the other hand the debate about the extensions and intensions (i.e. the denotations and connotations) of terms of (some) substantival expressions was not a debate about the ambiguity of a certain syncategorematic word, but, supposedly, about the dual function of all ordinary categorematic words that are used or usable in the subject-place in subject-predicate sentences. The connection between the two debates was, I imagine, this. Some people said that in 'all men are mortal' we are talking about or mentioning some men; others said that we need not be doing this, but only saying that there could not be any immortal men. The former were saying that the sentence was a categorical one, the latter that it was hypothetical. The former were committed to saying that the subject-term of their categorical sentence must, *qua* being a subject-term, name or denote some men. The latter were saying that the protasis of a hypothetical is not asserted for true and that the whole hypothetical could be true even though it was actually false that there existed any men, so no men were named or denoted by any part of the protasis.

The traditional doctrine erroneously took the two premises and the conclusion of any syllogism as isomorphous subject-predicate propositions and, out of deference to Barbara, took such supposedly bi-polar propositions as the standard model of all or of all respectable propositions. All such propositions are, it supposed, analysable into a subject-term coupled by a copula to a predicate-term. And what was predicate-term in one proposition could, with perhaps a little surreptitious re-wording, reappear as subject-term in another.

The subject-term was the name of what the proposition was about; the predicate term named what was affirmed or denied of that subject. Ordinarily the subject-term was supposed to name a particular (or a batch of particulars) and the predicate-term was supposed to name the attribute or property that was asserted or denied to belong to it (or them). Now though the predicate-term of a standard subject-predicate proposition could (it was wrongly thought) move over unmodified to be the subject-term of another proposition, still in the propositions in which it functions predicatively it does not do, what the subject-term does, namely mention the thing or things that the proposition is about. It is, roughly, only in their subject roles that terms are used mentioningly. (And even this does not hold in, for example, the propositions of fiction, where the subject-terms are used only quasi-mentioningly. It does not hold in affirmative or negative existence-propositions. It does not hold in all identity-assertions, or in definitions. And it does not hold in assertions of the pattern 'any S is P'.)

Where the subject-terms of such sentences are used mentioningly, be they names, pronouns, demonstratives or substantival phrases, we could say, if there were any point in doing so, that the things, persons or processes mentioned were the 'extensions' or the 'denotations' of those nominatives; and we could extend this to the things, persons or process mentioned by such other mentioning expressions as might occur in, for example, relational sentences like 'Caesar was killed by his friend Brutus'. But then it would be quite clear that other fragments of sentences such as 'is mortal' or 'was killed by' are not mentioning expressions and have no extensions or denotations in this sense. Nor would entire sentences have extensions or denotations in this sense. It should also be clear that the persons, things or processes so mentioned are not themselves parts of the meanings of the mentioning expressions. It would belong to the meaning of 'his friend Brutus', *that* it was being used to mention just this person, just as it is the present function of this hammer to knock in this nail. But the nail is not part of the present function of the hammer, and Brutus is not part of the use of an expression which mentions him. To understand the reference would be to realize that this was how it was being used. But Brutus could not be a way in which an expression was used.

On this interpretation, only a minority of expressions would have extensions; none of the standard syncategorematic expressions and none of the standard predicate-expressions would do so; no sentences or sub-sentences, and not even the nominatives of all subject-predicate sentences would do so; and even those expressions which are used mentioningly would not have the mentioned persons or things, but only the fact that they were mentioned, as parts of their meanings. In particular it is an error to suppose that predicatively used expressions like 'is omniscient' or 'is the friend of Caesar' can be transferred unaltered to the subject-place. For, for one thing, it is an important grammatical fact that since neither 'is omniscient' nor 'omniscient' can be the subject of a verb, a new nominative has to be constructed such as 'the omniscient being' or 'all omniscient persons'; and this is not equivalent to the predicate '. . . omniscient'. And this grammatical fact reflects a difference of employment; for 'the omniscient being' and 'all omniscient beings' are ordinarily used in the mentioning way, which was not how the predicate had been used. It is a corresponding error to suppose, as Carnap seems to do, that a 'predicator' is being mentioningly used in another way, namely as mentioning a property, e.g. a quality, a state, a relation or a natural kind. The predicate in 'Socrates is mortal' does not mention the property of mortality—we use the noun 'mortality' for that purpose. Adjectives and verbs do not do the same jobs as the abstract nouns that are commonly formed out of them and we have to know how to use adjectives, verbs, etc., for their own jobs before we can learn to use the corresponding abstract nouns for their quite different jobs. Only the sophisticated mention or talk about properties. It is not true, therefore, that predicators jointly mention properties and either the things that have them or (what is quite different) the class of things that have them. The truth is that they do not do either of these things; for they are not mentioningly used expressions.

One of Carnap's major concerns is to resolve the long-standing dispute whether predicate-expressions stand for (or denote) properties or classes. Believers in universals assert the former; believers in classes assert the latter. Carnap's eirenicon is to say that they do both at once. They have classes for their extensions and properties for their intensions. But the dispute was a spurious one. For the predicate-expressions alluded to are not mention-expressions or, more specifically, names, at all. We mention classes by such phrases as 'the class of . . .', and we mention properties by such expressions as 'jocularity'. The adjective 'jocular' is not used and could not grammatically be used to deputize for either. Nor could they deputize for it.

Carnap's way of (nominally) dispensing with the 'Fido'-Fido principle does not release him from the Frege–Meinong embarrassments about sentences. The sentences which he calls 'declarative' (which appears to mean what everyone else means by 'indicative'), while not described as names of subsistent truths and falsehoods, are none the less described as having such entities for their intensions. For their extensions they have some mysteries called 'truth values'. For sentences, having been classed as a species of 'designator', have to possess their significance in the ways prescribed generally for designators. And a designator, we are told in another connection (p. 107), 'is regarded as having a close semantical relation not to one but to two entities, namely its extension and its intension, in such a way that a sentence containing the designator may be construed as being about both the one and the other entity'. So though in fact only a minority of sentence-fragments, namely mentioningly used substantival expressions, can be said to have extensions, Carnap has to assimilate the jobs even of sentences to this special job of a species of sentence-fragments. And this is precisely parallel to the Frege–Meinong mistake of treating sentences as names. These theorists assimilated saying to calling; Carnap assimilates saying to mentioning. Yet both mentions and names (which are a species of mention) are ordinarily used only as fragments or sentences. They enable us to say certain sorts of things, but when we have uttered them by themselves we have not yet said anything.

Carnap flounders uneasily over the question How do false sentences mean anything? as anybody must who thinks that 'meaning some-

233

thing' is a relation-expression. He thinks that true sentences have propositions for their intensions, which propositions are cosily exemplified by facts. (I fail to see how a fact can be an example of a true proposition. Could there be several examples of the same true proposition and, if not, what does 'example' mean?) But a false proposition is not thus cosily matched. So Carnap has to say that a proposition is a compound of elements each of which is severally exemplified, though the compound of them is not. A sentence is, therefore, after all, just a list. 'Socrates is stupid' is equivalent to 'Socrates, attribution, stupidity'. Three entities are mentioned in one breath, but no one thing is said. Plato knew better than this, but then he paid some attention to saying.

Carnap generously, if somewhat airily, says that readers who are discontented with his account of the meanings of entire sentences need not let it worry them. The rest of his theory of meaning does not hinge on this particular bit of it. But surely, if his method of meaning-analysis does not apply to what a sentence means, this shows that there is something wrong with his method. And, worse than this, if the one section in which he tries to discuss saying (as distinct from naming and mentioning) is inadequate or wrong, it would be rash to feel confident in the merits of his account of the meanings of sentence-fragments. If the plot of the drama is bungled, the scenes and acts can hardly be well constructed.

Carnap more than once says that he is not guilty of hypostatization, though he has to find not one but two entities to be the correlates of every designator. The term 'entity' we are requested to take, leaving aside 'the metaphysical connotations associated with it', 'in the simple sense in which it is meant here as a common designation for properties, propositions and other intensions, on the one hand, and for classes, individuals and other extensions, on the other. It seems to me that there is no other suitable term in English with this very wide range' (p. 22). Shades of Meinong! Now by 'hypostatization' we mean treating as names or other sorts of mentions expressions which are not names or other sorts of mentions. And just this is the tenor of the whole of Carnap's meaning-analysis. True, he abjures certain mythological dictions in which some philosophers have talked about their postulated entities. True, too, he sometimes uses hard-headed (but none the less mythological) dictions of his own, as when he says 'the term "property" is to be understood in an objective, physical sense, not in a subjective, mental sense; the same holds for terms like "concept", "intension", etc. The use of these and related terms does not involve a hypostatization' (p. 16); and 'the term "concept" . . . is not to be understood in a mental sense, that is, as referring to a process of imagining, thinking, conceiving, or the like, but rather to something objective that is found in nature and that is expressed in language by a designation of non-sentential form' (p. 21). Whereabouts in nature are we to look for concepts? How are the properties 'Jocularity' and 'Primeness' to be understood in a physical sense?

My chief impression of this book is that it is an astonishing blend of technical sophistication with philosophical naïveté. Its theories belong to the age that waxed with Mill and began to wane soon after the *Principles of Mathematics*. The muddled terminology of extension and intension which belonged to the muddled and obsolete doctrine of terms is disinterred in order to help construct a two-dimensional relational theory of meaning, at a time when it ought to be notorious that relational theories of meaning will not do.

Carnap's influence on philosophers and logicians is very strong. The importance of semantic problems in philosophy and logic cannot be over-estimated. It is because I fear that the solutions of these problems may be impeded by the dissemination of his mistakes that I have reviewed so scoldingly the treatise of a thinker whose views are beginning to be regarded as authoritative.

15

LOGIC AND PROFESSOR ANDERSON

Reprinted from 'The Australasian Journal of Philosophy', vol. XXVIII, *1950, by permission of the editor*

Professor Anderson has, during the last quarter century, exercised a powerful influence on philosophical thought in Australia, and especially in Sydney. But since nearly all his published writings have been articles or reviews in *The Australasian Journal of Psychology and Philosophy*, contemporary European and American philosophers have learned little, if anything, of his views. Nor have their activities, during this quarter century, occasioned any conspicuous reactions in him. None the less there are certain interesting parallels to be found between some of his and some of their ideas, as well as certain equally interesting divergences.

I want to bring out and discuss, I hope provocatively, what I take to be the core of Anderson's philosophy. But I should make it plain from the start that I have only his published writings to go on (and not quite all of them). I know nothing at first hand of his unpublished teachings, and I have next to no idea to what extent he has abandoned or modified opinions expressed in his earlier writings. So I may ascribe to him views which his pupils know to be no longer his, and even treat as his abiding premisses what they know to be discarded errors. All my citations are from his articles, reviews and discussions in *The Australasian Journal of Psychology and Philosophy*. I normally refer to these by title and year.

(1) Anderson has been a consistent and strenuous campaigner against all sorts of philosophers' 'ultimates'. Championing a view which he entitles sometimes 'realism', sometimes 'empiricism', he crusades against various sorts of Idealism, Monism, Dualism and Rationalism. When philosophers postulate proprietary entities, such as the Absolute, subsistent universals, *a priori* principles, necessary truths, internal relations, *ad hoc* Faculties, ideas, sensa and the like, Anderson assails them. He is, in this respect, a fellow-deflationist with Mach and Ostwald, James and Schiller, the New Realists, Moore,

Russell and the Vienna Circle. He bombards some of these when they, in their turn, postulate or argue for factitious entities or principles. There are not any different levels or kinds of existence such that, for example, scientists explore one of them while philosophers explore another. Whatever exists or occurs exists or occurs in space and time. There is nothing other-worldly to describe. There are only brass tacks.

Were I trying to do justice to the whole of Anderson's thinking, I should have to expatiate on his numerous, very cogent, ingenious and original polemical arguments. His shot and shell do great damage to the positions that he is attacking. Platonic Forms, internal relations and twentieth-century sensa, in particular, receive an effective trouncing at his hands. But I am concerning myself not with the fate of inflationist doctrines which have been under fire for so long in both hemispheres, but with one position which is peculiarly Andersonian.

(2) On the other hand, though resembling some of these European thinkers in rejecting the idea that philosophy differs from the sciences in being the science of the other-worldly, he differs from them in refusing to draw a sharp distinction of any other sort between philosophy and science. Indeed, unlike them, he is not much interested in the domestic problem of the role and methods of philosophy. Where we in the northern hemisphere have debated, almost *ad nauseam*, the notions of analytic truths, clarification, philosophical analysis, meta-languages, logical syntax and the rest, Anderson seems content to suggest (surely falsely) that doing good philosophy is doing good science, and doing bad (e.g. metaphysical) philosophy is doing bad science. He says, in a review in 1935, 'This work [of extending the interest in philosophy] requires the rejection of both scepticism and "construction" in favour of *discovery*, and incidentally the removal of any postulated opposition between science and philosophy, which are both concerned with facts'; and, later, 'But the philosophical criticism of science is possible not because philosophy has its own province, "the province of the 'ultimate'", but because philosophy is science and has true statements to make about the very things any special scientist is examining —and he will know these things better, i.e. be a better scientist, if he knows their philosophical features'; and 'Further, what is called "method" is not something different from "findings"; method, which is the same in philosophical as in other science, consists in finding certain relations which things have (e.g. implication) . . .'

(3) The principle from which Anderson derives his *Gleichschaltung* of philosophy with natural science can be seen operating again, and

much more frequently, in his *Gleichschaltung* of ethical statements with scientific statements. Predicates like 'good', 'bad', 'right', 'wrong' and 'virtuous' must not be construed as signifying other-worldly qualities or relations; therefore, they must be construed as signifying ordinary, this-worldly qualities or relations. To say that something is good is to describe a spatio-temporal situation, just as much as to say that something is hot or red. We find out that things are good or bad in just the same ways as we find out that they are hot or red.

(*a*) In a moral judgment, as in any other, something is judged or asserted, i.e. some situation is said to have occurred; . . . [and] statements such as 'This is good' are made, and they must be met or supported in just such ways as would be employed in dealing with the statement 'This is sulphur'. . . . the logic of moral events is the same as that of any other events. ['Determinism and Ethics', 1928.]

(*b*) Extension of knowledge is possible, then, if we view things natura-listically and reject all conceptions of mysterious powers, of ultimates and higher realities. This applies as much to ethics as to any other science. If there is to be any ethical science, then ethical ultimates or powers, moral agencies above the historical facts, must be rejected. If we are to say significantly that ethics deals with goods, we must be able to exhibit goods as going on, as definitely located activities, just as we exhibit moving bodies or growing plants. . . . Ethical theory then is not a policy. It consists of propositions to the effect that such and such things are good and that they work in such and such ways. But, of course, a student of ethics may have a policy . . . . The question for ethics then is to exhibit the working of forces of a specific kind, not to call for approval or support for them. . . . Goods, as social forces, as forms of organization, are engaged in struggle and develop ways of working in that struggle. ['Realism versus Relativism in Ethics', 1933.]

(*c*) Two consistent attitudes can be adopted. One is to deny that good-ness is a quality, to take a purely relational view of it, e.g. that it is the demanded . . . . The other is to take good simply as a quality, to recognize goods as things existing in certain places and going on in certain ways. On this view, though not on the other, there will be a distinct science of ethics, but it too will be a positive or natural science. . . . This means that we can acquire a knowledge of good, in particular, only as something upon which we can act and which can act on us—only as something 'natural', present in our environment. Unless good is one description of certain things, helping us to recognize them just as their being green might do, we can have and communicate no knowledge of it—assuming, that is, that it is not something relational; . . . ['The Meaning of Good', 1942.]

(*d*) We learn about goods, as about other things, by observing them; . . . ['Realism and Some of its Critics', 1930.]

The principle is clear. Ethical predicates are not to stand for any other-worldly qualities or relations; therefore they have to be construed as standing for this-worldly qualities or relations. They signify ordinary, empirically ascertainable properties of things or occurrences or activities. The vocabulary of an encyclopaedia of the natural sciences will contain words like 'good' and 'bad' just as it contains words like 'sulphur', 'red' and 'growing'.

Like, for example, some members and followers of the Vienna Circle, Anderson begins by denying that ethical predicates stand for transcendent properties. But while they drew the consequence that ethical predicates do not stand for qualities or relations at all, but are merely emotive or hortatory expressions, Anderson draws the consequence that they stand for empirically ascertainable qualities or relations. Where they said that ethical pronouncements cannot express propositions, since they cannot, in principle, be verified or falsified by observation or experiment, Anderson says that they do express propositions, or describe spatio-temporal situations, and therefore that they are empirically verifiable or falsifiable.

(4) Anderson's general deflationist line of argument comes out very clearly in his early (and I hope outgrown) account of mathematics ('Empiricism', 1927). After attacking idealism and rationalism for making their distinctions between higher and lower truths, higher and lower realities, and the rest, he says, 'Thus empiricism regards it as illogical to make such distinctions as that between existence and subsistence or between the "is" of identity, that of predication and that of membership of a class; and still more obviously illogical to say that there *is* something defective about "is" itself'; and, later, 'Rejecting in this way the distinction between necessary and other truths ...'; and, later, 'And all this implies, I maintain, that science depends entirely on observation, i.e. on finding something to be the case, and on the use of syllogism, either for proof or testing; or, more generally, on observation in connection with, and in distinction from, anticipation. This means that there is no distinction between empirical and rational science. Since everything that can be asserted can be denied or doubted, since deduction and hypothesis are always possible, all sciences are observational and experimental.'

He then moves on to try to show that geometry is an empirical science. 'Our geometrical theorems are themselves the results of careful observation'; '... that geometry is, like all others, an empirical or experimental science, dealing with things of a certain sort, that there is nothing *a priori* about it, but that it is concerned throughout with fact.' 'Geometry, we may say, is concerned with empirical characters and relations of things in space and is a practical science, and Euclidean geometry consists not of "implications" but of propositions (connected to some extent, of course, by argument) which are either true or false.' The finale of this article runs, 'And therefore all ideals, ultimates, symbols, agencies and the like are to be rejected, and no such distinction as that of facts and principles, of facts and values, can be maintained. There are only facts, i.e. occurrences in space and time.'

In another context he says, 'And finally, unless we could find implication as a relation among propositions, i.e. unless implication were a *sensible fact* [A.'s italics], we should never know how to infer' ('Realism and Some of its Critics', 1930).

(5) What has gone wrong? Why, if Anderson justifiably rejects Platonic or Lockean or Meinongian or Hegelian stories, is he therefore driven to tell his equally impossible stories about mathematics, good and implication? We may approach at least part of the answer in this way.

There is obviously a certain affinity between Anderson's spatio-temporal situations and the atomic facts once patronized by Russell and Wittgenstein. Their completely elementary propositions assert that named particulars have specified qualities or else stand in specified relation to other named particulars. What, in the last resort, i.e. at the terminus of analysis, makes a non-analytic statement true or false is the obtaining of particular matters of fact; and each particular matter of fact is a value of 'S is P' or 'A is γ to B'.

But here an important difference is to be noticed. Russell and Wittgenstein did not suppose that all or most or perhaps any of the assertions that we actually make are atomic statements. They are, rather, cheques drawn against these solid coins. The statements that we ordinarily make are logically (not necessarily grammatically) highly complex and general. Explicitly or implicitly, they embody conjunctions, quantifiers and variables. So that whereas one atomic proposition can, apparently, differ in form from another only as a simple, singular, affirmative, attributive proposition differs from a simple, singular, affirmative, relational proposition, an ordinary proposition, on the other hand, can differ in form from another in a host of ways—as negative from affirmative, as singular from general, as singly general from multiply general, as conjunctive from disjunctive, as analytic from synthetic, as modal from categorical, and so on indefinitely. Perhaps the bank-till houses only pennies and shillings, but the cheques we draw on this hard cash can differ from these and from one another in an endless variety of ways.

Now Anderson seems to be oblivious of any logical differences save the difference between qualities and relations. His regular touchstone is the question 'Quality or Relation?' Is knowing (or willing) a quality? No; so it must be a relation. Is good a relation? No; so it must be a quality.

I do not wish to argue the question whether or not we can produce specimens of elementary propositions; or whether or not the possibility of exhibiting more complex and/or general propositions as compositions of (or operations upon) less complex and/or general propositions entails the existence of a stratum of perfectly simple and completely non-general propositions. Nor do I wish to debate the question whether Anderson is right in thinking that any elementary proposition is either an attributive or a relational proposition, or whether Aristotle was right in thinking that there were six, seven or eight other options. Somebody called 'Logic' seems to have confided the dichotomous answer to Anderson, and perhaps she has given him some good reasons for it.

The important thing is that Anderson seldom, if ever, finds occasion even to mention such propositional differences as those between negative and affirmative; conjunctive, disjunctive and simple; analytic and synthetic. The roles in arguments of such words as 'any', 'some', 'all', 'most', 'a', 'the', 'if', 'because', 'therefore', 'probably', 'may', 'cannot', etc., go undiscussed and for the most part unmentioned. Yet it is precisely those statements which incorporate these words, or could be reworded so as to incorporate them, that seem patently misconstrued when construed as reporting or describing spatio-temporal situations. Does 'John is not at home' describe the same situation as 'John is at the theatre', or a different situation? Does 'somebody telephoned' give you the same information as 'John telephoned' or different information? Does 'if the glass drops, there will be a gale' report a gale, or any other meteorological occurrence?

That Anderson does intend to construe all assertions after one model is shown by the statement already cited, 'In a moral judgement, as in any other, something is judged or asserted, i.e. some situation is said to have occurred.' Taken at face value, this assertion requires us to believe that we can never judge or assert that a situation has not occurred, that a situation will occur, that a situation might or cannot occur, that situations of a certain sort can be relied on to occur whenever other specified situations occur, that either situation A has occurred or situation B has occurred, or that either situation A has occurred or it has not occurred. For if we could assert such things, we should be asserting something other than that some situation has occurred. Furthermore, since, when we are told that something has occurred, it is always proper to ask when and where it occurred, we are, by implication, forbidden to make or understand statements to which these questions are not appropriate. But when told that sugar is soluble or that swans are white (as distinct from 'a piece of sugar dissolved' or 'there was a white swan'), we could not significantly ask 'When?' or 'Where?'—since 'anywhere' and 'anywhen' are already connoted by the (tenseless) verbs of such generalisations. So no generalisations or causal laws are true (or even, I suppose, false). It is true that in his discussion of Causality in 1938 Anderson does not merely allow but insist that particular causal statements rest on universal propositions. 'It *is* natural, then, that, to the question what causes a certain sort of thing, the answer should be "a certain sort of thing"; it appears that what we are all the time seeking to establish is a general connection, that is to say a universal proposition, to assert which is to assert that something happens invariably.' So, presumably, he has wisely given up his principle that in all judgements or assertions 'some situation is stated to have occurred'. He is here implying that at least one sort of general proposition is not to be construed as a report of a particular spatio-temporal situation or even as a batch of reports of particular spatio-temporal situations. (Why, indeed, should they be? Unlike Reuters, we do not want to learn only what has occurred.)

On the other hand, in 1930 ('Realism and Some of its Critics') he had said, 'It has therefore to be recognised that "This body is fiery", "This body is hot" and "Fire is hot" are propositions all of the same order, and their terms are all of the same order.' This was said in criticism of the Platonising view that 'the idea is of a different order to the thing compared, and cannot in any sense be regarded as another thing alongside these with which they can be compared'. So it may merely be an odd way of asserting, what is true, that the universal proposition 'Fire is hot' must not be construed as ascribing a temperature (not to these bonfires or those coal fires, etc., but) to a 'universal'. However, I think that Anderson does confuse the truth that universal propositions are not attributive or relational propositions about 'universals' with the falsehood that universal propositions can and must be construed as assertions that something has had a quality or a relation somewhere and somewhen. For in '"Universals" and Occurrences' (1929), to which he refers back in this argument, he says,

'But when these two propositions ['All lots of sugar are x' and 'All lots of sugar, which are introduced into a solvent, are dissolved'] as well as proposition (1) ['All things of the character x, which are introduced into a solvent, are dissolved'] have been clearly stated, we can see that they are all different, but that nothing has been said to show that they are not occurrences. And so with "potentiality" in general: if there is in any substance something that we can call a potentiality of it, then its having that potentiality *occurs* [A.'s italics]: .... Leaving aside potentialities then, and taking the proposition "Sugar is sweet", ... we can hardly avoid asserting that the sweetness of sugar occurs in space and time.' Anywhen and anywhere? Or on 12 May 1902 in London and 4 June 1910 in Sydney?

Certainly universal statements are not reports of other-worldly states of affairs; but nor are they reports of this-worldly states of affairs. For we report states of affairs in the idiom of—reports of states of affairs. And this is not the idiom of universal statements. Of course there is an important connection between the jobs of universal statements and the jobs of reports of states of affairs, just as there is an important connection between the jobs of spanners and the jobs of bolts. There would be no use for spanners if there were no bolts. But spanners are not bolts, any more than they are transcendent Bolts. The argument that spanners must be ordinary bolts *because* there aren't any transcendent Bolts would not take in a child— unless some ill-advised governess had trained him to think only of bolts when anyone mentioned implements, as 'Logic' apparently trained Anderson to think only of reports of things' having had qualities or relations when anyone mentions propositions, statements or judgements.

Anderson's logical alphabet is so exiguous that one wonders where he got his 'logic' from. Not from Aristotle, who investigates other inferences than syllogisms and has ten 'categories' where Anderson has two; not from the Stoic logicians who investigated the inferences that hinge on conjunctions; not from Boole, De Morgan, Frege or *Principia Mathematica*. One is at least forcibly reminded of Bradley, who, though he spells the world very differently, spells it out of the same penurious selection of letters. Indeed the connection is, perhaps, more than accidental. For if a philosopher allows himself only an artificially limited set of logical cupboards and pigeon-holes, then when he finds that a lot of his belongings will not readily fit into them, he is tempted to solve his storage-problem by high-handed devices. Either he *deems* his articles to be of the required sizes and shapes or, if intellectual scruples forbid this, he *deems* his cupboards and pigeon-holes to contain just those secret shelves and interior compartments which will afford the required fit. Sometimes repugnance for the latter device is the motive for resorting to the former, and then we get an Anderson. Sometimes repugnance for the former device, e.g. as practised by Mill, is the motive for resorting to the latter, and then we get a Bradley. The prudent householder has a different policy. He tries to provide his house not with the minimum quantity of storage-places that he can mention in one breath, but with the minimum number that will house the things that he wants or is likely to come to want to store. The question whether at any given stage he needs an extra shelf or cupboard or whether he needs only to be more careful and clever in packing is always an open one. What we can never say is that we have now, at last, been provided by logic (i.e. logicians) with all the cupboards and pigeon-holes that can ever be needed. Indeed, my own view is that though recent logic (i.e. logicians) has been relatively lavish in providing dockets for propositional differences, it has not yet provided nearly enough to cover the varieties of statements and arguments employed in science, law and ordinary life. Has it (have they) provided enough even to cover the propositions of pure mathematics?

It might be said on behalf of Anderson that though he does indeed betray little interest in most of the propositional differences which have occupied contemporary and past logicians, still this indifference does not actually matter. For study of the logic of 'some', 'all', 'any', 'a', 'the', 'and', 'or', 'if', 'can', 'probably' and 'not', etc., is not required for the elucidation of the terms that have concerned Anderson (save that of 'cause'). The realist account of 'John knows so and so' or 'John's enquiringness is good' is independent of these matters, since the statements cited do not embody any of these words. But this defence will not do. For, as Anderson recognizes for qualities and relations, grammatical similarities can go with logical differences, and grammatical differences can go with logical similarities. A one-verb sentence can express a disjunctive proposition, and a noun–copula–adjective sentence can express an open or variable hypothetical proposition. Why does 'John is my uncle, but he is not my mother's brother' imply that he is my father's brother? Because for John to be my uncle he must be the brother *either* of my mother *or* of my father. Yet 'John is my uncle' does not contain two clauses joined by 'or'.

Take for instance the verb 'to know'. An important part of Anderson's realism consists in his rejection of various idealist theories of knowledge and in their replacement by another, namely by the theory that 'know' signifies not a quality of the knowing person nor a quality of the thing or fact known, but a relation between the person who knows and what he knows. So, to say that John knows so and so is to assert a relational state of affairs concerning John and what he knows. And, in accordance with his general view of situations or states of affairs or facts, Anderson maintains that 'in speaking intelligibly of "knowledge", we are speaking of a certain state of affairs, the mental process which knows as connected with and distinguished from another state of affairs, mental or non-mental, which is known' ('Empiricism', 1927).

Now here, though I do not know that it matters much for his immediate ends, Anderson is quite patently wrong on one point. For 'know' is never used for a mental process or for what a mental process does. Singing and panting are processes, and if told that someone has been singing or panting, we can ask how long he has been singing or panting for and whether he has stopped yet. But we cannot ask how long someone has spent in knowing something; nor is knowledge something which can be interrupted or accelerated or resumed. We can say that someone has known the date of Easter for weeks, but not that he has been knowing it throughout the past three minutes, or that he is (or is not) knowing it now. In these and many other ways 'know' behaves like 'own', and not like 'sing' or 'pant'.

Of course there is the moment of transition from not knowing (or owning) something to knowing (or owning) it. We learn, find out, or are informed of things at specifiable moments, just as we acquire, inherit or are presented with things at specifiable moments. But as we own things from the moment of acquisition to the moment of destruction, sale, donation or distraint, so we know things from the time when we learn them to the time when we forget them or die.

To say that someone owns or knows something is not to say that at this or that particular moment something is going on. But it *is* to say that at *any* moment during the period of possession certain sorts of things *can* go on. The owner *could* give his watch away, pawn it, sell it, throw it away, take proceedings against a thief, and so on; and these would be occurrences. The knower *could* tell someone the date of Easter, scold someone who got it wrong, and so on; and these would be occurrences. But to say of someone that he *could* at *any* moment of a certain described period do something *either* of this sort *or* of that sort, *if* situations of this or that sort were to arise, is to use 'could', 'any', 'some', 'either–or' and 'if'. (And, of course, this expansion of 'knows' and 'owns' is only a promissory sketch. It is not nearly complex enough.)

So 'John knows the date of Easter' certainly does not report a spatio-temporal occurrence—and it does not report a transcendent (attributive or relational) state of affairs either. A theory of knowledge which is indifferent to propositional differences other than that between qualities and relations is without storage-room for those most familiar features of knowledge which control the ordinary grammar of the verb 'to know'.

The same sort of thing is clearly true of implication. To say that a given proposition 'p' implies another proposition 'q' is certainly not to affirm 'p-and-q', or even to deny 'p-and-not-q'. It is to say that it *could* not be the case that 'p, but not-q'. And whatever it is that is expressed by 'could not', at least it is not a 'sensible fact'— from which, of course, it does not follow that it is a non-sensible, Meinongian fact. For it does not report a spatio-temporal (relational) situation *or* report *per impossibile*, a transcendent (relational) situation.

Who knows if 'good' would not also yield to similar treatment, as it certainly does not yield to either the deflationist or the inflationist treatment in terms of qualities and relations?

(6) There remains to be mentioned one further important divergence between the course of Anderson's thinking and that of some European philosophers. When Russell came across the contradiction of the class of all classes that are not members of themselves, and then found the parallel contradictions of 'the Liar', etc., he was forced to look for a solution in some sort of theory of Logical Types. An essential part of this theory consists in the assertion that there can be grammatically well-constructed sentences, of orthodox vocabulary, which do not say anything true or false. They do not express propositions at all. Despite their perfectly regular verbal ingredients and their perfectly regular grammatical constructions, they are meaningless, nonsensical or absurd. And they are meaningless for assignable *reasons*—reasons of the kind which it has always been part of the business of logicians and philosophers to examine. This dichotomy between True-or-False (or Significant) on the one hand and Nonsensical on the other hand was, I think, regarded by Russell himself as of only local importance. It provided a way out of a few quite special embarrassments.

But Wittgenstein, as I construe him, and the Vienna Circle saw in this dichotomy the general clue that they required to the difference between science and philosophy. Science produces true (and sometime false) statements about the world; philosophy examines the rules or reasons that make some statements (like those of good scientists) true-or-false, and others (like metaphysicians' statements) nonsensical. Science is concerned with what makes (significant) statements true or else false; philosophy is concerned with what makes them significant or nonsensical. So science talks about the world, while philosophy talks about talk about the world.

In the *Tractatus* Wittgenstein maintained that the things which philosophy wanted to say could not be said. The conditions of significant (true-or-false) assertion could not be the topics of significant assertions. That sentences of different sorts observe or break the rules of significance can be shown but not stated or explained. This doctrine of the ineffability of philosophy was, perhaps, derived from Russell's Type-principle that a proposition cannot be a comment upon itself, or that what a sentence says cannot be a truth or falsehood *about* what it says.

To meet this point, Russell, in his foreword to the English translation of the *Tractatus*, pointed out that we, including Wittgenstein, obviously do succeed in saying a lot of the things which, according to Wittgenstein, were unsayable. He suggested that we should distinguish *orders* of talk. First-order talk is about the world; second-order talk is about talk about the world, and so on. No Type-rule is broken by a sentence which comments upon a sentence of a lower order than itself. So philosophical talk could be significant second-order (or higher) talk.

On this showing not all talk about talk would be philosophy. Grammarians, etymologists, teachers of rhetoric, etc., talk about uses of language, but they are not doing philosophy. Doing philosophy consists in discussing what can and cannot be *significantly* said, and not what can or cannot be elegantly or idiomatically said.

This view of philosophy proved the more acceptable since it at least seemed so nicely consonant with the actual philosophical practice of G. E. Moore. He, without saying much, if anything, in general terms *about* the procedure of philosophizing, had in fact for a long time been conducting his philosophizing by a special sort of examination of the ordinary uses of the words of ordinary language. Abstaining from anything like other-worldly speculations, he had been pertinaciously sifting the ways in which words like 'good', 'perceive', 'can', etc., are actually employed in our everyday (first-order) employments of them. He had been *doing* a special sort of linguistic analysis, and now the generalization of Russell's dichotomy between True-or-False and Nonsensical made it possible to *state* in general terms what sort of a task this was. 'Nonsense' ceased (or should have ceased, if it did not) to be a vague term of abuse, and became a logicians' category.

Now statements about other statements (when they concern the satisfaction or non-satisfaction by these of the logical conditions of significance) are patently *not* reports of natural occurrences—or, of course, of supernatural occurrences or states of affairs either. So the *Gleichschaltung* of philosophical with scientific assertions appears, on this showing, to derive from obliviousness to a new and cardinal propositional difference, that between first-order and higher-order propositions, when these higher-order propositions are (not reporters', etymologists' or commentators' propositions but) assessments of the logical propriety or impropriety of the construction of the lower-order sentences.

It would not be true to say that Anderson has nothing to say about the dichotomy between the significant and the nonsensical. Gasking (in 'Anderson and the *Tractatus Logico-Philosophicus*', 1949) makes a valuable and searching examination of the similarities and (much greater) differences between Anderson's and Wittgenstein's treatments of this subject. But it is true, I think, that Anderson does not regard the dichotomy as showing anything important about the differences between doing science and doing philosophy. And it is true, as the citations I have made in my second section show, that at least he used to think that there is no important difference between doing science and doing philosophy. Fortunately Anderson's practice of philosophizing has not been governed by his theory of it. Not one of his articles contains, so far as I can see, the reports of any experiments, the culling of any statistics, the description of any laboratory techniques, the results of any mensurations, or the application of any mathematics; nor is a single prediction vouchsafed, the verification or falsification of which would be a test of the hypothesis behind it. What he actually does is what all other philosophers (even idealists) do. He debates. And he frequently debates extremely cogently. Now cogent debating, of a certain sort, is doing philosophy well, and it is not what good entomologists or astronomers or sociologists necessarily do well.

But I fear that Anderson will reply that debating consists in reporting sensible observations of the occurrences of implications. For 'logic' tells him that implications must be relations, and as they cannot be unearthly relations, they must be earthly relations.

16

LUDWIG WITTGENSTEIN

Reprinted from 'Analysis', vol. XII, 1951, by permission of the editor

An original and powerful philosopher, Ludwig Wittgenstein, an Austrian who finally became a naturalized British subject, came to England shortly before the First World War to study engineering. In 1912, bitten by logical and philosophical problems about the nature of mathematics, he migrated to Cambridge to work with Bertrand Russell. During that war, he was in the Austrian army and ended up a prisoner of war. In this period he wrote his one book, the famous *Tractatus Logico-Philosophicus*, of which a not quite reliable English translation was published in 1922. He taught in an Austrian village school for some time, during which he came into close philosophical touch with a few of the leading members of the Vienna Circle. In 1929 he came to Cambridge, where the importance of his ideas had been quickly recognized. In 1939 he became Professor. For part of the last war he was a hospital orderly at Guy's Hospital. In 1947 he resigned his Chair. Besides the *Tractatus*, he published only one article.

In the last twenty years, so far as I know, he published nothing; attended no philosophical conferences; gave no lectures outside Cambridge; corresponded on philosophical subjects with nobody and discouraged the circulation even of notes of his Cambridge lectures and discussions. But with his serious students and a few colleagues, economists, mathematicians, physicists and philosophers, he would discuss philosophical matters unwearyingly. Yet from his jealously preserved little pond, there have spread waves over the philosophical thinking of much of the English-speaking world. Philosophers who never met him—and few of us did meet him—can be heard talking philosophy in his tones of voice; and students who can barely spell his name now wrinkle up their noses at things which had a bad smell for him. So what is the difference that he has made to philosophy?

It is vain to try to forecast the verdict of history upon a contemporary. I have to try to do this for one who has for about 30 years avoided any publication of his ideas. So what I offer is a set of impressions, interpretations, partly, of mere echoes of echoes.

From the time of Locke to that of Bradley philosophers had debated their issues as if they were psychological issues. Certainly their problems were, often, genuine philosophical problems, but they discussed them in psychological terms. And if they asked themselves, as they seldom did ask, what they were investigating, they tended to say that they were investigating the workings of the mind, just as physical scientists investigate the working of bodies. The sorts of 'Mental Science' that they talked were sometimes positivistic, sometimes idealistic, according, roughly, as they were more impressed by chemistry than by theology or vice versa.

However, fifty years ago philosophers were getting their feet out of these psychological boots. For psychology had now begun to be done in laboratories and clinics, so armchair psychology became suspect. But even more influential was the fact that logical quandaries had recently been exposed at the very roots of pure mathematics. The mathematicians needed lifelines, which they could not provide for themselves. Logicians had to work out the logic of mathematics, and they could not base this logic on the findings of any empirical science, especially of so hazy a science as psychology. If logic and philosophy were not psychological enquiries, what were they?

During the first twenty years of this century, many philosophers gave another answer to this question, a Platonic answer. Philosophy studies not the workings of minds or, of course, of bodies either; it studies the denizens of a third domain, the domain of abstract, or conceptual entities, of possibilities, essences, timelessly subsisting universals, numbers, truths, falsities, values and meanings. This idea enabled its holders to continue to say that philosophy was the science of something, while denying that it was the science of any ordinary subject-matter; to champion its autonomy as a discipline, while denying that it was just one science among others; to give it the standing of a science while admitting its unlikeness to the sciences. Thus the question 'What are philosophy and logic the sciences of?' received a new answer, though one with a disquietingly dreamlike ring. It was the answer given by Frege and by Russell.

In Vienna thinkers were facing much the same question, though from an opposite angle. Whereas here it had been widely assumed that philosophy was Mental Science, and therefore just a sister science to physics, chemistry, zoology, etc., in the German-speaking world it was widely assumed that philosophy stood to the other sciences not as sister but as mother—or even governess. Somehow professors of philosophy there enjoyed such a pedagogic domination that they could dictate even to the scientists. *Of course* philosophers were the right people to decide whether the teachings of Darwin, Freud and Einstein were true.

Late in the 19th century Mach had mutinied against this view that metaphysics was a governess science. By the early 1920s this mutiny became a rebellion. The Vienna Circle repudiated the myth that the questions of physics, biology, psychology or mathematics can be decided by metaphysical considerations. Metaphysics is not a governess science or a sister science; it is not a science at all. The classic case was that of Einstein's Relativity principle. The claims of professors of philosophy to refute this principle were baseless. Scientific questions are soluble only by scientific methods, and these are not the methods of philosophers.

Thus, in England the question was this: What are the special virtues which the natural and the mathematical sciences lack but logic and philosophy possess, such that these must be invoked when the former find themselves in quandaries? In Vienna the question was this: Given that philosophers cannot decide scientific questions, what are the logical virtues which scientific procedures possess but philosophical procedures lack? The contrast between philosophy and science was drawn in both places. In Vienna, where the autonomy of the sciences was actually challenged, the object was to expose the pretensions of philosophy as a governess science. Here, where, save for psychology, the autonomy of the sciences was not seriously challenged, it was drawn in order to extract the positive functions of logic and philosophy. Philosophy was regarded in Vienna as a blood-sucking parasite; in England as a medicinal leech.

To Wittgenstein the question came in its English form. And so he could not be called one of the Logical Positivists. Their polemics were not his; and his quest for the positive function of logic and philosophy was not, until much later, theirs. He was influenced by Frege and Russell, not by Mach. He had not himself felt the dead hand of professorial philosophy which cramped, and still cramps, even scientific thought in Germany and Austria. He, conversely, himself helped to fix the logical lifelines for the mathematicians.

I want to show how Wittgenstein transformed and answered what was all the time his master-question, 'What can philosophers and logicians do, and how should they do it?'

I have said that after a long imprisonment in psychological idioms, philosophy was, for a time, re-housed in Platonic idioms. But this was only a temporary asylum. For after a short period during which philosophers tried not to mind the dream-like character of the new asylum, something awoke them from the dream. Russell, in his enquiries into the logical principles underlying mathematics, found that he could not well help constructing statements which had the logically disturbing property that they were true only on condition that they were false, and false only on condition that they were true. Some of these self-subverting statements seemed to be inherent in the very basis which was to make mathematics secure. There was a major leak in the dry dock which Frege and he had built for mathematics.

Russell found a patch for the leak. Underlying the familiar distinction between truth and falsehood, there is a more radical distinction between significance and meaninglessness. True and false statements are both significant, but some forms of words, with the vocabulary and constructions of statements, are neither true nor false, but nonsensical—and nonsensical not for reasons of wording or of grammar, but for logical reasons. The self-subverting statements were of this sort, neither true nor false, but nonsensical simulacra of statements. Notice, it is only of such things as complex verbal expressions that we can ask whether they are significant or nonsense. The question could not be asked of mental processes; or of Platonic entities. So logic is from the start concerned, not with these but rather with what can or cannot be significantly said. Its subject-matter is a linguistic one, though its tasks are not at all those of philology.

In Wittgenstein's *Tractatus* this departmental conclusion is generalized. All logic and all philosophy are enquiries into what makes it significant or nonsensical to say certain things. The sciences aim at saying what is true about the world; philosophy aims at disclosing only the logic of what can be truly or even falsely said about the world. This is why philosophy is not a sister science or a parent science; that its business is not to add to the number of scientific statements, but to disclose their logic.

Wittgenstein begins by considering how a sentence, a map, a diagram or a scale-model can represent or even significantly misrepresent the facts. The isolated words 'London' and 'south' are not true or false. Nor can a single dot on a sheet of paper be an accurate or inaccurate map. The sentence 'London is north of Brighton' is true. The same words, differently arranged as 'Brighton is north of London', make a false statement. Arranged as 'South is London of Brighton' they make a farrago which is neither true nor false, but nonsense. For dots on paper to represent or misrepresent the direction of Brighton from London, there must be a dot for each town and they must be set out in accordance with some convention for points of the compass. For a statement, map or diagram to be true or false, there must be a plurality of words or marks; but, more, these bits must be put together in certain ways. And underlying the fact that the truth or falsity of the statement or map partly depends upon the particular way in which its bits are arranged, there lies the fact that whether a significant statement or map results at all, depends wholly on the general way in which the bits are put together. Some ways of jumbling them together are ruled out. What rules rule them out?

In the *Tractatus* Wittgenstein came to the frustrating conclusion that these principles of arrangement inevitably baffle significant statement. To try to tell what makes the difference between significant and nonsensical talk is itself to cross the divide between significant and nonsensical talk. Philosophizing can, indeed, open our eyes to these structural principles, but it cannot issue in significant statements of them. Philosophy is not a science; it cannot yield theories or doctrines. None the less it can be skilful or unskilful, successful or unsuccessful. It is in pursuing the activity itself that we see what we need to see. Rather like learning music or tennis, learning philosophy does not result in our being able to tell what we have learnt; though, as in music and tennis, we can show what we have learnt.

Now it is true that philosophical clarity is achieved in the acts of appreciating arguments rather than in propounding theorems. But it is false that all philosophical talk is nonsensical talk. Wittgenstein had himself said very effective things, and talking effectively is not talking nonsensically. What had brought him to this frustrating conclusion? When he wrote the *Tractatus*, he was, I think, over-influenced by his own analogies between saying things and making maps, diagrams and scale-models. Certainly, for marks on paper to constitute a temperature chart, or for spoken words to constitute a significant statement, the dots and the words must be arranged according to rules and conventions. Only if the zigzag of dots on the nurse's graph-paper is systematically correlated with the thermometer readings taken at successive moments of a day, can it represent or even misrepresent the alterations in the patient's temperature. Only if words are organized according to a number of complex general rules does a true or false statement result.

Suppose we now asked the nurse to depict on a second sheet of graph-paper, not the course of the patient's temperature, but the rules for representing his temperature by dots on graph paper, she would be baffled. Nor can the rules and conventions of map-making themselves be mapped. So Wittgenstein argued in the *Tractatus* that the philosopher or logician is debarred from saying what it is that makes things said significant or nonsensical. He can show it, but not tell it. After the *Tractatus* he realized that though saying things does resemble depicting things or mapping things in the respect for which he originally drew the analogy, it does not resemble them in all respects. Just as the nurse can tell, though not depict, how the temperature chart represents or misrepresents the patient's temperature, so the philosopher can tell why, say, a scientist's statement makes or does not make sense. What alone would be absurd would be a sentence which purported to convey a comment upon its own significance or meaninglessness.

The *Tractatus* has two distinct but connected aims. The first, which I have crudely sketched, is to show both what philosophy is not, namely any sort of a science, and what it is, namely an activity of exploring the internal logic of what is said, for example, in this or that scientific theory. The second, which I shall not even try to sketch, is to show what sort of an enquiry Formal Logic is. This brings me to a general point about the *Tractatus*. Wittgenstein's first interest had been in the logic of mathematics and thence in the logical paradoxes which were the big leak in the dry dock that Frege and Russell had built. He was, therefore, equipped and predisposed to squeeze whatever can be significantly said into the few statement-patterns with which the logic of mathematical statements operates. He used its terminology, its codes, and its abacus-operations in his task of exploring various philosophical issues, and, above all, his own master-issue, that of the nature of philosophizing itself. In consequence, the *Tractatus* is, in large measure, a closed book to those who lack this technical equipment. Few people can read it without feeling that something important is happening; but few experts, even, can say what is happening.

But this is not the end of the story. Maybe it is only the preface. For, after lying fallow for some years, Wittgenstein returned to philosophy. His teaching in this period differs markedly from that of the *Tractatus*; it even repudiates parts of the *Tractatus*.

First, he no longer forces all expressions into the favoured few patterns of the logic of mathematics. With this goes a revolt against moulds of any sorts. The rubrics of logical systems and the abstract terms of philosophical schools are like the shoes of Chinese ladies, which deformed their feet and prevented them from walking on them. Philosophical elucidation is still inspection of expressions, but it is no longer inspection through the slots of a logician's stencil or through the prisms of a scholastic classification-system. His diction has reverted from that of a Russell discussing esoteric matters with mathematicians to that of a Socrates discussing everyday ideas with unindoctrinated young men. Nor does he now elucidate only the propositions of the sciences. Like Moore, he explores the logic of all the things that all of us say.

Next, though I think that his master-problem is still that of the nature, tasks and methods of the philosophical activity, he no longer thinks that philosophers are condemned to trying to say the unsayable. But he now avoids any general statement of the nature of philosophy, not because this would be to say the unsayable, but because it would be to say a scholastic and therefore an obscuring thing. In philosophy, generalizations are unclarifications. The nature of philosophy is to be taught by producing concrete specimens of it. As the medical student learns surgery by witnessing and practising operations on dead and on live subjects, so the student of philosophy learns what philosophy is by following and practising operations on particular quandary-generating ways of talking. Thus Wittgenstein would rove, apparently aimlessly because without any statement of aim, from one concrete puzzle to its brothers, its cousins, its parents and its associates, demonstrating both what makes them puzzling and how to resolve them—demonstrating, but not telling; going through the moves, but not compiling a manual of them; teaching a skill, not dictating a doctrine.

One favourite procedure of his might be called the 'tea-tasting method'. Tea-tasters do not lump their samples into two or three comprehensive types. Rather they savour each sample and try to place it next door to its closest neighbours, and this not in respect of just one discriminable quality but along the lengths of various lines of qualities. So Wittgenstein would exhibit the characteristic manner of working of a particular expression by matching it against example after example of expressions progressively diverging from it in various respects and directions. He would show how striking similarities may go with important but ordinarily unremarked differences, and how we are tempted to lean too heavily on their similarities and hence to be tripped up by their latent differences.

For philosophers do not examine expressions at random. The quest for their internal logic is forced upon us by the fact that we find ourselves already caught up in unforeseen entanglements. Why do we slide into quandaries? Let me invent an example. We find ourselves talking as if, like a train, so time itself might one day slow down and stop. We divide a train into coaches and coaches into compartments. We divide a month into weeks and weeks into days. When a train is passing me, some coaches are beyond me, some are still to come, and one compartment of one coach is directly abreast of me. I look at its occupants through the window. Surely time is like this, Last week has gone, next week is still to come, but I can exchange glances with the occupants of Now. So, as trains always slow down and stop somewhere, what makes time puff on so tirelessly? Might not Now be the last compartment of the last coach? Yet surely not; there would still be something behind it, if only the empty wind. You see that it is tempting, but also that it smells like nonsense to speak of the last compartment of time. Why may we say some things about time which are very much like some things that we legitimately say about trains, when to some of the proper corollaries of what we say about trains there correspond no proper corollaries about time? To answer this question, we should have to examine the functioning of whole ranges of things that we say about trains, rivers and winds; about moving shadows, rainbows and reflections; about perpetual motion machines, stars, clocks, sundials, and calendars; about the series of numbers, days of the week and minutes of the day. And then we may see why we slid and no longer incline to slide from the proper corollaries of familiar dictions about trains to corresponding corollaries of somewhat similar dictions about time. We see that we had over-pressed certain analogies between ways of talking; and that we were so dominated by a favourite model, that we had gone on using it where it could no longer work. And now we know, in a way, what time is, though there is no shorter or better way of saying what time is than by going through again the same sort of process of linguistic tea-tasting.

I must conclude. Wittgenstein has made our generation of philosophers self-conscious about philosophy itself. It is, of course, possible for a person to be very thoughtful about the nature and methods of an activity, without being made any the better at performing it. The centipede of the poem ran well until he began to wonder how he ran. Maybe we have been made a bit neurotic about the nature of our calling. But Wittgenstein's demolition of the idea that philosophy is a sort of science has at least made us vigilant about our tools. We no longer try to use for our problems the methods of arguing which are the right ones for demonstrating theorems or establishing hypotheses. In particular we have learnt to pay deliberate attention to what can and cannot be said. What had, since the early days of this century, been the practice of G. E. Moore has received a rationale from Wittgenstein; and I expect that when the curtain is lifted we shall also find that Wittgenstein's concrete methods have increased the power, scope and delicacy of the methods by which Moore has for so long explored in detail the internal logic of what we say.

REVIEW OF LUDWIG WITTGENSTEIN: REMARKS ON THE FOUNDATIONS OF MATHEMATICS

Reprinted from 'Scientific American', vol. CXVII, *1957, by permission of the publishers*

The late Ludwig Wittgenstein was a deep and influential philosopher of science, yet outside the circle of professional philosophers little is known of the man and his work. This book is the second collection of his papers to be published since his death. The editors of *Scientific American* have asked me to take this occasion, not to review the book, which in any case is too specialized for the general reader, but briefly to describe who Wittgenstein was and what he did.

First for the man.

He was born in 1889 in Austria and died in 1951 in England. He was of Jewish origin, though he was brought up a Roman Catholic. He, with the rest of his family, was intensely musical. His father was a wealthy steel magnate. He himself was trained as an engineer, and was engaged in aerodynamical researches in England when in 1911 and 1912 he became perplexed about the logical and philosophical foundations of mathematics. Advised, apparently, by the German mathematician Gottlob Frege, he went to Cambridge to study under the author of *Principles of Mathematics*, Bertrand Russell.

During the First World War he served in the Austrian army, and ended up a prisoner of war in Italy. His rucksack contained the manuscript of the only book of his that was published during his lifetime, the *Tractatus Logico-Philosophicus*. This was published in 1922, with the German text faced by an unreliable English translation. It contains an introduction by Russell, but Wittgenstein disapproved of this. A revision of the translation should appear fairly soon. Wittgenstein became professor at Cambridge in 1939, succeeding G. E. Moore, and he resigned in 1947.

He was a spellbinding and somewhat terrifying person. He had unnervingly piercing eyes. He never used hackneyed expressions—not that he strove after originality of diction, but he just could not think in clichés. To his own regret, he could not help dominating his associates. He remorselessly excommunicated persons of whom he disapproved.

He loathed being connected with academic philosophers, and he avoided academic chores. After 1929 he attended no conferences; he did no reviewing for journals; only once did he attend a philosophical meeting in Oxford; he was inaccessible to visiting philosophers; he read few, if any, of the philosophical books and articles that came out during his last 25 years.

He was like Socrates in rigidly separating the philosopher from the sophist; unlike Socrates in shunning the market-place; like Socrates in striving to convert his pupils; unlike Socrates in feeling the need to conserve his genius by insulation. He was hermit, ascetic, guru and *Führer*.

What of the philosopher?

He had no formal training in philosophy. His ferments came from his own insides. I do not know just what shape his initial perplexities about mathematics took. Anyhow, he consulted Frege and Russell, and studied their logico-mathematical writings; the central problems of his *Tractatus*, though not the same as theirs, were clearly reactions to their doctrines.

Frege and Russell tried to show that all pure mathematics derives from the completely general truths of formal logic, i.e. that these truths stand to arithmetical truths as Euclid's axioms to his theorems. But what was the point of trying to demonstrate this continuity between logic and arithmetic? Surely the truths of mathematics are as well established as anyone could demand, so what is gained, except for tidiness, by underpinning them with an ulterior foundation?

At that time reflective mathematicians were in trouble. Their science seemed all limbs and no body. The very vigour of these branches was generating cross-purposes between them. The notion of number itself seemed to take as many shapes as there were branches of the science of number. Mathematics felt like a caravanserai, not a house.

Its external relations with other sciences also were precarious. John Stuart Mill had likened the truths of mathematics to those of the natural sciences: they are generalizations from experience, susceptible of overthrow by unexpected exceptions. It would be much more surprising to find an exception to $7 + 5 = 12$ than to find a black swan, but only much more. Which is absurd. For another thing, many thinkers, when asked 'Of what entities is mathematics the science?' were giving a psychological answer. The physical world contains countless sorts of things, but it does not contain numbers. There are nine planets, and the earth has one moon. But you cannot see 9 or 1. So, if numbers are not physical things, what else is there for them to be, save ideas in our minds or thoughts or something of the sort? But then arithmetic ought to make allowances for the differences between what goes on in lunatic and in sane minds; in visualizers' and in nonvisualizers' minds, and so on. Which is absurd.

Because mathematics needed, internally, coordination between its members and, externally, autonomy from the inductive sciences, especially psychology, its affiliation to logic felt like a rescue operation. Mathematics could be saved from internal discord and from external pressures by becoming part of the unchallengeable science of logic.

But what sort of science is this? What sort of truths are the truths of logic? What sorts of information does logic give us about what sorts of entities? That is, I think, the central problem of Wittgenstein's *Tractatus Logico-Philosophicus*.

The truths and falsehoods of the natural sciences are truths and falsehoods about what exists and happens in the world. Their truth or falsehood depends upon what is the case with things in the world. But the truths of logic give us no information about the world. 'Either it is raining or it is not raining' exemplifies a logical truism, but it tells us nothing about the weather. It is true whatever the weather. 'Socrates is mortal' gives us important information or misinformation about Socrates, but '*If* all men are mortal and Socrates is a man, *then* he is mortal' gives us an applied logical truth, which is true whether or not he is mortal.

The truths of the natural sciences are factual truths, while those of logic are purely formal. Their truth is neutral between the world as it is and as it might have been. This formal nature of logical truths shows itself in another way. The truism 'Either it is raining or it is not' remains true if for 'raining' we substitute 'snowing', 'freezing' or anything you please. For any proposition whatsoever, either it or its negative is true. The force of 'either . . . , or not . . .' is indifferent to the material fillings of the clauses that it links, so long as the clauses are the same. Hence truths of logic can be expressed most cleanly if we algebraize away all material elements like 'Socrates', 'mortal', and 'it is raining'. This leaves, for example, 'For any p, either p or not-p'.

Thus logic is unconcerned with the actual truth or falsity of the factual statements which can be draped on its skeletons. Nonetheless logic is essentially concerned with the truth-or-falsity of these statements, since it has to work out how the truth or falsity of one *would* follow, if another *were* true or *were* false. That Jack went up the hill would have to be true *if* Jack and Jill went up the hill; and from the falsity of 'Jack went up the hill' would follow the falsity of 'Jack and Jill went up the hill'.

Well then, why should we not answer the original problem by saying that the subject matter of logic consists of truths-or-falsehoods, and that it has to discover in them their formal properties which secure that one would be true if another were true? But then what sorts of entities are truths-or-falsehoods, and what sorts of properties are these formal properties?

When I say 'It is raining', my words convey something to you. You understand them even though you do not know that it is raining. They make sense, even if it is not raining. So the actual state of the weather is one thing; the truth-or-falsehood that it is raining is something else. In getting the meaning of my words, you are getting not what the state of the weather is, but what-it-is-being-represented-as-being. But what enables expressions to represent things as they are, or as they are not? What enables a complex of symbols to *mean* something *vis-à-vis* some actual matter of fact? Consider a simple map representing, truly or falsely, the relative positions and distances of three towns: A, B and C. The dot 'A' is one inch higher on the page than the dot 'B', and this is two inches higher than the dot 'C'. This map might tell you that the town A is north of B, which is north of C, and that B is 20 miles from C and 10 from A. How does it do this? By an understood code by which lettered dots stand for towns, the top of the page for north and an inch for 10 miles. It is the way in which the dots are situated on the page that says how the towns are related to one another on the ground. In this case the map, if true, is in certain respects photographically like the corresponding stretch of ground. But with a different code the same dots might represent or misrepresent the heights of three peaks, or the degrees below boiling point of three saucepans. Representation can, but need not, be photographic. The notes played by the musician are not *like* the black marks on his score, yet the arrangement of the latter, by a complex code, may faithfully represent the arrangement of the former.

The 'codes' which enable different arrangements of words to represent different states of affairs are enormously complicated, and they vary among different tongues. In English, if you wish to say that Brutus killed Caesar you must put 'Brutus' before the verb and 'Caesar' after it. Not so in Latin, which achieves the same result by different word terminations. But without applying some syntactical rule or other you cannot say anything, not even anything false. Symbol-structures can represent and misrepresent the structures of actual states of affairs because, though the representing structure is not usually *like* the represented structure, they are still structurally analogous to one another. A sentence has a meaning if its syntax *could* be the structural analogue of an actual state of affairs, even though, when false, it actually has no such factual counterpart. Caesar did not kill Brutus, but 'Caesar killed Brutus' makes sense, since there is, so to speak, room in reality, though unfilled room, for this uncommitted murder.

Not all complexes of words or dots or gestures convey truths or falsehoods. An unorganized jumble of words or dots makes no sense. Even a sequence of words with an orthodox grammar can make nonsense. Lewis Carroll concocted many such sentences; for example, 'The Cheshire cat vanished leaving only her grin behind her.' Sometimes serious thinkers inadvertently construct senseless sentences. Early geometricians seriously held that Euclidean points are round. A truth-or-falsehood, then, is an organized complex of symbols representing, by analogy of structure, a counterpart actual-or-possible state of affairs. It is, for example, a sentence, 'in its projective relation to the world'. To find out whether it is actually true or actually false we have to match it against its should-be counterpart state of affairs in the world.

Already we can see how Wittgenstein's account of what it is to make sense, that is, to be true-or-false, led to the famous principle of verifiability, by which the logical positivists ostracized as nonsensical the pronouncements of metaphysicians, theologians and moralists. Observation and experiment are our ways of matching the propositions of, say, astronomy against the stellar facts. Where observation and experiment are excluded, our pretended truths-or-falsehoods have no anchorage in facts and so say nothing. They are nothing but disguised gibberish.

What of the truths of logic, the status of which it had been Wittgenstein's main task to fix? Are these also disguised gibberish? Or are they salved by being classed with the most general truths of natural science? Wittgenstein steers between this Scylla and this Charybdis.

An everyday 'either-or' statement, like 'Either Jack climbed the hill or Jill did', leaves it open which climbed the hill; but it still rules out something that might have been the case, namely, the climbing of the hill by neither of them. But if we ask of an 'either-or' truism of logic like 'Either Jack climbed the hill or he did not'; what is ruled out by *this* assertion?, we see that the only thing ruled out is Jack's neither climbing nor not climbing the hill. And this is not something which might have been but just happens not to be the case. An ordinary factual assertion gives the 'yes' or the 'no' answer to a question; it invites us to select the one and to forswear the other. But a truth of logic gives us nothing forswearable to forswear, and so nothing selectable to select. It is factually empty, or 'tautological'.

It does not, however, follow that the truths of logic are of no use simply because they are uninformative. They serve to show up, by contrast with their own absolute hospitality, the ways in which ordinary statements convey, by their relative shut-doored-ness, positive information or misinformation.

The truths of logic, then, are not nonsensical, though they are empty of information or misinformation. Their business is to *show* us, by evaporation of content, how our ordinary thoughts and assertions are organized.

I pass over Wittgenstein's accounts of the connections and differences between logic and mathematics and between logic and mechanics, important though these are for showing up, by contrast, the positive nature of logic. But I must not pass over his account of the relations between logic and philosophy. For, as his title *Tractatus Logico-Philosophicus* hints, his book was secondarily concerned to fix the status of philosophy. What sorts of things can philosophers tell us—philosophers as distinct from logicians and from scientists? Are the truths of philosophy factual or formal truths?

Earlier philosophers, if they tried at all to place philosophy, had tended to treat it either as psychology or as non-empirical cosmology. But Russell and others realized that philosophy was neither a natural science nor yet a supernatural science. Russell had emphasized the close connection between logic and philosophy by treating all seriously philosophical questions as problems for 'logical analysis', as if logic supplied the lines of latitude and longitude, while philosophy had to fill in the geographical detail.

In partly the same way Wittgenstein, having separated off all philosophical from any scientific puestions, describes the positive function of philosophy as 'elucidatory'. Its function is to disclose that logical architecture of our ordinary and scientific thoughts which our vernaculars conceal but which the designed symbolism of logic would expose. But now there breaks out a seemingly disastrous difference between logic and philosophy. The formulae of logic, though they tell us nothing, still show us, so to speak, at their limit the positive force of the 'ors', 'ands', 'alls' and so forth on which our ordinary truths and falsehoods are built. But philosophical pronouncements are in a worse state, since their elucidatory mission is to *tell* us what sort of sense or nonsense belongs to the propositions of the sciences and of daily life; and this is not the sort of thing that can conceivably be told. The meanings, that is, the truths or falsehoods that we express, cannot then be lifted out of their expressions. We can talk sense, but we cannot talk sense about the sense that we talk.

Consider again my map in which the situations of three dots on the page told you, truly or falsely, the situations of three towns. Now I ask you to draw another map which is to tell me not about things on the ground, but about the information or misinformation conveyed by the first map. It is to tell me whether the first map is accurate or inaccurate, and especially it is to tell me the cartographical code by which the three original dots represent the compass bearings and distances of the towns. You will promptly protest that you cannot make a map of what another map says or of how it says it. What an ordinary map alleges about the earth's surface is not another bit of that surface and so a second map could not map it. The significance-conditions which an ordinary map exemplifies are not *stated* by these or any other maps.

Similarly, we normally know when a sentence expresses a truth-or-falsehood, and when it is nonsensical. We read the composition of an actual-or-possible state of affairs out of the composition of the sentence. But we are debarred from *stating* this correlation. Attempts to state it would be attempts to stand outside the significance-conditions of statements. They would therefore break these conditions, and so be nonsense.

Philosophical elucidation advances only over the ruins of its attempted articulations. The sort of clarity that we seek we achieve in becoming conscious of what makes us stammer. Critics quickly pointed out that Wittgenstein managed to say many important and understandable things. So perhaps the language of maps has limitations from which the language of words is exempt; and perhaps the notion of sense is wider than the notion of truth-or-falsehood to empirical fact.

Wittgenstein left many manuscripts which are now in process of being published. The first book to be so published was his *Philoso-phical Investigations*. This has the German text faced by a quite good English translation.

Philosophical Investigations differs from the *Tractatus* in presentation, subject and direction. The *Tractatus* consists of a chain of sentences or short paragraphs, prefaced by numerical and decimal index-numbers signalling both the train of the argument and the relative weights in it of the successive items. Each sentence seems to be the product of an almost Chinese process of pruning and recasting. Many of them mystify, but the reader cannot get them out of his head. In many stretches the *Tractatus* presupposes familiarity with mathematical logic. The *Philosophical Investigations* is more like a conversation. It is a dialogue between the author and his own refractory self, and it presupposes no technical sophistication. It is split up into relatively long paragraph-sections, the continuities between which are often hard to see. Indeed, they are not always there. Unfortunately the book contains no aids to the reader in the shape of table of contents, index or cross references.

Notoriously the *Philosophical Investigations* throws overboard some of the cardinal positions of the *Tractatus*. Some people assume that this exempts them from trying to understand the *Tractatus*. This is a mistake, since a philosopher jettisons what he has taught himself to do without, and we need just the same teaching.

Moreover, a great deal of the *Tractatus* survives, both in the later Wittgenstein and in us too. It comes natural to us now—as it did not 30 years ago—to differentiate logic from science much as Wittgenstein did; it comes natural to us not to class philosophers as scientists or *a fortiori* as super-scientists; it comes natural to us to think of both logic and philosophy as concerned not with any ordinary or extraordinary kinds of *things*, but with the meanings of the expressions of our thoughts and knowledge; and it is beginning to come natural to us, when we reflect about sense vs. nonsense, to take as the units of sense what is conveyed by full sentences, and not what is meant by isolated words, that is, with what is *said*, and not with what is, for example, *named*.

How does the later differ from the earlier Wittgenstein? First, his central problem is different. He is no longer exercised about the status of logic. It is philosophy now that is pestering him for justice. Next he had in the *Tractatus* been scanning the notions of sense and nonsense through the perforated screen of logic. Through its apertures he could see only elementary atoms of truth and false-hood being combined into molecular truths and falsehoods by the operations of 'and', 'or' and 'not'. The only discernible differences between sayables were in their degrees and patterns of compositeness. All their other differences had been algebraized away. But now he forsakes this screen. He examines those differences between sayables which will not reduce to degrees of compositeness. Where he had examined the algebraized skeletons of statements in which only the logical constants were left functioning, now he watches the functioning of the live expressions with which we say real things. One thing that he quickly remarks is this. Not all sayables are truths or falsehoods. The logician attends only to assertable premises and conclusions. But not all saying is asserting. There is questioning, advising, entreating, ordering, reassuring, rebuking, joking, warning, commiserating, promising, deploring, praising, parodying. We talk a lot to infants and dogs, but we do not make statements to them.

In the *Tractatus* we were told, in effect, that only those sentences made positive sense which could be the premises or conclusions of a bit of natural science. In the *Philosophical Investigations* the door is opened to anything that anyone might say. We are home, again, in the country of real discourse.

The central notion of sense or meaning has correspondingly thawed. In the *Tractatus* truths-or-falsehoods seemed to be icicles of printer's ink; and their coordination with states of affairs in the real world resembled the congruence between the structures of two crystals. But sentences are normally things said, not written, by one person to another. So now Wittgenstein constantly discusses such questions as 'How do children, in real life, actually learn to understand this or that expression?' and 'How would we teach a savage to count, or tell the time?' Talking sense and following the sense talked by others are things that we have learned how to do; so the notion of sense comes out of the fog if we constantly ask just what we must have learned, and just how we must have learned it in order to be able to communicate. Most of Part I of the *Philosophical Investigations* is concerned with questions about sense, understanding, grasping, mastering, interpreting, etc.

One device that Wittgenstein constantly uses is that of exploring imaginary situations in which people have to think up and teach ways of communicating. A builder, for example, wants his inarticulate assistant to pass him bricks and slabs. How would he teach him to distinguish between the orders 'Brick' and 'Slab'? How would he teach him to bring *two* or *five* bricks, that is, to understand number-words? Wittgenstein calls these imaginary lingo-creations 'language-games'. This is unfortunate because many readers think he implies that talking is a sort of *playing*. In fact the central idea behind the label 'language-game' is the notion of *rules*. Learning to communicate is like learning to play chess or tennis in this respect, that in both we have to master written or unwritten rules—and there are many different, but interlocking, sorts of rules to be learned in both. The chess-player has had to learn what moves are allowed, what moves in what situations would be tactical mistakes, and even what moves in what situations would be unsporting. A crude generalization of Wittgenstein's new account of sense or meaning is that the meaning of an expression is the rules for the employment of that expression; that is, the rules licensing or banning its co-employment with other expressions, those governing its effective employment in normal and abnormal communication-situations, and so on. The dynamic notion of rules to be mastered has replaced the notion of an imposed structural congruence.

With his new notion of meaning, Wittgenstein is in a position to say new things about the philosopher's task of meaning-elucidation. But in the main he avoids trying to give any general account of what sort of task this is, or why and when it needs to be done, though there are passages in which he does enigmatically give such an account. Rather, especially in Part II of *Philosophical Investigations*, he tries to demonstrate in examples what philosophical quandaries are like, how to get out of them and what sideslips of thought get us into them. He is trying to teach us methods of operation, rather than give us the answer to a question in an examination.

I do not think that anybody could read the *Philosophical Investigations* without feeling that its author had his finger on the pulse of the activity of philosophizing. We can doubt whether his hinted diagnosis will do; not that he has located, by touch, that peculiar and important intellectual commotion—philosophical puzzlement.

18

G. E. MOORE

Reprinted from 'The New Statesman', 1963, by permission of the publishers

Between 1919 and 1953 G. E. Moore entered a number of philosophical reflections into notebooks, most of which he himself entitled 'Commonplace Book'. Dr C. Lewy has now published these reflections in chronological order and with indication of their approximate dates of composition.[1]

Several of the entries seem to be the outcomes of contemporary discussions with Lewy, von Wright, Malcolm and others; several seem to be the outcomes of Moore's study of books and articles by Russell, Johnson, Frege, Wittgenstein and others. In general they seem to be consolidations of previously half-consolidated ideas, further hammer-blows on nails already pretty well home. They are not confessions, heart-searchings or gropings in the dark. They tell us no secrets. Moore would not have been the philosopher he was if there had been any secrets to tell.

Of the 190 odd entries a few run to half a dozen pages; most to a page or two; and quite a lot are only half a page or less in length.

In subject matter their distribution is of some interest. Less than ten of the entries have anything to do with Ethics; elaborations of points in the theories of Time and Sense-perception are very numerous; but nearly half the entries are discussions of issues well inside the field of Logical Theory, and of these a score, all belonging to the last decade of the notebooks, are investigations of the notion or notions of *if . . . , then*. The entries will be interesting, though not often exciting, to researchers into Moore's philosophy, as well as to philosophers and logicians tackling toolshop problems continuous with Moore's. They will not, unless for occasional essays, be of much use to students, who should consume their Moore, with their other philosophers, in large mouthfuls. To readers whose interests are

[1] G. E. Moore: *Commonplace Book, 1919–1953*, edited by C. Lewy (George Allen and Unwin, 1962).

limited to the personalities of philosophers Moore's *Commonplace Book, 1919–1953* will have no appeal at all. Moore is working, not conversing.

Moore's concentration, in his notebooks, on logicians' problems sets us considering this question. What were the affiliations between Moore's philosophical thinking and the work of the logicians? In his 'Autobiography' in Schilpp's *The Philosophy of G. E. Moore*, Moore acknowledges at length and with emphasis the great debts he owes to the logical writings and lectures of Russell, as well as to personal discussions with him. He also pays tribute to the influences of Johnson, Ramsey and Wittgenstein. Some of the entries in this *Commonplace Book* are careful examinations of things written by Frege. But despite this tutelage Moore himself initiated nothing in the theory or in the techniques of Formal Logic, save for some helpful distinctions and non-technical expositions. He would not have expected or hoped that his name should be mentioned in the Kneales' *The Development of Logic*.

What Moore did was to import into the ratiocinations of philosophy the form-discriminations that had newly been elaborated *in abstracto* by the logicians. In this respect, his vocation, equipment, rigorousness and rigidities were those of a Twentieth Century Schoolman. As the bones and the sinews of Aristotle's logic shaped and sometimes misshaped the metaphysics, ethics, psychology and biology of Aristotle and the Aristotelians, so the new Schemata of mathematical logic brace and sometimes cramp Moore's epistemological, ethical and semantic thoughts. It is not that Moore is an algebraizer in philosophy. He employed the logicians' new inference-patterns as his stencils, not as his fabric. It is a major part of the philosopher's task to select and disencumber just these natural and familiar expressions which are competent to carry precisely determined premiss-burthens and conclusion-burthens. Theory-tangles can and must be resolved by rendering completely unequivocal and completely specific the different questions to which answers are required, and by demarcating exactly what propositions are and are not entailed by all the suggested answers to them. To find the implications and compatibilities of one proposition is to distinguish its force from the forces of the adjacent propositions which might be confused with it or be wrongly treated as part and parcel of it. The philosopher has not to discard his native dictions, but only to take all possible pains to unclutter their inference-edges.

It may be that Moore relied too docilely on the new surgical tools, which had been cut for duties considerably different from those which he imposed upon them; and it may be that Moore's diagnoses of the *aporiai* to be resolved were too much controlled by the operations which these tools enabled him to perform. If so, it follows that Moore's canons of argumentative precision and cogency need to be emancipated from these controls, and not that philosophy needs to be emancipated from his standards.

Like Socrates, Moore was apt to suppose that his analytic operations would terminate, if ever successful, in some analyses or definitions of composite concepts. But, like Socrates, he produced very few such analyses. Nor does what we have learned from him consist in a repertoire of such analyses. He taught us to try to assess and how to assess the forces of the expressions on which philosophical issues hinge. It is a not very important accident that he, with many of his critics and champions, did not fully realize that, before these forces have been assessed, definitions can do no good, and after they have been assessed there is no more good for them to do, save the little good that mnemonics do. In his 'Autobiography' (page 33) Moore announces gladly and unenviously the drastic reorientation that Wittgenstein was giving to philosophical enquiries and methods. He realized, without any resentment, that the tide of interest was ebbing from the estuaries in which he had so pertinaciously dredged. He does not mention, and probably never mentioned to himself, how much Wittgenstein's sails needed the keel and the ballast that Moore provided.

For some of us there still lives the Moore whose voice is never quite resuscitated by his printed words. This is the Moore whom we met at Cambridge and at the annual Joint Session of the Mind Association and the Aristotelian Society. Moore was a dynamo of courage. He gave us courage not by making concessions, but by making no concessions to our youth or to our shyness. He treated us as corrigible and therefore as responsible thinkers. He would explode at our mistakes and muddles with just that genial ferocity with which he would explode at the mistakes and muddles of philosophical high-ups, and with just the genial ferocity with which he would explode at mistakes and muddles of his own. He would listen with minute attention to what we said, and then, without a trace of discourtesy or courtesy, treat our remarks simply on their merits, usually, of course, and justly inveighing against their inadequacy, irrelevance or confusedness, but sometimes, without a trace of politeness or patronage, crediting them with whatever positive utility he thought that they possessed. If, as sometimes happened, he found in someone's interposition the exposure of a confusion or a fallacy of his own, he would announce that this was so, confess to his own unbelievable muddle-headedness or slackness of reasoning, and then, with full acknowledgement, adopt and work with the new clarification. Good arguments, no matter whose, were there to be employed by everyone; bad arguments, no matter whose, had to be eradicated with blasting-powder.

Himself free from both vanity and humility, he saw no reason, and he taught us to see no reason, why matters of personal prestige or sensitiveness should be considered at all. He never pulled his punches, but he never bullied; he tore to pieces our bad arguments, but he never sneered at us. Sometimes he applauded and availed himself of our valid points; but he never complimented us. He never tried to score. He never cheated. He had no philosophical gospel to broadcast and no philosophical party to campaign for. His own darling philosophical cruces were not very numerous, and their cardinal teasers often seemed to us factitious. We came across few theses which we could cite as Moore's doctrines, and we felt no special tug to accept those that we could cite. None the less we left for home feeling full of fight, but also feeling firmly resolved to put better edges on our arguments next time.

He reminded one, in quick succession, of a Duns Scotus, a ton of bricks and one's farmer uncle on a holiday. Before quite wearied by the ant-like labours that he squandered on obviously unrewarding side-issues, we would be startled out of our skins by his indignant repudiation of a suggested *via media*; two minutes later we would find him radiating geniality and looking slightly naughty. What did he teach us? To care more whether our bridges were soundly built than for anything else whatsoever.

19

REVIEW OF 'SYMPOSIUM ON
J. L. AUSTIN'

Reprinted from 'The Listener', 1970, by permission of the editor

How did English-speaking philosophy get its linguistic slant?

(1) The inquiries of Frege and Russell into the foundations of mathematics met obstructions which demanded new logical tools. But seventy years ago logic and philosophy still lisped in Locke's idioms: both needed to be de-psychologised. Syllogisms and equations could no longer be dissected into what associations of ideas are associations of. Out of what non-mental things, then, are our premisses and conclusions made? Of Platonic entities? Yet 'Socrates is mortal' is true of Socrates, not of any deathless proxy for him.

Frege showed that what, for instance, a subject-term expresses or conveys is not the object, if any, that it designates. 'Evening Star' and 'Morning Star' convey different Senses, though designating the same planetary Object. '$\sqrt{289} = 17$' says more than '$17 = 17$'. What a truth or falsehood is composed of is not the objects that it is true or false of.

Russell showed that for a denial of existence to be true—for instance, 'the island of Atlantis never existed'—its nominative must be significant and must not have an island corresponding to it. What it signifies *is* not any island. He also showed, what proved crucial, that some nominatives, like 'the last even number', cannot denote. For assignable reasons of logic some grammatically permissible subject-phrases are nonsense; and some quasi-statements cannot significantly be even denied as false.

Wittgenstein generalised the issue. Sense/nonsense questions undercut any questions about things or happenings. Logic and philosophy, being concerned with meanings and unmeanings, have no objects to be about, whether Everyman's, Locke's, Plato's or even Occam's. Since only dicta and scripta make or fail to make sense, logic and philosophy are to this extent linguistic. But the sense and nonsense that expressions make are not themselves philologists' objects. Our question 'Out of what things are truths and falsehoods made?' was itself a nonsense question. Even if we answer 'Out of concepts', these cannot be denotable things, happenings or processes etc., even mental or phonetic ones.

(2) Though G. E. Moore pioneered the de-psychologising of logic and philosophy, he lagged behind Frege, Russell and Wittgenstein on questions of Sense/Nonsense and Sense/Reference. Nor did the Paradoxes exercise him.

On the other hand, (a) he re-fostered the Socratic idea that philosophy is a search for definitions. The definition of a complex concept, like *danger*, was its 'analysis'; simple concepts, like *yellow*, were indifferently 'indefinable' and 'unanalysable'. Since 'concept' was paraphrased by 'word-meaning', philosophers' definitions were soon, against Moore's resistance, half-equated with those of lexicographers. (b) Moore confessed that to him personally philosophical ideas came only out of recoils against the odd things said by other philosophers. Having no first-hand puzzles, he moved by exposing the confusions, vaguenesses, non-sequiturs and equivocations of others. Since the harvest of Socratic definitions was meagre, 'analysis' came to signify 'exposure of muddles'. His practice, despite his protests, suggested that philosophy just is linguistic unmuddling.

J. L. Austin took as little as he could after Wittgenstein, a lot after Moore—the un-muddler, not the definer. He too shied away from the Paradoxes, and from puzzles in general. Besides his fine scholarship, he had the nose and heart of a philologist. He was a protector of maltreated nuances and a stamp-collector of idioms. He would sweepingly reprimand philosophers *en masse* for our occupational insensitiveness to idiom; also, less confidently, for our ambitions to bridge abysses instead of cutting steps. He dreamed of reforming our lax fraternity into a researching task-force, and our puzzle-ridden debatings into disciplined semantic fact-findings. The title 'philosopher' irked him, as 'professor' irked Wittgenstein.

Probably he thought of his own, almost botanical classifications of locution-types much less as contributions to philosophy than as elements for a future *Principia Grammatica*. True, it was for an anti-Cartesian end that he had isolated his special little class of the performative affixes, like 'I promise . . .' and 'I hereby name . . .', by which speakers occasionally signal their concurrent communicative intents. The obviously unchallengeable 'I acknowledge . . .' should not be cited as an extra '*cognito*'-type truth. But Austin's interest swung away from these rather incidental signals of intent to the neglected multifariousness of the things that we are doing when we testify, insinuate, command, admit, apologise, promise, threaten, advise, sanction, christen, offer, remind, request, accuse, vote, conclude etc. These disparate, and generally unpropositional saying-types deserve their Linnaeus, whether or not his discriminations happen to meet needs of, for instance, jurisprudents or epistemologists.

Whatever the niche in *Principia Grammatica* of Austin's 'How to do things with words', it is not by this but—I can see him wince—by his philosophical essays that he will have altered the shapes of things. Nor—I can see his spokesmen frown—is it by his patient, ear-to-ground and usually just discriminations between the contiguous and overlapping concepts of everyday and law-court life. No, it is by his un-Moore-like impatiences with the traditional cruces of philosophy. For he would, with a grimace, snatch up the tangled old skein of Determinism, Freedom and Responsibility; or of Knowledge, Self-Knowledge and Belief; or of Sense-Perception, Appearance and Reality; and unceremoniously shake it inside out.

These brusquely inverted skeins had their own knots, twists and loose ends, but not the inveterate, obstinate ones. Fingers severely drilled in piecemeal unravelling might actually undo these fresh, unaggravated tangles. But it was the impatient shakes that made the difference.

During his tragically early last years, Austin was scanning a conceptual new-found-land of his own. His semi-philosophical work of classifying our multifarious communicative doings loaded him with problems about the very notion of Doing. Some of these were jurisprudential problems. Just why might the courts find that something was, or else was not, or was not altogether, my doing? But there were other problems; and even puzzles. Just how does the perhaps complex and long-term intention with which you do something render yours an altogether different kind of action from my muscularly indistinguishable movement? What more is there to doing than thinking what to do? Why is it absurd to say that I did exactly— or roughly—293 things yesterday? Is refraining doing something— or nothing? When I kicked and scored, did I do two things or only one? Which one? We cannot tell where Austin would have located the central ridge, if any, of his new terrain; or how, after sedulous, inch-by-inch team-reconnaissances, he would have assaulted it.

Symposium on J. L. Austin[1] is an admirable budget of papers about

[1] Edited by K. T. Fann (Routledge and Kegan Paul Ltd., 1969).

Austin, written by leading or will-be-leading thinkers. A few of these twenty-six papers are biographical, descriptive or expository. But several are critical, even fiercely critical, of Austin's ideas and methods; others are vigorously critical of these criticisms. Where we expected a vase of memorial tributes, we get a cauldron of peppered meats, all good and many very good. Austin's acerbities are frequently repaid in kind; and he, in his turn, is accused of linguistic insensitiveness, and even of philological amateurishness. Austin made not a stir, but a lot of stirs. This book is a simmer of these vortices.

20

JANE AUSTEN AND THE MORALISTS

Reprinted from 'The Oxford Review', no. 1, 1966, by permission of the editor

I

Jane Austen is often described as just a miniature-painter. Her blessed 'little bit (two inches wide) of ivory' has too often set the tone of criticism. I mean to show that she was more than this. Whether we like it or not, she was also a moralist. In a thin sense of the word, of course, every novelist is a moralist who shows us the ways or *mores* of his characters and their society. But Jane Austen was a moralist in a thick sense, that she wrote what and as she wrote partly from a deep interest in some perfectly general, even theoretical questions about human nature and human conduct. To say this is not, however, to say that she was a moraliser. There is indeed some moralising in *Sense and Sensibility* and she does descend to covert preaching in *Mansfield Park*. Here I do discern, with regret, the tones of voice of the anxious aunt, and even occasionally of the prig. But for the most part, I am glad to say, she explores and does not shepherd.

I am not going to try to make out that Jane Austen was a philosopher or even a philosopher *manquée*. But I am going to argue that she was interested from the south side in some quite general or theoretical problems about human nature and conduct in which philosophers proper were and are interested from the north side.

To begin with, we should consider the titles of three of her novels, namely, *Sense and Sensibility*, *Pride and Prejudice* and *Persuasion*. It is not for nothing that these titles are composed of abstract nouns. *Sense and Sensibility* really is about the relations between Sense and Sensibility or, as we might put it, between Head and Heart, Thought and Feeling, Judgement and Emotion, or Sensibleness and Sensitiveness. *Pride and Prejudice* really is about pride and about the misjudgements that stem from baseless pride, excessive pride, deficient pride, pride in trivial objects, and so on. *Persuasion* really is or rather does set out to be about persuadability, unpersuadability and over-persuadability.

To go into detail. In *Sense and Sensibility* it is not only Elinor, Marianne and Mrs Dashwood who exemplify equilibrium or else inequilibrium between judiciousness and feeling. Nearly all the characters in the novel do so, in their different ways and their different degrees. John Dashwood has his filial and fraternal feelings, but they are shallow ones. They do not overcome his and his wife's calculating selfishness. Sir John Middleton is genuinely and briskly kind, but with a cordiality too general to be really thoughtful. What he does for one person he does with equal zest for another, without considering their differences of need, desert or predilection. He would be in his element in a Butlin's Holiday Camp. Mrs Jennings, whose character changes during the novel, is a thoroughly vulgar woman who yet has, in matters of importance, a sterling heart and not too bad a head. Lucy Steele professes deep feelings, but they are sham ones, while her eye for the main chance is clear and unwavering. Like her future mother-in-law she has too little heart and too much sense of a heartless sort.

Marianne and Elinor are alike in that their feelings are deep and genuine. The difference is that Marianne lets her joy, anxiety or grief so overwhelm her that she behaves like a person crazed. Elinor keeps her head. She continues to behave as she knows she should behave. She is deeply grieved or worried, but she does not throw to the winds all considerations of duty, prudence, decorum or good taste. She is sensitive *and* sensible, in our sense of the latter adjective. I think that Elinor too often and Marianne sometimes collapse into two-dimensional samples of abstract types; Elinor's conversation occasionally degenerates into lecture or even homily. This very fact bears out my view that Jane Austen regularly had one eye, and here an eye and a half, on a theoretical issue. The issue here was this: must Head and Heart be antagonists? Must a person who is deeply grieved or deeply joyous be crazy with grief or joy? To which Jane Austen's answer, the correct answer, is, 'No, the best Heart and the best Head are combined in the best person.' But Elinor sometimes collapses into a Head rather loosely buttoned on to a Heart, and then she ceases to be a person at all.

Jane Austen brings out the precise kinds of the sensibility exhibited by Elinor and Marianne by her wine-taster's technique of matching them not only against one another but also against nearly all the other characters in their little world. The contrast between Lucy Steele and both Elinor and Marianne is the contrast between sham and real sensibility or emotion; the contrast between Willoughby and, say, Edward is the contrast between the genuine but shallow feelings of the one and the genuine and deep feelings of the other. Lady Middleton's feelings are few and are concentrated entirely on her own children. Her husband's feelings are spread abroad quite undiscriminatingly. He just wants everyone to be jolly.

I want briefly to enlarge on this special wine-taster's technique of comparative character-delineation. Jane Austen's great predecessor, Theophrastus, had described just one person at a time, the Garrulous Man by himself, say, or the Mean Man by himself. So the Garrulity or the Meanness is not picked out by any contrasts or affinities with contiguous qualities. Our view of the Garrulous Man is not clarified by his being matched against the Conversationally Fertile Man on the one side, or against the Conversationally Arid Man on the other. The Meanness of the Mean Man is not brought into relief by being put into adjacency with the meritorious Austerity of a Socrates or the allowable Close Bargaining of a dealer. By contrast, Jane Austen's technique is the method of the vintner. She pin-points the exact quality of character in which she is interested, and the exact degree of that quality, by matching it against the same quality in different degrees, against simulations of that quality, against deficiencies of it, and against qualities which, though different, are brothers or cousins of that selected quality. The ecstatic emotionality of her Marianne is made to stand out against the sham, the shallow, the inarticulate and the controlled feelings of Lucy Steele, Willoughby, Edward and Elinor. To discriminate the individual taste of any one character is to discriminate by comparison the individual taste of every other character. That is to say, in a given novel Jane Austen's characters are not merely blankly different, as Cheltenham is blankly different from Helvellyn. They are different inside the same genus, as Cheltenham is different from Bath or Middlesbrough, or as Helvellyn is different from Skiddaw or Boar's Hill.

Thus in *Pride and Prejudice* almost every character exhibits too much or too little pride, pride of a bad or silly sort or pride of a good sort, sham pride or genuine pride and so forth. Elizabeth Bennet combines a dangerous cocksureness in her assessments of people with a proper sense of her own worth. Jane is quite uncocksure. She is too diffident. She does not resent being put upon or even realize that she is being put upon. There is no proper pride, and so no fight in her. Their mother is so stupid and vulgar that she has no sense of dignity at all, only silly vanities about her dishes and her daughters' conquests. Mr Bennet has genuine pride. He does despise the despicable. But it is inert, unexecutive pride. He voices his just contempt in witty words, but he does nothing to prevent or repair what he condemns. It is the pride of a mere don, though a good don. Bingley has no special pride, and so, though a nice man, spinelessly lets himself be managed by others where he should not. His sisters are proud in the sense of being vain and snobbish.

Darcy is, to start with, haughty and snobbish, a true nephew of Lady Catherine de Burgh. His early love for Elizabeth is vitiated by condescension. He reforms into a man with pride of the right sort. He is proud to be able to help Elizabeth and her socially embarrassing family. He now knows what is due from him as well as what is due to him. Mr Collins is the incarnation of vacuous complacency. He glories in what are mere reflections from the rank of his titled patroness and from his own status as a clergyman. He is a soap-bubble with nothing at all inside him and only bulging refractions from other things on his rotund surface.

The same pattern obtains in *Persuasion*. Not only Anne Elliot but her father, sisters, friends and acquaintances are described in terms of their kinds and degrees of persuadability and unpersuadability. Anne had suffered from having dutifully taken the bad advice of the over-cautious Lady Russell. Her father and sister Elizabeth can be persuaded to live within their means only by the solicitor's shrewd appeals to quite unworthy considerations. Her sister Mary is so full of self-pity that she can be prevailed on only by dexterous coaxings. Lydia Musgrove is too headstrong to listen to advice, so she cracks her skull. Her sister Henrietta is so over-persuadable that she is a mere weathercock. Mr Elliot, after his suspect youth, is apparently eminently rational. But it turns out that he is amenable to reason only so long as reason is on the side of self-interest.

This particular theme-notion of persuadability was, in my opinion, too boring to repay Jane Austen's selection of it, and I believe that she herself found that her story tended to break away from its rather flimsy ethical frame. Certainly, when Anne and Wentworth at last come together again, their talk does duly turn on the justification of Anne's original yielding to Lady Russell's persuasion and on the unfairness of Wentworth's resentment of her so yielding. But we, and I think Jane Austen herself, are happy to hear the last of this particular theme. We are greatly interested in Anne, but not because she had been dutifully docile as a girl. We think only fairly well of Lydia Musgrove, but her deafness to counsels of prudence is not what makes our esteem so tepid. Some of the solidest characters in the novel, namely the naval characters, are not described in terms of their persuadability or unpersuadability at all, and we are not sorry.

I hope I have made out something of a case for the view that the abstract nouns in the titles *Sense and Sensibility, Pride and Prejudice* and *Persuasion* really do indicate the controlling themes of the novels; that Jane Austen wrote *Sense and Sensibility* partly, at least, from an interest in the quite general or theoretical question whether deep feeling is compatible with being reasonable; that she wrote *Pride and Prejudice* from an interest in the quite general question what sorts and degrees of pride do, and what sorts and degrees of pride do not go with right thinking and right acting; and that she wrote *Persuasion* from an interest—I think a waning interest and one which I do not share—in the general question when people should and when they should not let themselves be persuaded by what sorts of counsels.

I shall now become bolder. I shall now say what corresponding theme-notions constitute the frames of *Emma* and *Mansfield Park*, though no abstract nouns occur in their titles.

If cacophony had not forbidden, *Emma* could and I think would have been entitled *Influence and Interference*. Or it might have been called more generically *Solicitude*. Jane Austen's question here was: What makes it sometimes legitimate or even obligatory for one person deliberately to try to modify the course of another person's life, while sometimes such attempts are wrong? Where is the line between Meddling and Helping? Or, more generally, between proper and improper solicitude and unsolicitude about the destinies and welfares of others? Why was Emma wrong to try to arrange Harriet's life, when Mr Knightley was right to try to improve Emma's mind and character? Jane Austen's answer is the right answer. Emma was treating Harriet as a puppet to be worked by hidden strings. Mr Knightley advised and scolded Emma to her face. Emma knew what Mr Knightley required of her and hoped for her. Harriet was not to know what Emma was scheming on her behalf. Mr Knightley dealt with Emma as a potentially responsible and rational being. Emma dealt with Harriet as a doll. Proper solicitude is open and not secret. Furthermore, proper solicitude is actuated by genuine good will. Improper solicitude is actuated by love of power, jealousy, conceit, sentimentality and so on.

To corroborate this interpretation we should notice, what we now expect, that the novel's other characters also are systematically described in terms of their different kinds or degrees of concernment or unconcernment with the lives of others. Emma's father is a fusser, who wants to impose his own hypochondriacal regimen on others. But his intentions are kindly and his objectives are not concealed. He is a silly old darling, but he is not a schemer. He tries in vain to influence his friends' meals and his grandchildren's holiday resorts. He is over-solicitous and solicitous about trivialities, but he does not meddle, save, nearly, once, and then John Knightley properly loses his temper with him. Mrs Elton is silly and vulgar. Her fault is that of officiousness. She tries to force her services on other people. She is a nuisance, but there is nothing underhand about her; rather the reverse, she advertises too much the unwanted benefits that she tries to impose on her victims. John Knightley is somewhat refreshingly unconcerned with other people's affairs outside his own family circle. He is honest, forthright and perceptive, but, unlike his wife, her father and her sister Emma, he does not interest himself in things that are not his business. He is not brutal or callous, and only twice or three times is he even testy; but other people's affairs are not naturally interesting to him. Gossip bores him and social gatherings seem to him a weary waste of time. Mr Elton differs from John Knightley in just this respect, that Mr Elton affects solicitude without really feeling it, while John Knightley is frankly unsolicitous. By contrast, Miss Bates is an incessant, though entirely kindly natterer about other people's affairs. She cares very much about everybody's welfare, though her concern is, through no fault of her own, confined to talk. She is debarred from doing anything for anyone save her old mother, but all her little thoughts and all her little utterances are enthusiastically benevolent ones. She is the twittering voice of universal good will. Mr Knightley is like her in good will, but unlike her in that his is executive and efficient good will. He says little; he just helps. He does what needs to be done for people, but he does not do it behind their backs, nor does he shout about it to the world. Finally, Frank Churchill is matched against Mr Knightley in that while he too does things which make small or big differences to other people's lives, he often does surreptitious things. He does not hurry to come to meet his new step-mother; and when he does come it is because his crypto-fiancée has just returned to the village. He flirts with Emma, but does not let her know that he is only playing a game, and playing a game as a camouflage. He forces a piano on his fiancée without letting her know to whom she is indebted. He is not wicked, but he is not above-board, so many of his actions affecting others belong to the class of interference, and not of legitimate intervention. He is ready to make use of people without their knowledge or consent, in order to get himself out of difficulties. He is like Emma in being a bit of a schemer, but he is unlike her in that she tried to shape the whole life of Harriet; he tricked people only for momentary purposes. He did not want to make big or lasting differences to anybody's life, save his own and his fiancée's; but he was reckless of the danger of making such a difference without intending it. He meddled by covert gambling, she meddled by covert plotting. It is no accident that he was the adopted son of a domineering and wealthy old lady and her intimidated husband. In effect they had trained him not to be forthright. This theme-notion of *Emma*, that of *Influence and Interference*, is explicitly brought out in the conversation in which the heroine and hero first open their hearts to each other. These two abstract nouns both occur there, as they occur sporadically elsewhere in the novel.

Now for *Mansfield Park*, Jane Austen's profoundest, but also her most didactic novel. Its theme-notion is the connection, to use her own ugly phrase, between fraternal and conjugal ties. Here nearly all the characters are systematically described in terms of the affection which they feel, or do not feel, or which they only pretend to feel for their own flesh and blood. Their capacities or incapacities to make good husbands or wives are a direct function of their lovingness or unlovingness inside their own families. Fanny's devotedness to her brother William, her cousins, aunt and uncle gets its reward in happy marriage; while her coldheartedness at home results in marital disaster for Maria.

Jane Austen duly describes not only the major but also many of the minor characters in terms of their excellences and defects as brothers, aunts, daughters, cousins and parents. Sir Thomas Bertram is genuinely fond of his wife, children and niece. But he is too stiff and pompous to be intimate with them. He is affectionate at a distance. So his children do not love him and he does not understand them. Lady Bertram is drowsily fond of her family but is so bovine and inert that she seldom does anything or says anything to affect anybody. Her sister, Mrs Norris, is an officious and mischief-making aunt and an unforgiving sister. Her eloquent professions of love for the Bertrams are a mere cover for self-importance. With such parents and such an aunt, Tom, Maria and her sister grow up selfish and cold-hearted. Maria marries for the wrong reasons and destroys her marriage for worse ones.

The real hero of the story is Fanny's brother, William. He is gay, affectionate, vigorous, straight and brave, and he makes Fanny happy. It is their brother-sister love which is the paradigm against which to assess all the others. Fanny's love for her cousin Edmund had begun as a child's love for a deputy-William.

Henry and Mary Crawford have accomplishments, vitality, wit, artistic tastes and charm. But they speak undutifully in public about the unsatisfactory uncle who had brought them up; they resent the unexpected return of Sir Thomas Bertram from Antigua to the bosom of his own family, simply because it puts a stop to their theatricals; and even between brother and sister the relations are cordial rather than intimate. Unlike William, Henry never writes a proper letter to his sister. Nor does he mind setting the Bertram sisters at loggerheads by flirting with both at once. He has little personal or vicarious family feeling. Critics have lamented that Henry Crawford does not marry Fanny. But this would have ruined the point. He has indeed everything that she or we could wish her husband to have—everything save two. He lacks high principles, and he lacks filial and fraternal lovingness. He is without those very qualities which make William the ideal brother. Henry could never be what Edmund was, a deputy-William. Though by no means without a heart, he was too shallow-hearted for him and Fanny ever to be the centres and circumferences of one another's lives.

Northanger Abbey is the one novel of the six which does not have an abstract ethical theme for its backbone. I think that when Jane Austen began to write this novel, it had been her sole intention to burlesque such novels as *The Mystery of Udolpho* by depicting a nice but gullible teenager looking at the actual world through, so to speak, the celluloid film of Gothic romances. But even here Jane Austen's ethical interest came quite soon to make its contribution. For we soon begin to find that Catherine, though a gullible ninny about how the actual world runs, is quite ungullible about what is right and wrong, decorous and indecorous. Her standards of conduct, unlike her criteria of actuality, are those of a candid, scrupulous and well-brought up girl, not those of the unschooled, novel-struck girl that she also is. Jane Austen began *Northanger Abbey* just poking fun at factual gullibility; but she soon became much more interested in moral ungullibility. Jane Austen the moralist quickly outgrew Jane Austen the burlesquer.

II

Jane Austen did, then, consider quite general or theoretical questions. These questions were all moral questions; though only in *Mansfield Park* and *Sense and Sensibility* did she cross over the boundary into moralising. I am now going to be more specific and say what sorts of moral ideas were most congenial to her. I will try to bring out together both what I mean by this question and what its answer is.

In the eighteenth century, and in other centuries too, moralists tended to belong to one of two camps. There was what I shall call, with conscious crudity, the Calvinst camp, and there was what I shall call the Aristotelian camp. A moralist of the Calvinist type thinks, like a criminal lawyer, of human beings as either Saved or Damned, either Elect or Reject, either children of Virtue or children of Vice, either heading for Heaven or heading for Hell, either White or Black, either Innocent or Guilty, either Saints or Sinners. The Calvinist's moral psychology is correspondingly bi-polar. People are dragged upwards by Soul or Spirit or Reason or Conscience; but they are dragged down by Body or Flesh or Passion or Pleasure or Desire or Inclination. A man is an unhappy combination of a white angelic part and a black satanic part. At the best, the angelic part has the satanic part cowed and starved and subjugated now, and can hope to be released altogether from it in the future. Man's life here is either a life of Sin or else it is a life of self-extrication from Sin. We find people being depicted in such terms in plenty of places. The seducer in the *Vicar of Wakefield* is Wickedness incarnate. So he has no other ordinary qualities. Fanny Burney's bad characters are pure stage-villains. Occasionally Johnson in the *Rambler* depicts persons who are all Black; and since they possess no Tuesday morning attributes, we cannot remember a thing about them afterwards. They are black cardboard and nothing more. The less frequent angelic or saintly characters are equally unalive, flat and forgettable.

In contrast with this, the Aristotelian pattern of ethical ideas represents people as differing from one another in degree and not in kind, and differing from one another not in respect just of a single generic Sunday attribute, Goodness, say, or else Wickedness, but in respect of a whole spectrum of specific week-day attributes. *A* is a bit more irritable and ambitious than *B*, but less indolent and less sentimental. *C* is meaner and quicker-witted than *D*, and *D* is greedier and more athletic than *C*. And so on. A person is not black or white, but irridescent with all the colours of the rainbow; and he is not a flat plane, but a highly irregular solid. He is not blankly Good or Bad, blankly angelic or fiendish; he is better than most in one respect, about level with the average in another respect, and a bit, perhaps a big bit, deficient in a third respect. In fact he is like the people we really know, in a way in which we do not know and could not know any people who are just Bad or else just Good.

Jane Austen's moral ideas are, with certain exceptions, ideas of the Aristotelian and not of the Calvinist pattern. Much though she had learned from Johnson, this she had not learned from him. When Johnson is being ethically solemn, he draws people in black and white. So they never come to life, any more than the North Pole and the South Pole display any scenic features. Jane Austen's people are, nearly always, alive all over, all through and all round, displaying admirably or amusingly or deplorably proportioned mixtures of all the colours that there are, save pure White and pure Black. If a Calvinist critic were to ask us whether Mr Collins was Hell-bound or Heaven-bent, we could not answer. The question does not apply. Mr Collins belongs to neither pole; he belongs to a very particular parish in the English Midlands. He is a stupid, complacent and inflated ass, but a Sinner? No. A Saint? No. He is just a ridiculous figure, that is, a figure for which the Calvinist ethical psychology does not cater. The questions Was Emma Good? Was she Bad? are equally unanswerable and equally uninteresting. Obviously she should have been smacked more often when young; obviously, too, eternal Hell-fire is not required for her.

Let me now bring out my reservations. Jane Austen does, with obvious reluctance and literary embarrassment, use the criminal lawyer's Black-White process three or four times. Willoughby in *Sense and Sensibility* begins by being or at least seems to be, behind his attractive exterior, black-hearted. It turns out that he is only a bit grey at heart and not black. The latter shade is reserved for his fiancée, whom therefore we do not meet. In *Pride and Prejudice* Wickham and Lydia do become regulation Sinners, as do Mr Elliot and Mrs Clay in *Persuasion*. Fortunately London exists, that desperate but comfortingly remote metropolis; so Jane Austen smartly bundles off her shadowy representatives of vice to that convenient sink. It is in London that Henry Crawford and Maria enjoy or endure their guilty association. Thus Jane Austen is exempted by the width of the Home Counties from having to try to portray in her pastel-shades the ebony complexion of urban sin. Human saints and angels gave her no such literary anxieties. She just forgot that there were officially supposed to exist such arctic paragons, a piece of forget-fulness for which we are not inclined to reprove her.

As early as in *Northanger Abbey* Jane Austen explicitly relinquishes the Black-White, Sinner-Saint dichotomy. Catherine Morland, brought to her senses, reflects:

Charming as were all Mrs. Radcliffe's works ... it was not in them, perhaps, that human nature, at least in the midland counties of England, was to be looked for. Of the Alps and Pyrenees, with their pine-forests and their vices, they might give a faithful delineation; and Italy, Switzerland and the South of France might be as fruitful in horrors as they were there represented. Catherine dared not doubt beyond her own country, and even of that, if hard pressed, would have yielded the northern and western extremities. But in the central part of England there was surely some security of existence even of a wife not beloved; in the laws of the land, and the manners of the age. Murder was not tolerated; servants were not slaves, and neither poison nor sleeping potions were to be procured, like rhubarb, from every druggist. Among the Alps and Pyrenees perhaps, there were no mixed characters. There, such as were not as spotless as an angel, might have the dispositions of a fiend. But in England it was not so; among the English, she believed, in their hearts and habits there was a general though unequal mixture of good and bad. Upon this conviction she would not be surprised if even in Henry and Eleanor Tilney some slight imperfection might hereafter appear; ...

In *Persuasion* Jane Austen gives us what she would have been surprised to hear was a good rendering of Aristotle's doctrine of the Mean.

Anne wondered whether it ever occurred to him [Wentworth] to question the justness of his own previous opinion as to the universal felicity and advantage of firmness of character; and whether it might not strike him that like all other qualities of mind it should have its proportions and limits.

Not only was Jane Austen's ethic, if that is not too academic a word, Aristotelian in type, as opposed to Calvinistic. It was also secular as opposed to religious. I am sure that she was personally not merely the dutiful daughter of a clergyman, but was genuinely pious. Yet hardly a whisper of piety enters into even the most serious and most anguished meditations of her heroines. They never pray and they never give thanks on their knees. Three of her heroes go into the church, and Edmund has to defend his vocation against the cynicisms of the Crawfords. But not a hint is given that he regards his clerical duty as that of saving souls. Routine church-going on Sunday with the rest of the family gets a passing mention three or four times, and Fanny is once stated to be religious. But that is all. I am not suggesting that Jane Austen's girls are atheists, agnostics or Deists. I am only saying that when Jane Austen writes about them, she draws the curtain between her Sunday thoughts, whatever they were, and her creative imagination. Her heroines face their moral difficulties and solve their moral problems without recourse to religious faith or theological doctrines. Nor does it ever occur to them to seek the counsels of a clergyman.

Lastly, her ethical vocabulary and idioms are quite strongly laced with aesthetic terms. We hear of 'moral taste', 'moral and literary tastes', 'beauty of mind', 'the beauty of truth and sincerity', 'delicacy of principle', 'the Sublime of Pleasures'. Moreover there is a prevailing correlation between sense of duty, sense of propriety and aesthetic taste. Most of her people who lack any one of these three, lack the other two as well. Mrs Jennings is the only one of Jane Austen's vulgarians who is allowed, none the less, to have a lively and just moral sense. Catherine Morland, whose sense of what is right and decorous is unfailing, is too much of an ignoramus yet to have acquired aesthetic sensibility, but the two Tilneys have all three tastes or senses. The Crawfords are her only people who combine musical, literary and dramatic sensitivity with moral laxity; Henry Crawford reads Shakespeare movingly, and yet is a bit of a cad. Elinor Dashwood, Anne Elliot and Fanny Price have good taste in all three dimensions. Emma Woodhouse is shaky in all three dimensions, and all for the same reason, that she is not effectively self-critical.

III

So Jane Austen's moral system was a secular, Aristotelian ethic-cum-aesthetic. But to say all this is to say that her moral *Weltan-schauung* was akin to that of Lord Shaftesbury. Shaftesbury too had, a century before, assimilated moral sense to artistic sense, aesthetic taste to moral taste. A Grecian by study and predilection, he had followed Aristotle in preference to Plato, the Stoics or the Epicureans. A Deist rather than a Christian, he had based his religion, such as it was, on his ethics and aesthetics, rather than these on his religion. So I now put forward the historical hypothesis that Jane Austen's specific moral ideas derived, directly or indirectly, knowingly or unknowingly, from Shaftesbury. Certainly she never mentions him by name; but nor is any moralist mentioned by name, even in those contexts in which her girl characters are described as studying the writings of moralists. Anne Elliot does advise the melancholy Captain Benwick to read, *inter alios*, 'our best moralists'; Fanny Price tutors her young sister, Susan, in history and morals; that teen-aged bluestocking, Mary Bennet, makes long extracts from the writings of moralists, and regales her company with their most striking platitudes. But the word 'moralist' would cover Goldsmith or Pope as well as Hutcheson or Hume, Johnson or Addison as well as Shaftesbury or Butler. We cannot argue just from the fact that Jane Austen speaks of moralists to the conclusion that she has any accredited moral philosophers in mind.

My reasons for thinking that Shaftesbury was the direct or indirect source of Jane Austen's moral furniture are these:

(1) I have the impression, not based on research or wide reading, that throughout the eighteenth and early nineteenth centuries the natural, habitual and orthodox ethic was, with various modifications and mitigations, that Black-White, Saint-Sinner ethic that I have crudely dubbed 'Calvinistic'. Hutcheson, Butler and Hume, who were considerably influenced by Shaftesbury, all dissociate themselves from the Angel-Fiend psychology, as if this was prevalent. The essays, whether in the *Spectator*, the *Idler* or the *Rambler*, though I have only dipped into them, seem to me to use the Black-White process when very serious moral matters are discussed; but, perhaps partly for this reason, they tend not to treat very often such sermon-topics. The light touch necessary for an essay could not without awkwardness be applied to Salvation or Damnation. Fielding, who did know his Shaftesbury, was too jolly to bother much with satanic or angelic characters. There are many Hogarthian caricatures in his novels, but they are there to be laughed at. They are not Awful Warnings. That is, I have the impression that the secular and aesthetic Aristotelianism of Shaftesbury had not acquired a very wide vogue. It was not in the air breathed by the generality of novelists, poets and essayists. Perhaps there were latitudinarian sermons, other than Bishop Butler's, in which concessions were made to Shaftesbury and Hutcheson. I do not know. But I fancy that these ideas were current chiefly inside small, sophisticated circles in which 'Deist' was not a term of abuse and in which one could refer without explanation or apology to Locke and Descartes, Hobbes and Aristotle, Epicurus and Spinoza. So, if I am right in my assimilation of Jane Austen's moral ideas to those of Shaftesbury, then I think that she did not absorb these ideas merely from the literary, ecclesiastical and conversational atmosphere around her. I do not, on the other hand, insist that she got them by studying the writings of Shaftesbury himself, though if I was told that she got them either from Shaftesbury himself or from his donnish Scotch disciple, Hutcheson, I should without hesitation say, 'Then she got them from Shaftesbury.' Of Hutcheson's epistemological professionalisation of Shaftesbury there is not an echo in Jane Austen. She talks of 'Moral Sense' without considering

the academic question whether or not it is literally a Sixth Sense. Nor do I find any echoes in her from Butler or from Hume, who in their turn echo little or nothing of the aestheticism of Shaftesbury.

(2) Another thing that persuades me that Jane Austen was influenced fairly directly by Shaftesbury himself, besides the general secular and aesthetic Aristotelianism which she shares with him, is the vocabulary in which she talks about people. Her stock of general terms in which she describes their minds and characters, their faults and excellences is, *en bloc*, Shaftesbury's. Almost never does she use either the bi-polar ethical vocabulary or the corresponding bi-polar psychological vocabulary of the Black–White ethic. The flat, generic antitheses of Virtue and Vice, Reason and Passion, Thought and Desire, Soul and Body, Spirit and Flesh, Conscience and Inclination, Duty and Pleasure hardly occur in her novels. Instead we get an ample, variegated and many-dimensional vocabulary. Her descriptions of people mention their tempers, habits, dispositions, moods, inclinations, impulses, sentiments, feelings, affections, thoughts, reflections, opinions, principles, prejudices, imaginations and fancies. Her people have or lack moral sense, sense of duty, good sense, taste, good-breeding, self-command, spirits and good humour; they do or do not regulate their imaginations and discipline their tempers. Her people have or lack knowledge of their own hearts or their own dispositions; they are or are not properly acquainted with themselves; they do or do not practise self-examination and soliloquy. None of these general terms or idioms is, by itself, so far as I know, peculiar to Shaftesbury and herself. It is the amplitude of the stock of them, and the constant interplays of them which smack strongly of Shaftesbury. It had been Shaftesbury's business, so to speak, to Anglicise the copious and elastic discriminations of which Aristotle had been the discoverer. In Jane Austen Shaftesbury's Anglicisation is consummated without his floridity.

Given the stilted bi-polar vocabulary of, say, 'Reason and Passion' or 'Spirit and Flesh', then it is easy and tempting to reserve the top drawer for the one and the bottom drawer for the other. But given the copious, specific and plastic vocabulary of Aristotle or Shaftesbury, it then becomes a hopeless as well as a repellent task to split it up into, say, fifteen top-drawer terms and seventeen bottom-drawer terms, into a platoon of sheep-terms for angelic and a platoon of goat-terms for satanic powers, impulses and propensities. To the employer of a hundred crayons the dichotomy 'Chalk or Charcoal' has no appeal. For example, John Knightley's occasional testiness was obviously not a Virtue. But nor was it a Vice. At worst it was a slight weakness, and in his particular domestic situation it was even a venial and rather likeable condiment. Where the icing-sugar is too thick, a splash of lemon-juice is a welcome corrective. We would not wish to be surrounded by John Knightleys. But we would not wish to be without them altogether.

(3) There is one word which Shaftesbury and Jane Austen do frequently use in the same apparently idiosyncratic way, and that a way which is alien to us and, I think, subject to correction, alien to most of the other eighteenth- and early nineteenth-century writers. This is the word 'Mind', often used without the definite or indefinite article, to stand not just for intellect or intelligence, but for the whole complex unity of a conscious, thinking, feeling and acting person. I am not here referring to the philosophico-theological use of 'Mind' for, roughly speaking, the Deist's or Pantheist's God. We do find this use occurring now and then in Shaftesbury, as in Pope.

Shaftesbury and Jane Austen both speak of the Beauty of Mind or the Beauty of a Mind, where they are talking about ordinary people; and when Shaftesbury speaks of the Graces and Perfections of Minds, of the Harmony of a Mind, or the Symmetry and Order of a Mind and of the Freedom of Mind he is talking in his jointly aesthetic and ethical manner just of laudable human beings. Jane Austen employs a lot of analogous phrases: 'Inferior in talent and all the elegancies of mind', 'delicacy of mind', 'liberty of mind or limb' (all from *Emma*); '[he] has a thinking mind', '. . . in temper and mind', 'Marianne's mind could not be controlled', 'her want of delicacy, rectitude and integrity of mind' (all from *Sense and Sensibility*). In 'one of those extraordinary bursts of mind' (*Persuasion*, ch. VII) the word 'mind' perhaps means 'intelligence' or just 'memory'. Now I think that Shaftesbury used this term 'Mind' as his preferred rendering of Aristotle's ψυχή, for which the normal rendering by 'Soul' would, I guess, have had for him too Christian or too parsonical a ring. He does once or twice use the disjunction 'mind or soul'. Jane Austen is even charier than Shaftesbury of employing the word 'soul'; and she, I surmise, just takes over the Shaftesburian use of 'Mind', very likely without feeling, what I think most philosophers would have felt, that this use was an irregular and strained one. If the Shaftesburian uses of the word 'Mind' did not subsequently become current in literature, sermons or conversation, or even, as I am sure they did not, in the philosophical writings of Butler and Hume, then the fact that Jane Austen often makes the same and similar uses of it would be fairly strong evidence that she drew directly on Shaftesbury. But whether this is the case or not is a matter of philological history, in which field I am not even an amateur. I am primarily arguing for the general, if vague, conclusion that Jane Austen was, whether she knew it or not, a Shaftesburian. It is a dispensable sub-hypothesis that she had studied the rather tedious and high-flown writings of Shaftesbury himself. Shaftesbury had opened a window through which a relatively few people in the eighteenth century inhaled some air with Aristotelian oxygen in it. Jane Austen had sniffed this oxygen. It may be that she did not know who had opened the window. But I shall put an edge on the issue by surmising, incidentally, that she did know.

My Life
and Death
by
Alexandra
Canarsie

My Life
and Death
by
Alexandra
Canarsie

Susan Heyboer O'Keefe

𝛀

PEACHTREE

ATLANTA

A Freestone Publication

Published by
PEACHTREE PUBLISHERS, LTD.
1700 Chattahoochee Avenue
Atlanta, Georgia 30318-2112

www.peachtree-online.com

Text © 2002 by Susan Heyboer O'Keefe
Jacket illustration © 2002 by Michelle Hinebrook

Jacket design by Loraine M. Joyner
Interior design by Melanie M. McMahon

Manufactured in the United States of America

10 9 8 7 6 5 4 3 2 1

Library of Congress Cataloging-in-Publication Data

O'Keefe, Susan Heyboer.
   My life and death, by Alexandra Canarsie / Susan Heyboer O'Keefe.
      p. cm.
Summary: Escaping school and family problems in a cemetery, fifteen-year-old Allie begins attending strangers' funerals, which leads to her first real friendship and a mystery that she believes only she can solve.
   ISBN 1-56145-264-5
   [1. Family problems--Fiction. 2. Interpersonal relations--Fiction. 3. High schools--Fiction. 4. Schools--Fiction. 5. Funeral rites and ceremonies--Fiction. 6. Mystery and detective stories.] I. Title.
   PZ7.O41445 My 2001
   [Fic]--dc21
                                                                        2001007255

For Michael—now and always

Prologue

one of this would have happened, I suppose, if I had a normal hobby like skateboarding or hanging out at malls. But I don't do things like that. I go to the funerals of strangers.

Weird, huh?

Maybe I began going so I'd have something to put into the diary I'd always planned to start. I imagined that other people used diaries to keep track of their fabulously interesting lives. *I* needed to keep a diary because it would be the one place I could talk about things the way they *really* happened.

No matter how I explain something, Mom or Aunt Darleen or one of my teachers sighs and rolls his or her eyes and murmurs, "Well, you're the only person who saw it like that, Allie."

What does that mean? That it didn't really happen that way? That I didn't tell the truth, maybe didn't even *see* the truth in the first place? That makes me halfway think I should shut up and try not to attract attention, at least for a while. But sooner or later my wicked side twists and turns and breaks loose. In other words, I have to air out my tonsils and tell *my* side of things.

Aunt Darleen or Mom would say that going to the cemetery that first morning was just an accident or maybe bad luck. I say it was definitely fate...

Chapter One

It was June, and Mom and I had just moved again, the tenth time in six years. We were renting an old run-down trailer in Lost & Found Acres, in the town of Nickel Park. Lost & Found was pretty much rock-bottom living, the kind of place people on the "wrong" side of the tracks looked down on. Mom had grown up in Nickel Park, though not in the trailer park, so coming home had been really hard on her.

I guess she just had to spread all that good cheer around, because our first Saturday in the trailer, she stuck her head into my so-called room, which was about a sneeze bigger than a gym locker, and asked me a surefire, let's-start-to-fight question:

"You know, Allie, come September you'll be a freshman," she said. "High schools have so much more going on than junior high. Will you join something this year?" *This* year, as opposed to last year, and the year before that, was what she was really saying. She wore the painful smile of an optimist who never hears the word "yes" yet refuses to give up hope.

"Golly gee, Mom. There's so much that I just can't choose," I said brightly. "Maybe the school paper, drama club, chorus, and girls' softball team. It's all so exciting. Maybe I'll even try out for team captain!"

Her face pulled into itself, a contrast to the poster of Einstein I'd just hung up (the one where he's sticking out his tongue).

"Look, if you can't handle a crowd scene," she said tightly, "at least do something with math. Why don't you volunteer to tutor?"

Kill my one good subject wasting time on a moron? I mean, math was my easiest class. It was basic. $1 + 1 = 2$. A x B = AB. It was totally predictable, all memorization and logic, not like analyzing a poem. A math problem was always the same. A poem was slippery: it changed each time you read it. I got enough slippery stuff in life.

"I don't see any effort on your part to adjust," Mom nagged.

With so much effort I deserved a medal, I kept my mouth shut and rummaged through one of the moving boxes for a pair of shorts. As soon as I pulled them out, Mom switched gears without so much as taking a breath: "You're *not* wearing *those* today, are you?"

"Sure," I said. "It's a picnic, isn't it?"

The third annual Nickel Park Welcome Stranger Picnic, to be precise. Aunt Darleen, Mom's only sister, had lived in Nickel Park all her life. She'd told us the "tradition" started three years ago when the Tastee Treet Cookie Factory opened and Nickel Park's population exploded. The factory was where Aunt Darleen, and now Mom, and probably most of Nickel Park worked, at least the people who weren't milking or shucking or whatever it was hicks did. The town council decided it would be neighborly for all the newcomers who'd moved in during the past year to get together with the old-timers and meet and mingle.

In a town as small as Nickel Park, "population explosion" probably meant ten new people, being "neighborly" meant a chance to sell life insurance to the newcomers, and "meet and mingle" meant gossiping over the three-bean salad. I knew the last part made Mom nervous. People would talk if she went, but talk more if she didn't. And what was she anyway—a newcomer? An old-timer?

She'd left Nickel Park to go to the state university instead of just commuting three towns over to Deedy County's junior college. Her first semester, she declared herself a psych major; her second semester, she got pregnant. "One day," I once overheard her say, "I woke up and found I'd somehow become a college drop-out married to another college drop-out," as if how it actually happened baffled her. In the six years since the divorce, she'd gone through a string of jobs too embarrassingly long to fit on a résumé. What was the classification for a local girl who *didn't* make good?

Maybe all this had been going through her mind and that was why she was a bit touchy about my outfit.

"I really want to make a good impression," she said.

"Some impression," I countered. "If I wear a dress to a picnic, I'll look like a jerk."

"Wear shorts at our first public appearance, and *I'll* look like a bad mother."

"First public appearance? What are we, royalty?" I swung around to look at her. "Ow!"

I'd banged my arm against the sharp edge of the dresser. Everywhere I turned I bumped into what the rental agent called "conveniently placed furnishings." *Can you die from black-and-blue marks?* I wondered. Worse, none of the stuff tripping me was ours. It came with the unit. Another convenience, said the rental agent. More crap was what *I* said. Rips in the carpet had been smoothed with duct tape. The kitchen counter that doubled as the table was scarred with cigarette burns and worn down past the pattern. Everything looked gray and faded except for the flowery blue curtains Mom had bought new. They were such a lie they made me mad every time I saw them.

Still, I should have been grateful. Some of the trailers were subdivided into twos and threes. Aunt Darleen lived in one of those. I guess that made ours the deluxe model.

I'd end up killing my aunt if I had to live with her in such a tiny space. I'd had a taste of life with Aunt Darleen the week before. Mom had put me on the bus to Nickel Park a few days ahead of her while she put our things in storage. At least that's what she said she was doing. I think she really stayed behind to have a garage sale. She'd sold my life from under me. Now whenever I passed the blue curtains, I unraveled a bit of the hem. Three more days and they'd match everything else.

As I stood rubbing my sore arm, Mom snatched the shorts out of my other hand.

"Don't take all morning to get dressed," she said. "We don't want to miss the group introduction." This was the part of the picnic when all the new people marched up onto a ribbon-decked stage and let themselves be gawked at. "If we're not on time, we'll be introduced later all by ourselves, which I do *not* want. Just make yourself presentable."

Presentable. As if anything could be done with my tall gawky body and blah face. I have sandy hair, neither blond nor brown, and gray eyes, neither blue nor green. I felt like the kitchen counter, worn down past the pattern.

I took the shorts from her, flung them back into the box, and fished out a sleeveless denim jumper. This was as far as I'd go: jumper and sandals, no slip, no pantyhose. If I couldn't be presentable, I could at least be comfortable.

As I pulled off my jeans and top and pulled the jumper over my head, Mom launched back into her original let's-start-to-fight subject.

"You know, Allie, you're getting a brand new start here," she said. "It's a new town, at least for you, a new home, a new school. And Nickel Park has some wonderful teachers. Or they did back when I went. Maybe some will even still be there."

How could she talk like that, as if this was a great adventure for me? This dump was *not* my home. I'd never really gone to a school I liked, but my *home* was six years, ten moves, and several hundred miles back.

"It's high time you learn how to get along, young lady," she went on. "No more loner stuff. You've got to meet people halfway."

She crossed her arms and gave me a stern look. She was tall, slim, and sandy-haired, too, gray-eyed and gray-faced; she looked so much like me, it was like fighting with myself. Or like fighting with my future. Maybe that's why I did it so often.

"Meet people halfway?" I echoed. "Halfway to the mall? Halfway to Mars? I don't see *you* with crowds of friends, Mom. Maybe you should try going halfway yourself."

As soon as the words flew from my mouth, I felt small and ugly. Mom was always working so hard she didn't have time for friends. Up till now she'd been a waitress, which always left her too tired to do more than come home and soak her sore, swollen feet in ice water. But if you try to unsay what's been said, that's like twisting the truth to suit you, so I kept my mouth shut.

The phone rang.

As soon as Mom answered, I knew it was Aunt Lolly. She's my dad's great aunt and my great-great aunt. Though my dad disappeared after the divorce and was a forbidden topic, we always stayed in touch with Aunt Lolly. That was so she'd leave me something in her will. Mom would never admit that. She said we did it to be nice. *I* figured that *she* figured that Aunt Lolly was the only way I'd get to college, as I sure wasn't going on a scholarship. *I* was surprised I'd made it through junior high.

"Of course I have time to chat!" Mom said with fake delight. That annoyed me to the point of craziness. If she couldn't talk now, she should just say so and call back. Instead, she forced her mouth into a smile, drummed her fingers, and probably thought, *here's a good hour shot.*

I refused to put up with an hour's worth of silent commands to change into something dressier, so I stomped outside and slammed the door behind me. Out on the corrugated metal stoop, I looked around at my wonderful new home.

With a name like Lost & Found Acres, you'd expect old sagging trailers, skinny smudge-faced kids, pit bulls, and death-trap refrigerators abandoned out back. Well, our trailer *did* sag, there *were* lots of skinny kids, and the two German shepherds chained up about five trailers down set my heart thumping with their vicious bark. But one section was full of nice trailers with satellite dishes on top so big they threatened to tip the whole thing over. And a steady parade of shiny new RVs pulled in to dump their crap, fill up on gas, then take off to who knew where, throwing a cloud of dust behind them.

A veil of dust hung in the air even now. The rest of the world had all sorts of weather. I had quickly learned that the trailer park had just two—dust and mud—and it hadn't rained in three days. By the time I reached the road, my nose had started to itch and my skin had picked up a thin coating of grime.

I knew Mom wanted to leave for the picnic as soon as she got off the phone. I meant to stay close, I really did, but when I saw a splotch of green beyond the far end of the trailer park, I began to walk toward it. I ignored the curtains that twitched aside as I passed and the kids who begged for a dollar for candy. The green lured me, an oasis in a desert. Maybe it would end up a mirage and be just the corner of a hideously painted trailer. But I had to see.

The end of the trailer park bordered on a sparse patch of grass where the dust finally gave way to better soil. Some distance away, under the shade of a row of trees, stood an old crumbling stone wall and an iron gate. One of the doors hung tilted from a single hinge; the other had fallen off completely. Weeds had grown up between the bars. Rusty letters across the still-standing archway said "Evergreen Cemetery."

The back of my neck prickled as I stepped over the fallen gate.

Evergreen was everything Lost & Found was not: lush, dark, almost cool. The place was overgrown with grass, weeds, ferns, and wildflowers. I found a path of sorts between old twisted oaks draped with hanging vines and things equally creepy. Bushes that should have been pruned into front-lawn tameness spread up and out, pressing in on me as I walked by. The hot sunlight that made the trailer park a dust bowl barely penetrated the thick branches and leaves, creating a sort of perpetual twilight.

The cemetery seemed to have sprung up in the middle of the woods. Gravestones had pushed their way up beneath straggly rosebushes and sprouted like stone mushrooms on the hillside. Angels and skulls and strange-looking clawed creatures elbowed past trees and bushes and watched with cold marble eyes as I trespassed on their silent, secret world.

In the movie-set town of Springfield, the last place we lived, I don't remember any cemetery at all. It must have been hidden away, or else Springfield shipped off its dead, the way they shipped off the rest of their problems, like me. All Springfield cared about was that everything looked good on the outside. A cemetery would have been a wart on the ass of a beauty queen—okay as long as the judges never saw it. *This* cemetery looked as if it might take over the whole town.

I wandered through Evergreen till I came to its new section, where all the tree-filled hollows and hills leveled off to stretches of lawn. Grave markers, set in neatly measured rows, were upright slabs or small stone rectangles flat against the ground—not a carved skull in sight. A narrow paved lane cut through this newer part and led off to the west, where it probably came out onto one of the town's main roads.

In the new section, a funeral was taking place.

Most of the time I stay clear of any and all social activities, but that day I didn't. I walked closer to get a better look, then a little closer, until soon I was almost part of the group. I leaned against a headstone, closed my eyes, and listened to the minister.

"Did you know Mr. Franklin well?" asked a nearby voice.

An elderly woman in black stood next to me. Usually I can guess someone's story in about five seconds max. What I can't guess is easy enough to fill in—interesting details about things people have done, things they wished they'd done. On any other day I could have written this woman's life and handed it to her in a leather-bound book, from her Persian cat named Elroy to her bingo addiction. But being caught so close up, I suffered major brain freeze. I looked down at my sandals and shrugged. She took that as a yes.

"Well, thank you. It was so kind of you to come."

As I walked away, my mind raced with all the incredibly cool answers I might have given and how the old lady would have reacted.

And it didn't have to stop with today's visit.

> *TV Guide* listing for *The Girl in Black:* "Each week a
> mysterious young woman goes to the funeral of a
> stranger, setting off a chain reaction of dramatic,
> sometimes dangerous events."

The idea of having my own show—written by, directed by, and
starring me—was irresistible, even though normally I didn't watch
much TV. Nothing sucked more than counting on watching your
favorite show, only to discover that the set had been pawned yet again.
About the third time it happened, I decided TV was stupid anyway.

The main gate to the cemetery came out on Turkey Hill Road. It
took me a few moments to get my bearings. By the time I got back
to the trailer park, I'd been gone over an hour.

"What do you mean storming out like that?" Mom demanded.
"And where have you been? You know I wanted to leave."

"I went to a funeral at Evergreen," I said.

"A funeral? Whose? Who died?"

"I don't know. Just someone."

Red splotches popped out all over my mother's cheeks.

"You went to a funeral and you don't know who died?"

"I do now. It was a Mr. Franklin." Studying the floor, I heaved my
biggest sigh and said, "It was a very sad service."

"Alexandra Canarsie, sometimes I just don't understand you!" she
fumed. "I was worried sick. And look at you! What in the world were
you doing?"

My mother's hands fluttered about my jumper, picked off a couple of loose leaves, then brushed something from my hair. Suddenly
she tore open the bow at the neck of her own blouse, and I knew we
were skipping Nickel Park's third annual Welcome Stranger Picnic. I
guess she decided not showing at all was better than standing on
stage alone.

"Let 'em talk," she said. She kicked off the heels I knew must have pinched her feet. "I'm sure they've been yapping about me nonstop since I moved back anyway."

She leaned back in the trailer's one comfortable chair, sighed, and closed her eyes. She looked tired; she always looked tired. I figured she'd be asleep within seconds. I figured wrong.

"That was a horrible, morbid, intrusive thing you did, Allie," Mom said. She opened her eyes, sat up straight, and nailed me with a killer look. "Don't you *ever* do that again."

The very next day I began going through the obituaries in the *Daily Sentinel;* we read Aunt Darleen's copy when she was finished checking it for sales and engagement announcements for "the ones that got away." I was clearly justified in checking the obituaries, even provoked. Mom asked me three more times about joining an activity and keeping busy. Since it was only June, she began to push the summer rec program. I decided I wouldn't argue any more. It just wore us out, and she didn't need help from me in that department. Each morning she left for her new job, working alongside Aunt Darleen at the cookie factory. Each night she came home exhausted, smelling of vanilla and butter and sugar. I wanted to hug her, to bury my face in her white lab coat, and sniff my way back to some wonderful childhood place I imagined I knew. But too tired for even a hug, she would strip off the coat and collapse into the chair.

The middle of her second week on the job she seemed particularly beat.

"How Darleen can go from work to drinks and dancing is beyond me," she murmured, her hand over her eyes. "When did I get so old?"

"When you had me?" I offered.

"Must have been." She lowered her hand and gave me a "Mom" look. "So, did you spend the day reading again or did you find something more constructive to do? What about volunteering at the library?"

Volunteering? I'd stick with an activity that suited me: going to funerals.

The next morning I found several scheduled for Saturday burial at Evergreen. I studied them, then chose a name: "Ethel Claridge, 87, president of the garden club for ten years." The obituary was brief, there was no next of kin, and the funeral was likely to be small. I was doing poor Ethel a favor by showing up. That was my idea of service.

Ethel, Ethel…a good name for tragedy, I thought. *Her first and only love died in the war and her later marriage to Mr. Claridge was just for show on both their parts. Then somewhere in all their years together, Mr. Claridge fell for her, truly and deeply, while Ethel still pined for her dead love. They both died of a broken heart.*

Mrs. Claridge was being buried at ten o'clock Saturday morning. At nine Mom left for the community-center aerobics class, coaxed to join by Aunt Darleen. I circled Mrs. Claridge's obituary in black marker, put the opened paper on the counter, then walked to the cemetery. I was right: only three other mourners were there. No kin, the paper had said. Were these her friends, or just fellow members of the garden club?

When I got back, Mom and Aunt Darleen were sitting at the kitchen counter, their heads close together. They were both still dressed in their exercise clothes: Mom in an oversized navy T-shirt and tights, Aunt Darleen in glittery pink spandex and black bicycle shorts. Aunt Darleen was younger by five years. Maybe she'd seen her future in Mom, too, and decided she didn't like it. She dyed her hair whitish blond, wore teen fashions a year after they'd become stupid, and had long fake nails with smiley faces on each tip. I wanted to scream every time I saw them.

"Oh," said my mother stiffly when I came in. "How are you, Alexandra?"

Alexandra? I was in real trouble.

"Okay. Hi, Aunt Darleen."

"Hi, Allie. How was the funeral?"

I noticed Mom kicked her under the table.

"Why don't you change your clothes, Alexandra? Then you and I and Aunt Darleen can do something silly this afternoon. Maybe miniature golf."

I said sure, went into my sardine-can room, and stopped just inside the door to listen.

"Aren't you going to say anything?" Aunt Darleen asked.

"Shh, she'll hear you. I've been doing a lot of thinking. There's only one reason why she'd go off to the cemetery again this morning. I think she's mourning her father."

Hearing my father mentioned made my breath catch.

"Mourn him? But he's not dead!" Aunt Darleen said.

"He might as well be dead. Sometimes I think it would be easier for her if he *were*."

"Well, talk to her about it."

As desperate as I was to find out about my father, I didn't want Aunt Darleen to take my side. She was supposed to be the trailer-trash butt of my jokes, not my defender.

"I couldn't," Mom answered. "Talking would be much too painful."

"For her or for you?"

"For her! She's just a kid, she still needs protecting."

"Winnie, she's a teenager! Why, when I was her age—"

"I know what you were doing at her age," Mom said hurriedly. "But you're not Allie. I've got to do things my own way."

"Yeah, look how good *that's* working," Darleen answered. "I mean, if she was just at Evergreen visiting Mom and Pop's grave, that would be one thing. But she's going to strange funerals. That's plain weird."

Mom and Pop's grave? The grandparents I had never met were at Evergreen? My mother had said they'd been killed in a car accident years ago. A strange sensation crept over me. Mom really *had* come home.

"And if Allie *is* mourning her father," she asked, "how else can she act it out?"

"Give her his picture and a dart gun. At least she can do that in her room. You know how small this town is, Win. Burp and your neighbor says, 'Excuse me.' You've been back less than two weeks and people are already talking. It'll be Springfield all over again! It'll be worse than Springfield because they know you here in Nickel Park."

Worse than Springfield? Not likely. For once I'd almost been happy to move.

"You don't know anything about Springfield!" my mother snapped. "Springfield was a horrible town with a horrible school."

"Oh, unlike all the other towns and all the other schools the two of you have left."

"This time it's going to be different. It has to be."

My hands stung. I looked down and saw I was clenching them. The nails had dug into my palms. Tight stomach, tight fists. I slammed the door to my room and began to change my clothes. I gave Nickel Park three months, tops.

Chapter Two

All summer I worked on my new hobby. Whose funeral would I go to this week? What would I wear? Who would I be? This time I got to make up stories about *me*. Had I delivered the deceased's newspaper? Had I carried his groceries from the corner store? Or was I the silent, mysterious stranger whose presence created shocking rumors among the remaining family?

Each week I added to my outfit, rummaging through every yard sale within a couple of miles. By the end of July my uniform was complete: black skirt, white blouse, black tights, black ballet slippers, black shoulder bag and, lastly, a black beret. The look was so classic for a funeral, so retro, that tearful sincerity oozed from my every pore.

Saturday after Saturday, Mom would leave for aerobics while I shuffled around the trailer still in my nightgown. Saturday after Saturday, I'd come home from a funeral, neatly dressed in black, to find her waiting for me at the kitchen table. She said nothing—she was good at that—only stared at me with a stern expression.

I wasn't sure why I picked the funerals I did. Ethel Claridge's service was so small I almost fooled myself into believing I had done her a favor by just showing up. All the while I imagined a neon sign above my head spelling out *PHONY!* Afterwards I looked for funerals likely to pull a crowd. One week, there were no funerals at all at Evergreen, which actually ticked me off.

Come September, my choices would be limited to weekends. I supposed I could always cut class to keep going during the week. I'd cut class billions of times before, and for less reason than that. At the least, it would certainly give me an interesting topic for my sessions with the school psychologist.

But I had time left before September.

I'd never had a summer to myself before. The summers when my dad was still home were blurs—an argument here, an argument there, a week in a cabin, a week at the beach. Lately, summer was just a better time to move. By April, Mom and I would be hanging on by our fingernails—me to finish the school year, Mom not to quit before I finished. She said she'd rather quit than get fired. Since getting fired always seemed likely to her, she was always quitting. She had more waitressing jobs than I had schools. Maybe being fired as a wife had made her jumpy.

The phone calls from successive principals didn't help:

"Mrs. Canarsie, Allie is boycotting our unit on Native Americans because it would offend her Chickawawa grandmother."

"Mrs. Canarsie, Alexandra issued report cards to all her teachers today. Most of them failed."

"Mrs. Canarsie, your daughter has been in another fight."

My academic career deteriorated from cute to catastrophic. Somewhere along the line I also lost credit for a grade, between moving so much and cutting more. The year I had to repeat, I achieved circus status and became the world's tallest seventh-grader.

In Springfield, I never made it to the end of eighth grade, even without moving. Mid-May, I piped the juicier parts of a cable movie over the PA system—not the worst of my offenses, but the final straw. The school shuffled papers and officially declared me an eighth-grade graduate. This was right after they had unofficially declared me incorrigible, which was like a switchblade short of a juvenile delinquent. There was no need, they said, smiling, for me to return to class or to attend graduation.

Maybe Mom had guessed what Springfield High would tell me—
"Head right to the special-ed room; do not pass Go; do not collect
$200"—and didn't want that stigma on my record, as if it mattered
by that point. Or maybe she was just antsy and needed to quit again.

That meant the usual joy of being dragged to the library to help
her check classifieds in a dozen different newspapers.

"Hmm," she'd say, thumbing through the pages. "Not a single job
for a college freshman drop-out with no skills and no experience.
Now, why couldn't someone pay me just to sit around and look beautiful?" She never smiled when she said it, probably because reality
meant one more diner doing "hard time." That's what she called the
breakfast and lunch shifts—double-time service because everyone
was in a rush, and bad tips because people were pissed about going
to work. She once told me she'd like to apply for a cushy job as a
hostess in an expensive supper club. "I wouldn't dare, though," she
said. "Who'd follow me, even to their table?"

This time Aunt Darleen had galloped to Mom's rescue, her knight
in shining white spandex, miraculously producing a spot on the
assembly line at the Tastee Treet Cookie Factory and a trailer park
roof to put over our heads. Some rescue—slumming it in Nickel
Park.

Even so, from my end, things had looked good at first. I liked
moving during the summer, as I'd get to walk in the high-school door
for the first time with everyone else, instead of slinking in mid-
March, trying to find an empty seat somewhere. And no hot sticky
months sitting in summer school trying to cram in all the history or
English I missed during the year, no wasted time scouring newspapers on Mom's behalf while she worked. From June on, all I did was
go to funerals and shop for black.

I also read a lot. The alternative was to think and that made my
stomach hurt. I read everything, as long as it wasn't real: mysteries,
adventures, fantasies, westerns, even Mom's romances, if they didn't
make me gag too much. Aunt Lolly's big thing was biography. "What
could be better than what actually happened?" she asked me.

"How about what should have happened but didn't?" I said. Aunt Lolly didn't get it.

✳

Twenty-seven books and a dozen funerals later, it was August 18. In three days I would be fifteen. I asked Mom if I could have my ears pierced as a birthday present. She drove me to the mall in Cottersville, an hour away. This required great personal sacrifice on both our parts. I hated malls, which somehow compelled teenagers to roam in packs, thereby increasing their stupidity exponentially. No one else my age had the good sense to shop alone, like me. My mother hated driving in even a mist, and it was still pouring after a day of rain. Despite the weather, she took me out that very evening, as if afraid I would change my mind. Clenching both the steering wheel and her jaw, she told me she was delighted I was finally beginning to "pay attention to myself." I ignored her white knuckles, the heavy sheets of rain, and a twinge of guilt; *I* was delighted because simple pearl studs were a lovely complement to basic black, the perfect accessory for a sincere funeral goer. When I became a not-so-sincere student, I could later switch my ear-wear to safety pins, maybe fishing hooks.

By Thursday, my actual birthday, all my excitement was gone. I was fifteen. So what? Worse, Mom started in on me again over breakfast. Though it was the last few days of vacation, I'd gotten up early. We sat in silence as she drank her coffee.

"How do you feel today, Allie?" she asked quietly. The peaceful moment was over. She didn't look up as she stood to button her beige blouse, tuck it into her tan skirt, then tie the bow at her collar. I wanted to take a red crayon and color in flowers on the beige material. At least Aunt Darleen showed some flash and trash beneath *her* white coat.

"Hmm?" my mother asked again, pouring herself cereal.

How did I feel? Sick and desperate, because I hoped my father would call me today, the way every birthday I hoped he would call.

Last year I'd been stupid enough to tell my mother. Of course she wouldn't come right out and ask me about it now.

"Huh, honey?" she persisted. "Are you okay?"

She stirred her cereal until it was too soggy to eat. The bowl was plastic, one of the "conveniences" of the trailer. That meant it wouldn't break when poor trashy folks like us got riled up and threw dishes. Just seeing it made me want to fight.

"Honey, look. I'm only saying that I don't want you to be disappointed."

"I'm used to being disappointed," I answered. "My whole life disappoints me."

I saw the hurt in her face but couldn't stop. What would I do with my own hurt if I didn't give it to her?

"I hate this place, I hate it!" I yelled. "We move too often!"

"Would you have wanted to stay in Springfield?"

What could I say? I never wanted to leave any place, but I never wanted to stay.

"I left for your sake," Mom continued. "And I think you know that."

"But..."

But what if my dad tried to call? We'd moved ten times since the divorce.

I remembered him dressing up like a pirate to take me out trick-or-treating. The two of us shopping for groceries and coming home with five bags of marshmallows. He was my dad and I loved him. But he left six years ago and never came back. Did that mean my memories were wrong?

"Aunt Lolly always knows where we are," my mother said. She poured a second bowl of cereal and slid it toward me. "Look, I'm sorry I couldn't get the day off, but we'll have fun tonight. Aunt Darleen's coming over and we'll all go to Rocco's for pizza."

I didn't look up.

"Come on, Allie. Talk to me. Tell me how you're feeling."

I was fifteen and I felt like hell.

I pushed the bowl away fiercely, grabbed my house key, and ran out.

After ten minutes of being waved at (small-town folk would say "Hiya" to an ax-murderer), I headed toward Evergreen. The cemetery suited my mood.

I rambled up and down the wooded hills of the old section. The tombstones and pillars, the stone angels and stone-veiled mourners seemed to strain backward out of my way as I passed, then close in behind me.

I couldn't help but eye the place professionally, checking that weeds had been pulled, mausoleum doors tightly closed. I began to plan my next funeral visit. It gave my mind something to grab onto.

Maybe I should bring flowers, or carry a white lace handkerchief. I never cried, but the gesture would be nice—plus I needed something to do with my hands. Flowers, yes. Not a full bouquet. A single red rose. I liked that. Elegant, yet dramatic.

I imagined *my* funeral, the single red rose on *my* casket. Still classy. But I'd want armfuls of flowers everywhere else. No making donations "in lieu of." And no throaty altos warbling till everyone cried. Just bagpipes playing "Amazing Grace," like at Spock's funeral in that *Star Trek* video, the one old enough to be *Covered Wagon Trek*. And when they wheeled me out, everyone could sing the old hymn "Just As I Am," a good choice since it would be way too late for me to change.

Somehow, that idea wasn't as funny as it should have been.

What does a minister say when he's never met the deceased? Does he talk around the truth? Would I have a funeral of just three, like poor Ethel Claridge? And who would they be? Mom, Aunt Darleen—and one of my teachers, trying hard not to tap dance for joy? Certainly not friends. Even more certainly not my father. Or would it be just my luck for him to finally show up, a few days too late?

A splotch of white caught my eye and I looked down. Someone had thrown away an empty cigarette pack, and it had gotten wedged between a headstone and a vase of plastic flowers. I leaned over, picked up the pack, and shoved it in my pocket. Some people had no consideration.

All at once I saw myself in freshman English next week, writing the inevitable "What I Did During My Summer Vacation" essay. My black mood twisted like a dry leaf in the hot August wind. Stupid essays meant the stupid school year would have begun, and once more I'd be the stupid new kid in class. At least once I'd like to stick around long enough to let someone else be the new kid. Maybe then *I'd* end up being the new kid's friend.

How else was I ever going to do this friendship thing? It was impossible to break into a clique. Even the weirdoes and geeks, spazzes and gimps weren't like me. No one was. At first, I used to pretend it was sorta cool being the only one. This year I was ready for things to be different. And afraid they would be exactly the same.

I plopped down against a mausoleum. All around was summer, yet the threat of winter was locked inside the marble, icy against my back. All those lonely Januaries to come....

My grandparents are here already, somewhere.... They know all about lonely Januaries.

Goosebumps crept up my arms. From nearby I heard the lazy buzz of a bumblebee; from further away the whine of a lawn mower.

My father once said that when he eventually bought a house, the very next thing he would buy would be a lawn mower. To him, nothing said ownership more than mowing your lawn. But he never bought us a house. He left before he did.

Had my mother wanted my *father* to take me when he left? Instead of arguing because each of them wanted custody, had they argued because *neither* did?

I jumped up and began to walk again. As I headed toward the new section, the sound of the lawn mower grew louder, like a headache on wings swooping down to attack me. I pressed my hands to my ears. The position didn't block out the noise, it just threw me off balance. I tripped on a tree root and nearly fell.

I imagined hitting my head and blacking out. I could see the headlines:

TEEN FOUND IN CEMETERY HAVING FIT
Bizarre Behavior Traced to Over-Talkative Mother

The story, about how I was to be removed from the dangerous environment and placed with a foster family, followed on page three.

A different noise, deeper, almost grinding, drowned out the lawn mower. Curious, I walked beside the winding, crumbling-down wall that separated the old section from the new one, ducking my head below its shoulder height to get closer without being noticed.

Up ahead stood a piece of heavy machinery. A man sat inside behind levers and controls, while another stood outside. In front of the machine was a shallow hole; to the left of it a small mound of dirt. I still couldn't see what the men were doing, so I followed the wall till I was a few yards away.

It must have been a slow day for my brain. It wasn't until the huge yellow machine lowered its gigantic jaws into the hole and actually bit into the earth that I at last realized what I was seeing: a new grave being dug.

For all my interest in funerals, I never much considered the hole itself, about someone being put in the hole to stay forever. Here one was being dug right in front of me—and on a sunny summer's day.

I stood there, pinned to the wall by an unnamable emotion, and watched. The hole grew deeper, the pile of dirt taller. I was sweating, even though the shade from the closely knit trees was cool enough to make me shiver. Finally the hole was so deep I couldn't see the bottom from where I stood.

From behind me came a whisper:

"Is that Jimmy's grave?"

I yelped and swung around so fast my arm scraped the stone wall. A few feet away stood a tall thin boy with red hair and lots of freckles. He wore blue track shorts and a white sleeveless T-shirt and

21

carried a checkerboard towel over one shoulder. His eyes widened when I turned.

"You're not Janet," he said, stumbling backwards. Before I could say anything, he disappeared behind the bushes. I went back to watching the men work. I didn't stay much longer, though. The day had turned too creepy even for me.

That night I looked through the past few newspapers. It didn't take long to find out who Jimmy was. "Youth Drowns in Kinnewaska" headlined the article. A picture showed a smiling, bland-faced boy in a white baseball cap. The caption said, "Jimmy Muller at his birthday party last month, wearing a favorite present." James Muller, said the article, had drowned this past Monday while swimming at Lake Kinnewaska, which bordered the far side of Nickel Park. He was alone at the time. His body was discovered by local resident Ariella Canfield. Muller's drowning had been ruled an accident.

Jimmy, the only son of Frederick Muller of Nickel Park, owner of the Deedy County Ford Dealership and candidate for town council, and Beverly Stowe of Los Angeles, California, had just turned fifteen. Jimmy was an altar boy at St. Paul's Lutheran Church, a helper at the church's food pantry, a volunteer at the county hospital, and a paper-boy for the *Daily Sentinel.* At Nickel Park Middle School, he had been eighth-grade class president and president of the math club. Next week he would have been a freshman at the high school. The funeral was tomorrow. Graveside services would follow at Evergreen.

A fifteen-year-old freshman good at math? The similarities between us were downright spooky, though I doubted someone with all his credits had been kept back a grade like me for not serving enough time. What had happened to him?

I reread the obituary. Jimmy Muller had more credentials at fif-teen than many of the old-timers I'd buried. Despite this, we were candidates for a "separated at birth" article. We had both just turned fifteen. We were both only children. We would have both been fresh-men at the same high school, in a town so small we would have been in the same classes. We had both belonged to the same church. Well, St. Paul's *would* be our church if Mom and I went at Christmas; that's where she had gone as a kid. Jimmy and I had parents who were divorced or separated. And we both loved math. And here I was, reading his obituary in the copy of the *Sentinel* we shared with Aunt Darleen. We were probably on his paper route. It was as though I was meeting and losing my one and only friend all at the same time.

And while he'd been drowning, I had been planning to shop that night for pearl studs.

We were total strangers, but no one could have known me any better. Sure, he was good and civic-minded, and I was his evil twin, but that would have been part of the attraction. We would have looked at each other and seen all the "maybes" in life.

The next morning at Evergreen was different. It wasn't a hobby today. I was going to a real funeral. Sadness and confusion sat on my shoulders like twin vultures. People weren't supposed to die at fifteen.

The gravesite was crowded with teenagers. Jimmy's class, I guessed. These were the kids who'd be freshmen with me next week, the kids who'd measure me up in half an instant then ignore me the rest of the year. A mixture of expressions painted their faces, from a bored "who cares" and "my mother made me come," to wet, red eyes and blubbering grief. I fixed my own features into my routine solemn mask.

Jimmy's parents were easy to spot. They stood by the grave, both of them in dark glasses. Fred Muller had a hawkish face. His black suit looked expensive, but also rumpled and slept in. Stuff hay down his collar and sleeves and he'd be a mean-looking scarecrow. Beverly Stowe was flashier, with a ruffled gray dress, wide-brimmed gray hat on a bleached-blond head, and spiky high heels. Despite the fancy outfit, she looked genuinely upset. Still, I was angry. What was she doing in California, anyway? Trying to break into acting at her age? I could see her now, in a line of teens auditioning for some low-budget dog, mumbling the words to her part over and over.

Sure, she and Fred hated each other—they were standing five feet apart at their kid's funeral—but why couldn't she have moved to the next town? Why go all the way to California? She probably hadn't seen her kid in years. It was a little late to be sad now.

Phony kids, phony parents. I was disgusted with all of them. There'd been a hundred times more honesty among the three old ladies who knew Ethel Claridge.

But if it were *my* funeral and my dad had somehow known, would he have come?

Suddenly I saw that the casket wasn't in place yet over the grave. Even though the raw edges of dirt were covered with crayon-green mats, I could still see the big open hole, waiting. I wanted to slap someone. Shouldn't the casket have been in place before the Mullers were allowed out of the limo and led to the gravesite? Wasn't there someone whose job it was just to make things as pretty as possible? We didn't really have to look at the open hole, did we? I mean, Jimmy's parents were right here, and little kids, and weepy teenage girls. My body jerked with impatience.

Finally the casket was positioned with flowers around it to hide all trace of the darkness beneath. When the minister spoke, he had to work to keep his voice from cracking. It couldn't have been easy to bury one of his best altar boys. When he finished, the Mullers and the mourners closest to them each dropped a red rose onto the casket. As the Mullers stepped backward, people started to drift toward them, maybe to try to offer some sort of comfort.

"Hi."

I looked around. It was the tall, red-haired boy who had spoken to me the day before. He wore a navy suit so new I wanted to check for the price tag.

"I thought you were Janet Cleary yesterday," he said, shifting his weight between his feet, bending each knee in turn. "I found out later that she was away for the weekend. Not that she told me. Our moms play bridge together." He blushed so deeply it connected his freckles. "Sorry. I'm Dennis Monaghan. How did you know Jimmy?"

Meaning, I hadn't been in school with them.

"He...I mean I... " My voice was too shaky to trust, especially on

24

a lie. I found myself doing what I'd done at my first funeral: looking down with embarrassment.

"Do you know him from St. Paul's? I go to Our Lady of Victory."

I nodded at the out Dennis had given me. *Dennis Monaghan, Our Lady of Victory, red hair. Irish Catholic,* I thought, *with eight younger redheaded brothers and sisters at home.* Remembering the track shorts and checkerboard towel from yesterday, I decided that Dennis was bent on winning a track scholarship to college so there'd be money left over for the eight younger Monaghans.

"My name's Allie Canarsie," I said. "I'll be going to Nickel Park High next week. A freshman." My voice sounded quivery. "Like Jimmy would have been."

"Yeah, me too."

Dennis shifted from left foot to right, left to right. Behind him I could see someone leading Jimmy's mother toward a black limo. The minister was some distance away, talking to a woman who had no business cornering him on such an occasion.

"I guess this proves the value of the buddy system," I said, desperate to restart the conversation without me as its subject. "He shouldn't have gone swimming alone."

"Jimmy hated the water. He shouldn't have gone swimming, period," Dennis said sharply.

I nodded again as if I knew what I was talking about. "It was a tragic accident," I said.

Dennis opened his mouth but no words came out. He stared off toward the old section, empty of crowds and caskets and freshly dug holes. "Yeah, right," he said at last. He stuck his hands in his pockets, walked away hunched over, and left me with the feeling that I'd just said something very, very wrong.

Chapter Three

Dear Diary,
I'm so excited! I'm in a new home in a
new town and tomorrow's the very first day
of school! Lucky, lucky me!

I crumpled the paper and slam-dunked it into the trash.

Mom didn't look up. She was at the kitchen counter making dinner. Aunt Darleen was at the refrigerator, hunting for a diet soda.

There's an expression, "Fake it until you make it." To be happy, you should smile a happy smile and do happy things and think happy thoughts. Eventually you'll *feel* happy. In other words, "Fake it until you've fooled even yourself." But writing that I was excited and lucky had only set off mental sirens screaming "Liar, liar, liar!" Maybe that's why I'd started the diary on a sheet of loose-leaf, easy to throw out. The brand new journal I'd bought over a year ago was still in my bottom dresser drawer.

Tomorrow *was* the first day of school—Thursday morning, August 28—that alone was true. Nickel Park High (and probably its rug-rat version too) actually started its school year *before* Labor Day.

"I think it's pretty crappy that they start school so early in this hick town," I complained loudly from my seat in the living room.

"Oh, they're serious about education here," Aunt Darleen said. "School starts early and ends late."

"Well, hush my puppy," I answered. "Don't y'all need to keep the young'uns out in the fields sowin' and reapin'?" Nickel Park had several farms within its boundaries, one with an apple orchard. Small-town life was bad enough. Farms made me twitch.

Aunt Darleen squinted. I was supposed to be terrified or at least cowed by her expression. Ha, *cowed*. Score one for me.

"You'll be reaping the back of my hand," she said.

"Okay, okay," Mom interrupted, refereeing, but laughing as she said it. It was good to hear her laugh.

We actually had a pretty decent time eating dinner. Aunt Darleen wasn't as annoying as usual, and Mom even threw in a joke every so often. I almost let myself believe that starting school wouldn't be so bad.

The next day, though, the optimism I'd let creep in was gone. Mom was at the counter again, early-morning silent, making my lunch and packing it in a plastic bag saved from the last time we went to the drugstore. With today being the first day, she must have assumed that packing me a lunch would be a nice "Mom" thing to do. She usually pretended I bought lunch in the cafeteria and I usually pretended I ate it. Most days I skipped. The cafeteria was for losers.

"Talk to me, Alexandra," she said, her back turned as she folded a napkin into the bag. "It's a new school. You must be a little bit nervous."

"People get nervous when they don't know what's going to happen," I said. "I already know. My teachers will hate me. The kids will hate me. And I'll hate all of them back. So...nope, I'm not a bit nervous."

When my mother turned around, her eyes were shiny. For the billionth time in my life, I wished I could have kept my big mouth shut. Then the moment passed.

"You don't have to bluff," she said. "I know you're frightened. I would be, too."

"I'm not frightened! I said I'm not nervous and I'm not!"

I went to my room. Trouble was, in a trailer, my room was only inches away.

I could still hear her in the kitchen pacing, breathing, *thinking.*

Deciding to go with all black, I got dressed. Not my funeral uniform, just the basics: black jeans, black tee, black sunglasses, Doc Marten rip-offs, and my black bag. At the last I added a studded black dog collar, hopelessly out of fashion, I knew, but still guaranteed to annoy—especially when people got close and saw it had chew marks.

"I've gotta go now," she said.

I stuck my head out my bedroom door. She stood ready to leave, her white coat folded neatly over her arm.

"Don't forget your house key and don't forget your lunch," Mom said. She paused. "I love you, Allie. Good luck today." Then she was gone.

Minutes later I stepped outside and stood at the door for a moment. The day was beautiful, sunny and summery but with a sharpness in the air that made you know fall wasn't too far off. I locked the door and set out for Nickel Park High.

It was my first day of school, in a brand new school, in a brand new town, in a brand new state. I could be anyone here, I could do anything. I could try out for cheerleader, run for class president, become a model student. I could have tons of friends, sworn buddies who'd actually save me a seat at the lunch table. I could have teachers so impressed they'd be writing my college recommendations before freshman year was out.

Yeah, right. The past always caught up with people. With me, the past not only caught up, it ran me down. Me a model student? I was once, for about six nanoseconds in kindergarten. Teachers writing me recommendations? Must be time to up my meds.

Reality was Nickel Park, the unpaved lanes between the trailers, the shoulderless, single-lane roads, the combo video/deli/liquor/ drugstore that was the mega-hangout of town.

And then there was the high school, which I had just reached.

Three stories tall with a ground-level basement, it had been finished just last year, Aunt Darleen had said last night. It was white brick, which was supposed to look modern, but which even she admitted made it look plain weird, like an albino. I'd been in the high school once already, back in June to fill out forms and take a few tests. It had impressed me as being dinky. Yet Aunt Darleen bragged how it was twice the size of the old school, which had housed kindergarten through twelfth grade all in the one building.

"With Nickel Park growing so fast, the county built a brand new grade school *and* a brand new high school at the same time," she'd said. The high school boasted an indoor swimming pool, its own baseball field, and four brand new computers in the library.

I almost said, "I guess Nickel Parkers are so pleased they could spit," but I didn't, for Mom's sake.

Watching as students took their last breath of freedom, I couldn't help but wonder what this year would have been like if my dad had never left or if he'd taken me with him. I'd be going to a small posh private school in a city, I bet. Or maybe we'd travel and he'd get tutors for me whenever I had to pass one of those state exams meant to prove I wasn't being neglected. Dad had never really spoiled me while he was at home, but I knew he would if it was just the two of us.

But it wasn't, it was Mom and me, and I was here instead.

What had she done to force him out?

Maybe Dad can't *be here. Maybe he's a spy and has a secret life or maybe he ratted out a big-time gangster and had to join the witness protection program.*

I used to tell myself my own bedtime stories when I was younger. They always ended with a knock at the door and my dad's voice saying he was there to take me home. For a long time it was the only way I could get to sleep.

Normally, given my mood, I would have cut school. But I was so new that no one would miss me, so what was the point?

When I finally went inside, I found that Dennis Monaghan, the red-haired boy from the cemetery, was in my homeroom, along with twenty-six other students. We were one of only three freshman classes in this little town (and that's *after* the growth spurt Aunt Darleen was so proud of), so the chances of our being in class together had been good. *Jimmy, too,* I thought. *I bet I would have been in class with Jimmy.*

Dennis gave half a wave. The other kids looked at me with curiosity. Most of them were wearing jeans and T-shirts, but mixed in were plenty of polyester trousers and short-sleeve buttoned shirts screaming "Hicks!"

Up front sat a boy with a cast up to his thigh. Instead of shorts, he wore cow-pie brown pants, with one leg cut off.

"Pitchfork accident?" I asked, stepping over him.

"Huh?"

"Never mind."

I slumped down in the last seat of the last row. I kept my sunglasses on so anyone staring couldn't see me staring back. Some kids could go into a situation like this and look at all the new faces and wonder excitedly who was going to be their new best bud. I knew better than to think that. I never had time to make friends, just time enough to get people to hate me. At least it made leaving easier.

The teacher arrived as the bell rang. He rapped on his desk.

"Settle down, settle down." He was white-haired, wrinkled, and old, so old that, with any luck, I'd be burying *him* at Evergreen before the marking period was over. He was also thin and wore a baggy plaid sports jacket and a big red bow tie. He might have lost tons of weight, which was why the jacket was so baggy. Or maybe—this was better— maybe he'd poked through the racks at Goodwill till he'd made his find. "I'm your homeroom teacher for the year," he announced.

Great. When I get bored, I can count his wrinkles.

"I'd like to tell you freshmen that I'm new to Nickel Park and that I come here after a long assortment of jobs, including private detective, professional ice-skater, industrial spy, and cloistered monk."

I could smell a line ten miles away. Still, he was pretty good: he'd hooked the class into open-mouthed attention. He continued.

"I'd *like* to tell you all those things, but I can't. I'd be found out as soon as your older brothers and sisters—and your parents—told you that *they* had Mr. Wheatley, too."

"Oh, it's Wheatley," the kids murmured. "Yeah, Wheatley."

"Yes," he nodded, "your relatives all had Mr. Wheatley for freshman English years and years and years ago, and now it's your turn."

Here was my final proof of how small Nickel Park was: it not only had just one English teacher for all its freshmen, it apparently had just one freshman English teacher for the town's entire history.

Wheatley was still talking: "I'm sure your relatives will delight in telling you how old I was even back then. I guess that makes me ancient by now, but please keep in mind that I'm not dead. Not yet at any rate," he said, staring at me. I blushed, remembering I'd just been making plans to bury him.

With that, Wheatley launched into a regular first-day-of-school talk, which I didn't bother to listen to. Suddenly the whole class was looking at me and whispering.

"What?" I said angrily, sliding lower in my seat.

"I merely asked you to introduce yourself," said Mr. Wheatley. "I understand that, unlike me, you really are new to Nickel Park. Alexandra Canarsie, right?" he asked, referring to a slip of paper. "Should we call you Alexandra?"

"Allie."

"Very good, Allie. Why don't you tell the class a little about yourself. Where do you come from?"

"I'm from Springfield, Delaware, though the teachers there said I was the student from hell."

Shocked laughter broke through the class.

"Ah, a challenge," said Mr. Wheatley, straightening his back and rubbing his hands together. "I love a good challenge. And as the student from hell, what did you hate most about Springfield?"

"The people," I said slowly, considering. "Yeah, I hated the people. All of them. Especially my English teachers."

"Well, then, I'll try not to disappoint you. We might seem like a one-horse town, Miss Canarsie, or should I say, a one-English-teacher town. But we're still capable of surprises."

My cheeks burned at having my mind read not once, but twice. Oh, he was a cool one, that Wheatley.

While we were eyeing each other, the PA system crackled. At the end of the usual first-day announcements, Principal Saunders spoke briefly about the great loss to the student body that had touched everyone so deeply. It was a moment before I realized he was talking about Jimmy Muller. A brief memorial service would be held in school the next day, last period.

"Isn't one funeral enough?" someone whispered.

Gurgling noises came from the back as someone pretended to drown.

"That's cold, man. Quit it!" someone else snapped.

A girl to the left of me gulped down a sob.

As if in response, the principal added that if anyone felt the need to talk to a counselor, arrangements could be made.

Wow, I thought, closing my mind to the image of the carpet-lined grave. *Nickel Park doesn't have a shrink on staff. Now* that *is small!* I wondered whether I should go to the service tomorrow or cut. In a way, I owed it to Jimmy to go. He and I would have been friends, while everyone else here was obviously a world-class loser.

The first-period bell rang and Mr. Wheatley waved us off. *Okay, here's where he grabs me on the way out and gets me alone and says, "I've seen your file, Alexandra Canarsie. Your permanent record. And it's not a pretty sight."* He didn't. For a moment I didn't know what to do. I hurried out.

Dennis Monaghan stood in the hall. Was he waiting for me? I couldn't remember the last time someone had done that.

"Hey, Dennis," I called. My voice sounded loud and echoey. Half a dozen kids turned round, and he scowled. If he *had* been waiting, regret now flashed across his face.

"It's my first day," I said, jittery. "Talk to me." Stupid things were popping out of my mouth. I blamed it on Wheatley's not doing what I expected. "Talk to me, Dennis, I need to talk, talk, talk."

"What?" He looked at me strangely and backed off. "It's eight o'clock. I've got to get to class."

He turned and disappeared.

First period was math, which was bad because then I'd have no incentive to stick around for the rest of the day. To my surprise, when I found the room, Dennis was the only person from homeroom there. He seemed equally surprised to see me. Also surprising was how old the other kids were. For once I might have been the baby of the class. Some of the kids looked as though they were already shaving, girls included. I checked the printed schedule the office had given me to make sure I was in the right room. Yep. Room 221, Miss Barbosa.

Barbosa the Barbarian, I thought.

Then she walked in, and I changed the name to Barbie Doll.

Miss Barbosa was traffic-stopping gorgeous, tall and willowy, with long black hair. She also wore lots of makeup and fashion-magazine clothes. I'd try not to hold that against her; after all she was a math teacher. In an instant I had her story down cold: how she'd been a homely math Darryl most of her life, a Stephen Hawking groupie who couldn't figure out why cafeteria politics was more confusing than string theory. Then a lab accident led to major reconstructive surgery and her current face.

Yeah, that sounds about right, I concluded. *Math teachers don't look like that on their own.*

I took off my dark glasses, found a seat, and sat up straight.

"This is algebra II and I'm Miss Barbosa. Most of you are sophomores. I know many of your faces from passing you in the hall. I also know a few of you somewhat better than that."

Some of the older students groaned. I guessed they were juniors or seniors, repeaters who had failed the class last year.

"Along with our, uh, more experienced students, we have a couple of freshmen. This continues last year's experiment of accelerating individual students since we're too small to have honors courses. Freshmen?" she asked, waving the two of us to our feet. "You're

Dennis Monaghan, right? Class, while Dennis was taking algebra I
in the middle school, he also worked his way through geometry in
Mr. Iglesia's math club."

More groans. Dennis looked as if he wanted the floor to swallow
him.

"And you're Alexandra Canarsie," Miss Barbosa said to me. "I saw
the results of your entrance test but not where you'd taken geometry."

"I guess I sorta picked it up on my own."

"Oh, Christ, give me a break," someone muttered.

I turned around to give an icy stare. The blond-haired boy behind
me was older, obviously one of the repeaters. He was heavy, nasty
looking, and dressed in the latest style, a Pyramid-brand white
leather jacket. The brand mark, an inverted red pyramid, was on the
shoulder, so I knew it wasn't a cheap look-alike. The jacket probably
cost more than what Mom made all week. I bet he was one of those
snotty rich kids who got a bribe like that for finishing one night's
homework. My anger made it to my eyes. He gave me the finger in
return.

"Tom Creighton, that's enough," Miss Barbosa warned him. "You
can sit down, Alexandra."

"My name is Allie," I said.

"Okay, Allie. Now let's get started."

Whenever Miss Barbosa turned to write on the board, Creighton
kicked my chair. What was the use of putting me in an advanced
math class, then surrounding me with mental midgets?

As soon as the bell rang, I put my dark glasses back on and spun
round. "Cretin, oops, I mean Creighton, your leg is twitching pretty
bad there. Is that your Elvis impression or do you have to take a
leak?"

Dennis looked horrified, his cheeks nearly the color of his hair.
The other kids burst into laughter, then choked it down and turned
away. Creighton rose to his feet to leave, shoving my books to the
floor as he swaggered past me.

"Hey, freshman," a girl whispered. "Leave him alone."

"Who are you, his girlfriend?"

"No, just someone who's tired of funerals."

I shrugged, then bent down to gather my books. At the front of the class, Miss Barbosa pulled Dennis aside to speak to him. I fiddled with my things while I eavesdropped.

"I'm so very sorry about Jimmy Muller," she said. "I understand you were best friends."

Jimmy was Dennis's best friend? At the cemetery I'd made that stupid remark about the buddy system. No wonder Dennis had gotten all weird on me.

"Jimmy would have been in this class, too," Miss Barbosa said. "He sounded like an extraordinary student and I was really looking forward to having him. Again, I just wanted to give you my condolences."

Dennis didn't answer Miss Barbosa, just nodded, his eyes downward. All the while he swayed back and forth with that shifting motion of his. He was probably mentally warming up for his next sprint, and at a time like this, maybe mentally running away.

Miss Barbosa looked over and saw me. I thought she was going to say something about Creighton so I slipped out.

The rest of the morning was a waste: Spanish and gym—which I cut to explore the school and discover its best hiding spots—then lunch, so early they should have served eggs. Brand new or not, the cafeteria was like all the others I'd been in: plastic orange trays, plastic orange chairs, easy-wash tile floor, and cement block walls. There was the constant shuffle of feet, the occasional brown-bag missile, and beneath it all a warm meaty smell. Black kids sat on one side, geeks and freaks in one corner, cheerleaders and jocks in another, the rest spread out.

There didn't seem to be room for me, no room in anyone's eyes. Their closed-off expressions made me want to break through, to sit down somewhere, anywhere, and know I belonged. Impulsively I sat on top of the table closest to the soda machine, rested my feet on the bench, and pretended I was watching the entrance for a friend to arrive.

"Get down!" Dennis appeared, holding a brown bag and a carton of milk. He pulled me from the table to the bench. "Sit, Allie!"

"Why?"

"You attract too much attention up there."

"Oh, but I do it so well," I said, more pleased than I wanted to admit that he had come over on his own.

Dennis looked as if he'd never seen the likes of me before. And in this place, I bet he never had.

"So, you're a math whiz, too," I said.

He shrugged. "I do okay." He started unwrapping his sandwich.

"Freshmen don't eat at this table!" a voice boomed.

Dennis looked up. From his expression, I expected at least Attila the Hun behind me. When I turned, I saw only Tom Creighton and two other guys. Creighton wore his Pyramid jacket; the others wore jackets with sports letters. Creighton stood with his arms folded.

"Are you *deaf?* I said freshmen don't sit at this table."

Dennis tripped over himself, trying to scoop up his things.

"You should know better, Monaghan," Creighton said to him. "For old time's sake, I'll let you off with just a warning. And *you.*" He dismissed me with a sneer. "You're both pukey little babies and it's your first day. But now you know better, right?"

I opened my mouth to answer back, but with unbelievable speed Dennis dragged me away. He pushed me down onto a bench in a far corner.

"Are you crazy?" he asked, standing over me and glaring. "You weren't going to move, were you? *Plus,* you were actually going to talk back!"

"Never mind. You'll get used to my mouth."

"Will I? Maybe I don't want to."

He turned around and left.

I suddenly remembered why I usually skipped lunch.

Chapter Four

arth science is the study of the science of the earth. It's really, really important. If it weren't important, I wouldn't have a job because that's all I know—how earth science is the science of the earth. Real high school science teachers teach biology and chemistry and physics to real students. I get to teach dirt to kids who care less.

This was what Mr. Penn's opening lecture on Friday *should* have sounded like, if only he'd been honest. In reality, I heard him dare to utter the words "exciting," "important," and "fascinating"—words never before associated with earth science—and so I immediately zoned out. This was easy to do with the buzz of post-lunch snores in the background. We were having Mr. Penn for the first time because he hadn't been here yesterday for the start of school. Lucky him. *And lucky us,* I thought, *now that I've heard him.*

Mr. Penn was short and thin, with a bobbing Adam's apple and an expression as nervous as a cat whose tail has been pulled once too often. He was young, too, especially compared to a wrinkled-up mummy like Wheatley. I heard someone whisper that Penn was a first-year teacher.

Your success in this class depends on knowing how to sleep with your eyes open, how to use impressive-looking charts in any project, and how to take multiple-choice tests because they're the easiest to grade.

Within ten minutes I decided he should have been an accountant. That gave me permission—not that I really needed it—to take a mental vacation. As usual, my first thought was of my father. What was he doing at that very minute?

It was always easy to place my mother. Each time we moved, she took me to visit her new job. She had said it would help me during the day to visualize her—pouring coffee from behind a counter, serving up four plates of the daily special at once. So I'd already visited the Tastee Treet Cookie Factory during the summer and had seen my mother there. She'd looked so small and timid among the whirring machines, checking as miniature metal cow udders squirted out white icing onto chocolate wafers, dozens of black, then black-and-white circles passing her eyes on conveyor belts.

I never saw where my dad worked. I knew he commuted to the city and did something with computers. "Something with computers"— my mother's phrase. I bet he was so blindingly brilliant, that was all she understood. I got my math smarts from him.

After Dad had moved out for the third time, I left school one day during recess and tried to find where he worked. I wanted to tell him I was sorry for everything I'd ever done wrong that had made him leave. I wanted to find out what I had to do for him to come back.

I was only seven but I'd ridden the bus to the city before with Mom so I wasn't afraid getting on and paying by myself. I knew enough to stand close to the woman ahead of me so we looked as if we were together. But I didn't know enough to realize there were lots of buses and not all of them went to the same place. That one didn't go to the city. Instead, the route ended at an industrial park. I started to cry, not because I was lost but because I hadn't found my dad. The driver took me back to the bus station, where I called my mother.

"Don't you ever do that again, Allie!" Mom had said when she picked me up. The school had already phoned to say I was missing, so she'd been frantic. "Bad things can happen to people when they're alone."

Why was I remembering that now, my second day at a new school? It seemed like a bad omen. Annoyed, I pushed the image away and forced myself back to Mr. Penn's droning voice.

Remember that my favorite color is green. Posters and projects that use a lot of green automatically get an extra ten points.

When the bell rang, I nearly jumped out of my seat. I looked for Dennis in the hall. Today at lunch I'd wanted to sit with him again. It was so cool yesterday, having him come up to me like that in the cafeteria. *Lame,* another part of me argued. *Basically all he did was pull me off the table and yell at me.* Today he hadn't come over at all. He'd picked a table with only one seat left and sat there, eating in silence. After a few minutes I realized how pathetic I was being. I spent the rest of lunch in the girl's room.

Yeah, alone was my middle name.

Compared to Mr. Penn's bore-me-to-death drone, old Wheatley was downright electrifying. He had spent most of yesterday's opening class talking about what we'd cover in freshman English: the obligatory Shakespeare play, units in expository and creative writing, and of course the typically depressing choices found on most academic reading lists. Wheatley started class with a quick grammar quiz that covered everything we were supposed to know but obviously didn't. After quickly eyeballing the results, he decided we needed blackboard work.

"'The handsome young man in the white, three-piece suit strutted his stuff onto the dance floor to the wild cheers of the crowd.' Now, who'd care to take a stab at diagramming that sentence?" Wheatley asked.

"'Strutted his stuff onto the dance floor'?" repeated a boy from the front. "See, that's the problem, Mr. Wheatley. Diagramming and disco—they're both deader than dinosaurs."

"Really? Now, which Piccolini are you?" Wheatley said, referring to his list of names. "Are you George or Gerard?" The boy up front had an identical twin, who sat in the back, one seat over from me.

"I'm George."

"George, huh? Well, I can only take your word on that, so I think I'll refer to you by location and not name. From henceforth until eternity, or at least until next June, which will certainly feel the same, you in the front will be known as Mr. Piccolini North and you in the back will be known as Mr. Piccolini South. Which of you actually sits where is up to you."

The class laughed, though I didn't believe for one second that Wheatley was confused. He just liked delivering a line.

"So, Mr. Piccolini North, I'll ignore your comment—by the way, 'dead' has no comparative degree—and ask you to diagram this instead: 'The multi-pierced singer of indeterminate gender leapt off the stage and crowd-surfed across the room and back.' Sir—to the blackboard!"

It took most of the remaining period for Idiot Twin North to puzzle out the sentence.

"Homework," Mr. Wheatley called a few minutes before the bell. "And please, no moans. It's Labor Day weekend, so it's appropriate that I make you labor. Make up five sentences and diagram them. Points off for simple inanities like 'I want my MTV.' Bonus points if you manage to amuse me. Yes, Miss Canarsie?" he said at my upraised hand.

"So, you want us to be funny, like 'When the man failed miserably as a stand-up comic, he became an English teacher so he could subsequently torture his captive audiences.'"

I didn't look at Dennis as I spoke, though I was dying to know if he was laughing with the rest of the class.

"Hmmm…'subsequently.' Impressive, but somewhat redundant with 'so,'" Wheatley said, blunting my joke. "Yes, definite bonus points for that, Miss Canarsie, but remember there's a very fine line between amusement and insult. Cross it at your own risk."

Before I could make a crack about English teachers who used clichés, Wheatley added, "And remember, while *I* may slip into the occasional hackneyed phrase while talking, your writing has the opportunity of a second draft."

My mouth was still open when the bell rang. The guy was positively spooky.

Dennis didn't make his usual dash out the door.

I was grinning as I walked down the aisle toward him.

"Well?" I asked.

"Well," he said, his expression wary, "I'm wondering if you're going to be a pain in the ass to know."

"Maybe, but never boring," I shot back.

He grunted a neutral reply, then led the way to world civ.

My last two classes—art and study hall—were cut candidates a little lower than gym, but I decided to grit my teeth through both. Study hall was being replaced by Jimmy's memorial, plus I wanted to be visible at my locker around final bell.

In case of what?

In case one of the cheerleaders wanted to invite me to a slumber party? Or the president of chorus planned to ask me to join? Or Dennis Monaghan dropped by to ask what I was doing for Labor Day weekend?

I'm getting feeble. Next I'll be whining if I'm not elected homecoming queen.

After study hall, I walked right past my locker and out the door. Tomorrow was Saturday, and I had a funeral to go to.

✳

Josephine Ellers, 38, beloved wife of Darren,
devoted mother of Helen and Joy.

Last week, Jimmy Muller, 15; this week Josephine Ellers, 38. What was there, something in the water?

All summer I'd been planting old people, so these two back-to-back funerals were creepy. I mean, they were wrecking a perfectly good hobby. But I had no choice; Josephine Ellers was the only funeral at Evergreen scheduled for Saturday.

For the first time I almost stayed away. But what else did I have to do? Color a picture for Aunt Lolly to hang on her refrigerator? Maybe later I'd cut school during the week to get to a decent funeral, but for now the Ellers' service would have to do. I walked through the trailer park's dirt roads to the back entrance to Evergreen.

Grief, palpable even from a distance, poured off the crowd like heat from the summer pavement. It was an uncomfortable reminder of Friday's memorial for Jimmy. Held in the gym, the memorial had begun with a few words from the junior high principal, then the pastor of St. Paul's Church. Two girls read drippy poems about a flower being picked before it blossomed and a star falling from the night heavens. Their own original work, of course. I didn't know whether to laugh or gag. From the crowd came no jokes, no imitations of drowning, no remarks. Students wept, some openly, as well as a few teachers. If I had been by myself, say, watching the memorial on TV, I might have choked up. But I didn't allow it. I hated to cry in public. Mr. Iglesia, Jimmy's junior high math teacher and the math club adviser, spoke about Jimmy's love of numbers. Even then, I refused to let go and practiced multiplication tables in my head to block out his words.

Mr. Muller had attended the memorial too, alone and unannounced. If any of the teachers recognized him, they said nothing. He slipped in after the memorial started, stood silently in the back, and slipped out before it was over. Good thing. He missed the Nickel Park High School Choir murdering Eric Clapton's "Tears in Heaven." Jimmy's mother didn't attend. I supposed she'd returned to California and her acting auditions, or whatever it was she was doing out there.

I hadn't seen Dennis at the memorial service either.

The same kinds of intense emotion—grief, anguish, and anger—soaked through today's funeral for Josephine Ellers. Her daughters Helen and Joy were about ten and twelve, with stringy blond hair and eyes black with sorrow. They held hands like lost three-year-olds. I couldn't be sure who their father was, so many sad-eyed men stood close. Who were they all? Brothers? Cousins?

I realized the girls were partially orphaned.

So was I, in a way. My father was gone, as good as dead. Maybe he really was dead. Something terrible could have happened to him, a car accident, botulism, kidnapping. Again I heard my mother's words the day I'd ridden the bus to find him: "Bad things happen to people when they're alone, Allie." *I* was alone, half-orphaned, but my father was alone, too. What had happened to him?

Looking at the Ellers sisters, I decided I didn't want to know their story, didn't want to fill in any of the details. I left Evergreen and hurried home.

I changed from my black clothes to yellow shorts and a pink top, last year's Christmas present from Aunt Darleen. Not intending to enroll in clown college, I had buried the outfit in a bottom drawer. Today it somehow seemed right.

Once dressed, I walked over to the Nickel Park Library. I had to return the last of my summer reading. Or maybe I hoped to run into Dennis. *Get real,* I told myself. *It isn't as if he's falling all over himself to be nice. He's—what?—said "hi" a few times?* My entire social life consisted of "hi." Pathetic.

I just wasn't used to talking to people. Oh, I was a master at talking *at* them, then sauntering off while my crack still burned the air. But an actual conversation? I needed a course in that a lot more than I needed gym.

The library's air conditioning was a relief after the sweaty walk from the trailer, and I decided to hang out. Everyone had taken off for the Labor Day weekend. I had the place to myself. The air was cool, slightly dusty, and silent except for the comforting thump-shush of books being reshelved.

My favorite armchair stood in the corner past the Reference Department. Being allergic to nonfiction, I never used Reference.

But this time, as I walked down the aisle toward the chair, something caught my eye: a long row of Nickel Park High yearbooks. Idly, I wondered what Wheatley had looked like way back when the high school was a hut and an outhouse.

When I pulled out the first volume, a booklet wedged in next to it slid out and fell to the floor. I figured it was one of those invaluable little nuggets libraries so often had, like "The Identification and Termination of the Boll Weevil," written by a local agricultural freak. But it wasn't. It was the most recent yearbook for the Nickel Park Junior High School. Dennis would be in it.

Jimmy Muller would be in the yearbook, too. Jimmy, who, unlike Dennis, was sure to have been my friend. I wouldn't have had to make an effort with Jimmy. We would have gravitated toward each other like positive and negative magnets.

I grabbed a handful of recent years and took them back to the armchair. They were of miserable quality, little kids trying to be like the big kids, armed with just a photocopier. Still I could see the enthusiasm of whoever put them together. There were school photos of every student, with group shots of each club. In the most recent edition was a photo of students on either side of a smiling, dark-haired man, who held paper pentacles over two boys kneeling in front of him. I recognized his face from the memorial service before I read the caption: "In Mr. Iglesia's Math Club, the stars come out to shine." The boys in front were Dennis and Jimmy. Maybe the girl who'd written about a falling star had been thinking of this photo.

In the picture, Dennis was grinning. I'd seen him over the space of five days, counting our first two meetings in the cemetery, and he had yet to smile. Had the grin been for the camera, or had his mood permanently darkened since Jimmy's death?

Jimmy had the same bland, golly-gee pleasant expression as in his obituary photo. He was a model of good humor and perfection. If we hadn't immediately clicked, like missing halves of a whole, we would have spent all our time trying to convert each other; we'd be locked in the classic struggle of light versus dark, good versus evil, Luke versus Darth Vader, only to discover somewhere along the way that we were one and the same.

I stuffed the booklets into my knapsack, since reference books couldn't be checked out, then headed toward the entrance. There, running up the library steps just as I opened the door, was Dennis.

"Hey, Allie," he said. He stopped on the top stair.

"Hi. What are you doing?" I asked.

"Uh…going to the library." He answered slowly, as if it had been a trick question.

How's this for a diagramming sentence, Mr. Wheatley? "In just five words, the girl destroyed the last shred of doubt that she was an utter loser."

"I mean, what have you been doing this weekend?" I said, attempting a quick recovery.

"Not much. I've got a family picnic tomorrow, which is like the last thing on earth I want to do. But I have to go. Then maybe I'll get some practice in on Monday," he said, starting to shift back and forth between his feet.

"Practice?"

"Running. Down at the track. I mean I run every day, but not always at the track."

"Oh."

"The high school track, not the town track," he explained. "The high school track is brand new."

"Oh. Well, I guess if you're going to run, a new track is better than an old one."

"Yeah… See you."

He pulled open the library door. A wave of cool air washed over my burning face. *A new track is better than an old one?* I didn't know which was more shocking: that I'd actually made such a lame remark or that the Stupid Police hadn't pulled up, sirens blaring, to arrest me. Without my sarcastic one-liners, I was better off mute.

Why was it so hard to talk to Dennis? Maybe because he didn't give me any help. I didn't see why. If I'd have been Jimmy's close friend, and Jimmy had been Dennis's close friend, then I should clearly be Dennis's close friend, too, and able to talk to him. What could I do to make him come to the same conclusion on his own?

Chapter Five

I spent too much of Sunday trying to figure out Dennis's few words. Tomorrow he was going to run at the track—the high school track, he'd been careful to point out. Did that mean he was telling me where he'd be so I could show up? But he hadn't mentioned a time, and I sure wasn't going to sit in the bleachers all Labor Day from dawn to midnight letting birds nest in my hair. How pitiful would that be? Maybe he'd never meant for me to come at all. Maybe it had only been something to say till he could shake me.

It was almost enough to make me ask someone how to talk to boys. But who? Mom was so quiet, I didn't see her having much useful experience. That left Aunt Darleen. Then my aunt came over to visit. This was no longer the Platonic ideal of Aunt Darleen, full of wonderful, wise advice, but the real thing. And the real thing squealed when the screen door hit her in the butt, and that real butt was wearing lime-green shorts so micro they barely covered what legally had to be covered. Did I really want advice from the Tastee Treet Cookie Queen? I came to my senses and kept my mouth shut.

Why did I care anyway? Most people suffered extreme cases of Dumb Ass Syndrome and had nothing to say worth my listening to.

Instead, I spent most of Sunday locked in my room, studying the junior high yearbooks. Knowing Dennis was a way of knowing Jimmy, but the reverse was also true. Maybe if I knew Jimmy better, I'd know how to talk to Dennis.

What would it have been like being friends with Jimmy? Would he have asked me to take over his paper route the days he couldn't make it? Maybe I'd have agreed, but there'd be no way he could have convinced me to come to the food pantry or hospital. I wouldn't have done those sickly sweet things, not even for him.

But I'd have broken my rule against organized groups and joined the math club. Maybe I'd have beaten Jimmy for the presidency. After all, he had Mr. Iglesia lead him through geometry as an extracurricular, while I had done it purely on my own, proving my obvious math superiority. Mom had found a geometry text at a garage sale one day and tossed it on my bed, saying, "Here, Brainiac. A present. Knock yourself out." So I was one up on Jimmy at least on that point. He didn't like it.

I had to catch myself. He *wouldn't* have liked it. But I'd never know for sure because I had never met him.

It wasn't fair, it wasn't right. Why couldn't I have known Jimmy and then gone swimming with him that day so he wouldn't have been alone?

My mother's warning stuck in my head like the refrain of a bad song, only this time I heard the words as she'd really said them:

"Bad things can happen to kids *when they're alone."*

Jimmy was alone when he died, alone when he went swimming. I wasn't there to go with him. I could have been there, *should* have been there, if only we'd met a little sooner.

But we hadn't.

Suddenly I remembered something Dennis had said the day of the funeral, that Jimmy hated the water. How could I have forgotten it all this time? Remembering it, I had to then ask why a kid who hated water was out at the lake alone. I tried to think of an answer. There was none.

Bad things can happen to kids when they're alone.

Something very bad had happened to Jimmy.

※

48

On Labor Day, Mom, Aunt Darleen, and I drove over to the Cottersville mall for the grand opening of a Wal-Mart, which would undoubtedly become the new social hub of Deedy County. On the drive over, Mom asked dozens of questions about my new teachers. She and Aunt Darleen both had had Wheatley for English, of course, as well as the same gym teacher. And back then Principal Saunders had been vice-principal of discipline. He was one to watch, Aunt Darleen added. "*I* know," she said, winking. "You're more like me than you'll ever guess."

Sure. Next I'd be wearing glow-in-the-dark hot pants.

Was I walking in my mother's and my aunt's footsteps? Did that condemn me as well to life in Nickel Park? I refused to think about it and instead worked hard at being good. I tried on lots of horrible clothes, which made Aunt Darleen happy, as she had company in the dressing room. But I bought only black jeans and a black tank, both on sale, which made Mom happy, as her budget wasn't wrecked.

On the ride back, despite every promise I'd made myself the night before, I asked Mom to drive by the high school and drop me off in front.

"Oh?" she asked. "Gonna hang out with some kids?"

Biting back a crack about cheerleaders and jocks, I just grunted.

I waited till the car turned the corner, then I headed over to the athletic field.

Though I couldn't understand showing up at school on a holiday, there were about a dozen kids working out: running, doing long jumps, stretching or squatting to warm up. Dennis was on the far side of the track, moving in long, easy strides as if he could keep running forever. I walked to the home-side bleachers, found his checkerboard towel and water bottle, and sat down. He waved when he came round but ran three more laps before stopping.

"Hi," I said, throwing the towel to him.

He grabbed it, slung it around his neck, then bent down, hands on his knees, and gasped for breath. Sweat had darkened his hair to maroon.

"That looks painful. Why do you do it?" I asked, watching him flex his legs and jog a bit in place to cool off. I walked everywhere, no matter how far, because buses cost money, but that was pure need. The value of motion for its own sake escaped me.

"Why do I do what?" he asked, wiping off his face.

"Why do you run?"

"Because it's a sport where I won't get beaned with a fastball or tackled by three hundred pounds of concrete. I won't snap my neck being pinned, and I won't drown."

"Drown," I repeated.

The word just slipped out. Dennis hid his face momentarily in the towel. When he looked up, he was expressionless. He sat next to me and took a long drink of water.

"Tell me about Jimmy," I prompted.

He capped the bottle, gazed out at the other runners, then said, "Why should I?"

Because I need to know, I thought. *I need to know about the one person on earth who might have finally understood me.*

Recalling Miss Barbosa's words from the first day of school, I said, "Jimmy told me you were his best friend."

"He did? Really? When did he say that?"

I busied myself tying my sneaker.

"Was it during Youth Week at St. Paul's?" Dennis continued. "His dad made him go again this year even though Jimmy didn't want to. Did you go, too?"

"Nah, I never go to those things," I said.

Dennis nodded then lapsed into silence. He was a quiet person but not still. Jangles of energy streamed from him, as if he needed another ten laps just to calm down.

"Jimmy's death must be rough on you," I said, trying to get him to talk again. "I know it is on me." I picked at my shoelace. "He lived with his dad, but his mom lived in California. What were they—separated, divorced? Jimmy never said which."

"Divorced."

This was a natural place for me to say "like mine," but I kept quiet. I never talked about my parents. Never.

Dennis propped his elbows on the bleacher step behind him and stretched his legs in front. "Mrs. Muller left about three years ago," he said. "It probably took Mr. Muller a week to notice she was gone, he's always so busy. He's a big-time car dealer, biggest in Deedy County. He finally hired Mrs. Hidalgo to take care of Jimmy."

"Who's that?"

"Mrs. Hidalgo? She's the live-in housekeeper. I guess you never went over there."

I shrugged, my all-purpose cover-up. To distract him, I asked, "How did you two become best friends? Did you share a cubby in kindergarten?"

Maybe I'll learn something here, I thought, *like how to make a friend.*

"Jimmy moved to Nickel Park in fifth grade," Dennis explained. "By the end of the first day of school, kids were calling him a rich snot. Jimmy would answer, 'Yeah, I'm rich, but you're the snot.'" A smile softened Dennis's face. "The second day, Tom Creighton tried to take the rich kid's lunch money. I guess he figured Jimmy would be an easy target. Jimmy was short then, so short, he told me, that his mom had even held him back a year and made him repeat kindergarten, hoping he'd grow."

Aha. That explains why Jimmy was a fifteen-year-old freshman, like me.

"Anyway," Dennis continued, "Jimmy's parents never trusted him with more than a dollar or two. He figured it would just make Creighton madder if he didn't have any more than that to give him, so he decided to call his bluff and refused. Creighton made good on his threat and beat him up."

"And you rushed in and dragged him off?" I asked.

"See this?" Dennis bent his wiry arm and showed the smallest of muscles. "This is *after* I gained weight. I called the playground guard and let *her* drag him off. Creighton had it in for both of us after that."

"What did he do?"

"Beat us both up the next day. Neither of us wanted to go home all bloody. So we sneaked back into school, washed up as best we could, and wore our gym clothes to try to hide the mess. I didn't look too bad, and my parents believed me when I said I fell off the monkey bars. Jimmy's parents were fighting pretty regularly by then. They didn't notice him either night." Dennis scratched his head, thinking. "I guess a common enemy made us bond. Common fear and humiliation. It was the only time Creighton actually touched us, but he threatened us both just about every day. I was glad to be rid of him last year, at least for a while."

"Last year? He's a junior."

"We had a one-building school system till then," Dennis said, jogging my memory. "At least Jimmy doesn't have to put up with him anymore."

Even his own indirect reference to Jimmy's death silenced Dennis. He pulled in his arms and legs and sat up straight. I didn't want him to think it had been a mistake to talk, so I steered to an easier subject.

"Exactly how good was Jimmy in math? Could I have been Math Club president?"

"Maybe. Maybe not. The other day Miss Barbosa called him 'an extraordinary student.' She sounded disappointed not to be having him."

I thought I heard a hint of envy in Dennis's voice. Again he stopped talking.

"It must be tough to lose a kid like that," I said, encouraging him to go on. "I mean, a volunteer, a math whiz, teachers actually looking forward to having him. It's not like he was a smart-ass." *Would anyone ever regret not having me in class?* "I guess, all those times I didn't see him, he was hanging out with you," I finished.

"We hung out a lot," Dennis said, studying the tip of his running shoe.

"But not two weeks ago. Not when he'd gone swimming."

"Yeah, right." He grabbed his things and leapt to his feet.

"Did he do that a lot?" I persisted. This was the longest conversation I had had with Dennis—or with anyone from school, for that matter—and didn't want it to end. Besides, I was curious, no faking there. "Did Jimmy usually go off swimming by himself?"

"Jimmy hated to swim," Dennis said flatly. "I told you that."

"Then why—"

"End of story."

Dennis walked off toward the exit. I followed. Outside on the sidewalk, he said, "See you tomorrow," and turned left. I turned right to go home.

Something was wrong. It wasn't just that I'd been cheated out of a friend. Something more, but what?

✳

That night I couldn't sleep. I'd nod off, then half wake up, drifting between the dark around me and the dark inside my head. I kept remembering a movie I'd seen a few months ago. During the time I'd spent at Aunt Darleen's, I'd temporarily slipped back into the habit of watching TV, figuring she'd rather pawn a major body part than her set. One night I'd watched this old black-and-white film about a woman who died in a sailing accident. Weeks later her estranged sister showed up and revealed that the dead woman was afraid of the water and would have never gone sailing. So it couldn't have been an accident. She'd actually been murdered.

My knee-jerk reaction, of course, was that the same thing had happened to Jimmy, that he hated swimming and wouldn't have gone in the first place, much less alone. But the idea was just too ridiculous to take seriously. What was I going to tell people, *Well, it was just like this movie?* I had enough credibility issues as it was without adding stupidity.

The next day, even if I'd wanted to tiptoe around the possibility, I didn't get the chance to mention it to Dennis. Maybe he thought he'd said way too much at the track because on Tuesday all I got from him was a nod and a grunt. It really threw me. I did all the things I usually did at a new school—hunting down places to hide when I cut class, putting myself to sleep imagining my teachers' private lives, thinking of incredibly bitchy things to say to Tom Creighton, many of which actually flew from my mouth in his presence—but all the while I kept wondering how to get Dennis to talk to me.

Every day I showed up at the cafeteria, hoping he'd sit with me again. He didn't. Tuesday, Wednesday, Thursday, Friday—he either picked an already-crowded table and sat in silence, or else he tossed his lunch in the trash can, went outside, and jogged. School-wise, the week was just as wretched. Miss Barbosa kept treating Tom Creighton like he was human instead of the cretin he really was. Mr. Wheatley was auditioning for Teacher of the Year, or at least everyone's favorite uncle on a black-and-white sitcom. Meanwhile, Mr. Penn explored, and sometimes crossed, the very fine line between boring and dead. Some of these complaints and witticisms would have been much juicier if shared, but Dennis had become a fortress of silence.

Saturday I spent most of the day trying unsuccessfully to read my bad mood away. Sunday I just happened to walk by the high school track and hang out for a while, in case Dennis just happened to be there again. He wasn't. So I just happened to storm back home under a black cloud, kicking at stones, cans, and mailbox posts on the way.

When I reached Lost & Found, I found Aunt Darleen at our trailer. Neither she nor Mom heard me come in, they were arguing so loudly. Both of them were in the kitchen, Mom at the sink, my aunt a few feet behind her, their backs to me. As soon as I heard what they were arguing about, I wanted to throw up.

"You've only been here three months! How can you think about moving again?" Aunt Darleen yelled.

"I don't know," Mom said, banging pots around without purpose. "Mr. Berger left me a note on Friday, said he wanted to see me. I've tried to put it out of my mind, but I can't anymore. I know what he's going to say: 'Things don't seem to be working out.' Maybe I should save him the trouble and quit first thing in the morning."

"But *three months!*"

"It's not just me," Mom said quickly. "Allie hates her school."

"Allie hates every school. It's what teenagers do. It's in their job description."

"But this time she really—"

"What?" Aunt Darleen demanded. "Don't blame this on Allie."

"Yeah, don't blame it on me!" I shouted. "When were you going to mention leaving to *me,* Mom? I've got a life, too, you know. A crummy miserable life, but it's mine! You have no right to keep ripping it to shreds."

I ran to my room and slammed the door. How could she do this to me again?

I blocked out the argument and began to spin a story. In the story, Mom moved, but I ran away and came back to Nickel Park. I lived in the school in one of the hiding spots I'd found. I slept on a gym mat, showered in the girls' locker room, scrounged food from the cafeteria. I became a model student so no one would call my mother and find she was no longer in town. Then Mr. Wheatley discovered where I was staying at night, because he was a mind reader, at least with me. It turned out he had an incredible empathetic link with me because I reminded him of his own daughter, who had died dozens of years ago in a train wreck. He asked me to stay with him, of course, so I wouldn't be alone.

After a while, the scene slipped away, and I found myself thinking about Jimmy instead. It was easier to think about Jimmy than about myself.

About eight Mom and Aunt Darleen moved from the kitchen toward the door, their voices calm. I had missed dinner—and how the argument ended. Now they were talking as if they'd never fought.

"We'll go Wednesday then?" Aunt Darleen asked.

"We'll see. They're predicting rain, and you know I don't like to drive in the rain."

"Then *I'll* drive," Aunt Darleen said. "You can keep your eyes shut the whole time."

My stomach began to tighten. Not the tight, I'm-fifteen-and-I'm-already-getting-an-ulcer ache, but strange and queasy, as if I was flying upside down in a helicopter after eating pepperoni pizza. Maybe it was nerves from not knowing what Mom had decided.

A wordless thought was just beyond my grasp, something big, something important. It grew stronger until at last it screamed:

It had rained all that day!

The day Jimmy died, the day a kid who hated the water supposedly went swimming all by himself, had been cool and rainy. It had stuck in my mind because it was the day my mother—who hates to drive in the rain—had taken me out shopping for pearl earrings for my birthday.

The sense of wrongness I'd had all along about his death exploded in my mind. Just like in that old movie, someone who hated water would never go swimming alone in the first place. But now add to that a rainy day, and it became impossible. So what had really happened? What if he'd been lured out to the lake? What if his accident had been set up? *What if Jimmy Muller had been murdered?*

It would explain everything.

Excited, I sat up straight and considered the facts.

The paper had said it was an accident. An accident like that couldn't have happened. If Jimmy hated to swim in the first place, he would have hated even more swimming in a dark, muddy lake. Throw in bad weather and his being alone, and calling it an accident became absurd.

Jimmy had been murdered.

It took an outsider like me—but with the insight of being Jimmy's friend—to see what had happened. I could imagine the whole thing easily. God knew there were enough people who hated *me.* I could feel myself in Jimmy's place, being threatened, stalked, hunted down. And then...then...

Once I started to think about it, it was obvious. He'd been murdered, then his death set up to look like an accident.

My new question was this: If Dennis knew that Jimmy hated swimming, Mr. Muller probably knew too. So why hadn't either of them mentioned this to the police? Why hadn't either said Jimmy shouldn't have been at the lake in the first place? It was the one clue that should have created suspicion in everyone's mind. That clue added to the bad weather made the whole thing obvious. Yet it was being totally ignored.

But not any more. Now Jimmy had me.

Chapter Six

The next day I planted myself by Dennis's locker. My plan was to lead him slowly through my reasoning, until he came on his own to the same conclusion I'd come to. My patience evaporated as soon as I saw him.

"Jimmy's death wasn't an accident," I blurted out.

Dennis staggered as if I had punched him.

"You don't know what you're talking about!"

"I know Jimmy wouldn't have gone to the lake alone in a million years. And I know you didn't say anything to the police. Well, did you?"

His brick-red blush answered the question before he did.

"What's the difference? He's dead. It doesn't really matter where it happened."

"Of course it matters!" I said. "He shouldn't have been there. It was cold, it was rainy, he hated swimming. That can mean only one thing."

Dennis slammed his locker and walked away.

I shouldn't have shocked him like that, I thought. *Now he's in denial.* An accident was bad enough; murder was unthinkable. Dennis probably already felt guilty for not being there, the way I did. This news was too much for him.

But *I* couldn't hide from the truth.

Who did it? A murder had to have a murderer. Who would want

to kill a good-hearted, brainy, well-behaved kid? We weren't talking about me here, where everyone from my kindergarten teacher to the supermarket clerk would like to wring my neck. It had to have been a stranger. *Yeah, like a serial killer,* I thought. *Jimmy's lucky he hadn't been gutted and flayed.* The worst part was that whoever did it was still loose.

I couldn't catch Dennis's eye in homeroom or math. That distracted me so much I gave Miss Barbosa the wrong answer when she called on me.

"Good going, genius," Creighton said from behind. "You need tutoring?"

Actually, I had given the right answer, but it was for problem nine and we were only on problem three. Between working ahead on my own and trying to send meaningful looks to Dennis, I had lost track of where the class was. When someone later gave the answer for number nine, Miss Barbosa looked up at me sharply. At least now she knew I wasn't a total idiot.

I didn't hang around for her apology, though, but jumped up at the bell before Dennis could rush out. Creighton lurched up out of his seat at the same time. My head knocked the books from his hands to the floor.

"Ow, way to go, Cretin," I said, rubbing my ear. "Why do you even have those? It's a waste of natural resources to give you books."

"Oh yeah? It's a waste of air to let a loser like you breathe."

I didn't catch up with Dennis till lunch, where I found him at a corner table. "Please," I said. "You've got to listen to me."

"No, I don't." He got up and went out into the schoolyard.

Through the window I saw him chuck his lunch into a trash can, leave his backpack by the bike rack, then jog off. He returned before the period ended, red-faced and puffing as if he'd spent the entire time sprinting.

He was gone, of course, by the last bell.

It looked as if Dennis wasn't going to be much help. But I owed it to Jimmy to solve his murder. Friends had to watch out for each other.

I liked the idea of being a detective. Even so, I needed to calm down, get a neutral opinion. I hurried to the public library where there was a row of phones. It was three-thirty. Aunt Lolly would be in her kitchen, probably having a cup of tea.

Aunt Lolly encouraged me to call collect on my own every so often. I didn't know whether these calls were a way for Aunt Lolly to check up on Mom, or whether Mom had asked her to check up on me. I didn't care. The calls didn't make me Niece of the Year or anything. I figured they were a way to stay connected to my dad, even though Aunt Lolly never mentioned his name either. She looked a bit like him, in a white-haired, shriveled-up-old lady way. And I figured that sooner or later she'd let something about him slip out.

"Where are you?" she asked me. "I can hardly hear you."

"By the library. There's no booth, that's why it's noisy. They're too cheap here in Nickel Park to build phone booths."

"Allie, you're a brat. You used to be so sweet, but now... If I were younger, I'd wash your mouth out with soap then hang you by your ears to dry."

"Me sweet? Never," I said, startled. *Was I really once sweet? What had happened?* "You must be getting senile. You're confusing me with a long lost cousin I never met."

She sighed so deeply her breath almost passed through the wire. "Is there a purpose to this call?"

Her sharpness put me off. She usually just insulted me back.

"No, just general harassment."

"I'm sorry. My arthritis is killing me." Her voice softened. "Is there something you want? I'm not worth spit right now, but if there's anything I can do once—if—the medication kicks in..."

"No, nothing." Her hands were so crippled with arthritis she could have rented them out for horror movies. The pain had to have been brutal. "I wanted...I wanted to say hi, I guess."

"There's more than that, isn't there?"

Aunt Lolly was very old. Some days her mind was fuzzy, and some days it was sharp. Today must have been a sharp day. But if she was in too much pain for a little joking, I doubted she was up to discussing murder.

"That's okay. It can wait. I'll call you later."

"Are you sure? At least tell me how the new school is."

"It sucks big time, but I didn't expect different. So…I guess okay."

"In other words, your usual. How's your mother? How's her job? She didn't say much when she called Saturday. Is that a good sign or bad?"

I'd completely forgotten my mother's argument with Aunt Darleen yesterday, forgotten to ask about it this morning, forgotten even to think about it during the day.

"I don't know. She's…she's been talking about—" My voice shook unexpectedly. "Aunt Lolly, why does she quit all the time, why do we always move?" *Why did my father leave?* "I mean, is it me? Is everything my fault?"

"No, of course not, Allie. I know it may feel like that to you, but your mother probably feels that everything is *her* fault. I think the two of you need to have a good long talk."

"What are you, a shrink?" I snapped. Her silence hurt me more than any remark. "I'm sorry. Really. I hope you feel better soon."

"So do I."

I hung up more unsettled than before. I had a murder on my hands, and all I'd done so far was scare off my only potential friend in all of Nickel Park High *and* be mean to an old lady.

When I got to the trailer, I started supper. I made a vow to cook every day that week without fail. I still didn't know if Mom was going to move again or not. I wasn't sure if I wanted to know. But maybe she'd think my new devotion to domestic stuff meant I was happy. I couldn't leave Nickel Park now, not while Jimmy needed me.

So I scraped potatoes and carrots and chopped onions and peppers and zucchini, and while I worked, I thought. I kept returning to the picture that had run with the article on Jimmy's death. Setting the vegetables aside, I went through the recycling pile. Jimmy's obituary was still there. I clipped out his photo and memorized his face.

I could have recognized him blocks away. I mean, friends can do that—they know each other by the back of the head, a footstep, a single laugh. At least, that's the way I always imagined it.

Jimmy had an ordinary kind of face, though he was grinning so hard it hurt to look at it. He wore a white baseball cap, "a favorite present" the article said. Who had given it to him? The newspaper had said something about a birthday party. If Dennis asked why I didn't go, what could I say?

I was going through possible excuses when my mother—quiet, bland, beige Winifred Canarsie—*sailed* through the door, beaming.

"Guess what?" she said.

"What?"

"I've been promoted!"

"What!" I shrieked. I jumped up and grabbed her.

After a long tight hug, she pushed me away then balled up her white labcoat and tossed it into the kitchen trash.

"Good-bye, cookies. Hello, front desk."

"Front desk?"

"I'm the new receptionist—and that's just for starters." Shaking her head, she laughed at the wonder of it. "*Me.* I guess wearing dresses under that horrible white coat paid off."

"I thought you were worried about getting fired," I said, remembering what she'd told Aunt Darleen. "Didn't you say somebody left you a note?"

"Mr. Berger. I was worried he was going to yell at me. But when he called me in, the first thing he said was that they had an opening for a receptionist and he was offering *me* the job. He said I was so quiet, so dependable, I had to be a calming influence. He said I'd be good in the lobby. He'd had to leave early Friday, so he left the note for me to stop by his office today." Mom grabbed both my hands and looked at me excitedly. "He said that if the receptionist job went well, he might consider me for office manager in a few months—and get this—he encouraged me to take advantage of the company's tuition reimbursement plan. He said if I went back to college at night, they'll pay for it! Of course, it would only be an associate's degree from Deedy County Community, that's the only college nearby, but still... *a degree!*"

Has this happened at other jobs too, I wondered, *her running away just before her big break? How many opportunities has she missed?*

My mother pulled me to her and hugged me again. Her whisper was a dark confession:

"It has to work this time, Allie. We have nowhere else to go."

✳

The next day Dennis continued to avoid me. I could understand, what with my shocking news and all. But you weren't supposed to shoot the messenger, right? So I persisted, silently dogging him all Tuesday as we walked to class and hanging around his locker before and after school. On Wednesday, when I followed him to the cafeteria, he finally sat at an empty table. I took it as a sign that he was at least willing to listen. I pulled the newspaper photo from my bag and shoved it at him.

He pushed the photo aside and began to unwrap his lunch. Finally, he inched the photo closer and said, "Stupid kid. He had to be told you were supposed to wear the hat backwards. But he loved it. Never took it off."

"Did you give it to him?"

"Sure, a Pyramid cap on my allowance? Nah, it was a birthday present from his dad, though Mrs. Hidalgo decided on it and did the shopping. She moved mountains to get that hat. She'd do anything for Jimmy."

I stared at the photo. Something about it bothered me. Maybe it was the grin on Jimmy's face. He didn't have a clue how soon he'd be dead.

"Listen, Dennis," I said softly. "Jimmy is gone. There's nothing we can do to bring him back. But something's wrong here, and you know it."

"Don't start, Allie," Dennis said, half-rising.

"Why are you so scared to know the truth?"

"I'm not scared," he said.

"Then help me. Help me find Jimmy's murderer."

"Murderer?"

Dennis's face lost its color. I realized this was the first time I'd actually said the word.

"Yes, murderer." I leaned in closer for emphasis. "Jimmy was murdered."

Dennis stared down at a grease spot on the table. I couldn't see his eyes. "Why do you think Jimmy was…" His voice trailed off.

I listed my reasons. When I finished, I said, "Now it's up to us to solve the mystery." But his face had shut down again, the color returning.

"Even…even if you're right," he said, "shouldn't it be left to the police?"

"And if they're not doing their job?" I picked up his lunch bag and poked around among its contents to hide how pleased I was. Maybe I hadn't convinced him, but at least we were talking again. I fished out a box of raisins, a sure sign of a mom-made lunch if there ever was one. "Cops aren't that bright," I continued.

"They're probably a lot brighter than you."

"Thanks. But *they* say it was an accident. We know better. It's up to us—although actually…" My mind started to leapfrog from idea to idea. "The police station might be a good place for us to start."

"The police station?" Dennis looked up from his sandwich, alarmed.

"Maybe they know more than they're letting on." I shook out a few raisins. They looked like rabbit turds. I dropped them back into the box and wiped my hand. "In the movies cops always hold back crucial evidence to separate the real murderer from the crazies who confess to everything," I explained. "In this case the cops aren't saying it's murder. Maybe that's what they're holding back."

"And your plan is?"

My mind raced until it found the perfect setup.

"We fake our way into the police station and when the cops aren't looking, we go through their file on Jimmy."

"You're kidding, right?"

"We can do it. It wouldn't be that hard."

"*No!*" Dennis said angrily. "You'll never be able to fool the cops, and you'll wind up getting *me* in trouble."

"You're worried about getting in trouble? And you call yourself Jimmy's friend? Never mind, I'll do it myself!" I tossed the raisins at him and jumped up from the table.

I was so disgusted I didn't bother to cut earth science and used the period to take a nap. It was too short and only made me cranky. I pushed my way out of Mr. Penn's class and down the hall, wishing I could barb my elbows like a rooster in a cockfight.

Just across from Wheatley's door, Creighton stood in the hallway, scrawling on a piece of paper propped against the wall for support. The tip of his tongue, stuck out in concentration, couldn't erase the infinite dumbness smeared across his face. I had the perfect crack but before I could say it, someone from behind pushed me along into English class.

My butt hadn't warmed the seat one second when the fire bell rang. At first no one seemed to understand, because the bell for class hadn't rung yet. But the *ring-ring-ring* continued and we finally realized what it was.

"Class, proceed out the nearest exit up the hill to the flagpole," Mr. Wheatley said. Students began wandering around, talking. "C'mon, c'mon," he continued, "you've been doing this since you were babies." He grabbed one talkative boy by the shoulders, turned him around, and pushed him toward the door. "You all know the routine for a drill."

"A drill?" I said from the back of the room. "There was smoke in the hall."

"Smoke?"

"Yeah, smoke." I paused, a true master of timing. But before I could deliver the punch line—"It was the smell of brain cells burning: Tom Creighton was doing homework"—a boy up front shouted.

"You smelled smoke? She smelled smoke!"

"A real fire!"

Students rushed toward the door.

"Settle down, don't panic!" Wheatley called. "Leave in an orderly fashion! No, I don't know if it's real. No, you can't go to your locker. People, did you hear me?"

"Mr. Wheatley, no," I said, heading toward him. He interrupted before I could finish, shouting, "Go! Get out!"

Well, who cares, I thought. *It isn't a real fire anyway, so it's no big deal if he thinks it is. We're getting out of class all the same.*

I turned to give Dennis a thumbs-up but didn't see him. Maybe he had left already.

Then from the hall someone shouted "Fire!"—probably one of the kids from class who'd rushed out first. The call was picked up and echoed in increasingly panicky tones. The slow shuffle of bored students on a routine fire drill accelerated to a pounding race.

"No, I didn't mean—" I said.

Wheatley clapped as loudly as he could to get our attention but he could scarcely be heard as everyone ran to get out the one door. His hands were large and wrinkled, like his face. Looking from one to the other, I saw for the first time how pale he'd become.

"Ow! Watch it, get off me! Help!"

It was the boy in the cast, the one I'd accused earlier of being the victim of a pitchfork accident. One of his crutches had slipped. He lost his balance, dragging several students down with him. A girl screamed.

"Julie, get up and shut up. You're not hurt," Wheatley said sharply, pulling the girl up and almost falling himself as students banged into him rushing out. "Arturo, help Mac with his crutches. Wait till the worst of the crowd leaves, then walk him down the stairs. Yes, there'll be time." Mr. Wheatley stopped to catch his breath, laid his pale white hand on his chest, and gulped down air. "Edith, go ahead, I'll get them."

He waved off the student who had stopped to close the windows in good fire-drill routine and closed them himself, all the while rattling off instructions and getting paler by the minute.

"I'm serious, go!" His voice rose. "You!" he roared, pointing at me. "Outside at once!"

I was paralyzed, watching Wheatley's face drain to a sickly white. Wasn't that one of the signs of a heart attack? And shortness of breath too? Why did he have to get so upset? It was only a joke.

I forced my feet to move.

"Mr. Wheatley, I…" My lips opened but nothing came out. "I…I'm afraid I…"

"There's no reason to be afraid if you'll just go!"

He pushed me into the line of kids. I tried to step out, tried to say, "But you don't—" He pushed me out the door.

Swallowing my panic, I shoved forward until I saw a shock of red hair. I called Dennis's name. He stopped, fought backward through the crowd, reached out, grabbed my hand, and held it while he led me outside and up the hill to the flagpole. His hand was warm, and I thought I could feel his heartbeat through his palm. When we were a few feet from the rest of the class, he let go of my hand and dropped his backpack on the ground.

At first I said nothing, just stood and watched the school. Dennis paced, waiting, no doubt, for wisps of smoke or the flicker of flames. I was waiting for Wheatley. Finally he appeared at the door, clearing a path for Arturo and Mac, the kid on crutches, then he went back in to herd out stragglers. Soon I heard a wail of sirens, getting louder by the second.

I suppose the silence got to Dennis because at last he said, "How bad was the smoke you smelled? I didn't smell anything myself."

"There was no smoke."

"What do you mean, there was no smoke?"
"There was no smoke. It was a joke."
"It was *what?*"
"A joke. Just a joke," I said.
He backed away from me.
"You're crazy. You really are crazy."

Chapter Seven

"It wasn't my fault!" I shot back. "I was starting to tell a joke but everyone freaked before I could get another word in. Even Wheatley wouldn't listen." I shoved my hands in the back pockets of my jeans. "And so what? Nobody got hurt."

"That you know of."

"Nobody got hurt," I repeated. I squashed down the image of how sickly Mr. Wheatley had looked. "It's not the worst thing I've ever done in my life. Besides, it'll keep us out of class longer."

Both the police and the fire department had arrived, their multiple sirens winding down to quiet. Firemen jumped off the truck. Some stopped to speak to the principal, others raced into the building.

Dennis stood watching them. Without looking at me, he asked, "So what's the worst thing you did then?"

Make my dad leave? Mouth off to my mother? Be mean to Aunt Lolly? So many choices! I decided to stay away from my personal life.

"The school before this, Springfield Junior High." I could feel my cheeks grow red. "I got kicked out—sorta kicked out, because they only sorta knew I was the one who'd done it. I did stuff afterwards too, but this was the worst." Thinking the situation could use some humor, I added, "I guess we made a mutual decision that I leave the state."

"What did you do?"

"Set off an M-80 in the girls' room wastebasket. The top blew off and shot out a window."

"Allie, an M-80 is like an eighth of a stick of dynamite! You could have blown your arm off. Or someone else's."

"It was just a firecracker. And I waited till the bathroom was empty." I tried to grin. "So, does that make me delinquent or responsible?"

"Did you do that as a joke too?" he asked. "Here's a news flash: stuff like that isn't funny anymore. It never was."

Dennis strode away, leaving his backpack, leaving me.

I sat down hard on the grass, drew my knees to my chest, and hid my face.

It wasn't my fault! It wasn't! A shuddering breath so deep it seemed to come from someone else broke from my lips.

"It's all right, Allie. It's over. Things got out of hand, but in the end no one was hurt."

Wheatley. I was surprised he remembered my name. Then again, most of my teachers learned it right away.

"Are you okay?" he asked. I should have been asking him if he was all right.

Without lifting my head, I mumbled, "Sure."

"Really sure? Upstairs you said you were afraid. It appears you needn't have been. There was no fire. Perhaps someone had been smoking in the bathroom and you caught a whiff of it in the hall."

Was he giving me an out or hoping I'd confess?

"I don't really expect an answer," he said, making my neck tingle. "After all," his voice grew softer, "you weren't the one who actually yelled 'fire,' were you?"

"No, I wasn't!" I said fiercely, looking up. Wheatley's color was back, although his bow tie was lopsided and tufts of his white hair stuck out like wings. "I mean, if I say A, and somebody acts like a jerk and says B, and then a bigger jerk says C, that's not my fault, is it? I can't be responsible for the general stupidity of the world."

"Hmmm," he said, not giving me a clue. "Still, you might want to talk about it. We can if you want, or you can go home. School's dismissed for the rest of the day. The fire department wants to do a thorough inspection. In case there actually was smoke."

I didn't think I'd been staring, but Wheatley suddenly smoothed his white hair and straightened his bow tie in a few quick movements.

"Are you quite sure you're all right?" he asked again.

So much care and concern was starting to make me twitchy. I stood and began to look for Dennis.

"All right then," Wheatley concluded. "I'll see you tomorrow."

As he walked off, I called, "Hey."

"Yes?"

"Thanks."

He smiled, and a million wrinkles creased his face.

"For what?"

For not dying of a heart attack in class.

"For asking how I was."

"Anytime."

As Wheatley headed toward the school, I caught sight of Dennis. He was standing on the outside of a group of kids, not talking to anyone. I saw him look over at me. I decided to wait. It was another fifteen minutes before he gave up, climbed the hill, and sat on the grass next to me.

"I'm sorry," I said. This was at least half-true. I was sorry he was mad. I was sorry I'd almost sent Wheatley out in an ambulance. "I guess it wasn't the smartest thing I've ever done."

"No, you're saving that for when you try to fool the cops."

He turned toward me to say it. The nervous hitch of his breath against my bare arm was strange and shivery, and I jumped up.

"So, you've been thinking about my plan," I said, brushing grass off my jeans.

"I've been thinking about how to keep you out of trouble."

"Yeah?" A wisecrack dried up in my throat. "Why?"

"I don't know why!" he snapped. "Just because."

Gee, how articulate, I almost said, but didn't. I held my breath. When he didn't say anything else, I asked, "So, will you help me?"

Dennis sighed. Maybe he was resigning himself to my quirky charms. "At least let me hear your plan," he said.

"Yes!" I crowed, excitement returning.

I explained my scheme: Dennis and I would go to the police to say we'd overheard a plan to rob the Nickel Park bank. Once we were in the police chief's office, Dennis would pretend to get sick. While the chief helped him, I'd sneak into the files for the report on Jimmy's death.

"That is so unbelievably lame," Dennis said. "We wouldn't get past the front door. And besides, you don't have any idea where they keep the files."

"Oh yeah? Then you come up with something better."

He didn't answer, but he did walk with me toward the police station as far as the combo video/deli/liquor/drugstore. Then he stopped short and wandered off the sidewalk toward the picnic tables outside the store.

"You're really going through with this, aren't you?" His restless shifting kicked in: he was ready to take off, right now. "I thought you were bluffing." He hesitated. "I can't do it. We'll just get into trouble."

"It'll be okay. After all, we're not the murderer, right?"

"Will you quit saying that word!" He ran his fingers through his hair.

"Come on, Dennis, it's important that we know the truth. Look, even if we're caught, we won't get in trouble. We're only looking for information."

I grabbed his hand and tried to pull him a few feet but couldn't. It was a standoff. Dennis was not going to change his mind and I was not going to give up my plan.

"Okay," I said finally. "I'm going in."

"Alone?" he asked, staring at me.

"Yeah. I'll find a way to do it myself."

"You are even crazier than I thought."

I couldn't wimp out now, not after all my talk. I left Dennis standing there shaking his head and walked through the door of the police station.

In a town as puny as Nickel Park, I expected a lone officer, feet on the desk, fanning flies off his open-mouthed face with his hat. Instead, a long counter divided the room. Behind the counter were two men and a woman, each in a tan-and-chocolate uniform. The men were talking over a paper-strewn desk. The woman wore a phone headset and sat at the counter in front of a complicated telephone setup. Everyone looked busy.

"Excuse me," I said to the woman. "I'm Mary Johnson. May I speak to the chief of police?" Suddenly realizing how stupid the bank robbery story sounded, I said, "I'd like to interview him for the high school paper."

"I'm afraid you'll have to make an appointment. We're very busy. There was an incident at the school today, but you probably already know that."

"An incident? You mean, someone yelled 'fire' during a fire drill and started a stampede."

"'Stampede' is a bit of an exaggeration, but one of the teachers twisted her ankle during the rush, and we've had to handle a lot of calls from upset parents."

"I'm sure you have!" I said as earnestly as I could. "That is precisely one of the things I hoped to cover in my interview with the chief."

"No."

I gave her my best performance, telling her how terrifying the experience had been, then fabricating a tale about the kindness and bravery of the Nickel Park policemen. I finally took a long shot that she'd been a student here herself a few years back. "Mr. Wheatley especially wanted me to bring back a story for the school newspaper."

Sighing, the woman pushed a button and spoke into her headset. "Roy, up front, please." She glanced at me, smiled, and added, "I have a surprise for you."

A minute later the words "What is it now?" preceded the cop who walked into the room. He was short, stocky, and obviously much too young to be a police chief.

The woman introduced us: "Mary Johnson, Officer Roy Rivers."

"Officer?" I said. "I asked to talk to the chief."

"Maybe some day when you're a real reporter, honey. But since you're a junior reporter, you'll have to settle for a junior officer."

From the sour expression on Roy Rivers's face, he obviously did not like being a junior anything. His hair was blond, his eyes watered-down blue, and his mustache thin and almost colorless, like a smear of chalk on his upper lip. He looked at me as if I was the cause of his every problem in life.

"What's this all about?"

"I'd like to interview you for the school paper, Officer Rivers. About the fire drill gone bad."

"This is a joke, right? Marge, tell me this is a joke," he said to the dispatcher. "I'm doing kiddy interviews now?"

"Roy, the young lady asked for an interview, and I'm only trying to cooperate. We wouldn't want to be accused of trying to hide something from the press, now would we?" The two officers working at the desk laughed.

"Guys, I've been here six months," Officer Rivers said, exasperated. "When does the initiation end?"

"Excuse me," I said, insulted. "I am not part of an initiation. This is important, and I'd rather be talking to the police chief."

Half a curse escaped his mouth before he could muffle it.

Officer Rivers led me down the hall into an empty room. It held two card tables pushed together, three chairs, a row of file cabinets, and a bookshelf. Its walls were bare, its gray linoleum scuffed nearly white. Piles of papers were spread over both tables.

"Mary Johnson, huh?" Roy Rivers asked. I nodded. He sat down, pulling the buttons tight over his stomach. "I can give you five minutes, Mary Johnson. As you can see, I am very busy alphabetizing." He gestured grandly at the piles of paper.

I took out my notebook, paged my way to a clean sheet, searched my backpack for a pen, then fiddled with it for a minute. I glanced at the cabinets. The middle drawer of the second file was labeled Mi through Or.

"So, today's fire drill," I began. I stopped to cough, setting up my request to ask for water. "Can you give me any information on it?"

"No comment."

"You mean, it wasn't a routine fire drill to begin with?"

"I said no comment. That means no comment either way."

"Can you tell me what happened after someone yelled 'fire'?" I asked, coughing again.

"No comment."

"Do you have a suspect?"

"No comment."

"Gee, I bet I'm going to win the Pulitzer with this piece."

"Yeah, about as soon as I win a medal for bravery. This is a waste of time. You should go."

"Just a few *(cough, cough)* more *(cough, cough)* questions." I gave it all I had and launched into a full-fledged fit. "I'm sorry," I gasped. "Could I have some water, please?"

As soon as he walked out, I jumped up and pulled open the middle drawer. My fingers flew, searching for Muller. *Mistler... Munson...Ortega.* My hands shook. It wasn't there! I yanked out a handful of folders, hoping Jimmy's was stuck in between.

"What the hell are you doing?"

I spun round, scattering pages everywhere. Officer Rivers stood holding a paper cone of water. Scowling, he slammed the door shut and stood in front of it.

"I was just, I mean...I'm sorry," I said. "Let me clean this up." I gathered the papers, scanning them as I did, still hoping to see Jimmy's name. Rivers leaned over and grabbed the files from my hand.

"I had you pegged as a phony from the start," he said.

"What?" That was almost as upsetting as getting caught. "How?

"Maybe my baby sister is editor-in-chief of the paper and talks about her staff all the time," he said. "Or maybe you're just a lousy liar, *Mary Johnson*." He shook his head.

"You got me, I admit it, I'm not on the paper," I said, hoping I looked sheepish. "I'm a freshman. I thought a scoop on what happened today would get me on. You know what it's like. Everyone wants to be a reporter."

"Cut the bull before I start thinking *you* yelled 'fire' to get a story. I asked what you were looking for."

I stood up straight.

"Jimmy Muller's folder."

Whatever Officer Rivers was expecting as my answer, that wasn't it. He seemed shocked, then his expression softened.

"Jimmy Muller...that kid who drowned, huh? Well, you won't find him here. These are personnel files. What do you want to know?"

"It wasn't an accident. Jimmy Muller was murdered."

"Murdered?"

Officer Rivers handed me the paper cone then dropped into a chair. I gulped the water. My mouth had gone dry.

"What makes you think it's murder?" he asked, his brow furrowed, his eyes fixed on the edge of the table in front of him.

I crumpled the paper cone and planted my feet. "Let me see the file, then I'll tell you."

"You watch too much TV," he said, looking up. "Tell *me* what you know and maybe, *maybe,* I won't tell your parents you were here."

Parents with an *s.* Now who'd been watching too much TV?

I sat opposite him, which only made him get back up. He didn't want me there long enough to get comfortable.

"Jimmy Muller hated the water," I told him.

"You a good friend of his?"

"The best. And Jimmy never went swimming."

"Then that's why he had the accident," said Rivers, "because he wasn't used to it."

"No, you don't understand. Jimmy really hated the water. Hated it so much he was terrified of it." *And he* was *afraid, wasn't he,* I thought. *He must have been.* "He would never go to the lake. Never. And certainly never alone."

"Look, I'm sorry about your friend," he said gently. "Sorrier than you know. See, he was my first stiff on the job, I mean, my first death. The call came in on my shift. Some woman all excited about a body. Ninety-nine times out of a hundred it's an old tire, which is the only reason why I got the call in the first place." He shook his head in disgust. "If the others had thought for one second it'd been real, they never would have let me go. But they didn't, and I went, and I found a kid instead."

"And?"

His face hardened, and he waved toward the door.

"It's time for you to go. I've got work to do."

"I'm telling you about a murder and you're brushing me off!" My voice was louder than I intended. "Now you know why I was sneaking around. I knew you wouldn't believe me. I mean, why should you? I was only Jimmy's best friend."

"And he hated the water," the officer repeated.

"Plus it was raining that day," I added. "You can check back weather reports. Why go swimming at all?"

"Okay, so why didn't you report this when it happened?"

"No one asked. But Mr. Muller knew. Why didn't he say anything?"

"He's a grieving parent. He has bigger things on his mind."

"And murder isn't big?" I settled back in my chair.

"It wasn't murder. The autopsy found nothing to suggest it. No bumps, no bruises, nothing—just water in the lungs. The coroner figured the kid swam out too far, got a cramp, then couldn't make it back in."

"Don't you see?" I asked. "It was made to *look* like an accident."

"But why? Murder means motive. Who'd want to kill your

friend?" Officer Rivers opened the door for me to leave. "The case is closed." I could see his patience slipping. "Fred Muller has been through enough."

"You know Mr. Muller?" I asked.

"Sure, I bought my car from him. He doesn't need to hear talk that his son was murdered, especially coming from some smart-ass kid. Now please go."

"But what if it's true? You can't dismiss it because you think Mr. Muller has had enough," I said. "Somebody ought to go out there and interrogate him right away. He could be holding all sorts of clues and not know it!"

The officer's thick finger shot out and pointed at me. "Don't try any more phony interviews. I don't want to hear that you were bothering him."

I returned to the best argument I had: "But Jimmy hated the water!"

"All right, all right," Roy Rivers said, exasperated. "I'll ask about it, okay? And when it leads nowhere, I'll drop it."

"And if it leads somewhere?"

"Then I'll follow up. But I'm not expecting anything. And neither should you."

"What about the file? Do I get to look at it now?"

He laughed. "No. Go home. Do some homework. Go to cheerleading practice." He picked up my notebook, opened it, and read my name from the inside. "Leave this to me, Allie Canarsie. I don't want to hear *from* you or *about* you again."

Chapter Eight

The next day I cut gym again. There was no sense letting the gym teacher become familiar with my face. It would just give her false hope, because I intended to make like David Copperfield and pull a vanishing act for the year. It was hard enough to believe it was only Thursday of my first full week of school. With everything that had happened, I felt I'd lived ages the past few days. Making me drag through gym would be a violation of my civil rights, somewhere under the category of cruel and unusual punishment. I figured that by cutting class I was actually saving Nickel Park a messy lawsuit.

The first day of school, during the first gym class I cut, I'd discovered the basement storeroom. The school basement was really just its ground floor. The gym itself was down there, as well as the swimming pool, locker rooms, and showers. At the far end of the basement were a few small offices, a records room, some utility and equipment closets, and a big storeroom. The storeroom was a great place to hide. It was filled with beat-up desks and office furniture, old gym equipment, textbooks that predated the printing press—obviously leftovers from the old school that some bureaucratic penny-pincher couldn't bear to throw out.

After hiding there a couple of times, I found another prime spot. The art department had a darkroom at the end of a quiet hall. Luckily for me, photography wasn't being taught till the third quarter, and the school newspaper looked as if it only came out for emergency editions, like when cows stampeded the football field or something. The developing equipment and chemicals were still locked up somewhere, so for the moment, the darkroom was mine.

But I still needed a few more hiding places, so that day I headed up to the third floor to scout out possibilities. Several empty classrooms were up there, waiting, I supposed, for Nickel Park's continued growth spurt. The labs were up there too—bio, chemistry, and physics. Earth science didn't have a lab, of course, though maybe later in the year Mr. Penn would take us outside to make mud puddles. The band had practice rooms on one end, soundproofed, which was a good thing because the clarinets yowled like cats in heat. The rest of the third floor was quiet. The halls still had that freshly waxed smell and none of the lockers showed dents of frustration.

I decided on the girls' room, conveniently located next to a stairwell for quick comings and goings. First I taped an Out Of Order sign on the outside of a stall door. Then I locked myself in the stall and sat with my feet curled up Indian style on the toilet seat so no one checking underneath would see me. The position wasn't too bad. Before my circulation was cut off at the ankles, I finished my algebra homework for tomorrow, plus the extra credit problems Miss Barbosa had already assigned for the weekend.

Of course, as the school year dragged on, I'd need to find a few more havens of peace and quiet, free from stupidity. But these three were a start.

I was in a good mood by the time I went down to lunch. Even the open-mouthed gobbling of the other kids didn't annoy me.

I sat across from Dennis at the same corner table. Though he had heard my story about the police station yesterday, he wanted to run through it again now. He didn't seem to notice how many more details there were this time around. It felt so good to have someone listen to me.

"So the cop grabbed you by the arm and shook you hard?" Dennis asked.

"I was trying to run out of his office with Jimmy's file. I was fast, but he was faster."

"You didn't mention me, did you?" Dennis asked for the twentieth time.

"Nope, I gave no real names except for Jimmy." I skipped the part about Officer Rivers reading my name out of my notebook. Dennis was only interested in keeping himself out of it anyway. "I was Mary Johnson from the school paper."

Dennis shook his head. "What nerve. I can't decide if you're gutsy or plain nuts."

His admiration was begrudging, but I didn't care. It was there, if deep, deep down.

I shrugged as if I invaded police stations every day and began to unwrap my sandwich. Baloney and cheese, with lettuce even. Mom had made me lunch for the fifth straight day now. By that alone, I knew how much she wanted things to work out here.

Nickel Park was growing on me, too, like a fungus. I hadn't counted on staying, though. I'd already cut gym every day, plus ditched a couple of other classes as well. I'd made the acquaintance of the local police and had had a hand in creating a fire alarm stampede. All I had to balance that was doing a little homework and eating lunch in the cafeteria two weeks in a row. If we stayed, my future here was not going to be easy.

Dennis broke into my speculations. "I still can't believe you did it," he said. "You lied to the police and almost snatched Jimmy's file."

"Yeah. It's a shame I didn't get the chance to actually read it. But I did get some useful info—like not to hold my breath waiting for the cops to do anything. Can you imagine? I'm saying there's a murder and the cops are saying, 'Don't bother Mr. Muller.'" I pulled the soggy lettuce off my sandwich and tossed it back into the bag. "Like Jimmy's own father wouldn't want to know."

"Maybe he wouldn't. I mean, he's upset about Jimmy and all, but he's also the kind of guy who's hung up on what other people think. An accident is bad, but...you know." Dennis had yet to say the word *murder.* "That would attract the wrong kind of attention. Maybe he'd think it would reflect on the cars he sells, or even on him. During the summer I heard my mother say he's running for council. I guess now he'll get the sympathy vote."

"Well, he's got the police vote, that's for sure. And that doesn't leave us much to work with." I wondered what to do next. "Uh oh," I said, catching sight of a broad back in white leather. "Red alert! Jerk at three o'clock."

Without turning, Dennis knew who I was talking about.

"Why did you have to make him look so bad in math today?" he whispered, as if Cretin could hear him over the cafeteria's roar. "If he doesn't know the answer, don't you be the one to give it. Where Creighton is concerned, it's better just to *keep quiet!*"

"It's not my fault that he's stupid as well as obnoxious."

"Don't rub his nose in it. That would at least make *my* life easier."

Creighton walked away without ever turning toward us.

"Alert over," I said. "Pyramid leather in retreat."

Dennis rolled his eyes. "I don't understand why that brand is so cool. Sure, you can't find Pyramid clothes in Nickel Park. But even in the city people get into screaming matches over it. Jimmy's cap—the one he got for his birthday—Mrs. Hidalgo told me she took three buses into the city and waited in line an hour for it as a new shipment was delivered. Jimmy was so thrilled he never took it off. He probably slept with it on."

"I didn't think Jimmy was the fad type," I said, frowning. I certainly wasn't, which meant that Jimmy shouldn't have been either.

Dennis shrugged. "I think it was because it was a birthday present from Mr. Muller. Jimmy idolized him, in between hating his guts. All he ever wanted was for his dad to notice him. I bet Mr. Muller didn't even know he'd given Jimmy the hat for his birthday."

And now it's too late for either of the Mullers to pay attention to their kid. My mood began to sour.

Later, in English, I was relieved to see that Mr. Wheatley was still as animated as he'd been in homeroom, meaning he was fully recovered from yesterday's fire alarm. I didn't have to worry about him anymore. I couldn't, even if I'd wanted to. My baloney sandwich was an undigested lump making me bloated and sleepy. Wheatley was jabbering on about weird, unrelated stuff, like stone cutting and family relationships. I couldn't follow his words, so I propped my head on my hand and settled in for a nap.

Closing my eyes was like bringing the curtain down on everything around me. Maybe the next act would have a new scriptwriter, maybe new actors. I had to admit there were days I got sick and tired of everyone in the cast, including myself.

Suddenly I pitched forward.

"What?" I cried out. I grabbed the edges of the desk to keep from falling. The class was laughing. Wheatley stood in front of me, his hand on my elbow. I hadn't heard him come down the aisle.

"I was conducting a little experiment, Miss Canarsie, to see whether your head would remain upright without the assistance of your hand. Apparently not." He let go of my elbow. "If you'd remove your dark glasses, then I could see when you're asleep and would know better than to disturb you. And besides," he said, looking oh-so-smug, "sunglasses are like training wheels. They're not worthy of *your* talents. A competitive napper like you must rise to greater challenges."

"I was not napping. I don't feel well. Maybe I should see the nurse," I said, getting halfway out of my chair.

"The nurse isn't here. She ate in the cafeteria and went home sick. You'll have to tough it out. Now, since you *weren't* asleep," he tapped me on the shoulder to sit back down, "perhaps you could offer us your reaction to my opening lecture on *Jude the Obscure.*"

Who? That sounded like the patron saint of grammar teachers or something. *Obscure* was certainly the right word, as I had no idea what Wheatley was talking about.

"My reaction?" I said. "I'm going to hate it."

"I disagree with you. I think you'll actually like *Jude the Obscure,* because *it* hates everything. It's antireligion, antimarriage, antiestablishment—just your kind of novel, Allie. If Hardy were writing today, perhaps it would be anti–English teacher as well. In fact, that sounds like an assignment if I ever heard one."

The class groaned. Tossing the chalk up and down as he walked, Wheatley strolled up to the blackboard, then began to write.

> **What would Thomas Hardy protest against if he were writing today? Would the issues remain the same or would he have new institutions to shoot down?**

Wheatley turned to us. "Give me a three-hundred word essay by tomorrow. I am negligently overdue getting a sample of everyone's writing anyway."

"Thanks a lot, big mouth," someone said.

"Check his lesson plan," I snapped back. "He's probably given that assignment every year for the past hundred years."

"Only the past three," Wheatley smiled. "I had to fight hard to give *Jude the Obscure* to freshmen. I figured, why waste all that freshman hatred on something like *Animal Farm?* Instead, give 'em something that hates back. What do you think, Miss Canarsie?"

I scowled at him. Freshman hatred. Yeah, right. He was so pleased with himself. Well, he was wrong about me. This wasn't just a phase I was going through. This was me, this was my life! And teachers who thought they were so cool and so smart and so understanding knew nothing about me.

Refusing to answer, I slumped a little lower in my seat.

"Okay," Wheatley said to my silence. "I'll wait and get your considered opinion in writing."

I was still angry when I got to the trailer. To make it worse, Aunt Darleen, who had a spare key, was standing in our tiny kitchen with shopping bags all around her. What was it with her? We'd just gone shopping a week and a half ago on Labor Day!

Aunt Darleen wore black leggings and a pink stretch-lace sweater that barely skimmed her belly button. The price tag hung from the neckline. I must have caught her trying things on, as if the fifty times she'd tried them on in the store hadn't been enough.

"So what do you think?" she asked.

She swiveled her shoulders to show off the pink top. Her stomach was flat, but if I looked closely enough I'd probably see that her belly button had wrinkles. I'd come to think of my aunt as one of those magazine "Fashion Don'ts," clueless women whose faces are blocked out to save them further embarrassment.

"Nope, doesn't work."

"Oh."

Her disappointment poked at my conscience. She'd already bought the sweater. Would it have been so bad to tell her she looked good?

"How was school?" she asked.

I slammed my books down on the counter. "School sucked."

"I see you're your usual cheerful self. Maybe this will help. I spent my lunch hour shopping because, as we all know, after the holiday sale comes the clearance sale." She pulled a black blazer from the nearest bag and held it out to me. "Here. A belated birthday present."

A black blazer—exactly what I wanted. How had she known?

Three weeks ago, for my birthday, she'd offered to take me to the mall for a makeover, free with any purchase. I could get "beautified," she'd joked, while she and Mom could "watch and learn," and it would be great fun for the three of us. I told her that she had an active fantasy life. I guess she'd been disappointed enough to ask Mom what I really wanted.

But a *blazer!* All I could say was "Wow!"

I grabbed it and tried it on. It fit perfectly.

"Your mom told me you'd been hunting one down in garage sales."

"Yeah, black velvet, but this is really nice, too. Thanks, Aunt Darleen. Thanks an awful lot."

She looked at me with a puzzled expression, probably surprised by my politeness. Then she shrugged and gave me a quick hug. When she tried to pull away, I impulsively held on tight. I didn't want to fight with her all the time, I really didn't. She was my mother's sister and, despite her many flaws, the only really good person in Mom's life right now.

"Aunt Darleen, why do you—" The words "dress like trailer trash" almost popped out. "I mean, why don't you dress more like Mom?"

She laughed. "You mean, white on white, tan on tan? No thanks. When I'm an old lady in a nursing home, they better have sequined johnny coats. Life needs more color in it, not less. And you understand exactly what I'm talking about, don't you?" she asked, winking.

In a horrible way, I did.

"This, now." She held me away by the shoulders and looked me up and down. "Black or not, this definitely looks great. Are black blazers the hot new thing this fall?"

I looked at her blankly before I understood what she meant.

"Oh, no, it's not that," I said, stuffing my hands into the pockets. "I'll wear it to school, too. But the weather's going to turn cool soon. I need something that'll keep me warm and still look good at a funeral."

Her mouth fell open.

"I should have known! Honestly, Allie, you've been going to the cemetery all summer. Isn't it time to give that up? Give your poor mother a break. Try out for cheerleader, for heaven's sake."

It was the second time in two days someone had mentioned cheerleading. My image must be slipping.

"It's okay with Mom," I said defensively. "She doesn't give me much grief over it."

"If you were my daughter..." Glaring, Aunt Darleen left the threat unfinished.

"If I were your daughter, we'd end up killing each other."

"At least we'd both die happy," she cracked.

"Hey, that was pretty good," I said. "You're pretty funny for an old lady."

"Yeah, I'm a regular comedian." She sat at the table. From the change in her expression, I knew she was about to get serious. I tried to back away but she grabbed my hand. "As long as we've brought up the subject," she said, "why do you keep going to funerals? Your mother has *her* theories, but I'm asking you—why?"

"It's something to do."

She shook her head. "Knitting is something to do. Is it because of your father? Though she'd never tell you, that's what Winnie thinks."

It should have made me feel grown up to hear my mother referred to by name instead of "Mom," but it didn't.

"I know what she thinks," I said. "I heard the two of you talking that first day. You wanted me to use a dart gun on Dad's picture."

"I didn't know you were listening."

"But it's what you think," I said. "You never liked my father."

"No, I didn't, but I never disliked him either, at least not until the end. Joe was just…Joe." When her hands searched the air for the right words, it was as if the smiley faces on her nails were laughing at me. "He was a real charmer, sure, but he was all talk and not much else. Not a bad guy. Just not good enough for my sister—or for you."

"No! That's not what he was like!" Someone was finally talking about my father, and all I got was lies. "My father was wonderful and smart and funny," I said, "and he…he could do anything he wanted to do or be anyone he wanted to be!"

"Allie, I know you still love him and miss him, but he wasn't like that. He was a computer programmer, that's all. The one good thing was that he made enough money so that Winnie could stay home with you, but even that backfired because she never got an ounce of work experience in her life. She was the first of us to get to college, then she met him and blew her big chance. And I'm afraid she's gonna blow it again. She's got a job sitting down now at a desk instead of waitressing. And instead of sleazy strangers hitting on her at three in the morning, maybe she'll actually meet someone decent."

"Yeah, meet who? The Pillsbury Dough Boy?" I sniped.

"But is she happy?" Aunt Darleen said, ignoring me. "No. She was ready to turn tail and run last week. Maybe this week too, even after getting promoted. She just doesn't know how to handle good news. I think deep down she's waiting for an excuse, any excuse, to leave. So don't *you* give her one!" my aunt warned me, shaking her smiley-face finger. "She ruined her life over your father. And for what? He was nobody special."

"Nobody special?" I yelled. "Nobody *special?* Look who's talking—Little Miss Tastee Treet, the pride of Nickel Park." I tore the blazer off, threw it at her, and ran into my room.

Aunt Darleen followed but didn't come in.

"I'm sorry. That was a stupid thing for me to say. He was special, Allie, if for no other reason than that he had you."

A few minutes later I heard the trailer door close behind her.

Angrily I paced in my room, which meant one step forward, turn, one step back. Back and forth, back and forth, till I was dizzy from pivoting.

I grabbed my knapsack and pulled out paper and pen.

> Dear Diary,
>
> Everyone lies to me! Is it possible to hear lies so many times they become the truth? If I lose the memory of my father, all I'll have left will be what other people tell me—lies, lies, and more lies. Is there an adult anywhere who tells the truth? I hate living like this, not knowing what's real and what isn't. I just hate it!

I ripped the paper to confetti.

I pulled out another blank sheet and started over. What would Thomas Hardy hate today? Who cared! I only knew what I hated. Three-hundred words? Ha—I'd need a book to tell it all.

Ten scrawled pages later, I threw down my pen. *Let old Wheatley look at this. See if he still thinks he has me figured out.*

Drained, I wandered out to the kitchen. It was past time to start dinner. Mom would be here soon and I'd made myself that promise to cook. But I didn't open the refrigerator.

I found the phone directory, looked up the number of the Nickel Park police department, and dialed it.

"Is Officer Rivers in?" I asked.

"He's busy right now. Can I take a message?"

"No, I…he was going to find out something for me. I—look, tell him Allie Canarsie is on the line."

"I told you he's—"

"Could you please give him the message right now? Allie Canarsie. I was there yesterday. Ask him if he has anything for me."

A minute later I came off hold with a pop as if Officer Rivers had grabbed the phone from the receiver.

"Yeah, I got something for you. A message from Fred Muller."

"You spoke to Mr. Muller?" I said hopefully.

"You bet I did. I stopped over at his house last night. I was as subtle as possible, but it was still hell for him. And you know what he said? Do you know what Fred Muller said, Miss Junior Detective? He said his son never had any girls for friends. Not a single one. Certainly not one named Allie Canarsie. So who are you?"

"I was Jimmy's friend," I insisted. "I was."

"You couldn't have been. You don't know a thing about that kid. You want to know what else Muller said? He said his son *loved* to swim. Couldn't keep him out of the water. He said Jimmy was a champion swimmer."

"Champion swimmer?" I repeated slowly.

"Yeah. And Fred Muller said he has the medals to prove it."

Chapter Nine

All next day, "champion swimmer" echoed in my ears. I'd been so stunned to hear those words yesterday, I hadn't asked Officer Rivers the next logical question: how does a champion swimmer drown? Wasn't that even more proof that something was wrong?

Worse was knowing that Dennis Monaghan had lied to me. I kept sneaking looks at him during math, trying to puzzle out why he had lied and whether he'd lied about anything else. Most of what I knew about Jimmy, what I *thought* I knew, had come from Dennis. I had learned not to trust what adults said. Now I was discovering that maybe I couldn't trust anyone to tell me the truth. I would have to find it on my own.

"Allie!" Miss Barbosa's tone said she'd already spoken to me. She tapped her pointer sharply against the blackboard.

The seat of my chair was thumped sharply and I heard a snicker.

"I'm sorry. Could you repeat that?" I asked. With a sigh, Miss Barbosa asked me to solve the inequality she'd put on the board then turned to read off what she'd written. *Thump...thump...THUMP!* The last blow bumped me up into the air a few inches. I gritted my teeth and held onto the sides of my desk as I listened.

"I said, solve the inequality of $4 \leq -3x - 1 \leq 9$. C'mon," Miss Barbosa said impatiently. "This is supposed to be a quick review of algebra I before we get to this year's real work."

"Umm…" I squeezed my eyes shut to think. "-10/3 ≤ x ≤ -5/3."

"At *last!* Thank you. Please pay attention from now on. And stop wiggling around." She went onto the next problem.

"What's the matter?" Creighton whispered. "No snappy comeback?"

"I wouldn't waste my breath."

"Oh, I'm devastated!"

"Gee, a four-syllable word."

"Allie!"

"I'm sorry, Miss Barbosa. Tom wanted to know the difference between addition and subtraction. It's a little deep for him, I'm afraid."

"One more time and you'll be explaining it to him in detention."

A final *thump,* then I heard, "Catch you later, freshman."

"Why do you do that?" Dennis asked. Math was over and we were rushing down the hall; I was on my way to Spanish, while Dennis revealed his much higher academic ambitions by heading off to Latin, which he took in addition to French.

"Why?" I repeated. I wanted to ask *him* why, why he'd lied. But if he had been lying about Jimmy, he'd lie again now. It was better not to let him know what Officer Rivers had told me yesterday. I shook my head. "Why do we do anything, huh? Because it's there, Dennis. You know—like Mount Everest." I clapped my hand over my heart. "Tom Creighton is my Everest," I said dramatically. "I will not rest till I have climbed his north side and planted a flag on top of his pointy little head."

For the first time since we'd met, Dennis laughed out loud, a big open-mouthed laugh that let me see he had a back filling. For some reason, simply the sound of it was a relief.

After last period, Dennis stopped me in the hall. He asked if I wanted to walk with him over to Jimmy's house.

"A lot of my stuff is there," he explained as we left the school. "If I wait till tomorrow, Mr. Muller might be home. He works most Saturdays, but I don't want to take the chance and run into him."

"Why not?"

"He doesn't like me much. I was a bad influence."

"You, a bad influence?" Next to me, Dennis was a poster boy for charm school. "But you were Jimmy's best friend."

Dennis shrugged.

"I figured you guys did everything together. Classes, the math club. Did you volunteer with him at the food pantry or hospital?"

"Nah, he did all that because it looked good on his record. I think his father was prepping him for college from about age three. He hit the roof whenever Jimmy let his grades slip in his other subjects. All Jimmy really cared about was math. I think he was happiest when people called him a math genius."

"How about you?" I asked. "I'm so endearing, people are likely to strangle me before they find out I can count. But I bet people fuss over you, too."

Dennis' cheeks darkened. "This way." He pointed toward a side street.

As we walked, the houses became much larger and much older— the fancy kind of older that spelled haunted house if it wasn't kept up and big money if it was. Wide green lawns and towering shade trees surrounded each house. It was hard to believe we were in the same town where Mom and I lived in a trailer park.

Dennis stopped in front of an enormous two-storied white clap-board house. It had a wraparound porch with all sorts of fancy curlicue woodwork, three chimneys on top of its steeply slanted roof, and an old stone well out front. Neat flower beds and evenly trimmed bushes completed the scene. All it lacked was actors, a few movie cameras, and a musical score in the background.

"This is it."

"Wow! It's practically a mansion," I said.

"Come round back. Jimmy made me a copy of his house key, but Mrs. Hidalgo should be in now. She's usually in the kitchen."

"Mrs. Hidalgo?"

"The housekeeper. Don't you remember?"

Oh yeah. The housekeeper Dennis was surprised I had never met before.

At the rear of the house, he stepped up onto the porch and rang the bell. Then he turned away, mouth pulled so tightly it trembled.

A short moon-faced woman in a white uniform answered. Thick hair sat coiled on top of her head. It was hard to tell her age. The coil of hair was streaked with gray but her face was baby smooth and she was hefty enough to have entered a WWF cage match and won. I tried to remember her from the funeral but couldn't. I hadn't known at the time it might be important.

"*Sí?*" Her dark eyes glared from behind squarish silver eyeglasses. Her thin lips pulled down at the edges. "What do you want?" she asked in a Spanish accent.

Then Dennis turned around.

"Oh, it is you," she said softly.

She and Dennis stared at each other through the screen for a moment. She unlocked the door and stepped away from it, so that we entered on our own.

While the outside of the house looked old, the gleaming kitchen was completely modern. It seemed big enough to hold our entire trailer, but cold, like a picture from a catalog where no one really lived. No mess, no knickknacks, no dumb little kitcheny things people collect.

"This is Allie Canarsie," Dennis said. Would the housekeeper, like Fred Muller, declare that Jimmy never knew me? I held my breath as Dennis continued. "Allie knew Jimmy from St. Paul's."

"Jimmy..." The word escaped Mrs. Hidalgo's lips like a sigh. She turned her broad back to us, pulled out a handkerchief, and dabbed at her eyes. "I never expected to see you again, Dennis," she said. Her voice, choked at first, became steadier. "Maybe I never *wanted* to see you again." She stuffed the handkerchief back in her pocket and turned on him. "Why are you here now?"

"To get some of my things back. You know—video games and

tapes." He stared at the floor and shrugged. "Can I go up and get them?"

"Señor Muller would not be pleased to know you were here," she said. "He would not be pleased to know I let you upstairs in Jimmy's room now that Jimmy is…"

She bit her lower lip to keep it from trembling.

"But I've got to get my stuff," Dennis said. "Mr. Muller won't know unless you tell him."

She glanced at the wall clock.

"Please? There's…there's a library book up there, too," Dennis added. "I've got to get that at least. I'll be really fast."

"Go then. *Pronto!*"

Dennis slipped out of the room, looking relieved to get away. I wished I'd been able to go with him. It was awkward staying down here with Mrs. Hidalgo. Why had she said she never wanted to see Dennis again? And why hadn't Dennis seemed surprised by her words?

Lips quivering, back straight, Mrs. Hidalgo began to stride about the kitchen. She took out just one glass, poured milk into a tall pitcher, and placed an assortment of cookies on a fancy silver tray. She put everything on the table, then stepped back. "Please, have some," she said. "You are here, you should eat." She waited until I sat down. "You knew Jimmy from St. Paul's?" she asked.

"Yes, oh, mmmm, this is delicious." I said it quickly as a distraction, but it was the truth. The cookies were not just homemade, but knockout gourmet, which gave me an idea. "You know, Jimmy really liked your cooking," I said. "I can see why."

The tears filled her eyes again. "He said that to you?"

"Yes, often." How much should I tell her? Dennis had said—if I could believe him—that Mrs. Hidalgo would do anything for Jimmy. Even help find his murderer?

"It was a terrible accident, wasn't it?" I finally said. "I mean, I was just getting to know Jimmy. I'm new in town."

"He was a good boy," she said, nodding. "Not an angel. But in the end, good."

Not an angel? Jimmy had seemed almost too good to be real.

"He always seemed like an angel to me. But then," I said, checking first to make sure Dennis wasn't coming through the door, "I hardly knew him. What was Jimmy really like? Why do you say he wasn't an angel? Did he sometimes do bad things? Did he ever make people mad at him?"

Mrs. Hidalgo shook her head. "I do not like these questions." She turned for the pitcher and said, "You need more milk," though my glass was still half full.

I kept on talking. I was so nervous I must have sounded suspicious. There had to be a more subtle way to ask if Jimmy had any enemies.

"I guess Dennis would know better about those things," I said, wondering what was taking him so long. "They were best friends, after all. They hung out together every day, didn't they?"

"Hung out." Mrs. Hidalgo repeated the words awkwardly but nodded. "*Sí*, every day."

"Too bad they didn't hang out together that last day, right?" Reaching for another cookie, I sneaked a look at her. "I mean, if only Dennis had gone to the lake too, maybe Jimmy would be alive."

"If Dennis had gone to the lake..." Mrs. Hidalgo pulled the handkerchief out again, shoulders heaving. I squirmed in my chair. I hated to cry in public and wasn't thrilled when someone else did it. There was a place for stuff like that; it was called the bathroom.

I suddenly realized that Mrs. Hidalgo had stopped crying and instead was looking up at the ceiling. "If Dennis had gone to the lake..." she repeated softly. Her dry-eyed gaze stayed upwards for some time. "He should come down now," she said. "It's getting late."

"Can I go up and get him?" I asked impulsively. "I'd like to see Jimmy's room, if it's okay with you." I really did want to see his bedroom. Plus, I had to get out of there.

She hesitated, then gestured toward the door.

"Through there. Turn right at the top of the stairs."

I raced out before she could change her mind. I had a quick impression of the other rooms, packed with furniture that didn't fit the old house—oversized oil paintings, massive leather couches, chrome and glass tables—then I found the staircase and hurried up. To the right, one of the doorways spilled light out into the hall. Dennis didn't hear me. He was sitting on the bed, staring at a blank wall like he was auditioning for a zombie movie.

"Couldn't you find anything?" I asked.

"What?" he asked groggily. "No, I...I meant to look, that's what I came up here for, but..."

"But what? What's wrong?"

"I guess it just hit me. This is the last time I'll be here."

"Well, Mrs. Hidalgo wants you to hurry up."

The room was huge. On the right stood a four-poster double bed with a white chenille spread. On the left stood a heavy wooden dresser with a mirror and matching chest of drawers. An open rolltop desk sat opposite the door, next to a window. To the left of the desk was a stand holding a computer and printer. In the far corners of the room on either side were doors, probably to a closet and bathroom.

The bedroom might have belonged to an adult, except for the video game setup attached to the TV.

Dennis began to poke around halfheartedly, shuffling through a stack of books and papers on the desk. I opened a couple of drawers in the chest: underwear in squared-off piles in one, socks balled up by color in the other. I glanced over at the TV. Even the video games were alphabetized.

There was no sense that a teenager had lived here. I was disappointed. I'd hoped to be able to get a better feeling for Jimmy. Instead, it was the room of a stranger.

"I guess Mrs. Hidalgo cleaned the life out of this place after Jimmy died," I said.

"No, it was always like this. He claimed he kept it neat to keep her from messing with his stuff, but he was just as picky about his locker at school. Even so, he didn't like her much. He told me that in his diary he used to call her Señora HiDil— Well, take my word for it, it wasn't nice."

Goosebumps rose on my arms. "Jimmy kept a diary?" I asked. Like I'd always wanted to, had tried to so many times.

"It was a way to get revenge on paper, that's how he described it."

"Revenge for what?"

"I don't know. I never saw the diary myself," Dennis said. "Jimmy only told me the stupid stuff in it, like calling her Mrs. Hydraulic, Mrs. HiDildo." Dennis blushed and opened the door to the right onto a walk-in closet about as big as my bedroom. He stepped inside, looked at the blazers and hanging dress shirts starched and ironed to scissors sharpness, but touched nothing.

Maybe Mrs. Hidalgo had seen Jimmy's diary, I thought.

"What's she like?" I asked. "It's hard to tell right now, she's so weepy."

"She's strict. Mr. Muller told Jimmy that before she came to the U.S., she and her husband used to run a famous restaurant. She's a master chef, and in her kitchen, she was god. All the help was terrified of her. She liked it that way. It made for better service, she told Mr. Muller. What a comedown. Now *she's* the help."

"A master chef?" That explained the cookies. "So what happened to the restaurant?"

"It's complicated. I got it from Jimmy who used to listen in on conversations she'd have with Mr. Muller. Anyway, the Hidalgos became friendly with the wrong people, politically speaking. The government started hassling them, then finally shut the restaurant down. The Hidalgos left the country but Mr. Hidalgo died on the way here."

A heart-stopping story began to unwind itself in my head. "Did they have to sneak out with just the clothes on their back?" I asked Dennis. "Did they have lots of narrow escapes?" I grew more excited. "Was her husband savagely gunned down just as they were about to cross the border?" I saw it plainly: the image of a man caught against a barbed-wire fence, the bloody bullet holes in his body nearly black in the stark glow of a searchlight.

"Hey, why should I know? And what does it matter, anyway?"

"Details, Dennis, details. They're what make life interesting. What country was it?"

"I don't know that either. I asked Jimmy once. He said to pick one, all those South American countries are the same."

Mrs. HiDildo. Not an angel. All those South American countries are the same. There'd been a real love-fest going on here.

Dennis pulled one book off the shelves. I could see the library call number stamped on the spine. "I guess I don't want anything else," he said. "C'mon, let's go."

Back downstairs in the kitchen, Mrs. Hidalgo was waiting for us holding a clear plastic bag stuffed with clothes.

"Only that?" she asked, looking at the book in Dennis's hand.

"If it's okay, I'm going to leave the rest," he said. "I only took this because it's a library book."

"Then you do not want your...your..." She shook her head. "Your *camiseta?*"

"What?" Dennis stared hard at the plastic bag she was holding. A sticker on it said "Nickel Park Police Department."

"It must be in here," Mrs. Hidalgo said, gently shaking the contents of the bag onto the kitchen table. "After the police brought this, I never opened it and never showed it to Mr. Muller. Too sad."

Sniffling, she separated the items and laid them out lovingly: red bathing trunks, a pair of blue shorts, a black shirt covered with white math formulas, a towel, a balled-up pair of gray sweat socks, a pair of sneakers, a watch, a key ring, a penknife. Gently she picked up the black shirt.

"*Camiseta.* Undershirt."

"T-shirt," Dennis corrected her. "Jimmy had that T-shirt made for my birthday a few months ago," he explained to me. "A place on Main Street will print whatever you want. He liked the shirt so much he was forever borrowing it."

"And he wore it that last day," I said.

"Take it." Mrs. Hidalgo thrust it at him. "To remember."

Dennis pulled his hands to his side. His eyes were wide and full of pain, his face was chalk white. "No...I..." He saw that both Mrs. Hidalgo and I were staring at him. "Yeah, thanks." With a trembling hand, he reached out and snatched the shirt from her. "I mean, it was a gift from Jimmy and all. I should keep it."

"*Sí, un regalo,*" she murmured. She tucked the keys and penknife into the shorts pocket.

Dennis rushed out without saying good-bye, the shirt in his fist.

I stood there a moment longer.

"Thanks for the milk and cookies." My voice came out a whisper.

Mrs. Hidalgo never looked up from folding and refolding Jimmy's bathing trunks.

I hurried to catch up with Dennis, faster and faster down the path to the sidewalk and back toward the center of town. I didn't ask him why we were running. He didn't say a word until we were almost back at school, where he mumbled a quick good-bye and turned down a side street.

As I walked home, something began to bother me. I hadn't really learned anything new during my visit to the Muller house. Yet at the same time I couldn't help thinking that I'd missed something. I didn't know how or what, but I had missed something. It nagged at me the rest of the afternoon, something I hadn't seen and should have...or something I *had* seen but didn't recognize. It wasn't until late that night, lying in bed, that it hit me. Looking through the shelves, poking through the drawers, I hadn't seen a single swimming trophy or medal in Jimmy's room. Where were all the medals Officer Rivers had talked about? I tried to recall his exact words. Rivers hadn't seen the medals himself—now I remembered—he had only repeated Muller's claim that Jimmy had won them.

I'd blown it. During those few minutes I'd spent alone with Mrs. Hidalgo, while Dennis was upstairs and couldn't hear, I should have asked her if Jimmy was a champion swimmer.

Chapter Ten

Saturday morning was cool and breezy, but sunny as I approached the small group of mourners. A sunny funeral seemed false, like you could pull away the sky as easily as moving as piece of stage scenery and find just gray and black beneath. There was nothing sadder than a rainy funeral, but at least it was honest.

Autumn felt seconds away. Though the trees in the old section of Evergreen were just starting to turn, a few fallen leaves had skittered around in the wind and found their way into the new section. There the plain straight headstones made me think of stripped trees. Skeletal—wasn't that the word used to describe bare branches against the sky? The thin slabs of marble were skeletal in a more real way, hiding what lay beneath.

I was glad to have the black blazer Aunt Darleen had bought, though our argument still depressed me. Why couldn't she have said, "Here's a present, Allie," given me the blazer, and kept her mouth shut? Why bring up my father, tell me he was nobody special? Her words made the gift a lie, like a sunny funeral.

I was nobody special. That's why my father left or at least why he hadn't taken me with him. I wasn't worth taking, I wasn't worth a visit, I wasn't worth a postcard.

"Hey you!"

Startled, I looked up to see an old woman in black. She'd broken away from the group of elderly mourners and was marching toward me. Her eyes were angry. Her lips mumbled words I couldn't hear, then she called out again.

"I mean you, girlie!"

I stood there, not sure what to do. She hurried up to me and grabbed my arm.

"I know who you are," she said loudly. "You're that strange girl who goes to all our funerals. I know all about you."

What did she mean, she knew all about me? I tried to twist away. She was a tiny shriveled thing; I should have been able to break free but couldn't.

"We don't want you here! This is none of your business!"

"I…you don't…"

I couldn't get the words out to defend myself.

"I don't know what you think you're up to but it's no good!" she ranted. "This is an insult! Now go away and leave us alone!"

"Easy, Margaret, easy," said a voice at my ear. "It's okay."

Startled, I turned. A tall thin man in a black suit and black bow tie had come up from the side. It was Mr. Wheatley. I hadn't recognized him at first outside of English class. Without his red bow tie, which he'd replaced with a black one, he looked like a stranger.

"It's not right, John," the old woman protested. "She shouldn't be here."

"I don't think Harold would have minded, would he? 'The more the merrier.' Isn't that what he always used to say?"

Mr. Wheatley unfolded the woman's fingers from my arm. Murmuring to her soothingly, he took her hand and began to walk her back to the crowd.

"But she didn't know him," the woman said. She started to cry.

Mr. Wheatley put his arms around her. Looking at me from over the top of her head, he mouthed the words, "Wait for me." After a pause he added, "Please." Then he escorted the woman back to the gravesite.

I wanted to run away, but everyone's gaze nailed me to the spot. Besides, Wheatley wasn't done with me. I decided to get it over with now instead of waiting till Monday in school.

Once he joined the mourners, Wheatley blended in with the other old men, all dressed alike, black suits, black hats drawn low on their heads. They wore their uniform, as I wore mine.

Finally the minister was ready. He opened his prayer book and the men removed their hats—not one at a time, not in a wave from the front of the crowd to the back, but all at once, like dancers in a chorus line performing a single step, like something in a dream. The prayer book opened and every hat came off in one swoop.

I glanced at the old woman who had yelled at me. None of my business? My going to funerals was none of *her* business. Why should she go after me? I wasn't bothering her. I wasn't bothering anyone. All I ever did was watch.

Horrible. Morbid. Intrusive. Those were the words my mother had used the first day I went to Evergreen. Well, it was horrible and intrusive for some old woman to march up and grab my arm and claim she knew all about me. She knew nothing about me, and neither did Wheatley. Neither did Aunt Darleen, for that matter, and neither did my mother. They never understood me and they never would. I didn't want them to. I couldn't be special, but I could be weird. I wouldn't let them take that away from me.

After the service ended, I paced back and forth between a row of headstones. Wheatley shook a few hands, kissed a few cheeks. Then he put his hat back on and began to walk over. Twenty minutes earlier, after he'd pried the woman loose from me, I wanted to thank him. Now I was ready to strike out.

"So, what do you want?" I snapped.

He looked down at me. He seemed much taller than in class.

"I wanted to apologize," he said at last.

"Because your friend came after me like that?"

"What? Oh, no, for myself. I tried to catch you after homeroom yesterday and again after English, but you slipped out both times. I wanted to apologize for Thursday—when you were sleeping and I knocked your hand out from under your head."

An apology? The breath ran out of my next sentence. I kicked the side of a headstone. "It's your class." I shrugged. "You can do whatever you want."

"No, I can't. None of us can do whatever we want, not always. We have to think of the consequences. We have to think of other people. But I didn't. At the time it seemed like a good joke, but instead I only alarmed and embarrassed you. I'm sorry."

Wheatley was always surprising me. I didn't like it.

He straightened his back and let his gaze sweep over the cemetery. The other mourners had all left. Only the groundskeepers remained.

"I read your paper," he said, not meeting my eyes.

"And? Am I starting the year with an F? I'm used to it."

He smiled. "Well, I didn't notice a single mention of Thomas Hardy. However, I was also looking for a writing sample and you did give me that, many times over. Your writing showed a lot of, uh, energy."

"Gee, what a polite word for hate."

"How much of what you wrote is true?" he asked.

"Every word of it."

"Literally? Figuratively?" When I didn't answer, he asked, "Do you really hate everything and everyone so much?"

"Sure. Why not? Everyone hates me, so I hate them back. It's a natural reaction."

"I don't hate you, Allie." He said it so gently I had to look away.

"It's only September," I said.

"Maybe I'll surprise you."

I turned and started to walk away.

"Do your parents hate you?" he asked quickly.

I didn't answer. I didn't know the answer.

"Does Dennis Monaghan?"

"What about Dennis?" I asked, stopping to look back.

"He's your friend, isn't he? I had cafeteria duty these first two weeks. You ate lunch together almost every day."

Was I that obvious? Dennis was my friend. My only friend.

Not true, I thought. *There's Jimmy...my* best *friend.* It was easier to have him for a friend, despite the problem he had given me to solve with his death. Dennis had lied to me, Dennis had made things up. Dennis had gotten me—*me!*—to believe him.

For the first time I dared to ask myself what else Dennis had done. Thoughts tumbled out as if finally freed from a locked closet. From the beginning Dennis hadn't wanted me to investigate Jimmy's death. He wouldn't talk to me the first week and even afterward fought the word murder, refused to help me with the police, and tried to avoid me. Yet he also lied to me about Jimmy's hating the water, as much as confessed to being jealous of Jimmy, even took me to Jimmy's house where things felt so wrong, all guaranteed to make me more curious.

Curious—or suspicious?

It was as if Dennis desperately wanted me to leave Jimmy's death alone, yet at the same time was compelled to get me involved. Why?

There was really only one answer: because Dennis felt so guilty he wanted, *needed* to be found out. But why would he feel guilty? I couldn't even think the words. I leaned against a tombstone to catch my breath.

"What is it, Allie?"

Had my face gone all strange?

"It's nothing," I said, straightening. "Dennis is okay."

"Good. Talk to him then. Show him your paper. I doubt it's something you'll show your parents."

Parents, parents. Doesn't anyone live in the real world?

"Well, your mother at least," he said, as if I'd corrected him out loud. "Winifred, right? Winnie. I didn't make the connection at first because Canarsie isn't her maiden name."

"You remember my mother?" He had taught her, of course, I knew that. But I'd figured she had faded in time to just one of a crowd of faceless students.

"Of course. I saw her at the Seven Eleven just last week. Darleen, too. I can't decide which one of them you're more like."

"But they're complete opposites!" I protested.

"As I suspect you are."

His warm smile made me furious. I was beginning to understand his plan. I was going to be his pet project, all because he'd taught Mom and Aunt Darleen a million years ago. I bet he'd read my file—that's how he found out who I was—and had decided he was going to rehabilitate me. Well, just let him try. "Can I go now?" I asked impatiently.

"Of course. I'll see you Monday."

Wheatley headed off through the old section, so I went the other way. Before I knew what I was doing, I had walked to Jimmy's grave.

There was a raw look to it, though sod had been laid and a headstone erected since I'd been there for his funeral. The letters in the headstone looked sharp enough to cut my finger if I tried to trace them.

JAMES FREDERICK MULLER

BELOVED SON OF FREDERICK AND BEVERLY

JIMMY

I had lost him. I had lost my one great, my one *true* friend before he could give me anything but sadness.

It wasn't right that he was dead.

None of it was right.

It was up to me to fix it.

But how? And can I do it if Dennis stands between me and the truth?

✳

The next morning I scanned the paper and found the directory for the local churches. St. Paul's Lutheran Church offered Sunday School and coffee hour at ten, services at eleven. Everyone was welcome. I couldn't sneak off there by myself because it was in the next town of Bakersville. I'd need a ride.

"Mom," I said after she'd had her second cup of coffee. "You know how you've been meaning to call St. Paul's?" She had mentioned it maybe three times over the summer but neither of us had taken her words seriously.

"Yeah?" She was already suspicious. Church was not a topic I brought up often.

"I looked up the schedule. We have plenty of time. Might as well start now." I shrugged, trying to look indifferent.

"Why the sudden interest?"

"Well..." I thought fast. "There's this boy..." I gestured vaguely. It was the truth, since I was thinking of Jimmy, but I knew what Mom would assume.

"Oh. A boy."

Though she tried not to show how pleased she was, I could see the thought flashing across her face like a neon sign: *maybe my daughter is normal after all.*

"Oh," she said again, trying to match my indifference. "Who is he?"

"I haven't actually talked to him yet," I said, "but I was hoping at church..."

"Okay. Sure, church. How much time do we have?"

I began to regret opening my big mouth. Was it worse to lie about church than about school? My other lies were something Mom just had to sit back and listen to. This one involved pantyhose.

Church will be good for her, I argued. *She needs to meet people.*

But all along I knew the real reason why I wanted to go to St. Paul's.

We never made the coffee hour and were late for the service, which was usual for us. When you went to church only at Christmas and Easter, and sometimes not even then, it was easy to forget in between how long it actually took to pull yourself together and get there. By the time we arrived at the old stone building and slipped into a back pew, the entrance hymn had already been sung and the opening prayers already prayed.

Everyone around us smiled. There were about a hundred people in all. This would have been a puny handful anywhere else in the world, but here in Bakersville, which was about a fire hydrant bigger than Nickel Park, St. Paul's probably boasted about its thriving parish. I could see at once it was the sort of place where everyone knew your name, knew whether or not you'd come the week before, and if not, knew why.

Though I had an aisle seat, I saw mostly the backs of heads. I was beginning to give up hope when I spotted him up front—Mr. Fred Muller, Jimmy's father. I recognized his profile as he turned to accept the offering plate from the usher and pass it on.

Even without the dark glasses he wore at the funeral, I knew him. He had balding black hair and a big beaky nose like a giant hawk. He still looked like a scarecrow in a good suit. I didn't need Dennis's description of how Mr. Muller had ignored Jimmy except to nag him. It was there on his face. I tried to imagine his campaign poster for councilman, all smiles and cheerful slogans, but couldn't. I couldn't see him as a car salesman either. Mr. Muller looked like he didn't know how to smile. He looked like a sour-faced, tight-lipped miser, like it hurt him to let go of the collection plate.

I scarcely heard a word of the service. As soon as it was over, I dragged Mom out of the pew. The pastor was already at the back of the church. We suffered through handshakes and an invitation to register with the parish. A few old-timers broke in to welcome Mom back and to say how they remembered her from when she was just knee-high to a grasshopper.

Knee-high to a clodhopper is more like it.

Finally we were free. Outside I pulled Mom over and asked if we could wait. I turned back to the people behind us as they spilled down the steps.

"Was he here?" she asked.

"Yeah, he was," I said, searching the faces.

"Good. Point him out if you can do it without being obvious."

Realizing what Mom meant, I looked around, hoping to see a likely looking boy. There was no one the right age.

"Maybe he left by the side," she suggested helpfully.

"Maybe," I said. Then there he was at the big red double doors of the main entrance, talking to the pastor. Their heads were bent together, the pastor had his arm around Mr. Muller's back, and Mr. Muller was nodding. His miserly look had been scrubbed away and replaced by a rough, open expression. He probably didn't want to wear his miser's face in front of the pastor. Maybe he had even dropped some serious dough in the collection plate to impress everyone. After all, he was running for office.

Mr. Muller blinked a few times—it was windy that day—pinched the bridge of his nose, then pulled away from the pastor and walked down the steps to the front gate. Mrs. Hidalgo wasn't with him, although on the sidewalk several parishioners patted his shoulder, gave him a hug. He certainly had the sympathy vote in this crowd.

"I'll be right back," I told Mom and rushed off before she could say anything. I followed Mr. Muller along the sidewalk around the block until we were well away from the other churchgoers.

"Mr. Muller!"

He turned to see who was calling.

I waited till I was a few feet away then said, "Mr. Muller, I want to talk to you about Jimmy."

"Are you the girl Roy Rivers told me about? I told him Jimmy didn't know you, but I've had time to think now and…" His voice grew softer and he shrugged. "How can a parent know everything?" He offered me a very thin hand. "I'm Fred Muller."

I could feel his bones shift beneath my grasp. Two shakes and he should have let go; he didn't.

"Did Jimmy really know you?" he asked, holding on.

"I knew *him*." By this time it was true.

"How?"

"It doesn't matter."

I stopped, pulled away, and took a deep breath. There was no way to prepare Mr. Muller for what I had to say.

It'll probably be best to start slowly, I thought. *Maybe not mention my fears about Dennis yet. At least not until I'm sure.*

At the moment I was certain of only two things: Jimmy would have been my friend, and Jimmy had been murdered.

"I bet I knew Jimmy better than you did," I said. "It's okay. Teenagers are like that with their parents. And what I know is that Jimmy's death wasn't an accident."

An ugly expression worked across Mr. Muller's face. At first he backed away from me, then he stepped forward and grabbed my wrist.

"Who are you?" he demanded.

"Allie? Allie?"

At the sound of my mother's voice, Muller let go.

"Don't you ever talk to me again," he said, his words hoarse. "And don't you ever talk about my son again—to anyone."

Chapter Eleven

hat do you do when your only friend may be psycho? Be very, very nice.

That's how I decided to handle Dennis.

I hadn't slept much Sunday night, wondering about him.

Does Dennis only seem guilty, or is he really guilty? And of what? What has he done? Am I in any danger?

I decided to keep quiet for a while and be nice to him.

Monday morning before the first bell, when Dennis complained about his weekend biology assignment, I offered to do his homework for him. I was getting bored with earth science, I explained; maybe homework from someone else's class would be more interesting. Tuesday, Wednesday, and Thursday, trying to score higher on the niceness meter, I didn't raise my hand at all in math so that Dennis could answer all the hard questions himself. I didn't annoy Creighton either, not even once, because I knew how nervous that made Dennis. And on Friday before we left for the weekend, I insisted that Dennis first follow me downstairs to the basement storeroom.

"What's this?" he asked, peering around at the clutter.

"Where I spend third-period gym," I said. "Cool, huh?"

"You don't have third-period gym," he said. *"I* have third-period gym. You're not in that class."

"That's because I'm usually here. You can come too, if you want."

I'd never shared a hiding spot before. I was giving away a very special gift. "When you want to cut class, come down here."

Dennis looked at me strangely, shook his head, then ran back upstairs. Outside we parted in front of the school.

"Hey," he called. I turned back to face him.

"Yeah?"

"Um..." He looked away. "What are you doing this weekend?"

"I don't know. Stuff. Family stuff," I said quickly, as if someone else, a very nervous someone else, was working my puppet jaw.

"Oh. Well, I'll probably be running Saturday and Sunday," he said. "I mean, if you just want to hang out."

I nodded. It sounded good, but somehow it ended up being a very busy weekend. There was always something to do, from rearranging the furniture in my room, which took about five minutes, to finishing up the last chapter in my library book, which took about ten. *What if Dennis is really psycho?* I argued with myself as I moved Einstein's poster a whole two feet to the left. *Do I really want to hang out with him outside of school? There'll be fewer people around. Wouldn't that be dangerous?*

Monday I recovered some of my bravery and continued with my plans to be nice. First thing that morning, I slipped him the answers to our algebra homework in case he hadn't had a chance to do it. Then at lunch, I paid for his chocolate pudding and milk and, when we sat down, offered him my sandwich as well.

"What *is* it?" he demanded. "This has been going on for a week. You're killing me with kindness."

Killing *him*? It was all to prevent him from killing me. Jimmy used to be his friend, and Jimmy was dead. Now *I* was Dennis's friend. I could envision this whole terrible mess twenty years from now—every one of his best friends dead by mysterious accidents. The police wouldn't have figured it out, though all the while Dennis would be sending them anonymous notes signed "Buddy."

I took back my sandwich and pretended to be offended.

"You're acting weird," Dennis continued. "I mean, weird even for you, Allie. You're acting like some flaky fairy godmother."

I studied his puzzled face. Maybe it was getting carried away to call him psycho and to imagine him on a twenty-year crime spree. I wasn't even sure he'd done anything to Jimmy. If he had, it was probably a one-time thing, one of those crimes of passion you hear about. Maybe he'd been so jealous that one day his mind snapped. I could understand it. Jimmy had a big fancy house with a housekeeper, maybe even gardeners who rode around on those neat lawn mowers, plus he was such a brain that teachers had actually looked forward to having him. It was all so different from anything that *I* knew. Maybe it had pushed Dennis over the edge.

I was safe. I really believed that. But if I could make Dennis's life a little bit easier, maybe *I'd* be a little bit safer. So I was serious about trying to be helpful. Obviously I wasn't doing a very good job.

"You're my friend, Dennis. I'm just trying to do what friends do." I almost bit my tongue at that; what if murder was Dennis's idea of friendship? "I mean, I'm trying to be nice."

"Why?"

As I searched for an answer, I took a big bite of sandwich. Ugh, liverwurst. Mom's good-mother phase was lasting longer than was healthy. It was probably a good thing Dennis hadn't taken my lunch.

"Why are you being nice?" he repeated impatiently. "Tell me, Allie, why are you being so nice?"

"Because I like you, Dennis," I snapped. "That's why."

His face grew so red his freckles disappeared. Then I realized what I'd said, what he thought I'd said, and I suddenly knew that I'd meant it the way he thought I meant it. My own cheeks grew hot. I threw my sandwich down and jumped up.

"Let's not both be jerks about it," I said sarcastically.

I ran up to the third floor girls' room and locked myself into a stall.

I liked Dennis. I hadn't known I liked him till the words popped out. Wheatley had practically said as much on Saturday in the cemetery—

that I liked Dennis—but I hadn't figured it out. It bothered me that Wheatley had me nailed when I didn't understand myself.

I liked Dennis, and that was a big problem. I'd never had a real friend before, much less maybe a boyfriend. I'd always been so busy mouthing off and getting in trouble and making sure everyone hated me. And now when I finally did like someone, he just happened to be my best suspect for murder.

What do I do now?

If Dennis really was the murderer—there, I'd said it—and I ignored the facts, I might be starting my own life of crime. I could see it so plainly: I'd end up as his moll and we'd spend our lives fleeing from place to place as desperately hunted fugitives. I'd have to dye my hair and change my name. He'd have to dye his hair, too, and get an unlicensed doctor to bleach those freckles. It would be an endless series of dirty motel rooms and fast food restaurants. We could trust no one but each other, and some days not even that.

I had to admit, it was appealing.

Maybe that was because deep down I couldn't believe Dennis would hurt anyone, not even in a once-in-a-lifetime crime of passion. When I stood toe-to-toe with Creighton, it made Dennis turn green, and merely talking about an innocent firecracker had really thrown him. Plus, he'd become my friend these past couple of weeks, sorta, or at least he'd allowed me to hang around—this while most people still hadn't said hello. How could he be that sensitive and that cold-blooded at the same time?

Maybe it's easy, and I'm fooling myself.

I wished I could talk to my father. I could ask him how to tell when a boy was lying or telling the truth. My dad could reveal the secret code that guys use against us girls. Then when Dennis looked me in the eye and said, "I'm not the murderer," I'd know whether to believe him or turn him in.

But how could I possibly turn him in, even if I found definite proof? Now that I'd said I liked him, I'd be a traitor if I did.

Do you know how much I like you, Dennis? I could hear myself saying. *So much, I'll wait for you while you're in the slammer.*

But did Dennis like me back?

The rest of lunch period was a nightmare. Curled on the toilet seat, my legs cramped up right away. Then a couple of cheerleaders came into the bathroom. I knew they were cheerleaders from the complexity of their conversation:

"Absolutely not! 'Go, team, go' definitely sounds better than 'Go, go, team.' Plus the accent is way clearer to cue our splits!"

These were the girls who were never alone, never without friends, never not laughing.

Where was a voodoo doll when you needed one?

Just when I thought they were leaving, they began to gossip about the color guard.

"Tracie's always out of step."

"Stacie's so fat all her sequins are gonna pop."

"Casey's so ugly she should march with a bag over her head."

I had two choices: either puke up my liverwurst or go to class. As they gaped, I slammed out of the stall, ripped the Out of Order sign off the door, glared at them, and rolled my eyes. Unfortunately, the full effect was lost behind my dark glasses.

Earth science was miserably boring again, but I was sorry when the bell rang and it was time to face Dennis. Worse, I had to face him in English, and Wheatley knew I liked Dennis. I hung around the hall till the very last second, then rushed into class just as the bell rang to avoid embarrassing non-conversations and non–eye contact.

Wheatley was his usual all-knowing self, which annoyed me no end. He had finally graded the Thomas Hardy papers. After reading a few of them out loud in class, he returned them. He didn't read mine, of course, though he gave it a B+. When I saw the grade, I got really mad. The paper was filled with ranting and had nothing to do with the topic; Wheatley had said so himself. He'd given me a good grade so he could pat himself on the back about how well his pet project was progressing.

Dennis didn't say much at all the whole afternoon. I wasn't sure if he was avoiding me or if I was avoiding him. In the next class, the one time I happened to look at him and he looked back, he blushed that terrible red color again. It was so noticeable the world civ teacher asked if he needed air and opened all the windows wider.

As soon as class ended, Dennis jumped up and ran out. That left only art and study hall for me, while he had journalism and French. I didn't have to worry about seeing him, or not seeing him, I wasn't sure which. He either stayed late after French or left school at the speed of light. In any case, he never showed up at his locker after the final bell.

Why is he so upset? I wondered. *Is it because of what I said at lunch or because I haven't talked to him since then? Does he know that I suspect him a little? Is he afraid I'm too close to the truth? Or is it something else?* My stomach began to hurt. *Maybe the idea of being liked by me is creepy.*

As I walked home, my head pounded. I was so tired and angry and miserable that I didn't have any fear left for the howling German shepherds, strangling themselves on their choke chains to get a piece of me.

When I let myself into the trailer, the place seemed smaller than usual, as if it had been subdivided in my absence and all the furniture squeezed into a smaller fit. I could move from one end to the other by turning my head, it seemed.

I saw how shabby everything was, despite Mom's efforts: the new curtains she'd bought, which I'd deliberately frayed; the wobbly lamp, which she swore was Art Deco but was only a flimsy imitation; the pillows on the couch, which were more to cover stains than to decorate. The whole place was bogus. Cheap and fake. I didn't have a real house, I didn't have a real family, I wasn't even a real person. All my life I'd been pretending to be something I wasn't—human. No wonder Dennis had been weirded out when I told him I liked him. No wonder my father had left.

I slammed around the trailer, knocking my books to the floor, kicking doors shut, punching the pillows on my bed. Nothing made me feel real.

I slumped to the floor and sat there, breathing hard. The phone rang. Startled, I jumped and whacked my head on the doorknob. Near tears, I let the phone ring again and again, then finally got up and went into the kitchen to answer it.

"Hello."

"Allie, is that you? It's Aunt Lolly."

"Oh, hi."

"My goodness, Allie, I just called to say hello, but what's wrong?"

I guess she could hear how miserable I was.

"Nothing, I, that is— " I took a deep breath and tried to calm down. This was Aunt Lolly, I reminded myself, a sweet old lady caught in the middle of things. No need to upset her. "I'm okay. Really. How are you?" I remembered how much pain she'd been in when I called her last week, so I asked, "How's your arthritis?"

My polite words came out like lines from a script, but she answered anyway.

"Oh, thank you, dear. I'm better. The doctor changed my medication and the new stuff seems to be kicking in."

"That's good. That's really good."

"It is. I was so afraid I'd have to give up break dancing."

"Break dancing?" I couldn't hold back a smile. "Nobody does break dancing anymore."

"You know how old-fashioned I am, as outdated as dot matrix your father used to—" She swallowed up the last word but it was too late.

At last she'd let his name slip!

"My father?" I prompted. "What about my father?"

"Never mind, dear."

"Aunt Lolly," I twisted the phone cord around my fingers, "there's something I've been wanting to ask you for the longest time."

"Oh." Her voice dropped. "It sounds serious."

"It is."

"Oh," she repeated.

There was a long silence. She wasn't going to make it easier. She was going to force me to say the things we never talked about. For years I'd wanted to scream out my questions. Now that I was about to whisper them, I was afraid.

"I...uh...I want to know about...him." The next words rushed out. "Do you ever hear from him, Aunt Lolly? Did he ever tell you why he left? Do you at least know where he is? Or can you find out? It's really important that I talk to him, so important—"

"Allie, Allie," she said. "Slow down. One question at a time."

"It's a matter of life and death," I finished.

MY life and death. I had begun this conversation wanting to talk to my father so he could reveal the secret code guys used against girls. Then I'd know whether to trust Dennis. Then I'd know how to solve the mystery of Jimmy's death. Now I wanted to talk to my father to solve the mystery of my life. Everything was all mixed up in my mind. If I could only talk to my father, it would all be different.

"Oh, my," Aunt Lolly said. "This is certainly quite, *quite* unexpected." I could imagine her fanning herself rapidly, flustered, her face screwed up with worry.

She's an old lady, I thought again. *Funny and sweet, but just a helpless old lady. She probably doesn't know any more than I do.*

"Allie, did you tell your mother you were going to ask me?"

"No. I wasn't expecting it to come up. Can't this be between us?"

I didn't want my mother to know. Deep down, beneath all the lip I gave her and all the trouble I made, I knew she was trying hard to be everything to me. My asking about my father was like telling Mom she wasn't enough—that she hadn't tried hard enough or wasn't good enough. She wouldn't understand that my needing him had nothing to do with her. I just needed him. I needed him to say that he needed me too.

"Mom doesn't have to know, does she? Find out where he is, then the next time you call, you can say his number several times. I'll memorize it, so I won't have to write it down while Mom's watching."

"I can't guarantee anything, dear."

"I know." I'd twisted the cord so tightly my fingers were starting to turn purple. I let it loose and wriggled my hand. "But you'll at least try, won't you?"

"You should talk to your mother about this first, Allie. I don't want to do anything or even say anything unless she knows," she said. "Promise me you'll talk to her."

"But you're the only one who can help me."

"I'll see what I can do," she said. "But don't get your hopes up."

"Okay." I was disappointed. "Thanks for calling."

I hung up, feeling foolish. Even if Aunt Lolly put me in touch with my father, it would take weeks or months before we were so used to talking to each other that I could ask him about trusting Dennis.

And where would I slip that question in, I wondered, *before or after asking why he had left me, why he had never called, what I'd done in the first place to make him never want to see me again?*

This was a dead end. I wasn't going to learn anything sitting here. There had to be another way. *And there is,* I thought, *at least another way to get information about Dennis.* I had to go back to the Muller house alone and talk to Mrs. Hidalgo. This time I'd ask her all the questions about Dennis and Jimmy that I hadn't asked last week.

I looked up at the clock on the wall. Mom wouldn't be home for at least another hour. Without giving myself time to think, I grabbed my key and left.

Chapter Twelve

Mrs. Hidalgo? It's me. Allie Canarsie." It was impossible to tell whether Mrs. Hidalgo was surprised when she opened the door. She looked beyond me to the backyard.

"The boy is not with you," she said in her accent. It took me a moment to realize who she meant; last time she'd referred to Jimmy as a boy, "a good boy."

"No, I'm by myself," I said. "Could I ask you a few questions?"

Wariness flickered in her eyes. She hadn't liked my last questions. "I'm busy."

"Just for a minute? There are so many things I don't know and…and…" I was surprised at how shaky my voice sounded. "I think Dennis needs help—to get over things," I added, not wanting to betray him. "And Jimmy was *my* friend, too."

Mrs. Hidalgo said nothing.

"I have no one else to talk to. Please?"

Pursing her lips tight, she pushed open the screen door and let me pass. She walked to the side counter and stood before a pile of vegetables and a cutting board. She was making dinner, which was what I was supposed to be doing.

I stood awkwardly in the middle of the kitchen. Her back was to me. It was thick and broad and it stretched her uniform tight across the shoulders.

"You have questions," Mrs. Hidalgo stated, addressing her words to the wooden cabinets in front of her. She began chopping carrots with a large knife, enough carrots to stock a soup kitchen, chopping so quickly I was afraid she'd nick her fingers. "And now you come without Dennis to ask these questions."

"It's a hard thing to talk about."

"It has been a hard thing to live through."

I had to be careful. I had to remember she'd come here as a refugee and a widow, with no one of her own, hired to replace Jimmy's mother. Over time she'd become motherly toward him herself, possessive even. She might not see that I had a right to the same feelings.

"I'm sorry," I said. "I guess with everything that's happened, no one's been thinking of you."

"I am only the housekeeper. A servant to Señor Muller." The knife paused its machinelike chopping, and she stared at the cabinets. "A good servant." She sighed. "Please, sit down."

I pulled out a kitchen chair, sat at the table, and got to the point.

"Mr. Muller doesn't like Dennis, does he?" I asked.

"No, he does not. And lately I can see why." The words burst from her. "Dennis did not come to the, the—what is your word for it—the *wake*. He did not call Señor Muller to say he is sorry. He did not even write a few words on a card. And at the funeral he stayed at the back like a stranger." Her words slowed, and she turned around and squinted at me. "Like a curious stranger."

Had she heard about my visits to Evergreen? I shook off the possibility and continued my questioning.

"What do *you* think of Dennis? Do you like him? Or did you, before these past few weeks?"

The question caught her off guard. It wasn't till she had turned back to the vegetables that she said, "I think the boys did not always bring out the best in each other."

In Mr. Iglesia's Math Club, the stars come out to shine.

Two math whizzes working together. How did they not bring out the best in each other?

"What do you mean?"

"Señor Muller is a good man, a very good man. What he wants for his son is what the son should want for himself. The father should be the strongest influence, no one else." She worked methodically as she spoke, transforming the carrots into piles of orange coins.

"And Mr. Muller wasn't the strongest influence? Who was then, Dennis?"

"So many questions!" she said, half-turning to me. "What is the one question you really want to ask?"

One question? Last night, I had wanted to ask whether Jimmy was a champion swimmer, but now… Could all the worries and suspicions in my mind be answered by one question?

Blood pounded in my ears, then faded, to be replaced by the tiny sounds that lay beneath the kitchen quiet: the hum of the fluorescent light, the drip of the faucet, the tick of the clock.

I rested my hand on top of the kitchen table. Maybe Jimmy had sat in this very spot his last day; certainly he'd sat here countless times before that. Did the table and chair remember? Was there something of him still left? I knew he loved irrational numbers but hated graphs. Preferred old-fashioned ghost movies to slice-and-dice horror. Could be really, really stupid at times and refused to see what was best for him. Somehow, I knew all this.

What had he done to get himself murdered?

I asked Mrs. Hidalgo my one question: "What happened the day Jimmy died?"

She wiped her thick hands on her apron, crossed the room to get a pot, and began to fill it with water from the sink.

"The day did not seem special. They never do at the time. Only afterwards, _sí?_ It was Monday, like today. Mondays I shop in the morning for the week. Tuesdays, Wednesdays, I am off. Thursdays, I clean this very big, very empty house. Fridays, I shop again, for the weekend. Saturday, Sunday, I cook fancy meals that no one eats." Her words had become a soft chant, as the pot in her hand overflowed beneath the faucet. "Such is my life now," she finished. She shut off the faucet, poured out half the water, then swept the carrot slices from the board into the pot.

"And the day Jimmy died?" I reminded her.

"I was late getting out. I like to shop early, before the vegetables pass through so many hands. But that Monday I was late." She looked out the window above the sink, stared into space. "All morning Jimmy was in his room. About ten o'clock, he said he was leaving, but he did not say where. I did not know if he was meeting Dennis or not. But maybe not, I thought, because the night before the boys had a ... a *riña.*"

"A what?" I asked.

"*Una riña, riña,*" she said, her hands gesturing. "*Un argumento.*"

"They had an argument?" My throat tightened beneath invisible fingers. Dennis had never mentioned an argument. But why should he? It would just make him seem even more guilty. If I didn't already suspect him, that would clinch it. "What did they fight over?" I asked.

"I do not know. They argued very hard, very loud, but too fast for me to understand." She tapped her ear with her finger.

"So you didn't know Jimmy was going to the lake."

"No."

"Were you surprised to hear that he drowned?"

"I could not believe it," she said, her voice edged with tears.

"Because he had died, because of the way he died, or because he had even gone to the lake?" I asked, leaning forward. "Was Jimmy a good swimmer, a great swimmer? Did he even swim at all?"

"Too many questions!" Mrs. Hidalgo said impatiently, banging the pot on the counter. Water splashed over the sides. "I have no more time. You should go now. I say no more."

Officer Rivers was the only adult I'd told that Jimmy was murdered. Would it be a mistake to tell Mrs. Hidalgo? Would she immediately suspect Dennis and get him in trouble before I could discover the truth? Right now, the truth looked bad for him.

"Mrs. Hidalgo, I don't think we know everything that happened that day," I said. Before I explained anything, I first wanted to see how she'd react to this hint.

Before she could answer, we heard a door slam. Startled, Mrs. Hidalgo looked from me to the doors leading to the living room, and back again.

A man's voice grew louder and louder as it moved toward us.

"Hi, Blanca, I'm home early." The swinging doors flew open and Mr. Muller stepped into the kitchen. His tie had been pulled loose and his collar was open. "I couldn't concentrate again today, but I guess that—"

I was paralyzed. Even my mind froze.

"You!" he yelled.

He started toward me. I leaped up so fast the chair toppled over and clattered to the floor. I ran across the kitchen, yanked open the screen door, and ran down the driveway.

Halfway to the street I looked over my shoulder to see if he was following. Mr. Muller had stopped at the open door and stood there, staring.

What if I had tripped? What would he have done?

I didn't know whether to tell him I was sorry or to grab a rock and toss it through his kitchen window.

I only knew I was in real trouble now.

Chapter Thirteen

That night until about eleven and again early the next morning, I waited for something to happen. Mr. Muller would call either my mother or Officer Rivers and I'd get yelled at, grounded, and condemned to forced physical labor. They'd make me do something stupid like mow Mr. Muller's lawn with a pair of scissors, busy work to occupy my hands while my mind was supposed to meditate on how hurtful, intrusive, and let's-not-forget morbid I'd been. I'd refuse, of course, and things would get messy. Sooner or later I'd end up back with a school psychologist, though the closest thing this hayseed town could probably scrape up would be the local vet. Mad cow disease, mad girl disease—close enough.

And they say that self-knowledge is the key to happiness. *Yeah, right.*

I'd heard nothing by the time I was ready to leave for school, though my mother had looked at me strangely during breakfast. I wanted to have it out with her right then. We hadn't had a good screaming match all summer—not since we'd left Springfield in May—and here it was the last week in September. We were way overdue. Plus, I still wasn't sure whether we were staying in Nickel Park, or whether Mom was as antsy as Aunt Darleen had said. When she got her promotion, Mom had confessed she had nowhere left to go. But I knew there was always a sleazier diner, a shabbier boarding house, always someplace cheaper, lesser, lower to go.

Did she still want to move? I refused to ask. A fight bubbled inside me, and the needle on my thermostat inched toward the red zone. My internal furnace was rattling and hissing, popping bolts and splitting seams as the moment of explosion grew closer. That morning, the pressure gauge was approaching the danger level. My mouth started to yap on its own.

"I hate Nickel Park!" I declared at breakfast. Words needed action, so I shoved the cereal bowl away and glared at my mother. "You're right, things aren't working out. I'm ready to move again."

That wasn't true. I didn't know why I said it, maybe just to push her into reacting. I *hated* moving. Each move not only took me that much further from my father, but it also guaranteed that I was the new kid again. I guess I had allowed myself to believe that maybe, just maybe, after I got past all the unbelievably dumb things I always said and did in a new place, this time I'd actually settle down.

Besides, Jimmy was in Nickel Park, and he needed me. Dennis was here too.

Mom didn't take the bait. One eyebrow rose at my outburst but she said nothing. When I huffed and crossed my arms, she ignored me. She put both our cereal bowls in the sink, ran water in them, handed over yet another brown-bag lunch, and told me to try to have a good day. Then she left.

I couldn't figure it out. Hadn't anyone called her about my bothering Mr. Muller? Had she decided to let the school handle the whole thing? Or maybe she hadn't heard about it at all. Why hadn't Mr. Muller complained about me?

I wondered about it all morning, at least until Dennis walked into homeroom. All he said was "Hi," but his ears burned like red signal flags. Obviously he was remembering I'd told him I liked him. *I* was remembering that he and Jimmy had argued the day before Jimmy died. I didn't know whether to turn Dennis in or go all girly and start to giggle. Instead I gave him a snappy salute but refused to speak. *Lie low for the day*, I decided.

I stuck to my plan for all of twenty minutes. In first period math, everyone in class was called to the blackboard one by one to work out the homework problems on slope. I was returning to my seat as Tom Creighton was swaggering up the aisle for his turn and he tripped me. I swung but missed, then Miss Barbosa yelled it had been an accident and to calm down. Creighton smirked. I figured I'd had enough of this idiot.

It took him forever at the board, of course. He only had to say if the equation showed whether the lines were parallel, perpendicular, or neither, but he had no idea what he was doing, though it was his second time around in this class. Miss Barbosa gave up, told him the answer, and said he could sit back down. I uncapped a black marker and gripped it like a knife.

"Allie, don't!" Dennis whispered. He must have been monitoring my every move.

"Shut up."

"Allie!"

Creighton walked by. Just as he did, I slashed an ugly black mark on the back of his oh-so-fashionable white leather Pyramid jacket.

The kids behind him gasped. The dumb look on Creighton's face deepened for a second before he realized what had happened. There was a really funny moment when he kept turning around to see what I'd done, looking for all the world like a puppy trying to catch its own tail.

Finally he tore the jacket off to examine the back. His mouth opened and closed stupidly, and he backed up in disbelief. His mute reaction drove me crazy—all that fishy gulping over a stupid leather jacket. It was probably a spontaneous little surprise his parents had bought him. I got little surprises from my Mom, too, like a candy bar.

I had to prod him one more time.

"I was trying for a Z like Zorro, but you moved, Cretin."

That did it. Creighton bellowed, then bent over and charged. I jumped up to meet him. His head thumped me hard in the chest and knocked me backward. I kicked out as I fell, tangled his legs with mine, and he tumbled to the floor on top of me.

"Fight! Fight!"

I hadn't gotten in one good punch before Miss Barbosa pulled us apart. She barked instructions to the class and then dragged us into the hall.

"What is going on with you two?" she demanded.

"He tripped me. It wasn't an accident."

"So trip me back!" Creighton yelled. "I pumped gas all summer for that jacket. I worked like a dog!"

"If you were smart enough to work like a person, it wouldn't have taken so long." The crack was out before I realized he'd bought the jacket himself.

"Both of you shut up!" Miss Barbosa jumped in. "Look, Allie, I don't care how early in the year it is or how bright you're supposed to be. I can suspend you for this, so if you're looking for trouble, you're going to get it! And you, Tom, you're already hanging by a thread."

"Yeah, and you got the scissors." The words should have been said with a sneer, but instead his expression had turned gloomy.

"Coach is ready to toss you off the team," she said.

"But I need football for college, Miss Bar—"

"You should have thought of that before. This is it. Stop fighting. If you so much as scowl at yourself in a mirror, you're off."

"But it was her f—"

"It was both of you from the first! Now get back in there. And you can both see me in the principal's office after school."

We returned to class. Miss Barbosa told another student to switch seats with me. As I leaned down to get my backpack, Creighton whispered, "I'll get you for this."

"Don't count on it." I answered without emotion. I'd been filled to bursting for so long that only fighting would relieve the tension. So why didn't I feel better? Because it hadn't really been a fight, just a scuffle? I guess it had released just enough pressure to ward off an explosion for the time being but not enough to give me real relief.

"Are you okay?" Dennis asked, at my side as soon as the bell rang.

I slipped away from him and spent both Spanish and gym in the girls' bathroom. I stayed for lunch, earth science, and Wheatley's class as well, though by then my bottom was permanently dented from the toilet seat. Afterwards, for a change, I headed down to one of the great hiding spots in the boiler room. Maybe meditating on an actual furnace would inspire me. But the world civ teacher saw me in the hallway, and I had no choice but to go with her. She didn't say "Aha!" so I figured the cut sheets for the earlier classes hadn't arrived yet.

In world civ, Dennis made all sorts of where-were-you? gestures.

After study hall and the last bell, I went to the principal's office: wood paneling, fake plants, water cooler, framed diplomas and certificates. If you've seen one, you've seen them all—and I have. Creighton wasn't there yet, neither was the principal. Miss Barbosa was.

"You'll get two full weeks of detention, starting next week," she said sternly. She sighed and looked at the ceiling. "Just what was going through your head, Allie?"

I said nothing.

"Look, we've all seen your record, we know you've had problems with school in the past, but we wanted you to get a fresh start here."

Oh, great. The official WE. Is any school without one?

Barbosa continued: "We hoped the accelerated math program would challenge you enough to keep you out of trouble, but maybe we were wrong. Being smart won't be enough to keep you in my class, Allie. You have to show emotional maturity as well. Can you do that from now on?"

I shrugged. I had messed up in the only class I cared about and in front of the only teacher I wanted to impress. Half of me was furious, the other half was numb.

"For now, this will stay between you, me, and your mother," Miss Barbosa said. "I'm giving you detention for 'disrupting the class.' If I say you were fighting, that has to involve Principal Saunders. He won't be satisfied with detention, not for you, and certainly not for Tom. But I won't hesitate to tell him if this happens again. Is that clear?"

I nodded.

"All right. I spoke to your mother a few minutes ago. I told her what happened and that your detention starts next week. Also, I told her that financial compensation should be made as soon as possible for the jacket's damage."

Financial compensation? I hadn't counted on that. Mom's mac-and-cheese paycheck couldn't be divvied up any more.

"Your mother wants you to call her back right now. You can use the phone in here. Dial nine for an outside line. I'll be in the hall waiting."

My mother hated getting personal calls at work, so I knew I was in serious trouble if she wanted to talk to me right away. *Financial compensation.* She'd already spent too much over the years paying off broken windows, lost textbooks, jammed VCRs, and the like. Usually I could plead that what had happened was an accident. Not today.

"Hi, it's me."

"And?"

There was a long silence. Was she waiting for me to explain? To apologize? It wasn't fair. I was the one who had to put up with Tom Creighton. Just because I didn't knuckle under to his constant bullying like everyone else, I was being blamed.

But money to pay for his stupid jacket could only come from Mom.

"Aren't you going to say anything?" she finally asked.

"No…Yes…" I cleared my throat. "I'm sorry."

"I thought things were going to be different here."

"Why should they be? I'm still the same."

"Maybe that's the problem, Allie. The problem is you."

"It always is, isn't it? Not you. Even though *you* were the one who said things weren't working out."

"And I dropped it and haven't mentioned it since. This morning you said that *you* wanted to move. Was this your way of making it necessary?" Her sigh was long, deep, and pained. "Look, I'm tired of this kind of thing, and I'm tired of having to pay for the cleanup, but I don't want to argue over the phone," she continued in a restrained voice. "And I don't want to argue when I get home because Aunt Darleen is coming for supper. You know how you should behave, so do it."

"Gee, that's great advice, Mom," I said. I could picture her at her receptionist's desk at the cookie factory, sitting a little straighter, pressing her lips a little more tightly, trying hard to keep her face unreadable. Knowing she couldn't answer me back made me feel safe and reckless all at the same time. "I guess you finished that course in parenting you've been taking," I said. The words were razor sharp. "What did you get? An F?"

"Allie."

"Or maybe you've been listening to Aunt Darleen more."

"I don't want to bring her into this."

"Why not?" I couldn't stop, the words poured from me. "She butts in whenever she wants to."

"Darleen told me about last week. She also said that she'd already apologized."

"She should have apologized to *you*, Mom, not me." I was hanging onto a greased rope over a cavernous hole. No matter how hard I gripped, all I did was slip down farther and faster. "Aunt Darleen said Dad was nobody special. What does that make *you* for marrying him?"

My mother's shock burned me through the phone lines. I would have given anything to have taken the words back, but I couldn't. We hadn't said my dad's name for over a year and now I was throwing it in her face.

"Allie, this phone call is about *your* behavior."

"Yeah, right. *My* behavior." I was sorry for what I'd said, but angry she was going to ignore it the way all these years she'd ignored the fact that I still had a father. "Not your behavior. Not Aunt Darleen's. I'm the one with the problems. Sorry. I forgot that for a minute."

"Look, Allie, I have to get off now," Mom started, "But we can—"

I slammed down the receiver.

When I left the office, I saw Creighton lurking in the hallway, head down, hands in his pocket. I was amazed he had bothered to show.

"Your turn," Miss Barbosa said to him. Maybe she had used up all her exasperation on me because she seemed calmer, almost understanding. "Your aunt's waiting for your call. Then you and I are going to sit down and have a long talk. There *is* a way through this, Tom, but you're going to have to really work at it."

He made a face as he passed me.

Outside, Dennis was waiting on the front steps.

"Hi," he said, looking everywhere but in my eyes. Why was *he* embarrassed? I was the one who'd made a fool of myself. "Where were you most of the day?" he asked.

"Hiding in the girls' room."

"They'll catch you there."

"Then I'll find someplace else."

Still upset from the call with my mother, I walked away. Dennis followed.

"Did Miss Barbosa come down hard on you?" he asked.

"Detention for two weeks starting Monday." I slowed a little so he could pull even. "I guess it could have been worse."

"She likes you, that's why it wasn't."

"She *likes* me?" I said, surprised. "That's news."

"No, she does. Can't you tell? She likes Creighton, too, even though he drives her up the wall. What about him? What she'd do?"

"I don't know," I said. "She wanted to have a long talk with him. But first she told him to call his aunt."

Which means what? I wondered. *That he has no parents? That his home life is as messed up as mine?* I didn't like the bit of sympathy that popped out before I could squash it.

"He said he'd get me," I told Dennis.

"You'd better be careful."

"I'm always careful. You saw how careful I was this morning. I carefully uncapped my marker, then I carefully scribbled on Creighton's jacket so we could carefully fight." Describing it like that made what I did seem mean, made *me* the bad guy. Why couldn't the jacket have been a gift from incredibly rich parents to their incredibly spoiled son?

Dennis tugged at my arm and we stopped walking.

"You could have been hurt, Allie."

Now I blushed. Afraid girly giggles would turn my brain to soup, I pulled away and started to cross the street.

From behind us came a low throbbing rumble, undercut by a squeal. Rounding the corner sharply was an old black sports car, no muffler, lots of rust-pitted chrome.

Dennis grabbed my arm and practically pulled me to the opposite sidewalk.

"I guess the crossing guard ducked out early," he said. He kept his hand tucked into the crook of my elbow. That felt weird, so I pulled free again and ran ahead. I turned to give the car a dirty look as it passed by.

Only it wasn't passing by. The car had crossed the yellow line. It was going to jump the curb and hit me head-on!

The moment spun out forever. The sports car was small and pointy-shaped and had dark mirrored windows. It looked like a big black insect coming to sting me. I tried to run, to back away, but my every movement was slow and thick. I couldn't move faster and I couldn't tear my eyes away.

"Allie!"

This has to be a nightmare. Everything will be all right in the end. No one ever gets hurt in a nightmare. I'll wake up before anything bad happens. Won't I?

"Run, Allie, run!"

Thump! Suddenly I was flying.

Chapter Fourteen

Whoever was in that car was trying to kill me!" I insisted. Dennis nodded, pale and wide-eyed. I knew he never really believed Jimmy was murdered. But less than twenty minutes ago he had shoved me out of the way of a car that sure looked like it'd had my name written on its fender. If Dennis hadn't reacted so quickly, I would have been its new hood ornament. My back was still sore where he had pushed me, and my chest from having the wind knocked out of me.

I didn't believe in coincidences. There was only one possible explanation: even if I didn't realize it, I was getting too close to the truth about Jimmy's murder.

Shaken after the black car zoomed off, Dennis had taken me to his house. We sat in his room, drinking soda and wondering how close a call we'd actually had.

Dennis's home was more like mine than Jimmy's. It was a tiny bungalow with peach-colored shingles and rust-colored trim, set on a patch of closely mown grass, on a block lined by similar small houses. The street would have been where upwardly mobile trailer-park people moved if they made good.

The house must have been a tight fit for the eight younger brothers and sisters I'd given Dennis, though I saw no evidence of them— no big wheels, no swing sets, no one-armed dolls lying in the bushes. I mentally whisked them off to Ireland to stay with their grandmother. I'd decide why later.

The inside of the Monaghan house was neat enough to pass Mrs. Hidalgo's inspection, from the stack of magazines in the living room squared off at the corners, to the table in the tiny dining room already set for dinner. "Mom" and "Dad" mugs sat at two of the three place settings. The mugs were sweet enough to make my teeth ache. I'd been comfortable in the bungalow till then, more comfortable than among the chrome and leather trappings at Jimmy's.

Dennis's room was obviously his own turf. Once past the door, the floor was wall-to-wall books and clothes. He kicked a pair of purple pajamas under the bed, mumbling they'd been a gift, then moved books from the desk chair to give me someplace to sit other than the unmade bed. On the wall Einstein stuck his tongue out at me, proof of either some complicated physics theory of bi-location, or else proof that all math nerds thought alike.

"You saved my life pushing me out of the way," I said, sitting down. "You could have been hurt yourself. You jumped right in front of the car to save me!"

Sprawled on the bed, Dennis screwed his freckled face into a squint. "Talk is cheap. I figure you owe me big, Allie Canarsie. Real big."

"Sure. Anything." For once I didn't joke. What had happened was serious, so serious that—

As Aunt Lolly would say, Dennis would have had a canary if he'd known what I intended to do next, so I leaned over, picked up the phone, and dialed without asking.

"Is Officer Rivers in?" I asked. "This is Allie Canarsie."

Sputtering exploded from Dennis. Like a first-grade teacher, I raised my finger for silence. Without so much as a single question, the woman who answered the phone put me through. *Aha,* I thought, *my legend is growing.*

"Yes, what is it now?" Officer Rivers said sharply.

"Someone in a black sports car just tried to run me down," I told him. "You know what that means, don't you?"

"You were jaywalking?"

I could imagine his pale mustached mouth smirking at his own joke.

"No, the car practically jumped the curb! I tell you, it was heading straight at me! If my friend hadn't pushed me out of the way, I'd be dead."

"No names!" Dennis hissed, waving his hands.

"So why are you telling me?" Officer Rivers asked.

"Don't you see? Someone was trying to shut me up."

"Gee, I wonder why."

"I know too much. You can't deny that now."

"Any witnesses to this near-accident?"

"It wasn't an accident! But no, no one else saw it, just my friend."

"Miss Canarsie, I suspect you crossed the street too close to an oncoming vehicle and panicked. In short, you have an overactive imagination. Don't bother me again."

He hung up.

Dennis was freaking out. "I can't believe you did that! You've got to be the craziest person I've ever known. Come on, Allie," he pleaded. "You've got to stop all this."

I shook my head at him. "Don't you see? Someone wanted to stop me from snooping into Jimmy's death."

It was so clear what had really happened. The car must have been driven by either the murderer himself or a hired hand.

Why wasn't Officer Rivers pursuing this lead? And why hadn't he mentioned my going to the Mullers' the day before? Obviously Mr. Muller hadn't reported the incident to him. Why? Things just weren't making sense.

At least I knew one new thing: putting himself in danger to save me meant that Dennis couldn't have been the murderer. But I still had questions for him.

I cupped both hands around my soda, a cold damp prop.

"Tell me more about Jimmy," I said.

"I give up!" Dennis said. "You're not only crazy, you've got a one-track mind." He picked up a Game Boy from the bed and started to play. "Why do you always want to talk about *him?*" he asked quietly.

"You're jealous, aren't you? I mean, *were* jealous."

"He got all the attention. Still does, even now."

"Did Jimmy know how you felt? Did you ever fight about it?"

Dennis shrugged.

"When did you fight? What was the last thing you fought about?"

Dennis looked so small sitting on his bed, so pale.

He's just a kid, I thought, *and so am I. Maybe I should let it drop. No matter what he's done, if anything, he has the rest of his life to make it up. He saved* me *today. That's a start.*

A part of me wouldn't let go, so I repeated, "When was the last time you had a fight with Jimmy Muller?"

After a long time Dennis said, "The day before he died." He concentrated on the game and didn't look up as he spoke. "It was the only time we'd ever fought in all the years we were friends, but it was a horrible fight...so bad I took off the shirt he'd given me—you know, the one with the math symbols—and threw it at him. I told him he could keep his lousy present."

"So that's why you were spooked when Mrs. Hidalgo said Jimmy had been wearing it when...when he went to the lake."

Dennis seemed reluctant to say more. I kept my voice soothing and asked, "What was the argument about?"

"Mrs. Hidalgo, of all things. Jimmy used to read her mail and listen to her phone calls to her friends and her son."

"She has a son?" I asked. Now instead of two people running to stay just ahead of the searchlights, bullets, and dogs, I saw three, the third one small between the two adults, dragged, nearly carried to keep up with them.

"Yeah, Mateo. He lives in Chicago. He came to this country long before she did. She stayed because of her restaurant."

The image shattered. It had been no good to begin with, anyway. Given Mrs. Hidalgo's age, her son would have been grown by now.

And without the image to distract me, my brain caught up with what Dennis had just said.

"Jimmy would read her mail? Listen in while she was on the phone?"

"Both. He was convinced Mrs. H. had her eye on his father, to marry him for his money or something."

"But she's old enough to be Mr. Muller's mother," I protested.

"That's why Jimmy thought it was disgusting. And that's why she was so nice to *him*, he said. Not for himself but to get in good with his father." Dennis threw the Game Boy onto the bed, riffled through the pages of a paperback, threw that down too. "Sometimes I think it was just an excuse so Jimmy could spy on her. He loved being sneaky, tracking people, listening in on conversations. He always bragged about doing stuff like that. It really annoyed me."

"Why?"

"It just did," Dennis said, shrugging.

Now *I* got annoyed. "Why did you care?" I asked. "You and Mrs. Hidalgo didn't look like best friends the day we went over there."

"No, but she adored Jimmy. He still stabbed her in the back. Everyone said he was so good, and he really *was* good, most of the time. Then he'd do creepy things that no one would ever know except me and that no one would ever believe. He would mock the people at the food pantry or imitate the old folks at the hospital. He volunteered for that stuff just to put on his résumé. His father had said that if he didn't get into one of the big three for college— Harvard, Princeton, or Yale—he couldn't go to college at all, he'd have to work in the car showroom with him."

"That's pretty harsh, isn't it?" I said. "I mean, let the kid finish junior high first before nagging about Harvard."

"You know what?" Dennis wrinkled his face, looking puzzled. "Jimmy once said that he agreed, that if he couldn't go to the best, he didn't deserve to go at all. This past year, I felt like I hardly knew him. He'd do nice things for people, cut them down afterward, then do something even nicer. Some of the good stuff was public—like sucking up at the Welcome Stranger Picnic. I'm sure you saw him there…"

Jimmy had gone to the Welcome Stranger Picnic? It was good I was sitting down because my legs turned to pudding. I scarcely heard Dennis's next words.

"But it wasn't all for show," he continued. "Jimmy would do other stuff, too. He'd help some second-grader finish his math home-work on the playground before school, put money in parking meters about to run out so people wouldn't get a ticket. Last winter he stayed after school and helped mop up because the janitor was com-ing down with the flu. Nobody told Jimmy to help the guy, and nobody ever found out. He just did things like that sometimes."

Jimmy had gone to the picnic. All along I'd been thinking that if I'd only met him, how different things would have been. Without knowing it, I'd had my chance and had blown it. If I hadn't fought with my mother that day, if I hadn't wandered off to Evergreen, if I hadn't gone to a funeral and been late coming back—we would have gone to the picnic too. We would have gone, and Jimmy and I would have met, and Dennis and I wouldn't be sitting here now, having this conversation. Maybe I could have seen that Jimmy was in trouble, that someone was out to get him. Maybe I could have saved his life.

"What is it, Allie?" Dennis asked. "Are you okay?"

Suddenly the soda can buckled beneath my grip, splashing cola on my jeans. I jumped up and brushed at the wet spot. Meanwhile my mouth was too dry to answer. I took a long drink of what was left, sat back down, and cleared my throat.

"Then what?" I asked, trying to remember how this had started. "You were going to tell me about your fight."

"We never used to fight. We were always on the same side of things," Dennis explained. "But I was getting tired of all the Jekyll-and-Hyde stuff. When he was mocking those people behind their backs, maybe he was really mocking me. We were always different on the outside, you know? Big house, little house; kinda rich, not so rich; that kind of thing. Now we were different on the inside too. So when he told me about reading the latest letter from Mrs. Hidalgo's son, I lost it. There he was, that Pyramid cap on his head, tearing down the person who'd waited hours in line to get it for him. Jimmy wasn't really bad," Dennis said, as if trying to convince himself, "but at the time I was just so tired of his crap."

"What did you say?"

"We were yelling by then. I said he was a big phony and a rich spoiled brat. He said I was jealous, that I was a leech trying to live off him. He said I was really second-rate and would never be as good as he was at anything. Especially math. Then I..." Dennis took a deep breath. "I said if he was so good, why did his mom live all the way in California? I said I bet she moved so she didn't have to see his ugly face every day. 'Who'd want a kid like you?' I screamed."

Who'd want a kid like you?

I didn't want to talk any more.

Dennis never noticed my reaction. "That's when I took the shirt off and threw it at him," he said, "then I left." Dennis didn't know how much he'd just hurt me. But he knew what a terrible thing he'd said to Jimmy because his next words were, "I told you, it was a bad fight. My best friend, and that's how I said good-bye. I guess...I guess you don't like me much anymore, do you?"

"I still like you." I made myself smile. "You didn't know you were saying good-bye, that's all."

Like he didn't know what he'd just said to me.

I was tired and weak. Lately the littlest things made me want to cry. The big things made me want to curl up inside myself and disappear. But I had one more question, only one, then maybe I'd finally have the truth, at least about Dennis.

"Remember what you told me at the funeral?" I asked. The day seemed so far away I could scarcely remember it myself. "You told me that Jimmy wouldn't have gone to the lake. You said he hated to swim."

"And?"

"Officer Rivers said Jimmy was a champion swimmer, even had medals."

I searched Dennis' face for signs of lying. All I saw was confusion. "I said Jimmy hated to swim," he answered. "I didn't say he couldn't." "But I don't get it."

"It's not that hard to understand," Dennis said. "Mr. Muller swam in the Olympics a thousand years ago but washed out in the first heat. Jimmy was supposed to get the gold that he never got."

"Yeah? He never once mentioned swimming to me." I could hear Jimmy's voice—couldn't I?—rambling on about math or complaining about his volunteer work, but never saying a single word about swimming.

"Maybe he was sick of talking about it. He and Mr. Muller fought about it all the time. Mr. Muller had forced Jimmy to learn to swim when he was two but he could never force him to like it. The swimming itself wasn't so bad; it was the constant practice and pressure and the nerve-wracking competitions that got to Jimmy. He was always begging to quit, but Mr. Muller didn't care. He didn't care that Jimmy hated it. He didn't care that Jimmy was better at other things, like math. He didn't want an Einstein for a son, he wanted Mark Spitz or Matt Biondi—someone with multiple gold around his neck."

Dennis stopped to finish off his soda.

"Two years ago," he continued, "Jimmy cramped up doing laps. He'd been horsing around right before that, so his coach didn't take him seriously. He said he nearly drowned before anyone realized he wasn't faking. It scared him so badly, he ended it right there. He figured he was too old to be forced to do anything. Besides, his mother was long gone; he didn't need to give in anymore to keep peace. So he stopped swimming on the spot."

"And Mr. Muller still fought with him about it?"

"Sure, about everything from Jimmy's wasting his talent to his making Mr. Muller look bad by quitting."

"Oh." Rubbing my eyes, I started to back away toward the door. "I guess I'd better go. Thanks again," I said. "I mean, it's not everyday I get my life saved."

"What?" a woman asked from behind me.

I turned around. A shorter, softer, frizzy-haired version of Dennis had appeared at the door. She must have just come in from work as she was dressed in a suit and still carried her pocketbook.

"Nothing, Mom," Dennis said quickly, getting to his feet.

"Don't be so modest," I said. "He saved my life, Mrs. Monaghan. A car almost hit me and Dennis jumped in its way to push me to safety."

Only when my mouth had stopped flapping did I catch the frantic "shut up" signals Dennis was making. It was too late. Mrs. Monaghan's freckled skin had grown chalky.

"Dennis jumped in front of a car?" she asked.

"To save me."

"Allie's exaggerating, Mom. A lot. You know, I never introduced you. Mom, this is Allie Canarsie. She's new this year."

"Dennis, are you sure you're all right? Did the car actually touch you? Did you report it? Did they catch the driver?"

"I'm fine, it was nothing. Some guy just swerved a bit, that's all. He was probably just changing CDs. There was no reason to report him."

"Are you sure? Can I get you anything? Do you have any aches or bruises? Can I get you an icepack?" She leaned over and put her hand on his forehead, then his cheeks. How being nearly hit by a car would give Dennis a fever, I didn't know. His face burned brightly from her attention.

"I'll see you tomorrow, Dennis. Good-bye, Mrs. Monaghan. It was nice to meet you."

"School tomorrow?" Chewing on the nail of her thumb, she looked at Dennis. "I don't know. Will you be up to it?"

"Yes, Mom. I told you everything's fine," Dennis said, his voice between anger and pleading. When his mother turned, he gave me a see-what-you've-done expression.

Suddenly I remembered what he'd said when I asked him why he ran: *Because it's a sport where I won't get beaned with a fastball or tackled by three hundred pounds of concrete. I won't snap my neck being pinned, and I won't drown.* He'd been telling me that his mother was over-protective, but all I'd heard was his words about not drowning.

The realization made my skin crawl. All along people had been telling me things I hadn't heard. What else had they said? Had I already been told all the clues I needed to solve Jimmy's murder but had just been too deaf to hear them?

Chapter Fifteen

The next day was gray and dismal, and, sure enough, Dennis was absent. His overprotective mother was probably afraid the dampness of the fog, coupled with yesterday's near miss, might give him some horrible, life-threatening disease like appendicitis. A girl in homeroom told Wheatley that Dennis's mother had made a distraught call to the school first thing that morning. No, the girl didn't know why—though *I* could guess. She'd just overheard the office secretary telling someone else. Passing me in the hall on the way to math, Creighton muttered it was a damn shame the driver had missed. Word was getting out faster than I expected. By noon, the whole school would know that Dennis and I had nearly been killed by a black sports car.

Without Dennis, even Miss Barbosa's class dragged. Simply knowing he wasn't in the building slowed the clock till each tick of the second hand tortured me. When the bell rang, I was too twitchy to go to Spanish. Who could sit for another forty-five minutes? I headed downstairs, meaning to rummage around in the basement storage room, but when I hit the ground floor and saw a red exit sign, the temptation was too great and I left the building.

At first I planned to go to Dennis's house to try to spring him for the rest of the day, but after walking my first block in the fog, I knew there was really only one place to go. I stopped by a newsstand, picked up Wednesday's *Daily Sentinel,* and turned to the obituary section.

I lucked out. Evergreen had a funeral at ten o'clock.

Cutting school for a weekday funeral had been in the back of my mind for some time. Without making a conscious decision, I had worn my uniform that morning—white blouse, black skirt, black tights, black shoes, and black blazer. My mood was sharp and jittery, but the thick gray air blunted my pointed edges till after a while even the inside of my mind was cottony. The fog blurred the corners of buildings, cut off rooftops; it made everything look only half-made. Then I thought I saw the shadow of a black sports car, thought I heard a low rumble muffled by the heavy air, and everything became barbed and bright again. I waited a moment, holding my breath, but the shadow faded into the fog.

The funeral was for Bernard Melander, age sixty-eight. Survived by his wife Queenie. A short obituary, one of the shortest I'd seen. No children were listed, no siblings, no occupation, no activities, no honors. I was performing a community service by going.

To pass the time beforehand, I circled the cemetery from inside the wall, where I'd be less obvious. Evergreen ranged from old to new, unkempt to mown, hilly to flat, ornate to plain. It was like walking a map of my mind.

Eventually I found a prepared grave and waited nearby. A little before ten a hearse and a single limo drove up, three cars behind them, headlights like wandering eyes in the fog. After the coffin had been set in place, the chauffeur helped from the limo an elderly minister, then a tall, thin woman in a black dress and veiled hat. The people from the other cars stood apart from each other, like strangers.

The minister wasn't as brief as I expected, given the short obituary. He droned on and on, his words a low rasp, all about life and death, man's expectations and disappointments, our earthly troubles and our heavenly rewards. He never mentioned Bernard Melander's name, and it seemed obvious to me he hadn't known him.

During the long sermon, the woman, who had to be Queenie Melander, glanced at me repeatedly. I refused to leave. I would not be bullied again. Even when she began to walk toward me, I stood straight and ground my heels into the soft damp earth, took a deep breath, and prepared to defend myself.

"Got a cigarette?" she asked when she was closer.

I shook my head, startled into silence.

"Damn." She took off her veiled hat and shook her hair loose. It was shoulder length, its color a mixture of sand and gray. Her lined face was narrow, matching her body with its flat unyielding surfaces. She gave me a close, head-to-toes inspection. "Shouldn't any kid cutting school have cigarettes on 'em?"

"I don't smoke."

"But you *are* cutting, aren't you? What did you tell the teacher, that Bernie here was your grandfather? Be careful of that, you only got two. Uncles are better. Though I *am* surprised to see you here. I thought kids made up funerals, then went shopping or something."

I didn't answer.

Moving farther from the minister and the tiny group of mourners, she threaded her way through a few rows of tombstones, then sat on a low urn. She crossed her legs and looked out at the stretch of graves in front of her, away from the one she'd just left.

I walked over to the headstone next to the urn. "Are you mad I'm here?" I asked. People who didn't do what I expected always made me say more than I meant to.

"No." She sat up a bit. "What harm is there?" She waved her hand in my direction. "Bernie would have liked it, some sweet young girl showing up for him."

"I'm not sweet!"

She looked me over again. "No, I guess you aren't." She turned her attention back to the other graves. "Are they finished?" she asked, not looking behind her to the funeral.

"Yes, but now they're just standing there. They're not going to leave without you." She didn't respond. After a moment, I inched round to face her. "What are you waiting for?"

"What? Don't look at me!" she said, annoyed, quickly wiping her eyes. "I've never let *anyone* see me cry, never! And I'm not starting now!"

"I'm sorry. I only asked what you were waiting for."

"Jesus, kid, I'm waiting to know what to do! I'm waiting to know what to feel!"

She doesn't know what to do. She doesn't know what to feel. She could be me.

"You're Queenie, aren't you?" I asked.

"How did you—" She eyed me more intently. "Did you really know Bernie?"

I wanted so much to say, yes, I had known her husband. But what would I have said next? That he had been wonderful, that he'd been a real creep? That he'd plucked me from the streets and paid for my drug rehab, that I'd been teaching him to read, that I was his secret daughter?

"I read the obituary," I said. "This was the only funeral scheduled for today. Your name was mentioned."

"Oh." She stood up and faced me. "Yeah, I'm Queenie. Mrs. Melander to you."

"I'm...I'm very sorry about your husband, Mrs. Melander, I mean, even without knowing him, I'm sorry."

They felt like the only true words I had ever spoken in my life.

She nodded. "Thanks." She wiped her eyes one more time. "We're going out to eat now. I mean, that's the expected thing, right? Do you want to come?" Her smile was crooked. "You'd be the only person I know there, which is saying something, huh?" She looked over at the three people who waited with the minister, the chauffeur, and the cemetery workers.

I shook my head. "I should be getting back to school."

"Okay, then. Good-bye." Her eyes watered, and her hands rose a few inches from her side. *She wants to hug me,* I thought, *but doesn't know how, maybe hasn't hugged anyone in years.* I leaned forward and drew her to me. She smelled of baby powder.

I let go and hurried away blindly, bumping into headstones as I walked, nearly tripping on flower stands and the low curb of the paved path that wound through Evergreen. It had been so easy to hug her, easier than hugging Aunt Darleen or even, sometimes, my mother.

By the time I got back to school, I had missed Spanish, gym, lunch, and enough of earth science not to bother with it. Wheatley's class I spent looking out the window onto the blur of foggy playing fields.

Who was Queenie? What kind of life did she lead that no one had shown up at her husband's funeral, not even for her sake? I was torn between imagining the details and just letting her be what she was—someone I would never, ever know.

Why did I even care?

Suddenly I wished I had someone to talk to. Sure, I'd talked a lot about Jimmy with Dennis. Maybe I was ready to talk about myself. I mean, I thought I was, though the idea alone made my stomach queasy.

"I said, are you all right?"

Mr. Wheatley stood over me, concern multiplying the wrinkles on his face. The room behind him was empty, and no one had come in for the next class.

"Where did everyone go?"

"English is long over, Allie."

I started to jump up, but he motioned for me to stay.

"I'll write you a late pass. Just tell me what's going on." With his bony fingers, he fussed with his bow tie. "Though I don't know well that that well, I don't consider you the quiet, brooding type. You're more inclined to fast talk and fast action. So something must be bothering you. The near hit-and-run?"

He had heard, too, of course. I nodded.

"But you weren't really hit, and you and Dennis are both fine. Is it something else? I mean, I know it was a close call and it must have been terrifying, but you seemed rather stressed even before that."

"Stressed?"

He smiled. "Would you prefer bratty? So, do you want to spend this period talking? I'm free now." *That's why no kids have wandered in,* I thought. Wheatley reached inside his ugly plaid jacket for a pen and a pad of passes. "Or do you want to leave now and stop by later?" he asked. "For all the talking you do, I wonder if you ever say what you really want."

It seemed so easy. I could tell him everything—from my messed-up life and parents who hated me, to Jimmy's murder. Then I could let Wheatley take care of it. But he was an adult, like my mother, like Officer Rivers. The battle lines had been drawn.

"I know you think I'm useless because I'm an adult," Wheatley said. "Worse, I'm a *senior citizen,*" he added, mocking himself. "But you might want to give me a chance. Even if you don't think I can do anything, speaking your thoughts aloud might help you sort things out for yourself."

The idea put a lump in my throat. I shook my head.

"You got me in trouble yesterday with that cut slip," I said.

"I'm not the one who skipped class."

"You're the one who reported me."

"Apparently I wasn't alone."

"So if everyone knows I just went through this big trauma, why don't they give me a break?"

"You cut all those classes *before* the car, not afterwards."

He was right. I'd cut classes almost all of yesterday after my *other* trauma, that puny little excuse for a fight with Tom Creighton.

"C'mon, Allie," Wheatley said. "Was it really so awful? Or was it the final straw, the icing on the cake—whatever phrase you young people would use nowadays?" He capped the pen and leaned back against the desk behind him. "Perhaps you and I *should* talk."

Shaking my head, I gathered my books and stood up.

"I'll take that pass now."

"Remember, Allie, when you're ready, I'm ready. Always. Just name the time and the place."

I wanted to tell him so badly the muscles in my mouth twitched. *Talk to him,* a little voice urged. *Not about the murder. Just anything.*

Tell him about almost meeting Jimmy, about almost saving his life. No? Then tell him about Queenie. There'd be no harm in that. He'd be easy to talk to, I bet.

I said the word before I even knew it: "Maybe."

His smile made me panic.

"But not now, not here," I said quickly, grabbing the pass. I needed time to make up my mind about what and how much to say.

"When? What about last period? I'm free again then."

"Okay, last period. That's good. I just have study hall then," I said, as if it really mattered what class I skipped. "I'll get a pass and meet you by the girls' room on the third floor."

"Why not here in my classroom? Or the office?"

"Too crowded last period," I explained. "Look, maybe talking isn't such a great idea after all."

"No, no, third floor, last period. I'll be there."

But I wasn't. Last period I walked halfway up the staircase, then got so nervous I almost puked. So I turned around and ran down to the basement. It was too bad, Wheatley hanging around, by the girls' room of all places. But if I went up to say I wasn't coming—well then, I'd be up there, wouldn't I? And he'd *make* me talk.

In the storeroom, I made my way through its dimly lit maze of splintery hockey sticks and dented filing cabinets till I found a wobbly desk in the far corner. Though the pool was at the other end of the ground floor, I could smell the fresh bite of chlorine. I sat, imagined the sight of a younger Jimmy swimming laps, and made up snotty excuses for tomorrow when Wheatley asked where I was.

Me talk to a teacher? Sure. I'd be bringing in apples next.

Chapter Sixteen

Maybe ditching Wheatley gave me the guilts, because after school I didn't head straight to the trailer park. I wandered around the neighborhood across from the playing fields. The thickening fog muffled my footsteps then threw the sound back at me. Once I thought I heard a car approaching from behind, the way I had on my way to Bernie Melander's funeral. Without even turning to look, I left the road and began to sprint through people's backyards, sure a car would never follow me there. I ran through yard after yard, across huge plots that backed onto scraggly fields and around prissy little flowerbeds, never once glancing over my shoulder. With the fog, I might not have seen anything anyway.

I ended up back at Evergreen. I wasn't surprised. The funeral today was unfinished business, though I didn't know how coming back would change that. I felt comfortable in Evergreen, safe, probably the safest I felt anywhere in Nickel Park.

I stopped to catch my breath.

It was about four o'clock but the mist made it look like dusk. I was in the new section. The even rows of graves headed by straight slabs faded into a wall of fog only yards away, a barrier so thick I could almost touch it as it tightened around me. There was no hint of the cemetery's surrounding acres, its hills and valleys, trees and ornate statues. There was only a small circle of flat wet ground and a dozen headstones, with no way into the circle and no way out. Still panting, I leaned against a tombstone and slid to the ground. Moisture from the cold marble soaked through the back of my blazer. My skirt was dirty and hiked up and my tights had at least three runs. It had been a rough day on my uniform, far beyond the normal wear and tear. It was time to get black pants, at least for the winter.

"Stupid jerk!"

"Says who?"

Though the words sounded distant, they brought me up to a crouch.

"Shut up, you're both jerks."

I knew that third voice. Curious, I crept in its direction, slipping from headstone to headstone. The wall of fog seemed to move with me, and I still couldn't see who was talking. The voices started coming closer. I hid behind a double tombstone and peered through the mist. Still nothing, but the voices were clear.

"Ooooooo," someone groaned. "I vant to drink your blood!"

"Shhh! The caretaker will hear us. Sounds carry in the fog."

"Nah, nobody can hear us, nobody can see us. C'mon. Let's do it."

The last voice was Creighton's, which meant the other two had to belong to his fellow thugs. *Creighton.* I'd already had a couple of run-ins with him today. On the way to math this morning, he had made that crack about the sports car missing me. All during class his sneering look had drilled a hole in the back of my skull. When I passed him in the hall after world civ, I'd bumped his elbow and sent his books crashing to the floor. His jaw had tightened, but he'd lifted both hands in surrender and backed away, leaving his books there. Creighton refuse a fight? He hadn't fooled me for an instant. He was waiting for the right time and place.

And I had given it to him, running into him here, an isolated foggy graveyard, with two of his friends to back him up. *The prudent thing, kiddo, would be to skedaddle,* Aunt Lolly's voice whispered in my mind. No one had ever accused me of prudence, but this time I knew I'd better not push my luck.

Just as I turned to creep away, I heard one of Creighton's goons crow, "Man, we're on a roll this week! Borrowing my cousin's 'vette was a stroke of genius. Did you see that bitch's face when I gunned the car straight at her?"

"I told you to shut up," Creighton said.

I started to shake with fury. So that's how he knew so fast this morning that I'd almost been hit. A snarl rose in my throat and my fingers curled to claw his eyes. But there were still three of them and one of me.

Scarcely breathing, I moved cautiously, close to the headstones. Then there, just visible, three eerie shapes materialized, Creighton and the two others. Creighton looked particularly spooky, edges blurred where the mist nibbled at his image. He was all in white— white cap, white Pyramid jacket, faded jeans, white hightops— strange and unreal, a ghostly figure in the ghostly fog.

He pulled cans from inside his jacket and tossed them to the ground.

"Time for art class."

Spray paint. The three of them scooped up the cans, fighting over the colors, then they were off, Creighton in the lead. They squirted slashes of paint on this gravestone and that—Xs, smiley faces, swastikas, upside-down crosses, question marks, curse words, the names of rock stars, and a few squiggles I couldn't make out—all the time running as if the point was to deface as many graves as they could in the shortest possible time. They kicked away flowers to get at the stones, knocked down markers, and stomped on a fresh grave, leaving it raw and trampled.

I hurried after them as best I could, clutching my books to my chest, hiding behind monuments as the boys moved on to each new place.

This is my secret place, mine! They have no right to be here.

"Hey look," one of them said. "It's that kid."

"What kid?"

I stopped short, held my breath. A thrill of fear jolted down my spine, and my legs tensed to dash away as I waited to hear my name.

"That kid who drowned—what?—a week ago, two? His headstone."

"Oh yeah, the rich kid."

All at once I realized we were near the place where Jimmy had been buried. Staring hard through the mist, I could see Creighton standing on the grave, addressing Jimmy's headstone.

"Well, rich kid, you found out your money makes no difference here, didn't you?" Creighton's voice was scornful. "Bet you're getting bored by now. Bet you're looking for something to do."

The *sssss* of paint. I bit my lip to keep myself from screaming.

"We're all worm food in the end," he concluded.

"Don't be getting so philosophical," one of his friends protested.

"C'mon, let's go to the Van der Hoff mausoleum," said the other, "see if we can break in."

"Or at least paint it. Man, that's so big I could write my life story on it."

The other shot back, "You don't need much room to write 'I was born a dickhead.'"

Creighton broke into the laughter. "This is getting old. Let's drive over to Hector's, get a beer. His old man's gone for the week."

Reversing direction, the first two passed within yards of my hiding place. Creighton followed. He stopped right in front of me, wariness stamped onto his profile. He tilted his head as if sniffing the air. *Does fear stink?* I couldn't swallow. Then he faded—white on white, a ghost within a ghost—into the fog. As I watched him disappear, I saw the scrawl of my black magic marker and the red inverted Pyramid triangle—first there, then gone.

A few minutes later I crept over to Jimmy's grave. Creighton had played a fast game of tic-tac-toe with himself, red *X*s, red *O*s. The red puddled in the carved letters and dripped as if Jimmy's name was crying blood. I wiped the paint off with my bare hands, cleaned them on the grass, then wiped some more. The stone was left mottled and streaked, but it was all I could do.

If only I'd known Jimmy sooner…if only I'd gone to that stupid picnic…he'd be alive now, not here, defenseless against whatever jerk passed by.

Without warning, the sight of the red staining my hands sucked the breath from me. Shuddering, I dropped to my knees before the headstone. The evening was cold and wet. Jimmy lay only a few feet beneath me, colder and wetter than I could ever imagine. Shapeless thoughts slipped and slid inside my mind, refusing to be caught and framed in words. For a long time I'd known that I'd missed something. I didn't know what it was, but I knew that it was important.

I pressed my palms flat against the headstone.

"Help me, Jimmy. Help me, so I can help you."

Then it hit me, like a flash of lightning from the stone to my mind: The inverted red triangle I'd just seen disappearing into the fog hadn't been on the jacket.

A second flash, to my heart:

Who had personally tormented Jimmy for years?

Who had tried to scare me off by running me down?

Who—my head started to ache—was suddenly wearing a white leather Pyramid cap, just like the one Jimmy had been given for his birthday? Just like the one I had *not* seen in the bag of clothes returned by the police?

Tom Creighton was Jimmy's murderer.

Chapter Seventeen

By that night, I had a surefire trap to catch Creighton. But by the next morning, my head swirled with doubts: *Am I doing the right thing? Isn't it dangerous? Shouldn't I call the police?* I picked up the phone a dozen times and a dozen times hung up, remembering Officer Rivers's cold voice when I'd tried to tell him about the black sports car. I had lied to him trying to steal Jimmy's folder. Now everything I said or did was just another lie. *Only Dennis can help me now,* I thought, as I hung up the phone a final time and left the house.

When I reached the high school, I didn't see the usual crowd hanging around the parking lot. I was late! I ran the rest of the way, up the stairs and down the hallway. I burst into homeroom like a crazy woman, hushing the class to abrupt silence.

Dennis wasn't there. My last lifeline was yanked away. Suddenly I was afraid. Ignoring the stares of the other students, I collapsed against the wall, gulped down air, bent over to ease a stitch in my side.

"In training for the marathon, Miss Canarsie?" asked Mr. Wheatley. I shook my head. "Then please take your seat."

Wheatley! I'd said I'd meet him yesterday in front of the upstairs girls' room. How long did he wait for me? Did someone call him a pervert? Was he mad now?

I flopped into my chair and laid my head on the desk. I'd been so busy planning how to catch Creighton I'd assumed Dennis would be back today. Dennis was part of the plan. I couldn't finish this alone.

I suffered through the PA announcements, as well as Wheatley's contributions to the day's news. Finally the bell rang. When I started to get up, he gently pushed me back into my seat. He waited till everyone left, then folded his tall thin frame into the desk across from me.

"You didn't show yesterday," he said. His voice was neutral. I couldn't tell whether he was ticked off or not.

"I suddenly didn't feel like talking."

"But you very much wanted to talk to Mr. Monaghan this morning, didn't you?"

"How did you know that?" I demanded, goose bumps creeping up my arms.

"Maybe because your eyes darted to Mr. Monaghan's desk the instant you ran in. Maybe because you deflated like a popped balloon when you saw he wasn't there." Wheatley shook his head. "I don't read minds, Allie. I don't have to, not with *your* body language. You know, Dennis isn't the only person you can talk to. I'm willing to forget being stood up. Why don't we start over again? This is my prep period but after fifty-odd years of teaching, I can wing it just this once."

I studied the cover of my math book. I needed to get to class right away to get my plan rolling, but Wheatley's voice was soft, low, soothing. He made me want to listen. He made me want to answer back.

"You look pretty alone," he said. "Talking could help."

Alone. He knew what buttons to push.

"Allie, I'm not going to let you off this time. Talk."

He wasn't the first teacher who'd tried to help me, but there was something different about Wheatley, something that tugged at me. Maybe I was just a sucker for bad jokes and loud sports jackets. Yet no matter how tempted I was, I couldn't help wondering if it was really me he was interested in.

"If you hadn't taught my mother, would you be trying so hard with me now?" I looked up at him. "Tell me the truth."

"The truth? What's the truth? Cleverer men than I have pondered that." He leaned forward and pitched his voice low: "'When my love swears that she is made of truth/ I do believe her, though I know she lies.'"

I pulled back, started to stack my books to leave. My voice was expressionless. "Why don't you come right out and say no? You're just quoting someone else to do your dirty work for you."

"Shakespeare," Wheatley said. "And I'm just trying to say yes *and* no." He shrugged and held out his hands. "I found out right away that Winifred is your mother, so how can I say for sure that's not part of it? But I can say—and this *is* the truth—that I'm trying primarily for *your* sake, Allie. Winifred is not my student now, hasn't been for years. You're my student. Now *you* tell *me* something," he dared. "Tell *me* the truth. Were you responsible for the panic at last week's fire alarm?"

"No!" I said right away. My eyes burned as I stared him down. *His* eyes were blue, not the soft blurry blue you usually see in old people, but hard and dark, like cold water. Why hadn't I noticed them before?

"And yes," I added slowly.

He beamed, the smile of a patient teacher with a slow student. I felt both pleased and stupid, as if I'd just sounded out the word "cat" for the first time.

"Often truth is neither black nor white, but gray...a little of each," he said, straightening his bow tie. "But sometimes it's black *and* white—at the same time. That's how we hurt each other with the truth. That's how we can love someone, like a mother, at the same time that we hate her. Or how there can be a grown-up truth and a teenage truth about the same thing. They're completely differ-ent, yet both true." The lecturing tone disappeared and his voice became earnest. "Talk to me, Allie," he urged. "Keep talking. It's going to sound corny as all get-out, but what is the truth of your life right now?"

I was late for math. With each second my plan to catch Tom Creighton as the murderer was ticking away. I had to make up my mind. I couldn't tell Wheatley everything, but I couldn't let him go away empty-handed, either. In a way, he might even be able to help, now that Dennis was absent. I couldn't do this alone.

I looked Wheatley straight in the eye so I wouldn't miss his reaction.

"I guess it really all began when I started going to the funerals of strangers."

Good old Wheatley never blinked.

✳

When I finally stopped talking, there was barely enough time in the period to go to math and give Miss Barbosa my pass. The bell rang as I was handing it to her. Then I backed up and stood by the door while kids flew out of the room. Creighton would have had to cross my path to leave, but he didn't try. He stood up and waited by his desk. I didn't move either. It was the first I'd seen him since yesterday, since I'd realized he was Jimmy's murderer. The answer to the mystery had been there all along in his thick-featured Nazi face.

"Allie?" Miss Barbosa asked.

"Yes?" I answered, staring at Creighton.

"Is there something else?"

"No, Miss Barbosa."

"Then you can leave."

"I will."

I didn't move from the door. Creighton didn't move from his desk.

"Allie, come here. I forgot to give you the homework assignment."

I never took my eyes from Creighton's. His fists balled and unballed like a machine.

"You can tell me the homework," I said. "I'll remember."

"No, I *want* you to come *here* for it."

I crossed to her desk. At a nod from her, Creighton left. We never got closer than ten feet.

"Look, Allie, he's willing to try, he really is, because this is his last chance and he's got an awful lot to lose. But I'd better see some work on your end, too," Miss Barbosa warned. "Don't push him. And don't push me."

I made my expression blank. "The homework?"

I spent second-period Spanish hiding in plain sight. The inner door to the nurse's office was locked, but the front room was open. I lay down on one of the cots, pulled up a blanket, and drew long deep breaths that were supposed to calm me but didn't.

I was jumpier than an ant on an electric grill. What had Creighton been doing since math? *I* never did what people expected; why should he? My eyeball challenge might have been a huge mistake. Had it tipped him off?

Even before it was time for third-period gym, I was up from the cot and out the door. I hurried downstairs to the basement to put the final touches on my trap, which involved taping over the storeroom's light switches, then pushing heavy bookshelves and filing cabinets in front of them. I was out of breath when the bell rang for fourth-period lunch. I ran back upstairs, raced to the cafeteria, threw my bag and backpack onto the table by the soda machine, then hopped up to sit on top of the table. My feet danced nervously on the bench.

"You never learn, do you?"

"Dennis!" I was so surprised I nearly hugged him. "I thought you were absent!"

"No, not today, just really, really late." Sliding his fingers beneath the collar of a too-heavy sweater, he said, "My mother didn't want me to catch cold and waited till the last of the fog had burned off. She also gave me a note to skip gym." He rolled his eyes but I could tell he was blushing. "I was in the vice-principal's office trying to explain the connection between skipping Wiffle ball and *not* getting hit by a car."

"Doesn't matter," I said, grinning. I was so happy to see him. I told myself it was because I needed him for the trap to work.

He tried to pull me from the table.

"Creighton's here! Quick, get down before he sees you."

"No, that's the whole point," I said. I batted his hand away then snatched it back and held onto it. "Listen, Dennis, there's no time to explain. Trust me. Remember the basement storeroom I showed you last week? The room with the old desks and gym stuff? Go down there right now, hide in the back, and wait for me."

"What?" He shook his head as if he hadn't heard right.

"It'll be dark in there, so be careful. I fixed it so no one can get to the light switch."

"Allie, I don't know what in the world you're talking about."

"Creighton's the murderer. I'm going to get him to admit it to me downstairs. I need you to witness his confession."

Believing Dennis to be absent, I'd also asked Wheatley to go downstairs during our talk in first period. I hadn't told him my suspicions about Creighton. Wheatley would never have helped me lay a trap for a killer, so I had needed another way to get him downstairs. An idea had come to me as yet another kid tapped on the window of the closed classroom door and waved.

"I can't talk anymore," I'd told him. "There are too many people here and you're Mr. Popularity." At that point I was genuinely jumpy.

"The period's almost up anyway," Wheatley answered. "Can we continue this later?"

That was when I'd had my idea. The records room opened onto the basement storeroom. I asked Wheatley to meet me in the records room during fourth-period lunch.

"Fourth period I'm proctoring study hall this week," he said, shaking his head.

"Please? If I have to wait till later, I'll chicken out, like when I left you up by the girls' room."

"I don't know, Allie," he said, frowning. "Ever hear the saying, 'Fool me once, shame on you; fool me twice, shame on me'? If I have someone cover for me then go downstairs and you don't show—"

"I will, I promise, I have so much more to tell you, some...some pretty bad stuff…life-and-death stuff." I let my lower lip quiver then stopped as Wheatley raised a skeptical eyebrow. Melodramatics didn't work with him. I decided to try weird and mysterious instead. "I don't even know if I can be in the same room as you when I talk…I… Could you—this is going to sound really, really strange, but—could you sit in the records office down there and just listen? Just listen to whatever you hear, and say nothing, *absolutely nothing*, no matter what?"

"You mean like a confessional?" Wheatley whispered, leaning closer.

"Exactly! A confessional!"

He sat back, his eyes narrowing. "Then I assume I'll get to give you penance," he said dryly.

He had me. I guess it was only fitting, after all. Here I was, half-lying to him right after his words about the truth.

"Doesn't the end *ever* justify the means?" I asked.

"It depends. I presume your 'means' are this heart-wrenching little song-and-dance routine. What's your justifiable end?"

"Getting you downstairs fourth period," I said.

"Why?"

"Because I need you there. I really do. I need you to hear something, just to hear it."

"Hear what?"

I shook my head. "I can't say."

"Then I can't say I'll be there," he replied. Maybe my song-and-dance-routine face dissolved into genuine panic because he added, "I'll think about it."

"Please," I begged him.

"I said I'll think about it," he repeated with an annoying smile. Did he think he was calling my bluff? Or was he bluffing himself and planned to spend fourth period with his feet up on his desk, throwing spitballs at the study-hall dummies?

The truth was, I needed him, even though Dennis might go along with my plan. A teacher made a much more believable witness than a student.

All these thoughts rushed back into my mind as I realized that I still hadn't convinced Dennis to go downstairs.

"What did you just say to me?" Dennis asked. His lunch sat unopened before him on the table.

"I said, Creighton is Jimmy's murderer. I want you to hide in the storeroom and witness his confession."

"Allie, is this a joke?" Dennis asked. "'Cause it isn't funny. I don't understand." He obviously didn't, or else he'd have flung himself at Creighton.

I glanced across the cafeteria. The Cretin was nearly at the cash register. He was buying only a carton of juice, which could mean he wasn't going to stay. I had to catch him before he left.

"Dennis, just do it!" I pushed him toward the exit. "Right now! Don't make me go down there alone!" I was sure he would keep arguing with me, but he nodded and ran out.

I turned around and watched as the Cretin paid for his juice in pennies. The cashier tapped her foot, while his friends poked him repeatedly and laughed.

Even standing still he swaggered.

I was angry when I'd seen Creighton in class this morning, but hadn't known how furious I was until that moment. My hands started to shake and sweat prickled my upper lip. Before I realized I was moving, I was shoving my way through the crowd to where he stood.

"Hey you!" I called.

I smacked the juice carton out of his hand. It spun through the air, hit a wall, and split open. Roars of annoyance erupted as people got sprayed, then they hushed as they saw what was happening.

"I've had it with you!" Creighton bellowed. His friends grabbed him by both arms as he strained forward.

"She's not worth it," one of them muttered.

"I don't care!"

"Oooh, I'm petrified." I grinned uneasily, knowing if I held out my hand it'd be trembling. I walked closer, let the phony smile drop from my face. Lowering my voice, I said, "I know what you did."

Creighton stopped struggling. His friends loosened their hold, and he leaned forward.

"What did you say?"

"I said I know what you did." The crowd inched closer, straining to hear. I feinted a sudden jab at Creighton's left shoulder; he side-stepped it right into the slap of my other hand, nothing much, simply a prick to his ballooning ego. "I know, and I'm telling!" I said.

I skipped away as he lunged, fury making him clumsy. Over the heads of students I saw Miss Barbosa and Mr. Penn approaching from separate directions to see what the trouble was. *I have to do this now,* I thought.

"You and me, downstairs, this minute," I said. When his two friends started to follow, I taunted, "Can't do this on your own?"

No time left.

Before the teachers made it through the crowd, I turned, slipped out the exit, and ran down the first flight of stairs to the landing. I hoped Creighton would do the same. When I saw him at the top of the stairs I called out, "You want me, you got me!"

I ran down the second flight, satisfied he was following. But I wasn't satisfied with the rest of my plan. Now it seemed so stupid, stupid, stupid!

What if Dennis changes his mind? Or comes out in the middle of things and tries to talk to Creighton himself? And what about Wheatley? It's no good without Wheatley as a witness. What if he decides to stand me up like I did to him? What if Wheatley and Dennis run into each other before I get there?

It was too late. Creighton was after me.

At the bottom of the stairs were doors that led to the girls' and boys' locker rooms, as well as to the hallway that ran past the gym teacher's office and the swimming pool toward the gym. The basement storeroom was on the other side of the building.

"You made a big mistake yesterday," I said.

My voice echoed in the cinderblock hallway. From the gym I could hear boos and cheers, the heavy tramp of feet, the shrill blast of the gym teacher's whistle. Beneath that I heard a chant of "One, two, three, four," probably a different class in a different section of the gym doing calisthenics. I walked backwards, my eyes on the hall behind me. Where was Creighton? At this rate, Miss Barbosa would show up before he did.

"Do you know what that mistake was?" I called.

Creighton jumped at me from a side door, much too close. He must have gone through the boys' locker room. He grinned as I backed away.

"My mistake was not shutting you up the first day."

I couldn't outrun him down the long corridor toward the store-room, so I wheeled round and fled through the double doors leading to the pool. The odor of chlorine stung my nose, made my eyes tear. Light from the ceiling skittered across the water's bobbing surface. The floor, too, was wet. Though the pool was empty now, kids had been swimming here just the period before. I slowed down to walk across the slippery tile. All the phys ed classes for this period were in the gym or maybe outside in the playing fields Would anyone hear me if I screamed?

Behind me the doors crashed open with a gunshot-like crack. Creighton rushed in, saw me, and ran along the walkway, either not noticing or not caring about the wet floor. I tried to hurry, but he grabbed me by the arm.

"Am I about to have a swimming accident too?" I asked. "Like Jimmy Muller?"

The shock on Creighton's face was what I'd hoped for. In that brief second I kneed him as hard as I could, then shoved him. Doubled over in pain, he was thrown off balance and skidded crazily on the wet tiles. As quickly as I dared, I made my way to the door on the opposite end.

I was back in the hallway. I headed past the gym, ducking below its door windows, moving away from the safety of crowds to the danger of the storeroom at the far end. As I walked, I once more backed through the corridor, but this time every so often glancing over my shoulder at utility and equipment closets to make sure I wasn't surprised again. But no—the door from the pool swung open at last. Creighton stood silhouetted against the dancing reflections of light. Then he started after me, one hand still clutching his crotch, a loping monster from a horror movie.

"Come back here, Canarsie," he called. "I won't do anything. I just want to talk to you."

I waited till he was closer, then I ran the final distance down the hall and into the storeroom.

"You want to talk to me, Creighton?" I said loudly as I crossed the doorway. "You talked to Jimmy Muller, and now he's dead." I wanted my first words in the storeroom to be dramatic, so dramatic Wheatley would be willing to sit still and listen once he realized I wasn't really there to have another heart-to-heart with him.

The storeroom was dark. The filing cabinet still blocked the light switch, just as I'd arranged it earlier. This meant the tape was also still in place over the switch, so Creighton couldn't wriggle his hand in behind the files.

Dennis had gone ahead of me, I was sure. And the lights were still out, so he'd be hidden. This should give Creighton plenty of time to spill his guts as he fumbled around in the dark. But was Wheatley here? I couldn't call out to check without giving myself away.

The only light came from the hallway and from the small records office at the far side of the room. I knew from my many previous trips that the deep shadows were thrown up by old desks, empty file cabinets, rolling blackboards on wobbly frames, and piles of used sports equipment.

I was pretty deep into the storeroom when Creighton appeared. He groped around, trying to find the light switch. With a lot of effort he might have been able to push back the file and pry off the tape, so I had to get him moving at once.

"I said, Jimmy's dead, Cretin, and I know what you did."

Creighton waited, maybe to let his eyes get used to the dark.

"Who's this Jimmy you keep talking about?" he asked. "C'mon out and tell me."

I didn't answer. At last he began to move into the room. From the light behind him, I saw him reach out to feel his way.

"Why did you do it?" I asked. "Yesterday at Evergreen—all those graves, and you end up at his."

"I don't know what you're talking about. This Jimmy guy, now Evergreen. I wasn't at Evergreen yesterday, no way. I was home doing homework."

As he talked, he pushed his way in, moving more quickly than I'd expected and he still hadn't admitted a thing. *I should have waited*, I thought, *should have talked this through first with Dennis*. But once I saw Creighton in the cafeteria, I'd reacted blindly. I couldn't let him get away with murder.

"I know everything," I said. "I know it was you in the black car. I know you and your moron friends trashed Evergreen last night. But that's nothing compared to what you did to Jimmy." I had to make him confess. I inched toward the middle of the room, away from the light where it was more difficult for him to see, but difficult for myself as well. Were the bookshelves where I remembered? I wanted them between myself and Creighton.

"All right, Canarsie. It was us in the car, I admit it, but it wasn't me driving and it wasn't my idea. It was payback, you know, for the jacket."

"I'm telling."

Thump! Sssss! Thump! Creighton was shoving boxes aside to get to me.

"You'll never make anyone believe you," he said. "It'd just be your word against mine. Besides, you weren't hurt."

"I know everything, and I'm telling."

I slipped behind a desk and circled away. From this angle I could see the outline of his figure. When he realized I had moved, he spun around, arms wide, searching the darkness.

Crack! Suddenly his silhouette dipped—was he bending over? Maybe he'd rapped his shin on a desk corner.

"Why, Canarsie?" he asked. He straightened with a grunt, arms close to his side. Was he holding something? The shadows made it impossible to see. "Why do you have it in for me? What did I ever do to you?"

"Not me, *Jimmy.*"

"That's it. You're crazy." He rushed toward me.

I bumped into a blackboard, steadied it with my hands, rolled it between us. But when I looked round the other side, I saw nothing. Creighton had moved away from what little light there was, then had stopped moving.

I stared until colored points danced before my eyes. Saw nothing. I stopped breathing to listen to his. Heard nothing.

Desperate to end it, I said, "Did you have to wear the cap so soon? Did you think no one would notice?"

"What cap?"

His voice was much too close. I swallowed.

"Jimmy's Pyramid cap," I said. "I saw you wearing it at Evergreen. *That* was your mistake: wearing it too soon. You murdered him for it. But it wasn't enough, was it? You had to go spray-paint his grave, too!"

"Murdered? You're crazy! I'm not getting put away for a freak like you!"

All at once, voices from all sides—

"Allie, behind you!"

"Everyone, out!"

"Somebody turn on the lights!"

"Put it down, son."

Creighton whirled toward the last voice, the closest, swung in that direction instead of at me, and smacked Wheatley hard with the bat. Even in the dark, I could see Wheatley crumple to the floor.

"Oh God, no!" cried Creighton. He dropped the bat and tried to run but in his frenzy fell over a desk.

Miss Barbosa rushed in, shoved the already-fallen Creighton flat on the floor, and pressed her knee to the back of his neck. Dennis pushed forward from the very back of the room to where Mr. Wheatley lay. Mr. Penn ran in, panting, followed almost immediately by the janitor, the two of them shouting, "What's going on? What happened? I can't see!" Miss Barbosa yelled at the janitor to call 911 and the police. He and Mr. Penn ran out. Penn returned with a huge flashlight. I made my way over to Dennis. He was crouching over Wheatley, who lay very still, staring at the ceiling, biting down against the pain. There was a horrible bulge in the arm of his shirt and a growing dark stain; when the baseball bat hit, the bone must have broken so badly it jabbed through the skin.

Dennis carefully took off Mr. Wheatley's red bow tie and loosened his collar.

"I am so sorry," I whispered. "Mr. Wheatley? I am so sorry." He couldn't hear me.

Mr. Penn waded in through the mess. When he aimed the flashlight at us, I saw that the blood soaking through Wheatley's left sleeve had trickled onto the floor.

"Joe, did you get through to 911 and the police?" Penn called back over his shoulder. There was a shout from Creighton. Penn positioned the flashlight on a desk and hurried to help Miss Barbosa.

"I didn't mean to hurt anyone," Creighton yelled, struggling. "I was only trying to shut her up! She's crazy! She's out to get me!"

Creighton's words infuriated me.

"I'm out to get *you*? Look what you did!" I screamed. "You killed Jimmy! You tried to kill me! And you almost killed Mr. Wheatley!"

"I don't know a Jimmy, I didn't kill a Jimmy!" Creighton insisted, his face pressed to the floor by Mr. Penn. "I keep telling you that."

"You did! You killed him for his cap! *His cap!* This isn't a game! You can't push the start button, give us all three more lives. This is real, this is *real…*"

My legs were shaking so badly that crouching was too much. I slipped to the side and sat on the floor. I clutched the seat of a chair to keep from falling over completely.

"His cap... What else do you want? How about this?" I tore the watch from my wrist and threw it at him.

I missed widely in the dark. The only light shone on Wheatley, an actor spotlighted in a bad play. He breathed hard, as if trying to remember his lines. Dennis, kneeling before him, opened and shut his own mouth wordlessly, as if he were the prompter but had forgotten the script.

"Or how about my sneakers, Cretin?" I continued, tearing at the laces. "They're five-dollar specials. Want those too?" As I tried to pry off one of the shoes, a cold wet hand grabbed my wrist. Though the grip was weak, it stopped me instantly. Wheatley. I lost my breath.

"For his c-cap," I finished, looking down at him.

"It's over now, Allie," he whispered. "All...over."

All over.

Jimmy.

"I couldn't let the Cretin get away with murder," I tried to explain. "Don't you see?"

But did *I* see? I'd almost been killed. Wheatley had been hurt, was in horrible pain. Was the truth worth all this?

"Shhh." He patted my arm like I was the one who needed comforting. "Tom Creighton...didn't murder Jimmy...for his cap."

"What?" Dennis and I exclaimed at once. I tried to pull away but Wheatley grabbed my wrist again, as if preparing me for the words to come, as if he knew I would bolt and never stop running once I'd heard them.

"He couldn't have," he said. "Jimmy wore the cap...till the very end...I saw him...at the wake...in his coffin. He was buried in it."

Then Mr. Wheatley gasped, a terrible choking noise. His good hand flew up and clutched his left shoulder. The choking stopped, his eyes closed, and his head fell forward.

I started to cry.

Chapter Eighteen

The end-of-period bell rang while Miss Barbosa was taking me upstairs and through the halls to Principal Saunders's office. Kids rushed out of their classes in a solid crowd, which then broke in two to let us pass. I didn't care how they stared. As I walked, numbness crept over me, first my feet and legs, then my body, then the inside of my head. I couldn't be hurt if I wasn't there to feel it. A train could have materialized in the hallway and run me down, and I never would have flinched.

Saunders was about to let loose a million questions, but Miss Barbosa shook her head and motioned the principal out into the hall. She led me to his inner office, brought me a paper cup of water, and set it on the desk. I'd sat in this same spot days ago, screaming at my mother on the phone about what a lousy parent she was.

Seconds later I heard twin sirens, no doubt the ambulance and police. Miss Barbosa ran out, while I stayed, listening to the shriek rising and falling.

Silence.

The sirens stopped so abruptly that an echoing void filled their wake. *Of course.* A pinprick of an idea slowly worked through layers of flannel. *They don't need a siren for Mr. Wheatley. Not anymore.*

I saw my bag and backpack on the lost-and-found shelf in Saunders's bookcase. Someone must have brought them from the cafeteria. I grabbed my purse, then, turning again, saw the cup of water that Miss Barbosa had left on the desk. A red thumbprint marked the paper cup. I raised my hand to block the sight, and there, on the long sleeve of my white shirt, were large bloody handprints. At some point after Wheatley had grabbed his broken, bleeding arm, he must have patted mine, trying to comfort me. I hadn't seen the stains when Miss Barbosa was leading me down the hallway. No wonder we'd gotten everyone's attention.

Like a robot, I rolled my sleeves up past the blood and walked out. Everyone was busy trying to discover why the police and ambulance were here. I wheeled round in the opposite direction and left. This time no one noticed me.

Several blocks from school, I realized how warm it had become. The sun was slanting into my eyes with the intensity of a day at the beach. *Mrs. Monaghan is probably happy about that,* I thought. This morning she'd been so upset about Dennis catching a chill in the fog that she almost hadn't let him come to school. *The fog. Parents worry about such stupid things. Not lakes. Not black sports cars. Not baseball bats.*

The scene in the storeroom replayed in my mind. My whole plan for avenging a death had succeeded only in causing one.

Wheatley's dead.

My legs caved in. Suddenly I was sitting on the sidewalk in front of a barbershop, crying.

How could I have been so wrong? The night before, planning my trap, everything had been obvious—from my finally solving Jimmy's murder to my being honored afterwards by the Nickel Park Police Department for my cleverness and persistence. I had imagined it so clearly that I'd smelled the bouquet Officer Rivers had presented me.

I had imagined it so clearly...

Did I imagine everything?

No! Because then...

The more I thought, the more it seemed that I was the only real murderer.

The barbershop door opened, letting out layers of smells, warm and dark and masculine. Wheatley had worn Old Spice. I could smell it in class, most strongly in homeroom when he was fresh from scraping off his bristly old-man beard and patting on aftershave.

When I had daydreamed about Wheatley taking me in—after my mother had moved from Nickel Park and I'd run away and sneaked back and was living alone in the school—I hadn't really given us a daily life. I just replayed his invitation over and over in my mind: "You can live with *me*, Allie. I was a father once, long, long ago. Let me be one again." So we'd be doing each other a kindness, my moving in with him.

I tried now to see us together. Maybe I'd gripe about his gross whiskers in the bathroom sink because he didn't rinse them all after shaving, or maybe he'd nag that I wasn't doing enough homework, one of the dangers of agreeing to live with a teacher. But I couldn't. I saw nothing, just an empty house with empty rooms, filled with overstuffed furniture, yellowing lace doilies on arm rests and sofa backs, the smell of mothballs, the faint sound of old music, maybe Big Band or Swing, the tick of a clock made louder by the silence. I walked through every room and never found Wheatley. He was gone, dead, and I was all alone, even in my mind.

I realized people were staring at me, sitting there in the middle of the sidewalk. I pulled myself up, walked a few yards, then ducked into the shadow of an alley between the Good Eatin' Diner and the Main Street Drugstore. The alley was cool and dark and empty. I rested for a moment against the brick wall. The cold brick brought up a memory: leaning against a mausoleum at Evergreen the week before I had started school, before I had met Dennis, before I had heard of Jimmy, before Wheatley had lost the big lottery of life by ending up with me in his class. Eons ago, back when the world was still safe from Allie Canarsie.

For a moment I tried to defend myself, saying that Wheatley was old, that he'd looked sickly during the fire drill last week, that he probably would have died soon anyway. A harsher voice argued back: it wasn't simply the fire drill but the panic caused by me that had made him sickly. He was well enough to still be teaching a full day. People didn't automatically drop dead at a certain age.

Look at Aunt Lolly. Queen of the Break Dancers.

After a few moments, I pushed away from the brick wall and left the alley. This time I headed toward the town green that bordered the shops. The municipal building and post office were on one side, a phone booth, water fountain, and public rest room on the other. I needed to talk to someone I hadn't hurt, needed to know that such a person existed.

"Aunt Lolly, it's me." *Should I tell her about Wheatley? Or just let her talk and listen to her voice?*

"Allie, dear, I've been expecting you ever since I spoke to your mother Monday night."

"What? You spoke to Mom?" I asked.

"Didn't she mention it when she talked to you?" Aunt Lolly said hesitantly. "She *did* talk to you about your father, didn't she? She said she would."

My father. Aunt Lolly had finally said the words deliberately, no accident.

Numbness fled, replaced by pins and needles as my whole sleeping body woke up. Now I remembered: I had begged Aunt Lolly to find my father and to tell me where he was. She must have found out but instead called my mother with the news. Now Aunt Lolly wanted to make sure I'd heard the news first from my mother's lips.

"Sure, Mom already talked to me," I lied. "She told me about him." Would Aunt Lolly know I wasn't telling the truth? Could she hear the tremor in my voice? "But afterwards she said to talk to you, too," I added, "that you could explain everything better."

"I don't know what there is to explain," Aunt Lolly answered, sounding confused.

"Just go through it all again, in case Mom left something out," I said.

"Well, personally I never understood why your father cut the two of you off like that," she said. "I was furious with him. Of course now, with his new family, he says he wants to forget the past. But it's still not fair, especially to you, and it's absolutely no excuse for his behavior six years ago or for dodging child support all these years."

"His new family?" I bit down on the inside of my mouth to keep from screaming. "I mean, Mom told me and all, but how many kids was that again?"

"A girl, nine, from his new wife's first marriage, and of course now the baby."

A girl nine years old? That was how old *I* had been when Dad left. He'd found a better daughter.

"It was real hard…for Mom to tell me." I blinked fast, clearing my eyes of tears. "Was she shocked much when she heard?"

"At first," Aunt Lolly said, warming to her subject. "But she's had two years to get used to it."

"Two years?" My breath whooshed out. "She's known for two years?" For two years my mother had sat before me every day and not told me the single most important thing in life I needed to know. I swallowed hard and tried to keep my voice steady. "I mean, I had thought that when you called her, you were telling her for the first time."

"No, I was asking her once again when she was going to tell *you.*"

Fighting my rising voice, I asked, "Two years ago, did Mom find out about Dad through you? Or did he contact her?" *To contact me,* I hoped, *to ask about ME.*

"I found his whereabouts by accident," Aunt Lolly said, "and told her as soon as I knew. I felt you should know as well, even two years ago, but that was your mother's decision to make, not mine, like not taking him to court for back support once she'd found him was her decision, too."

Still clutching the phone to my ear, I looked around. The grass was as green, the sky as white-blue as seconds before. Toddlers played in a sandbox while mothers stood by, chatting, one eye on their kids. An ice-cream truck, trying to prolong summer, slowly cruised around the common and rang its bell.

In other words, life went on, because life didn't give a rat's ass about me. If I hadn't learned that earlier in the basement storeroom, I was sure learning it here in this phone booth.

"Was Mom ever going to tell me?" I finally asked.

"She's told you now."

I cleared my throat and tried to sound as if this was a routine question on a checklist. "What she didn't really say was where he is."

"Oregon."

Oregon was light-years away, just above California, where Jimmy's mother had moved....

"When can I see him?" I asked.

"Oh, Allie." My aunt's voice folded down into a whisper. "She didn't talk to you about that part?"

"No."

"Honey, I'm so sorry. The last time I talked to him, he said all this crazy stuff about only now discovering who he really is and what he really wants, that he's starting a brand new life out there, and that he wanted to put all the stupid things he'd ever done behind him."

"That means me," I said flatly.

"No, it doesn't. Oh, he can make his words sound modern and with-it, but in the end, it's plain old selfishness. Your father does whatever he wants, damn the consequences. He always has. He was a very selfish little boy, and he grew up to be a very selfish man. He used to jerk your mother up and down like a yo-yo, tomcat around as if he were the last man on earth, and think that damned smile of his would make it all worthwhile in the end. He really believed that. For a while, so did your mother. Maybe that's why she kept moving, afraid he'd show up on her doorstep one day, smiling, married or not, and she wouldn't be able to help herself." Aunt Lolly stopped abruptly, then cleared her voice. "I'm sorry. I didn't mean to be so blunt. But never once in your father's life did he stop to consider who he might be hurting."

I couldn't answer. It was easy for Aunt Lolly to say things like my father was selfish; *she* wasn't the one he had left behind. Now my dad had a new nine-year-old daughter and he could try all over again. Maybe he'd be luckier with this kid. Maybe she'd be good.

"Thanks," I said. Everything seemed strange—the sky, Aunt Lolly's voice, my own body—strange, dizzying, and distorted. Only the phone was real, and I was about to hang up. "Thanks for telling me the truth."

"Allie?" Her voice filled with doubt. "You'll call again?" she asked. "Have your mother drive you down for a visit soon. We all need to talk about this much, much more."

Without answering I hung up.

Once my hands left the solid touch of the phone receiver, something inside me snapped loose and flew away. I began to run, not knowing if I was running to catch whatever had broken loose or running to escape it. I ran through the common, down past the library, street after street, until all the play-toy blocks of Nickel Park's houses gave way to greater and greater stretches of land. I ran and I ran, and I thought of Dennis running the track, and Creighton running after me, and Wheatley, too—how could I have forgotten him for even an instant?—Wheatley running toward fate, to die on a cold basement floor.

Eventually my steps slowed to foot-dragging exhaustion. The sidewalk had long ended and the traffic had become light. I walked on the dirt shoulder of the road. Every so often there was a billboard planted in the grassy fields that lay on either side.

Aunt Sophie's Country Cookin', Best Food for Miles Around! said one.

Genuine Indian Moccasins, Belts, Purses. Leather Luxuries, Three Miles on Rte. 90, read another.

When I saw the billboard that said Tastee Treet Cookies, A Smile in Every Bite, One Mile, I finally knew where I was headed.

I could smell the place before I saw it, the warm sweet smell of home that both turned my stomach and made me want to cry with longing. Chain link fencing surrounded the parking lot but the gates were wide open and I walked right in, through the rows of cars and into the big gray building.

When I passed through the doors of the cookie factory, I felt both raw and numb, inside and out. I threaded my way through people in the lobby to the front desk where my mother sat behind a huge phone console and a fake potted plant. My heart jumped when I saw her, like a dog straining at its leash when its master returns. I wanted to curl up in her lap and go to sleep in the warm sweet smell.

"Tastee Treet Cookies," she murmured into the phone. "May I help you?" Her index finger hovered over a row of buttons, waiting to push one.

"What—these guys too cheap to get voicemail?"

The words were supposed to be a joke but they sounded so sharp and mean my mother jumped. I didn't want to be mean to her, even though I'd just found out that she'd lied about my father. Maybe later we would fight about it, because it certainly deserved a fight, but right now all I could think about was Mr. Wheatley. I wanted my mother to take one look at me and wrap me in a hug.

"Allie! What are you doing here?"

How could so many emotions show on one person's face so fast? She settled for anger.

"The school called." Looking around, she lowered her voice. "What in God's name were you thinking?"

Her attack threw me. I fumbled for words. "I, I—"

"You can be so crazy and stupid sometimes! I just don't know what to do with you!" She lowered her voice again. "How much more irresponsible are you going to get?"

"But I was only trying to—"

"No buts. I don't care what you were trying to do. When are you going to realize that life is not all about you, Allie?"

"I know that, Mom, I really do now. I am so sorry."

She shook her head. "Oh, *now* you know it, *now* you're sorry. It's a little late for that, isn't it?"

If she says Mr. Wheatley's name out loud, I'll break down and scream.

"Mom, please," I begged.

She froze, straightened her back, and smiled stiffly at an older woman who stared at us as she passed. Between clenched teeth, my mother's voice dropped back to a whisper.

"You know how much I hate getting calls at work, you know it! And such petty crap as this. A month's worth of cut slips already— and that's only gym! They're still adding up all the others. Plus a lot of talk I didn't understand about a fire drill. I don't want to even think about that."

"What?" I asked. Why was she talking about cut slips?

She doesn't know!

The school must have called first thing this morning, I realized, before the whole terrible thing with Creighton and Wheatley had happened.

"Mom, please, it's not what you think."

"Don't give me that." Closing her eyes, she pressed her fingertips to her temples and massaged them.

"But you don't understand—" I insisted.

"I understand that once more I quit my job and moved for nothing. Well, that's it," she said. All the pain in her head seemed to shoot out through her eyes. "It's our last move. No more fresh starts. I've finally got something decent here, and it's a good thing too because I'm out of choices, this is my last chance." For one instant her anger slipped, and she looked lost and vulnerable. "Don't you see, Allie? I can't do this any more, I can't keep it up." *It*—moving, being homeless, solving our every problem by leaving town. Her face hardened again. "This time you've got to live with whatever mess you've made, no matter how badly it stinks."

"The way *you* have?" I finally shot back. "Like all those moves weren't really for you each time, to get further and further from Dad? Like you weren't talking about leaving again just last week? Guess what, Mom, it doesn't matter. Dad probably never looked once for you, not then and certainly not now. Aunt Lolly says he's got a happy new wife now, and a happy new daughter, and a whole goddamn happy new life out in Oregon. And no matter how far you run, you can't run from knowing that he dumped you!"

My mother's cheeks paled to stark white, then a single bee-sting appeared on each.

She stood, ignored the people who had stopped to listen, and dragged me into the ladies' room.

"Please leave," she said to a woman standing at the sink. "*Now.*" The woman took one look at us and hurried out, her hands still wet and soapy. The door hadn't completely closed when my mother grabbed me by the shoulder and shook me hard.

"Don't you ever dare talk to me like that again!"

"Like what?" I jerked away. "You mean, tell the truth for once?

"You don't know the truth about anything. You don't know anything about your father, anything real, and you don't know anything about what it was like being married to him."

"I do so," I declared. "*You* were dumped, and *I'm* paying for it."

"Is that your excuse? That your father was Prince Charming and Bill Gates rolled in one, and I cheated you of some sort of dream life? And now you're going to get even with me by tearing through schools as fast as pantyhose? I don't buy it. There's no excuse for your behavior. None."

She meant my behavior in general; I heard my behavior today and cringed. I turned toward the mirror; an angry stranger scowled back. How could I look so furious on the outside when inside I was so sad and sorry? I didn't want to yell. I wanted to talk about Jimmy and Mr. Wheatley and what I'd done and whether I'd ever be able to live with myself again. But my insides and my outsides were all scrambled, and my voice was still harsh when I snapped, "When were you going to stop lying to me?"

"I haven't been lying to you," my mother answered. She stood beside me in front of the mirror. We yelled at our reflections instead of at each other. It wasn't easier. "Your father…wasn't always a nice man," she continued. "I've only been trying to protect you."

"How long were you going to protect me? Till I was ninety?"

"Don't change the subject. This is about you and school. You've been going to strangers' funerals all summer, cutting about every class you have, and now creating panic with false fire alarms. Doesn't it ever get real for you?"

Too real: Wheatley lying on the floor.

"This kind of behavior has to stop right now!" She tugged at me to face her. "Do you hear me, Allie? You're ruining your life."

For once I agreed but habit forced the words from my mouth:

"No, *you* ruined it six years ago when you drove Dad away!"

My mother slapped me. Then she froze, her palm an inch away from my burning cheek, and stared at her hand in wonder. She'd never hit me before. And she didn't even know what I'd really done.

When she lowered her hand, it was trembling and her eyes had filled up.

"Go outside, wait by the car." She turned away. "It's in back. I'll be out in a minute."

We had so much to say to each other, so of course we drove home without speaking. In the great dark silence I seemed to hear every word Wheatley had ever spoken to me, down to his saying that Jimmy had been buried in his cap...followed by that horrible choking sound he made at the very end.

My mother pulled into the rutted drive of the trailer park, bottoming out as she always did by the German shepherds, which made them go wild. When we passed Aunt Darleen's end of the subdivided trailers, I saw a curtain twitch. She must be on nights this week. I wondered how much time I'd have before she was at our door to see why Mom had left work early.

We turned the corner onto our lane. A police car was parked in front of our trailer.

My mother's hands tightened around the steering wheel.

"Oh my god, Allie," she said quietly. "What have you done now?"

Chapter Nineteen

As soon as Mom and I got out of our car, Officer Rivers left his. The passenger door of the patrol car opened as well, and Miss Barbosa stepped out. Startled, I turned away to avoid seeing the look on her face.

Mom motioned for them to come in. Rivers sat in the easy chair, perched on the edge, as if he shouldn't relax on duty. Miss Barbosa sat on the loveseat. She had brought my backpack from school. Her clothes were rumpled and her makeup smeared, her fashion-model look destroyed by the day's events. I stood. Mom stood too, head down, arms folded, shoulders hunched against the coming blow.

Officer Rivers spoke first. "Miss Canarsie, would you like to explain why you left school right after the incident?"

"What incident?" asked my mother.

Not answering, Rivers said to me, "Miss Barbosa here was worried when she discovered you'd left the premises. She insisted she come along. Ordinarily, I'd say no, but...." He smiled at her. Even bedraggled, she was gorgeous. "Well," he continued, "let's just say you're mighty lucky we all know each other in Nickel Park. Sometimes we do things a bit informally. Anyway, we have a lot of questions only you can answer."

Questions only I can answer? All I know is that I left Mr. Wheatley lying on the storeroom floor, and he's dead because of me.

The image was burned into my brain—Wheatley's face and shirt white even in the shadows, the stain of blood black then suddenly bright red as the flashlight turned on us. My brain couldn't shape my thoughts into words; how else could I share this picture? If the others could peer into my mind, they'd scream in horror.

"What happened, Allie?" My mother's voice sounded far away. "What did you do?"

I couldn't answer.

"Miss Canarsie," Officer Rivers asked, "did Thomas Creighton carry the baseball bat into the storeroom with him or was it already there when you had your confrontation?"

"Confrontation?" my mother repeated.

"Or perhaps—" Rivers's eyes narrowed. "Perhaps you placed the bat there yourself, Miss Canarsie? Did you think that supplying Creighton with a potential weapon would better make your point?"

"Hey, what kind of questions are these?" Miss Barbosa protested.

"Miss Canarsie, did you know that Mr. Wheatley had a heart condition when you asked him to meet you in the storeroom?"

"No!" I shouted.

Liar.

Hadn't I known? Hadn't I suspected? But why hadn't I thought about that when I asked him to meet me downstairs?

"Mr. Wheatley?" my mother asked. "What about Mr. Wheatley? Is he all right?"

No, he's dead, and it's all my fault. How could I have forgotten how sick he'd looked the day of the fire alarm, herding the students out of the room, concerned for *their* safety?

"Will someone tell me what's going on!" my mother yelled.

Officer Rivers cleared his throat, pulled a notepad from his pocket, and thumbed through a few pages.

"After questioning some other witnesses," Rivers said, "we were able to put most of the story together. Correct me if I have anything wrong, Miss Canarsie."

He began at the beginning, or at least the beginning he knew. He said that I'd come to the conclusion that a classmate's recent accidental death had been murder, and that last week I'd gone to the police station to steal their case file on the accident.

"At some point your daughter then decided that the school bully who'd been bothering her had also murdered this classmate. At lunchtime today," Rivers went on, "Miss Canarsie provoked the bully, trying to force a confession from him. The bully retaliated with a baseball bat, but the blow meant for her badly injured a teacher who was trying to intervene, and the teacher subsequently suffered a heart attack."

My mother and I gasped, she at the words "baseball bat" and me at the word "suffered." Not died, but *suffered.*

"Mr. Wheatley…is he…is he alive?" I asked, not allowing myself to hope.

"No thanks to you," Officer Rivers answered.

Yes! Yes, he's alive!

My next breath was the purest and sweetest I'd ever known. I wanted to grab Rivers and kiss him, to thank him for the news, to thank God.

I swear to be good from now on, to keep my big trap shut, to consider other people first, to think before I act, to show Mom how much I really love her, to—

A tidal wave of doubts rushed over me:

Does Wheatley hate me now? Or pity me as a pathetic loser? Will he eventually come back to class? How will I ever be able to face him?

I must have started to look shaky because Miss Barbosa had me sit next to her on the loveseat.

And how close had Dennis been standing? I wondered. *Had he come between Creighton and me? What if Creighton had swung the bat the other way? Has Dennis considered that? If he doesn't today, will he tomorrow? Will he hate me then too?*

The roller coaster inside my heart rose and plummeted so many times, I didn't know whether to giggle or puke.

My mother's voice slowed me down and pulled me back into the room. "Will Mr. Wheatley be all right?" she asked, lifting her head.

"They didn't have to operate, so they're optimistic."

"He's alive," I repeated.

"And in more pain than he ever bargained for! He's in intensive care right now with a serious heart condition and a compound fracture from the blow of the bat." Smoothing his pale mustache with his thumb, Rivers stared at me. "You've got a lot to answer for. You might even be facing charges yourself before all this is over."

"Allie...charged?" my mother asked. "What for? She didn't swing the bat."

"If there's no statute on the books for criminal provocation, there should be. Maybe a year or two in juvie hall would do her good, straighten her out."

"That's why you're here?" Mom asked. "To take Allie to the station?"

"If that's not just hot air, say it right now, Officer," Miss Barbosa said coolly, "and let these people call a lawyer. You didn't hint at anything like this back at the school."

Face reddening, Rivers clamped his mouth shut.

Miss Barbosa put her arm around me. I wanted to pull away. It was bad enough I had messed up in her class. I had messed up in life, too. How much bigger of a jerk could I get in her eyes? But what did it matter? All she probably saw in me was someone like Creighton, someone who oh-so-desperately needed her help. She must have majored in math, minored in social work.

"Allie, Tom's been arrested for assault, maybe attempted murder. He's seventeen, so he'll probably stand trial as an adult," Miss Barbosa said. When I tried to look away, she took my chin and turned my face back to hers. "This last time you pushed him too far."

"I didn't swing the bat," I said, echoing my mother.

"Tom wouldn't have swung it either, if you hadn't goaded him."

"But you know him!" I blurted out. I shrugged her arm off my shoulders and stood up. "He's crazy, the littlest thing sets him off!"

"Tom says the very thing about you."

The words silenced me. They were true, weren't they? Creighton had accused me only of all the things I'd just sworn not to do anymore. But the roller coaster was at the peak of a hill again, ready to go flying down the other side. I couldn't stop it.

"You've seen what he's like, Miss Barbosa. He was going to hurt someone sooner or later. That someone ended up being Jimmy."

"Look, Allie," Miss Barbosa said, "there's no proof at all that—"

"No proof?" I asked, trying to hold back the tears. "Then why did he try to run Dennis and me down? Why did he spray-paint Jimmy's grave?"

"Tom says it was a coincidence," Miss Barbosa explained. "He admits scaring you with the car. He even admits vandalizing the cemetery. But he insists he didn't single out any one grave. When you taunted him in the lunchroom, he thought you were going to turn him in for the cemetery, that's all. But that was enough. He figured he'd be arrested and would lose his last chance at a sports scholarship. So he went after you to shut you up. Tom is an emotionally agitated young man who didn't think he had any options left."

"Tom, Tom, Tom!" I chanted. "What is he, your boyfriend? His name is Creighton. Creighton the Cretin."

"Allie, be quiet," warned my mother.

"But I never did anything to this guy, Mom!"

"No?" Miss Barbosa said. "What about his jacket? Didn't you ruin his leather jacket because you thought he murdered Jimmy?"

No, I thought. *But it's better than the truth: I ruined Creighton's jacket* before *connecting him to Jimmy's murder.*

Jimmy's murder.

I put my hands together and spoke to each person one by one, begging.

"Look, I'm sorry I've been a pain in class, Miss Barbosa. And I'm sorry I lied to you and tried to steal your file, Officer Rivers. And Mom, I'm sorry for...for every minute that I've ever been awake. But don't you see? None of this changes anything. Even if Creighton didn't murder Jimmy, *someone* did."

Six eyes stared at me, three mouths gaped.

"The killer is still out there," I finished.

"I do not believe you just said that." Officer Rivers's lips pulled tight.

"But Jimmy hated to swim! He shouldn't have been at the lake!"

With a heavy sigh, Rivers pushed himself from the chair.

"She's out of control, Mrs. Canarsie," he said, as if I'd gone deaf, dumb, and blind. His thick fingers pinched the air. "She is *this* close to stepping over the line. If she keeps this up, someone is bound to press charges against her." He shook his head. "What a shame, to have your life over at fifteen."

I set my jaw. "Yeah, tell that to Jimmy."

"Allie." Miss Barbosa also stood. "I heard you tell Tom that this isn't a game. That goes for you, too. You've got to drop it, do you hear me? Let the police handle it."

I backed up a step, found myself against the wall.

Officer Rivers addressed my mother. "You *will* tell Mr. Canarsie, won't you, ma'am? In the end, it does no good to hide these things."

"There is no Mr. Canarsie," she said. She looked at me, as if daring me to comment. "We're divorced. We...we don't keep in touch."

"Ah." His eyes glittered. Of course. That explained everything. I was the depraved product of yet another broken home.

I followed Rivers and Miss Barbosa to the door as they said their good-byes. Outside we had an audience, a few Lost and Found residents sitting on their stoops or standing idly in the road.

Well, let them gawk! I don't care. I tried caring, I cared for someone who couldn't care for himself, for Jimmy, and look where it got me.

As soon as the door shut, my mother said, "We've got to talk. Right now."

Her voice came from behind me. I already knew what I'd find—her face full of pain and sadness, sorrow edged with anger—and so I stayed at the door, my breath clouding the window till I could see neither my own reflection nor the empty road beyond it.

"I'm sorry about your father, Allie," she said. "And I'm sorry that I didn't tell you sooner and that you had to find out on your own."

She was trying not to yell. It didn't matter. We were so overdue for this fight I don't know how we hadn't burst our seams with waiting.

"You were young at the time, and I had lots of reasons for not explaining. I guess I just got in the habit of protecting you."

Her footsteps backed away then returned.

"Not telling you was a mistake. We all make mistakes, like you did today. But what you did is very serious, and we need to talk about it right now."

"Oh sure, after all these years of keeping your mouth shut, now you want to talk."

From the corner of my eye, I saw her reach out. "I understand how upset you must be," she said.

"You don't understand anything!" I turned and slipped past without touching her. "I hate you. Do you understand that? I hate you!"

"I understand you're upset, and I'm sorry. Your father's leaving is between him and me. His not visiting is between him and me. You got dragged into it. It's wrong and it's not fair, I know, but there it is." She took a step toward me. "We still have to talk about what you did."

"No!" I turned round and round, looking for someplace else to go to get away from her. There *was* no place. The trailer was too small. The anger whistled from me like air from a balloon, leaving me cold and empty. "I never asked to be born to such crummy parents," I said. "I never asked to be born at all. I wish I was dead."

"No, shhh, you don't mean that," she said, reaching out again.

"I do mean it!" I batted her hands away. "I mean everything I say. I'm not a liar like you! I mean it: I wish I was dead!"

The trailer was a prison. The only place left to go was into my cell.

"Alexandra, you come back out here this second and talk to me!"

Whatever hold she'd had on her anger broke.

"I don't know what else to do!" She thumped on my locked door. "I have pampered you, disciplined you, ignored you, and smothered you. I've given you responsibilities, I've taken away responsibilities. Nothing works! Do you hear me, *nothing works!* Why is that, Allie? Maybe the problem isn't on my end but yours. Maybe it's not that you need a better mother but that I need a better kid!" she screamed.

Sure, why not? Dad needed a better kid, why not you?

Pots and pans started to bang. Mom muttered under her breath, every so often walking to my door and ranting loudly, then moving the three inches back to the kitchen.

"And I don't believe, after everything that happened," she said, "you still insisted that boy was murdered. How stupid are you?"

As stupid as I was bad, I guessed, which meant pretty stupid.

On and on she nagged, jumping back and forth between what my father had done and what I had done. How many years had I wished she'd talk about my father? Now I just wished she'd shut up. It was bad enough my parents were divorced, but they weren't supposed to be creeps, too. I didn't want to know how the divorce had been a nightmare, how before that he'd cheated on her, how she'd threatened to leave and how he'd wheedled and whined for her to stay. How *he'd* left, then come back, then cheated on her again. How he'd even hit her.

I clapped my hands over my ears. These were not my parents she was talking about! These were ugly strangers!

My head ached, my stomach knotted. How could she dump this on me all at once? After six years of silence? For six years I'd thought I had a wonderful father. Instead, he was a monster.

After a while the horror and pain faded.

So what if my father's a creep? At least he's been up front about it. At least he never pretended to have done anything for my good, not like every other adult. Everything he did was only for his own benefit, all to help him on his wonderful road to self-discovery.

"From now on I want to know where you are every minute of every day," my mother yelled from the kitchen. "And from now on, you will go to every class every day. That includes gym. I don't care if you have double pneumonia and two broken legs, do you hear? *Every single day!* And after school you're to come and wait for me at the factory."

I needed to calm down, look at things objectively, get some distance and perspective. Sitting cross-legged on the bed, I pulled a sheet of paper from a notebook.

Dear Diary,
I nearly killed someone today, nearly got him killed.
And I'm the one who's supposed to be looking for a murderer. Maybe I should look closer to home.

I shuddered and crumpled the paper into a tight ball.

"Are you listening to a word I'm saying?" Mom shouted. Her voice cracked with the strain. "No more going to funerals. And no more nonsense about fake murders or fake fires or fake anything!"

Fake murders? Maybe I was wrong about Creighton. But Jimmy was still dead and it couldn't have been an accident. If everyone could just get past being mad at me, they'd see that.

I took out another sheet and titled it "Things I Know to Be True about Jimmy Muller's Death." It didn't take long to come up with a list.

1. Jimmy hated the water and wouldn't have gone swimming by himself in the lake.

2. His father couldn't care less what Jimmy hated, and they fought all the time about swimming.

3. Jimmy was a champion, so even if he had gone swimming, he shouldn't have drowned.

4. Everyone thought Jimmy was an angel, but he was a fake and had a huge bad streak.

5. Mr. Muller didn't want to know that Jimmy was murdered when I tried to tell him.

6. Mr. Muller wouldn't want to know about the bad streak, either, especially since he's running for office.

7. Dennis was jealous of Jimmy.

8. Jimmy was spying on Mrs. Hidalgo.

9. Mrs. Hidalgo had a grown-up son Mateo.

What could I deduce from these facts? What suspects, what motives were hidden in this list? I had to admit that from the first I should have been looking for an adult.

"And another thing, young lady—" Mom rapped on the door. "Are you listening? Finding out about your father isn't going to get you any sympathy from me. I ran out of sympathy for you long ago! Things are going to change around here. From now on, you'll—"

I put my hands over my ears.

What if Mateo, Mrs. Hidalgo's son, is in this country illegally? And what if Jimmy found out? What if he had tried to blackmail Mateo? Excitedly I jotted Mateo's name in the margin. Mateo…a successful businessman and community leader with a dark secret, willing to go to any lengths to keep from being deported back to the country that so savagely slaughtered his father, a country where all the wealth he'd accumulated here would be stolen. *A great motive.*

But what if Mrs. Hidalgo discovered her son was being black-mailed? I kept seeing her thick strong hand holding the kitchen knife. Mothers did crazy things to protect their children, or at least, that's what I'd heard. She'd seemed protective of Jimmy. How much more protective would she be of her own blood? Enough to murder to keep him safe? I imagined her steely eyes behind their silver eyeglasses calculating what had to be done, then doing it as ruthlessly as pulling the head off a chicken for dinner.

I jotted her name down beneath her son's.

"And I swear," said my mother, "if I get one more phone call from school, that's it. You know, they send boys off to military school when they're troublemakers. There are places I could send you, Allie. It would break my heart, but I can't deal with this anymore."

Who else should be on the list?

My mind started to whir so fast I grew dizzy, my heart hammered wildly, and there was a roaring rush in my ears.

Who got all freaked when I started to talk about Jimmy's death?

Who threatened me when he caught me still talking about it?

Who should have complained to Officer Roy Rivers about me, but didn't?

Fred Muller.

What was his motive?

"Do you know what it's like to get these kinds of phone calls, Allie? I mean, they're bad enough as it is, but then to get them at work? Do you realize how much and how often you embarrass me?"

Muller was a parent. Jimmy was a teenager. Listening to my Mom, hearing how angry she was, I figured that was motive enough. Plus there was all that stuff about Jimmy letting his father down because he hated sports. He embarrassed him, Dennis said. Like I embarrassed my Mom. Embarrassment was something a political candidate had to avoid at all cost. And think of all the sympathy votes he would get when his beloved son drowned so tragically.

Fred Muller.

My hand trembled as I wrote his name.

"Are you listening to me, Allie?"

"He was your father, Jimmy, your father!" I whispered fiercely.

"Your mother left you. Your father was the one person you should have been able to trust." My voice broke. "Look what he did to you."

I swept the paper and pen to the floor, stood up, and leaned against the door. The veneer still vibrated with my mother's harsh words.

I'll get him for you, Jimmy. I swear I will.

Chapter Twenty

The next morning, Friday, I stayed home from school. Maybe no one expected me to go anyway. Maybe no one wanted me to. It didn't matter. I had things to do, and staying away saved me the trouble of cutting classes.

I figured Dennis had stayed home as well. Even if he hadn't realized how close he'd come to death yesterday, his mother would have, so I called his house, knowing she hadn't let him go in.

"Hello?" he answered.

"Hi, it's me."

There was a long, terrible silence. I was afraid he would hang up on me. He didn't. He didn't talk, but he didn't hang up either. I listened to his breathing for what felt like forever and found a thousand different meanings in its uneven pace.

"Have you heard anything about Wheatley?" I finally asked.

"Just that he's in serious condition." Dennis paused. "What about you? Are you okay?" I nearly collapsed with relief.

"I guess."

"What happened to you yesterday, Allie? I mean, afterwards. I looked for you."

"I...I went home. I got my mother from work and went home."

"Then what happened?"

"Not much." *As long as I don't count almost being arrested, humiliating myself in front of Miss Barbosa, discovering my father is a first-class bastard, and having the fight to end all fights with my mother.*

"Anything happen to you?" I asked.

"I think my mother's ready to quit her job to homeschool me."

"Is she there now?"

"No. Allie, you sound weird. Are you sure you're—?"

"Do you still have your key to Jimmy's house?" I asked before he could finish.

"Um…yeah. No one asked for it back yet. Why?"

I told him I'd explain everything if he'd bring the key and meet me a block away from the Muller house. I hung up before he could ask any questions.

On my way there, passing Evergreen, I stopped on the sidewalk for a minute and looked at the cemetery in the direction of Jimmy's grave. He was there, somewhere, waiting for me to finish what I'd started for him.

I walked toward the school, walked past it, then walked across town toward the Muller house. Mr. Muller would have left for work by now. And Mrs. Hidalgo said she shopped on Fridays. A good housekeeper would shop early, wouldn't she? To get the best, the freshest food? I counted on her being gone. While the house was empty, Dennis and I would search it for evidence that Fred Muller had killed his son.

All last night my thoughts had jumped from idea to idea. What would incriminate Fred Muller? There was no gun to match with bullets, no vial with traces of poison. So what should I be looking for?

The answer had exploded in my mind, and I'd bolted upright in bed.

I was looking for a witness, a silent witness: *Jimmy had kept a diary.*

In his diary, Jimmy had called Mrs. Hidalgo names. Maybe Jimmy had called his father some things in it, too. With luck the diary would accuse Mr. Muller. Perhaps some not-so-accidental accidents had happened to Jimmy in the past. Or perhaps he had suspected his father of wishing him harm. If I could find that diary and give it to the police, as well as a report of everything else, they would have to believe me!

My pace slowed as I approached the Muller house and saw Dennis standing on the corner. It was awkward seeing him again for the first time since yesterday. A million years seemed to have passed since we were both in the basement storage room, crouched over Wheatley. At first Dennis didn't say anything when I walked up to him. He stood with his hands in his pockets, looking off down the block.

"You want to go in there, don't you?" he said, his gaze on Jimmy's house at the bottom of the dead-end. "Tell me why, and it had better be good, good enough to make me go with you."

"It's simple: I have to know what happened to him. And you have to know, too, don't you? We already looked for the answer on the outside. We have to look inside."

"What are we looking for?"

"For whatever we find," I said, not ready to reveal my suspicions about Mr. Muller.

"And if it's not there, if we find nothing?"

"Then this will be the end of it."

It has to be the end. I made all those promises yesterday; once I know the truth about Jimmy, I mean to keep them....

Maybe the details weren't important, or maybe Dennis had come to his own conclusions about Mr. Muller. He nodded once, then we walked down the block together.

The house was dark. Wanting to get away from the front in case anyone drove by, I hurried down the side path, Dennis close behind. Jimmy had given him a key to the kitchen door, not the front door. I knew it, just the way I knew Jimmy. At the back I paused to peer in the window. The kitchen, too, was dark and deserted.

I held out my hand. Dennis stepped onto the porch, gave me the key, and I unlocked the door. We slipped in and shut the door behind us. No security alarm buzzed, no rottweiler growled, no neighbor yelled through the bushes.

Okay.

Though I'd been here twice, everything looked unfamiliar in the faintly lit room. Only the oven clock glowed, flashing *12:00, 12:00,* like a warning. The power must have surged in the night and no one had reset it. The hanging copper pots, the counters, the knives in their long wooden rack gathered what little light there was and gleamed softly, almost lit from within, making the kitchen alive and watchful. One pot swung an inch as if moved by a breath. I backed into a chair, and a gasp of panic escaped my lips. Dennis pulled me close to steady me. Silently I turned in his arms and pointed toward the hallway. We tiptoed past the counter, through the open kitchen door, down the hall, and upstairs to the bedrooms.

At last, in Jimmy's room, Dennis whispered, "Okay, we're here. Now what?"

It touched me to think how far he'd come on faith alone.

My answer was as quiet as his. The silent house and especially the bedroom seemed like a shrine to Jimmy, sacred space, and even though I was about to tear it apart, whispering seemed appropriate.

"I want to search for evidence," I said. "I bet there's something here in this room that will clear everything up."

"Like what?" Impatience tinged his voice. "We know Tom Creighton didn't kill Jimmy. Who else could have done it? And why would the evidence be here?"

"I want to find Jimmy's diary."

Dennis stepped back too quickly and almost tripped.

"We can't read his diary!" he said, so fiercely it surprised me.

"Listen, Dennis, if life was normal, I'd agree; we'd have no business reading it. But life isn't normal. I'm positive Jimmy's death wasn't an accident. I think…" The words I'd thought so freely stuck in my throat. "I think his father killed him."

The room faced west, its windows opposite the morning sun. In the thin light, Dennis's features were drained of color like an old photograph. His lips moved a moment before his voice caught up.

"Mr. Muller? Are…are you sure?"

Instead of the anger or ridicule I might have expected, instead of demands for explanations, there was something else in his voice, a

sad longing just short of hope. Maybe he had suspected all along but
had shoved the suspicion down because it was so horrible. Or maybe
he just wanted the whole thing to be over, or to know the truth at all
costs. What could I say to such expectation? Yes, I was sure—as sure
as I'd been that Tom Creighton had been the murderer? As sure as I'd
been, for the briefest second, that Dennis himself had killed Jimmy?
But to be *unsure,* to admit doubt, robbed me of my right to keep
looking, so I nodded.

And Dennis accepted it.

He had never actually seen Jimmy's diary, had no idea where it
was kept. So one by one we pulled each book from its shelf and held
its spine to the window, not wanting to turn on any of the lights.
Mathematics, history, novels, science, all alphabetized by title. Where
should we look? Under "D" for diary? "S" for secret stuff? Maybe the
diary had a fake cover, a phony book title to throw off busybodies. I
started to get frantic, yanking out books I'd already looked at, this
time to open them up and fan through their pages, checking for
handwriting. Soon I was slamming them back onto the shelf, then
finally not bothering to do even that, tossing them to the floor, not
caring how I left the room. I only wanted to find Jimmy's diary.

Next I rummaged through the dresser, sliding my hand between
cool cotton T-shirts and underwear in the top drawer, under sweaters
in the middle, and among a jumble of odd-shaped objects in what
was obviously a bottom catchall. Here at last were the swimming
medals, ribbon after ribbon, all tangled together, but no diary. I
opened the rolltop desk, pulled out every drawer there, looked in
every pigeonhole, pressed corners and ridges for a secret panel.

Meanwhile Dennis got down on his knees, pulled up the bedspread, looked under the bed, and searched deep under the mattress.
Then he disappeared into the walk-in closet at the foot of the bed.
He examined the floor, looked into boots and shoes, checked for
loose boards, poked around the top shelf, then patted down the
clothes themselves for a lump in one of the pockets.

Nothing.

The diary has to be here—it has to! I tried to calm down. *Where haven't I looked? What am I not seeing?*

My eyes fell on the computer. Of course! What more natural place for Jimmy to keep his diary than on his PC?

I fumbled for the switches, watched the machine boot, then called up the directory. There on a long list of files was most likely what I'd been searching for: Dear Pythagoras.

"Got it! Dennis, this has to be it!"

I pulled up the first screen of text. What would Jimmy's words be like? Had he written my autobiography? Nervous, excited, sad, I began to read.

```
Saturday
    This feels really weird. I mean, I named
this "Dear Pythagoras," like that's supposed to
help, right? Like I'm really plugged into the
great P, maybe sending him cosmic e-mail. Who
am I kidding? Pythagoras is The Man, while I'm
nothing, nobody, and never will be. And isn't
this basically talking to myself? They lock you
up for that, don't they, for talking to your-
self out loud? Why is writing to yourself any
different?
    I'm not so sure about a diary now anyway.
But one thing at least. If I do write stuff
down, this is the place to keep it. Mrs. H. is
still in the fifteenth century, except in the
kitchen. I mean, her cooking tools could nuke,
shred, or liquefy the world. Meanwhile, she won't
learn to drive because she says she doesn't
understand it. Forget computers. She won't
touch them.
    And Dad isn't interested in anything I do if
it doesn't involve swimming. He wouldn't care
if my diary held plans for a bank heist.
Oh—unless he could invest the take in a new
car dealership. So this is the safest place for
me to be.
```

```
    Besides, if I do feel Big Brother is watch-
ing, I can always move the whole thing online
for electronic storage. The archives of James
Muller. Or better yet, post it daily as
Jimmy's Blah Blah Blog! for everyone to read.
I like that.
    Wouldn't they all be shocked to know who I
really am? They'd better find me out before
it's too late.
```

The entry was dated a year and a half ago but felt so real Jimmy might have been whispering in my ear: *They'd better find me out before it's too late...*

I wanted to read straight through but didn't have time. I was there to examine Jimmy's relationship with his father, to discover what had happened that made Muller want to kill him. What had gone on these past months? Were there attempts before the actual crime? How much had Jimmy known or feared? I jumped to the end of the file to read backwards.

The last entry was dated the day of his murder. Mrs. Hidalgo had said he left around ten. I could see him sitting at his PC in Dennis's black math-symbol T-shirt. Had Jimmy known, had he suspected at all? Or had the final betrayal shocked him?

Here I was, in the same spot, sitting in his chair, typing at his keyboard, breathing his air.

As I was scrolling to find the last entry, I heard a faraway whisper: "What does it say?"

I realized that Dennis wasn't eagerly reading over my shoulder. He still stood in the closet, deep in its shadows, his face hidden from me. I got spooked. Had I been wrong again, when I eliminated Dennis from my list? Is that why he had even now protested my looking at the diary, because he knew it would betray him? From what I could see, he looked like a condemned man, head low, eyes down, shoulders curled inward. Even the silence sang out his guilt. Did I really need to read the words that Jimmy had written? Then his grave, dripping with red paint, flashed before me.

I've come too far to stop now. For Jimmy's sake. For my own. I have to keep going.

"Nothing so far," I told Dennis. "I'm reading the last entry now."

```
Monday
    Dad and I had another fight last night. Like
I really need that, especially with Dennis mad
at me and no one to talk to. I could say the
fight was the same old stuff, but each time it
hurts like it's brand new. 'So what's wrong
with swimming?' he says. Everything. I've
already told him a thousand times I'm scared,
but he laughs. 'Don't be such a baby. Fear is
something to be conquered.'
    I am afraid, but there's so much more to it
than that. How can I tell him the rest? That
swimming is just one more thing to make me look
good while all the time I'm nothing, I'm crap.
Why can't he like me the way I am? Why does he
need the medals? Because he knows. He knows
there's nothing inside me. Mom knew. So does
Dennis. We're friends only because he feels
sorry for me. Yesterday, while we were scream-
ing at each other, I had the nerve to say he
was jealous—of all people, Dennis jealous of
me! He's the one who's real. He's the one with
a real family, real feelings. He wears his real
face. All I have are medals and not even that
any more. And I called him second-rate, like
double-daring him to call my bluff. For a
moment, I thought he would. For a moment, he
was close, so close, when he asked why my
mother never visited a creep like me. But he
held back from saying those final words. It was
pity, I'm sure.
    Sometimes I feel so miserable I could die.
    All right. Dad wants me in the water, he'll
get it. I'll show him. I'm going down to the
lake right now. He'll be sorry.
```

200

My hands flew off the keyboard, my throat closed.

All right. Dad wants me in the water, he'll get it. I read the sentences again. *I'll show him. I'm going down to the lake right now. He'll be sorry.*

What did it mean? What did the words mean?

Sometimes I feel so miserable I could die.

I tried to catch my breath, couldn't. I'd made a fool of myself, gotten into all sorts of trouble, had that horrible fight with my mother, risked my life and Dennis's life, put Mr. Wheatley in the hospital, only to discover *this.*

Jimmy had killed himself. Why hadn't that ever occurred to me? How could I have not known? We were so much alike, but then... I stared at the computer screen and reread the words.

How could he have done this to me? I thought he'd been stolen. Instead I discovered he'd run away and left me, left us all.

"What is it, Allie? What does the diary say?"

Dennis whispered as if someone had hands around his throat. I was right, he *was* weighed down with guilt and with the fear of his guilt. The hands round his throat were Jimmy's, blindly searching for help as he went down for the third time. But Dennis hadn't been there, hadn't gone to the lake that day because they had argued. They had had the very first fight of their friendship, and the next day Jimmy had died. This must have been what Dennis was afraid of all along.

Suddenly the overhead light snapped on. I twisted round in the desk chair to look behind me. Mr. Muller stood in the doorway, a heavy golf club raised in both hands. His face was tight and mean, black circles under his eyes, two deep creases along his thin mouth.

"Oh God, it's you." Mr. Muller dropped the club and sagged against the doorframe. "I thought you were...but that would be...so you had to be a burglar." He put his hand to his chest and breathed deeply. "I was going to..." He shook his head. "What are you doing here? Why the hell won't you leave me alone?" He held out both hands. Not getting an answer, maybe he settled for an easier question: "How did you break in?"

"I d-didn't, I…" I stammered over the words, aware of Dennis, standing so close but unseen in the closet. Would he show himself? Should I reveal his presence? "I had a key," I said finally. Heart thumping, I swallowed twice before I had enough spit for the next sentence. "I have a really good reason for being here."

Mr. Muller looked at the PC monitor, nodded, didn't ask what my reason was.

"I…I didn't mean to scare you," I added. "I thought you'd be at work or maybe out campaigning." Like that was any better.

"I quit the campaign the day of the funeral. And I don't go to work much these days. In fact, I don't do much of anything, except sit in the dark. Which is what I was doing when I heard noises from up here. You sounded so much like him."

The words licked my spine with a cold tongue.

Mr. Muller started to pick his way through the books Dennis and I had torn off the shelves. I started breathing again only when he sat on the bed. His scarecrow frame was so thin he barely dented the mattress.

"I'm sorry about the mess," I said. I stood up and picked up a few books, nudging the closet door partially closed with my hip as I did.

"No matter. He'd do the same himself sometimes, pull the books all out, then put them back."

I wanted to scream, to tear my hair, to jump out the window. I'd been caught like a thief in Muller's dead son's room, with Dennis hiding in the closet, right after finding out that the dead son had killed himself, and Muller was telling me about Jimmy's cleaning habits. The conversation was like an artsy film where six people read lines from six different scripts.

"Why are you here?" Muller asked again.

I put the books on a shelf and sat back down at the computer. "Jimmy was my friend, and it wasn't right, his dying," I said. "I…I had to find out why."

"And the reason is in there?" Muller pointed to the PC as if it was a ravenous lion. "I...I thought so, too. Was afraid so. I thought I'd go through his files. I wanted to, I really did. To find out, you know? But I haven't touched even his clothes. How am I supposed to deal with what he wrote?"

How would *I* deal with it? I'd come here to prove Muller a murderer. I could still do it, just by saying that it was *his* fault, that *he'd* driven his son to suicide, pressuring him to swim, nagging him about his grades, making him volunteer. Every rotten, senseless, traitorous thing Muller had ever done to his kid added up to death. I understood that. I understood rotten parents. I understood being betrayed.

"One day the door to his room was open," Mr. Muller said, "a rare occasion. He was sitting there at the keyboard." Muller's left hand fingered the tufts of the chenille bedspread; I thought of myself unraveling Mom's kitchen curtains thread by thread. "I asked what he was doing," Muller continued. "He told me he was writing a story for English class. But he answered in a strange, high voice and said his story was about a character whose friends and family accepted him even though he was a pathetic piece of crap."

Muller stopped, looked toward the doorway. No one was there.

"Then?" I prompted, though I wasn't sure I wanted to hear the rest.

"Then I asked him what the hell kind of story that was." Quoting Jimmy, Muller's voice became high and weird: "'It's a story about diversity and tolerance, Dad, so that's why it's so very happy, happy, happy. In truth, though, there's an epilogue, too tragic to be brought to school, in which everyone finally does realize the character is just a walking piece of crap, and they flush him down the toilet. Flush, flush, flush, and he drowns.'"

As Muller chanted in a high voice "flush, flush, flush," water flooded my lungs, rushing in after a last, long-held, burning breath was finally, willingly let go. It hurt so much—the held breath, the cold water instead of air deep within, the harsh words of countless arguments ringing in my head. I didn't know which hurt the most.

My shoulders curled in, my back curved. My body wanted to roll into a tight little ball around my soft middle. I knew that inside the closet Dennis had disappeared, shriveled up to a dry pinpoint of grief.

Who was talking? I recognized the pain but not the person. Or maybe I recognized too many, all of us, all in the one voice.

Muller's eyes drifted from mine. His lips worked silently. His hand came to rest on Jimmy's bed pillow. When he finally looked back at me, he smiled.

"Don't cry," he said.

"I'm not." Who would I be crying for? But hot tears slid down my cheeks. "Then what did you do?"

"I walked downstairs, poured myself a cup of coffee, and congratulated myself for not being dragged into yet another fight with my teenage son. I never once thought…I mean, if anything, maybe I should have wondered if he was on drugs. Maybe the extra attention, though I'd have been wrong, would have been enough. But I didn't, and he left me," Muller whispered, talking more to himself now. "First she left me. Then he left me."

Then he left me.

Muller knew the truth yet was afraid of it. Suddenly telling him that he was to blame for his son's death was the most important thing to me in the whole world. The truth was an absolute good and should always be told, right? I had to let him know what crummy parents did to their kids.

With determined anger, I turned to him, turned *on* him—and saw for the first time that he wasn't dressed and still wore pajamas. There wasn't much left of him, loose white skin, flapping white clothes. His feet were bare, narrow, bloodless except for two tender pink bumps just below his big toes. A dozen pictures then, a thousand feelings: Mom with bunions from years of diner waitressing, so happy now with this much better job, which she really wanted to keep even if she wasn't completely sure yet; Aunt Lolly with a broken hip, her long narrow feet sticking from beneath a white hospital sheet; my father in a white T-shirt and pajama bottoms running outside barefoot after my mother the one time *she'd* left *him,* tried to leave, taking me with her.

If Mr. Muller was guilty of murdering his son, was Dennis also guilty for having fought with Jimmy the night before? Was Jimmy's mother, for having left him years ago? Was *I*—for having skipped that picnic and missing the chance to become the one friend who might have helped?

All of us were guilty, and not guilty, all at the same time. Or did things sometimes just happen?

And another thought: If Jimmy had meant to kill himself, why did he bother bringing a bathing suit and towel? Maybe he had *wanted* his death to look like an accident, so he wouldn't hurt his father any more than he had to. Maybe Jimmy hadn't been calling out to me from his grave after all.

I clicked on `Dear Pythagoras,` deleted the file, emptied the wastebin, then immediately turned the computer off so the deletion would seem part of shutting down.

"Your son didn't leave you, Mr. Muller," I said. "It was an accident. There's no real reason why."

"No? You mean, you didn't find...?"

I thought he'd break down right in front of me.

"No, I didn't find anything. I read it all and I found nothing. It was a stupid, stupid accident." I stood up, wiped my own tears, and handed him Jimmy's key, the one Jimmy had given Dennis. "Sometimes terrible things just happen."

Mr. Muller stood, picked up the golf club that had fallen to the floor. His words were thick and trembling. "I'm going to go to the bathroom now. Wash my face. When I finish, you'd better be gone. Because later, when I stop to think about this, I'm going to be very, very angry that I found you in my son's room. So go."

He moved silently into the dark hallway. When I heard the bathroom door click shut, I opened the closet, leaned into the darkness, and quickly kissed Dennis's wet cheek. Then I grabbed his hand and we ran downstairs.

Chapter Twenty-One

I messed up, Mr. Wheatley. I messed up real bad." With Dennis at my side, I whispered the words to the motionless, white-sheeted form before us. Mr. Wheatley was sleeping, although I didn't see how he could, between the constant clamor in the hospital hallway and the multiple electrodes and wires that led to beeping machines. Hypnotized, I watched the pulsing green line of his heartbeat. Wheatley was very pale—white skin, white bristles roughening his unshaved cheeks, white hair against the white pillow. His left arm was in a cast to just above the elbow. An IV ran into his large, wrinkled hand.

Painkillers, I hoped. *Maybe that's how he's able to sleep.* Or maybe not. He was in a semi-private room, though the other bed was empty right now; he'd been moved from intensive care just this morning the nurse had said—which should have been good news. But he was so pale, so very still.

"Dennis, you don't suppose he's in a coma, do you?"

"Wishful thinking, Miss Canarsie?"

Wheatley's eyes moved beneath their lids, opened, shut, stayed open.

"You're awake!"

"And you're observant."

Though weak, his voice was clearly sarcastic. It had never felt so good being insulted.

"How did you get in here, Miss Canarsie, you and your comrade in crime? What did you tell the nurse? That you're my long-lost children?"

"More like great-great-grandchildren," I said.

"Allie!" Dennis protested.

"Don't worry, Mr. Monaghan. I'm much tougher than I look. After all, I teach freshman English."

I took a deep breath. I had something to say before I lost my nerve.

"I'm sorry, Mr. Wheatley. I messed up, and bad things happened as a result. Bad things happened to *you*, and it was my fault. But I never meant for you to get hurt." I swallowed. "For me to hurt you. I only wanted..."

It seemed so foolish now, I couldn't finish.

"You only wanted to catch a killer?"

I nodded.

"I'm sorry, too, Mr. Wheatley," Dennis said. "I mean, if I'd thought twice about what we were doing, maybe I could have talked her out of it."

"Logic and reason in the face of an unstoppable force? You never had a chance." Wheatley's voice grew softer, and his eyelids fluttered. He'd be back asleep soon. Eyes closed, he murmured, "Just tell me why, Allie."

"What?"

"I asked why." He spoke slowly, pacing himself. "Why did you do it? I don't mean why you accused Tom Creighton. Before that. Why did you see a murder where there was none?"

I had wondered that too, over and over, ever since reading Jimmy's diary. Maybe because I refused to see his death as an accident, as blind chance...or because I was so convinced Jimmy and I were alike, I didn't let him have his own feelings, his own deeper pain.

"And if there had been a murder," Wheatley said, "why did you believe that you were the one who had to solve it?"

Once my words might have come out defensively. Now they just sounded tired: "I did it because I thought that no one cared, and I know what that's like."

Maybe this wasn't the absolute truth. It wasn't at the beginning. But it was true by the end.

"Are you really as alone as you think you…" His voice faded to silence, then his breath became slow and heavy.

I was glad he had fallen asleep again and that I didn't have to answer. It didn't seem like a good time for self-examination.

"I care, Allie," Dennis said. "*Cared*—about what happened to Jimmy," he added quickly, blushing. "I mean, even though you didn't—" He stopped.

"Though I didn't what?" I asked.

"Nothing."

"What?"

"Even though you and Jimmy…you never…"

I hung my head, grateful Mr. Wheatley was dozing and didn't hear that I'd never met Jimmy, that it had all been a lie.

"How long have you known?" I asked Dennis.

"Always."

His answer startled me.

"Then why did you let me go on? And why did you believe me about the murder?"

"I don't know. I believed because…because I needed to believe." His own head dipped low. I heard what he didn't, couldn't say: that he needed to believe in something other than suicide; he needed to believe in something other than his own guilt. Someday he'd ask me the question outright; he'd ask me what I read in Jimmy's diary. I'd have to tell him the truth then and could only hope that by the time he was ready to hear the words, I'd be ready to say them.

"Believing in the murder kept you around, kept you talking," Dennis said softly, "even if you were always talking about *him*. And besides, I liked you…. Do like…"

Do like—present tense, despite all the terrible things I'd done the past few weeks. Tears filled my eyes, spilled over.

"So?" I snapped, pulling away and straightening my back. "This doesn't mean I'm sticking around for your senior prom or anything!"

"Coward," Wheatley murmured.

"You're supposed to be asleep!" I said.

"Who can sleep with all this ruckus?"

"Dennis Monaghan?" A nurse stuck her head behind the curtain. "Your mother called. There's a pay phone down the hall. Time's up anyway." Dennis ducked out, but the nurse stayed and fussed with the monitors and IV bag, maybe to make sure I left as well.

"Please," Wheatley asked. "Just a minute more with my great-great-great-great-great granddaughter."

The nurse bit her lip. "You just made yourself about two hundred years old, Mr. Wheatley, but okay. One more minute," she said sternly.

"So," Wheatley said when we were alone.

"So," I answered. His eyes were too direct. Hadn't he just been asleep? Maybe he had faked it, to listen as Dennis and I talked. I blushed, remembering. "So, are you coming back to class?"

"Of course."

"When?"

He shrugged. "I'm not sure. I imagine sometime between the end of your inevitable suspension and the end of Christmas break. There's a lot of leeway in there. Give me a call in the meantime though, Allie. I'm in the book. You wouldn't want your barbed wit to get rusty, waiting for me."

"I'm sorry," I said, my eyes filling up again.

"I know. I'm sorry, too." With his good hand, he patted mine. "Things will be different when I get back. Now that I know your talents…" He gave my hand a light squeeze. "I'll be expecting A papers from you, especially in creative writing."

"That's cold, Mr. Wheatley," I said, though I knew he was letting me know we were still friends. "Isn't it past time you retired?"

"Not while there's a breath left to breathe and a freshman left to torture."

I left a few seconds later. Dennis had called his mother, who had phoned home and found him missing. The hospital had been her first guess. She was running over now on her lunch break to drive Dennis home. I shook my head at his offer of a ride. I doubted that his mother would be happy to see me right now; she probably associated me with car accidents, broken bones, and heart attacks.

The day was overcast. It should have been depressing, yet inside I felt more strange and happy emotions than I knew the names for. I was like someone who'd tasted only salt and pepper all his life then finally discovers coriander, rosemary, and turmeric, which sounded like girls in one of those snotty cliques I loathed, but were really herbs and spices and stuff. Mr. Wheatley was alive. And Dennis liked me, even though I had lied to him about knowing Jimmy and had gotten him into a lifetime's worth of trouble. It seemed more than I deserved. I'd figure out the rest as I came to it.

Walking home from the hospital, I found myself back at Evergreen, back where it all started. The distance from the street into the cemetery to Jimmy's grave seemed too great to cross and I sat on the curb instead.

I was exhausted in every part of my body and soul. I could barely think about everything I'd done since we'd moved to Nickel Park. I'd screwed up in so many ways. Had I done anything right? Remembering Mr. Muller's face when I told him I'd found nothing in the diary, that small flicker of hope becoming just a birthday candle brighter, I guess I had to say yes. Maybe not much more than that, though.

I still found it hard to believe how wrong I'd been about Jimmy. I'd thought we were almost twins in a way: liking so many of the same things, having a parent who took off and never visited, connecting at so many invisible points. Yesterday, I'd even said I wished I was dead. But that was before I knew what he'd actually done, before I knew that sometimes, when we say words like that, we find a way to make them come true.

My teeth began to chatter, then my whole body shook. Before I knew I was going to cry, long hiccuppy sobs burst from my mouth. I dropped my head to my arms and bawled like a little kid.

After a long time I caught my breath and looked up. From the corner of my eye, I saw a boy standing several yards away, motionless, as if all along he'd been waiting for me to lift my head. For one brief second I thought it was Jimmy, then realized it couldn't be.

I wiped my face and began to get up.

"No, stay there."

"Mom?"

I hadn't recognized her. She was wearing faded jeans, a blue windbreaker, and sneakers, and had tucked her sandy colored hair under a baseball cap.

"The school called," she said, when she'd walked closer. "They weren't really expecting you in, and you weren't supposed to go anyway, but since neither of us phoned, they wanted to check. They tried the trailer first. No answer, so they called me. I left work and stopped by home to see if you were there. Then I headed over here to look for you."

"Am I going to get you fired?" I asked.

"No. Luckily, Mr. Berger has three teenagers. He said he understood. Besides, I shouldn't have gone in today myself. I don't know what I was thinking. You were nearly killed yesterday."

She sat next to me on the curb. For a few minutes, neither of us spoke. But it wasn't like yesterday's silence on the way home after our fight, or all the silences of all the years before that. It was the silence of wanting to talk, of getting up nerve to talk, of trying to know what could possibly be said to heal the hurt between us.

It had to begin with two words.

"I…I'm sorry, Mom, I'm sorry… Yesterday, I said it to try to talk you into something, but now I'm saying it because it's true. I'm sorry for just about every minute I've ever been awake." Tears poured from me all over again, and I covered my face with my hands. In a sharp stabbing instant, I saw myself the way other people must. "Whatever happened to me, whatever happened to…to everyone else, happened because of my own fault… I'm not a good person…and I'm a horrible daughter."

She circled my shoulders with her arms for a hug and whispered in my ear, "Shh, that's not true. Listen to me, Allie. You're the daughter I want." I tried to pull away but she held me firmly. "Honey, are you okay?" she asked, taking my face and turning it to mine to look into my eyes. Her image was blurred by tears.

"No, no, don't answer that," she said quickly, shaking her head. "It's a stupid question. I know you're not okay. Look, Allie, I want to say something and to do something, and I want to say it and do it now before we go back home and you start yelling and I start yelling and things get as mean and ugly as they were last night." She took a deep breath. "I know we have big problems. You have your problems, I have mine, and together we have a whole different set. Miss Barbosa strongly suggests counseling, but I figure that even with outside help for both of us, these problems may feel unsolvable, especially at first. Things will probably get worse between us before they get any better." She looked away and studied the dirt at her feet as she continued: "But I want you to know that I love you, and that I will always love you, no matter what. Nothing either of us says or does will ever change that."

My throat closed up again. *I love you too, Mom.*

All I could do was think the words. It had been so long, my lips had forgotten how to say them.

Last night Officer Rivers had told her to tell my father about me, had said there was no good in hiding these things. How would my father have reacted? Would he have yelled and screamed the way Mom did last night? Would he then have come after me today to tell me that he loved me anyway, the way she did? I would never know because he had left me. And after everything my mother had said, maybe it was the best thing he could have done.

He had left me. But my Mom hadn't. She was still here. She had taken me with her. The one time she'd tried to leave him, she had taken me with her even then. I suddenly knew she always would.

"Listen, about yesterday," she said softly, "when I told you your father hit me?"

I nodded. As if I could have forgotten.

"That part's true. He did hit me. At the very end. But it was just the once," she said. "Just the one time. I got so scared, scared for us, scared for him. Scared he'd do it again, scared I wouldn't be able to leave him if he did. I was afraid I'd become one of those poor, miserable women you read about. Maybe it scared him, too, because that's when he left for good." Breath blew from her mouth in a big sigh. "But even after he left, I stayed scared for a long time. I thought I saw him hanging around the diner where I worked after the divorce. That was why I moved the first time. I thought he was stalking me. The first couple of times we moved, it was because I thought I saw him, though I was never really sure. Then at some point we began to move just because it seemed the easiest thing to do whenever we got into trouble, me or you."

She shifted position on the curb, inched away from me, looked away.

"In the end I wound up wondering if I hadn't bolted that first time for no good reason, if it maybe hadn't been him at all." Her shoulders sagged, her head lowered. "Lately I've also been wondering about being afraid for so many years. He hit me once. It was absolutely wrong, it will always be wrong, and there is never a way to justify something like that. But did that make him a wife beater? Or was it only my thinking that made it so? I hit *you* yesterday." She held out her hand and stared at it. I grabbed it from the cold air, held it close, and warmed it against my face. She started to cry then, and I did too, and we held onto each and rocked back and forth.

"I might be wrong about him, at least that part. I probably am. I guess it's time for you to make up your own mind about the rest." She reached into her pocket and pulled out a slip of paper. "Maybe I should wait till we've talked to someone before giving this to you. Maybe they'll jump up and down and scream and say, 'You did what!' But here—I'm giving it to you now."

I stared at the scrap of paper for a long time without unfolding it.

"What is it?" I asked. But I already knew.

"Go ahead," she told me.

In Mom's small neat handwriting was an Oregon address and phone number, no name. My father.

"Are you sure?" I asked.

Was *I* sure? I had wanted this for years, my mother had fought me at every point, and now I didn't know. I'd been wrong so many times lately I needed higher math just to keep count.

"I'm as sure as I'm ever going to be, which isn't a lot," Mom answered. "But Aunt Lolly is sure, and Darleen is, too. She's the one who finally convinced me."

"Aunt Darleen?"

"She said it would be all right, safe, for you to call or to write him. She said you wouldn't start moving forward till you stopped being pulled back by the past." Mom gave an embarrassed cough. "Uh, she said the same thing about me too. She said I've been looking for a geographical cure by moving all the time, but moving all the time just makes things worse."

"Aunt Darleen said that?"

I wanted to make a wisecrack about there being more to my aunt than big hair and smiley-face nails but the words didn't come. Aunt Darleen was family—close family, if I'd only let her. And my Aunt Lolly, too, Queen of the Break Dancers.

Once more Wheatley had me nailed: I wasn't as alone as I thought I was.

But even having so many people behind me didn't make the scrap of paper I held less scary. My fingers squeezed it tightly, as if it would bite me if it got loose.

"What should I do, Mom? Should I call him now? Should I wait?"

My mother smiled, an expression so filled with surprise, wonder, and delight I half-expected to turn around and see that Santa Claus had landed his sleigh behind me.

"What?" I asked.

She shook her head. "Nothing. It's just that I can't remember the last time you asked me for advice. But I guess I haven't have had much to offer lately."

"I wouldn't have taken it anyway," I said, not wanting her to cry again. "You know me."

"Do I? Not yet, not for a long time even, but maybe sometime." She fished a tissue out of the windbreaker's pocket and blew her nose.

"Meanwhile, what should I do with *this?*" I held out the scrap of paper with the phone number and shook it. I wasn't sure whether I wanted to burn it or tuck it next to my heart. "What if I lose it before I call? Should I memorize it? But I don't want it running through my head like a bad song. I can see me answering an algebra problem with a ten-digit number."

"Shhh, take it easy," Mom said, hugging me. "I've written it down in my address book. You can look it up whenever you want. Or Aunt Lolly will give it to you anytime you ask. Or, now that you know the city, you can call Information."

Call Information for my father. How strange—all this time he'd been available to anyone who asked the phone company, but not to me.

My hands shook when I refolded the paper and put it in my pocket.

"So, are you going to call him?" my mother asked.

I shrugged. I'd rushed into so many things during my short career that I was, as one school shrink had put it, the poster girl for poor impulse control. I didn't want to be stupid about this, too. When I finally talked to my dad, I wanted it to be because I'd thought about it and made a decision, not because I was reacting to something somebody else did or said.

Besides, I wasn't sure how I felt about him any more. Actually, yes, I did know. I hated him. I had always seen him as the innocent victim, driven away by my mother. Now I'd discovered he'd done some pretty mean things. Even at best, he was the cruel and heartless father who had abandoned his poor wife and kid. He had left me—*me!* But maybe my hate right now was the blind opposite of everything I'd felt before. I'd have to wait a while to find out if there was a middle.

Maybe I could talk it over with Dennis. It was time I told someone about myself.

"I don't know what I'll do," I said to my mother. My hand slipped back into my pocket and fingered the paper. "I don't know anything anymore."

This week a huge piece of me had died, but which part was gone and which part was left? And why had I come to Evergreen, of all places, to figure it out? I had buried so many strangers here. Now, in a way, I was burying part of myself.

Maybe I've gone to my last funeral for a while. Though perhaps not my last visit to Evergreen. My grandparents are up there. Not people I have to pretend to know, but people I should have known. Family. The next time I visit, that's where I'll go. Maybe my mom will want to go with me.

"You know what, Mom?" I said, ducking my face so she wouldn't see I was still crying. "I've been doing some serious thinking."

"We all have," she said.

"And from now on there's gonna be a brand new me," I promised.

"You don't have to change totally," she said. "I love you already. Just a few improvements here and there, you and me both."

"No, no, I mean it." What started as a simple sincere comment became a sudden brainstorm. "But a brand new me needs a brand new identity."

"What?" she asked warily. She was probably wondering, *What now?* After all, things had been quiet for, oh, maybe all of five minutes. Much too long for peace with Alexandra Canarsie around.

"I've been giving it a lot of thought," I said. And I had, at least fourteen nanoseconds' worth. "And I've decided I should change my name."

I tried to stand, found my legs had gone to sleep, pushed my mother up, and let her pull me after her. "I always liked the name Florence," I went on, wondering how I would sign it. An ornate *F*, a looping *l*, then an unreadable scrawl. "Florence," I said softly, tasting the word. "Is that a student council president's name or what? But never, ever Flo."

"Florence?" she repeated. "Student council president?"

"No, you're right, student council president is too much too soon," I admitted. It was better to start off small. "Maybe president of the Nickel Park Biker Club. Bet you didn't know there was one, did you? I'll need to dye my hair green, though, or at least shave it."

"Shave?"

"Just the left half of my head. Probably get a tattoo, too, like a scorpion."

"A scorpion?" my mother repeated yet again. Obviously the shock of the new me had robbed her of independent speech.

"Mom, you've always been after me to do more, fit in."

She pushed me in the direction of the trailer park.

"Alexandra Canarsie," she said, laughing, "you are grounded for so long for what you've done, you'd better have the name of your nursing home tattooed on you, not a scorpion."

"Grounded?" I shrieked. "I'm grounded?"

"Of course, you're grounded. What did you expect after this— that I'd raise your allowance?"

"But I almost got killed this week!"

"And if it had happened, I wouldn't be grounding you," she said, wiping away a final tear from my cheek. "But it didn't, and I am, and you are."

We were going to have the worst fight of our life about this, I just knew it. But not now. Not now. Now I just leaned my head against my mother's shoulder and let her take me home.